Praise for *Gettysburg Requiem:*
The Life and Lost Causes of
Confederate Colonel William C. Oates

"LaFantasie has done a terrific job of telling Oates's tale, and of using him as a tool to delve into the greater issues that filled Oates's own life and times. . . . This fine biography does him the justice denied him in times past."—George C. Bradley, *The Civil War Courier*

"Exhaustively researched and elegantly written, this captivating biography is a signal contribution to Civil War historiography. . . . In LaFantasie's penetrating analysis, Oates becomes the avatar of everything both objectionable and laudable in the antebellum and postwar South as well as in the intervening Civil War."—*Library Journal* (starred review)

"Until now, Confederate Colonel William C. Oates is remembered—if he is remembered at all—for losing to the celebrated Joshua Chamberlain in the fight for Little Round Top at Gettysburg. Here at last is Oates in full dimension, a fascinating, Faulknerian figure out of the Old South."—Stephen W. Sears, author of *Gettysburg*

"In LaFantasie's absorbing and penetrating account, Oates emerges as an iconic figure to mirror the urbane Chamberlain . . . offering 'a fascinating—and sometimes unsettling—portrait of Southern manhood and the dynamics of violence, heroism, and memory.'"—Michael Kenney, *The Boston Globe*

"William C. Oates and Joshua Lawrence Chamberlain faced one another in a storied confrontation on Little Round Top at Gettysburg. This fine biography demonstrates that Oates's life fully matched his more famous opponent's in drama and importance. LaFantasie's perceptive narrative uses Oates to explore major themes relating to the Civil War, the turbulent postwar years, and the struggle to shape the memory of the conflict."—Gary W. Gallagher, author of *The Confederate War*

"Beautifully written and superbly researched . . . Oates's story is a richly compelling one, set against the most dramatic period in United States history."—Joan Waugh, University of California at Los Angeles

"A candid and penetrating biography. . . . Lyrically written, challenging in its conclusions, this is an important book about the wartime generation of southerners and how they adjusted to the realities of the post-war South."—Craig L. Symonds, author of *Decision at Sea: Five Naval Battles That Shaped American History*

"A brilliant example of diligent research and skillful writing. . . . William Oates's life, before, during and after the battle of Gettysburg, illustrates his times better than that of grander figures whose public virtues and sins overshadow their inner complexity. But never until now has anyone as talented as LaFantasie taken the pains to do it right."—Ernest B. Furgurson, author of *Freedom Rising: Washington in the Civil War and Chancellorsville 1863*

Other works by Glenn W. LaFantasie

Twilight at Little Round Top

*Gettysburg: Colonel William C. Oates, C.S.A. and
Lieutenant Frank A. Haskell, U.S.A.*
(editor)

The Correspondence of Roger Williams
(editor)

Gettysburg Requiem

The Life and Lost Causes of Confederate Colonel William C. Oates

Glenn W. LaFantasie

OXFORD
UNIVERSITY PRESS

OXFORD
UNIVERSITY PRESS

Oxford University Press, Inc., publishes works that
further Oxford University's objective of excellence
in research, scholarship, and education.

Oxford New York
Auckland Cape Town Dar es Salaam Hong Kong Karachi
Kuala Lumpur Madrid Melbourne Mexico City Nairobi
New Delhi Shanghai Taipei Toronto

With offices in
Argentina Austria Brazil Chile Czech Republic France Greece
Guatemala Hungary Italy Japan Poland Portugal Singapore
South Korea Switzerland Thailand Turkey Ukraine Vietnam

Copyright © 2006 by Glenn W. LaFantasie

First published by Oxford University Press, Inc., 2006
198 Madison Avenue, New York, NY 10016
www.oup.com

First issued as an Oxford University Press paperback, 2008
ISBN 978-0-19-533131-8

Oxford is a registered trademark of Oxford University Press

The Library of Congress has cataloged the hardcover edition as follows:
LaFantasie, Glenn W.
Gettysburg requiem : the life of William C. Oates / Glenn W. LaFantasie.
p. cm.
Includes bibliographical references and index.
ISBN 978-0-19-517458-8
1. Oates, William C. (William Calvin), 1833–1910.
2. Soldiers—Confederate States of America—Biography.
3. Confederate States of America. Army—Biography.
4. Governors—Alabama—Biography.
5. Gettysburg, Battle of, Gettysburg, Pa., 1863.
6. Confederate States of America. Army. Alabama Infantry Regiment, 15th.
7. United States—History—Civil War, 1861–1865—Campaigns.
I. Title.
E467.1.O18L34 2006
976.1'061092—dc22
2005035271

1 3 5 7 9 8 6 4 2

Printed in the United States of America
on acid-free paper

For Oatsie

CONTENTS

Acknowledgments ix
Illustrations xv
Introduction xvii

1

Rough and Tumble Days 1

2

Baptism by Fire 27

3

An Unchristian State of Mind 49

4

Ragged Jacks 69

5

Boulders Like Gravestones 89

6

In the Purple Gloom 111

7

Gone to Flickering 137

8

The End of Chivalry 155

9

Before the Bar 173

10

The One-Armed Hero of Henry County 193

11

Striking to Hurt 223

12

A Soldier in His Heart 245

13

Stumbling Toward Equality 263

14

Requiem 287

Abbreviations Used 311
Notes 315
Selected Bibliography 367
Index 397

ACKNOWLEDGMENTS

"Writing, at its best, is a lonely life," affirmed Ernest Hemingway, and he was right, but I have found nonetheless that this book could not have been written without the help of my loving family, many close friends, a bevy of fellow historians and writers, and scores of librarians and archivists. During the decade-and-a-half that I worked on this book, which was many times interrupted when other projects and responsibilities required my attention, I have come to rely on the steadfast support and kind services of people I know well, others whom I have met as a result of this project, and still others whom I have never met in person, but who gave me their unselfish help anyway. I thank them one and all.

For someone who is not a writer or an editor, my wife, Donna A. LaFantasie, has a keen sense of what works on paper and what doesn't—and, thank heaven, she has never been meek about telling me so. Donna has also given me hope when all else seemed lost; trust, when nothing seemed certain; love, when she had nothing else to give. Our children have stood by me as well, when all they really wanted was a father instead of a writer in the house. My eldest daughter, Donna M. Hayes, helped me with research and, more than once, in a reversal of roles, saved her mother and I from the jaws of unexpected calamity. So did our son, Ryan T. Hayes, the most giving man I have ever met. Our youngest child, M. Sarah LaFantasie, grew up with this book, did research with me in libraries, walked battlefields to the point of exhaustion, took awful bus tours with me around the Gettysburg battlefield, and made me laugh all the while. When she was still living at home, she would stop by my study to say goodnight while I burned the midnight oil. She may never know how much those little visits, and our nonsensical chats, really meant to me. All of our children have now grown into adulthood. I am proud of them all—and I trust this is not the only time or the only place I have said so.

Northern families, unlike their Southern counterparts, are not known for their solidarity. But my family has always given me support in ways that William Oates could have fully appreciated and understood. The entire Fulfold family—Nancy, Robert, Tom, and Sue—have been heroic in cheering me on. All of them have given their love unsparingly, but Robert and Nancy know why my wife and I are especially in their debt. My mother, Edith Wynaught LaFantasie Jenkins, and my father-in-law, Donald H. Dignon, both made loving efforts to make sure this book was completed; tragically, neither of them lived to see it published. Nor did my father, Warren, who died when he and I were both too young for such a thing to happen. The late Wendell Jenkins, my stepfather, always believed in my dream to be a professional historian. My sister, Terry Lynne Pezzi, has shared the wonderful journey through the past that my parents began for us with family trips to historic sites in New England, the South, and the West. She is one of the very few people who truly understands what the writing of history means to me. My niece, Nicole Douglas, and my nephew, Raymond Pezzi, are now closer to me than all the miles and waves have ever implied. Muriel and Diane Bartlett, aunt and cousin respectively, have always gotten the rest of the family through our worst crises.

This book is dedicated to Mrs. Marion Oates Leiter Charles, the granddaughter of William C. Oates. For those who know her, Oatsie Charles is a force to reckon with. She is outspoken, outgoing, and often outrageous. But she is, hands down, the most interesting person I have ever met, and I marvel over the fact that we have become friends, despite the fact, as she has often reminded me, that I am a damned Yankee by birth. Besides many other favors, Mrs. Charles granted me exclusive use of the Oates Family Papers while they were in her possession. Her generosity has been unbounded. She has never once asked to review anything that I have written about her grandfather; she would never stoop to such behavior. In the end, I hope that I have done justice to the man she calls "The General." I have enjoyed getting to know him. But I must say in all honesty that what I have enjoyed the most, apart from the immense joy I had in writing this book, has been my coming to know what a very special person Oatsie Charles is. Her late husband, Robert H. Charles, took particular interest in this project. I am grateful, too, to her daughter, Victoria Leiter Mele for support and encouragement. On Mrs. Charles's staff, I owe a great deal to Charlotte Price, Anne Wilson, and Thelma Café for their kind assistance. In June 2005, Mrs. Charles donated the Oates Family Papers to the Alabama Department of Archives and History.

Good friends sustained me while I labored at understanding William Oates and his world. Barbara Benton and Ira Meistrich have been more than friends to me; they are family. But our friendship goes deeper still, down into the bottom of my heart. I thank them for their love and support. In dark nights, they are always there with a lantern; in bright days, they are always there with a smile. With her sharp editorial eye, Barbara read the manuscript in an early iteration and gave solid advice about how to improve it. Ira is the kind of friend who never questions, never doubts; he just keeps giving. Ian Brier has also been able to use his keen intelligence to find humor in situations both ridiculous and sublime. Other friends in Gettysburg also deserve thanks for their steady support and jovial fellowship: Terry Burger and Sue Tanner, Sal and Gail Prezioso, and Barbara Williams.

In Virginia, several friends deserve my thanks, particularly the late Frank Black, Brenda Branscome, Philip Cato, William C. Davis, Ernest B. Furgurson, Nick Kotz, Michael Lacy, Charlie Maddox, Kathy Read, and Susan Wyatt and Robin Anderson. William and Virginia McLaughlin were always patient and understanding. My friends at Barnes & Noble, Manassas, never stopped believing in me, and I thank them all, including Marc Cessna, Madeleine Ellison, Geoffrey Holscher, and Dorothy Hudson. Other friends also deserve mention for supporting the cause: Linda and Kevin Cooney, Peter Cozzens, John and Helena Farrell, Jennifer Farrell, Josef Ruth, and Lee Walker. In Rhode Island and Massachusetts, I am grateful for the all the encouragement I received from Joel A. Cohen, Mario DiNunzio, Kate Dunnigan, Maury Klein, Pamela Kennedy and Robert McMahon, Shelley Roth, Nancy Rowell, Elizabeth Stevens, and Sharon Strom. I do not know what I would do without the friendship, the unconditional love, of Marcia and Bruce Read; they are a bedrock in my life. I must single out Gladys Wyatt for a special thank you—she offered her roof (and her soothing good cheer) at a crucial moment. In Montgomery, I am particularly grateful to Rodman and Martha Nachman, Kathy Reich, and the late Virginia Durr.

Amy Kinsel and I share an interest in things Gettysburg and in the ever-puzzling question about how best to reach our students, but her friendship means more to me than our similar academic endeavors. She has helped me keep going, focus my efforts, and sharpen my thinking. Evelyn Furse, who is a member of our family by acclamation, not by birth, is steadfast in two things: loyalty and love. She has helped my family and me in so many ways, including her remarkable generosity, that it is impossible to keep count of her kindnesses. We may have lost count, but we will never forget.

This book has profited from close readings of all or parts of the manuscript by Linda Crist, Gary W. Gallagher, James M. McPherson, John Y. Simon, Joy Tutela, Michael Vorenberg, Joan Waugh, and Gordon Wood. Several groups of Professor Waugh's students at UCLA got to hear me talk about Oates during tours across the slopes of the Little Round Top. As my dissertation director at Brown University, Mike Vorenberg let me benefit from his deep scholarly understanding of the South, the Civil War, slavery, politics, legal and constitutional history, and American society in the nineteenth century. His editorial recommendations, which were always pertinent and often provocative, went beyond the call of duty. I don't know how I can ever repay the debt I owe him. From his example, I learned that being a good historian involves more than just knowing one's subject; it also entails compassion, generosity, kindness, sensitivity, and mercy. Professor Vorenberg made it possible for me to finish my studies at Brown, and he helped turn this book into something better than it was before he read it. Needless to say, if any shortcomings or errors still remain between these covers, it is in spite of Professor Vorenberg's devoted efforts, not because of them.

At Brown University, I received extraordinary support and collegial encouragement from Mary Beth Bryson, Abbott Gleason, Timothy Harris, William Heindel, Amy Remensnyder, William P. Tatum III, Michael Vorenberg, and Gordon S. Wood. Several colleagues at the University of Maine at Farmington have given me help, advice, and encouragement: Allison Hepler, Stephen Levine, Kenneth Orosz, Allen Berger, and Robert Lively. I am particularly grateful for the support and interest in my work of UMF President Theodora J. Kalikow. For two memorable semesters spent at Gettysburg College, I am grateful to Michael Birkner, Timothy Shannon, and William Bowman. As always, Gabor Boritt was a source of support and inspiration. The participants of the annual Civil War Institute heard early versions of my chapters dealing with Oates's experiences at Gettysburg and walked the field with me on Little Round Top. Over many years, members of the Gettysburg Discussion Group pitched their ideas and shared their considerable knowledge of the battle.

Other scholars and friends have given me aid and comfort over the many years it took me to research and write this book; all these fine people tried their best to make my work easier and reduce my labors, which, through no fault of theirs, became unconscionably protracted. My sincere thanks go to Stefan Brodsky, Thomas A. Desjardin, Jeff Hall, Faith Healy, Sean Healy, Paul A. Hutton, Terry Jackson, Julian and Maggie Kaiser, Robert K. Krick, Gary Laine, Judith Barrett Litoff, the late John J. Pullen, Richard A. Sauers, David C. Smith, Diane Smith, and Timothy Smith.

Research for this book was facilitated by the marvelous efforts of knowledgeable and generous librarians, archivists, and manuscript curators. Edwin C. Bridges, Norwood Kerr, Deborah Pendleton, and Linda Overman have answered my every request and have pointed me to crucial sources at the Alabama Department of Archives and History. At the Library of Congress, Manuscript Division, I received expert guidance and friendly assistance from James H. Hutson, John R. Sellers, Jeffrey Flannery, and Paul Smith. At the Woodrow Wilson International Center for Scholars, I enjoyed borrowing privileges from the stacks of the Library of Congress that put countless rare books into my hands. I could not have found all the many treasures buried in the National Archives had it not been for Michael Music and Michael Pilgrim. In Maine, Eric Jorgensen and Julia Oehmig of the Pejepscot Historical Society, Brunswick, showed me the gems contained in the Alice Trulock Collection and in their Chamberlain collections. At the Hawthorne-Longfellow Library, Bowdoin College, my endless questions were answered gracefully by Susan Ravdin and Dianne M. Gutscher.

Over the years, many different gifted historians and archivists have helped me with my research at Gettysburg National Military Park, especially D. Scott Hartwig, Kathleen Georg, John Heiser, Eric Campbell, Darrell Smoker, Karlton Smith, Robert Prosperi, Winona Peterson, and Superintendent John Latschar. In particular, Supervisory Historian Hartwig saved me from many errors, large and small. At Chattanooga and Chickamauga National Military Park, James Ogden answered every question with skill and led me to useful sources about the battles and the creation of the first national military park in the United States. I am grateful to Richard J. Sommers and the staff of the U.S. Army Military History Institute, Carlisle Barracks, for promptly responding to my requests for information concerning two different wars of the nineteenth century. At the Musselman Library, Gettysburg College, David T. Hedrick and Karen Drickamer provided friendly assistance. My thanks go to Dr. Jack Anderson, John D. Glasscock, Charlton Oates Pingel, and the late Abbott Spear for sending me photocopies of documents in their private collections. David Guest sent me an old newspaper clipping that sparked my reconstruction of an important episode in Oates's later life. Jeff Stocker, a very capable Civil War historian (and a very capable attorney as well), engaged me in conversations that enlightened me about the Alabama Brigade and little-known facts about Little Round Top.

This book could not have been written without the able assistance of librarians at the Fauquier County Public Library in Warrenton, Virginia, and I wish particularly to thank Catharine Ogilvie, Ann Alexander, and Jenny Lyons. At Lord Fairfax Community College Library in Warrenton, I received valuable assistance and friendly support from librarians Laura Leftwich and Linda Harper. I also wish to thank the friendly librarians at the Blanding Public Library, Rehoboth, Massachusetts. For help with illustrations, I am particularly grateful to John Heiser, Cynthia A. Luckie, Arthur W. Bergeron, Jr., and Holly Reed. George Skoch has, one more time, translated my scribbles into comprehendable maps.

A grant from the National Endowment for the Humanities provided travel money for research in Montgomery, Alabama.

At Oxford University Press, I benefited from the wise guidance of one of the best editors in the business and a man I greatly respect: Peter Ginna. Furaha Norton gave the manuscript a thorough reading with a critical eye that helped ultimately to improve it immensely; she also kept this project on track—no mean feat, given the author's missed deadlines and feeble excuses. In the production department, Ruth Mannes turned manuscript into bound books with grace and much patience. Jen Simington was bold and kind in her copyediting; mostly I am grateful to her for catching mistakes in grammar and consistency that would have otherwise resulted in embarrassing prose. My former literary agent, Thomas C. Wallace, stuck by this book during the dimmest of days, when no light seemed willing to break through the clouds. I am grateful for the good efforts he made for me and for his faith in this book. By being my friends, three men made me a better historian—and, I believe, a better human being—than I otherwise might have been had I never known them: Richard K. Showman, Cranston Jones, and William G. McLoughlin. They are all gone now, and I miss them.

Writing may be as lonely as Hemingway claimed. But all these kind people tend, in my case, to prove otherwise.

ILLUSTRATIONS

1. Colonel William C. Oates, March 1864

Little Round Top
2. View of Big Round Top, Gettysburg
3. Joshua Lawrence Chamberlain
4. Little Round Top
5. The Confederate attack on Little Round Top

Oates's Confederate Commanders
6. Robert E. Lee
7. Thomas J. "Stonewall" Jackson
8. Richard S. Ewell
9. James Longstreet
10. John Bell Hood
11. Evander M. Law

Home and Family
12. Exterior of William Oates's house, Abbeville, Ala.
13. Doorway, Oates's house, Abbeville
14. Interior, Oates's house, Abbeville
15. Another exterior view, Oates's house, Abbeville
16. Sarah Toney Oates ("T") on her wedding day, 1882
17. Oates in the 1880s

18. T Oates in the 1880s
19. William C. Oates, Jr., on his first birthday, 1884
20. Oates giving an outdoor speech, ca. 1894
21. T Oates, ca. 1894

Political Friends and Rivals
22. James L. Pugh
23. Reuben F. Kolb
24. John Tyler Morgan
25. Joseph Forney Johnston
26. Edmund W. Pettus
27. Booker T. Washington
28. Willie Oates, fourteen years of age
29. President William McKinley
30. Brigadier General Oates, 1898

The Last Decade
31. T in a photograph given to Willie, ca. 1900
32. Roseland, the Toney plantation house outside Eufaula, Ala., ca. 1890
33. William C. Oates, Jr., in cadet uniform, U.S. Military Academy, ca. 1900
34. Joshua L. Chamberlain in later life
35. Elihu Root, secretary of war
36. President Theodore Roosevelt
37. Rufus B. Weaver
38. Oates's grave monument, Oakwood Cemetery, Montgomery, Ala.

INTRODUCTION

In the days and weeks following the death of William C. Oates on September 9, 1910, obituaries and shorter notices of his passing appeared in major newspapers throughout his home state of Alabama, the South, and the nation. "A great figure in our history has passed," declared the Birmingham Ledger. The *Montgomery Advertiser* agreed: "Alabama loses, in the death of William C. Oates, one of its ablest and most patriotic citizens. His name is inscribed high in that list of men who made Alabama's history; it is a name that will loom larger as the years pass." In far-off California, the *Sacramento Union* called Oates "a brave leader" and "an ardent champion of the rights of the Southern people." The *Chicago Post* described him as "a constructive statesman" and a "high class public man." In the pages of the *New York Tribune*, he was remembered "as a man of independence and character, who lived up to the traditions of the old South, and was always ready to sacrifice himself to those traditions."[1]

Yet all this high praise at the time of his death did not make Oates's name loom larger in history as the twentieth century wore on. Today he is hardly remembered at all, except by Civil War students and enthusiasts who know him as the Confederate colonel who led his regiment against the very famous Joshua Lawrence Chamberlain and the 20th Maine Infantry at Little Round Top, south of Gettysburg, on July 2, 1863. His other achievements in life, his other endeavors, have mostly been forgotten. In Alabama, he was once known as "The One-Armed Hero of Henry County," and everyone understood that his heroism had been performed during the Civil War and that he had earned his first laurels as a soldier for his state and for the Confederacy. Today, Oates is still considered a hero in Henry County, down along the Chattahoochee in the southeastern portion of the state, but elsewhere in Alabama his name is rarely recognized or honored.

It's too bad that Oates is not more well know, for his life offers us a fascinating—and sometimes unsettling—portrait of Southern manhood and the dynamics of violence, heroism, and memory in the nineteenth century. Oates was a good deal more than just a Civil War colonel. As a young man, he ran away from home as a fugitive from justice, believing that he had killed a man in a brawl. A decade later he became a pillar of the community, practicing law and running a small newspaper in Abbeville, the county seat of Henry. During the Civil War, he served in more than twenty-five engagements and was wounded six times; his last wound resulted in the loss of his right arm. During Reconstruction, he resumed his law practice and turned to politics. After Alabama reentered the Union, he won election as a Bourbon Democrat to seven terms in the U.S. Congress. He served one term as governor of the state but failed to achieve his highest ambition, a seat in the U.S. Senate. In the Spanish-American War, he commanded troops as a brigadier general, although he complained about not seeing combat before the conflict came suddenly to an end. At the Alabama Constitutional Convention of 1901, he made a sincere and impassioned plea in favor of black suffrage rights. In his final years, he accepted President Theodore Roosevelt's appointment to serve as the federal commissioner to locate and mark Confederate graves throughout the Northern states.

The highlights of his career, however, do not reveal the whole man. Oates was a man of many parts, a complex individual who seemed on the surface to be simple and honest and totally uncomplicated. He could be generous, giving, and kind. When he walked into a room, heads turned, hands reached out to greet him, and people huddled around him. Yet he was a very private man, a man who struggled with a pronounced violent streak, an abusive temper, and a tendency to withdraw from those who loved him most. He strived all his life to be an honest man, but he often confused outspokenness with honesty, personal opinion with truth. Too often he justified his own dishonesty and hypocrisy as a means to fulfilling his own ambitions, for he was able, like many politicians then and now, to rationalize that the ends he personally wanted were the same ends the public should desire.

Although he was devoted to his wife and son, he often alienated them with his bullying. And while he condemned African Americans as inferior beings, he fathered a child with a black woman who may have been his slave or a paid servant. His relationships with women, including his mother, his wife, and his paramours, were complicated by Southern masculine mores and his own inability to see the women in his life as anything other than an extension of himself. He was, in his own way, a caring man—he cared deeply for his family, especially for his younger brother who died at Gettysburg, for his mother and his other siblings, and for his wife and son. In the Civil War, he cared about and provided for his men, and while many of his comrades saw him as ambitious and dangerously impetuous, it is quite evident that his troops respected him and considered him an able and honest leader. He was a generous man, sometimes taking family members under his own roof and supporting them financially for long periods of time. Oates was always a hard worker, and after the war he reaped monetary rewards for his labors that far exceeded anything he had ever anticipated. Always frugal with a dollar, he spent his money prudently but not miserly. He swore off liquor at a young age, avoided dairy products because he was allergic to them, and enjoyed nothing better than a tall, cool glass of water.

He was also courageous without being overbearing about it. Oates carried his bravery well as an inner trait and never flaunted it or tried to make it into more than it was (except, perhaps, when he was on the political stump). He loved war, hated battle, and admitted often that he had been deeply frightened by the horrors of combat on more than one occasion. Oates called himself a colonel until he achieved higher rank—a brigadier generalship—in the War with Spain, but he technically never rose above the rank of lieutenant colonel in the Confederate service, and his claim that he was about to be commissioned a brigadier general when Appomattox ended the Confederacy forever appears, on its face, to have been more pipe dream than reality. But no one ever questioned William Oates's mettle as a soldier or an officer. He was a born warrior, even though he came to know—and fear the fact—that all war is hell.

These and other numerous contradictions set him apart from his fellow Confederates and white Southerners. Although he served the Confederacy with honor, he held nothing back when it came to criticizing the South's war leaders or admitting how inglorious the war actually was. Two decades after Appomattox, when North and South began to embrace one another in the warmth of an overwhelming reconciliation sentiment that pervaded the nation, Oates spoke the rhetoric of reunion and restoration, but revealed nonetheless his own deep resentment toward the North and his steadfast unwillingness to renounce the principles of secession or even, for that matter, of slavery. He was not simply an unreconstructed Southerner. Instead, he seems to have felt a strong ambivalence toward the North. But he did not always embrace the South fondly, either, particularly when he remembered the costly blunders committed by his fellow Confederates on and off the battlefield. Oates's example, at the very least, suggests that historians might have to reconsider their conclusions about how smoothly or how lovingly the two sections reconciled their differences in the years between 1880 and 1910. In so many respects, Oates could not put the Civil War behind him after Appomattox. The war—and particularly the battle of Gettysburg—would both consume and haunt him for the rest of his life.[2]

Nevertheless, he firmly believed in Southern institutions and ideas, such as white supremacy and black inferiority. Like many other white southerners, he seemed untroubled about keeping African Americans in subservient roles while exploiting them for personal gain and even sexual pleasure. Thoroughly a xenophobe, Oates was convinced that the rise in European immigration during the last three decades of the nineteenth century threatened the nation's social order and ethnic purity. His heart was constricted by his hard attitudes toward blacks, immigrants, Northerners, Republicans, Populists, and practically anyone who was unlike him. He was, as one Alabama historian describes him, "a conservative among conservatives."[3] In many respects, that's putting it mildly.

In fact, Oates's political ambitions, his virulent racism, his pronounced sense of masculinity, his personal violent streak, and his persistent memories of the war fused together to define the contours of his world after the Civil War. Like so many other Southern men of his time, Oates sought to dominate the people around him, including the family members whom he loved and those who loved him. But he could never quite manage to dominate anyone as completely as he desired—not his alcoholic father, his clairvoyant mother, the soldiers he commanded, the young woman he married, or any of his sons, legitimate or illegitimate. Nor could he control the events that drew him in, like the swirling catastrophe of the Civil War, or the rather feckless way that happenstance often played havoc with his life. Oates hoped for victory at Gettysburg, but earned defeat and personal loss instead. In his political life, the office he wanted most—a seat in the U.S. Senate—eluded him completely and left him wondering why his greatest political desire had been denied him. Mastery was something that he sought in every sphere of his life, but it was something he could never quite attain. One of the pervasive effects of slavery was the notion, so prevalent among white men in the South, that one should—and could—achieve control over one's own life and destiny. Oates was not the only white Southerner to discover that mastery was only an insidious myth.[4]

Oates never became as important to others as he believed he should be or deserved to be. Having been raised in poverty, he later took on the pretensions of the Alabama gentry and married up to secure his social status, but he always remained rough around the edges and unimpressed by the formal code of honor that motivated the prestigious planters—cavaliers, he liked to call them—whom he otherwise tried to emulate. Nevertheless, Oates spoke the language of honor and lived according to various honorable principles that governed the behavior of white males in the South, although Oates's sense of honor tended to be brash and wild, not polished or refined. Here was a man of modest origins who assembled great wealth by the time of his death but who, despite all his achievements, never became readily accepted into the Alabama aristocracy. In that sense, his life offers us a picture of a Southerner who shared the aristocracy's ideology and world view, who regarded himself as a member of the elite, but who genuinely did not care what others might think of him.[5] In the end, his strong sense of self served him well and allowed him to venture beyond the narrow confines of his time and place. Oates was no social visionary, by any means. But toward the end of his life, his thinking began evolving, and he pondered solutions to problems—particularly racial problems—that were, for many other white Southerners, anathema.

His personal violence was one indisputable trait that he shared with the slaveholding planters. Even so, he had no qualms about confronting his adversaries with threats or fists without paying heed to the planter conventions of honor or the decorum of duels. Oates never fought a duel, but that may have been because he let his fists fly before his opponent could articulate a proper challenge. Although most of his brawling occurred during his youth, before he settled down in Abbeville in the late 1850s and became a respectable attorney and newspaper publisher, Oates could not completely control his violent streak in his more mature years. He once engaged in fisticuffs on the steps of the Alabama State House; on another occasion, he shot and killed a man who had just murdered one of his servants. For Oates, violence was a physical means of emotional expression that erupted when words failed or when he simply could not contain his anger. Like other white Southerners, Oates probably believed that violence was synonymous with power; but just the opposite was true. His violence, which was tightly intertwined with his Southern and frontier conceptions of honor, revealed his utter frustration in those moments of his life when he lacked the power to control events or the people around him. When Oates resorted to violence, including the strikingly effective and no less damaging verbal violence he sometimes used on his loved ones, he was not demonstrating his power over his victims, but his powerlessness. His violence, then, was an offshoot of his quest for mastery, but by using violence he ensured that any mastery he truly sought would ultimately elude him.[6]

To be sure, Oates was no Billy the Kid. He did not live by the gun or die by the gun. Yet precisely because of this, his brand of violence possessed a banality all its own. American violence, in its many forms, has been perpetuated by its prevalence, by its everyday occurrence, and by a widespread cultural acquiescence to its expression and effects. "What is impressive . . . about American violence," wrote Richard Hofstadter nearly thirty years ago, "is its extraordinary frequency, its sheer commonplaceness in our history, its persistence into very recent and contemporary times, and its rather abrupt contrast with our pretensions to singular national virtue." On the surface, Oates's violence can be regarded, perhaps, as fairly unexceptional in his time and place. There were men whom Oates knew who were far more violent than he ever was or ever could be. Yet violence molded him and shaped his world, not as some prosaic social force that influenced him from afar, but as a distinguishing quality of his unique personality. Even the Civil War provided him with a "legitimate" outlet for his violent streak, although the brutality and horror of the battlefield became too much for even him to bear. Significantly, violence ran through his experiences and through the heart of the nation during his lifetime.[7] Violence was something that defined who William Oates was.

His memory, though, was his greatest inner demon. Memory, wrote Oscar Wilde, is the diary each of us carries about. For William Oates, personal memory was a journal of the soul he often wished he could discard.[8] Although his memories of the war, most completely rendered in his 1905 book, *The War Between the Union and the Confederacy and Its Lost Opportunities*, revealed that the conflict had been the high point, indeed the turning point, of his life, those same memories often manifested themselves in dark recollections, shrouded and cold, of lives sadly broken and comrades forever lost, particularly his beloved brother John, who was mortally wounded at Gettysburg. Every year after 1863, William Oates dreaded July 2, the anniversary of Little Round Top, and December 24, his brother's birthday, for those two dates brought doleful reminders of how much he had actually lost in the war—and that loss, no matter how it might be measured, always seemed to outweigh whatever it was he had gained as a Confederate officer.[9]

Oates participated more buoyantly in the concoction of a patriotic and public memory that honored the Confederacy's righteous cause and its stand against Northern political domination, sectional aggression, and military invasion. While he balked at celebrating the leadership of Jefferson Davis, whom he held in extremely low regard, or mindlessly praising Lee for every order the general ever issued on the field of battle, he did become an enthusiastic believer in and promulgator of the Lost Cause and all its tenets. By doing so, he succeeded in temporarily sublimating his very worst memories of the war and substituting in their place the more glorious recollections of a mythical romantic war fought bravely by the finest sons of the South against the most rapacious devils of Yankeedom. In the end, though, the terrible memories always seeped through, like ink stains through paper, as they did so often and so poignantly in his book and in his private letters. Memory for William Oates was both public and private. But it required great energy, which he repeatedly expended, to keep the private memories from view.[10]

Memory embodies power.[11] The act of remembering involves not simply the retrieval of data from a mental file cabinet; remembering profoundly encompasses all at once the past and the present in its image of an event or a face from yesterday. The power of private memory had tremendous significance for Oates, especially when one considers how he struggled so arduously and failed so completely to gain mastery—self power—over his own life and over the world that surrounded him. In the same sense, he also failed to achieve control over his private memory. The specters of his recollections—particularly the ghost of his lost brother John at Gettysburg and the gray phantoms of his many lost comrades in the war—eventually overpowered him, and he could only succumb to private sadness.

Public memory contains power, too, and Oates learned—as did so many other white Southerners—that the past could be reshaped and manipulated to great purpose and for formidable political benefit. Out on the hustings, Oates was an effective campaigner and public speaker, and he did not hesitate to use his combat record and his empty sleeve to great political advantage. Over and over, he praised the courage of his fellow Confederate soldiers, painting their sacrifices and their devotion to duty in idyllic terms that had little to do with the realities of the war. Even at Appomattox, he wrote, his fellow soldiers "were still ready to march into the jaws of death, where the hellish din of battle drowned the shrieks of the wounded and the groans of the dying." There was nothing, he said, "for any old Rebel to be ashamed of." The soldiers of the Confederacy had "stood by their colors with unflagging courage when ruin, carnage and death reigned supreme."[12]

For Southerners, though, the war was something not to be remembered as it had been experienced; it was to be remembered as they thought it *should* have been experienced. In the collective Southern memory, the Civil War became a vivid romantic picture that artfully blended reality and myth into a *created* memory rather than a retrieved recollection. The Southern remembrance of things past emphasized the sad passing of the plantation way of life and the bravery of Confederate soldiers who had died for a noble cause—a cause fought in the name of states rights, not in the defense of slavery. Oates was a true believer when it came to the Lost Cause. From the close of the war until his death, he proclaimed the tenets of the Lost Cause with passion and faith: that the war had been caused by radical abolitionists (whom Oates identified as "puritans") who sought to impose by force, if necessary, their own sense of morality on slaveholding white Southerners (whom he called "cavaliers"); that Robert E. Lee and Thomas J. "Stonewall" Jackson were brilliant military leaders who might have achieved victory had Jackson not died, had Gettysburg been won, and had Lee's army not been overwhelmed by the superior numbers and resources of the Union army. By claiming that the war was not fought over slavery, the Lost Cause and its champions—including Oates—succeeded in suppressing African American memories of the war and its meaning. In time, the Lost Cause appealed to white Northerners as well and allowed for a sentimental reconciliation between the sections that stood on the foundations of a social amnesia—an insidious, and occasionally deliberate, forgetfulness that sought to cast into oblivion any cognizance of the Civil War as a contest over slavery, emancipation, and civil rights for African Americans. By the first decades of the twentieth century, the triumph of the Lost Cause was practically complete and perfectly astounding. Across the land,

a deafening silence kept Americans from acknowledging that race had anything at all to do with the fiery war that had claimed 620,000 lives.[13]

The Lost Cause stimulated Oates's individual memory, prompting him
to recall events and people within a context he might not otherwise have had;
it also supplied him with a validation of his memories and his interpretations
of the past. People remake their recollections to suit their present circumstances. So do societies. An individual's memories depend on interaction with
others to frame and select which episodes in the past to remember and which
to discard. As historian David Thelen has explained, personal and collective
memories work together to provide individuals with a shared identity by "iden-
tifying, exploring, and agreeing on memories." The common memories—
collective memories—are constructed by individuals who see their own
memories as matching or resembling the memories of others. In the postwar
South, the Lost Cause provided Oates and other white Southerners with a
theater of memory that allowed them to search their own individual memories in an effort to substantiate what they came to believe was the *truth* of the
Lost Cause by drawing on their recollections of experiences during the war as
evidence; in this sense, public and private memory merged for many, if not
most, white Southerners in the decades following the Civil War. Oates is a
good example of a prominent Southern figure (although he occupies a lesser
tier than, say, Jefferson Davis, Robert E. Lee, or even Nathan Bedford Forrest)
whose memories of the war were shaped to fit the ideology of the Lost Cause.
But his individual memories contributed to the shared experiences, the collective memories, that became the mythology of the Lost Cause.[14]

Not long after the war, Oates wrote a letter to Edward Porter Alexander,
Lieutenant General James Longstreet's former artillery chief in the Army of
Northern Virginia, that revealed how neatly his own personal memories already had blended with the primary elements of what would later emerge in
the South as the Lost Cause ideology. "I am one of those who do not believe
that the cause is wholly lost," Oates affirmed. "I believe that it is only stifled
by force & rests in obeyance & will again lie revived & ultimately triumph,
but perhaps in a different form. It may be clad in new habitments, but the
principles—which were truth & can never perish—will be triumphant in the
end." The "principles" to which he referred were states' rights and white
supremacy. "And now that I am fighting for the Democracy [i.e., the Democratic Party]," Oates continued, "it is but a continuation of the great conflict
with this difference: the other was for constitutional liberty as bequeathed to
the American people by Washington & his compeers, outside of the Union—
the present issue is for the same principle within it."[15] As early as 1868, Oates's
memories had become one with the Lost Cause.

Yet his memories did not necessarily sooth his soul. Like William
Tecumseh Sherman and countless other veterans, Oates was torn between
his private and public memories of the war. He could never quite decide if the

war had been horror or adventure, nightmare or lark. As a result, his writings—most tellingly in his book, *The War Between the Union and The Confederacy*—reveal both the starkness of war's brutality and the amplitude of its romance. Oates wanted all of his comrades in arms to be heroes; but when he came to writing the biographies of each man who had served in the 15th Alabama, he could not help setting the record straight by disclosing who had shirked their duty, who had let their messmates down, and who had deserted from the ranks. He did, however, usually find something good to say—sometimes sounding a flourish of trumpets with his praises to heroism—about nearly all the men in his regiment who had died of disease or in battle. His ambivalence about the war made it more difficult for him to put the conflict behind him. He liked those blaring trumpets; but the ghosts came to him far too often.[16]

Memory can also *empower* whoever is doing the remembering. Oates's book offered him the opportunity to remember the war in all its fullness—the gore and the glory, the triumphs and tragedies.[17] Perhaps it is not surprising that his book starkly reveals his profound indecision over whether the war was a great adventure or a horrible nightmare. But writing the book enabled him to face the past more directly than he otherwise might have done or, perhaps, even wanted to do. Although the war was for him, in so many respects, an endless one that had failed to close when Lee surrendered at Appomattox, the act of writing his book took him deeper into the past than any of his ruminations and memories and published articles and private letters had done thus far. He seems, in any case, to have confronted the past more honestly, more straightforwardly, more doggedly, than many of his contemporaries had done or were willing even to try. As a result, his book differs in style and content from most Civil War memoirs written by the aging veterans of the Blue and the Gray around the turn of the century. One gains the distinct impression that the book was a cathartic experience that allowed him to unleash his emotions and embrace the past, no matter how much anguish and pain might result from reliving the war yet one more time.

To be sure, his Civil War memoir is unlike any other. Oates called it "a new venture in historic production, combining regimental with general history," and so it was, except that it actually combined a history of the 15th Alabama, the regiment with which Oates saw the longest service during the war, and an account of his personal experiences in the war. There were a few chapters that amounted to a "general history" of the war, one on Lincoln, another on economic conditions in the South during the war, and some accounts of battles in the western theater and descriptions of generals he did not know personally or serve under, but mostly the book was devoted to the 15th Alabama and to his own memories of the war. To combine these elements into one, Oates needed a great deal of space, so the book is a massive tome, a magnum opus written by a man who made "no pretense to scholarly attainments" and who "lacked the advantages of a classical education."[18] The book also includes a complete roster of every soldier who served in the 15th Alabama replete with a short biographical sketch. All in all, the work offers an epic narrative that paints a candid personal portrait of the vicissitudes of war set against the broader canvas of the nation's most bloody and fiery trial. It is Oates's masterpiece, although it cannot be ranked as a literary masterpiece. His clumsy writing style severely hobbles the book's literary merits. Oates does not express himself eloquently; his prose is invariably plain, but it is also powerful and passionate. The intensity of his writing makes his book so compelling and so refreshingly different from the often stylized accounts that fill the rather abundant bookshelf of published Civil War reminiscences. More than anything else, it is Oates's distinctive voice that gives the book its literary uniqueness and its remarkable realism. Reading his words, one fairly hears the Civil War; in countless passages, Oates makes his readers *feel* like they are there beside him, experiencing the war's drama as it transpires. Like Oates himself, his book is a pure American original.

His book was not, however, a complete record of what had happened to him and his men during the war. It was not humanly possible to set down every memory of every significant—and insignificant—event that had taken place while he and his command served in the Army of Northern Virginia. In some cases, he included what he thought was important; in other instances, his memory failed him and he could not remember every particular or even every soldier's name who had marched with the 15th Alabama. To overcome his own lapses of memory, he researched events—sometimes by consulting published sources such as the *Official Records* or *Battles and Leaders of the Civil War*—and tracked down former soldiers who had served in the regiment by publishing newspaper announcements or writing to local postmasters throughout Alabama. He was diligent in making his history as complete as he could. Oates told what he knew, the things he could remember, and he refreshed his own memory by communicating with his fellow veterans. He became happily reminded of them and their personal experiences during the war by reading their letters or meeting them unexpectedly on the streets of Montgomery, the broad avenues of Eufaula, or the narrow lanes of Abbeville. As such, he created a treasure chest of memories that helped to spark the individual memories of others and forge their shared memories as Confederate veterans.

The things that Oates forgot—including the things that he could not remember, no matter how hard he tried; the things he willingly forgot; or the things he suppressed in his memory, willingly or not—were just as important (or, at least, provocatively suggestive of significance) as the things he did recall and record for posterity. This biography, however, does not systematically try to reconstruct what Oates could or would not remember; nor does it attempt to lay bare what he kept hidden in his subconscious. However, scholars should regard historical forgetfulness with as much seriousness of purpose as they do historical memory. On several occasions in his life, Oates displayed a very convenient failure of memory—a delinquency that may simply demonstrate his humanness. Yet when Oates, late in life, told Joshua Chamberlain that he did not recall having corresponded with him about the battle of Gettysburg a few years earlier, when Oates in fact had included a long account of the battle for Little Round Top in an earlier letter to the former Maine governor, there may have been forgetfulness involved or perhaps something a bit more deliberate.[19] I suspect the latter was the case.

There is no accounting for some of Oates's memory lapses, just as there is no reasonable explanation why he believed with complete certainty the testimony of a subordinate officer who claimed that Elon J. Farnsworth, a brigadier general in the cavalry corps of the Army of the Potomac, had committed suicide at Gettysburg on the afternoon of July 3, 1863. After the war, Oates spread the story of Farnsworth's alleged suicide with such effectiveness that other former Confederates took it up and claimed to have witnessed the event when they were nowhere near the scene of the Union general's death. As a result, Oates became the promulgator—if not precisely the originator—of one of the Civil War's most persistent myths, what we today might call an "urban legend." In telling and retelling this story, Oates's memory would fade in and out from one version to the next, occasionally supplying details that he would later controvert or admit were assumptions, if not outright fabrications. When faced with indisputable medical evidence that Farnsworth died from bullet wounds that could not have been self-inflicted, Oates refused to see the light and steadfastly maintained until the end of his life that the Union general had in fact killed himself.[20] In other words, he sometimes believed what he wanted to believe, and there was no convincing him otherwise, facts or no facts. But in this instance, his beliefs may have been shaped more by his commitment to honor, his own sense of manliness, and the effects of his war experiences than by whether the suicide story was actually "true" or not.

So he held on to the past, even though he sometimes held it at arm's length, for fear that it might lunge out at him and consume him. He fought rather strenuously to live in the present, and he usually succeeded. But, in the end, the past did consume him, no matter how much he tried to keep his distance from it. Even if he wanted it to, the past—the Civil War—simply would not end for him. It kept beating its drum in his mind, kept offering up scenes he preferred to forget, kept awakening him and drawing him back to its incessant reveille. There was no escaping the war, no matter how many years passed by. Or so it seemed. A few months before he died, though, he finally found the key for putting the war, and all his troubling memories, to rest. Having found it, he realized that he could at last enjoy some peace, some inner tranquility. He could never have reckoned that fulfillment—saying goodbye to his memories and finally letting them go—would result from coming to terms with the past, rather than from hurling lightning bolts of power at others and longing for utter control in his life.

For Oates, the power of violence and memory did not accomplish what he most longed for in life—mastery, control, authority, dominion. He gained some of these things—or at least he thought he did—but never to the degree that would satisfy his yearning for security, for calm, in a turbulent world. But to press the point too far is probably imprudent. Unquestionably, he did achieve a good deal of mastery in his public and private lives. His accomplishments do reveal how he often gained control over his life and shaped it to his own desires: As a young man, he decided to abandon his roguish ways and become an attorney and respected citizen; he successfully raised a company of soldiers in Henry County to serve in the Confederate army; he served as a distinguished officer in the Alabama Brigade of Lee's Army of Northern Virginia; through hard work he established a very successful and prosperous law practice after the war; he rose in local and state politics and became a skilled politician who repeatedly won reelection to office; he served with honor, despite his peaceful assignments stateside, as a brigadier general during the Spanish-American War; he took on the mantle of an elder statesman who was known for sticking to his principles; and he provided financial security and a stable household for his family. In fact, he probably succeeded in most things he set out to do, which encouraged him to think that he could attain total control with ease over *all* the different spheres in his life.

But Oates lived his life lacking a firm conception of contingency or of unexpected and unintended outcomes, what modern social scientists call the unanticipated consequences of purposive action.[21] When things did not go his way, he was often left stunned or befuddled. Nor could he ever quite understand why so many of his attempts to control others ended in failure; or worse, they wound up putting him less in control than when he had started. Twenty-five years after Gettysburg, while pondering his own arguments against giving suffrage rights to African Americans, he declared that he felt no animosity toward blacks. "I was raised among them and played with them in my childhood," he wrote. He acknowledged owning "a few when they were slaves." But then he added, with more purport than he could know, "or rather they owned me." Throughout his life, Oates repeatedly missed the fundamental truth that the German philosopher Hegel had explicated so effectively—any attempt to dominate another must ultimately end in sorry failure. In his desperate search for control and order, Oates experienced the frustration so commonly felt by Southern white men of his time and place, whether they owned slaves or not: Controlling one's self was just as difficult, and sometimes more so, than controlling others or the events that unfolded in one's world.[22]

Out of his frustration, and out of a good many other sources that lay deep inside him, Oates's anger came forth—perhaps the same kind of anger that persuades individuals to believe that their section of the country is being threatened by another or that leads men to enact secession resolutions or that convinces volunteers to take up arms against their countrymen. His anger toward the North translated easily into violence, just as it did for so many other Southerners at the time. The truculent decade of the 1850s revealed how treacherously anger, violence, and sectional animosity could flow together into a single river of ruin. This confluence of private emotion, sectional enmity, and unbridled violence was perfectly, and savagely, demonstrated by Preston Brooks when he caned Charles Sumner on the floor of the U.S. Senate in May 1856.[23] The resort to violence did not belong exclusively to Southerners, as John Brown made plain in Kansas and at Harpers Ferry before the outbreak of war between the North and South, but there seems to have been something in the Southern temperament that transformed anger rather quickly and disastrously into violence and then armed conflict. Just after the surrender of Fort Sumter, William Howard Russell, the English journalist, reported that among the Charlestonians there was "no sign of shrinking from a contest: on the contrary, the [South] Carolinians are full of eagerness to test their force in the field. 'Let them come!' is their boastful *mot d'ordre*." And while Oates never caned a U.S. Senator, he did get into at least one brawl in the Henry County Court House over the issue of secession. Often his anger, like the rage of other white Southern males, touched off a spark that exploded a powder keg within him, producing violent actions and reactions in the flash of a moment. All things considered, it is not farfetched to argue that Southern anger and violence, which the correspondent Russell described in all its "fury and animosity" in South Carolina, joined rather swiftly and tragically together in Charleston Harbor to set off the Civil War on April 12, 1861.[24]

As a man on the make, Oates always looked to the future, but he rarely could understand his present without referring to the past. For that reason, such issues as racial relations—including segregation and the disfranchisement of blacks in the 1890s—seemed in his mind to be natural policies that had grown out of old traditions, even though the uncertainties of modernity in the New South probably had more to do with the establishment of racial prohibitions after the war than had slavery or any of the antebellum presumptions of race. When faced with choices in his life, he weighed the possibilities, placed himself and his own welfare above all other concerns, and made his decisions according to his understanding of prevailing forces and defining realities. After the Civil War, his pragmatism, political talents, survival skills, and entrepreneurial vigor led him into the power halls of the rising new elite—the Democratic party leaders and the successful businessmen, many of whom began as lawyers, who eventually displaced the planter class in the New South. These "new men," as some historians have called them, were a lot like Oates. He fit in well with them and into the political and economic turbulence that became a hallmark of the South after Reconstruction. Oates rode the rising tide of the new men; for as long as he remained in agreement with them, he profited from the association, financially and politically. There was a great deal about Oates that reflected the exigencies of the "New South." He became a full-fledged member of the ruling class, despite his lack of blood connections to the old Alabama aristocratic planters and to what some in that state still refer to as "real money." After the war, and particularly after Reconstruction, he stood shoulder-to-shoulder with the white men of his state who ran things, who controlled the government, who managed the economy, who exploited others for their own gain, and who took advantage of political and economic fluidity to keep themselves on top. But, significantly and paradoxically enough, it was that very fluidity that would make William Oates ponder possibilities that, ever so briefly, ever so tentatively, would challenge the very foundations upon which the ruling elite governed the New South.[25]

These, then, were some of the contours of Oates's life—some, but not all. What makes Oates so intriguing a figure, in my estimation, are the multiple layers of his experiences as he rose from obscurity to renown. In death, though, he has become what Leon Edel, the biographer of Henry James, calls a "figure under the carpet."[26] Oates never mastered the art of self-awareness; his introspection always floated on the surface, never sinking to any significant depths in the ocean of his experience. Yet like Robert Penn Warren's Willie Stark, there was always more to William Oates than met the eye. Oates never gained the broad popularity of Warren's fictional political titan or even of the real Huey Long, upon whom Warren based the character of Stark. But given Oates's own sense of self-importance and his driving ambition, his lack of fame in our own day—even within his native state of Alabama—stands as a sad and ironic legacy. Although newspapers and periodicals across the nation took notice of his death, and predicted his lasting place in the Southern hall of heroes, he actually passed rather quickly and thoroughly from public view, almost as soon as the final volleys had been fired over his grave. In life, he had gained high status, considerable wealth, some power, a good deal of influence, and even public esteem. But he would not be widely remembered. For the most part, his story has not been told.

Oates's biography is a Southern story—as much a part of the South, in its own way, as the hard destruction of the Confederacy, the sentimental poems of Paul Hamilton Hayne, the horrid injustices of Jim Crow, the white supremacist bombasts of Theodore Gilmore Bilbo, the agonizing childhood of Richard Wright, the suffocating heat of Yoknapatawpha County, the stars falling on Alabama, and the tidewater mornings of William Styron. It is the story of how one white Southern man from the humblest of backgrounds rose to great heights but failed to achieve lasting glory or immortality. It is the story of a very ordinary man who possessed some extraordinary talents and who, despite all his best efforts, could not escape his past.

Biographies of Confederate colonels are few in number. Most of the attention is usually focused on the generals in gray of the Army of Northern Virginia who forged what Bruce Catton has called "the Confederate legend"—Robert E. Lee, Stonewall Jackson, J. E. B. Stuart, and to a much lesser extent, because of the controversy that still swirls around him, James Longstreet.[27] Recent biographies of Civil War figures also tend to concentrate on the war years and not much else. While this biography of Oates does shine a spotlight on his Civil War experiences—and particularly on his role at Gettysburg, the turning point of the Civil War and the turning point in his life—I have tried to give as much consideration to his life before and after the war as the sources allow. In that sense this is not a military biography, although the reader will find a fair amount of military history in it.

As for Confederate officers, some good modern biographies have been published for a small muster roll of Southerners who held the lower rank of colonel: E. P. Alexander, William R. J. Pegram, and John Pelham—all artillerists in Lee's Army of Northern Virginia; John S. Mosby, the famous partisan; and Henry K. Burgwyn, Jr., who commanded the 26th North Carolina and fell at Gettysburg.[28] This biography expands the roll, although some might argue that this work is as much a biography of a Southern politician, or a brigadier general in the War with Spain, or a backwoods brawler and gambler, as it is a life of a Confederate colonel.

Oates led a colorful life that contained its human share of triumphs and defeats, joys and sorrows, drama and melodrama, loves and losses. He was flawed and demanding and domineering. He was also loving, steady, and loyal. Most of all, his enthusiasm for life—his robust ebullience for the world and its pleasures, his sincere interest in people and their concerns—made him attractive to others and drew them closer to him, for they enjoyed the one great power he did possess and could readily share: the ability to live life to the fullest. If nothing else, it is easy to agree with the obituarist who approvingly summed up Oates's life by proclaiming: "He was full of pluck."[29]

Gettysburg Requiem

We used to wonder where war lived, what it was that made it so vile. And now we realize that we know where it lives, that it is inside ourselves.

—Albert Camus, 1962

1

ROUGH AND TUMBLE DAYS

The library in the house on North Ripley Street in Montgomery, behind the towering marble bulk of the Alabama State House, was ornate, garish even, and did not suit the style of a plain man. Around the room were high shelves of books that showed off the impressive shiny spines of first editions and endless leather volumes of great works. Furniture and paraphernalia filled up the rest of the room—giant urns with cat-o'-nine tails and potted plants stood near the long windows, books and papers sat stacked on the floor in piles, and American Indian art and artifacts from New Mexico and Arizona took up whatever empty spaces existed on the shelves, on the end tables, and on the floor. Near a window, through which a stream of white light poured into the room, there was a large partner's desk of oak, and seated at the desk was a huge man with white hair, a full white moustache, and no right arm. The man was writing with his left hand, and he was fully engrossed in his work.[1]

William C. Oates was trying to set down his life story for his son—or so he said. The year was around 1902. His son, William, Jr. (called Willie), was nearing twenty, and Oates felt it was time for the young man to understand what his father had seen in the world, how he had come to live his life, and what he had accomplished so far. He wrote the story out in longhand, every page of it, and it almost seemed as if the autobiography were writing itself. Oates's devotion to detail suggests that his purpose went beyond the memoirist's standard device of writing for one's offspring. With great determination to recover his past, to conjure up memories before they could be totally forgotten, Oates seemed to be writing his autobiography for himself.

"When I am dead," Oates wrote in the introduction to his life's story, "I want my son . . . to know at least the outlines of my career—my successes and failures—my mistakes and correct conduct, my good deeds and bad ones that he may profit by following in my good example and be happy by avoiding my errors." But he also hoped that others would read his autobiography and learn from it. "The young people who read it," he said, "will find, not in the style of writing, but in my course through life[,] food for reflection." For inspiration, he drew on the models of Benjamin Franklin's autobiography, which the sage of Philadelphia had ostensibly composed for *his* son, David Crockett's memoirs, and Joseph Glover Baldwin's comic picture of frontier life, *The Flush Times of Alabama and Mississippi*. In a sentence he purposely phrased to sound like a kernel of Franklin's own wisdom, he declared that "the habit of telling the truth, the naked truth, which is truth without any fringe of imagination or fiction[,] will soon become so firmly implanted in the mind that an invasion by the arch evils of the truth—exaggeration, prevarication, lying—are not apt to enter."[2]

Stirring the ashes of his memory, he found some of them still smoldering and some barely glowing. Through all the smoky haze and hurry of his prodigious life, he had been known in fact to remember his own birthday imperfectly, sometimes getting the day and year completely wrong, but now, sitting in his quiet library, his mind drifting back over the years, he managed to set down the date of his birth with clarity and precision. William Calvin Oates was born—as he noted with care—on November 30, 1833, in Pike County, Alabama.[3] It was a momentous year, not only because of his entry into the world, but because of an astronomical event that happened two weeks before his birth. For three days a meteor shower over North America lighted up the skies with shooting stars and balls of fire, probably as many as 10,000 an hour. The phenomenon was particularly visible over the Southern states, and slaves came to refer to the event as "the year (or night) the stars fell." Many blacks would later mark their own birth dates specifically as having occurred either before or after the meteor storm. The event in some places sparked religious revivals among both black and white Christians, especially in the South.[4]

In the immediate aftermath of these falling stars, Oates was born to parents who had little time or opportunity to gaze at the heavens, even when the sky was all ablaze. Oates's father, also named William, was an industrious but poor farmer who put down stakes out in the middle of nowhere on a high plateau that proved to be a challenge for growing cotton or, for that matter, just about anything else. The elder Oates, whose parents came to America from Wales before the Revolutionary War, grew up in South Carolina and moved to Alabama in his twenties. He was a pure product of the Carolina backcountry rather than the genteel society of its coastline. Once, in a fight, he broke a man's skull with a stick, spent time in jail, and stood trial for his crime (he was acquitted).

After the death in fairly rapid succession of two young wives, he moved to Pike County in February 1833 and married the petite Sarah Sellars. The pretty young woman, a North Carolina native, had a civilizing effect on the man—most of the time. She could read and write very well. Oates's father could only read an almanac and, when he had to, a Bible, which he opened infrequently in his younger days. He could barely sign his name.

In time, as the family grew, William Oates Senior found it more and more difficult to make ends meet. Sarah Oates gave birth to eight children, four boys and four girls, although not all of them survived to adulthood. As the eldest child in this large family, which resembled so many other families on the frontier that required the labor and productivity of their children just to survive, William Junior carried the heaviest load of responsibility. In his own words, he later said that he had been raised "to plow and hoe and do other farm labor." His father worked hard and tried his best, but he could never quite provide all that the family needed. Yet, in the son's opinion, his father had deeply loved his wife and children. The man's only fault, said William, was his hair-trigger temper.[5]

The senior Oates, as it turned out, was a very violent man. "When he became angry," his son remembered, "it was a word and a blow[,] and sometimes the latter came first." His rage, which would manifest itself without warning, was exacerbated by his alcoholism. More than once William was caught pouring the bottle dry (with the intention of filling it with vinegar), and his father punished him severely with floggings that the boy never forgot.[6]

In Oates's world, home was not the only place where violence could be found. It was part of the atmosphere, part of life in every cabin, part of the woods and meadows in the wiregrass country, where men did not think twice about punching, biting, stabbing, and shooting for the most minor offense—or for no offense at all. Oates was raised, in fact, in a rough-and-tumble hinterland. In the mid-1830s, Pike County in Alabama was still an untamed frontier, which meant that it existed mostly on the fringes of law and order, and that its inhabitants usually had to find their own way to conquer whatever might be threatening their lives and livelihoods.[7]

Every day they confronted great uncertainty and danger. Deep in the backwoods, where the thick pines and cedars made daylight look like moonglow, the settlers got by on what little they could grow themselves and whatever fortune came their way, good or bad. Usually they worked a few acres of land, growing corn and root vegetables with a few rows of cotton and tobacco. In most cases, they owned only a meager number of livestock—a milch cow, some razorback hogs, and maybe a lean horse. To bring in food for themselves and their families, the men hunted and trapped game in the piney woods. Despite their poor circumstances, these frontier families some-times owned one or more slaves who would help till the soil, round up the livestock, or perform domestic duties for their masters.

The white men on the Alabama frontier lived from one day to the next, many of them drunk or useless; others, like the senior William Oates, scratched out a living from the land but never really succeeded at it and certainly never prospered. It was a crude society, one that developed its own rules and mores and conventions. The men told tall tales to prove their manhood and hide their inability to control their own lives. Life was hardest on the women and children. Many died young. Sometimes diseases swept through the little com-munities and cut down old and young, the frail and the feeble. It was a hard, hammer-pounding-granite kind of existence.[8]

Life was precarious. One black night, when all had been quiet and still around the crossroads and everyone had begun to fall asleep, a rider pounded suddenly down the road and galloped past the Oates cabin in a cloud of dust, sounding the alarm that two men had been killed by Indians at Union Springs, just a few miles to the north. Not only the Oates household but every family in the immediate vicinity poured out of their homesteads and into the dirt road, shouting, screaming, and wailing in their plight. They evacuated Oates's Crossroads, hiding in the woods a few miles from the settlement. Oates's father lifted young William up in his arms and grabbed a gun in his other hand; his mother bundled up and carried away Oates's infant brother, John—the only two children in the family at the time. In the morning, when it was clear the danger had passed, the families returned to their homes. Fifteen or twenty men—Oates's father among them—rode north to find the Indian cul-prits. What they found instead were the two dead white men at Union Springs. The Indians had vanished without a trace.

The raid had occurred in the waning weeks of a conflict called the Creek War of 1836, a series of small engagements that ended tragically, though predictably, for the Indians. One of the several tribes in the southeast that had been ordered to remove themselves from their land and resettle in Indian Territory beyond the Mississippi River, the Creeks resisted efforts made by the federal government and the surrounding state governments to relocate them by force. Although Oates, a lad of four, did not actually witness the raid that dark night in Pike County, he did get to see the panic that ensued in the community from just the news that Indians had struck nearby.

Such a memorable tumult remained vivid for Oates even as an old man. Even though the community of Oates's Crossroads generally lived in har-mony, with the local settlers relying on one another to ensure their collective survival, Oates tended to remember the upheavals—like the Creek Indian raid or tavern free-for-alls—that divided the settlement, created boisterous turmoil, and left one with the impression that life was constantly uncertain. Commenting on his youth, and on the unpredictable and perilous nature of frontier life, Oates wrote that he "often wondered how I was any account when I recall the soundings of my youth."[9] Although this sounded like a statement of humility, Oates really meant that but for his frontier childhood, with all its uncertainty and violence, his life might well have turned out differently. What Oates wanted the readers of his autobiography to understand—and to believe unquestioningly—is that he overcame great odds, soared over great hurdles, to become an important and worthy man in his adulthood. In many respects, he was right; he did rise above his humble origins. But in other respects, in aspects of his life and character that he could not readily perceive or understand, he would always remain a pure product of the frontier.

Danger and hardship were not all he ever knew in his youth. Like most boys, Oates spent a good deal of his time romping through the countryside, over cotton fields and wooded hills and bubbling streams, with a gaggle of friends and his closest companion, his younger brother John. William and his brother were inseparable. They played together, they worked together, they went nearly everywhere together. Only two years separated them in age, so the boys felt more like playmates than brothers. The younger brother was the spitting image of William, only smaller in size, and they might have passed for twins. John looked up to his older brother, adoring him for his mighty abilities and wanting to emulate him in all things. In return, William felt a special closeness to John, a protective big-brother affection that made the younger boy feel safe and that gave William a noble purpose in life. "No brothers loved each other better," remembered William as an older man.[10]

Along with their good friend, Barnett "Bud" Cody, the boys played in the same ways that most country boys do: hiking through the woods, wading through the creeks, fishing, hunting, exploring, and getting into mischief. "My daily business when not at work," said Oates, "was shooting snakes with a little shot gun." Sometimes William and John would wander over to the crossroads, where the local characters—tinhorn gamblers, horse racers, and "whisky suckers"—assembled daily to spin yarns and lie about their achievements in life. "Brother John and myself were greatly amused," Oates recalled, "as country boys naturally would be at the rich, rare and comical sayings and doings of that crowd." William received praise from his mother for his truthfulness, but he actually had developed great talents as a liar; the other boys always chose him to come up with the most plausible lie they could offer up to their parents as an explanation for their misbehavior.

On Sundays, Oates and his friends would frequently pretend to be born-again Christians enraptured at a revival meeting (a game that young Cody, the minister's son, must have felt particularly at home with). William Oates would be cast in the role of the preacher, cajoling the assembled crowd and condemning them for their sins, while his friends feigned all the body gyrations—the moving and the shaking—that had become associated with camp meetings along the frontier during the Second Great Awakening, a religious revival that spread like wildfire through the backwoods of the South in the first few decades of the nineteenth century. Even when William and John played by themselves, the camp meeting game became a favorite activity under the shade of the trees near their father's "humble cottage" or in a grove deep in the woods, where without inhibition they could mimic the prayers and sermons of the stump preachers.

Acting the part of a minister was in stark contrast to Oates's favorite child-hood activity—"playing at Cards." At a young age, he became an adept gam-bler, often hustling his young friends out of prized possessions like toys and pocket knives. His mother never knew of his sinful behavior (or so he thought). She always trusted and believed him; as he grew older, he felt some deep pangs of guilt for having purposely taken advantage of her faith in him.[11] To a great degree, these feelings remained with him, long into his maturity. His burden of guilt defined his dealings with women for the rest of his life, so much so that he would conscientiously avoid—either by will or circumstance—enter-ing into a lasting relationship with another woman during the first four decades of his life. The separate spheres assigned to men and women in nineteenth-century America, and particularly in the South, where men placed women on a pedestal, allowed Oates to deal with women on his own terms without getting overly involved or romantically entangled with them. Only once, while he was still in his teens, did he claim to have fallen in love with a woman, but the relationship was ended when he discovered she had been unfaithful to him.

His relationship with his mother rested on more than guilt, however. "A better woman never lived," he said of her. She had little schooling, but she was extremely intelligent and well read. Pious in her devotion to God and to the Baptist faith, Oates's mother regarded the Bible as the greatest of all books. She had an incredible memory, said Oates, and it seemed as if "she never forgot anything." Her even temper helped to calm the senior Oates when he went on his rampages, and her intervention saved the children from larger doses of the father's violent hand. And yet there are vague hints that Oates was more afraid of his mother than he was even of his violent father. Perhaps she smothered him with affection; perhaps, despite her temperate and loving manner, she was overly controlling or manipulative. There is no doubt that Oates loved his motherly deeply and sincerely. But the rest of his life revealed his inability to deal with women without dominating them—perhaps as he wished he could have done with his mother.

Bolstered by her Christian faith, she also had a gift that occasionally brought her into the realm of the angels: she was, as Oates called her, "a prophetess," someone who possessed "second sight" and who saw "visions." She could see things that others could not, could feel forces that others could not sense, and could experience the supernatural in ways that mystified her family and her neighbors. Oates was convinced his mother was a clairvoyant, even though he rejected claims by others—including itinerant mediums and spirit communicators who gained public notoriety during the Spiritualism that emerged in America during the late 1840s and 1850s—of special occult powers or endowments. In Oates's opinion, his mother's inexplicable spiritualistic talents only made her more remarkable, more wonderful. Remembering her in later years, he wrote: "No boy, no man, ever loved his mother more dearly or tenderly than I loved mine."[12] But he must have always wondered if she could actually look straight into his heart and see the truth that lay hidden inside. If she could, or if he *thought* she could, the realization must have unnerved him.

As he grew older and entered his teens, he turned his attention to the young women who lived in the vicinity of Oates's Crossroads, the frontier community of scattered cabins and hardscrabble farms in Pike County named for his father. These young neighbors often seemed as magical to him as his mother, though it was their feminine charms, not Christian spiritualism, that mesmerized him.[13] Even at a young age, he was extremely comfortable with women. He learned quickly how to talk to members of the opposite sex and how to use his own charms on them. In his teenage years, he developed an eye for the ladies—a trait he took pride in for the rest of his life. He was rather boastful of the fact that he liked women as much as he did and that they liked him back. In one of his fondest memories, he recalled the dances of his youth that shook the shingles on his neighbors' dogtrot cabins out in the wiregrass country. At those dances, he learned how to flirt with women and, quite simply, how to have fun with them.

Tall in stature, robust in build, with thick black hair and mysteriously gleaming dark eyes, Oates won the hearts of ladies wherever he went. They thought him handsome (or so he himself claimed), but there was also a quality about him, an air of danger and recklessness, that made many women cast longing glances in his direction and swoon in his presence. Something about him—the boldness of an adventurer, perhaps, or the swagger of a pirate—attracted women to him. There was a look of defiance about him, to be sure, but that was not all. One could also see ruthlessness in those Cimmerian eyes.

He was a favorite partner at the dances held around Oates's Crossroads. At one dance, he "kicked up" with a slender, red-headed, freckled-faced girl of about seventeen years named Polly Hart. Quite pleased with himself, Oates rambled across the dance floor with Polly, who was "as spry and leaped as gracefully as a young deer." But as the dance went on and on, Oates began to tire from the back steps and double shuffles, and he caught his toe in a crack in the floorboards, although he managed to keep his balance all the while. Everyone there laughed at his clumsiness, and his awkward behavior was embarrassing enough to stay in his memory—and for him to replay it in his mind—many long years after his pratfall occurred.[14]

On other occasions, Oates showed that he could be more sure footed. He had learned to stand on his own two feet at a very early age and not under the best of circumstances. In later life, he made much of the fact that he came from such a poor background and equally humble surroundings. Indeed, his lack of formal education was a sore point with him. When Oates was working for his father and for the family, he and his brother John attended school infrequently with their friends. He liked school, understandably preferring it to the endless chores that faced him at home, but he never became a very good student. His teachers relied almost exclusively on recitation and repetition to instruct their students. Inside the schoolhouse, said Oates, the result was "a perfect babel of sounds and voices, and everyone had to be loud or he could not hear himself."

To control the students, most of his instructors relied on a hickory switch, which they did not spare. The violence of the frontier spilled through the chinks in the log walls of the schoolhouse near Oates's Crossroads, just as it spilled into the lives of everyone who lived there, and the teachers doled out punishments for breaches of decorum as well as failure to know one's lessons at recitation time. In response to a teacher who had beat him, Oates, by now a strapping boy of fifteen, once loaded a gun and waited for the right chance to shoot his instructor. He never did, but it was not the last time Oates wanted to kill a man.[15]

Like the effects of a fire or flood, violence—the force that seemed to be a very part of the nature of the frontier and of Oates's world—set the young man on an unintended path. On evening, in the autumn of 1850, his father got drunk and unruly, and he took all of his rage out on William, whipping the boy for some unrecorded offense. When his father finished the flogging, Oates told him that would be the last time "any man would ever whip me." Oates packed his things, which could not have amounted to much, and moved out of his father's cabin. Looking for any work he could find, he hired himself out to neighbors and worked as a laborer on their farms. He used his meager savings to pay his tuition to a three-months' school during the following summer. In the winter, after his father turned penitent and his mother begged him to come home, Oates moved back with his family but paid his own keep by organizing a little school of his own, a class for very young children who had never attended school before.

Violence, however, kept getting in his way. In March 1851, he got into a fight with a fellow named Crauswell, "a great old bully," who thrashed Oates "pretty badly," but did not, according to Oates's own definition of the term, "whip" him. "I had it in me for years afterwards to kill him," Oates admitted many long years after the episode, "but I never got a chance." A few months after being assaulted by Crauswell, Oates attended a seance at the cabin of a neighbor named Post, whose daughter claimed to be a spiritual medium. She communicated with the dead by asking them specific questions; in answer to the questions, the spirits would make the table rise and let it fall to the floor with a rap. Oates, always the prankster, leaned on the table during the seance with his two hands and made it descend without much effort, pointing out as he did so that the girl was a fraud. The girl's father ordered Oates off his property and picked up a board to make sure the young man obeyed. A fight broke out, Post came at him wielding a board, and Oates defended himself with a hoe and struck the man in the head. Post went down with a fractured skull, and Oates believed he had killed him. The man's wife and daughters came running out of the cabin, screaming and waving their arms hysterically. From this maelstrom of confusion and flying accusations, Oates retreated to his family's cabin at the crossroads, where he told his parents about the incident. Then he stuffed some of his possessions into saddle pouches, got his three-year-old pony ready for travel, and took off into the night.[16]

He followed the roads that fugitive slaves frequently used in their flights to Florida, where they would end up living in the everglades with the Seminole Indians. Through a blur of haunting images and nightmares of the dead Post and his bloody wound, Oates headed south to his uncle's house in an adjoining county. Despite his familiarity with violence, the young Oates was nervous and frightened. Shortly after his arrival, his father showed up and informed him that Post was not dead, although he was still under a doctor's care for his brutal head wound, and the sheriff had issued a warrant for Oates's arrest. On foot, Oates headed for the warmer—and, he assumed, safer—climes of Florida.

After failing to make much money selling cigars and painting houses in Milton, Florida, Oates traveled on to Pensacola, a fine old Southern town where swaying palm trees lined the streets. He signed on for one month with a schooner that plied the Gulf of Mexico. More than any other experience in his life, his time as a sailor taught him the meaning of hard work. Out on the rough waters of the Gulf, with the tiny schooner being tossed like a cork from one giant wave to the next, Oates put up with a brutish first mate, a mean captain, and the drudgery and loneliness of being at sea. His only friend on board, he said, "was a big long negro." They took their meals together, sharing their food in a single tin pan. At night, when the Gulf winds blew a bone-chilling cold, they also shared a blanket and slept together to keep from freezing. In his later years, Oates remembered his dark-skinned shipmate fondly, without any apparent tinges of the racial prejudice that held white Americans—and especially white Southerners—so tightly in its grip (and that, in later life, would become so manifest in his pronouncements about slavery and blacks). Like so many of his fellow white Southerners, his opinion of African Americans was extremely complex, occasionally contradictory, and notably ambivalent. On one hand, he regarded them as honest, hard-working

people who regularly demonstrated their own sense of responsibility and trust-
worthiness. On the other hand, he saw them as biologically inferior beings
who required close supervision, stringent control, and incessant tutelage.
Either way, he expected them to be obedient and submissive. To demonstrate
his sincere concern for their care and welfare, Oates offered African Americans his paternalistic attitudes about their need for superintendence and their
inability to enjoy the fruits of freedom. Paternalism, in fact, made Oates's
ambivalence possible, for it enabled him to comprehend blacks in completely
racial terms while it also allowed him to praise, with an air of condescension,
their hard labor and their contributions to the Southern economy. Even in
his youth, when he could not possibly have owned any slaves himself, his
racial attitudes resembled those found pervasively among the planter
slaveholders. Out on the wave-tossed schooner, though, Oates's racial ambivalence became subservient to his need for friendship and his longing to
stay warm.

After three trips out on the stormy waters of the gulf, he quit the schooner and gave up a sailor's life for good, telling his captain and the mate that if
they would care to go ashore with him, he would give them the whipping
they deserved. They declined the offer. Back in Pensacola, he made some
money, got a hotel room, and then became deathly ill with yellow fever. The
sickness made him weak and listless, and he felt like "all my bones would
break." An old sailor and ship's carpenter named Lawton took Oates home
with him and cared for him with the help of his wife and two sons. Oates's
fever raged for five days, and at one point he slipped into such a deep uncon-
sciousness that his caretakers thought he was dead. They called in a doctor,
who began daily visits, and Oates slowly started feeling better. Unfortunately
Lawton himself caught the fever and lay on a pallet all day cursing old "yellow jack." Sometimes, rolling in a foggy delirium, Lawton would scream out:
"Jesus Christ and Andrew Jackson, two of the greatest men who ever lived!"
Eventually both men recovered.[17]

As winter came blowing in over the gray Gulf waters, Oates made his way
to Mobile Bay, where he was more impressed with the beauty of the Spanish
and Creole ladies there than he was with the shimmering harbor and its fleets
of schooners. From Mobile, he continued his journey aboard a steamer to
New Orleans, a city he called "Frenchy" and filthy, although he thought the
French Market a wonderful place that was "well worth seeing." Unable to
find a job in the Crescent City, he headed north on a Red River steamboat for
Shreveport.

Trouble followed him like a shadow. Oates met a young woman aboard
the steamboat that brought him to Shreveport, and they carried on a love
affair until her father, a slave stealer, interrupted them one night while trying
to hide from a local posse. Oates's romantic interlude ended abruptly, the
woman's father was taken by the posse into the night, and Oates slipped back

to town with the hope that he could stay out of trouble. He found work straight off as a house painter, a trade he could now claim as his own, but when he wasn't paid the wages owed him, he attacked his employer, holding the man's throat in a vise hold with his left hand while hitting him in the face eight or nine times with his right fist. One of Oates's friends finally intervened before Oates could kill the man. The next morning, Oates learned that a warrant had been issued for his arrest, so he ducked out of Shreveport and headed to Texas. Like so many other Alabamians who had pulled up stakes in their home state and moved to Texas (including Oates's personal hero, William Barret Travis, who had died within the adobe walls of the Alamo in 1836), Oates slung his carpetbag over his shoulder and headed toward the western horizon, where neither the Alabama nor the Louisiana authorities could get their hands on him.[18]

After walking twenty miles a day in the Texas heat, he came to a place called Marshall, a boom town that seemed to be growing almost daily, with buildings going up everywhere and people jamming the dusty streets from morning to night. With all the construction going on, and wood and brick houses popping up like daffodils in springtime, Oates had no trouble finding a job as a house painter and a carpenter. He stayed five months in Marshall, where, as he recalled, "I became much addicted to gaming at cards." His departure from the town, predictably enough, was precipitated by a fight he picked with a fellow worker who insulted him.

Still traveling on foot, he headed toward Nacogdoches County, where he successfully located several of his cousins, the children of his father's brother, Wyatt, who had set out for Texas a few years before but had only gotten as far as Grandico, Natchitoches Parish, Louisiana.[19] There Wyatt Oates and most of his family were struck down by cholera. The surviving children were taken to Texas by the family's slave, who raised the little ones and tried to control the older ones. It was from this branch of the family, perhaps at first through correspondence and later in person, that Oates must have first heard stories about Travis and the brave Alamo defenders. The eldest of the Texas Oates clan was also named William—"Bill" Oates—and he took a liking to his Alabama cousin almost immediately. When Oates left Nacogdoches, his cousin Bill tagged along, much to Oates's displeasure. His cousin, he said, complained all the time: His feet hurt, his baggage weighed too much, he wanted to rest. "He was," groaned Oates, "a spoiled child."[20]

Through the scrubby flatlands of Texas and westward across the Trinity River, the two cousins made their way to Waco, a small village of three or four stores, an inferior hotel, two or three bar rooms, some gambling houses, and, a faro bank—a place where the card game of faro is exclusively played. After a Texas Ranger was gunned down in the streets, the Oates cousins decided that

Waco was not the town for them, but before they could leave, William Oates stumbled into an encounter with one Dr. Baldwin, who took offense at something Oates said and held a gun to his head. Oates escaped with his life, but he went back to his hotel determined to get his own gun and blow the doctor's head off. He finally cooled down, though, and decided to "pocket the insult" rather than to wind up dead in the streets of Waco, like the ranger he and Cousin Bill had seen murdered. Later that night he learned that Dr. Baldwin was a gambler who had previously killed three men and went around town "half crazy" on morphine most of the time.

Eventually the two cousins found themselves in prosperous Port Lavaca on the blue waters of Matagorda Bay. By this time, though, Cousin Bill had had enough. He announced it was time for him to go home, and Oates was not sorry to see him leave. In Port Lavaca, Oates fell in love with a young woman, a redhead with a beautiful smile, and seriously considered marrying her until he caught her in the arms of another man. It was this betrayal that may have wounded him so deeply and kept him from falling in love with another woman until he had reached his late forties. By avoiding romantic involvement (although he certainly did not curtail his sexual adventures), he spurned one facet of manhood—courtship and marriage—that Southern white males regarded as a safe haven for their emotions. At the same time, he also could not live out his dreams through the admiration of a submissive and sympathetic fiance or wife as most Southern white men either did or expected to do as they gained a public reputation and assembled their personal fortunes. Oates's unrequited love affair, in other words, sent him down a different road than most other Southern men followed in search of their manhood. His road would be shaped by ambition, a trait he shared with other Southern men, but it would also become defined by his frustrated attempts to achieve mastery over the different spheres in his life.[21]

Heartbroken in Port Lavaca, he resumed his travels across the broad state of Texas until he found himself in Henderson, Texas, about forty miles north of Nacogdoches. While he was walking the streets looking for work, he saw a familiar face—almost his own mirror image—heading toward him. It was, of all people, John Oates, his adoring younger brother, who had traveled from Alabama to find William and bring him home. John's own perseverance and his youthful optimism had enabled him to maintain his quest through the dusty state of Texas until he succeeded in his goal. Embracing his brother on the street in Henderson, William Oates decided it was time to go home.[22]

Back in Alabama, Oates hid in his father's house because a warrant was still pending for his arrest. In a couple of weeks, he moved to Henry County, in the Chattahoochee River basin, where he was determined to make a new start and where he knew he was beyond the reach of the Pike County authorities. He enrolled in an academy in Lawrenceville, a small village of fifteen or twenty families located a few miles north of Abbeville. Having discarded old habits, he was now a good student and learned quickly, but he was mortified at having to sit in class with all the younger boys. He became a good student of English, could read Latin well, and advanced in mathematics and geometry.

At the age of twenty, he attempted to assume a more dignified demeanor and to pursue more respectable goals. Writing a few years later, he observed: "I have already learned the difficulties to be encountered in eradicating vicious and licentious habits contracted in youth, and in securing harmonious action of the moral and intellectual faculties principally by endeavoring to produce such effects in my own character." He vowed not to let his own "natural talents" go uncultivated or allow them to dissipate.[23]

He kept that vow by studying law. When he was an old man looking back over the years, he claimed it was his experience in a debating society at the Lawrenceville Academy that convinced him to become a lawyer.[24] But his choice of a career was probably more complicated than that. Taking up the law as a profession put him worlds apart from his father's occupation. It was the thing that could truly distance him from his sordid past.

In a sense, the law was a perfect profession for him. Having more than once fled from its clutches, he would now embrace the law as his own, take up its mantle as a personal crusade, and strive to find truth and justice for every one of his clients. Idealistic and ambitious, he thought striving for pure principle made perfect sense—not in a quixotic way, but as something tangible he could wrestle with and bring to the ground. He liked quoting Shakespeare about the place truth should occupy in the heart of every individual: "This above all: to thine own self be true; and it must follow, as the night the day, thou canst not then be false to any man."[25]

A thick cloud of dust flew into the air on the Clayton road as a stagecoach sped into Eufaula, a prosperous town of two-storied virgin pine and red brick buildings along a wide main street situated on a high bluff above the Chattahoochee River. In the center of town, which thrived from the cotton trade, Oates stepped out of the coach and walked to Mrs. Barrett's boarding house, a respected establishment known for the high caliber of its tenants. Oates was embarking on a new phase of his life, a new beginning.

On the day after his arrival, sometime during the autumn of 1856 or 1857, Oates went to the law offices of Pugh, Bullock and Buford, which he later claimed was the most prominent firm in town and in all of southeastern Alabama. He was probably right. James L. Pugh, the senior partner, was born in Georgia but spent his childhood in Pike County, living poorly and learning how to do without. Like Oates, he had experienced some sort of epiphany that led him to overcome his youthful indiscretions, find the desire to improve himself, and pay his way through school by delivering mail. Someone once said of Pugh that he was "the most emphatic man" he had ever met. By the early 1840s, Pugh had established himself as a distinguished lawyer.[26] Under the guidance of Pugh, Bullock and Buford, Oates would learn the profession of law, and he would also get his earliest training in the art of Southern politics.

Using his considerable charm and sharp wits, Oates fell in with these formidable attorneys and won their respect. He particularly enjoyed Pugh's blustery style, and the two became lifelong political allies, but he singled out Edward Bullock to be his mentor. Bullock, whose family came from Rhode Island before moving first to South Carolina and then to Alabama, graduated from Harvard College in 1843. He set up his law practice in Eufaula, where he also edited a newspaper. Oates called him a genius, "a man of superb ability, geniality and wit." A young man in his early thirties, Bullock was known for his formidable bursts of profanity, but Oates said he was the only man he ever knew who could swear without offending. One day, said Oates, the local Presbyterian minister saluted Bullock on the street and asked how he was faring. "Parson," Bullock answered, "mentally, physically and morally, I am remarkably well, but financially I am off Cape Hatteras in a hell of a gale."[27]

Oates received his earliest tutorials in politics from these ambitious attorneys. In the late 1840s, Pugh had supported Zachary Taylor, the Whig candidate from Virginia who handily won the presidency. But as the political controversy over slavery heated up between North and South—made even more fiery by the Compromise of 1850, the resistance of Northern antislavery activists to a new Fugitive Slave Law, and the passage of the Kansas-Nebraska Act by Congress that ignited a civil war between proslavery and antislavery settlers in Kansas—Pugh increasingly became a Southern extremist in his political attitudes, eventually embracing the views of Senator John C. Calhoun, the South Carolinian who forcefully defended the institution of slavery against all its assailants and who advocated secession if the North tried in any way to circumscribe the peculiar institution. When Calhoun died in 1850, Pugh threw his support first to Franklin Pierce and later to James Buchanan, two Northern Democrats who showed a pronounced sympathy for the South during their respective presidential administrations.

When Oates began his law training, Pugh and his partners were already key players in a faction known as the Eufaula Regency, a group of states' rights Whigs who believed in Calhoun's brand of southern nationalism, the protection of the slave institution against federal interference, and the expansion of slavery into western territories. Although Whig in background and anti-Jacksonian in its stance, the Eufaula Regency had decidedly Democratic leanings. Over time, as the sectional dispute between North and South worsened, members of the Regency became outright secessionists; in Alabama, they were the most vocal faction in favor of secession throughout the 1850s. Among the Regency's most famous supporters was the Alabama fire-eater, William Lowndes Yancey.

It was in Eufaula, in the law offices of Pugh and his partners, that Oates met models of the man he wished to become; it was there that he learned from watching the examples before him how white Southern men—professional Southern men unlike his uneducated and rough father—were expected to hide their emotions and develop an outward appearance, a mode of expression, a style *and* a substance, that made their private persona indistinguishable from their public one. Such an amalgamation of stifled emotions and pronounced outward masculinity became easily manifested in the arena of politics. In the South, politics was a manly and noble calling—the one place where passion could be openly demonstrated without fear of ridicule. Politics also allowed some Southern men to fulfill the manly trait of ambition—the desire to make something of oneself, to contribute to the advancement of one's family, the betterment of one's community, and the protection of one's region. While spending his days reading Blackstone's *Commentaries* and watching Pugh and his two partners in flamboyant action, both inside and outside of the courtroom, Oates gained an invaluable education in how to be a Southern man.

Oates had found himself three very capable teachers. All of them were politically active and equally committed to promoting the Southern cause through political means. Pugh himself had run for Congress in the late 1840s, although he lost the race despite Yancey's direct involvement in the campaign. In 1857, Bullock ran for the state senate and won. But the most politically active—and the most fiery—man in the law firm was its eldest partner, Jefferson Buford, whom many considered the real leader of the Eufaula Regency. Buford was another South Carolinian who had come to Eufaula after living in the primitive backcountry of Pike County. The people of southeastern Alabama respected him as an attorney but considered him too eccentric to be a truly effective politician. Nevertheless, he and his fellow members of the Eufaula Regency gained considerable political ground during the sectional crisis of the 1850s.

Buford saw in the actions of the North a pattern of discrimination against the South and its way of life. He became convinced that the United States contained "two separate, dissimilar and hostile systems of civilization"—one in the South, where racial distinctions and control prevailed, and the other in the North, where excessive democracy was reaching toward "communism and agrarianism." In time, mainline Democrats, such as John Cochran, John Gill Shorter, and Eli S. Shorter, joined with Buford and the Eufaula Regency and embraced its Calhounite ideology.

But Buford was not content with mere political action that resisted the policies of the North. During the political controversy that raged over "Bleeding" Kansas in the mid-1850s, Buford led an ill-fated expedition of Alabamians to that territory to rescue it from antislavery "jayhawkers." But the antislavery majority prevailed and Buford's expeditionary force disbanded when his attempts to raise support in Washington for Kansas proslavery colonists failed. Buford returned to Eufaula disappointed and almost penniless—he had spent his own fortune financing the futile expedition. His failure in Kansas did not improve Buford's feelings toward Northerners.[28]

Oates worked hard under the guidance of these able and influential lawyers. He put his every effort into grounding himself in the legal profession, and he often studied sixteen hours a day during the week and ten hours on Sundays. His diligence ultimately paid off. On a dark night in October 1858, he appeared at the Barbour County Court House in Clayton and survived the grilling of a committee of lawyers who had been appointed to administer his bar examination. The questioning lasted two hours. When the examination was over, Judge Dougherty of the circuit court proclaimed to the other committee members: "Gentlemen, the young man has undoubtedly stood the best examination I ever witnessed; give him his license."

With license in hand, Oates went to Abbeville, the seat of Henry County, about twenty-five miles south of Eufaula, and opened his practice around the first of December. A short time later, Oates joined in a partnership with William A. Clark, who had been one of his teachers at the Lawrenceville Academy. The firm of Oates and Clark did not thrive. At best, Oates remembered, the two lawyers only ever did "a starving business." To supplement his income, Oates bought a weekly newspaper, the *Abbeville Banner*, from a local minister, and took over as publisher and editor.[29]

Business for his law practice improved, perhaps as a result of his higher profile in the community that came with owning the newspaper, and the local sheriff began to throw clients his way. His first case involved a dispute between a husband and wife over some hogs. Oates represented the wife and won the case before a justice of the peace. If a woman was a party in a lawsuit, Oates always tried to take her side—because, he said, women "are usually right." Reflecting the dynamics of male patriarchal assumptions, which were even more pronounced in the South than in other regions of the country, Oates was voicing an opinion widely held by most men. In male eyes, women were weak, emotional, irrational, and vulnerable. Men stood at the top of a natural social hierarchy as lords and masters; in the South, this hierarchy included slavery as well as gender relations. The same pyramid hierarchy, in fact, was mirrored throughout the Southern institutions of politics and family life. The rich, white man occupied the apex of the pyramid; others—including women, children, yeoman white farmers, other laboring whites, poor whites, and black slaves—took up their rightful places beneath him and obeyed his patriarchal authority in all matters. Men were to offer women security, comfort, and protection. Women, in return, displayed subservience and admitted to their weaknesses. Or at least in men's minds that was how things were supposed to work. Yet women had a way of asserting their belief that they were actually stronger than men, especially when it came to bearing up under the strains of emotional turmoil or other kinds of crises. During the 1850s, when Oates began his law practice and decided that he preferred female clients, Southern women had already begun to express more audibly their discontent with the prevailing patriarchy.

Nevertheless, Oates's preference reflected how thoroughly patriarchal ideas pervaded Southern society and influenced male behavior. He liked to take women's legal cases not only because he was an irrepressible roué, which he most assuredly was, but also because female clients gave him the opportunity to offer his male protection to them, letting him play out the expected masculine and patriarchal role through a business, rather than a personal or romantic, relationship. By those means, Oates managed to steer clear of romances and marriages while still operating in a manly—and patriarchal—manner. In fact, Oates enjoyed taking care of women more than entering into meaningful relationships with them. For Oates, care and protection constituted the extent of a meaningful relationship with most of the significant women in his life, including his mother (after his father died and left her a widow), his sisters, the mother of his illegitimate children, and his wife. After providing for their comfort, he could not quite comprehend what else was—or should be—expected of him. Without fail, he was always proud of the way that he provided for the women who meant the most to him.[30]

Most of his concentration, though, was focused on the law. He kept his practice going on his own until late in 1860, when his brother, John, became his partner in the firm of Oates and Oates. It was William's example that had led John to study law and, rather predictably, follow in his older brother's footsteps. William was glad to have him in the business. John, he said, was "very bright and popular," and it is likely the younger brother attracted his own clients and helped to expand the firm's business.[31]

Even as grown men, the two brothers closely resembled one another. Like his older brother, John had black hair, dark eyes, and devilishly good looks. Both young men were brawny: broad in the shoulders, wide through their chests, narrow in the hips, and solid in their stances. Although William stood six-feet-two-inches tall, John was some five inches shorter. Perhaps that was why John always seemed set on never letting William get too far ahead of him—or get the better of him, if he could help it.

John was the quieter of the two. His older brother, who in their youth had taken the part of preacher in their revival mockeries, bellowed with a deep voice and could be deafening. Withdrawn to the point of retiring, John often kept his own counsel, spoke less frequently than his brother, and seemed to be holding back quite a bit behind his brooding eyes. There are hints that John was his mother's favorite among her sons. Some clues point to the fact that he might have been sickly as child and needed his mother's closer care and attention. Later, during the war, their mother worried more about John and focused her thoughts on his welfare rather than on William's, if the admittedly sparse evidence is any reliable indication of how she responded to their soldiering. Perhaps she knew that William could take care of himself. Or perhaps her preference for John was one of the wounds that shaped William's reticulate relationship with her. Despite John's own independent streak, a trait that ran in the family, he never refused the brotherly protection that William always offered him, whether he needed it or not.

One talent did make John the better of his brother. He could write more felicitously, with more grace and style, than William could, and the words seemed to flow smoothly on the page whenever he took pen in hand. He may have had the benefits of more schooling than William ever had, especially during those years when William was fleeing from the law and roaming through muddy gulf ports and dingy Texas towns. All in all, John also seems to have been the better speaker in public. He was a man of decidedly fewer words than his brother, but John's presentations in the court room were clear and concise and dignified, without the boisterous pyrotechnics that his brother favored. People tended to take him a bit more seriously than they did William, despite the older brother's significant and serious accomplishments.[32]

With his star on the rise, William Oates took a keen interest in politics and the worsening sectional controversy, and his newspaper gave him a voice in Henry County that sounded his political beliefs in the most public way possible. His rise to professional status enabled him to achieve respectability in his community, but it did not diminish his pugnacious tendencies. Oates was not afraid to speak his mind, even on the issue of secession, which was beginning to set the nation on fire.

As sectional passions flared between North and South during the late 1850s, many Southerners called for secession from the Union, but the movement gained little ground until John Brown's raid on Harpers Ferry in October 1859. Brown's raid put the fear of slave insurrection into the heart of nearly every slaveowner and convinced disbelievers of the radical, militaristic intentions of Northerners. Southerners increasingly assumed that anyone who took a stand against slavery, including vocal leaders of the Republican Party like Abraham Lincoln and William Henry Seward, wanted to eradicate the peculiar institution by force, just as Brown had planned to do.

Many Southerners, including Oates, rejected the overt radicalism of the fire-eating secessionists like William Lowndes Yancey and preferred the "National Democrats" faction, headed by James L. Orr of South Carolina. Although he rejected the Southern extremists, Oates's political views began to carry weight in his community. In 1860, he attracted the attention of Democratic leaders in southeastern Alabama, and they managed to win him a seat in the state Democratic convention that year. In the presidential election of 1860, Oates publicly gave strong support to John C. Breckinridge of Kentucky, a states' rights extremist who had been nominated by an anti-Douglas element

in the Southern Democratic Party on the election platform of protecting slavery in the territories with a federal slave code. The Breckinridge faction,
which harbored a good number of secession proponents, tried to lure mainstream Democrats into its ranks by spreading outrageous stories throughout
the South of impending slave revolts and subversive plots being masterminded
by Northern secret agents. Its success was extraordinary—enough so that the
Breckinridge Democrats eventually led Alabama to secession.[33]

It is doubtful that Oates argued against secession in his newspaper, although his neighbors in Abbeville branded him an opponent to secession
probably because he was unwilling to embrace the idea of immediate withdrawal from the Union. As a conservative, Oates wanted the Southern states
to proceed with care and great deliberation; but as a die-hard Southerner,
Oates defended the constitutional right of secession for the rest of his life.
The argument over secession brought more than heated debate. General
Alexander C. Gordon, who had been stolen by Indians as a boy and had been
given the name "Crazy Bear," led the local political attack against Oates, but
the young lawyer deftly parried and lunged, finally labeling the general an
outright liar in print. In the Abbeville Court House one day, as Oates presented a case before the registrar in chancery, General Gordon came storming into the courtroom, leaped over the bar, and brought Oates down to the
floor. The two men rolled around and struggled with one another, but the
result of the fight was inconclusive. According to Oates, they "carried pistols
for each other" thereafter and refused to speak to one another for three or
four years.[34]

Like many other Southerners, including George Fitzhugh, the famous
antebellum apologist for slavery and the Southern way of life, Oates believed
that the root cause of secession lay in the hands of fanatical Northern "Puritans" who habitually put "their noses into the business of other people"—and
had done so since the days of the Pilgrims in Massachusetts—by denouncing
slavery as the sum total of all villainy. If Northerners had left the institution
of slavery alone, if they had not "pretended that it was a great moral wrong,"
if they had not encouraged lawlessness in Kansas by "Puritan" radicals like
John Brown, then the South would not have been forced to exercise its legal
and sovereign right—guaranteed, in Oates's opinion, under the Ninth and
Tenth Amendments of the U.S. Constitution—to quit the Union and form
its own confederation. When the Northern states elected Abraham Lincoln,
Southerners, in Oates's opinion, recognized a "common danger": that "their
ancient and well-defined right to govern and regulate their own internal and
domestic affairs in their own way would be overturned and denied to them."[35]

But secession also represented something more to Oates and many other
Southern white men. The eruption of open political conflict between North
and South, the emergence of the market economy dominated by the North,
the success of the Republican Party and particularly Lincoln's election to the

presidency, the apparent loss of Southern power and influence in the halls of Congress—all these factors, which fire-eaters emphasized over and over again in their strident speeches, convinced Oates and others like him that national politics had become corrupted by the loss of virtue, that old republican ideal so cherished by America's revolutionary generation. To remain in the Union meant polluting the South's politics and degenerating into the same morass of self-interest that seemed to motivate Northerners and their scheming politicians. Honor demanded that Southerners maintain their independence from such corrupting elements. But just as the relationship between masters and slaves in Southern society ultimately revealed not only how slaves were dependent upon their masters but, more significantly, how masters were dependent on their slaves, so too was there an inherent paradox in the nature of Southern politics—a paradox that prized the independence of the region's statesmen while, at the same time, depriving those statesmen of any real independence because of their constituents' specific political demands. Virtue and honor became elusive, but Southerners came to believe that they could reclaim those attributes for themselves by freeing their states and regions of the evil of Northern corruption that threatened to leak southward. Thus, these Southerners thought, their statesmen might achieve true independence by separating their states from the Union. Secession, in that respect, was not a victory of Southern partisan politics; it was an action taken in desperate response to the failure of party politics.

Party politics, in Oates's opinion, had badly served the South. The split in the Democratic Party during the campaign of 1860 ensured the fact that "slavery was doomed." What's more, state politicians, particularly Governor John Anthony, had demonstrated a pronounced lack of statesmanship in the Alabama Secession Convention by letting his "ill temper" take charge and by "losing his head" to such an extent that the extremists, led by the more capable Yancey, won the day. None of this seemed to Oates, or to many white Southerners, how the politics of virtue and honor were supposed to work. Indeed, events proved rather conclusively to many that an infection of corruption had spread throughout the South and that Southerners had better perform a drastic procedure—the surgery of secession—to cut off the cancer before its malignancy poisoned everything. To succumb to the North meant that the South must sacrifice its honor; sacrificing its honor meant that the South would be dominated by the North; the result would turn Southerners into slaves under the complete control of Northern masters. It is not difficult to see how this syllogism made Southerners, even moderates like Oates, embrace secession rather than give up their liberties and become what they most despised within their own midst—slaves. The intent of the North was plain, said Oates. It hoped to convert the federation of states into a strong centralized national government "with power to govern the States by force." Oates knew the effects of violence and force very well; so did every white Southern man, whether he owned slaves or not. Coercion was something that was applied to slaves, not to free Americans. As a result, secession was the only way for white Southerners to avoid being placed in bondage by the North.[36]

For as much as Oates complained about the failure of politics and the divisiveness found in the Alabama Convention, the political act of secession achieved a unity throughout the South that had otherwise eluded the region for decades. Such unity—or, more precisely, the illusion of unity that came in the immediate aftermath of the secession of the Deep South states—reinforced the belief that the South was justified in breaking away from the North and gave a sense of relief to white Southerners that Northern corruption had been successfully averted. Even though Oates wanted his state to approach the issue of secession with caution, he had no patience with Unionists and did not see the need for defending his own support for secession in Alabama. Those who opposed secession, he said, hid behind the cloak of "the old flag." Once the South had decided on its course of action, said Oates, it was necessary to make the peaceful separation from the North complete by forming a confederated government to protect the sovereign rights of the Southern states. In his estimation, secession upheld a strict interpretation of the Constitution of the United States. He saw no irony in stating this openly.[37]

After Lincoln's election, Oates wholeheartedly supported secession; he believed that caution and deliberation were no longer necessary. So, too, did other Breckinridge Democrats. As he joined the ranks of the growing secession movement in Alabama, he found himself carried along by an energetic tide of youthful political activists. Throughout the South, but particularly in Alabama and the other Deep South states, secessionists were represented by "young wealth"—a rising elite already distinguished by its accumulation of money and property. "Cooperationists," those who sought a compromise solution with the North and expressed strong Unionist sentiments, came from an older generation of political leaders, many of whom had been born in the Upper South before migrating to such states as Alabama and Mississippi. At twenty-eight, with his professional activities as an attorney and a newspaper publisher earning him money and prestige in Abbeville, Oates could feel right at home with other secessionists from around the state who were also in their twenties and thirties. These young men, like youthful males everywhere, felt that they had something to prove and wanted to make their mark in the world. They were ambitious, and their ambition fit well into the patriarchal society that rewarded men for assertiveness and leadership. Although Oates did not condemn the cooperationists, and he even suggested that their policy might have been "wise," citing Virginia's cautious deliberation over the question of disunion, he nevertheless praised the young men in Alabama who, like himself, wanted to "secede before breakfast," for it was these men—though hampered to some degree by their impulsiveness and "hot-headed" temperaments—who were "good and true" and who took up "the laboring oar." These were the movers and shakers, without whom, said Oates, the secession movement would have collapsed.[38]

On December 20, 1860, South Carolina passed its ordinances of secession, and in quick order six other Southern states, including Alabama, followed the Palmetto state out of the union. Oates fully supported Alabama's secession ordinance, and years later he published the document in its entirety in his memoirs, as if to enshrine its wisdom and validity. Criticizing Lincoln and other Northerners who claimed that secession jeopardized the survival of the United States, Oates believed that the Southern states had not destroyed the Union. All they wanted, said Oates, was "peaceable separation"—something Lincoln was unprepared to let them have. Like other Southern politicians, Oates regarded the secession of the South as both a revolution and a conservative response to the Northern threat aimed against Southern liberties and states' rights. He interpreted secession in terms of how he understood the American Revolution to have been a "conservative" revolution. Yet he denied vehemently that Southerners had engaged in rebellion or were themselves "rebels." His argument was repeated by a good number of other Southerners who cried out for "revolution" and "conservatism" in the same breath.

In separating themselves from the Union, the Southern states succeeded in carrying out a revolution of sorts, yet they also worked ardently to retain and buttress the political society—the patriarchal republic—that had existed throughout the antebellum period. Secession brought about what might appear at first to be a rather peculiar contradiction: The political structure of the Southern states would be preserved intact because the secession revolution was actually a revolt to maintain the established order. But the contradiction was seen by Southerners as no contradiction at all. Secession was not a rebellion, as Oates so thoroughly agreed, for it sought to preserve and stabilize the South's patriarchal society, protect slavery, and rid the region of the threatening political corruption of the North. But those goals could only be achieved by reconciling the political tension that existed between the South's slaveholding political leaders and the majority of voters who owned no slaves. What might have otherwise been a revolutionary response to the North became, in Oates's estimation, a conservative reaction to defend liberty—something that whites who owned slaves and those who didn't held equally dear. Southerners, he declared, "have always claimed that secession was not rebellion, but a peaceable means of withdrawing from the Union under the reserved powers of each State." Pointing to one of the consensual assumptions that enabled the obvious divisions between slaveholders and nonslaveholders to be overlooked in the secession crisis and that brought various contending factions into agreement throughout the South, Oates tellingly referred to secession as "the natural inclination of mankind to adhere to old institutions." Oates saw the secession of the South as the first step in the creation of a new nation.[39]

Like many Americans at the time, Oates oversimplified the causes of disunion and the events that brought on war, but he did understand that slavery was at the core of the crisis of the Union. As a loyal Southerner, he blamed the North for precipitating the struggle over slavery and argued that the South should have been left alone to deal with the peculiar institution as it saw fit. He claimed in later life—at a time when his political and social prestige would have been enhanced by such an assertion—that he had owned a few slaves before the war, although there are no hints in his papers or in any records that he actually did. Whether he did or not, he must have had an extensive familiarity with slavery in his own considerable routine dealings with black people. Although Pike and Henry counties were not counted among the thriving "black belt" of Alabama's cotton lands, at least a quarter of the population in the southeastern portion of the state was comprised of African Americans in the 1830s; by 1860, nearly thirty percent of the population in Henry County was black. Out of 4,454 African Americans residing in Henry County in 1860, only 21 of them were free.[40]

For the most part, though, Oates was brought up without taking slaves or black people into much account. He accepted and took for granted that African Americans existed on the bottom rung of the South's social ladder, which is where he felt they belonged. To a great degree, Oates was so unquestioning about what he considered to be the natural order of things that he didn't pay much attention to black people one way or another, which is not to say that slavery had no effect on him or did not shape his world. Slavery influenced Oates profoundly, made its mark on him as a man and as a Southerner, determined how he viewed the world and his own place in it, just as it did so many other whites throughout the region, all of whom—whether slaveowners or not—seemed just as willing to rush to the defense of slavery and secession as Oates had been. Even though they owned few slaves or none at all and had little direct contact, if any, with the slave economy of the South, Oates and other whites from the poor wiregrass section of Alabama did have a common bond with the middle-class and wealthy slaveholders of the South: They were, quite simply, white.

Just as significantly, Oates was also a man, which in the patriarchal society of the antebellum South meant that he enjoyed a distinctive status as "master"—the ultimate authority figure—shared among planters, professionals, and yeomen alike. In the hierarchical pyramid of the Southern social structure, white males stood at the top, although those who owned slaves possessed a higher status than those who didn't, which is precisely why Oates may have claimed after the war that he, too, had been a slaveholder. All white men, however, were equally invested in the patriarchal structure that pervaded society, politics, religion, and slavery. The strands of white male authority in the public and private spheres were so tightly woven that yeomen farmers with few or no slaves readily lent their support to the fire-eaters and aristocratic

planters who sought to protect the institution of slavery from Northern interference. White men found themselves too heavily invested in the existing
social structure to voice any serious challenges to it. That included challenges
to the prevailing ideas about race and slavery.[41]

Oates was solidly a man of his time and place. He was fond of black people
(so he said) and could, as he did while sailing aboard the gulf schooner in his
youth, befriend them and treat them kindly. But there was, in his own mind,
a great divide that separated white from black. Negro inferiority was a cor-
nerstone of the social order through the South, and it allowed white people
to conclude—without much effort and with a good deal of relief—that they
were better than any slave because their skin was not black. Oates regarded
slavery as a benign institution, one in which masters, for the most part, provided all they could for their slaves and in return received loyalty and affection for their kindness. Looking back on slavery from the vantage point of his
later years, Oates wrote: "While denied education and intellectual improve-
ment of the schoolmaster, because [such things were] inconsistent with their
state or condition, yet they [the slaves] were cared for in sickness, housed and
fed, and made more comfortable than a majority of them have been as freedmen, save the one consolation which freedom bestows." His view of African
Americans, like that of so many white Southerners, rested on a paternalistic
air of superiority.

Yet Southern society was not a classic "herrenvolk" or racial "democracy" that drew whites together as the "master" race and pitted them against
blacks, slave or free. Various gradations of freedom and unfreedom, equality
and inequality, and persistent class, gender, and racial issues made the South
a turbulent sea of patriarchal republicanism that was hardly egalitarian or
democratic in its multiple dimensions. Power more than race shaped white
Southerners' understanding of why one man was a master and another a slave,
just as whites in the South understood that only a man could be head of a
household, while women and children (and black slaves) always occupied lesser
stations beneath him. To Oates and other Southerners, these relations of
domination and subordination—so intricately blended in the public and private spheres of life throughout the South—reproduced the "natural" order of
things, which were dictated not only by the forces of nature but by God himself. Inequality, in other words, was a natural thing. As for blacks, Oates firmly
opposed the "enforced equality of an inferior race." His attitude toward
women, whether white or black, relatives or paramours, differed little from
his views on African Americans. How Oates understood the role of women and
blacks—who occupied key subordinate places in the patriarchal hierarchy—
depended fully on how he grasped his own masculine role, his manly independence, and the virile authority he wielded over dependents and inferiors.
It was crucial to men like Oates to keep blacks, women, and disenfranchised
whites in their place, or else he might have to face the possibility of the exist-

ing structure of authority being unraveled or toppled from below. The foundation of patriarchal hierarchy and Southern republicanism had to be sustained. The very definition of manhood depended on it.[42]

Like many Southerners, including the prominent sons of Virginia, Thomas Jefferson and Robert E. Lee, Oates said he detested the slave institution, for "no man by the law of Nature had the right to own or control the labor of another, except for a just compensation." In Oates's opinion, however, compensation for their labor and their condition had been given to the slaves, not as individuals but as a race. African Americans would never have found their way "into the sunlight of civilization," he wrote, "except through the institution of slavery." Oates was living at the center of the American paradox: Liberty could only be maintained for whites so long as blacks remained in bondage. In explaining many years later why Southerners fought so desperately for the Confederate cause, he said: "We fought in the same spirit of our Revolutionary sires who bought with their precious blood the liberties we all now enjoy." Oates ostentatiously used the rhetoric of democracy throughout his entire political career, incessantly speaking about freedom and liberty and rights. Beneath the surface, though, he feared democracy because it, too, might dislocate the existing social and political structure of the South. In his words Oates professed to be a true democrat; but in his heart democracy frightened him, as it did many Southern power holders. Like other Southerners who supported secession, like other power brokers in the region, Oates did not crusade for equality, white or black. He may have sincerely believed that the South seceded and fought a bloody war to preserve its liberties. But in the end Oates wanted those liberties reserved to the white men on top who, in his opinion, deserved them the most. Most assuredly, those same liberties could not be extended to unworthy whites or to women or to blacks who were, as Oates put it so bluntly, only beginning to see the sunlight of civilization.[43]

2

BAPTISM BY FIRE

Rebellion swept through the South like a hurricane. Denouncing Unionists, who hid their Southern loyalty behind the old flag, William Oates looked on approvingly as the Confederate government organized itself in Montgomery, Alabama. He even traveled north to the capital city from Abbeville to see the Provisional Congress, which was composed of delegates from all the seceded states, assembled for the first time on February 4, 1861. He stayed on in the city to witness Jefferson Davis's inauguration as provisional president some two weeks later. Oates considered Davis "a great man in many respects." But he did not think he was up to the task of running a country. He believed that Davis might have made a good president in peacetime. But the Confederate leader, in Oates's opinion, "was not equal to the exigencies of the great office he held in a revolution." Oates thought Davis should have kept the bureaucracy in Richmond small, taken greater care in the appointment of generals, and placed the welfare of the nation's soldiers first. Instead, said Oates, Davis blundered his way through the war. The Confederacy needed a Napoleon or a Frederick the Great. It got Jefferson Davis instead.[1]

Despite his enthusiasm for the new Confederacy, Oates did not rush out after the surrender of Fort Sumter and Davis's subsequent call for volunteers in April 1861 to enlist in any of the numerous militia companies that began popping up throughout the South like blossoming rows of spring tulips. His younger brother John did, however. For once, John did not wait for William to take the lead. Setting aside any concerns about the fate of the Oates law firm, John enlisted for a year's service in May 1861 as a private in the Henry Grays, a company raised in Abbeville.

John Oates soon learned that soldiering was not what he thought it would be. His company, under the command of Captain Alexander C. Gordon (the lawyer with whom William Oates had tussled in the Abbeville court house), was mustered into the Confederate military as Company A of the 6th Alabama regiment. John endured the hardships of army life and managed during the first few months of the war to avoid contracting the deadly illnesses—such as measles, mumps, and typhoid—that savagely reduced the ranks of the Confederate army even before its regiments saw combat. The 6th Alabama was a rough outfit: Men wearing coonskin caps served along side officers smartly dressed in green coats. John and his comrades missed seeing any fighting at the battle of Manassas (called Bull Run in the North) on July 21, 1861. The regiment stood ready, not far from the banks of Bull Run creek, but it never received orders to advance against the enemy. After the battle, the 6th Alabama settled down into the routine—and supreme boredom—of camp life.[2]

Meanwhile, William delayed making a decision about whether to enlist or not. He wrote a friend saying he was anxious to go but did not want to do so if it meant giving up his business entirely. Within several weeks, he had changed his mind. He tried raising a company to serve for twelve months, but failed to get support from the governor. By the end of July, he successfully worked out the details for enlisting a three-month company with Governor Andrew B. Moore. He had no difficulty convincing the men of Henry County and the surrounding region to volunteer. An outpouring of wild patriotism swept through the South, and Henry County proved to be no exception. In July of 1861, Oates and his neighbors felt the heat of summer and the fires of zeal. Boys all over the South were volunteering to go fight the Yankees, and the spirits of the young men in Henry County were flying high with war fever and dreams of glory. "It was not a question who would go," remembered one recruit who would later stand in line to be mustered into Oates's company, "but who would stay . . . to take care of the home folks."[3]

Word of the Confederate victory at Manassas made the boys of Henry County even more eager to serve and see "a wild Yank" for themselves. It looked as if the Confederacy would win its independence with one or two more swift blows. Many feared that if they did not enlist soon, they would miss the fight altogether without getting "to smell gunpowder much less burn any," as one young Henry County volunteer put it. Others thought the war was already over, but they wanted to join the army anyway, just for fun.

On July 24, just three days after the Manassas battle, Oates gathered together his volunteers, and the little town of Abbeville overflowed with patriotic sentiment and high hopes. Youngsters calling themselves "Secessionists" strutted about, proudly displaying badges of red, white, and blue pinned to their chests. Oates's company was to be named the Henry Pioneers, although they were not the first volunteers from the county to march off to war. They would not be the last, either.

Most of the men who joined the Henry Pioneers were farmers, and some were as young as fifteen. Of the 121 men who enlisted in Oates's company, 5 were 40 years old; 1 was 49 years old; only 13 men were married. Dressed in their faded jeans and their old field hats, they formed up in front of the Abbeville court house and tried to act like soldiers even though most of them had no inkling how a soldier should behave. Oates joined the cause and took up the sword because he passionately wanted to see the Confederacy become its own nation among the nations of the world. His support of the Confederacy, his belief in the necessity of war to achieve Southern independence, and his willingness to fight personally for Southern rights were all sharp-edged components in his fierce devotion to Southern nationalism; as such, his ideas and feelings matched those of countless other Southerners who expressed similar sentiments and who were willing to give their lives for their new nation. The recruits in the Henry Pioneers enlisted for a variety of reasons, including a fervent nationalism that resembled Oates's own zeal, dreams of glory, peer pressure, a desire to impress young women, yearnings to escape from home, a hankering for adventure, and a youthful curiosity about the world that existed beyond the borders of Henry County. Patriotism and ideology formed core beliefs that inflamed Southern passions and, not incidentally, ignited a desire for a violent reckoning with their Northern foes. A strong Southern sense of duty and honor stimulated enlistments as well, although a commitment to honor may have been less powerful than other factors proved to be in attracting Henry County's farm boys, clerks, and laborers to war. Honor, however, certainly motivated the officers of the company, including Oates, who regarded Northern aggression as a test of Southern honor and who, as a scrambling professional hoping someday to achieve the higher status of a gentleman planter, took on the attributes—including duty and honor—that he associated with the ruling elites. But it was ideology that, for the most part, sent these young men off to war. Oates and his comrades in the Henry Pioneers all professed a willingness to give up their lives for the sake of their new country, for Southern rights, for independence, and, most significantly and ironically, for liberty.

But like other Southern recruits, these enthusiastic volunteers had yet another reason to join Oates's company and fight Yankees. A pervasive fear that the North threatened white supremacy in the South compelled these young men to sign their names to the muster sheets of the Henry Pioneers. Even without owning slaves themselves, they worried about the preservation of their region's racial equilibrium and about the radical ideas of Northerners, like Abraham Lincoln and other "black abolitionists," that might topple the slave society they knew so well. At stake was not only whites maintaining control over blacks and slaves, but the fundamental ordering of Southern society and its political economy. Southerners, Alabamians, and the young men of the Henry Pioneers were afraid that unless they fought against Northern aggression and domination, they would be subjugated. With subjugation, Northern "radicals" and African Americans and perhaps even women would be on top, white men on the bottom.

In the South's complex society, which consisted of various interpersonal relations of domination and subordination, the threat of any new layers of power—worse still, *Northern* power wielded over Southern interests—or a revolutionary change in the social structure that placed subordinates, including blacks, on any level higher than even the lowliest white man was simply too unthinkable to imagine. Subordinates must be kept in their place. The young white men of the South could not abide the prospect that if they did not fight in this war they might become subordinate to someone—Yankees, African Americans, women, or *anyone*—who was not already their superior. Their racial views, then, were bound up far more in an overwhelming acceptance of Southern notions of patriarchy than in any shared herrenvolk ideology that promoted white supremacy among differing classes throughout the region in an egalitarian battle against Northern racial hegemony. More than race, more than the fear of white slavery imposed by radical Northerners, more than any fear of the political enslavement of Southerners by Yankee abolitionists and mudsills, white Southerners—including the young white men of the Henry Pioneers who came from all classes and stations in Alabama society—mostly feared the loss of their male independence and the abrogation of their patriarchal mastery over their present subordinates within the South's fixed and solidly defined society.[4]

So they assembled into orderly ranks as best they could in the shadow of the Abbeville court house. Among the young men and the teenaged boys in the Henry Pioneers were Bud Cody, the young, well-educated son of a Baptist minister who had known the Oates family since his boyhood and who had decided to quit school and join the army, and William A. McClendon (called Gus by his friends), eighteen years old, a young farmer who itched to get into the war and whose sunny disposition made him fond of the tune "Bonnie Blue Flag" and belied his stern advocacy of secession, states rights, and the good "old South." Both Cody and McClendon were convinced that the men of the Henry Pioneers would be "tough stuff" and "hard to drive" on the battlefield. To the ladies of Abbeville, who had made a special flag for the Henry Pioneers, Oates delivered an "eloquent and patriotic" speech, assuring them that the men of the company would live up to the trust that had been placed in them.[5]

On July 25, the company received orders to report to Fort Mitchell, an old fortification on the Chattahoochee River that had been constructed during the Creek Indian war of 1813. Two days later, Oates assembled his men, got them into column as best he could, and marched them out of town on the road to Franklin, where the company would get river transport to Fort Mitchell. The crowds waved Bonnie Blue flags and cheered as the men passed by. Gus McClendon's father told his son to stay safe and then, amid all the noise and excitement, turned to Oates and said: "Captain Oates, take care of my boy."[6]

On the way upriver by steamboat, Oates decided to hold an election for company officers. To no one's surprise, including his own, the men "proclaimed" him captain; he was not actually "elected," he explained years later, because he already had been recognized by common consent as the leader of the company, having raised it in the first place.[7] After purchasing uniforms for his men with his own money, Oates took pride in the new bright red shirts and gray paints that each member of the company wore. The men called themselves "the Red Shirted boys from Henry," and it felt like they were getting steadily closer to becoming real soldiers as their journey north progressed.[8]

At Fort Mitchell, where a few dilapidated buildings still stood, Oates and his men settled into the routine of camp life. Nine other companies had arrived from around the state, and the open fields, surrounded by lush shade trees, were lined with orderly rows of white tents. Every morning the men awoke to reveille; every evening they participated in dress parade and "tattoo." Many of the soldiers thought that war was a very agreeable thing—or at least that's what they remembered thinking during these early quiet days of the conflict. "We would sit around our camp fires at night, tell old tales, sing old songs, box, wrestle, run, and jump, turn somersaults, pat and dance, and do everything imaginable for fun and frolic," remembered Gus McClendon.[9]

For Oates, the days at Fort Mitchell seemed less than golden or serene. He disagreed vehemently with the decisions made at the fort about the organization of the 15th Alabama regiment, the state unit to which the Henry Pioneers and the other companies had been assigned. The 15th had been the brainchild of Colonel James Cantey, a dashing lawyer and planter with a generous handlebar moustache and a distinguished salt-and-pepper goatee. He looked the part of a perfect Southern officer and gentleman. Cantey knew more about legal codes and cotton than he did about military affairs, although he had seen action as a captain and had been wounded in the Mexican War. Although Cantey would prove to be a fine officer, Oates declared that he did not like the man. He thought the colonel lacked the ability to organize the troops under his command simply and fairly.

It was certainly true that the command structure for the 15th Alabama had come about in a peculiar manner. Through some shady manipulations, Cantey had managed to elevate three captains—Alexander A. Lowther, Isaac B. Feagin, and William N. Richardson—to company command with seniority over the regiment's other captains, including Oates. Oates suspected favoritism and especially resented Cantey's preferential treatment of Lowther. In a lottery held to assign companies, Oates chose the letter "G," and the Henry Pioneers would henceforth be known as Company G, 15th Alabama. The letter designation placed Oates low on the seniority list, but he kept his outrage to himself— a rare moment of restraint that he would later regret. To his credit, though, Oates said that Cantey's unorthodox organization of the 15th Alabama was partly the fault of the company captains themselves—"we all acquiesced in it and thereby waived the right to subsequently object."[10]

After spending less than a week at Fort Mitchell, the men of the 15th Alabama packed up their belongings and boarded a train for Richmond. "We were going to the war at last," said a private in Oates's company with gushing enthusiasm. But in Richmond, the war still seemed very far away. The regiment spent its time marching and drilling in a mosquito-infested camp overlooking the James River, later the site of Chimborazo Hospital. Every night the mosquitoes descended on the camp in great, thick clouds. "Talk about the plagues of Egypt!" one soldier wrote. "I will compromise for any amount of frogs or locusts, and take fleas by way of variety, but defend me from mosquitoes."

Before the end of August, the 15th Alabama received orders to move to Manassas, where the bulk of the Confederate army held the ground along the grassy swales above Bull Run creek. On August 18, the regiment left Richmond by train, after listening to a dull speech by Jefferson Davis and a more rousing one by John Gill Shorter, the governor-elect of Alabama. All along the way to northern Virginia, young girls cheered as the troop train flew down the tracks.[11]

Oates and his men eventually set up camp at a barren place called Pageland, about five miles from Manassas Junction and two miles west of the Bull Run battlefield. Soon the fields and meadows, usually bright with the yellow and white wildflowers that dotted the Virginia landscape in the latter days of August, became studded instead with row after row of canvas tents.[12] Some of the men in the 15th Alabama had already begun to think of themselves as true soldiers, even though they had yet to glimpse any enemy troops or encounter the realities of battle. "Tell all of those boys that went back home to get in the band box and stay in there until the war is over," Private G. E. Spencer wrote to a friend in Alabama, "and then we will come and take good care of them." Other men acknowledged that drudgery dominated their lives, but they believed nonetheless that discipline and hard work could have their rewards. As one soldier wrote, they were developing "a hardihood and robustness" that prepared them well for "the arduous marches, the great privations, the scanty rations[,] and the threadbare clothing and equipment that resulted as the war progressed." But he was more comprehending than most soldiers. Oates's Alabamians still had no real idea what they had gotten themselves into.

Many of the men blamed their captain for making things tough. A few soldiers, for instance, considered Oates too aggressive and ambitious for his and their own good, though they seemed to recognize that his sometimes stern and distant demeanor simply reflected qualities that most officers were supposed to have. A good many people in Abbeville had predicted that Oates would turn out to be tyrant. They thought his desire for promotion would carry him away and put the lives of his command in jeopardy. Others saw him as too imperious to lead men effectively into battle. Still others simply dismissed him as having no apparent military abilities or experience.

He surprised them all. Showing great concern and kindness for his men, Oates taught them how to march, how to follow orders, and how to behave on the battlefield. He admitted he was strict with his men "when on duty," but otherwise allowed his men "the largest liberty consistent with proper discipline and the good of the service." Bud Cody told his family not to worry about him: "I have a good captain to attend to me." When kindness was warranted, Oates extended it to his men, urging sick soldiers to rest or report to a surgeon and encouraging others to do their duty despite their fatigue or boredom.[13]

Oates knew that war had lessons to teach, even to men who had not yet experienced combat. In late August 1861, about a month after the first battle of Manassas, he took his company on a tour of the scarred battlefield. It was a memorable occasion. The low Manassas hills, where the fighting had taken place, were a grisly sight. Burial mounds over shallow graves had washed away, exposing rotting corpses and severed limbs. The men could see hands and feet extended from the dirt of the flattened mounds. Mixed with the smell of putrefying flesh was the aroma of mashed fennel and pennyroyal—distinctive fragrances the men could not readily identify, so they assumed that Yankee bodies gave off strange odors. Overhead buzzards circled the battlefield like swirling dark clouds; on the ground, hogs roamed about snorting and looking for human grub.

Some of the men considered the outing an almost pleasant diversion, although they admitted that the decomposing corpses created a startling sight. It was like a picnic, said one of the soldiers. Many of the Alabamians picked up souvenirs to take home with them. Someone had erected signs and posts around the field to guide tourists to places where important events had occurred. Despite the holiday atmosphere, a few Alabamians grasped the deeper significance of what they saw before them. Wrote Samuel D. Lary, a private in Company B, to a newspaper back home: "The field is covered with the half decaying and partially devoured carcasses of man and beast—all of which speak in dumb eloquence of 'man's inhumanity.'" The tour of the Manassas battlefield became a turning point for the men of Company G, 15th Alabama, one that put them on the road toward the deadly realities of war and soldiering.[14]

It was at the camp in Pageland, not on the battlefield, that the men began to die. What Oates called "the worst enemy of our army"—the measles—struck their camp and swept through the ranks like a vicious scythe. The water in the camp was contaminated. The men suspected the water of spreading disease, but they had no other sources for fresh water. Everyone had to make do with what flowed through the fields in tiny, tainted rivulets. Oates complained about the army policy that kept the sick in camp, which only helped to make the entire encampment a sea of contagion. Even as the sickness ran rapidly through the camp, and as infected men became weak and useless, the army continued to enforce the requirement to drill four hours a day; meanwhile, the ranks became more and more depleted.

It was, as Oates described it, a "great folly." In less than six weeks, the 15th Alabama lost more than a hundred men to disease. For each man that fell, a burial had to be performed, and military funerals became a ritual of daily life at Pageland. The sick and dying longed for home. "No one, however humbled or renowned, is willing to be numbered with the dead of a stranger land," observed Samuel Lary. Friends watched friends die and couldn't believe the awful truth. There had been no battles, no charges, no wounded, no victories. And still men died, and it appeared as if this enemy—now more dreaded than the Yankees—could never be stopped.[15]

Finally someone in the army decided to abandon Pageland and find a more suitable place near Centreville for an encampment. About 300 of the 15th Alabama's sick were moved to Haymarket, Virginia, a little village about fifteen miles west of Centreville. As the Alabamians continued to die, they were buried in unmarked graves in the yard of St. Paul's Episcopal Church; some 200 men from Oates's regiment still rest beneath the tall shade trees around the church. Haymarket was not unique in the autumn of 1861. There were hospital sites just like the one at St. Paul's near practically every army camp on both sides from Virginia to Texas. The hell faced in Haymarket by the men of Oates's company and the entire 15th Alabama was experienced by thousands of soldiers, blue and gray. Few of the men who got sick in their camps recovered from their illnesses; most who contracted the measles or mumps or typhoid—or any of the highly contagious and lethal diseases that sliced through Civil War armies—died without ever really understanding what had happened to them or why they had to die. Over the next four years, disease continued to take its toll in the Confederate and Union ranks, and the terrible scenes that had taken place at Haymarket repeated themselves across the American countryside until the war, and all its hard suffering, finally ended.[16]

What William Oates and the boys of Company G learned at Pageland and Haymarket in the autumn chill of 1861 was a lesson as old as time. War is all misery, cruelty, and hell. And, all too often, young soldiers—brave and innocent boys—give their lives for no good reason at all.

By November, as leaves dropped from the trees and the winds turned brisk, the 15th Alabama settled into a new camp outside of Centreville, a rather worn and dilapidated Virginia village, taking over a huge field where Union soldiers had previously pitched their own tents. The field offered no protection from the harsh winds. As a result, Oates reported, the Alabamians got used to smoky fires that made their eyes water. Around these campfires, he said, no one could read or write or converse. "You could do nothing but cry and curse or pray, and I am of the opinion that very little of the latter was done."[17]

His company spent the long, cold winter fighting off boredom and despondency. For Oates, the bleakness of camp life was enlivened by the arrival of his brother, John, who had transferred from the 6th Alabama. It seems likely, in fact, that William arranged for his brother's transfer, perhaps to keep a better eye on John, or perhaps because John's health was beginning to decline. In the 6th Alabama, John had served as a private; he was moved into his brother's Company G as a second lieutenant—quite a leap in rank by any measure. John joined Bud Cody's mess, which delighted his old friend. The ties of old friendships, the sight of familiar faces, the bonds of community— just knowing that the boys around the campfire were from Abbeville and Henry County—must have given Oates, his brother, and the other young men of Company G some reassurance as they all tried to endure the bitter cold.

Like soldiers in both armies, Oates's Alabamians were experiencing the hardening process that would turn them into soldiers. Whether they steeled themselves against the horrors of decomposing dead on a battlefield or the loss of all too many friends from disease or the bone-chilling winds that swept across the broad plains at Centreville, they survived the challenges thrown in their way, just as all new soldiers must do in every war. Captain Oates and his boys were young and green and benighted. Oates had recently turned twenty-eight, his brother was twenty-six, and Bud Cody was seventeen. The median age of Civil War soldiers on both sides was 23.5; nearly three-fifths of the men were 21 or older at the time of enlistment. In the Henry Pioneers, the average age at the time of enlistment was 23.3; the median age was 24.5. Approximately 51 percent of the men were 21 years old or younger, which means that these boys from Henry County and the surrounding area were much like other recruits throughout the South—they were younger than their Northern counterparts. These young men, so many of them still boys, had powerful lessons to learn in becoming soldiers. They came of age in the midst of war and disease and death. Small wonder Oates and his comrades would never forget the ordeal for as long as they lived.[18]

Under Virginia's ominous gray skies, there was little to do except sit and march in the cold and try not to think too much about home. The Confederate forces, under the command of General Joseph E. Johnston, froze around smoky fires waiting for the Union army to make the first move. Meanwhile, the Union army, now under the command of Major General George B. McClellan, froze and waited for the Confederate army to make *its* move. Clearly no one was moving. And neither army appeared as if it really *wanted* to move. Johnston, a West Point graduate who had seen action in the Seminole War and the Mexican War, had achieved the rank of brigadier general in the Old Regular Army. He resigned his commission in April 1861 and commanded the Confederate troops that won the field at Manassas in July. He spent the autumn and winter in a bitter quarrel with President Davis over his seniority as a general. While he bickered with Richmond, his men sat idle in northern Virginia.[19]

Command changes broke some of the monotony for Oates's Alabamians, for with a shift of commands came a change in camp. Since mid-October, the 15th Alabama had been in the same brigade with the 16th Mississippi, the 21st Georgia, the 21st North Carolina, and the 6th North Carolina. That brigade, which was part of Major General Gustavus W. Smith's division, came under the command of Brigadier General George B. Crittenden, a dour-looking man with scowling eyes who happened to be the son of Kentucky's famous statesman, John J. Crittenden.[20] By the end of October, Crittenden was promoted to major general and sent west, and he was replaced by Brigadier General Isaac R. Trimble, a West Pointer from Maryland with a walrus-style moustache who, at fifty-nine, was among the oldest generals in the Confederate service. In his deep-set eyes, one could see fire and cold resolve. As part of the reorganization, Trimble's new brigade was reassigned to the division commanded by Brigadier General Richard S. Ewell, a born fighter despite his quiet demeanor, bird-like appearance, remarkable eccentricities, and noticeable lisp.[21]

In December, Trimble's brigade, including the 15th Alabama, moved to winter quarters in an oak grove located between Bull Run creek and Manassas Junction. Oates instructed his men to construct huts of logs and canvas, which they gladly did, seeing as the weather had turned increasingly nasty with regular bombardments of snow, sleet, and freezing rain. Despite the cold and snow, things started looking up for Oates and his company. With the change in camp, daily life was almost bearable. They enjoyed good food at last—even some Virginia turkeys and a steady supply of local beef—and ample delicacies that arrived in packages sent from home. Oates called the winter "long and disagreeable," but he seems to have been referring more to the inactivity that beset the Confederate army than to the discomforts of winter or the lack of adequate provisions. In his opinion, "the men had no cause to complain."

Though complain they did. Their most arduous duty consisted of going on picket patrol for two days every few weeks or so, but even this seemed more than the men could tolerate. Minor irritations became major grievances, and the men just could not be made to feel satisfied with their lot in

life. Lice became a common source of grumbling, and the men could not rid
themselves of the vermin no matter how hard they tried. Mostly it was the
weather that made the Alabama boys feel out of sorts. Some men thought
their huts too cold; others considered them too hot. Only Oates seems to
have believed they were just right.[22] Sickness continued to take its toll in the
winter camp. Gus McClendon, wandering in the woods near the frozen camp
one day, came upon poor graves with simple plank markers of two men from
the 6th Alabama regiment who had died of disease and had been buried without much care. McClendon knew these men well, and he was deeply saddened to have come upon their graves like that, suddenly and without warning,
realizing in the loneliness of the empty woods that he would never see his two
friends again.

Death was not the only reason the 15th Alabama's ranks were thinning.
Some men, too old and feeble to make it through, were involuntarily discharged and sent home. A few men could not see their way clear to remain in
regiments they regarded as poorly led and managed. Major John W. L. Daniel,
who had served as a delegate to the Secession Convention before joining the
army, was one of them. He and Colonel Cantey could not get along, and the
personality clash rankled him and impeded his effectiveness as an officer. Finally, after his health began to decline, Daniel resigned and returned to Alabama, where he reenlisted in another unit and became a captain.[23] To take
Daniel's place, Cantey appointed Alexander Lowther to the rank of major, a
promotion that irked Oates for its blatant favoritism. Lowther was, in Oates's
words, the colonel's "warm personal friend," for the two men had served in
Mexico together. At the root of Oates's anger over Lowther's promotion,
however, was his conviction that he would have been elected major by a two-
thirds majority if the decision had been given to the men to make, according
to military procedure. Oates called Cantey arbitrary and a poor judge of men,
but confessed, as he had in the past, that he did not bother officially to protest
Cantey's actions.[24]

So while Joe Johnston fumed about his seniority as a general, Oates stewed
over Lowther's promotion. Fuming and stewing can be commonplace activities for soldiers, especially when they have little else to do, but the problems
over rank and standing in the Confederate army, and the degree to which
such issues took hold of officers high and low, suggest that the Confederate
military may not have been quite as democratic as some Southerners thought
and some later historians have insisted. Favoritism took hold of the Confederate command system, and for officers like Oates and Johnston, there was
little they could do to change the faults of the military establishment or the failings of their superiors who preferred to promote others above them, whether
they deserved the elevation in rank or not. But it must be noted, for neither
Oates nor Johnston did so themselves, that if they had been the beneficiaries

of such favoritism, they probably would not have filed a protest or aired a complaint.[25]

As the long winter of 1862 bore down on them mercilessly, William Oates and his company must have believed that spring would never arrive. In March, warmer weather finally returned to Virginia, and the months of inactivity and boredom ended with rumors about the Federals advancing on the Confederate lines. General Joseph E. Johnston, nervous as ever, became convinced that the Confederate defensive positions in northern Virginia could not be held, so he ordered the army to withdraw south to the Rappahannock River. Hearing the news, the 15th Alabama hurried to cook rations, break camp, and get itself on the road. What the army could not take it burned in huge bonfires whose flames licked the sky and whose smoke spread the delicious smell of cooking bacon over the hills and down the creek runs. Oates thought the destruction of such good materiel smacked of lunacy, and it made him doubt General Johnston's ability to lead an army. He was not alone. Around this time President Davis was having some serious doubts of his own.

Under fair skies and with high spirits, Trimble's brigade took to the roads that led toward Richmond at a leisurely pace, following the line of the Orange and Alexandria Railroad. On March 10, the Alabamians crossed the Rappahannock River at the railroad bridge near Rappahannock Station, a whistle stop on the Orange and Alexandria. On the southern side of the river, Trimble's brigade formed a defensive line and waited for an expected Federal attack. The attack never came. Boldly, Ewell, now a major general, sent the 15th Alabama back across the river to Bealeton, a small community with a very busy railroad depot, to tear up the tracks there. As the regiment nervously went about its work unspiking the rails and lifting them off in sections, a Union division approached, commanded by Brigadier General Samuel P. Heintzelman, a brave man who rarely showed much initiative as a general. This time, though, Heintzelman was demonstrating more initiative than Oates and his fellow Alabamians ever cared to see. The Union general ordered his batteries to open up on the Confederates.

Promptly, and wisely, the Alabamians dropped what they were doing as they heard the whistling shells pass overhead. The regiment broke for the rear, made it back to the river, and crossed over to the safety of the opposite bank, where, high above on a bluff overlooking the river, Ewell was placing his division in a defensive line along the high ground. The two forces exchanged desultory shots across the river until Ewell, perched above the fray and not at all happy with what he was seeing, ordered the bridge burned. As the bridge went up in smoke, Heintzelman became discouraged and withdrew his men back toward Manassas. It was the closest the 15th Alabama had come to actual combat, and not every man was pleased with what he had seen.

Those whistling shells, which pursued the regiment all the way from Bealeton to the bridge at Rappahannock Station, resulted, said Oates, in "wild looks and low dodging all along the line."

Among the wide-eyed Alabamians who retreated to the bridge were twenty or thirty new recruits who had joined Company G, 15th Alabama, just a few days before, when war had seemed something more like a lark under the sunny skies of Virginia. Now they had a different idea, and all of them—the veterans who had come into the war last summer as well as the untested boys straight from home—were wide-eyed alike and worried if the next screaming shell might be the last one they ever heard. Oates, coolly, walked up and down the line, shaking hands with the new recruits and welcoming them to the company. His bravado was a purposeful act to demonstrate his personal courage under fire. As Oates went along, pumping hands vigorously, one recruit stepped out of line and told him that if they all stayed where they were some of them might get killed. Everyone in earshot broke into nervous laughter, but Oates—undeterred by artillery shells or humor—continued shaking hands with the new men.[26]

Winter returned to Virginia without warning, although it was mid-March and everyone had been hoping for sun-drenched days and dry nights. They got neither. A heavy snow fell on March 12, and the weather for the rest of the month turned out to be mostly precipitation of one kind or another—snow, cold rain, or sleet. Oates remembered years later that the mud was "shoe-mouth deep." The shelling from the Federals across the river continued annoyingly, and the shells would come screeching overhead and occasionally explode close to the Alabamians. Miraculously no one had been wounded, despite all the iron and lead that had been thrown at them.[27]

By the beginning of April the winter storms broke, the overcast skies finally cleared, and spring at last had arrived. The countryside was transformed from gray to green, and with the change in weather, the men's spirits began to lift, too. It was time, once more, to pull up stakes. About the middle of the month, Ewell's division marched across the Rapidan River toward the Blue Ridge and on to Gordonsville, a shady, bustling town and a junction for the Virginia Central and the Orange and Alexandria railroads. Two weeks later, Ewell's troops were on the move again, this time marching a short distance to Stanardsville, below the high rounded crest of the Blue Ridge Mountains. While the Confederates camped there, another cold front moved through Virginia, bringing rain and freezing winds—a brutal reminder that winter simply refused to give up its grip that year. Many of the men caught pneumonia; a large number of them were shipped off to Chimborazo hospital. Others had contracted—and died from—what Oates called "camp fever" (probably typhus).[28]

On April 30, after a cold rain and sleet had pelted the men through the night, Ewell's division formed a marching column, four men abreast, and started up the winding road that passed through Swift Run Gap, between the heavily wooded peaks of the Blue Ridge, and down into the Shenandoah Valley. Oates remembered the march vividly, even after long years had elapsed and visits to Europe had shown him mountains more than three times as high as those along the Blue Ridge. The beauty of this Virginia vista took his breath away: "On top of the mountain you could look over the country that lay behind us to the Potomac, and before lay the beautiful valley of Shenandoah. . . . In the midst of that valley the Massanutten Mountain rears his crest into the clouds, and miles and miles beyond the beautiful valley extends to the foot of the Alleghenies." But, as usual, it was the girls of the valley who really caught Oates's eye. The young ladies were "numerous and pretty," he said. He reported that many Alabamians found sweethearts in that section of the Shenandoah and that the married men "wished they were not."

The men soon discovered that Ewell's division, by moving over the mountains, had joined Stonewall Jackson's command in the Shenandoah—a fact that gave them renewed hope of seeing some action soon. News had also reached them that the Union Army of the Potomac was attempting to push its way toward Richmond up the Virginia peninsula, and suddenly the war involved high stakes and momentous crises. When Ewell's division was ordered down the valley, while Jackson led his troops along a parallel route on the other side of Massanutten Mountain, Oates was stirred by the warm reception he and his men received from the ladies of Luray, whom, he said, were "the most perfect beauties my eyes ever beheld." Inspired by the Shenandoah women, he quoted his favorite poet, Robert Burns: "Their cheeks looked like lilies dip't in wine, their teeth like ivory." Said Oates many decades later, "I felt that I was marching to a carnival of death, through the portals of Heaven, and that the angels were singing and cheering me on." His comments about the ladies revealed how much he enjoyed the attention that soldiers always receive from young women, no matter what war is being fought, but his waxing romantic by quoting Burns also demonstrated how he deftly manufactured and crafted his memories in later life, shaping them according to Southern manly ideals. One need not doubt that he imagined that the angels were cheering and singing as he and his company marched through the Shenandoah. But it is significant that he remembered the young women and the angels, and not the brutal march that left Jackson's men footsore and fatigued. In memory, war's hardships can sometimes be so easily forgotten— or so conveniently suppressed. Remembering the ladies was the Southern way of transforming memory into sentimentality.[29]

At Luray, a market town built on a gentle hillside with shops and grain mills and livestock pens, the two wings of Stonewall Jackson's army came together on May 21. With his army united, Jackson took the lead of the column. He rode several times from the rear to the front of his army, and as he did, the shouts would travel along the line, getting louder from the back and moving steadily forward, and as the shouts broke into cheers, the marching men would divide into two lines, one on either side of the roadway, and let the general gallop down the center. The enthusiasm of the men for this fantastic flying general expressed their admiration and their unlimited confidence in his leadership.[30]

In Oates's opinion, Jackson was "a military genius," and he liked the general—despite Jackson's relentless driving of his troops—for his energy and efficiency. Later, Oates compared Jackson to Napoleon, praising the Shenandoah campaign for a strategic brilliance rivaled only by the Corsican's Italian campaign in 1796 and 1797. Jackson, wrote Oates, "was not egotistical and never volunteered opinions or advice to his superior in rank." For Oates, Jackson was a model soldier, the perfect officer, and the foremost field general in the Confederate army. "His whole soul, mind, and strength were addressed to the discharge of duty," remarked Oates long after the war. Yet Oates was totally unlike Jackson on the field of battle. As an officer, Oates was competent and brave. But he was extremely impetuous, sometimes ignoring orders and using his own judgment, not always with caution or wisdom. Jackson, on the other hand, "received his orders without question or comment, and executed them to the letter of superb ability." It was too bad that Oates could not have learned from Jackson while under the great general's command. He might have become a better field officer.[31]

Mile after mile the men of Stonewall's army marched. During several of the hot battles that took place in the great Valley campaign of 1862—Front Royal on May 23, Winchester on May 25, and Strasburg on June 1—Oates and Company G of the 15th Alabama looked on from afar. They were not directly engaged, although once or twice the regiment came under threatening artillery fire or participated in mopping-up operations. Though not always under fire, the Alabamians nevertheless began to see what war was all about. In between the battles, they marched and marched down country roads, mostly through rain and in knee-deep mud. "I was never so tired and sleepy," Oates recalled many years later. As he marched along he occasionally fell asleep while walking, and the company's orderly-sergeant would catch him by the arm, shake him, and arouse him out of his slumber.[32]

On June 6, the 15th Alabama and Jackson's rear guard reached Harrisonburg, where Jackson and the main body of his army had left the turnpike the day before and set out for Port Republic to the southeast. Ewell's division took the same turn, and followed the Port Republic Road for about six miles to the Keezletown Road; there, at Union Church, a small village of scattered houses not far from Cross Keys, a tavern one mile farther south on the Keezletown Road, the 15th Alabama went on picket duty and spread itself across a wedge of ground shaped by the numerous roads that came together in the vicinity of the church. Except for a heated fight that evening along the Port Republic Road, where Brigadier General Turner Ashby—one of the Confederacy's brightest stars—was killed trying to rally his troopers during a

rear-guard action, the rest of the night remained peaceful. It was clear, however, that separate Union columns under Major General John C. Fremont
and Brigadier General James Shields were moving closer as they drove up the
Valley in hopes of trapping Jackson. The quiet extended into Saturday, June
7, and Oates and his men got some badly needed rest lounging in the grass
and lingering at their bivouacs.

Meanwhile, Jackson's division made camp near Port Republic, at the head
of the south fork of the Shenandoah, about seven miles from Union Church.
Random rifle shots from time to time told Oates and Company G that the
enemy was out there—hidden in the darkness or kept from sight by hills or
ridges. It was easy for some of the men to forget why they were all there,
boiling their coffee and cooking their bacon in the lush fields strewn with
wildflowers, all purple and pink, that reached all the way to the base of the
Blue Ridge. Every once in a while, however, loud bursts of gunfire would
remind the Alabamians that the Federals—who outnumbered Jackson's troops
by two to one—were pursuing them and probably coming up fast, hoping at
last to get Stonewall Jackson in their grip.[33]

Early on June 8, a Sunday morning, with blue skies and a bright sun
overhead, three companies of the 15th Alabama went out on picket duty around
the Union Church near Cross Keys, a tiny town located a mile south of the
Alabamians' bivouac. At about 9:00 A.M., while the coolness of the morning
still lingered in the woods and the fields, Lieutenant Colonel John Treutlen
saw two regiments of Federal sharpshooters advancing through a field near
the old log church. Suddenly Treutlen and his Alabamians were hit by volley
fire, but the Confederates, as Treutlen later remarked proudly in his report,
gave not "an inch of ground." Within no time, the entire regiment was engaged and eventually all of Trimble's brigade was swept into the fight.

The Alabama skirmishers fell back to the regiment's position, which
Colonel Cantey had placed along the crest of a little hill with a great open
field to its front. Out of the woods at the edge of the field came a determined
and grim-faced line of Union skirmishers. Cantey yelled out a command to
withdraw, which the regiment did through a wheat field and over some rail
fences, taking several casualties as the Federal skirmishers pursued the 15th
through the Union Church cemetery and on across the crossroads. During
the retreat, Sergeant William Toney—the brother of Oates's future wife—
fell mortally wounded.

The 15th Alabama fell back to the protection of Trimble's brigade line
behind a fence that bordered an open field of buckwheat and looked out on
some woods, about 150 yards away. At around 10:00 A.M., the long blue lines
of the enemy came through the trees and into the field, a sight to behold,
marching with great precision and ease. Many of the Alabama boys, anxious
to get off their first shots of the war, fired too quickly, before the Yankees had
even gotten in range. "Keep cool, Alabamians," the officers whispered to their

men. Taking advantage of the fence, the men of Trimble's brigade—including the boys of the 15th—lay down in the grass behind it and tried, as best they could, to get a bead on the approaching Federals.

Finally, someone shouted out the order to fire, and Trimble's brigade—spread along the whole length of the fence—opened with a devastating volley of flame and lead. Sporadic firing, deadly and loud, continued for a while, and Captain William Richardson of Company H, caught up in the excitement of the fight, stepped up on a log and screamed out, "Boys, give them hell!" The boys did just that with a second volley, and the Union force finally broke into pieces, fell back to the protection of the woods, and reformed its lines. After pulling itself together, the Federal troops left the woods and marched into the fields at an angle that made their intentions to flank the 15th instantly clear. Unknowingly, the Federals blindly walked straight into the blazing guns of the 21st Georgia, which mowed down the blue ranks with a single volley. At the fence, Company G suffered its first combat casualties—one man shot in the foot, another shot in the hand.

To check further the enemy's effort to flank the Confederates, Trimble ordered the 15th to take up a new position by the right flank around the fence and down a hollow, dividing the regiment in two and placing Treutlen on a hill on the left and Cantey around the right to capture a harassing Federal battery. Company G followed Cantey to the foot of a hill where a Union battery, its guns flashing and booming above the Alabamians, was causing great trouble for Trimble's brigade. But Cantey, riding up the hill enough to see that the Federal guns were supported by a full Union brigade, tried to pull his men out of an impossible situation. The Alabamians, including Treutlen on the left, kept up their fire as best they could, but the 15th was being hit hard, its men were falling everywhere, and the Yankees, firing canister, laid into them without remorse. Under the circumstances, the Alabamians panicked, and Treutlen attempted to keep order among his men. He failed. Much of the regiment—justifiably frightened by the chaos—fled in confusion. When they reached the bottom of the hill, Oates and the other officers successfully reformed their ranks and pulled the regiment back together.[34]

Another order to advance rippled down the Confederate line, and General Trimble himself arrived to take charge. The Alabamians smartly formed a battle line and moved out, this time supported by two other regiments in Trimble's brigade. Together the combined Confederate forces struck the Federals with great force, like a gray ocean wave crashing on a beach; the Alabamians took the lead in the assault, and drove the enemy—the Pennsylvania "Bucktail Regiment"—from its hilltop position. The Union battery, however, had already withdrawn from the hill. Old Trimble, his white hair gleaming in the sunlight and the fire glowing in his eyes, took command of the 15th, swung his horse toward the front, and led his men forward, steadily pushing the surprised and outmaneuvered Federals on Fremont's left flank back toward the Keezletown Road. Elsewhere on the battlefield, Ewell's other troops held their own against the confused Union regiments. Trimble asked Ewell for permission to keep on pushing the enemy. Much to his displeasure, Ewell thought they had accomplished enough for one day, and he told his brigade commander to sit tight.[35]

The battle of Cross Keys was actually a series of scattered skirmishes, none of which amounted to much, except that the engagement prevented Fremont's column from uniting with Shield's, which was significant in itself. Cross Keys, however, had a greater importance for the 15th Alabama: it was its baptism by fire, and, by any measure, the regiment had done pretty well. Later, when the officers sat down to write their official reports, the Alabamians fared particularly well, earning high praise for their part in the Cross Keys action from both Ewell and Trimble.

But there was something else. The men of the regiment had, for the first time, lost friends in battle and had seen comrades fall, and that experience was more than an initiation rite; it was a shocking, sorrowful, and humbling event that transformed these Alabamians, as much as the actual experience of combat had transformed them, into real soldiers. The regiment left at least seven dead, and perhaps as many as twenty-eight wounded, on the Cross Keys battlefield; several of those who were reported wounded later died.[36]

The night after the battle was unsettlingly noisy with the echoes of death. From where they lay on their arms, not far from the Union Church where the battle had begun, Oates and his men could hear the Yankees talking all through the night. As the sun rose above the Blue Ridge in the morning hours of June 9, Trimble received orders from Jackson to come up to Port Republic as quickly as he could, and Trimble responded without delay. "No brigade," remarked Oates, "ever marched five miles in a shorter space of time." From across the North and South rivers, sparkling in the morning light, Oates could hear the battle heating up on the wide plain that stretched from the South Fork to the foothills underneath the hazy outlines of the blue mountains.

Hastily, Trimble directed men over a covered bridge that spanned the North River and led directly into the town. After getting his brigade across, Trimble fired the wooden bridge by igniting two piles of hay at either end. The 15th Alabama, and the rest of Trimble's brigade, then crossed the South River over a makeshift—and rickety—bridge that Jackson's men had constructed by laying planks over some wagons. On the green plain, Oates and the other officers formed their men into battle lines, readied them for combat, and expected to be thrown in at any moment, but by the time the brigade had gotten on line, the sounds of fighting had died down in the distance. Although the outcome had not been certain for most of the day, Jackson and his men had finally prevailed, and Shield's battered Federals retreated down the Luray Valley.[37]

After resting for a week, Jackson's army was called east by General Robert E. Lee, who needed the Valley troops to defend Richmond against an invasion up the Peninsula by Major General George B. McClellan's Army of the Potomac. The men of the 15th Alabama walked with few stops from the Shenandoah Valley to the vicinity of Richmond, a distance Oates calculated to be about 140 miles. As they crossed over the Blue Ridge, the Alabamians caught sight of the entire Valley army arrayed from one end of the mountain gap to the other, a long column of soldiers in gray and butternut, their bayonets glistening in the bright sunlight, the bands playing to mark each step.[38]

Across the girth of Virginia, Jackson's army marched rapidly toward Richmond to link up with the Army of Northern Virginia—now under Lee's command—that was holding back McClellan's Union army on the outskirts of the Confederate capital. Lee told Jackson where he wanted the general to strike and when, but Jackson—beaten down with fatigue—followed unfamiliar roads and experienced delays that he had never encountered in his famous marches through the Shenandoah Valley. On June 26, Jackson delayed and maneuvered, but he did not launch an attack on the Federal right as Lee and his subordinates had expected him to do—and as he promised he would. The next day, which started out hot and hazy and only got worse as the day wore on, Jackson led his column toward the battle that had erupted about a mile from Gaines Mill, a gristmill on the plantation of William Gaines, an ardent supporter of the Confederacy.

By Ewell's order, General Trimble himself led the brigade onto the field, the 15th Alabama taking the lead in the column. As the Alabamians advanced, shot and shell exploded over their heads. Trimble called it "a perfect sheet of fire." Moving up to the crest of a hill, minus Colonel Cantey, who had managed with some others to get separated from the main body, the regiment received a galling fire that sounded like a continuous, rolling roar. Shells were bursting, rifles were spouting flames, solid shot was careening through the ranks, and the officers were shouting commands that mostly could not be heard. Oates went diligently about his duties, telling the men to buck up, making sure they kept up their fire, reminding everyone to aim low. The Alabamians faced steady volleys from a red-legged Zouaves regiment, but they moved forward across a road and kept their heads down as they tried to withstand the relentless storm of lead. Private Samuel Dickerson of Company G took a bullet in the head; he was the first man of Oates's company to die in combat. The Alabamians ascended a small hill, unstoppable in their determination to reach the top. Reaching the top was one thing; staying there was another. Men were falling everywhere; the firing was so intense that the ground seemed the safest place to be. A few men broke through the storm of minie balls to get within paces of the blazing Federal line, and one Alabamian

stepped up to a Union soldier, pointed his revolver at the man's face, and
fired point blank.

Clouds of smoke tumbled by, like rolling waves of morning mist being
chased by the warmth of the sun, but mostly the smoke clung to the ground
and created a thick fog through which little could be seen or recognized. The
Alabamians learned that a target, otherwise invisible in all the smoke, could
be discerned by listening to the effects of one's previous shot; if the bullet
struck home, a moan could be heard. The secret, then, was to aim toward the
place where the moans and groans were coming from. Along Oates's portion
of the line, his company's rifles grew burning hot from rapid fire, too hot to
hold and to aim, but many of the men, as Oates remembered it, simply picked
up muskets that had been dropped by the dead or wounded and tossed their
own faulty weapons aside. For nearly an hour and a half, the Alabamians kept
up their fire, which slackened only when the regiment began to run low on
ammunition.

At this point, Ewell came riding up, his hat in hand and his bald head
exposed to the glaring sunlight, and asked why the 15th had stopped firing.
John Oates, standing brave and erect, was there to explain the ammunition
shortage. The general was furious. His eyes wide and bulging, he told Lieutenant Oates to have the regiment fix bayonets, though the 15th's bayonets
had already been fixed. Ewell thundered off without fully understanding the
circumstances on the field. An ammunition detail showed up soon after Ewell
rode off, and the Alabamians hurriedly refilled their cartridge pouches. The
men were still replenishing their ammunition when the 5th Texas, sent by
Ewell to assist the Alabamians, came up from behind. All around, remembered Gus McClendon, "the canopy of smoke was so thick that the sun was
gloomily red in the heavens." With great style and flourish, the Texans
marched to the top of the hill, formed their line of battle, and fired a devastating volley into the Federals below. Then, as if in one motion, they reloaded
and fixed bayonets. Shortly the advance was ordered, the rebel yell rang out,
and the Alabamians and the Texans rolled down the hill in a single, deadly
wave. The Federal battle lines melted away, and when the Confederates
reached the bottom of the hill they discovered that they had not simply repelled their Union foes, they had annihilated them. A bayonet charge would
later figure prominently in Oates's battlefield experience, when the circumstances would be reversed and he and his fellow Alabamians would learn,
much to their dismay, precisely what it felt like to be on the receiving end of
a descending wave of glinting bayonets.[39]

That night, a few men carried torches out on the field to see if they could
find missing comrades. They discovered a scene of ghastly horror. The field
was covered with dead and wounded. Captain Peter Guerry of Company C
("a brave man," said Oates, "and a Christian gentleman") had been killed
leading his men into battle. Captain Lock Weems (Oates called him "a model

officer")—who had been appointed to command Company A when Alexander Lowther, Oates's rival, had been promoted to major of the regiment—was mortally wounded and died a few days after the fighting. Captain George Y. Malone of Company F (one "of the best officers in the regiment," said Oates) took a bullet in the thigh and was out of the war. Captain Lee E. Bryan of Company L was also seriously wounded and discharged from the service. The official reports, according to Oates, showed total losses for the 15th Alabama at Gaines Mill to have been 34 killed and 110 wounded.

What Oates now realized, what he had not realized about Cross Keys, was that he, like his fellow captains, could easily be struck down. It wasn't fear of dying that necessarily haunted him, although Oates was never reluctant to admit that battles frightened him as nothing else could. Rather, it was the fragility of life that haunted him, how human existence itself could be swept away in the flight of a conical lead ball or in the explosion of a tin canister. Oates contemplated the casualties at Gaines Mill and gained, perhaps for the first time in his life, a fundamental understanding of his own mortality. Of the 15th Alabama's role in the battle of Gaines Mill, he said simply: "It made a glorious record, but at a frightful cost."[40]

3

AN UNCHRISTIAN
STATE OF MIND

Like a great storm at sea, the war took its own course. The men who
had put it in motion, unleashing its rolling thunder and its flashing
lightning bolts, could not control its fury or its violence. With every
battle, every clash of the two mighty armies, the war grew more intense, more
brutal, and more unpredictable. No one commanded the tempest or its wrath.
William Oates was swept up in it, just as every American was, floating wherever the storm's current surged and ebbed, bobbing on its terrible waves like a
tiny cork. The war was now determining the fate of two nations and two peo-
ples, pounding away at them mercilessly. That is the way with all wars. They
elude control; they bring about unwanted change; they advance in inconceivable directions. Mostly, though, they ensure—in all their destructiveness, in
all their savagery—that nothing will ever be the same again.

No sooner had the Seven Days' campaign ended when Oates and Company G, along with the entire 15th Alabama, received orders to march toward
another uncertain destination, another uncertain fate. As they slogged along
Virginia's narrow highways, kicking up dust and wearing out boots, Oates
bristled when he heard news—which must have passed like quicksilver down
the column—that Major Alexander Lowther, his great rival, had been placed
in command of the 15th Alabama regiment, following Colonel Cantey's return home on sick leave. Lowther, who also complained of ill health and extreme fatigue, had submitted his resignation to the brigade command on July
12, but General Trimble refused to accept it and later succeeded in getting
Richmond to nullify it. The one consolation for Oates was that he became

acting major of the regiment. On July 17, the 15th Alabama—now under Lowther's leadership—drove on to Gordonsville, where it remained with Jackson's corps until the first week of August, observing the build-up of Major General John Pope's Union Army of Virginia in the green and brown hills surrounding Culpeper. Jackson moved toward Culpeper on August 7 and 8, but turned his force in the direction of Cedar Mountain (also called Slaughter's Mountain), south of Culpeper, where, on August 9, he ran into the right wing of Pope's army under Major General Nathaniel P. Banks, one of his adversaries in the Valley.[1]

In the ensuing battle, the 15th Alabama was detached from Trimble's brigade and moved up to a ridge near the mountain's summit to place itself in support of a battery of artillery. From this vantage point, Oates and the men of the 15th could see the battle unfolding below them, as if they were witnessing a circus performance from bleachers. As the Confederate cannon opened up on the enemy below, Oates heard the scream of a woman intermingled with the whining of artillery shells overhead. An instant later, several women— whose demeanor, according to Oates, "indicated culture and refinement"— came out of the woods and appealed to him for assistance. Their farm, they said, was down in the valley, precisely where the Union and Confederate troops were fighting. Oates instructed them to move over the ridge to a farmhouse where they could find safety and shelter. Before they left, the ladies (Catherine Crittenden, a widow, and her daughters) begged him to look after one of their number who had fainted on the way up and had been left in the care of a slave. Oates went down the mountain a short distance and found her—"as perfect a beauty," he said, "as was ever reared on the soil of the Old Dominion." He helped her get over the ridge to where her mother and sisters were, and then he left her "and never saw her again." Later the 15th advanced to the foot of the mountain, where it came under fire and Oates had the unnerving experience of having a shell explode in his face, although he was uninjured. Remaining on the fringe of the heavy fighting, the 15th Alabama that day lost only one man killed and seven wounded. The Yankees retreated from the field, and Jackson could claim yet another victory.[2]

Several days afterward, Jackson's entire corps—and the 15th Alabama with it—began a long, strenuous march in an effort to swing around the right flank of Pope's army, which had been concentrated north of the Rappahannock River. As Pope retreated north, with Lee's army also in hot pursuit, he deployed Union artillery along the Rappahannock to slow down the rushing Confederate tide. During an artillery duel between both sides on July 20, Oates was hit in the left arm by a shell fragment, which tore his coat sleeve and caused some profuse bleeding, but the wound turned out to be slight.

A driving rain impeded Jackson's progress, for the roads became thick with mud and the rivers and streams began to rise. On August 22, the 15th Alabama was thrown into a fight with retreating Yankees who were trying desperately to cross the Hazel River while being cut down by Confederate fire. Some drowned in the river, Oates remarked after the war, and others were shot in the water. But he passed the engagement off as a minor affair, even though the official records gave the 15th Alabama's losses as four killed, thirteen wounded, and one missing. In his later years, Oates disputed the figures, saying they were too high. He also pointed out rather caustically that Major Lowther was in command of the regiment that day, implying that either Lowther had mishandled the firefight with the Federals or that he had lied about the regiment's casualties, or both.

By August 26, as the summer heat made the air thick and almost unbreathable, Jackson's corps passed through the hazy Bull Run Mountains at the narrow passage of Thoroughfare Gap, where Indians had long ago blazed a winding trail between high cliffs of granite and limestone. On the following day, the 15th Alabama and Jackson's corps arrived in Manassas Junction, where the men wrecked trains, tore up track, and filled their stomachs and knapsacks with food that had been stored there for the Union army. For no good reason, other than as an expression of their racial animosities, the men also broke up an African American camp meeting, driving off the worshipers and donning hats that the ladies had left behind in their haste. After chasing a routed New Jersey regiment for a couple of days, and zigzagging back and forth over Bull Run creek, the regiment went into battle line at the edge of some woods behind the little crossroads of Groveton. The second battle of Manassas (known also as Second Bull Run) was about to open.[3]

Almost a year ago to the day, Oates had guided his untempered company around these gruesome plains, where the first battle of Bull Run had been fought on July 21, 1861. Now, as the men of the 15th Alabama waited in battle formation just to the north of the Warrenton Turnpike on a high ridge in front of an unfinished railroad cut, they could hear the distant sound of guns reverberating through the night. Later they learned that the firing came from Thoroughfare Gap as the Yankees tried unsuccessfully to stop Longstreet's portion of the Army of Northern Virginia from getting through the Bull Run Mountains. Pope's men were thrown back from the gap, and they withdrew up the Warrenton Turnpike toward Bull Run creek. In the darkness, Jackson ordered Ewell's division forward, and the Confederates burst out of the woods and took the retreating Yankees completely by surprise.

"Within a minute" after the Confederate attack, Oates remembered, "all was enveloped in smoke and a sheet of fire seemed to go out from each side to the other along the whole length of the lines." It was so dark that the Yankees could only be seen by the flashes of their muskets. The Alabamians drove the Union troops back to a fence in the blackness of the night, but it was impossible to know the positions of friend or foe, and men began aiming at the flares of muskets and even the glint of brass buttons—anything that shined and moved in darkness. Oates told his men to keep up their fire, which they did, and soon the exchange of volleys tore the fence into splinters.[4] For an hour the fight continued, men firing blindly into the night, until the Union troops, with shouts of huzzah, withdrew and left the field to the Alabamians. Someone went forward and struck a match. The ground was covered with Yankee dead and wounded. Among the boys of the 15th Alabama, the losses were great and terrible. In Oates's company alone, five men were killed, but some thought there might have been more. For the regiment as a whole, the returns showed fifteen men had died and thirty-eight had been wounded during the fight on the night of August 28. As for the high command, both Ewell and Trimble were severely wounded that night.

In the morning, the sun rose bright and hot, and in the light the men of the 15th Alabama saw before them, like dark stumps scattered across an uncleared field, the bodies of thousands of dead and wounded, Federal and Confederate. In Oates's memory, it was "the most sickening" carnage he ever beheld during the entire war. Some of Oates's men started a little fire on the edge of the thicket where they had fought the night before, and he joined them for what they all hoped would be a restful cup of coffee. But the smoke from the fire caught the eye of Yankee artillerists, who threw a shell in the fire's direction. Hitting the ground about fifty yards from Oates and his men, the shell bounced with great force toward them and landed in their fire. Some of the Alabamians ran, while Oates threw himself to the ground and tried, pawing at the earth with both hands, to make himself the smallest target he could. When the shell exploded, two of Oates's men were wounded from its fragments. Oates, miraculously, was not hurt, but he did admit that he was "very much frightened."

Jackson reformed his lines, and the 15th Alabama took up a new position behind the unfinished railroad embankment, using it as breastworks to defend themselves against an imminent attack by the Yankees. Oates was not doing well. The scenes of "blood and suffering" across the battlefield had made him nauseous, and he did not look forward to another bloody engagement with the enemy. He mounted his horse and roamed for a while, eventually finding a farmhouse occupied by "hospitable Virginia women" who made him breakfast, filled his cup with rivers of coffee, and let him nap on their front lawn while his horse grazed around him.

Oates awoke with a start when he heard the booming of guns in the distance, sprang to his horse, avoided a Union cavalry patrol, and galloped back to the Confederate lines. He rejoined his regiment in time to defend the railroad embankment as the Yankees launched yet another assault against Jackson's corps. The fighting went on for more than two hours, with the musketry never ceasing and some of the Confederates, who had run out of ammunition, picking up rocks and using rifle butts to stop the Union onslaught. By nightfall the two sides occupied nearly the same positions they had held when the day began.

On August 30, Pope ordered 10,000 men forward against Jackson's lines, only to be met by volley after volley of devastating artillery and musket fire from the Confederate flanks. "What a slaughter! What a slaughter of men that was," remembered a private in Oates's company. The Union troops fell back once more, but this time Lee saw a great opportunity and decided to take advantage of it. The Confederate commander told Longstreet to advance with his corps—about 30,000 men all together—and to drive the Union forces off the field. For about an hour, Pope tried to hold his ground in a desperate defense, but around 6:00 P.M. his lines broke and the Confederates pushed him all the way to Henry House Hill, where the outcome of the first battle of Manassas had been decided in 1861. As darkness spread over the battlefield, the fighting petered out at last, and the Second Battle of Manassas was over.[5]

At the beginning of the campaign, Oates's Company G had a total strength of about sixty men. After Second Manassas, only twenty-five or thirty men answered the roll call. On August 31, the regiment marched off the battlefield and down the dirt highway called the Little River Turnpike. A pouring rain began to fall and the Confederates spent a wet night bivouacked by the side of the road. Hoping to cut off Pope's retreat, Jackson kept his men moving down the turnpike on September 1. Near Chantilly Farm, at a place called Ox Hill, the Confederates crashed into a Union force under the command of Major General Philip Kearny and Major General Isaac I. Stevens. As a great thunderstorm boomed overhead, and a cold rain poured down in buckets on both sides below, the fighting raged on for several hours into the early evening. At one point, the Confederates panicked and the lines broke away, and the graybacks ran for the rear in utter disarray. Among the stampeding Confederates were the men of the 15th Alabama, who could not be stopped or rallied, despite the efforts of Oates and other officers.

In the confusion, Oates was hit in his shin by a ball or a piece of shell, which knocked him off his feet. A Georgia captain approached Oates and screamed at him to get back in the fight. Oates brushed off the Georgian by telling him he had no authority to order him to do anything, and he went to Captain Isaac B. Feagin, who commanded the regiment in Lowther's absence, to report the incident and find out what he should do next. Captain Feagin, chagrined over the Alabamians' inglorious retreat, ordered the regiment—or what remained of it—back into the battle, and when Oates and the 15th moved forward other Confederate regiments followed them. As night fell, the Confederates pushed the Yankees back, killing both Kearny and Stevens and crumbling the Union lines. Losses in the 15th Alabama were slight that day, but the memory of the drenching rain and the regiment's dishonorable flight from the battlefield stayed with Oates for the rest of his life. He could never rid himself of the shame he felt for his company and his regiment.[6]

In fourteen harrowing months, William Oates, now twenty-eight years old, had learned how to be an officer, and his men had learned how to be soldiers. They had traveled great distances, survived awful hardships, and engaged in horrible battles. The bloodletting they had witnessed—up and down the Shenandoah Valley, on the Peninsula, from the hilltop at Cedar Mountain, across the old battlefield at Manassas, and in the disheartening mud of Chantilly—made them give up any lingering dreams of glory, any misconceptions about war as a valuable, manly experience.

For Oates, the violence of the war and the human toll it was taking shocked him and exceeded his wildest imaginings. This was a violence unlike anything he thought possible and certainly different from the kind he had experienced in his youth, the brutal, personal violence of a father's lash or a man-to-man brawl on the frontier. Accustomed to impassioned mayhem and bloodshed from his days as a desperado, Oates was nevertheless appalled by the mass murder that was taking place on one battlefield after another.

Yet for all its destructive force, something about the war appealed to Oates and made him feel whole. One of his men in the 15th, while observing that Oates was "a handsome and brave leader," also remarked: "He was regarded by many as too aggressive and ambitious but he usually was well to the front and did not require his men to charge where he was unwilling to share the common danger." The war, in its legitimization of violence, had provided a socially acceptable channel, an outlet, for Oates's own violent streak.[7]

The disgraceful conduct of his company and of the entire regiment at Chantilly put Oates, he said, in "a very unchristian state of mind."[8] There was little he could do but let his blood boil. As they went into camp on the evening of September 1, 1862, while the rain continued to soak them to the skin, and the rolling thunder reminded them of the terror that had made them run that day, William Oates and his fellow Alabamians could not know that worse horrors awaited them down twisting county roads that never seemed to end.

From the very beginning of the war, the Confederates boasted of their prowess as fighting men. On plantations and in barrooms, in farm fields and in court houses, Southerners fiercely maintained that a single Confederate could easily whip ten Yankees—or more. After the first battle of Manassas, that assumption faded away when it became clear that the Yankees could fight and that it would take more than one battle to win the war, but the fact remained that the Confederate armies in the eastern theater under Robert E. Lee and Stonewall Jackson kept winning victories, one after another, throughout the spring and summer of 1862.

Apart from the earlier brags and puffed-up poses, there did seem to be something special about the Southern soldier after all. Undisciplined, disrespectful of authority, disorderly in appearance and on the march, these men nevertheless possessed a fierce spirit of independence and an iron determination on the battlefield and off. Lieutenant Colonel Arthur J. L. Fremantle, a British officer traveling with Lee's Army of Northern Virginia as an observer, remarked of them in 1863: "The Confederate has no ambition to imitate the regular soldier at all; he looks the genuine rebel; but in spite of his bare feet, his ragged clothes, his old rug, and tooth-brush stuck like a rose in his buttonhole, he has a sort of devil-may-care, reckless, self-confidant look, which is decidedly taking."[9] What's more, these men marched like the wind, lived on poor rations or no rations at all, and won amazing victories, sometimes against overwhelming odds.

If Confederate soldiers were becoming a legend, William Oates and his men did not yet know it. Endless marching occupied their attention, as did the aching in their bones and their unsatisfied yearning for sleep, while Lee's forces moved from one battle to another under a warm September sun. Given their rout at Chantilly in the rain, the men of the 15th Alabama could not have been thinking of themselves in legendary terms. Fear in battle was enough to peel away the veneer of heroism among even the finest soldiers. The men of the 15th Alabama were hardened veterans now, but none of them could quite believe they were legends.

And now they were moving north. On September 5, Oates and his regiment waded across the Potomac River into Maryland at White's Ford while a band played the tune "Maryland, My Maryland." From there they marched to the Monocacy River, near Frederick, where they made camp and rested for a few days. Oates rode into town to look around and concluded from what he saw that the good citizens of Frederick were patriotic Confederates itching to support the Southern cause and join Lee's army. Unfortunately, just the opposite was true. The Marylanders living in and around Frederick were ardent Unionists for the most part, and Lee's hopes of recruiting Maryland volunteers into his army during the autumn invasion fell flat. Lee issued a proclamation to the Maryland people, telling them grandly that the Army of Northern Virginia was now on their soil to save them from the injustices of the Lincoln administration. But only the Southern sympathizers in western Maryland believed him.[10]

From the flatlands near the Monocacy, the 15th Alabama moved out with the rest of Jackson's corps on September 10 and marched to the west. For the first hour, no one in the ranks knew where Jackson was heading, but during a rest break they were told that Harper's Ferry was their destination. Lee had expected the Union garrison at Harper's Ferry to evacuate the town after he had crossed the Potomac. When that did not happen, Lee decided to divide his forces and send a portion of his army to invest the stronghold at the confluence of the Potomac and Shenandoah Rivers. One column under Major

General John G. Walker approached Harper's Ferry from the east and south, positioning itself on Loudoun Heights, which overlooked the town from the Virginia side of the Shenandoah. Another column commanded by Major General Lafayette McLaws marched west and south toward Maryland Heights. Jackson, with the third Confederate column, faced a more complicated mission. He and his men first marched west over the Cactotin Mountains to Martinsburg, which he captured by forcing its Union defenders to retreat to Harper's Ferry, his final destination. Coming at the town from the west, Jackson took up a strong position on Bolivar Heights.

On September 13, the Confederates closed in. The following day, Confederate artillery bombarded the town in a deadly barrage that lasted nearly all afternoon and into the night. When Jackson received word from Lee that the Union army was in hot pursuit of the Army of Northern Virginia, he pressed the siege on September 15, outflanked the Union troops on Bolivar Heights, and captured the town that morning.[11] Although Oates didn't say so, he and the rest of Jackson's men must have felt a great deal of satisfaction at having so successfully brought the Union garrison to its knees in the town where John Brown—the old "Puritan abolitionist," as Oates called him—had conducted the raid that, in the minds of many Southerners, had started the war.

Despite Jackson's victory at Harper's Ferry, neither he nor Lee knew that a copy of the orders dividing the Army of Northern Virginia and directing the capture of Harper's Ferry had fallen into McClellan's hands, giving the Union general the advantage of knowing where each portion of the Confederate army was located. What Lee did know, however, was that the Army of the Potomac was about to bear down on him and that he must, at all costs and with great haste, bring together the various wings of his far-flung army. As a result, Jackson—leaving behind Major General A. P. Hill's division to parole the Union prisoners—led his men out of Harper's Ferry and up the Potomac River to rejoin Lee soon after midnight on September 16.[12]

For Oates and the 15th Alabama, all the marching and fighting were taking their toll once more. During the march from Frederick to Harper's Ferry, straggling had increased significantly, and it was becoming physically impossible to keep up with Jackson's required pace—which he had set at three miles per hour with ten-minute rest breaks every hour. Trimble's brigade did not set out for Sharpsburg, where Lee wanted his army to reunite, until late in the morning on September 16, probably because of traffic jams along the line of march. Oates's regiment reached Shepherdstown that afternoon, and the men of the 15th crossed the Potomac by stripping naked, carrying their clothes and equipment over their heads, and wading to the other side, where they dressed and moved on toward Sharpsburg.[13]

But Oates was not with them. Having almost reached Shepherdstown, he collapsed from an undisclosed malady and let his company and his regiment march on. He was placed on sick call by a surgeon and ordered to bed in the house of "an old Dutchman" on the road between Harper's Ferry and Shepherdstown. Although Oates never revealed the nature of his debilitating illness, it is likely that the wound in his leg, received during the battle of Chantilly, began to bother him and made it impossible for him to walk. He remained at the house outside of Shepherdstown for almost a week. Because of his disability, he was about to miss the bloodiest single day of the Civil War.[14]

The butcher's bill at Antietam was enormous. During the battle, almost 23,000 Northerners and Southerners were killed, wounded, or missing. But the 15th Alabama survived the battle relatively unscathed, except for the unusually high rate of casualties among the regiment's officers. Of the 300 men in the 15th Alabama who fought in the battle, 9 were killed and 75 were wounded (no report was issued on the regiment's missing). Some of these casualties occurred in the early morning hours of September 20, when the regiment got caught in a disastrous firefight at Boteler's Ford on the Potomac as it withdrew from Sharpsburg with the rest of Lee's army. Among those severely wounded that night was Captain Feagin, the last captain left standing in the 15th Alabama after Antietam. His wounds would keep him out of action for the rest of the year. Oates, who had heard the roar of battle from his sick bed in Shepherdstown and who watched the wounded streaming down the road to the army's rear, called the casualties of the 15th Alabama at Sharpsburg "considerable."

Although still not fully recovered, Oates caught up with the Army of Northern Virginia on September 21 at its camps on the Opequan River. He was dismayed by what he found. The ranks were depleted, the men worn out and hungry. Lieutenant Morris of Company G was in command of the regiment, for there were no captains left to take Feagin's place after he was wounded. Knowing that he could still not walk, but could ride, Oates obtained a horse and took command of the regiment.

As the army moved south and crossed the Shenandoah River, Oates and his regiment worked with the rest of Jackson's corps tearing up railroads, especially the tracks of the Winchester and Potomac Railroad that ran to Harper's Ferry. Stragglers and men back from sick leave rejoined the ranks of the Confederate army, which swelled during the autumn months. Around October 1, Major Lowther returned from sick leave and assumed command of the regiment. Setting up camp near Bunker Hill, Virginia, about seven miles north of Winchester, the 15th Alabama—and the rest of Lee's army—finally got some much-needed rest.[15]

That autumn, while Lee's army regained its strength, a religious revival swept through the Army of Northern Virginia's camps like a tornado. Evangelical preachers visited the army, and the soldiers enthusiastically attended Protestant services and camp meetings of various kinds. Casting out the sins of the world and finding one's place in God's realm had, by the end of 1862, become extremely important to the men in Lee's army. It also helped to assuage the loss of morale that came from the failure of Lee's invasion of Maryland and other Confederate defeats in 1862.

The Christian conversion, or "born-again" experience, gave new meaning to the soldiers' rag-tag existence, their war against Satan's horde from the Northern states, and their personal sufferings and losses. Prayer meetings also helped the Confederates, during this time of renewal and recommitment to the cause, to define more precisely their individual relationship with God— to come to terms, in other words, with their Maker. For the soldiers in Jackson's corps particularly, their new-found religion mirrored the ostentatious piety of their general and enabled them to understand the war itself as a holy crusade. With God on their side, Jackson was another Oliver Cromwell, and the army itself was another New Model Army fighting battles in the name of Jesus Christ.[16]

Bud Cody reported that camp meetings sometimes lasted three or four nights in a row, with preaching going on by firelight and candlelight. "There is a good deal of excitement," he wrote home to his minister father, "[and a] Large number of moaners every night." He did not say how many men in the 15th Alabama underwent a conversion experience (that process by which an individual gained God's grace), if any did at all, but he did observe that "large crowds attend[ed the] preaching."[17] As religious enthusiasm swept through the camp, no one bothered to recall that on the eve of Second Manassas a few soldiers from the 15th had maliciously broken up an African American camp meeting with an air of merriment that denigrated the spiritual significance of the gathering. No one among the Alabamians, so far as the record shows, suffered a guilty conscious from the incident, and even Oates reported it as if the whole affair had been a laughable bit of whimsy. But now the hardened veterans of the regiment humbled themselves before the same God, fell to their knees, begged for salvation, hungered for numinous rebirth. The longer the war dragged on, sounding its thunder and hurling its lightning bolts, the more soldiers became concerned with the state of their souls. Of course, no blacks came to disrupt *their* meetings.

It's unlikely that the awakening made any impression on Oates. Having long ago rejected the fervor of his mother's Baptist faith, he continued to keep religion out of his mind and heart. In his unbelieving state of mind, he was still very much the boy who had made fun of preachers while playing with his brother John and who had, into his adulthood, viewed organized religion with deep skepticism and grave doubts. For Oates, prayer meetings were not the means for his deliverance, either into the hands of God or out of this ungodly war. He relied, as he also had done, on his own individual powers and his own mastery, not on the Almighty's. His fate was in his own hands. If a bullet should find him on the battlefield, it would simply be the result of bad luck. God would have nothing to do with it.

Even as religious evangelism rose to a pietistic crescendo that fall, the army still had its work to do. After breaking up railroads in the peaceful surroundings of Bunker Hill and finding new sustenance in the word of God, Jackson's corps marched first to Culpeper, crossing the Blue Ridge once more, and then on to Port Royal along the banks of the Rappahannock, south of Fredericksburg, where his divisions laid out their camps. Winter came early that year. "A biting cold wind" blew in from the north, Oates recollected, "and it was all we could do to keep from freezing around great log fires." By this time, Major Lowther took sick again and went to the rear, so Oates assumed command of the regiment once more. Lowther's sickness, in his estimation, was a sure sign that another battle would soon take place.[18]

As the Army of the Potomac, now under the command of the bewhiskered Major General Ambrose E. Burnside, began to concentrate around Fredericksburg in December 1862, Lee ascertained the Union general's plan of crossing the Rappahannock undetected and advancing south to Richmond. Placing Jackson's corps on the right of his long line that stretched along the Rappahannock from Fredericksburg south to Port Royal, Lee waited patiently for Burnside to make a move during the first weeks of December. On December 10, the 15th Alabama received orders to cook three-days' rations and get ready to move. The following day, Union guns on Stafford Heights, overlooking the city of Fredericksburg, open fired on the town in a long and loud bombardment that reverberated between the hills on either side of the river. Down the Rappahannock, Oates and his men could hear the booming guns off in the distance, rumbling through the fog, like low thunder coming through a mountain hollow.[19]

On December 12, the Army of the Potomac crossed the Rappahannock in force and occupied the town of Fredericksburg, and the Union soldiers looted private homes and stores with a carefree abandon that seemed not to bother their officers or anyone in high command. Early the next day, which began in a heavy fog, Jackson's corps—including the 15th Alabama—deployed on the right of Lee's battle line at Hamilton's Crossing, about five miles south of Fredericksburg. Through the mist, the Alabamians could hear the Federal army across the river moving into its assault positions. "All was feverish with expectation," remembered one of Oates's men.[20]

By 9:00 A.M., the curtain of fog began to lift in front of them, revealing the magnificent—and terrible—sight of line after line of bluecoated troops arrayed across the plain, ready for the advance. Almost at once, far off on the right flank, the horse artillery under the command of young Major John Pelham roared into action and belched shot and shell into the compact Union ranks, tearing them apart. With only one Napoleon gun, which he moved quickly from place to place, Pelham tore huge gashes in the Union lines and delayed the general advance. The Union troops, forming a straight blue line like tin soldiers on a table top, were easy targets. It was, as Gus McClendon later recalled, "murderous work."[21]

For the first time under fire, Oates was in full command of the regiment. Ewell's division was now under the direction of Brigadier General Jubal A. Early, an irascible general who lacked Ewell's charm and experience. Colonel Robert F. Hoke of North Carolina took command of Trimble's old brigade, which included the 15th Alabama regiment, just before the battle. Hoke's brigade held the right of Early's defensive line on Prospect Hill, and the 15th Alabama was to the extreme left of Hoke's battle line. To the front was Major General A. P. Hill's right flank; to the rear was Major General D. H. Hill's division, acting as the reserve.[22]

After the Union guns delivered a devastating sheet of iron and lead into Jackson's lines, the Federal troops moved forward from their muddy plain toward the tracks of the Richmond, Fredericksburg and Potomac Railroad and the Confederate defensive lines beyond. As if on dress parade, the long rows of Federal soldiers advanced in perfect order and without hindrance. But Jackson's artillery crews were ready. They waited for the enemy lines to come into range and then pulled their lanyards. Caught in a deadly crossfire of precisely aimed guns, the Federal infantry wavered for a moment and then continued to move on. Behind them, the Union guns barked again, opening an artillery duel with Jackson's batteries that turned the battlefield into a hellish inferno.[23]

Off to the left of the 15th Alabama and Hoke's brigade, the Confederate line splintered and the Federals rushed into a gap between the brigades of Brigadier General James J. Archer and Brigadier General James H. Lane. Another Union thrust widened the break in the Confederate line by smashing into Lane's brigade of North Carolinians, while Archer—desperately calling for reinforcements—tried in vain to hold back the Union tide. At the same time, Jubal Early responded to Archer's plea for help and to the crisis that now confronted Jackson's divisions. Disregarding an order from Jackson to move toward the railroad, Early sent Colonel Edmund N. Atkinson's brigade into the fray, and above the din of battle the Rebel Yell could be heard as Atkinson's Georgians hit the Federals like a howling hurricane. In a swirl of confusing orders, Oates marched the 15th around the bewildered 13th Georgia, and the Alabamians took their place on the right of Hoke's battle line.[24]

As Confederate wounded streamed past the 15th Alabama toward the rear, Oates relayed Hoke's order for the brigade to fix bayonets. After firing a volley, the Confederates lunged forward, raising the Rebel Yell, and hit the Yankees full force with their bayonets lowered and murder in their eyes. Surprised and overwhelmed by the ferocity of Hoke's counterattack, the blue line wavered and broke. "The brigade," wrote Oates later, "swept everything before it in handsome style." One of his men reported that the Union troops "did not take time to give us a single fire, but retreated in confusion to their batteries[,] which were about seven or eight hundred yards from our rifle pits."[25]

Hoke's brigade—and Oates's Alabamians with it—would not stop. "The charge was kept up for a quarter of a mile," Oates remembered later, "just as though we were going through Burnside's lines to the river." Atkinson's brigade charged at the same time, making the Confederate surge unstoppable. Down the hill and into the railroad cut, Hoke's men pushed the Federals back and captured hundreds of prisoners who were frantically waving white handkerchiefs. Still the Confederates rolled forward, Oates and his men among the vanguard on the right of Hoke's battle line. "We had men in front a-going," Oates recalled, "and there was no halting."

Beyond the railroad cut, the Confederates reached a ditch, where they discovered more Federals than they had expected to find. Suddenly Hoke realized his brigade had stepped into range of the Union artillery, but it was too late. The Federal guns opened a killing fire on the Confederates. Oates saw Hoke's horse go down to its knees, throwing the general from the saddle. When the horse rose and ran, it dragged Hoke—whose foot was caught in a stirrup—for some distance before it could be stopped. Hoke, said Oates, "seemed addled for the moment by his fall," but quickly regained his composure. Hoke ordered the 15th Alabama and the rest of his brigade back to the vicinity of the railroad.[26]

Meanwhile, the battle raged farther north, where Burnside had ordered one of his Grand Divisions to attack Marye's Heights, a promontory overlooking the town of Fredericksburg. Longstreet's corps was huddled behind strong defenses on the heights, including the formidable defense provided by a sunken road and a stone wall that ran along the base of the high ridge. All afternoon and into the evening, in a series of assaults that even today seem shockingly wasteful and stupid, the brave men in Major General Edwin V. Sumner's division tried to break through the Confederate line, but only came within 150 yards of the sunken road. The repeated Union attacks accomplished nothing, except the slaughter of thousands who had attempted to achieve the impossible. That night a blue carpet of dead and wounded covered the ground beneath Marye's Heights, and the wails of the maimed could be heard from one end of the battlefield to the other in the cold darkness.[27]

Back along the far right of the Confederate line, where Jackson contemplated his situation and mulled over the possibility of a counterattack against the Federals, Oates and his men found scant protection in a shallow ditch. Almost as soon as the regiment reached the ditch, and the men crouched low to avoid being easy targets, the Confederate artillery behind them fired repeated salvos that soon were answered in kind by the Federal guns. "The position of the Fifteenth," said Oates, "[was] as perilous and disagreeable as well could be." Randolph Smedley, a sergeant in Company I, later wrote home that "there was not even a sprig to shelter us from the ball, grape, and canister which was being poured into our ranks from the enemy's batteries." Around sunset, the last artillery duel of the day ended; later the 15th Alabama retired to the protection of the railroad cut, where Oates and his men spent an uneasy night. As the night grew colder, the men of the 15th prowled around, looking to steal whatever they could find from the Union dead. Oates came upon two barefoot Alabamians who sat next to a wounded Federal, arguing over who deserved the man's boots as they waited for him to die. Oates settled the argument by taking the Federal's boots for himself and giving his wornout pair to one of his barefoot men.[28]

All during the next day, December 14, Lee and his generals waited for another Union assault that never came. So did Oates and his men, who continued to occupy the railroad cut and who thought for sure that the Yankees would attack them again. That night, the 15th Alabama was finally relieved and sent to the rear. It rained and snowed all night, but the men of the 15th celebrated the fact that for the first time in forty hours they were now allowed to build fires, walk around, and talk as much as they wanted. In the morning, another foggy day along the Rappahannock, the 15th Alabama marched to within three miles of Port Royal and happily began to set up the regiment's winter quarters. Despite the fact that the 15th Alabama had been in the thick of the fighting at Fredericksburg, its casualties were fairly light—three killed and thirty wounded.[29] All in all, Oates and his men had been extremely lucky.

It was a miserable winter that brought rain and snow and more mud to Virginia. The 15th Alabama—like every other regiment in the army—staked out its camp site and built crude log huts for its winter barracks. One of Oates's men remembered that four or five inches of snow stayed on the ground for most of January, and everyone experienced and complained about the bitter cold.

The winter of 1863 brought changes to the Army of the Northern Virginia. Implementing a law passed by the Confederate Congress requiring brigades to be organized by states, Lee ordered in mid-January the transfer and exchange of various regiments—including the 15th Alabama—into new brigades, divisions, and even corps. Oates's regiment was reassigned to a brigade under the command of Brigadier General Evander M. Law, a twenty-six-year-old native of South Carolina who looked considerably younger than his years. Law's new brigade, which consisted of the 4th, 15th, 44th, 47th, and 48th Alabama regiments, was placed in Major General John Bell Hood's division in Longstreet's First Army Corps. None of this sat particularly well with Oates and his men, who regretted having to leave their comrades in Trimble's old brigade and disliked being taken away from Jackson's command. "We were greatly attached to 'Stonewall' Jackson," wrote Gus McClendon, "for he had never known defeat."[30]

It did not take long, however, for the 15th Alabama to become acclimated to its new brigade. Toward the end of January, a huge storm spread snow several inches deep across the barren landscape, and the idle Confederates—including the 15th Alabama—took part in snowball fights that started on a small scale, involving men from one or two regiments, then grew in size as more and more men became caught up in the mock battle. Two or three thousand men on each side were soon flinging snowballs at one another. Off in the distance, Professor Thaddeus Lowe's observation balloon hovered in the sky trying to collect intelligence for the Army of the Potomac. Instead its operators witnessed probably the greatest snowball fight ever to occur in North America.[31]

Morale among the Confederates remained remarkably high. The religious revival, which had been interrupted by the battle of Fredericksburg, resumed in earnest in the camps, and one soldier in the 15th Alabama remembered passing the time singing "old time sacred music songs." Despite the tedium of camp life, which included daily drilling and occasional picket duty, the men of Lee's army kept up their spirits, endured the harsh winter, and hoped for a quick end to the conflict. Many believed that it would only take one or two more victories to win the war. Such beliefs, however, sprang from an optimism that reflected little more than wishful thinking. President Jefferson Davis had expressed similar optimism in an address to Congress in January: "By resolute perseverance in the path we have hitherto pursued, by vigorous efforts in the development of all our resources for defense, and by the continued exhibition of the same unfaltering courage in our soldiers and able conduct in their leaders as have distinguished the past, we have every reason to expect that this will be the closing year of the war."[32]

But there was no real end in sight. If anything, the war was to become more intense, more brutal, more protracted in every way. Fredericksburg, with all its blood and horror, seemed to be evidence of the emergence of a new war that could not be won overnight or even by the armies fighting a few more battles. Out of the fog and blood at Fredericksburg, the conflict between North and South was becoming a hard war—an all-out conflict that would engage the resources of both nations, bring their armies into hard-fought and devastating battles, draw heavily on their economies for sustenance, damage as much as possible their enemy's means of supply, assault each other's morale, engage in diplomatic contests involving foreign powers, and leave no one on either side untouched by the war's inconceivable destruction or its excruciating human suffering. Although no one could quite see it as yet, the war was becoming harder, more savage, more ruinous for everyone concerned, and it would not be over soon. Ahead lay a long road of battles, death, and sorrow.[33]

Other changes that winter shaped the new war and how it would be fought. On January 1, Lincoln issued the Emancipation Proclamation—a war measure, as the president called it—that freed all the slaves in the Southern states still in rebellion against the United States (with some exceptions, including places like Tennessee, several counties in Virginia, and parishes in Louisiana occupied by Union troops). Southerners furiously denounced the proclamation as proof that Lincoln and his political allies were as radical in their stand on slavery as the South had long maintained. Confederate leaders, including Jefferson Davis, also condemned the Lincoln administration for its intention to recruit black soldiers into the Union army. For Davis, and for many other Southerners, the Emancipation Proclamation meant that "a restoration of the Union has been rendered forever impossible by the adoption of a measure which from its very nature neither admits of retraction nor can coexist with union."[34]

Captain William Oates and his Southern brethren damned the proclamation, pointing out that it confirmed that Lincoln was nothing more than a black abolitionist at heart. But he also recognized that the use of black troops by the Federals would only magnify the shortages in manpower that the Confederacy was experiencing. To do something about the South's diminishing pool of recruits, Oates—presumably on his own authority—went to Richmond for four days in February 1863 to convince the Confederacy's leaders that slaves should be allowed to enter the Southern army "on such terms as would make them friends of the South." It is not certain to whom he offered his ideas, but he later claimed, and there is no particular reason to doubt his word, that he proposed enabling slaves to fight for the Confederacy in return for their full freedom after their term of service. What's more, he said to the Richmond officials, the freed slaves should then receive a bounty of eighty acres of public land as a homestead. If the same law provided for the gradual emancipation of the slave soldier's wife and children, the Confederacy would gain both good soldiers and good citizens.

For a young man already skilled in the art of politics and courtroom discourse, Oates seriously misunderstood the political climate—and the Southern racial ideology—surrounding the issues of emancipation and the use of black soldiers in the Confederate armies. By proposing that the Confederacy should fight fire with fire, Oates stepped into the flames himself. In response to Oates's proposal, an Alabama congressman insisted that slaves would never fight and would desert to the Union army. But Oates tried to explain that desertion would be averted if the Confederacy offered its fighting slaves their freedom after the war. Confederate congressmen from the border states of Missouri and Kentucky thought Oates's idea had some merit, but representatives from the other Southern states, where slavery still thrived, opposed even "the slightest experiment in that direction." In disgust, Oates noted that some slaveowners preferred that their own sons, rather than their slaves, do the fighting. Congressman James L. Pugh, one of Oates's old mentors and a leader of the Eufaula Regency, told him bluntly: "If we free the negroes to make soldiers of them, that is simply throwing aside the bone of contention, and we had as well stop the war at once." Obviously Oates saw the issue differently. His views may have resembled the later opinions of Robert E. Lee, who in January 1865 made plain his belief that white supremacy would continue to keep blacks in their place even if they should win freedom by serving in the Confederate military.

In the end, Oates's journey to Richmond produced shock, disbelief, and impolite sneers among the legislators with whom he met. Only General Ewell, with whom Oates discussed the question of slaves in the military, responded favorably to his plan. Ewell, in fact, had proposed to President Davis the idea of freeing slaves and arming them for service in the military as early as the summer of 1861. Davis, at that time, thought Ewell's suggestion was madness. Oates found a similar response among the Richmond leadership in the winter of 1863. The authorities, he reported, "treated my suggestion as the vagaries of a young man's enthusiasm." How many enemies he made among the politicians in Richmond because of his proposal is anyone's guess, but it seems likely that they viewed him with suspicion and distrust. Oates blamed their reaction on their ineptitude and their lack of vision. He firmly believed that if the people of the Confederacy had been given the choice between giving up slavery or giving up their new nation, "the people would have said, 'Let slavery go.'"[35]

Given all that he experienced in Richmond, it seems improbable that the South would have ever let go of slavery as easily as Oates surmised. It was for slavery and its preservation that the South was fighting; it was for slavery and its preservation that the South was seeking its independence. Slavery was an essential ingredient in the Confederate national identity and in the South's political structure. To have removed slavery from the Confederate cause would have, for thousands of Southerners, eliminated their primary reason for risking their lives on the battlefield and sacrificing their own welfare on the homefront. It would have threatened white Southern males with their loss of mastery, whether over slaves in their possession or other subordinates in the region's patriarchal dominion. Manual labor, which had become almost exclusively associated with blacks, would be left without a workforce to perform it. The hierarchical social structure would have its base obliterated, and the rest of society's layers would crash down on top of one another. Without slavery, the South simply would no longer be the *South*.

Obviously Oates misjudged the mindset of the political leaders in Richmond, but his biggest miscalculation was his timing. His trip to plead for black recruits came when the civilian authorities lacked any deep awareness of the dwindling manpower in the Confederate armies and finite numbers of qualified recruits throughout the South, although these issues should have been of top concern. Less than a year after Oates's Richmond sojourn, Major General Patrick Cleburne and several officers of the Army of the Tennessee issued a memorandum urging the Davis administration to enroll black soldiers. Recommending gradual emancipation and the legalization of slave marriages, Cleburne expressed the fear that the war would soon "exhaust the white race." Like Oates, Cleburne was naive and unprepared for the harsh reactions his proposal received in the army and in Richmond. Most white Southerners dismissed the idea as inherently containing the seeds that would destroy their own liberties. Despite the unpopularity of the idea, the debate over using slaves as soldiers continued in the Confederacy. By the end of 1864, even President Davis—who hoped everyone would forget his condemnation of the Emancipation Proclamation—and his cabinet voiced support for such a plan, but opposition throughout the South remained strong and boisterous. Lee, the South's great hero, finally gave his consent to the idea, arguing that slaves who fought for the Confederacy should be emancipated. In March 1865, as the war sped to its conclusion, the Confederate Congress narrowly enacted a bill to enlist black soldiers without granting them freedom. But it was too little, too late. The Confederate government did practically nothing to implement the act before the great finale occurred at Appomattox.[36]

Promising an end to slavery, as the Emancipation Proclamation did in early 1863, Lincoln played a wild card—the trump card—of the war. The proclamation changed everything. Lincoln, with the stroke of a pen, had ensured that the war, which had previously been fought to preserve the Union, or to win Southern independence, or to defend constitutional rights, or to end slavery, or to sustain the old thirty-four star flag, would henceforth become—and would irrevocably remain—a Northern war for black freedom and a Southern war against it. The Emancipation Proclamation redefined the nature of the war for both sides. From the Northern and foreign perspective, the proclamation meant that the Union cause was now aimed at freeing the slaves and enlisting African Americans in the fight. From the Confederate perspective, the war remained a struggle for *white* freedom, but it also became what Southerners had predicted it would be from the very start: a war over the fate of slavery. After January 1863, it became increasingly unlikely for the South to be able to lose the war and still hold on to slavery. If it *won* the war, the South could surely prolong the life of slavery.

It was the Emancipation Proclamation that had shifted the war's focus, subtly yet dramatically; indeed, Lincoln's document altered the war's very purpose, North and South. To win the war, the South now had to fight against the prospect of black emancipation. Everything, from every angle, pointed back to the peculiar institution. On the firing line, Oates and his fellow Confederates might like to believe—might insist repeatedly and forcefully—that they were fighting for white liberties, for state rights, and for Southern independence. But it was becoming harder and harder to declare, and at the same time to believe in one's heart, that this war was about anything other than the destiny of slavery. In that light, Oates's pleas about enlisting slaves in the Confederate military *had* to be rejected or ignored in Richmond. To arm the slaves, and to grant them their freedom, would have required a repudiation of the Southern cause—a cause fully devoted to preventing the abolition of slavery and the emancipation of every black slave.

And so the monster storm increased its gusts and churned the seas. It bore down equally in all its madness on the Union and the Confederacy. The tyrannical clouds raced across the darkened skies. Bewildered and frustrated, adrift like a shipwrecked sailor, Oates returned to his regiment and waited for the next wave, the next whitecap, to toss him about and put him once more in harm's way.

4

RAGGED JACKS

Whenever the 15th Alabama rested in camp, or went on the march, or stood fighting in battle line, William Oates had more to worry about than just himself. As commander of the regiment—even a temporary commander—the welfare of his men became his primary concern. But his awareness was particularly acute because his younger brother was serving as a lieutenant in Company G of the regiment. It was difficult for William not to have his eye on John, watching out for him, looking over his brother's shoulder, protecting him if he could, keeping him out of harm's way. John's presence was both a comfort and a source of grave apprehension for William.

In battle, the heat of the moment generally required William's attention elsewhere, but he must have gone into every fight wondering how his brother was faring and worrying about him getting hurt. Likewise, John must have shared the same concerns about William. These brothers enjoyed an exceptionally close relationship—it's no exaggeration to say that they were each other's best friend—and combat must have made them wish they could be in sight of one another or even fighting side-by-side. Sometimes that was possible when William was serving as a captain only of Company G. But in assuming direction of the entire regiment, the elder Oates would have taken up a position in the battle line that kept him toward the rear of the regiment's advancing lines and well behind his brother.

For the Oates brothers, and for countless other young soldiers in both armies, the Civil War was a family affair. Unlike modern military units, Civil War companies and regiments often contained fathers and sons, brothers, cousins, and sometimes in-laws and more distant relatives as well. These citizen soldiers joined the army by enlisting in units drawn from their local communities and surrounding areas. Not only did they know one another, having grown up together in the same towns or on neighboring farms, but they typically had deeper ties through blood and marriage. No restrictions in the Union or Confederate armies prevented family members from serving in the same company or the same regiment. The men who fought the Civil War often referred to it as "a brother's war," which emphasized the fraternal dimensions of a war that pitted Americans against Americans. Sometimes brothers did actually fight against each other, one for the Union, the other for the Confederacy, as did the famous Crittenden brothers of Kentucky, sons of Senator John J. Crittenden. But for many more brothers, the Civil War was fought brother *with* brother, one consanguine brother marching shoulder-to-shoulder into battle with another. Brothers could be found in nearly every Civil War regiment and company on both sides.

William and John Oates were not the only brothers or men from the same family who served in the 15th Alabama. Morris Holmes and his two sons, Pulaski and William, enlisted together in the Henry Pioneers, the unit William Oates had raised with recruits from Abbeville and Henry County. After the Henry Pioneers was mustered into service as Company G of the 15th Alabama, Morris and his sons served until the father and his eldest son, Pulaski, died of disease before seeing any combat; the remaining male member of the family, William, served until the surrender at Appomattox. Other fathers and sons saw service in the regiment's eleven other companies.[1]

It was brothers, though, who made up a huge portion of the soldiers in Company G. Three Griffin brothers had enlisted in the company; one of them received a disability discharge, one died of disease, and the other died of a wound received at Fredericksburg. As Company G's first lieutenant, John Oates gave his commands to an astounding number of men who were related to one another: three Riley brothers (originally there had been six, but three had died of disease); three Kirkland brothers (there had been four, but one died at Second Manassas); three McLeod brothers (there had been four, but one received a medical discharge, returned home, and then reenlisted in another unit); three Shepherd brothers; three Stone brothers; two Galloway brothers (there had been four, but two had died); two Renfroe brothers and two Smith brothers (there had been three each, but one Renfroe brother received a medical transfer to a desk job and one Smith brother took a medical discharge); two Enfinger brothers; two Balkcom brothers; two Melvin brothers; two Miller brothers; two Parish brothers; and two Woodham brothers. There would have been more, except that only one of the five Roney brothers was still alive or on active duty by 1863, one of two Trawick brothers had died of disease, one of the two Whatley brothers returned home to recover from a serious wound; two Sumner brothers had died in hospital, and the three Watson brothers had all died between October 1861 and August 1862.[2]

In the nineteenth century, brothers were often each other's closest friends and comrades. The military units of the Civil War reflected that familial bond, literally and figuratively. For many soldiers, their company and sometimes their regiment became surrogate families; for brothers serving in the same company or in the same messes, their units were extensions of their real families. Comrades who were not related by blood became new members of a family, a band of brothers, who marched together, ate together, played together, fought together, and, too often, died together. Familial bonds enhanced unit cohesion, making soldiers feel like brothers, even if they really weren't. Commissioned and noncommissioned officers commanded their companies with an air of authority that resembled fathers, uncles, and older brothers. Conventions of Victorian manhood required that obedience and respect be shown to older male family members. A young man was also expected to fulfill his kinship duties and prove his loyalty to his family. Those values carried over into the hierarchy of leadership and obedience in Civil War companies. Soldiers frequently used the language of family to describe their experiences during the war, particularly when they interpreted the character traits of their officers. Metaphors of family communicated actual ties of affection that existed between officers and their men. Officers spoke of their troops as "their boys"; when an officer fell in combat, enlisted men sometimes felt like they had lost their "father." The deep affection bound officers and soldiers together in a reciprocal relationship that resembled ties of kinship. In the ranks, soldiers hoped their officers would command with the hand of a gentle father; the officers expected their troops to obey and show all the heroism of a favorite son.[3]

But the familial nature of companies and regiments meant that these bands of brothers also experienced the contention—the bitter, competitive feuds—that sometimes divide fathers and sons and set brother against brother. When, as in the case of the Oates brothers, one held a higher rank than the other, the relationship between actual brothers could occasionally become strained. John Oates, for example, had a stubborn streak as pronounced as his brother's. Given his own imperious manner, William found his younger brother's independence a source of annoyance and a growing cause for concern. Sometimes John simply would not obey William's brotherly commands, although the younger brother apparently never failed to heed his military orders. For all their closeness, and for all their sincere devotion to one another, John tried diligently to escape from under William's shadow, as younger brothers frequently tend to do. Lieutenant Oates wanted his accomplishments to be his own, without his brother's assistance, and he avoided seeking favors or special treatment from William. He took pride in the fact that he had reenlisted in the army before any bounty law had been passed by the Confederate Congress and that he had served the first twenty-two months of the war without missing a day's duty and without ever taking a furlough. In January 1863, he was promoted to second lieutenant, not as the result of any favoritism shown by or to his brother, but because resignations and transfers necessitated the filling of officer vacancies in Company G.

John learned, however, that he could not make his way in the army entirely on his own. By the winter of 1863, while freezing temperatures and blankets of snow in Virginia kept him shivering and brought on the discomforts of rheumatism, John no longer felt himself; illness and fatigue slowed him down and made him more dependent on William's good graces. Observing that his brother needed rest, and recognizing that the 15th Alabama's ranks had become depleted from casualties, sickness, and desertion, William Oates decided to send his brother on a recruiting mission back home to Henry County. The elder Oates assigned a sergeant to accompany John on the trip to Alabama. In February, John left Virginia and returned home, grateful to have the rest and to do some good for the regiment all at the same time. Back in Abbeville, John found his neighbors in good spirits, although it was certain that "the novelty & enthusiasm of the war [had] worn away." Hope for foreign recognition of the Confederacy and a quick Southern victory no longer "delude[d] the people." Farmers were planting crops and raising stock to feed the armies, convinced that the war would last as long as Lincoln remained president of the United States.[4]

As the first signs of spring appeared in Virginia, Hood's division was on the move again. In the wake of the Fredericksburg campaign, President Davis, Secretary of War James A. Seddon, and Lee all saw—in somewhat different terms—the threats that existed if Union forces again attempted to take Richmond. Responding to the potential threat, the Confederate leadership instructed Longstreet to deploy two of his divisions—Pickett's and Hood's—to block any possible Union invasion from the southeast and, at the same time, remain close enough for easy rail transport to defend against the Federals if they decided to push across the Rappahannock. They also recognized the value of having Longstreet's divisions forage for badly needed food in an area that, as yet, had not been picked clean by both armies. Longstreet established his headquarters in Petersburg and moved Pickett's and Hood's divisions to Suffolk, sixteen miles west of Norfolk, where he hoped to box-in 17,000 Federals who defended eight forts and fourteen miles of entrenchments while his foraging parties collected what they needed from farms nearby and in North Carolina.[5]

On April 1, Hood's division—and the 15th Alabama with it—marched through Petersburg and turned southeast toward Suffolk. On the way, they passed through shabby-looking Jerusalem, the Southampton county seat, where Nat Turner had led a slave insurrection in August 1831, killing about sixty whites. Not that Oates mentioned the fact in any of his writings: He seems to have been unaware of the area's historical significance. But it was Turner's rebellion, probably more than any other historical event, that made so many Southerners wary of making soldiers out of slaves—as Oates had recently proposed in Richmond.

Near the Nansemond River, Oates and his men bivouacked very close to the Union batteries not far from Hill's Point on Longstreet's left flank, after having pushed back some Federal skirmishers into Suffolk in a firefight that resulted in very few casualties on both sides. There they lived an uncomfortable existence without fires and without much sleep—the Union guns were active and noisy, as were the skirmishers on both sides. The Confederates built their entrenchments and dug their rifle pits in this low, piney woods country, but rain and the Federal artillery—especially shelling from the gunboats on the Nansemond—occasionally impeded their progress and frequently kept them all miserable and weary.[6]

John Oates returned from Alabama with the new recruits for the regiment, but the rheumatism in his right hip, thigh, and leg had now become severe and practically immobilized him. His pain, which he attributed to "prolonged exposure in camps," grew so extreme that he sent a request to Congressman James L. Pugh for an appointment as a judge advocate of court martials, an assignment John believed would enable him "to take care of myself for a while," even though his recent leave at home had done little to improve his health. He refused to think about quitting the service. Pugh recommended his appointment to the secretary of war, but young Oates never received orders to transfer out of the 15th Alabama. Like so many other men who found the Suffolk siege a test of endurance, John lived with his discomfort and tried to cope with an illness that steadily grew worse and worse. His condition made William more fretful, more doting and anxious as the dreadful Suffolk campaign went on day after day.[7]

It was spring in Virginia and time for the war to erupt again in earnest. Union soldiers splashed across the Rappahannock River on April 29, when Major General Joseph Hooker, who had replaced Burnside as commander of the Army of the Potomac, began to move his troops in an ambitious and impressive offensive against Lee's army. Lee, feeling particularly vulnerable, sent telegrams that day to Davis and Seddon informing them of Hooker's initiative and asking them for the return of Longstreet's two divisions; privately, though, Lee knew that these divisions would probably not reach him in time. Seddon forwarded the messages along to Longstreet, urging him to break away from Suffolk and rejoin Lee as quickly as possible. But the siege could not be lifted quite that easily and Longstreet's supply wagons—which could not be sacrificed—were still in North Carolina completing their foraging missions. It was not until the evening of May 3 that the Confederates were able to abandon their entrenchments and move back across the Blackwater River toward Petersburg. By that time, Lee had fought Hooker in the battle of Chancellorsville, winning another great triumph, even without Longstreet's two divisions.[8]

With Longstreet's withdrawal from Suffolk, Oates and his Alabamians came close to escaping the siege practically unscathed. But the regiment was ordered to guard Hood's rear as the division pulled out of its entrenchments. On the night of May 3, the Federals, who had not ascertained Longstreet's intention to retreat, decided to attack the Confederate lines that night along the Providence Church Road. Oates and his men fought a sharp engagement as they tried to hold their position against the advancing Federals, but ultimately, after a back-and-forth fight in the forbidding darkness, the 15th Alabama withdrew to the protection of some woods, where the regiment remained until midnight. Then it joined the retreat march through the night. On the march from Suffolk, Oates and the 15th Alabama learned that Stonewall Jackson had been seriously—perhaps mortally—wounded at Chancellorsville.[9]

Since September, Oates had gained invaluable experience as a regimental commander and had demonstrated his talents as a leader of men. In early May, he received news that he had been appointed a colonel in the Provisional Army, C.S.A. (his commission was to date from April 28) and assigned officially to command the 15th Alabama. He replaced Colonel James Cantey, who had been promoted to brigadier general, and Lieutenant Colonel John Treutlen, who had resigned. Both men had been absent from the regiment on sick leave since the summer of 1862. Captain Isaac Feagin was promoted to lieutenant colonel; even though he actually outranked Oates, he said that he preferred not to assume the regimental command. Major Lowther, who remained on sick leave, was passed over, mostly because Generals Hood and Law, according to Oates, believed the vacancies in the regiment "should be filled by the captains who had so long performed the duties of colonel and lieutenant-colonel." The decision angered Lowther, who swore—despite his frequent illnesses and absences from the army, and his apparent lack of desire to participate in the war—he would do everything he could to win back the command of the regiment.

Unfortunately for Oates, the Confederate Senate never confirmed his commission as colonel, for reasons that are unclear. The legislators did not reject Oates's appointment; rather, they simply failed to act, as they did in other instances regarding commissions and promotions. Technically, he was still a captain. However, because he did not know that the Senate had neglected his confirmation, he assumed the rank and title of colonel.[10]

Later that month, the 15th Alabama moved with Hood's division to Raccoon Ford on the Rapidan River, where it was assigned picket duty at the river crossing. Oates had the regiment set up camp in a grove of chestnut trees and a clover pasture about half a mile in the rear of the ford. From the very start, the men of the 15th Alabama liked the camp site. "Here," said Oates, "we were most pleasantly situated." The likelihood of a Federal incursion seemed remote at best, the birds sang joyously in the trees, warm spring days lifted everyone's spirits, the soldiers dropped fishing lines into the clear waters of the Rapidan, and Oates and his men thought of their time at Raccoon Ford as "a happy retreat."

Oates had the best time of all. Not far from the ford lived the Porter family, a notable clan in this region of the Rapidan. The Porters owned a fine, stately home on the south bank of the river and graciously opened their doors to Oates, who lived the high life for the time his regiment remained bivouacked at Raccoon Ford. Even more appealing than the family's cordiality, however, was the Porter's fetching daughter, Miss Fannie, who, Oates remarked years afterward, was "a charming young lady" with a talented singing voice. She sang him "the sweetest songs," he recalled, and spent endless hours entertaining him and keeping him company. A good soldier through and through, he admitted nevertheless that he would have been "willing to have remained at that camp to the close of the war." As on other occasions when the romance of the war flooded his emotions, Oates called to mind some lines written by his favorite poet, Robert Burns: "But pleasures are like poppies spread, you seize the flower, its bloom is shed."[11]

On June 5, Hood's men—including Oates and the 15th Alabama—watched from atop a railroad embankment as Major General J. E. B. Stuart, commander of Lee's cavalry division, put his horsemen on review at Brandy Station, north of Culpeper. The review of nearly 10,000 mounted Confederates was done up with all the finery and flair that Stuart, a master showman, could muster. "It was a beautiful affair," Oates remembered. The train brought carloads of civilians from Charlottesville and beyond, including Thomas H. Watts, a lawyer from Montgomery whom President Davis had appointed attorney general of the Confederacy.[12]

Shortly after dawn on June 9, while General Stuart's cavalrymen were still asleep after having conducted another spectacular review for the benefit of General Lee, scattered firing could be heard coming from the direction of Beverly Ford on the Rappahannock, a few miles from the cavalry's main camp on Fleetwood Hill at Brandy Station. Union cavalry had thrust itself across the river in a surprise attack that caught Stuart's men napping and groggy. What ensued was the largest clash between mounted cavalry ever to take place on the North American continent.

South of Culpeper, Oates's men could hear the distant firing that came from the direction of the cavalry encampments along the Rappahannock.

Expecting a Union attack from the direction of Stevensburg, Hood's division was deployed in battle line near a place called Flag Mountain, about a mile behind Fleetwood Hill on the road to Culpeper Court House, but the enemy assault never came. Oates thought the infantry had scared away the Union cavalry. "If there be anything thoroughly dreaded by cavalry," he wrote, "it is infantry." Finally, after nightfall, when all the noise of battle had ceased, and Stuart had successfully beaten back the Federal cavalry, the 15th Alabama and the other infantry regiments retired to their camps.[13]

While Stuart paraded his troops and defended his ground around Fleetwood Hill, Lee had been at work getting his army into shape for his next move against the enemy, a second invasion of the North. Lee's plan was to strike into Pennsylvania, pushing as far above the Mason-Dixon line as he could get, drawing the Union army out of Virginia, and giving his army an opportunity to feed off the Keystone State's abundant farms. A decisive victory on Northern soil might even reopen the question of foreign recognition of the Confederacy, or, at the very least, encourage war-weary Northerners to settle for peace. A victory, in short, might end the war.

To compensate for the loss of Jackson, who had died on May 10 from an infection triggered by the wounds he had received at Chancellorsville, Lee reorganized his army into three corps consisting of three divisions each. The First Corps was to remain under Longstreet's command. But Lee replaced Jackson with two of his lieutenants, putting the Second Corps under the command of Lieutenant General Richard S. Ewell and the Third Corps under Lieutenant General Ambrose P. Hill. Six cavalry brigades were placed under Stuart's overall command. The artillery reserve was abolished, and five artillery battalions were assigned to each of the corps. All told, the Army of Northern Virginia had about 75,000 men in its ranks. Among the regiments least affected by Lee's reorganization was Oates's 15th Alabama, which remained where it had been in the official roster—in Law's Alabama brigade, Hood's division, Longstreet's First Corps. With an estimated 600 men and 42 officers, the 15th Alabama was, as Oates later testified, "the strongest and finest regiment in Hood's division."[14]

On June 10, Ewell led the march to the north with his Second Corps, which headed toward the Shenandoah Valley through the mountains at Chester Gap. Five days later, on a bright sunny morning, while the temperature climbed steadily and the day became a scorcher, Oates and his men formed into columns, marched through the streets of Culpeper, and took their place in the ranks of Longstreet's corps on its way toward the Blue Ridge. North they marched through Virginia's lush countryside. Everyday was hot, and the men began to wither under the blazing sun. Some men fainted, others fell behind. On June 17, Hood's division marched only fifteen miles that day, "up hill and down dale," until it found comfort for the night in a grove of oak and hickory near Upperville.[15]

The following day, William Oates led his regiment across the Shenandoah River, where the men plunged into the ice-cold water fully clothed and carrying their muskets over their heads. That night a cold rain poured down in torrents as Oates and his regiment tried unsuccessfully to stay dry in their camp on the western side of the mountains, near Snicker's Ferry. A rainy dawn greeted the soaked men of Hood's division. Reports of Federal cavalry forced Law's brigade to recross the river and bivouac up on the slope of the mountain, almost reaching its summit. There it spent the night as Oates and his Alabamians shivered in the dense fog, cold rain, and stiff breezes that swept over the mountain.[16]

The Federal cavalry never got as far as Snicker's Gap, for J. E. B. Stuart successfully halted the blue horsemen west of Middleburg on June 19. After daybreak on June 20, as the rain kept falling, Law's brigade of Alabamians left the soggy notch at Snicker's Gap, retraced their steps along the Shenandoah, and crossed the river yet one more time. The rain, however, had swollen the river and had made it almost impossible to ford. A detachment of cavalry positioned itself a short distance below the ford to catch any soldier who might lose his footing and be swept downstream. Chilled to the bone, Oates and his fellow Alabamians went into bivouac on the other side of the river, fully convinced that they would never be warm again. But that night, the men cooked rations for the first time in days, the rain stopped, and while the heavy mist continued to shroud Hood's division in a gray cloak, most of his troops began to feel better.[17]

One of the exceptions was John Oates. Although there are no specific surviving reports of his condition during Lee's march north, it seems fairly certain that forced marches, damp weather, and repeated crossings of the Shenandoah River did him little good. One of Hood's veterans, writing nearly forty years after the Gettysburg campaign, pointed out how the heat and cold and wetness of that march contributed to the permanent ailments of many a soldier: "Now, when you see these poor old Confederate soldiers, all crippled up with rheumatism and suffering so many aches and pains, you will see . . . that it is the result of a suffering and hardships that the present generation have no idea of. Treat them kindly, when they all pass away, you will never see their like again on earth." For John Oates, the severe pain of his rheumatism would not wait until old age. His suffering must have been nearly unbearable with every step he took with his regiment.[18]

Rain was falling hard in the early morning of June 26 as Oates and his 15th Alabama headed toward the Potomac with the rest of Law's brigade. Around 8:00 A.M., they reached the swollen river at Williamsport and saw that wagons, men, and horses had clogged the pontoon bridges so completely that nothing was getting across. Hood's men, therefore, got themselves ready to ford the deep water. Oates led his men across the Potomac, with the river nearly up to their chins, as military bands played "Dixie" and other patriotic tunes. Everyone was in high spirits. Mitchell Houghton of the 15th Alabama thought the crossing was "the grandest military display I ever witnessed." General Hood became inspired by the exuberance of the soggy soldiers who waded the river. "Never before, or since," he wrote in his memoirs, "have I witnessed such intense enthusiasm as that which prevailed throughout the entire Confederate army."[19]

On the other side of the river, Hood's division was given a generous ration of whiskey captured from the Federals. "The consequence," reported Oates, "was that there were quite a number of drunken officers and men." He was not pleased. A teetotaler who remained one of the few sober men in the division, Oates saw that his men had become indolent from the whiskey, but the march for the day had not ended. He indignantly forced the men back into column as Hood's command continued its march north across the small sliver of Maryland and across the Pennsylvania border. Many of the soldiers gleefully remarked that they had eaten breakfast in Virginia, dinner in Maryland, and supper in Pennsylvania.[20] That night, Law's brigade camped south of Greencastle near a large spring.

Oates was as little fond of his soldiers' mistreatment of civilians and their property as he was of their drunkenness. Some of the men went out foraging that night, despite Lee's orders prohibiting such activities by individual soldiers. The foragers got less than they might have had it not been pouring, but even in the rain many Alabamians came back with food and other treasures found on farms in the area. Oates and his adjutant, Lieutenant De Bernie Waddell, rode out into the rain and the darkness to prevent what Oates called "depredations" against the local citizens. They found men from the regiment milking cows into their canteens—and doing it with such ease that Oates realized this was not the first time the men had obtained fresh milk in this fashion. Oates posted a guard at the farm to protect the owner's property, and in return the family invited him to join them for supper.

The conversation at the table was stimulating and educational. Oates urged the family members—all "very loyal people to the Union"—to speak freely about the war. Oates was shocked. In almost every way, his hosts appeared to be educated people. But when it came to the war, he said, they were "remarkably ignorant" and regarded the conflict largely "as a personal contention between two ambitious men" who wished to gain supremacy. One of the ladies, Oates recounted, called for both Davis and Lincoln to be hanged and the war ended. "The same measure of ignorance existed in the minds of two-thirds of the people in the Northern States," Oates wrote in disgust. Much of their ignorance, he suspected, could be blamed on the foreign roots of so many Northerners, like these "Dutch" farmers who shared their supper with him. Oates called the Germans and Irish who fought in the Union army the "hireling paupers of Europe." It was against this "trash," he said, that the "chivalric" Southerners were waging their noble cause.[21] His xenophobia, which would blossom more fully during his political career after the war, found fertile ground in Pennsylvania. Suspicious of anyone who looked or acted or spoke differently than he did, Oates thought the German American farmers peculiar and eccentric. And he did not think their women were attractive.

Unlike the nativists who had founded the Know-Nothing Party in the 1850s, and who feared Germans and Irish for their Catholicism, Oates's belittling of foreigners, including the German Americans of Pennsylvania, who were mostly Lutherans, seemed to flow from his firm belief in the superiority of Anglo-American ethnicity. Enthralled by the myths and symbols that emphasized a distinctive American way of life, Oates thought that white Anglo-Americans—and particularly those who had settled the South—had created a nearly perfect society in the New World, one that no foreign nation or people could rival. At the same time, though, he admittedly did not much care for German and Irish Catholics, even though his own Protestant faith tended to remain mostly hidden from view. For Oates, Lee's invasion of Pennsylvania confirmed all his worst suspicions of the North. Above the Mason-Dixon line, Northern citizens were mostly ignorant foreigners who lacked the correct ethnicity to be good, solid Americans. They did not fit Oates's picture, shared by his fellow Southerners, of a socially constructed white national identity. The influence of immigration on the North thus gave Southerners even more incentive to achieve their independence, for reconciling with the Northerners would ultimately mean diluting the perfection of an Anglo-American culture that could only be preserved, only handed down in all its fullness to posterity, in the more ethnically pure South.

But Oates could only think these thoughts and believe that they mattered by denying what he otherwise knew to be true. He had traveled extensively throughout the southeast and the southwest before the war, and he had seen for himself how ethnic pluralism worked, in places like the Florida panhandle, Louisiana, and Texas. More to the point, the ethnic purity of the South could only rest on a perpetuation of slavery and white supremacy, and a suppression of foreign immigration, all of which Oates enthusiastically favored, but his recent attempt to persuade Confederate authorities to enlist slaves in the army did not harmonize well with his ethnic illusions. If the slaves went free after serving in the military, someone would have to perform the South's hard labor—and eventually immigrants would have to augment the region's labor supply. No doubt Oates had not sorted out the fine analytical points in what seemed to be more an emotional, than a rational, response to foreigners. At the same time, he also grudgingly admitted that some of the Irish soldiers in his regiment were among the best fighters. All in all, Oates's opinions of foreigners, like so many of his other ruminations, did not constitute a fully integrated system of thought. It was, rather, a hodgepodge of conservative reaction. In the end, though, he ate the "Dutch" family's food without hesitation or complaint.[22]

The Southern tide, carrying the bobbing Oates brothers and all the weary men of the 15th Alabama, continued to flow north. Around noon on June 27, Law's Alabama brigade reached Chambersburg, Pennsylvania, a large and thriving market town in the heart of the Cumberland Valley, just west of the imposing Appalachian Mountains. Oates observed that the buildings in the town—houses, stores, hotels, and taverns—were closed up tight as he and his regiment marched down its tidy streets. "The people stood in crowds on the sidewalks and the upper story windows," he recalled, "to see the 'rebels pass.'" Some of the local inhabitants boldly waved American flags at the invaders and a few laughed openly at the scraggly appearance of Hood's troops, whom Fremantle himself called "ragged Jacks," but the Confederates took no particular offense at the jibes and answered them with jokes and cheers and laughter. Yet there were some serious exchanges, too. One lady in the crowd remarked to a companion in something more than a stage whisper: "They are the ones who have killed so many of our soldiers."[23]

The Alabamians passed through Chambersburg and camped in some shady woods about two miles outside of town. For the next two days, while rain fell on and off, Oates and his men rested comfortably in camp and roamed the countryside looking for food, clothes, and whatever supplies appealed to them. No doubt John Oates savored the halt and hoped that the break from marching might ease his worsening aches and pains.

"It was a delightful rest," wrote William Ward of the 4th Alabama. The men, he said, had been carefully instructed to stay out of "mischief," but their search for provisions could not be stopped. Oates tried his best to curb his men and their foraging expeditions to neighboring farms, where apple butter and light bread could be obtained in abundance. Two privates from the 15th Alabama managed to bring a dog and two beehives full of honey back to camp; the dog, complained an irate farmer the next day, was supposed to guard the hives from plunderers like the two Alabama privates, but "the scoundrels stole the dog, too."[24]

On June 30, Law's brigade received orders to march east through the rain and mud into Fayetteville and on to New Guilford, a tiny hamlet of a handful of houses. The brigade, including Oates and the 15th Alabama, arrived there on the morning of July 1, and set up camp in an oak grove just off the pike that led to Gettysburg. Here Oates gave up trying to stop his men from foraging throughout the countryside and granted permission for them to go out in search of food and other plunder. His troops found ample supplies of apple butter, bread, and fat chester pigs. During the day, Oates and his regiment could hear the distant rumble of artillery off to the east in the direction of Gettysburg. When the muffled sounds of war continued to echo into the afternoon, flat noises floating through the dead summer air, the men knew that a major engagement had begun somewhere over the hazy summits of South Mountain. Around nightfall, orders came for Law's brigade to rejoin Hood's division, which had moved forward with McLaws's division of Longstreet's Corps. Oates passed the word along for the men to cook three days' rations and to be ready to march at 3:00 A.M.[25]

A full moon broke through the clouds during the night, bathing the countryside in a silvery light. No one in the 15th Alabama got much sleep in the cool darkness, knowing that a battle was waiting tomorrow over the blue mountains. John Oates must have spent the night in dread. Even though the regiment was hardened now with veterans who knew what to expect in the fire and smoke of battle, feelings of fear and uncertainty passed through the ranks as they did on the eve of every engagement. "We were not all of us as brave as Caesar," William Oates wrote long after the war, "nor were men, with few exceptions, at all times alike brave."[26] Each battle brought a new and different trial of courage, new terrors, new tribulations. Tomorrow, on a steep hillside south of the town of Gettysburg, William Oates's own courage would be sorely tested, as would the bravery and fortitude of every man in the 15th Alabama Infantry.

Word arrived for the regiment to make ready and assemble for the march. The men moved like black specters in the moonlight. After breaking camp, Oates and his regiment stood ready to advance with Law's brigade. It was three in the morning on July 2. Oates tried to keep his men calm and steady during the hour it took for the brigade to step off down the road toward Gettysburg. The Alabamians were uncharacteristically quiet on this march under the bright moon and scattered clouds. Occasionally one heard the sharp crack from a bushwacker's gun or the startling shout of an order, but mostly the only sound that drowned out all others was the recurrent slapping of soles on the hard macadam pike. The brigade stepped quickly without making any stops for the men to rest or catch their breaths. Everyone, including Oates and his Alabamians, knew this would be a fatiguing march, a march to remember.[27]

From New Guilford, the Gettysburg road followed a winding route up and down endless rolling ridges and through the middle of expansive corn fields that stretched as far as the eye could see, which was a considerable distance in the bright moonlight. Beyond Fayetteville, a small village of houses clustered on either side of the road, Oates and his men began to climb higher hills as they grew closer to South Mountain. Five miles out of New Guilford, now well into the mountain passes, the men silently pondered the smoking ruins of an iron furnace at Caledonia owned by the radical congressman, Thaddeus Stevens. On June 26, Jubal Early had ordered his troops to set the place on fire in retaliation for Stevens's abolitionism and his uncompromising hatred of the South.[28]

On through the night marched the Alabamians, up to the gentle summit of South Mountain, over its crests, and down steep slopes into the lush farmland

surrounding Cashtown, eight miles west of Gettysburg. In the darkness, the
15th Alabama lost three men, deserters who decided that this would be their
last march through the uncertainty of night and into the horrible certainty of
battle waiting up ahead. Oates thought that at least two of these deserters
might have been ambushed by local guerrilla fighters.[29] At the moment,
though, he was less concerned with keeping track of his stragglers or watching for enemy militia than he was about the well-being of his brother John.

The night march was precisely what John Oates did not need. Dampness
in the night air made his rheumatism unbearable, and he could not keep up
with the regiment. His brother noticed that he had fallen behind, so he sent a
horse back for John and brought him up to the head of the column. Clearly
John was in bad shape. He must have been suffering considerable pain that
night, probably joint pain and muscle fatigue in his right hip, thigh, and leg.
No treatment was available to sooth his agony or alleviate his discomfort. He
simply had to do the best he could astride his brother's extra horse.[30] The war
had boiled down to a test of individual endurance—for the men of the 15th
Alabama who struggled across South Mountain on this forced march, for those
whose stamina had run out and who could take no more marching or fighting, for John Oates and his aching body, and for Colonel William C. Oates,
who felt personally responsible for each and every one of them.

As Oates and his men drew closer to Gettysburg, treading by the tidy
brick houses in the picturesque villages of Cashtown and McKnightsville, the
sun came up and they could see the Confederate field hospitals by the road-
side, where the wounded of yesterday's fight at Gettysburg and thousands of
Union prisoners waited for their fates to be decided.[31] It was not an inspiring
sight for the Alabamians, who could sense that their hurried march was but a
preliminary to today's battle; come this evening, many of their own number
would be dead, wounded, or in the hands of the enemy. Gettysburg was up
ahead, and already the stench of battle—the putrid aroma of the dead—was
in the air.

Between noontime and 2:00 P.M., Law's brigade reached Herr's Ridge,
about a mile west of Gettysburg, and got some much-needed rest after its
grueling twenty-mile march from New Guilford. Longstreet later said that
Law's forced march was "the best marching done in either army to reach the
field of Gettysburg." The men searched desperately for water, for they had
emptied their canteens on the long march, but they discovered that fresh
water was in short supply. Oates realized that the march had been more strenuous than he had realized, for he had lost a number of men who collapsed from
exhaustion or who fell behind as stragglers. His regiment was tired, hungry,
and thirsty. No one knew what the next move might be. They were told that
Lee and Longstreet were conferring up ahead, near a seminary on a parallel
ridge across a lush glen. Oates looked to his men and to his brother, whose

illness had grown worse throughout the morning, and he waited anxiously for orders to move forward.[32]

He did not have to wait long. Shortly after 2:00 P.M., Oates and his regiment were on the march again, following the brigade column with the entirety of Hood's division. Longstreet was trying to move two of his divisions—Hood's and McLaws's—to the far left of the Union line, where he and Lee hoped his troops could roll up the flank of the Army of the Potomac as they had done last September at Second Manassas. To do so, the divisions had to march from Herr's Ridge to the south and west behind Seminary Ridge and deploy along the Emmitsburg Road across from the Round Tops. Nothing seemed to go right that morning. Poor reconnaissance, conducted in the morning by Captain Samuel R. Johnston, failed to let Lee and Longstreet know precisely where the enemy had established its lines. Shoddy staff work by the aides of both Lee and Longstreet hampered the job of putting the Confederate troops where they belonged to launch the assault. A long delay resulted when Longstreet decided to wait for Law's brigade to arrive in Gettysburg before putting all his columns in motion; at the same time, Longstreet's sense of caution made him worry that his divisions would be spotted along their route by Federal signalmen on the summit of Little Round Top. When it became likely that the column had been detected by the signalman, Longstreet ordered a countermarch that took precious time to accomplish. As a result, the halting approach march—and countermarch—turned two miles into four. In an understatement, which revealed how thoroughly the deployment of Longstreet's divisions had become blurred in his mind, Oates recalled that "there was a good deal of delay on the march, which was quite circuitous."[33]

The afternoon wore on, hot and sultry. Sometime before 4:00 P.M., Hood's division emerged out of the trees on Seminary Ridge and deployed along the nearly bare crest of Warfield Ridge, straddling the Emmitsburg Road. The Alabamians were placed in the center of the brigade line. From where they stood, they could easily see the Slyder farmhouse, its orchard, and its surrounding fields. Ahead, just beyond the Slyder farm, stood Big Round Top, impressive with its thick woods and towering heights (General Law called the hill "a huge sentinel" rising up before them). Oates and his regiment occupied the center of the brigade line, with the 44th and 48th Alabama regiments to his right and the 47th and 4th Alabama regiments to his left. In support of the main line, the brigades of Brigadier General George T. Anderson and Brigadier General Henry Lewis Benning stood about 200 yards to the rear.[34]

Yet even as Hood's troops readied themselves for battle, it became evident to Longstreet and his division commanders that the situation along the Emmitsburg Road was radically different from the one Lee had anticipated in drawing up his battle plan that morning. Instead of facing an enemy arrayed along the low heights of Cemetery Ridge to the northwest, Longstreet and

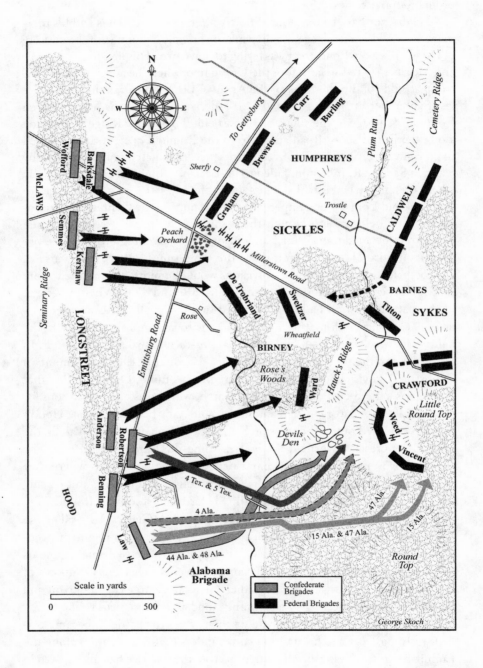

his men saw an entire Federal corps—Sickles's Third Corps—in their front, arranged in a salient near a peach orchard on the Emmitsburg Road. While Longstreet had been making his long and slow countermarch in the open country between Willoughby Run and Marsh Creek, Major General Daniel E. Sickles—acting against orders—had moved his entire corps forward from the shank of the Union "fish hook" line to the high ground around the Sherfy peach orchard, which would forever after be known as *the* Peach Orchard. In so doing, Sickles exposed the left flank of the Army of the Potomac, but he also presented a formidable obstacle along the Emmitsburg Road that the Confederates had not expected to find. Sickles's presence at the Peach Orchard caused confusion and hesitation among the Confederates. Accordingly, the battle plan was revised to reflect the reality of the new circumstances, particularly Sickles's unexpected forward deployment, but Longstreet insisted on following Lee's instructions for the assault along the Emmitsburg Road, much to the dismay of his division commanders.[35]

As Hood's men were forming into two battle lines, with Law's brigade in front on the right and Robertson's brigade in front to the left, Hood received word from his scouts that Big Round Top mountain was unoccupied by Federal forces and that the Union supply train was parked behind it to the east. Hood immediately notified Longstreet of this fact and asked for permission to swing his men around the mountain and take the Union line from the rear, but Longstreet refused to approve the maneuver and declared that he would follow Lee's battle plan as ordered. Distraught, and fearing that a perfect opportunity for victory was being ignored, Hood formally protested his commander's decision, but to no avail. After a flurry of messages sailed back and forth between the two generals, Longstreet finally rode up to Hood, reined in his horse, and told him flat out: "We must obey the orders of General Lee."[36]

While the generals argued among themselves, Oates and his men lay in the grass and contemplated the battle to come and their own prodigious thirst. Federal artillery opened on Hood's lines, and while the Texas boys to the left of Law's brigade took most of the heat, some of the shells found their way into the ranks of the Alabamians. Captain James Reilly's North Carolina battery was already in position in front of the Alabama lines, and as soon as some of Law's pioneers chopped down trees in the woods ahead of them, the Confederate guns let loose their reply to the Union cannon. In a short time, the cannonading became severe, and the men in the ranks impatiently tried to keep still as the howling shells flew overhead, some of them exploding directly above them. Across the valley before them, they could see fleecy puffs of smoke from the Union cannon near Devil's Den. Their ears ached from the banging of the guns. The artillery exchange took their minds off the impending battle, but not entirely. One soldier in Hood's division described the peculiar feelings as one awaited the order to go into battle: "The heart is heavy; the blood feels as if it was congealed; the breath comes short and quick." When the order finally does come, "it is a relief to move on."[37]

While trying to calm his men as the Union shells came crashing down around them, Oates came upon his brother John on the ground in the rear of his company. He put his hand to John's forehead and discerned that his brother was running a high fever. As far as he was concerned, that was enough to put his brother out of the battle. Oates told John that when the line advanced, he was to stay where he was and not make the assault. John sat up and said, with flashing eyes: "Brother, I will not do it. If I were to remain here people would say that I did it through cowardice; no, sir, I am an officer and will never disgrace the uniform I wear; I shall go through, unless I am killed, which I think is quite likely."[38] Oates probably should have insisted that John stay behind, but this was a romantic age when words of valor were accepted at face value and honored to the letter. For good or ill, John would go with his company into the assault.

While the guns continued to pound and the smoke grew thicker across the breadth of the ridge, Colonel Oates had more than just his brother to worry about. His men's throats were as dry as parchment, for they had long ago consumed all the contents of their canteens during the strenuous march over South Mountain. Recalling that he had seen a well near a house to the rear of the battle line, Oates ordered two men from each of the eleven companies in the 15th to take canteens and fill them. The water detail went off with the canteens clanking and thudding and the men of the regiment waiting expectantly for a cool drink as their thirst became even worse under the hot afternoon sun.[39]

Then the order to advance came. With great determination, and a healthy dose of reluctance as well, the men stood up, shedding their blanket rolls and surplus baggage. It was too late to call back the water detail. Oates knew that his loss of those twenty-two men could prove to be crucial in the coming battle. His only hope was that the detail would later catch up with the regiment, filled canteens in hand and none the worse for wear. Under the circumstances, the attack order infuriated him. "It would have been infinitely better to have waited five minutes for those twenty-two men and the canteens of water," he commented long after the battle, "but generals never ask a colonel if his regiment is ready to move." There was nothing he could do now. Given the overpowering thirst of his men, he had made the right decision— one that placed the welfare of his men above all other considerations—by sending the detail off to fetch water. But the decision would prove to be very costly in the fight to come.

Along the entire length of the brigade line, officers screamed out the order to advance. Firing and yelling like demons, the Alabama brigade made a mad rush down through a wheat field as enemy artillery among the boulders of Devil's Den blasted the gray lines. One Alabamian recalled that "in the din of battle we could hear the charges of canister passing over us with the noise of partridges in flight." A Texan in Robertson's brigade, which advanced after Law's men had stepped off, described the charge down into the valley of Plum Run, below the Round Tops: "On we go with the same speed, jumping over and plunging through creeks, pulling through mud, struggling through underbrush, still keep[ing] up the loud, irregular and terrible Confederate yell. Shells and grape shot, canister and minie balls, came hurtling through our ranks, bursting, screaming, whistling." Yet nothing could stop the "wild, reckless, unhesitating rush" toward the enemy. "No time for shining shoes," dryly commented another Texan.[40]

Oates and his men ran down the hill into the valley full fury, and the daunting Confederate advance successfully scattered Federal sharpshooters—green-uniformed members of the 2nd U.S. Sharpshooters, better known as Berdan's Sharpshooters—who had been posted around the Slyder house and who had been peppering Hood's division with musket fire ever since its arrival on Warfield Ridge. Law's own skirmishers, comprised of three companies taken from the 47th Alabama, had failed to scare off the Federal sharpshooters because they had managed, rather ineptly, to veer off to the east through Slyder's meadow, cross Plum Run, and get lost in the woods south of Big Round Top, thus taking themselves entirely out of the battle. The Federal sharpshooters, unnerved by the Confederate lines sweeping toward them, scrambled away from the Slyder farm by heading toward Devil's Den to the north and Big Round Top to the east. In short order, their green coats blended into the thick foliage that hugged the slopes of Big Round Top.

But the Confederate onslaught was less menacing than the greencoats had assumed. As the main battle line of Law's brigade rolled forward, many of the Alabamians found they were too weak to continue the charge. Soldiers fell out of the advance not only from wounds but from sheer exhaustion. Some men, fearing the advent of battle one more time, feigned wounds and went to the rear. But the butternut lines rolled forward over boulders and through thickets toward the Round Tops, which now could no longer be seen through the yellowish-white smoke that covered the fields.[41]

Moving through the valley toward the Round Tops, Hood's division was spread out, as Oates put it, "like the outer edge of a half-open fan." It was not easy going. The uneven terrain—including countless swales, dry creek beds, thickets, small stands of woods, boulders, and other obstacles—made it impossible for the men to keep in formation as they ran forward; the lines became disordered and bent, less like the fan Oates described and more like wavy lines scribbled across a page.[42]

Across the rough ground, John Oates somehow kept up with his company, even while others with sounder bodies fell behind from fatigue and dehydration. William Oates, at the head of his lines, must have tried to keep his brother in sight, but he could not have been able to focus his attention on the front and rear at the same time. Through brambles, briars, and thick undergrowth, Oates led his regiment until they passed through a small piece of woods and emerged—in more or less good order—into a large meadow of grass and hay. Up ahead of them, to their left and north, stood the empty Slyder farmhouse, silently keeping watch as the butternut soldiers moved at the double quick across the fields of green. Sounds of battle—the rattle of muskets and the thunder of artillery—floated toward the Alabamians from over the rooftops of the Slyder house and barn.

Straight ahead of the Alabamians loomed Big Round Top and its wooded slopes. Oates and his men hopped across the dry bed of a small stream, a branch of the larger Plum Run that could be seen ahead of them, cutting along the base of the large hill. Crossing the dry creek allowed the Alabamians to regain some order in their lines and slow their advance; there was nothing in their front to assault anymore, now that the Federal sharpshooters had been dispersed, so the battle lines assumed the rhythm of quick step as they approached the banks of Plum Run. But the noise of battle, growing more intense by the second, could still be heard beyond the ridges and trees to their left. Oates, hoping that John had managed to keep up with the pace of the advancing lines, tried to restore order in his regiment, all the while letting the course of events draw his men, his brother, and himself deeper into a battle that none of them would ever forget.

5

BOULDERS LIKE
GRAVESTONES

As William Oates tried to restore order among his men, General Law, the brigade commander, galloped up out of nowhere and reined in his horse at Oates's side. Law, who was three years younger than Oates, was an energetic and ambitious brigadier. He had a narrow face, high cheek bones, wistful eyes, a thin mustache, and a bushy van dyke that tried unsuccessfully to conceal his youth. Law was brave in battle and a competent officer, but there was something about him—perhaps his air of self-importance—that made some of his men dislike him. Oates admired Law and trusted him. He considered him sometimes negligent, though, especially when it came to filing battle reports and taking care of necessary paperwork.[1]

Law now seemed in a tizzy. Robertson's Texas Brigade to the left had encountered stiff resistance from Federal troops in the vicinity of Devil's Den; this had caused a gap between the Texans and Law's Alabama Brigade. Law had decided to reinforce the Texans with Benning's Georgia Brigade, which had been held in reserve, and he was about to pull his two right regiments—the 44th and 48th Alabama—out to eliminate a pesky Union battery atop Devil's Den that was effectively thinning Law's brigade with well-placed shells and canister. As Law discussed the situation with Oates, the 44th Alabama began slowly to drop back out of the advancing lines and move left on the oblique toward Devil's Den. Next the 48th moved in the same direction, leaving Oates's 15th Alabama on the far right of the Confederate advance.

The problem was, however, that Oates did not fully understand what was taking place. Law told him that the 15th was now "on the extreme right of our line" and he ordered him to "left-wheel" the regiment and "hug the [western] base of Great Round Top." Oates and his men, said Law, were to go up the valley between the two mountains and advance until they found the left of the Union line; the regiment was then to turn the enemy line "and do all the damage" it could. Law informed Oates that the 47th Alabama would be ordered to hold tight to the 15th's left flank and to advance with it. If, for any reason the two regiments became separated from the rest of the brigade, the 47th Alabama was to be under Oates's direct command. Otherwise, the 47th would remain under the orders of Lieutenant Colonel Michael J. Bulger (the regiment's commander, Colonel James W. Jackson, had collapsed during the advance and had been taken to the rear).[2]

But as Law spoke, the 44th and 48th regiments were still off to Oates's right and just beginning to move to the rear and left. The "saddle" between Devil's Den and Big Round Top was not yet fully visible, and a left wheel would have moved the 15th away from the base of Big Round Top rather than toward it. Moreover, the 47th Alabama was crowding Oates on the left, making a left wheel impossible to accomplish. Under the circumstances, Law's orders made little sense. Nevertheless, Law quickly bounded away and left Oates to deal with what he understood his orders to be. What he could not know at the time was that Law failed to give Bulger the same orders he had just given Oates. Unclear orders shrouded even more by the fog of war were not unusual in this conflict, especially since so many of the officers were citizen soldiers rather than professional military men or graduates of West Point. However, Law had studied at the Citadel and had taught in several military academies in the South before the war began; under the circumstances, lacking faith in the attack from the start, and with the Confederate assault already unraveling before it could even strike the enemy, he clearly wasn't performing at his best.[3]

Almost at that moment, Oates and his men reached and crossed Plum Run, their lines breaking apart as they scrambled into the stream's deep ravine and up its dusty banks to the other side. Two things happened next. From Oates's right, Federal sharpshooters in their distinctive green coats—members of the 2nd U.S. Sharpshooters who had earlier retreated and had taken cover behind a stone fence located a short distance up the slope of Big Round Top—opened fire on the 15th Alabama with devastating effect. At the same time, Oates looked over his shoulder to see that the 44th and 48th Alabama were now gone and that his right flank was dangerously exposed.[4]

As the 15th Alabama continued to assemble itself on the east bank of Plum Run and resume its advance, it was hit by another volley from the sharpshooters, and this time two men were killed, another enlisted man went down wounded, and Lieutenant Colonel Isaac Feagin fell with a severe wound to his right knee. Oates now faced a difficult decision. He could not know the size of the enemy force firing down on his regiment, but he did know that if he continued his advance along the bottom of Big Round Top, he would lose more men and would leave this enemy force in his rear, where it could inflict even more damage. Oates could either obey his orders and continue his advance or he could do something about the sharpshooters on his right flank. He chose the latter course, which, in the end, proved to be a military mistake.[5]

Oates halted his regiment. "Change direction to the right," he ordered, and his men wheeled about to face the enemy on the hillside. As the 15th Alabama swung around to the right, the 47th Alabama, still crunching into the 15th's left flank, followed the maneuver and remained in battle line on Oates's left, exactly where Oates expected it to be, given Law's otherwise perplexing orders. The movement to the right separated the two Alabama regiments from the rest of Law's brigade, but Oates believed he really had no choice in the matter.[6] He had to eliminate the enemy threat on his right flank. But in so doing, he disobeyed Law's orders and reduced the size of the Confederate force headed toward Devil's Den and Little Round Top and delayed the speed with which his troops could reach the destination Law had ordered them to reach. As the confusion of battle so often ordains to those caught up in its turbulence, Oates had few good alternatives and practically no time to make his decisions. Whatever he did—obey Law's orders and have his men be cut down by enemy sharpshooters or disobey the orders and protect his flank—became a losing proposition.

Behind a stone wall on the western edge of a clearing on the hillside was the Old Indian Field, the open pasture where the Slyder family grazed their cattle. From here Federal sharpshooters continued to riddle Oates's ranks with well-aimed shots. Oates ordered his lines forward, but his men found it rough going. The climb up the hillside to the Old Indian Field was formidable, and the men tripped and fell over rock outcroppings and thick underbrush. There were no orderly lines—in some places, no lines at all. Oates later described the difficulty of the ascent: "My men had to climb up, catching to the bushes and crawling over the immense boulders, in the face of an incessant fire of their enemy, who kept falling back, taking shelter and firing down on us from behind the rocks and crags that covered the mountain side thicker than grave stones in a city cemetery."

What's more, the 47th Alabama had double-quicked around in an arc to try to keep in line with Oates and his regiment, but in doing so it squeezed the left of the 15th and created a tangle in the lines. A sergeant yelled to Oates: "Colonel Oates, make Colonel Bulger take his damned concern out of our regiment!" Shortly the lines straightened themselves out, but even the Federal sharpshooters noticed the confusion caused by the unintended confluence of the 15th and 47th.

Despite the jumble, the Alabamians climbed higher and higher, pushing the sharpshooters back through the Old Indian Field and then farther up the steep slope of Big Round Top. Luckily for Oates and his men, the sharp-shooters mostly fired over their heads, although the constant zipping of minie balls through the air provided no comfort to the Alabamians. Oates could not see the sharpshooters, whose green uniforms blended in well with the sur-rounding woods and who deftly darted from tree to tree and from boulder to boulder. About halfway up the hill, however, the firing from above ceased suddenly, and Oates saw the Federals divide into two parties, each of which scurried into the woods and around the hill—one to the left, the other to the right. The sharpshooters who retreated to the right fired a few final shots at the Alabamians, but when Oates detached Company A to protect his right flank, the Federals disappeared from sight "as though commanded by a magician."[7]

Having come this far up the hill, Oates decided to lead his men to the top—another choice that could have benefited from more careful thinking. Even though he had wasted time chasing the elusive sharpshooters, he might have led his men back down the hill and tried to catch up with the rest of his brigade. Instead, he urged his men on as they climbed up the rugged hillside, which by now had become heavily wooded and strewn with insurmountable boulders. At one point, Oates and his men had to scale a veritable cliff that stood in their path. How John Oates managed to scramble over boulders and up the rock face of the hillside is unfathomable. Perspiration dripped into the men's eyes and made the climb even more difficult. They went on, though, even as some of the Alabamians fell out of ranks with exhaustion and thirst that could no longer be endured. Up and up they climbed, gasping to catch their breaths, until they finally reached the summit and collapsed on the rocks and ledges that covered the hilltop. Oates was aware of their suffering and proud of their achievement. "Greater heroes never shouldered muskets than those Alabamians," he said many years later.[8]

Oates allowed his men to rest for a few minutes. Probably he checked to see how John was holding up. Standing on the highest ledge on the hilltop, he got his bearings and tried to assess his situation. The view from the rocky summit was spectacular. The finest panorama was toward the south, where the green fields and hills of Maryland seemed to stretch on forever. To the west, the peaks of South Mountain were a vivid blue. Looking northward, he could plainly see the town of Gettysburg through the foliage.[9]

From down below, the roar of battle rose up like a madman's symphony from Devil's Den and the Valley of Death. Like the day itself, the battle was getting hotter and hotter. Under the cool shade of huge red oak and shagbark hickory trees, Oates and his men spent a few moments of the battle in a kind of suspended animation. For a brief time, the war suddenly seemed very far away. Then the sharp rattle of musket fire echoed once more over the hills and through the dense trees from far below, awakening Oates to the reality of war and his proximity to its flaming hell. Realizing he was atop the highest elevation on the battlefield, Oates pondered holding the hill and hauling artillery up to its ledges to catch the Army of the Potomac off guard and rake their lines with a devastating enfilade fire from the summit. The more he thought about it, the more he became convinced that Big Round Top was the key to victory on this Pennsylvania battlefield.

But he was most likely wrong. As he and his men had just experienced, trees and boulders covered the steep hillside, which would have made moving artillery up to the summit an arduous undertaking—not impossible, necessarily, but requiring a great deal of time that the Confederates did not have as the late afternoon slipped away. Even if guns could be placed on the hilltop, their field of fire would have been blocked by trees and treetops. Pioneers, the Civil War equivalent of the engineer corps, would have to be deployed with axes to chop down trees. But to what advantage? Unless the guns were rifled Parrotts, their range would hardly be effective for sweeping devastation through the Union lines stretching north like a river of blue along Cemetery Ridge. It is doubtful, as the Union gunners discovered on the summit of Little Round Top, that the artillery barrels could be depressed enough to fire on Devil's Den or Houck's Ridge or the Wheatfield. Oates's belief that Big Round Top was the key to a Confederate victory at Gettysburg revealed his lack of artillery training, his poor assumption that high ground necessarily meant superior ground, and his wishful thinking—all of which, actually, may have occurred to him in retrospect, as he gazed back upon the past.

He soon discovered that his own appraisal of the situation didn't much matter. The clattering sound of hooves scraping rocks interrupted his thoughts, and Oates looked down to see one of General Law's aides, Captain Leigh R. Terrell, approaching the summit on horseback. Terrell—a fastidious and bellicose adjutant who had once challenged a fellow officer to a duel with sawed-off shotguns—was furious. Why, he demanded, had Oates led the 15th and the 47th up to the top of this hill, and why had he halted? Oates carefully explained why he had done so, emphasizing the threat he thought had been posed by the sharpshooters and his men's need for a rest after the strenuous climb. Terrell explained that Hood had been wounded and Law had assumed command of the division. Law's specific orders, said Terrell, were for Oates "to press on, turn the Union left, and capture Little Round Top, if possible, and to lose no time."[10]

But Oates—whose greatest shortcoming as an officer was his occasional delinquency in obeying his orders to the letter—challenged Law's orders and made his case that Big Round Top should be occupied by Confederate forces. In fact, he tried to convince Terrell that he should be allowed to stay where he was and defend the position from any enemy force that attempted to capture the hilltop. "Within half an hour," Oates told Terrell, "I could convert it into a Gibraltar that I could hold against ten times the number of men I had." Terrell replied politely, but sharply, that Oates might be correct, but orders were orders, and Oates was required to obey the ones he had been given. For his part, Terrell explained, he had no authority to change Oates's orders, but he would be willing to express Oates's opinion to General Law as soon as time permitted. Meanwhile, Terrell reiterated that Law himself had ordered him to find the 15th Alabama and tell Oates to lose no time. Now, as Oates argued about the Gibraltar-like qualities of Big Round Top, precious minutes were being wasted. Terrell's point was simple: It was time for Oates to move off this hill and obey his commanding general's direct orders.

Finally Oates came to his senses. "I considered it my duty to obey the order communicated to me by Terrell," he stated in his later writings, but he failed to explain why it had taken him so long to reach this conclusion as the battle raged below him. Once stirred, however, there was no stopping him. He got his men on their feet and ready to move out. All this while, Bulger, in command of the 47th, had been resting his men farther down the slope of the hill, and he, too, ordered them into battle line. To avoid a sheer cliff on the north side of Big Round Top, just below the summit, Oates commanded both regiments to move to the left "and then . . . by the right flank forward." The men, he explained, "passed to the left oblique entirely down the northern side of the mountain." The Alabamians executed the maneuver with something less than grace, given their exhaustion and the fact that the natural obstructions— boulders and outcroppings—were as plentiful on the northern slope as they had been on the western.[11]

Crashing down through the woods on the hillside, Oates and his command could hear the cacophony of battle growing louder with every step. The ranks lost all semblance of order as the butternut lines descended the hill, rent asunder by trees, stumps, rocks, and defiles. As a result, the battle lines dissolved into clumps of men moving tentatively down the slopes, four or five men making their way together around obstacles and giving up entirely the effort to keep the long line connected. The 47th Alabama, linked to the 15th's left, experienced as difficult a time coming down the hill in the direction of the saddle that lay between Big Round Top and Little Round Top. Oates probably tried to dress his lines as his men reached the bottom of Big Round Top, for there was no telling when they might come in contact with the enemy. Meanwhile, it could not have been easy for John Oates as the Alabamians passed over such rough and broken ground. It was just as hard descending the hill as it had been ascending it, perhaps harder. The steep slopes made the soldiers want to run. The sergeants and the line officers held them back. William Oates must have spent part of his time looking over his shoulder to see if John was still with Company G.[12]

Between the two Round Top hills, the sparsely wooded hollow formed a natural passageway from the Taneytown Road west to the open fields below the western face of Little Round Top. Before reaching the hollow, Oates

Left: Colonel William C. Oates, March 1864. This photograph, the only one to exist of Oates as a young man in his early thirties, is taken from the frontispiece of his published memoirs, *The War Between the Union and the Confederacy* (1905). The original glass-plate negative and print, probably shot by a Richmond photographer, are lost. *Library of Congress*.

Little Round Top
Bottom: The attack of the 15th Alabama on Little Round Top, as depicted by an unknown engraver, ca. 1880s. Under the trees in the background can be seen the defensive lines of the 20th Maine. *Gettysburg National Military Park*.

Top Left: Little Round Top. In this photograph, taken after the battle by the famous Civil War photographer Mathew Brady, the craggy and scrubby slopes of the western face of Little Round Top are plainly visible, with Big Round Top, which Oates briefly thought might serve as the battle's Gibraltar, rising to the right in the somewhat hazy background. Neither Brady nor the other photographers who arrived on the battlefield in the days following the fighting snapped any pictures of the southern slopes of Little Round Top, where Oates and his 15th Alabama saw action. *Library of Congress*.

Top Right: Joshua Lawrence Chamberlain, in a photograph taken after he had received his star as a brevet brigadier general in 1864. As a colonel, Chamberlain commanded the 20th Maine at Gettysburg and successfully repulsed Oates's repeated assaults against his line. *Library of Congress*.

Bottom: The Confederate attack on Little Round Top. From a drawing by Edwin Forbes, the noted newspaper artist for *Frank Leslie's Illustrated Newspaper*. Forbes traveled with the Army of the Potomac, so this view of the Confederate assault against the western slope of Little Round Top, through what later became known as the Valley of Death, is Forbes's conception (rather wildly imagined) of what it must have looked like. Forbes even added a hill behind Big Round Top that does not exist. *Library of Congress*.

Oates's Confederate Commanders

Top: Robert E. Lee. Like most soldiers in the Army of Northern Virginia, Oates adored Lee and considered him a military genius, but he did come to believe that the Confederate made colossal errors at Gettysburg that might have, in the end, contributed to the Confederacy's defeat in 1865. *Library of Congress*.

Right: Thomas J. "Stonewall" Jackson. Oates and the 15th Alabama fought with Jackson's celebrated army in the Shenandoah campaign of 1862. Jackson was a pious Christian warrior who led his men relentlessly—in most cases—to remarkable victories in which Oates was proud to have participated as a combatant. With the rest of South, Oates deeply mourned Jackson's death after Chancellorsville in the spring of 1863. *Library of Congress*.

Left: Richard S. Ewell. The 15th Alabama, as part of Brigadier General Isaac R. Trimble's brigade, was under Ewell's division command when it received its transfer to Jackson's Valley army in April 1862. *Library of Congress.*

Bottom Left: John Bell Hood. Hood's division, which included the 15th Alabama in its ranks, stepped off first in Longstreet's assault against the Union left at Gettysburg in the late afternoon of July 2, 1862. Shortly after the attack began, Hood suffered a serious shrapnel wound that took him out of the fight and left him without the use of his right arm for the rest of his life. *U. S. Army Military History Institute, Carlisle, Pennsylvania.*

Bottom Right: James Longstreet. Oates was no admirer of General James Longstreet. He blamed Longstreet for many of the Confederate errors made at Gettysburg, but he did so after the war with considerably less venom than many other former officers of the Army of Northern Virginia. For the most part, Oates acknowledged that Longstreet was an able corps commander who often showed moments of brilliance on the battlefield. *U. S. Army Military History Institute.*

Left: Evander M. Law. The boyish but capable Law took over command of Hood's division on the afternoon of July 2, after Hood fell from a severe wound. Oates enjoyed serving in Law's Alabama brigade and, later, under Law when he assumed the permanent command of Hood's division. Nevertheless, Oates believed that Law sometimes was lax as an officer in completing reports and other paperwork. *Alabama Department of Archives and History.*

At Home in Alabama

Bottom: Exterior of William Oates's house, Abbeville, Ala. Oates lived in this house and probably maintained his law office in one of the front parlors, perhaps even before the war, but most certainly after he left the Army of Northern Virginia to recuperate from the amputation of his right arm in the late summer of 1864. This photograph is one of a series taken by photographer W. N. Manning in 1934 for the Historic American Building Survey. Even at that late date, the house probably looks very much like it did when Oates resided and worked there. *Historic American Buildings Survey.*

Right: Doorway, Oates's house, Abbeville. This doorway appears to lead from the south section of the house to the north section, connected by this hallway. *Historic American Buildings Survey.*

Below: Interior, Oates's house, Abbeville. The house had a fireplace in each room, which, given its overall compactness, must have kept the building snug in the wintertime. This photograph, also taken in 1934, shows interior decorations that no doubt belonged to its current owner and not necessarily to Oates or any of his relatives, who remained in the dwelling for many years after Oates relocated to Montgomery. *Historic American Buildings Survey.*

Bottom: Another exterior view, Oates's house, Abbeville. The house, now demolished and the site of a gasoline station (when last visited in 1992), appears to have been constructed in two stages and consisted of two halves—a northern structure with an added shadow house to the south that together resembles, to some degree, the famous and more primitive "dogtrot" log cabins that dotted the Southern frontier in the first half of the nineteenth century and in which Oates himself was probably born and raised. *Historic American Buildings Survey.*

Right: Oates in the 1880s. This photograph, of unknown origin, shows Oates as he appeared at the height of his political power while serving as a U.S. Congressman from Alabama. *Samford University Library*.

Bottom Left: Sarah Toney Oates ("T") on her wedding day, 1882. The wedding dress still survives, now kept in the treasured possession of a family descendant. T, as Oates called his bride, was nineteen years old when she married Oates; he was forty-eight. *Oates Family Papers*.

Bottom Right: William C. Oates, Jr., on his first birthday, 1884. The senior Oates was proud of his son, whom he hoped, as many fathers do, would follow in his footsteps and pursue military and political careers. *Oates Family Papers*.

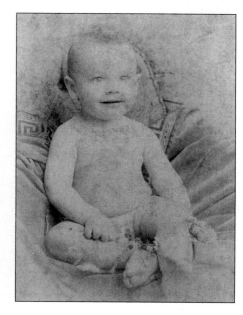

Left: T Oates in the 1880s. She was a popular hostess in Washington, and she gained a reputation for holding some of the best parties in the nation's capital while Oates served his seven terms in the House of Representatives, from 1880 to 1894. *Oates Family Papers.*

Bottom: Oates giving an outdoor speech, ca. 1894. Even from this poor photograph, now old and worn, one gains a striking sense of Oates's powerfully effective talents as a public speaker. *Oates Family Papers.*

spied something of importance to the east of Little Round Top, down in the furrowed flatland at the base of the hill. Stretched out in great array no more than 300 yards away was a Federal ordnance train of canvas-covered wagons, acting as a supply depot. Oates realized that this was the rear of the Army of the Potomac. Taking immediate action, but forgetting the direct orders he had just received from Terrell, he told Captain Francis Key Shaaf to lead Company A—about forty men—down the hill and "surround and capture the ordnance wagons."

What Oates failed to weigh, however, as he headed toward the shattering sounds of battle was that he had already lost a few men from sharpshooter fire, more than twenty men in the water detail, and an untold number who had collapsed from exhaustion or thirst; under the circumstances, he could ill afford to divide his forces in the face of the enemy. Yet that is precisely what he did, and off went Shaaf and Company A through the dark woods in pursuit of wagons that neither Oates nor the Army of Northern Virginia really needed at the moment. Eventually the detachment would be discouraged from completing its mission by the threat of Federal sharpshooters in the woods and reserve troops near the Taneytown Road, although the Alabamians apparently did get off a few shots in the direction of the Jacob Weikert house behind Little Round Top.[13]

Coming down off the hill, Oates could not see the line of the 47th Alabama off to his left through the trees, so he could not know that the slope of the terrain had caused the 47th to reach the saddle of land between Big and Little Round Top before the 15th did. As Lieutenant Colonel Bulger and his seven companies of the 47th emerged from the thick woods of Big Round Top, they encountered heavy enemy fire from the rocky ledges of Little Round Top as the 83rd Pennsylvania and the 20th Maine, under the command of Colonel Joshua Lawrence Chamberlain, poured deadly, raking volleys into the ragged line of graybacks. To the left of the 47th, the 4th Alabama was reeling back from its own unsuccessful attack against the Federal defensive line in the rocks on the southwestern slopes of Little Round Top. Just as the 47th got into formation and stepped off on its own advance, one of General Law's aides came galloping up to tell Bulger to attack. Bulger—a white-haired, fifty-seven-year-old former member of the Alabama legislature who was one of oldest officers in Law's brigade and one of its toughest fighters—needed no such order and felt he was moving against the entrenched Federal position as best he could. He was about to push to the front of his battle line to lead the charge in person.[14]

Off to the right, Oates must have been overwhelmed by the conflicting exigencies—great and small—that demanded his rapt attention. Enemy musket fire cut down his men. Minie balls zipped through the air. Smoke obscured his vision. He must make all the right decisions now. How could he make any decision when he couldn't see clearly to his front or to his flanks?

What should he do next? What did his instincts tell him? His men were counting on him. General Law was counting on him. Everyone back home had
placed their faith and trust in him. He had promised to take care of their sons
and husbands, fathers and brothers. And where was John? Had he made it
over the big hill? Was he with his company? What would he do if something
happened to John?

He had no answers, only racing thoughts and endless questions as his
heart pounded wildly in his chest. Probably the questions never formed themselves into conscious thoughts. Like most soldiers in dangerous situations,
Oates concentrated on doing his job, though the tasks before him must have
seemed monumental. At last he and his regiment reached the floor of the
hollow amid utter confusion, billowing and blinding smoke, and deafening
noise coming from every direction. Events began to be measured in split seconds. As his lines moved forward rapidly and approached the slopes of Little
Round Top, Oates could see no enemy in his front. Then, while he and his
men ascended the southern rocky hillside, all hell broke loose. Enemy musket fire directed at the 47th Alabama, to Oates's left, burst forth from behind
a ledge above the Alabamians. The high sound of rifle fire rose to a new
intensity as Federal volleys next hit the 15th Alabama, and Oates remembered that the enemy "poured into us the most destructive fire I ever saw."
The blast stopped the Alabamians in their tracks, but Oates and his officers
worked to close the gaps caused by the heavy casualties. Then the Alabamians, firing as fast as they could handle their muskets, returned the enemy
fire—"most spiritedly," as Oates put it.[15]

Oates could see through the heavy masses of smoke that the enemy was
perfectly positioned about 150 feet above him and hidden behind, in his words,
"an irregular ledge of rocks—a splendid line of natural breastworks running
about parallel with the front of the Forty-seventh regiment and my four left
companies, and then sloping back in front of my center and right at an angle
of about thirty-five or forty degrees." The Federals had piled small rocks
along the ledge to improve their defenses; where ledge and rocks offered no
protection, the enemy had taken cover behind trees on the hillside.[16]

Even though Oates could see the Union troops through the infernal fog,
he could see nothing at all to his right or left, where the 47th had become
unhinged from the advancing battle lines of the 15th Alabama. The smoke,
settling thicker and thicker, sank to the floor of the hollow between the hills
and gathered there into a thick cloud like meadow fog on a summer's morn.
Exactly where Oates was standing as the 20th Maine and his Alabamians fired
their first scorching volleys at one another cannot be determined, but it would
seem that he had positioned himself on the left wing of the regiment, near his
old Company G, which always took up a place in the battle line between
companies K and B.[17]

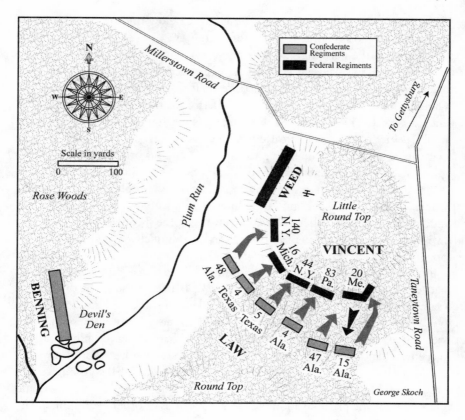

George Skoch

He should have been closer to the center of his lines, but his fondness for the old Henry Pioneers, the company he had raised himself in Abbeville, and his concern for his ailing brother kept him anchored for the time being toward his left flank. It was also the place where the fighting was the hottest and the deadliest. There he could stay as close as possible to John.

Little did Oates realize that the sheets of acrid smoke and the rocky, uneven terrain would ultimately determine the outcome of the battle. The volley blasts from the 20th Maine came through the blinding smoke with deadly effect. In minutes—seconds, really—Oates's casualties were piling up, and he must have known that his regiment's return fire could not possibly be inflicting the same kind of damage in his foe's ranks, if only because his men had to fire upwards, up the hill, thus increasingly the likelihood that they were firing too high, over their enemy's heads. The 15th was also taking blistering fire from the left companies of the 83rd Pennsylvania, catching the Alabamians in a slaughterhouse crossfire. Oates later mourned that it was during these moments of the battle and in this place below the southern slopes of Little Round Top that he lost most of his men.[18]

Through the haze, he saw blue soldiers moving behind the trees toward their left, and he surmised—rightly, as it turned out—that the Federals were extending their battle line to protect their left flank. To meet this maneuver, Oates ordered seven of his companies to perform a half wheel and overlap the enemy's left. On his own left flank, Company B was pinned down among some boulders at the base of Little Round Top's southern slope, while his other companies on the left—including Company G and his brother John with it—joined with the 47th Alabama for an assault on the 83rd Pennsylvania.

Oates's companies on the right successfully completed the "circular wheel," as he called it, but his battle lines were disintegrating into pockets of men rather than any cohesive or concentrated force. From above, the enemy fire was cutting his regiment to pieces. An unending chaos of violence enveloped the hillside. His men hugged the ground, half-dazed by the waves of noise that grew louder and louder, adding to the confusion and the frenzy of battle. In the smoking madness, the noise of battle was so great that few of Oates's men could hear him. He gave the order to advance, but it was drowned out by the steady rattle of musketry. Captain J. Henry Ellison of Company C, wearing a fine new captain's jacket that Oates had presented him as a gift, placed his hand behind an ear and asked Oates to repeat the order. But within seconds a bullet passed through the young officer's head. Ellison's men gathered around him, despite the hail of bullets that zipped through the air, and Oates took some precious moments to get his lines in order again. Finally he ordered a charge again and managed to get his left companies part way up the hill, where they shook the enemy's defensive line and pushed it back from a low, rocky ledge. The Federals held fast, however, along Oates's left, where his men were now partially jumbled together with the 47th Alabama.[19]

Nearly at the same moment, Bulger led his men forward without informing Oates of his intentions or worrying about the present circumstances of the 15th Alabama to his right or the 4th Alabama, huddled behind boulders; to his left. The Alabamians went screaming ahead like devils, Bulger standing atop a boulder waving his men on with his sword. Almost at once, though, Bulger was hit by a minie ball that struck his chest and lodged under his left shoulder. With Bulger wounded and out of the action, the desperate attack of the 47th faltered badly, and the Alabamians soon realized that they had rushed into a small defile that enabled three different Union regiments—the 44th New York, the 83rd Pennsylvania, and the 20th Maine—to fire down on them from three different directions. Panic-stricken, the 47th Alabama went all to bits in the heavy fire, broke ranks, and flew for the rear.[20]

From behind the ledge that the Federals had abandoned, Oates could now see the battlefield more clearly. He dashed over to the left, dodging the heavy rifle fire from above, to rally the men of the 47th. But it was like trying to hold back a tidal wave, and all he could do was watch the 47th Alabama disintegrate before his eyes. Quickly he returned to the ledge on his right, where the 15th Alabama kept up a galling fire against the 20th Maine. The air was alive with bullets. With the 47th gone, Oates worried about the safety of his left flank, but he rejoiced when he saw the Federals' right companies dissolve and fall back in confusion from the position they had been holding so firmly on the southern slope of the hill. The Union line, which had been shaped like a horseshoe, now bent itself back so that it more closely resembled a hairpin.

Oates concluded—wrongly—that his left regiments had been successful somehow in turning the Federal right flank, so he took advantage of the situation by ordering his men forward again, this time to drive the enemy entirely off the hill. "My men obeyed," he remembered years later, "and advanced about half way to the enemy's position, but the fire was so destructive that my line wavered like a man trying to walk against a strong wind, and then slowly, doggedly, gave back a little." As his line fell back in the smoke and confusion, the Federals seemed to regain composure on their right and the companies that looked before like they were withdrawing stood steadfast once more on the ground they had been defending.[21]

Five times the Federal and Confederate lines surged back and forth, up and down the rocky slopes of the hill. Some of the charges consisted of clusters of Alabamians—just handfuls of men—pushing their way forward through waves of smoke and murderous fire and battle thunder, only to be torn to pieces and forced back again by a Federal counterstroke. In between the attacks, the men on both sides fired sporadically at each other. Through it all, in the wild chaos of smoke, flame, thunderous noise, and yelling men, it was hard for Oates to tell where his Alabamians really were, for his lines could not be maintained in any kind of order. Men were crouched behind rocks and trees, ten here, two or three others there, and companies had become hopelessly tangled ever since the descent from the summit of Big Round Top.[22]

No one, not even the most skilled combat officer, could have followed the military textbooks while engaged in fighting of this kind. The broken terrain defied any proper formation of assaulting battle lines—or, for that matter, the establishment of any solid line of defense by the 20th Maine. It was the intensity of the struggle, though, that made all the difference, that prevented anyone from behaving as the Napoleonic primers and the West Point manuals dictated. In a total war, as this one was becoming, the soldiers had to put their complete energy into combat, devoting every muscle, every thought, every ounce of courage to the goal of destruction and victory. Within the firestorm of such relentless and deadly combat, the soldier and the war become one. The Civil War was what Lincoln in 1861 had predicted it would be: "a violent and remorseless revolutionary struggle."[23] For the men on the firing lines of the 15th Alabama and the 20th Maine, this was a fight that could only end badly with too many dead and too many wounded, no matter which side ended up winning. Oates knew the stakes. He was set in his determination to win, knowing that the price of defeat would be too high. But the situation went beyond his individual resolution, beyond his proficiency as an officer, beyond the best of his abilities as a citizen soldier. In hard wars, all-out wars that channel every effort into killing and destruction, sometimes there is no way of knowing what you are supposed to do and how, precisely, you are supposed to win. So you just keep moving forward and firing your musket and hoping for the best.

Oates discovered that moving his men forward under these conditions was extremely difficult, to say the least. Choking smoke blanketed the hillside and went rolling down into the hollow. For quite a while, sharpshooters—the men of the 2nd U.S. Sharpshooters who had earlier dispersed halfway up Big Round Top and had now taken cover behind a stone wall about 150 yards to the east of Oates's position with one detached company of Chamberlain's 20th Maine—picked off Alabamians in Oates's ranks without him comprehending that the shots were coming from behind him and not from the Federals in his front.[24]

Realizing, as he said later, that "to stand there and die was sheer folly," he decided to order another assault. Oates was still lingering near Company G, more toward his left flank than toward his right, and he knew that one of the biggest obstacles he and his men faced was getting over the daunting ledge of rocks that protected them from Yankee musket fire. When the moment came to attack, Oates—with his charcoal eyes gleaming and his face all red from exertion and smudged black from powder smoke—leaped from behind the cover of the ledge, scrambled over the rocks, and fired all six shots in his revolver into the face of the enemy. No one followed him except a solitary private from Company G, William R. Holloway, who joined him on the ledge and, kneeling, fired his musket at the enemy after taking careful aim. Within an instant, however, a bullet struck him in the head. Oates caught Holloway in his arms, laid him carefully on the rocks, picked up the musket, and coolly and deliberately fired a few rounds toward the enemy lines.[25]

It was the kind of courage—what one historian calls "courageous demonstration"—that officers were expected to show on the battlefield, displaying coolness and calm under fire so their men would follow their example. One might wonder if Oates was inflating this episode, either unconsciously in his memory or deliberately for the benefit of the postwar public, by making himself more heroic than he actually may have been. But there is nothing to suggest that he inflated anything in his account of the battle or in his telling of this anecdote about Holloway. Oates, in fact, didn't think too highly of such things as "courageous demonstration" or showing off how brave one could be in a deadly situation. Such displays, in his opinion, usually got one killed. For Oates, courage was something located deep inside, something he really didn't think about, something that happened naturally out of the pressing exigencies of the moment. He was more than willing to admit how frightened he could become on the battlefield. But Oates could also be incredibly brave and selfless, as he was when Holloway fell and he fired off some musket shots in anger at the enemy—his only means at hand for letting the Federals know just how he felt about Holloway's death. Sometimes, as on Little Round Top, his courage resembled what one twentieth-century combat veteran has called "the glaze of war," an ability to separate oneself psychologically from the events, including the danger, that one faces on a battlefield. Under this glaze, Oates performed acts that appeared to be courageous, but which might have been perceived as foolish or even stupid by someone else. The glaze of war operated like a narcotic that kept the battlefield distant in a soldier's consciousness, allowing one to do things quite out of the ordinary. In Oates's case, though, he was also motivated by his feelings for Holloway when he picked up the musket and fired away. "Poor Holloway," Oates wrote long after the war, "was a good man," Then he added, sadly: "He was killed instantly."[26]

The attack failed because Company G could not scale the ledge in its front, especially while the Federals showered lead down on the Alabamians. Holloway's death was bad enough, but Company G lost many other men during those short, deadly moments when Oates stood bravely on the ledge and urged his regiment forward. As Company G attempted to get up on the rocks, Federal volleys had cut down some of the company's finest soldiers. Captain Henry C. Brainard's last words were: "O God, that I could see my mother!" Lieutenant Bud Cody—the Oates brothers' boyhood friend—went down mortally wounded from a Federal volley. But the greatest loss for William Oates personally was when his sickly brother John fell after being wounded six times by Federal bullets.[27]

Oates seems not to have known his brother had fallen until he climbed down from the ledge, finally giving up on the assault from that direction. When John slumped to the ground, struck in the hip and legs that already ached from his rheumatism, Lieutenant Isaac Parks, a fellow officer who— like Bud Cody—had been one of the brothers' playmates, dragged him through the dirt to a large boulder, not far below the apex of the Federal line. As Parks laid him down behind the rock, a seventh bullet tore into Lieutenant Oates's hand, ripping off a little finger. Parks pulled him to safety behind the boulder, making sure the enemy could no longer see him from their position. Then Parks rejoined the battle and left John to fend for himself. Unable to move, and no doubt in shock, John had to know his wounds were severe. He was in great pain, and he was losing lots of blood.

William Oates also must have been in agony. His beloved brother, the man he regarded not only as a sibling but as his closest friend, was dying on the bloody rocks of Little Round Top, and he could not go to him or comfort him or protect him from death's ominous shadow.[28]

In the shelter of the ledge, William Oates moved farther to the right and searched for an opportunity to swing things in his favor. The air was ablaze beneath the smoke. He found his chance when he decided to attack the Federals once more, this time by advancing his right wing against the Yankee left. As the sound of rifle fire rose higher and higher, he walked along the broken battle line, waving his sword and bellowing, "Forward, men, to the ledge!" The companies on the right rose up, staggered a little from the scourging enemy fire, and advanced, pushing the Federals back once again across the rocky terrain toward the brow of the hill. Straight up the hill, the Alabamians bent low and lunged over rocks and through timber, shouting the high falsetto of the Rebel Yell as they laid down a killing fire. The heated air was full of billowing smoke and whining bullets.

Bounding forward, his huge frame breaking through the battle smoke like a mad bull charging through a dense fog, Oates tried to reach a boulder halfway up the slope, but he could only get within ten paces of it. The Yankees counterattacked with savage power, and hand-to-hand fighting broke out all along the front. Using their bayonets and their muskets as clubs, the Alabamians tried to stave off the Federal counterblow. Oates saw that his regimental colors, waving proudly in the heavy smoke, were only a step or two from the boulder. A Yankee attempted to grab the staff of the Alabamians' flag, but Sergeant Pat O'Connor of Company K drove his bayonet through the Union soldier's head. Years later Oates would acknowledge that "there never were harder fighters than the Twentieth Maine men and their gallant Colonel."[29]

But there was only so much the tired soldiers of the 15th Alabama could do. Throughout the day, they had been ground down unmercifully. Now the horrible shock of hand-to-hand combat and point-blank fire was simply too much to endure. Although the Alabamians briefly held their ground near the boulder, they were being smashed and splintered on the gloomy hillside. Captain De Bernie Waddell of Company G, who was then serving as the regimental adjutant, suggested to Oates as the bullets cut the air all around them that he take about fifty men from the right wing and try to outflank the Federals. Oates agreed to let him do so, but the decision could not have been more poorly timed. Waddell led the fifty men off to the right, fought hard to overlap the left flank of the 20th Maine, but managed only to keep up an enfilading fire that menaced the Yankees without rolling up their line. Oates, who was attempting to maintain his regiment's advanced position, could not afford to lose from his front the men Waddell took with him. With their numbers reduced, the Alabamians hung on near the boulder for a time, but then had to withdraw down the rugged slope of the hill.[30]

Beneath the ledge once more, Oates realized his situation was desperate. His regiment had been mangled. He finally became fully aware of the Federal fire—the combined musketry of the small contingent of 2nd U.S. Sharpshooters and the 20th Maine's Company B—coming from behind a stone wall to his rear. With haste, he sent a message to the 4th Alabama, way over around the hollow between the Round Tops, to ask for reinforcements, but his messenger returned quickly with bad news: The 4th, now more than 200 yards away, could not be found and it looked like the Federals were about to overrun Oates's right flank.

Meanwhile, two of his officers—Captain Frank Park and Captain Blant Hill—told him they had spotted enemy troops closing on the 15th's rear. Oates sent Park to find out the strength of the enemy force coming from behind. The captain returned saying he had seen two battle flags, so it appeared that two Federal regiments were advancing from the east toward the Alabamians. Taking a closer look beyond his regiment's rear, Oates watched in horror as Stoughton's sharpshooters, protected by a stone wall, cut down his men. As Oates later recalled: "While one man was shot in the face, his right-hand or left-hand comrade was shot in the side or back. Some were struck simultaneously with two or three balls from different directions."[31]

The shadows of the late afternoon were lengthening across the slopes of Little Round Top, and the light was getting weak. For Oates and his men, the situation had grown precarious. All around them was a hideous spectacle. Dead and wounded Alabamians lay everywhere on the ground, intermingled with Federal casualties from the Maine and Pennsylvania regiments. Between the lines on the hillside, the wounded called out for water and for assistance from their comrades. As Oates remembered many years later: "My dead and wounded were then nearly as great in number as those still on duty. They literally covered the ground. The blood stood in puddles in some places on the rocks; the ground was soaked with the blood of as brave men as ever fell on the red field of battle." Park and Hill now urged Oates to order a retreat, but he hesitated because he still hoped he could find reinforcements somewhere and turn the tide of the battle. Moreover, he simply could not conceive how a retreat was possible under the circumstances. He told the captains: "Return to your companies; we will sell out as dearly as possible." Hill was stunned and did not reply. Park simply smiled pleasantly, gave Oates a proper military salute, and said, "All right, sir."[32]

More than he could have consciously realized, Oates's decisions on the battlefield were being influenced by an ethos of honor—an aspect of Victorian masculinity and not just a trait of Southern manliness—that compelled

Civil War officers to do everything in their power to avoid appearing *dishonorable*. One of the easiest ways to heap dishonor on one's self was cowardice—running away in battle or retreating precipitously before the outcome of the engagement had been truly decided. A soldier could not demonstrate honor in a tangible fashion, for honor was ethereal; either an officer was honorable or he was not. So soldiers, and especially officers, displayed their honor by proving their courage. Absolute courage became the best means for maintaining an honorable reputation. Officers were generally held to a higher standard of honor—and thus courage—than enlisted men. A good officer would go out of his way to exhibit his bravery under fire, even if it meant purposely exposing one's self to murderous enemy fire. Because of the emphasis on honor, some officers—like Joshua Lawrence Chamberlain, Oates's enemy on the upper slope of the hill—thought of war as knightly and chivalric. Oates condemned any suggestion that war was a knightly contest, a joust for the sake of honor, a clash between gentleman. But his thoughts and his values were shaped, nevertheless, by the prevailing conventions of his time, and in facing his dilemma on Little Round Top he could not avoid weighing honor and dishonor, and the fate of his manly reputation, as he formulated his next step.[33]

Almost as soon as his captains rejoined their companies, Oates began to have second thoughts about his decision. The battle raged on, his men were fought out, the entire regiment was low on ammunition, and every man under his command was desperate for water and rest. His companies were scrambled. Organizing another attack uphill was next to impossible. The men kept up a brave fire from behind the rocks and trees, but there was no weight behind it. The whole war seemed to come down to this one moment. "I saw no hope of success," Oates recalled, "and did order a retreat." His decision was all the harder to make because if the 15th Alabama abandoned its ground, it would have to leave behind its dead and wounded, including John Oates, who remained hidden behind a large boulder.

Knowing that it would be impossible to withdraw from the regiment's position in any orderly fashion, Oates sent word to his officers and the clumps of men hiding behind boulders and trees that they should retire when he gave the signal. It was about 5:45 P.M. Oates, who probably had no watch, knew that the sun was getting ready to set. Just as he gave the signal for the withdrawal, the Federals—with a monstrous clamor of clanging metal and shouting men—came streaming down the hill with bayonets fixed and the glint of victory in their eyes. How many of Oates's men heard or saw his signal cannot be determined, but for those who had not begun to retreat on his command they were now being greeted by the most compelling reason of all to quit this hill—the Yankees were sweeping down the slope and, this time, the Alabamians had no more fight in them.[34]

"We ran like a herd of wild cattle," Oates wrote in his later years. They broke in unruly flight and went streaming for the rear. On Oates's extreme right flank, Waddell and his detail of fifty men were edging through the woods in hopes of turning the enemy flank, but the Federals came rushing straight down the hill toward them and chased them to the east, in the general direction of the Taneytown Road. Many of these Alabamians ran into the clutches of the 20th Maine's Company B and the Federal sharpshooters who were behind the stone wall. Waddell and some of his men managed, despite these obstacles, to elude pursuing Federals and work their way toward the saddle of land between the hills. But many Alabamians were not so lucky. They were grabbed by the collar, pushed to the ground, or halted at the point of a glistening bayonet.

Across the rest of Oates's front, the enemy drove down toward the Alabamians and swung from Oates's right to his left. Large groups of Oates's men were surprised by the suddenness of the Federal charge and were immediately captured. Others ran into the hollow between the two hills and scrambled up the steep and tangled slopes of Big Round Top. A few, miraculously, helped wounded men get away from the frenzied onslaught of the enemy. Oates remembered that he and his men raced through a line of dismounted cavalrymen—or Federals he *thought* were cavalrymen—and captured three of them as they sprinted through the woods. He also recalled that near him ran an enlisted man who had been wounded in the throat, and Oates could hear the whistling noise of the man breathing through his trachea and could see the blood spraying out of the man's neck every time he exhaled.[35]

As Waddell and a few of his men entered the hollow, they encountered the long lost Company A, which rambled out of the woods looking stunned and bewildered. Waddell, taking command of the company from Captain Shaaf, who seemed not to have his wits about him, ordered Company A to form a defensive line up on the slopes of Big Round Top to stop the juggernaut advance of the 20th Maine. It was a brave and timely act, for the Federals were in hot pursuit of the Alabamians and seemed perfectly willing to chase them up and over Big Round Top, if they had to. Waddell got the company in line and let fly a volley at the enemy. The holding action stopped the Yankees in their tracks.[36]

Oates himself was not having an easy time of it. As his men scampered up the steep slopes of Big Round Top, he tried to halt them and reform his lines, but the attempt failed because his troops were too scattered, too terrified, or too preoccupied helping their wounded comrades up the hill. Overcome by heat and exhaustion, Oates teetered for a moment, the world spinning round him, and then fainted and fell. Two of his burliest men picked him up and lugged him to the summit of Big Round Top, where the regiment's assistant surgeon revived him. For the rest of his life, Oates was grateful to the two men who, with no small effort, had saved him from falling into the hands of the enemy, something he dreaded more than being killed on the battlefield.[37]

Heat and exhaustion took their toll on all of the Alabamians, but Oates's fainting spell probably had as much to do with the emotional stress he was experiencing as it did with the physical fatigue that had worn him down. Whether he consciously realized it or not, he had made numerous mistakes that day as a field officer—errors that had led to the retreat of the 15th Alabama as much as the thick smoke, difficult terrain, and hard fighting of the 20th Maine. He would later argue that if he had had another regiment at his disposal, he could have taken Little Round Top, but the fact was—and this he could not admit to himself—that if he had not repeatedly divided his force in the face of the enemy, if he had obeyed Law's orders to the letter, if he had properly guarded his rear as he should have done, he might have won the day. Even so, he was clear-headed enough in the years after the war to realize that even if he defeated the 20th Maine and captured the southern slopes of Little Round Top, there was no way he and his Alabamians could have held the hill for more than a few minutes. The entire Sixth Corps of the Army of the Potomac, which had arrived on the field in midafternoon and was being held in reserve, probably would have moved up quickly to remove the 15th Alabama regiment and any other Confederate unit from the top of the hill.[38]

Oates's greatest distress was having to leave his brother severely wounded on the battlefield. He had abandoned John in his brother's moment of need—something John had never done to William, not in Texas, not in Alabama, not on any other field of battle. John, however, was simply too badly wounded to be carried from the field, especially on the run. William had had no choice but to leave his brother behind.

When William Oates regained consciousness, somewhere up near the summit of Big Round Top, he turned temporary command of the 15th Alabama over to Captain Hill, instructing him to withdraw the regiment to an open field on the Slyder farm, next to Plum Run. Night was falling, and the fighting between the sides had tapered off to a little intermittent firing. A massive cloud of smoke dulled the twilight. In the pale darkness, just before nightfall, the 15th Alabama made its way noisily down the treacherous southern slope of Big Round Top, through the trampled grass of the Old Indian Field, and down to the meadow beside the stream. Near the Slyder house, Oates and his men bivouacked for the night.[39]

There, in the open field, Oates resumed command and ordered the roll for the companies called. The day had been dismal enough, but now the roll call brought to mind every man who was not there. As the names were called out, the Alabamians who had survived this ordeal of death over the Round Tops thought of all the men now left behind—John Oates, Bud Cody, Henry Ellison, William Holloway, and all the others. Even the high-ranking Lieutenant Colonel Michael Bulger, of the 47th Alabama, believed to be mortally wounded, had been left to be captured sitting under a tree, sword in hand, bleeding profusely.[40]

For the first time, Oates realized the high cost of the day's fighting. In the deep night, with the fireflies sparkling all around, Oates knew that when the battle had started four hours earlier, "mine was the strongest and finest regiment in Hood's division." Going into the fight, the 15th Alabama had about 400 men (or slightly less than that) in its ranks. Now only 223 enlisted men and 19 officers answered at roll call, which meant that more than half of the regiment's officers had been left on the field. During the course of the night, as the dreadful sounds of the wounded could be heard, some of the missing men of the 15th Alabama straggled into camp and tried to explain where they had been.[41]

"It certainly was a very solemn and lonely night," wrote one of Oates's enlisted men. The ghost of defeat hung over the men of the 15th Alabama, as did the knowledge that they had lost so many comrades in the day's fighting. "There was no disturbance or interruption by the enemy," continued the private, "everything being as quiet as a graveyard." Oates ordered his pickets forward, close to the enemy lines. The night was not really as quiet as some would later remember it. The noise of the Federals building breastworks on Big Round Top, the sharp clatter of rocks being thrown together as the Confederates in Plum Run Valley did the same, and the monotonous pleas of the wounded broke through the stillness of the night and created a chorus of sounds that could not be ignored. Sometimes faraway voices could be heard slicing through the night.[42]

Some of Oates's men could not bear the thought of their wounded friends suffering through the night, so several of them volunteered to return to Little Round Top and drag as many wounded back to camp as they could. Oates later claimed the men on this patrol went forward without orders, but the fact that they hoped specifically to carry John Oates back into the Confederate lines makes it unlikely that William Oates knew nothing of the plan beforehand. The volunteers crept through the Federal lines without detection and managed to move some of the regiment's wounded officers a short distance from where they had fallen, when suddenly they were discovered by Federal pickets and shots rang out in the hollow. The patrol, barely escaping capture, returned crestfallen to the 15th Alabama's camp, carrying with it only Lieutenant Bud Cody's knife and notebook.[43]

Death is a night without end. That was precisely how it felt to be at Gettysburg on the night of July 2, even for the living. Some soldiers later remembered hearing the awful moans of the wounded throughout the black night; others thought the utter silence of the night to be unearthly. No matter how used to death, as a reality of life, Americans of the nineteenth century claimed to be, they could not adjust themselves to the overwhelming tragedy of death that the war brought to the nation's hills and farm fields and, when the battles were over, to nearly everyone's door. The death of a family member at home, surrounded by loved ones, was nothing like a battlefield death, far removed from family and friends. Even the sad deaths of children in nineteenth century America at least did not entail the anonymity of battle deaths, when so many soldiers fell without anyone at all to comfort them in the last moments, when so many died without anyone knowing who they were or where they had fallen. Nor could Americans reckon with the numbers of dead produced—one is almost tempted to say *manufactured*, because of the efficiency of Civil War weaponry—by each clash on the battlefield, especially since the casualty figures simply grew larger and larger after every successive battle. When Northerners and Southerners finally learned the terrible price that had been paid at Gettysburg they were shocked and, at the same time, numbed by the statistics. The violence of the war kept escalating, and the dead kept multiplying. And the war kept grinding down the soldiers.

Out in the darkness, the dead and dying lay strewn across the landscape, hidden from view under the somber curtain of night, but very present in the minds of the soldiers—men like William Oates—who had survived the days's fighting and now craved to know what it might all mean. For Oates, it meant defeat—not an ignoble defeat, by any means, or a dishonorable one, either. But his failure to capture Little Round Top was just that, a failure, and that reality would stay with him for the rest of his life. There were worse things to bear in this veil of tears. He had left his brother on the field of battle. Oates must have known that John's life hung in the balance, for he had learned that his brother had been hit not once, but several times before falling and being dragged to cover. Civil War soldiers, in most instances, could not survive multiple wounds of the kind that had brought his brother down. So Oates faced reckoning with the guilt and the uncertainty that had come from the crush of events, compelling him to withdraw his troops and leave his wounded brother behind. Why had he helped John transfer into the 15th Alabama? If he had remained in the 6th Alabama, perhaps he would now be unhurt. Why had John insisted on joining the assault? Was he still alive this night? Were Yankee doctors attending him? Had he been ignored by his Yankee captors? Would he die under the moonlight of a Pennsylvania sky? Would he never see his beloved brother again?

A popular Civil War song tried to deal with the sorrowful anonymity of battlefield deaths. Despite its overly maudlin sentiments, the song, "Somebody's Darling," written and published in Georgia in 1864, captured well the impact of soldier deaths on those survivors who lamented the loss of their fallen heroes:

Somebody's watching and waiting for him,
Yearning to hold him again to her breast;
Yet there he lies with his blue eyes so dim,

And purple, child-like lips half apart.
Tenderly bury the fair, unknown dead,
Pausing to drop in his grave a tear;
Carve on the wooden slab over his head,
"Somebody's darling is slumbering here."
Chorus:
Somebody's darling, somebody's pride,
Who'll tell his mother, where her boy died?

At home in Alabama, Sarah Sellars Oates, the mother of William and John, later claimed to have dreamt—her senses perhaps enhanced by her clairvoyance or simply by a mother's second sight—that grave misfortunate had befallen young John. On the battlefield, William Oates knew more than his mother did. He spent the night in torment, racked by guilt and anxiety, wondering about John's fate and hoping for the best. It was the worst night of his life.[44]

Such human misery was what hard war brought to the soldiers who fought it. It killed them in droves, and it made others—in the ranks and back at home—mourn the terrible loss and ponder their own mortality. Hard war took its high casualties on the battlefield, but it also wounded many soldiers in less visible ways, emotionally and psychologically, deep inside where feelings and thoughts intermingled. It demoralized them and left them dazed. Guilt over abandoning John tore Williams into small pieces. As an officer and as an older brother, Oates had been powerless to do anything differently; he was powerless now to do anything that could reverse the last few hours and restore his brother to his side. For a man who was used to wielding power, rather than being its victim, Oates must have found his lack of control over the situation unbearable. There was nothing he could do about it. If there had ever been a time when Oates missed John, when he longed to have him close, when he yearned to hear his voice, when he craved to see him, it was this long night, a night that belonged to the wounded and to the dead.

Even as the dreadful night passed into the early morning hours, it stayed warm and sultry. Overhead the full moon made everything look blue and white. Moonlight and low-hanging smoke created an eerie effect, a land of deceptive shadows and dim shapes, especially around the Slyder farm, where men and horses moved about as if they were gliding in the spectral light. It's doubtful that Oates or any of his men got much, if any, sleep that night. Everyone knew that the battle would be renewed tomorrow and that the end of fighting was nowhere in sight. Nearby, a Texan in Hood's division remembered that bleak night as a phantasmagorical horror. "If the old Satanic dragon has ever been on earth since he offered our Saviour the world if He would serve him," the soldier wrote years later, "he was certainly at Gettysburg that night."[45]

6

IN THE PURPLE GLOOM

Morning broke on July 3 with fog and smoke from countless camp-fires smoldering in the vicinity of the Round Tops. William Oates greeted the dawn with the same dull sensation—one could call it a fog of despair—that he had felt all through the night. The war, this very hard war, was upon him in a manner that had seemed inconceivable in the summer of 1861, when he and the other exuberant young men of Henry County had formed a company of soldiers to fight Yankees and win independence for the South. His regiment's unsuccessful attempt to capture Little Round Top revealed a war that was different in scale from the one he had experienced so far. Having missed the battle of Antietam, he had avoided the war's bloodiest single day. But having charged five times up the slopes of Little Round Top, having lost so many of his friends and comrades, having left behind his severely wounded brother John in the hands of the enemy, having used every means within his power to win a victory—all of these things felt beyond reality, beyond the realm of possibility. Defeat was something officers and soldiers must surely face from time to time, but *this* defeat seemed so costly, so personal, that it paled in comparison to any loss Oates, or the Army of Northern Virginia, had previously experienced on the field of battle.

It was not just his brother John, or even Bud Cody, although these losses were certainly enough to make any man—even a crusty, pugnacious fellow like William Oates—shudder in despondency. It was also the three Bagwell brothers. John Bagwell, twenty-one years old, had died from an illness in May 1862. A month later his older brother William, twenty-two, had also succumbed to disease. And now James, the youngest of three, was dead on the hillside of Little Round Top at twenty-one years of age. More brothers gone from Company G. Oates would have to write James's parents—the third such letter they would receive from a commander of the 15th Alabama over the past fourteen months. The letter would try to console James's parents by telling them he was a good soldier, that his comrades liked and appreciated him, that he had died bravely, and that he had selflessly sacrificed everything for the Confederate cause. Yet there were so many other dead and wounded and lost besides James Bagwell. In the next few weeks, Oates would be writing many similar letters to other parents and the wives of the fallen men who now lay hidden in the morning fog that cloaked the slopes of Little Round Top. There was one letter he dreaded the most. What could he possibly say about his brother to his own mother and father? That would be the hardest letter of all to write.[1]

Below the western face of Big Round Top, amid a persistent fog that lingered well after daybreak, Law's Alabama brigade held the extreme right of the Confederate line. The 15th Alabama moved to a spot in the brigade line halfway up the slope near the treeline, not far from where the Federal sharpshooters had dispersed into the woods the day before, and there the regiment built up a defensive wall of rock and deadwood. Oates's right extended beyond the stone wall, and his skirmishers formed a line to the west, at a right angle with the battle line so that it connected with the skirmish line of the 1st Texas, which occupied ground about a hundred yards south of the Slyder farmhouse. Oates and every other Confederate that morning presumed that if fighting broke out, it would be in the direction of the Federal defenses farther up the slope of Big Round Top or toward Little Round Top, now also heavily defended and fortified by Union troops.[2]

Just as the morning fog and smoke lifted, revealing bright sunlight and some scattered clouds, Federal cavalry maneuvered itself behind the low hills southwest of Big Round Top, not far from where Oates and his regiment had been posted. The Confederate high command seemed unaware that any sizeable force of Yankees was threatening the flank below Big Round Top. Shortly after 1:00 P.M., however, as the earth reverberated from the thunderous artillery duel that was a prelude to Pickett's Charge, which would be launched from the middle of the Confederate line, General Law realized that Federal cavalry was on his flank, and he took quick action to position batteries and infantry to fend off any impending attack. Law's batteries, which stood on Warfield Ridge, opened with grapeshot against the Federals, halting the enemy's progress for the time being. But Oates and the 15th Alabama, who listened carefully to every musket volley and artillery blast with grave concern to ascertain if the noises portended an approaching battle, did not know exactly what was taking place or if they should be preparing for a fight.[3] What Oates could not know was that the remorseless war, the hard war that was so quickly transforming itself into a total war, would again pull the 15th Alabama briefly into its path, but this time it would soon compel Oates to ponder questions about war and honor, courage and fear, in a different light.

Around 5:00 P.M., the Alabamians heard close at hand the popping of skirmish firing behind them as Union cavalry commander Brigadier General H. Judson Kilpatrick's dismounted troopers began to push in the Confederate pickets. Oates must have worried about the security of his own lines, including the skirmish line to his right. Desultory musket fire continued for about half an hour, when, out of the woods near the base of Bushman's Hill, Federal mounted cavalry, under the command of Brigadier General Elon J. Farnsworth, burst from the woods. Oates and his men jumped the wall in front of them and faced toward the west, braving the smattering of Federal fire from atop Big Round Top. It was the second day in a row that the 15th Alabama had to suffer from enemy fire front and rear. Farnsworth's horsemen approached at a fierce gallop, flashing sabers in hand, horse hooves pounding. The Union cavalry smashed through Oates's skirmish lines and rammed past the 15th Alabama, receiving a long sheet of flame from the muskets of the Alabama brigade. Soon the blue troopers ran headlong into the 4th Alabama, which had been ordered to move forward and block the Federal advance.[4]

Suddenly Farnsworth's horse went down, but most of his men rode on, finally turning south again to find safety in the woods on Bushman's Hill. Taking a trooper's horse, Farnsworth swung himself into the saddle, but instead of following his men back to Bushman's Hill, he and a few of his troopers decided to return the way they had come. In the meantime, Oates and his men crossed Plum Run at the double quick and unexpectedly encountered a small contingent of Union cavalry—Farnsworth and his returning entourage—bearing down on them. Farnsworth, pistol in hand, reined in his horse and ordered Oates's skirmishers to surrender. The Union officer was answered with a burst of volley fire, which knocked him, his horse, and another trooper to the ground, wounding them. Badly hurt, Farnsworth still grasped his pistol and tried to get to his feet. The other Federals, Oates reported, "dashed away." The lieutenant commanding Oates's skirmishers, John D. Adrian, cautiously approached the Union general and said, "Now you surrender."[5]

What happened next has been hotly disputed by eyewitnesses and historians down through the years. Oates did not witness the events himself, so he later had to rely on what Lieutenant Adrian told him had happened. According to Adrian, Farnsworth replied to his surrender demand by saying, "I'll be damned if I do," aimed his pistol at his heart, and fired. He slumped over dead, while the Alabamians stood there in total amazement. Oates kept this story to himself until after the war, when he repeated it widely; former Confederates believed the story (having assumed that Oates was actually an eyewitness to the suicide) and, in turn, mentioned it often in their accounts of

Gettysburg. In first telling this tale, Oates claimed that Farnsworth had shot himself in the head and had blown his brains out, but when Federal veterans—including the doctor who examined the general's retrieved body—revealed that Farnsworth had no head wounds, he changed his account to have the Union general kill himself with a bullet to his chest.

Former Union soldiers argued that the story was simply untrue and that Farnsworth had died of the wounds he received from the skirmishers' volley. Some said that the Confederates must have seen a different Union officer commit suicide, but Oates insisted that the man who had killed himself was Farnsworth, for he had taken the general's shoulder straps (removed by one of the Alabama skirmishers) and a letter addressed to Farnsworth that had been found in the dead officer's pockets. Oates tore up the letter (which he said was from a woman) and later lost the shoulder straps.[6]

Given the available evidence, including the accounts of Federal doctors who examined Farnsworth's body immediately after the battle and took stock of its wounds, it is unlikely that the Union general could have possibly committed suicide. Why, then, did Oates believe for the rest of his life that Farnsworth had taken his own life? Why did he repeat the story so many times that it actually became part of the folklore about the battle of Gettysburg? As with most aspects of Oates's life, the answers are not simple.

Suicide, as Oates must have known, did occur occasionally in battle. The reported instances were few, so it is difficult to calculate how many soldiers might have been pushed to take their own lives in the midst of combat, but Union records indicate that approximately 400 soldiers killed themselves during the war. Probably the actual number was much higher. It is not known how many of these suicides took place in camp, on the march, or on the battlefield. Nor is it certain how many Southerners may have committed suicide during the war. The most prominent case, which received heavy coverage in newspapers on both sides of the Mason-Dixon line concerned Brigadier General Philip St. George Cocke of Virginia, who had commanded the Fifth Brigade at First Manassas, but fell ill and, according to the *Charleston Mercury*, became "flighty" in the mind. He took his life in December 1861, but not while engaged with the enemy.[7]

Far more frequent were the reports in Northern newspapers of Union soldiers, officers *and* enlisted men, who committed suicide for various reasons, but the prevailing assumption was that these soldiers either suffered from delirium caused by sickness or a "fit of insanity." All of these suicides, as reported to the public, occurred in camps or barracks, while the armies refitted between campaigns. It is not particularly surprising that newspapers reported these deaths, given their lurid appeal, but it is remarkable how often—usually at least a few each month—such stories appeared in the major Northern papers, typically as small items attached to general war reports or as sensational sidebars.[8] One report, noting the suicide of a soldier who had been charged with disobedience of orders, stated that the man "was so prostrated by the disgrace that seemed impending, that he deliberately shot himself."[9] Suicide, in other words, held no honor for Northerner and Southerner alike. It was the coward's way out, unless a mitigating circumstance, such as a fatal disease or utter shame about to tarnish one's good name, turned the suicide into a heroic gesture.

Nevertheless, suicides in the Civil War might have been one way for some soldiers to express their own sense of honor. Some of them, especially the cases of battlefield suicides, may have believed they could die with honor by taking their own lives, if they were facing circumstances—such as capture, incarceration, and even execution by the enemy—that meant they could no longer live with honor. In Oates's case, he was more afraid of being captured and sent to languish in a Northern prison camp than he was about being killed in battle. When he heard Adrian's account of Farnsworth's death, he may have simply assumed that the Union general was avoiding capture much in the same way that Oates might try eluding his potential captors. For Oates, killing oneself to stay out of a prison camp was neither dishonorable or cowardly; in fact, he probably thought that Adrian's story made all the sense in the world.

It is harder to explain why Oates continued to believe that Farnsworth committed suicide long after he learned that the medical evidence conclusively disproved any such possibility. Why did Oates think that Farnsworth's suicide was so significant? What did it represent for him that was so vital, so central to his understanding of the Civil War's deeper meanings, that he could not stop believing it, even when objective evidence revealed that the suicide simply could not have happened? Farnsworth's "suicide"—unlike other suicides reported during the war—was important to Oates precisely because it was unique and involved circumstances other than insanity or impending death due to illness. The suicide challenged everything he thought he understood about the Civil War. At Gettysburg, his comprehension of the war and its meaning became immensely altered. His experience on that battlefield taught him what this hard war was becoming—a war of anomalies, a war in which people killed themselves rather than surrender, a war in which loved ones died, a war that left the survivors to face guilt, remorse, moral dilemmas, and profound sadness. From Oates's perspective, Farnsworth's taking of his own life broke all the rules, turned everything upside down, and revealed fully how the war had assumed its own course and had become something that no one could control. By committing suicide, Farnsworth had left everyone—especially his enemies, the Alabamians—stunned and befuddled. What kind of a war was this, that officers took their own lives rather than give up? In holding on to the Farnsworth myth, Oates disclosed how very much he believed that the war had transformed itself into something vicious, ungentlemanly, and morally bankrupt. The war, in short, had become unrecognizable; it was now a very different war from the one that had begun in 1861.

On the field, the Confederates remained in their positions as they watched the Federal horsemen retreat. Torn to pieces without having accomplished anything, the Union cavalry—now minus its brigadier general—withdrew into the woods, the musket and artillery firing sputtered out, and Oates and his men sat down for a rest along the southwestern base of Big Round Top. Later, when the skies opened up and poured down a torrential rain, he moved his men to a veritable no-man's-land south of the Round Tops. There he waited for orders that never came. Forty years later he remembered the uneasiness of the night: "The surroundings presented the most weird and lonely appearance. The dead lay scattered through the dreary and somber woods; the fast-scudding clouds overhead shut out all save just enough light, at short intervals, to get a glimpse of the solemn scenes around us. Not a sound was heard; the stillness was awful." After nearly getting shot by a Federal sniper, he decided to "abandon the post without orders, and get out of there." Fortunately, through that black and cheerless night, he and his men stumbled upon Law's brigade on the right of Longstreet's line.[10]

Independence Day arrived ingloriously under brooding gray skies. Across the bloody fields and hills of Gettysburg lay ample proof that this war between North and South had become something more than just a brothers' squabble. Strewn everywhere on the landscape and sheltered in makeshift hospitals were more than 51,000 casualties, the grim price of a war fought without bounds, without limits. The two armies had crashed together in a mighty collision. The sickening piles of corpses, the endless moans of the wounded, and the charred field of battle demonstrated how totally each side was committed to victory. The wasteland around Gettysburg revealed in horrible certainty that the armies—and their soldiers—had passed beyond courtly notions of romantic warfare, even though such notions infused their memories of the war long after it was over.

Behind breastworks of fence rails and earth near the Emmitsburg Road, Colonel William C. Oates and his men peered out on a desolate landscape that looked like a giant tornado had moved across the earth from one end of the battlefield to the other until nothing remained except for a stand of trees here, a few houses there, and some broken sections of fence posts and rails scattered all about. It was a cold summer morning, and the Alabamians warmed themselves by getting as near as possible to the burning Currens house, which had been torched by the Confederates because it blocked their view of the Union lines in the vicinity of the Round Tops.[11]

Inside the Confederate lines, the dead had been buried and the wounded removed to field hospitals—most of them set up in houses and barns on the surrounding farms—but there were still thousands of Southern wounded suffering without assistance all over the battlefield. Although they could not be seen from the 15th Alabama's vantage point along the Emmitsburg Road that morning, the casualties—dead and wounded—from the fighting two days ago still lay between the rocks and under the trees of the Round Tops. Already the stench of death—the sickening aroma of putrefied blood—permeated the air in and around Gettysburg.

Oates spent part of the morning trying to gain a better sense of who was present and who was missing from the regiment. His brother was gone, he knew all too well, but other soldiers kept drifting in and filling in the ranks behind the Confederate entrenchments. Oates went about his duties like a man in a trance. Weighed down by depression and a deep sorrow, a reaction not uncommon among combat veterans in the Civil War (including those who had *not* lost their brothers in battle), he could not stop thinking of John and the fact that he had been forced to abandon him on the slopes of Little Round Top. He felt, as he later explained in a heartfelt letter, "discomfited and exceed[ing]ly gloomy—even reckless and miserable." By "reckless," he probably meant, as the word was defined at the time, negligent and careless, overwhelmed by his dark thoughts and painful heartache. But it is also possible that he had lost his bearings and felt reckless enough either to do harm to himself, as he believed Farnsworth had done, or to avoid saving himself if some danger confronted him. What seems fairly certain is that he could not concentrate on the moment at hand, and he found it impossible to take his mind off his brother and the disastrous consequences of the fight for Little Round Top. His spirits sank lower and lower. Never before had he experienced such a total feeling of emptiness. He had, as he later phrased it so simply, lost his "dearest relative on earth."[12]

Around midday on the Fourth of July, thunder crashed overhead and lightning streaked across the sky as a series of violent summer storms descended on Gettysburg. It was almost predictable, in Oates's view, that great rains should come pouring down as they did, for rain invariably followed "a heavy battle." Lee ordered his long wagon train to begin rolling toward the Potomac. Although the rain fell in torrents that day, flooding the streams and turning the already muddy roads into bogs, the wagons, loaded with wounded, left Gettysburg around 4:00 P.M. Later that evening, Hood's division received orders to prepare to march. Behind the soggy entrenchments along the Emmitsburg Road, Oates and his men got their belongings together and tried to stay dry in the downpour that continued throughout the remainder of the day and night.[13]

It was still raining in the early morning hours of July 5, when Law's brigade moved out of its defenses, found its way to the Fairfield Road, and marched away from Gettysburg for good. Before the 15th Alabama took its place in the column, however, Oates rode over to the brigade's field hospital, where he visited the regiment's wounded and bid farewell to Lieutenant Colonel Feagin, who had been cut down on the Slyder farm by the Federal sharpshooters. Still depressed and overwrought with feelings of guilt, Oates found it hard to say goodbye to Feagin, who had "barely rallied from the shock of amputating his leg." Oates was feeling personally responsible for the calamities that had befallen his men, including his brother John and Feagin, one of his closest friends in the regiment. With Feagin now out of the war, Oates was losing a friend and "a brave officer." He had been, said Oates, "courageous and faithful," and it took a great deal of effort for Oates to hold back his emotions and say goodbye. Oates also had to force himself to accept that the army would be leaving Gettysburg, aborting the Pennsylvania invasion, and returning to Virginia. Leaving Gettysburg meant leaving John to a uncertain, unknowable fate. Drenched to the skin, Oates rejoined the regiment and led his men away from Gettysburg, slogging along the Fairfield Road toward South Mountain. He ordered them to close up ranks and warned them not to straggle. They moved like a long, dark funeral procession through the rain toward Hagerstown, Maryland.[14]

A few days later, Hood's division received word of the fall of Vicksburg. An infantryman in the Fifth Texas wrote: "Some few soldiers in the army and some people at home believed that Lee's retreat from Gettysburg and Pemberton's surrender at Vicksburg on the 4th of July, the anniversary of the Declaration of American Independence, was a providential warning to the South to give up the fight; maybe it *was* the handwriting on the wall." For Oates, though, the role of Providence in the battle was negligible. After the war, he declared: "I do not worship a God who takes sides in battle and gives the victory to the heaviest battalions, greatest numbers and best equipped with arms and implements of war without regard to whether the cause be just or unjust." At Gettysburg, said Oates, "God had nothing to do with it." Perhaps he might have felt differently if God hadn't seemed to turn on him at Gettysburg, striking down his brother and leaving his regiment shattered.[15] Oates didn't want to believe that God could have purposely inflicted the miseries of Gettysburg on Lee's army, the good men of the South, his brother, or himself. It was bad enough that John lay dead or dying somewhere beyond Oates's reach. To say that the Almighty had ordained such a horrible judgment on the young officer was too much for William Oates to accept or bear. Even to think such a thing meant that a providential God had turned his back on Oates and, equally distressing to contemplate, on the South.

William Oates could not know that his brother John had survived. On the rocky slopes of Little Round Top, John Oates had endured an unimaginable ordeal in the aftermath of the fighting there. Not far away from him, Bud Cody and other wounded men of the 15th Alabama lay in agony, wondering whether they would live or die, wondering if they did live, what would happen to them. Up and down the hillside, which was covered with a blanket of dead and wounded, the cries for help and for water went out into the thick darkness. One Alabamian later wrote his wife that "it was an awful scene to see and hear the shrieks and groanings of the poor dying soldiers on my right and on my left and before and behind and all around me."[16]

If Lieutenant John Oates were conscious during the night of July 2, which seems doubtful, he would have heard the chorus of voices lifted up across Little Round Top as wounded men prayed for deliverance, water, or even death. It is not known how long he, Cody, or the other wounded men of the 15th Alabama lay there among the rocks before Union soldiers found them and carted them away to field hospitals behind the lines, probably on July 3, when the nearby Confederates—including the 15th Alabama—fought off Farnsworth's cavalry charge.

At first Oates and Cody were taken to one of the makeshift aid stations behind the Union lines near the Taneytown Road. Later, when the seriousness of their wounds became apparent, the Alabamians were transferred to the Army of the Potomac's Fifth Corps, Second Division, hospital—the same hospital where wounded of the 20th Maine received their medical care. About 800 wounded—including a good number of Confederates—occupied this corps hospital, which had been set up on the farm of Michael Fiscel, about a mile and a half east of the Round Tops. Eleven surgeons were on duty.[17]

The hospital was bedlam and slaughterhouse combined. Piles of amputated limbs could be seen everywhere, attracting flies and giving off a sickening odor. Only some of the wounded could be comfortably accommodated on hay beds in the buildings and in several tents; many of the suffering men lay in long lines under the hot sun with no protection over them at all. The groans of the wounded blocked out most of the other sounds around the Fiscel farm, except for the occasional screams of men who could not bear their pain any longer. Rain storms that came after the battle put the men in more agony, turning the hay into damp straw and drenching the wounded soldiers to the skin. East of the barn, in a field overlooking a stream, the men who died from their wounds were buried in shallow graves that gave off an eerie phosphorescent glow at night.[18]

John Oates and Bud Cody were among the seventy-five wounded Confederates who received care in the three hospitals of the Fifth Corps that had been established in the vicinity of the Fiscel farm. As prisoners of war, the Alabamians had to wait their turn to receive whatever medical care the Union doctors were willing to give them. The Union doctor who treated Oates and Cody was J. A. E. Reed, the surgeon of the 155th Pennsylvania, a kindly and skillful physician from Lancaster, who, with the other Federal doctors, worked tirelessly to ease the misery of thousands of wounded. Reed found that his efforts with the two Alabama lieutenants were largely useless. Yet in an era before the modern Geneva Convention on the fair treatment of prisoners of war, Union and Confederate doctors generally followed prevailing principles of honor that enjoined them to treat wounded prisoners of war with decency and kindness. Reed and his colleagues treated hundreds of Confederate wounded after the battle, and they did so with as much care and professionalism as they devoted to any soldiers dressed in blue.

Hoping to make two Alabamians more comfortable, Dr. Reed moved them to a hospital tent and placed them on separate cots. It was Reed who told John Oates that he was dying, that nothing could be done to stop the spread of pyemia—blood poisoning accompanied by multiple abscesses—throughout his body. Besides running a high fever and shivering with the chills, John also suffered from jaundice. These afflictions, coupled with the extreme pain of his rheumatism, must have kept him in constant agony. Dr. Reed's wife, his sister-in-law, and a woman friend of the doctor's wife—a Miss Lightner—took a special and heartfelt interest in the dying young man and his friend Cody. Throughout the next three weeks, the women paid daily visits to the two Alabamians, got them to talk about home and family, gave them "delicacies" of food and drink when they could be obtained, read to them, laughed with them, and generally kept the wounded men company through the long ordeal of their final days.[19]

Soaked and footsore, Law's brigade passed over South Mountain in a leisurely march and reached Hagerstown, Maryland, on July 6. It was still raining when they got there, moved through the town, and took up a position a mile or so to the west. Colonel Oates and the 15th Alabama did their share of the labor throwing up defensive works outside of the town in expectation that the Army of the Potomac would soon be speeding toward the Potomac in pursuit of Lee. But the Yankees decided not to attack and instead fortified their lines facing the Confederates. Lee could not cross the Potomac because of high waters, but Major General George Gordon Meade, commander of the Union Army of the Potomac, was reluctant to commit his forces to an offensive action against the entrenched Army of Northern Virginia. If the Confederates felt trapped, with the deep and wide river behind them, they did not show it. Oates and his regiment—like the rest of Lee's army—were ready for a fight, if it came to that.

For more than a week, the Confederates manned their defenses, waiting for an attack. Finally, late in the day on July 13, Lee decided the river could be safely crossed. A makeshift pontoon bridge was laid across the river at Falling Waters, and Longstreet's corps moved across the seething Potomac in the dark and rain. As Law's brigade passed over the crude bridge and made landfall on the other side of the river, they looked up and saw on a high embankment, behind a shimmering veil of pouring rain, Lee sitting astride his horse Traveller, a silent gray ghost in the darkness.

All through the night, knee-deep mud impeded the progress of the withdrawal and river crossing. When a lightning flash lit up the entire sky, one soldier in the Texas brigade remarked, "Hell is not a half mile from here." The last of Longstreet's divisions went over the river while the rain still poured down around dawn on July 14. Later the Confederates fought off a spirited attack by the Federals, who had caught the last portion of Lee's army still waiting to cross the river, but the remnant of the Army of Northern Virginia made it across the pontoons and cut the anchoring cables so that the bridge floated off downstream with the current. The Gettysburg campaign was over.[20]

On July 21, Bud Cody died of peritonitis, a result of the wound he had received in his left groin.[21] Two days later, on a fine summer's evening, the end also came for John A. Oates. The day had begun in Gettysburg with a bright sun and blue skies. Before sundown, Mrs. Reed, the doctor's wife, and Miss Lightner visited his bedside and tried to bring some cheer into his day. But they could see he was doing poorly, struggling with his pain more than he had ever done before. As they tried to comfort him, he seemed to grow weaker with every breath. John asked the women to sing for him. They sang a hymn, "Jesus, Lover of My Soul." They all recited the Lord's Prayer. When the prayer was finished, Oates turned to the women and said: "Tell my folks at home that I died in the arms of friends." Then, as the sun dipped below the horizon, he died.

He was buried in a wooden coffin near the hospital, in a field overlooking a gentle stream on the Fiscel farm. A headboard with his name and rank marked the mound of dirt that covered him.[22] He was laid to rest 850 miles from home. John Oates was twenty-seven years old.

In their small house near Oates's Crossroads, 850 miles south of Gettysburg, William and Sarah Oates—the parents of William and John—went to bed early that evening and slept soundly into the night. Suddenly in the darkness, Sarah shook William violently and woke him out of a deep sleep. She was sobbing and crying. Through her sobs she insisted that John, their son, was dead. He had been in a great battle, she said, and had just died. She could not control her weeping, and William could not calm her down. He reminded her that no news of any kind had been received about a battle in which John could have fought, and no casualty lists had been posted for weeks. Surely, he said, she must have *dreamed* that their son had died. It was a nightmare, and nothing more. No, she replied, it was not a dream.

She described how she had seen her son, had seen him take his last breath, and had seen him laid out for burial. Her husband could say that it was a dream, but she knew better. No one would ever make her believe otherwise. She knew her young boy was dead. Sarah wept through the night, inconsolable in her grief and anguish.

Two days later, on July 27, word arrived in Oates's Crossroads that John had been wounded in the battle of Gettysburg. Sarah shook her head. "He is already dead and buried," she said. And so he was.

This was the story as William Oates told it several decades later, when he wrote his autobiography and included this intriguing anecdote about his mother. By relating this incident, he hoped to emphasize his mother's special spiritual qualities, her emotional sensitivity, and her precognitive abilities, but he also wanted to stress the great shockwave that John's death had produced in the Oates family. It was a devastating blow to his mother, his family, and, most importantly, him. Having had no such image of John on his deathbed in Gettysburg, but longing for a connection of any kind to his lost brother, Oates firmly believed that his mother had experienced a supernatural vision of John at the moment of his death—an image of unearthly significance that had manifested itself in her sleep.

His certainty that his mother had somehow seen John die could have been reinforced by the fact that many people, including individuals who never participated in a battle or resided anywhere near a battlefield, dreamed about the war before it occurred or while it was taking place. Abraham Lincoln's dreams have become famous in the annals of the Civil War, if only because they overflowed with great symbolism and ominous foreshadowing, but less famous individuals—ordinary people trying to live ordinary lives—sometimes dreamed vividly of the war and its intractable anabasis. These dreams, the memory of which often seemed strikingly real and tangible, enabled noncombatants to experience emotions similar to the ones felt firsthand by the soldiers doing the fighting: fear, anger, horror, sorrow, and, most significantly, helplessness. Like a dream, a terrible nightmare, the war was out of anyone's power to control. And it insidiously permeated every aspect of American life, along the battle lines and on the homefront. There was no escaping it—not in one's wakeful hours or in one's sleep.

Even for the soldiers themselves, the men who actually witnessed the fighting and who by their own hands had killed their enemies and caused unimaginable devastation across the landscape, the war became something of a dream, a vast panorama of events and places that seemed unconnected to reality. Could this horrible bloodletting be real? Surely this unthinkable catastrophe in the history of the American people must be an awful dream. It had to be a dream because it could not be connected, could not be explained, by what had come before it. The war, in all its perfect maleficence, could not be comprehended; it had no connection to the quotidian experiences of ordinary people, the conventional manner in which life had been lived, before the shells exploded in the darkness above Fort Sumter. For most of William Oates's life—during the days immediately following the battle of Gettysburg and for every other day thereafter—he wished that the Civil War *had* been nothing more than a dream; and in the morning, when he awoke, John would be there at the breakfast table, and all would be right again.[23]

By August 1863, Law's brigade was encamped along the Rappahannock River, near Fredericksburg, where William Oates and his regiment regained their strength and got back to the routine of military life between campaigns. Drilling took up a good amount of time every day, although the men hated marching around in circles under the blistering August sun. Occasionally the Alabamians moved across the river, where the Army of the Potomac had taken up its former positions, and sparred meaninglessly with the Federals.[24]

For the remainder of August, Oates worked hard in his job as a regimental commander, making sure that he completed requisite paperwork, like filing his official report for the battle of Gettysburg and taking care of his men as best he could. Oates's men respected his leadership, admired him as an officer, and generally praised his actions as commander of the 15th Alabama. In describing his war record in *The War Between the Union and the Confederacy*, the book he published in 1905 as a combined memoir and regimental history of the 15th Alabama, Oates wrote (in the third person): "He gave his men as good care and attention as any captain in the service possibly could. He always contended strenuously and doggedly for their rights." His men agreed and showed real fondness toward him. William Jordan of Company B remembered that Oates had been particularly kind to him during the retreat from Gettysburg, when Oates allowed Jordan to drop back to the rear when he was feeling poorly. Gus McClendon, a veteran of Company G, praised Oates for locating shelter for a sick man. McClendon said that "this was only one of the many kind acts" Oates had showed for his men "whenever an opportunity presented itself."

Yet why, in describing his accomplishments as an officer, had he written that particular passage in the third person? For about a page-and-a-half, this third-person account functioned as the introduction to a roster and a collection of biographical sketches of the men who served in the Henry Pioneers. Throughout the rest of the book, Oates wrote of his war experiences in the first person without self-consciousness; only in these few paragraphs did he use the third person to describe himself. He seems to have had two purposes. The first was stylistic: He wanted to make his own biographical sketch consistent with the others that appeared in this appendix to the book's main body. The other purpose, however, was more deceptive and reflected his concern with how he would be remembered in the future: He sought to strike an apparent air of objectivity in relating his record, which he painted in glowing terms, to the public. In doing so, he probably hoped the reader would think that someone else had written these complimentary words about him and that every word must be the truth; instead, without intending to do so, he revealed some self-doubts about his own service in the Confederate army, particularly concerning how his men thought of him. Beneath the surface, and despite his own high opinion of himself, Oates was not entirely sure that everyone in the regiment followed him willingly or considered him a capable officer.[25]

He had good reason. Oates, in fact, made his share of enemies among the men he led, and some of them expressed their views in forceful language. Long after the war, a former private in Company H said of him: "Oates was a tyrant to the men when in command of the regiment. . . . [W]hen I was suffering from a wound which caused the amputation of my leg, he tyrannized over me and treated me cruelly." Another soldier once "poured out vials of wrath on the colonel" when Oates declined to give the man a furlough, the sort of complaint most soldiers would have made under the circumstances. Others probably kept their views to themselves or expressed their displeasure with him privately in letters written home to family. After the war, public criticism of Oates had to be tempered because of his influential standing as a politician, an honored war hero, and a respected attorney. In the decades after the war, the ideology of the Lost Cause made it difficult for any Southerner to cast aspersions on Confederate veterans who had seen combat, unless one wanted to argue about the relative incompetence of the army's generals (so long as Lee and Jackson remained unsullied).[26]

To be sure, Oates was not universally loved by his men. He could often be hard on them, pushing them to extremes as Jackson had done with his troops in the Valley Campaign or showing favoritism in promotions or plum assignments. Although he demonstrated repeatedly that he genuinely cared about his men and their welfare, sometimes by even using his own money to buy them uniforms or supplies, he enforced military discipline without flexibility and sometimes with the ardor of a martinet. Unable to keep silent on the issues of the day, including his scorn for civilian leaders in Richmond, his strong opinions probably offended some of his men or led them to believe he was perennially bad-tempered. Oates had a habit of expressing his views openly and forcefully, as if no one else could possibly hold an opposing opinion. No master of diplomacy, he often shouldered—and occasionally blundered—his way along without any regard for tact or proper comportment. Nor did he suffer fools gladly. When it came to anyone he suspected of supporting his regimental rival, Alexander Lowther, he showed no mercy. Even men who did not much care if Oates or Lowther led the regiment sometimes felt Oates's sting.

His men probably never understood, whether they liked him or not, that Oates's style of leadership mirrored the hard war they all were fighting and the total war they all would eventually fight. The brutality of combat necessitated every soldier, including officers, to harden themselves for the bloody work of killing Yankees and putting their own lives at risk, time after time. They lost their innocence, which meant saying goodbye to those unsullied boys who had joyously mustered into Oates's Henry Pioneers when the war promised romance and glory. Now they had come of age and embraced manhood by looking into the face of death and becoming men of war. Oates took to the war with a natural ease at first. Already accustomed to violence and its bloody effects, his first months of combat experience did not really faze him; he found the death of his troops from disease far more unnerving than the casualties of battle. But the rising human cost of every battle, especially after Gaines Mill and the Peninsula Campaign, altered his feelings. He became increasingly sorrowful, and even noticeably morose, about the losses in his company and, later, after he assumed command of the 15th Alabama, in the entire regiment. The battle of Gettysburg, Oates's unwilling but necessary abandonment of John, the transformation of a limited war into a hard war, and eventually the emergence of total war, made him focus his attention more readily on the high price of the war, even though he had become a seasoned veteran and, like other hardened soldiers, somewhat inured to the slaughter of every battle. On the surface, seasoned soldiers acted like death was an ordinary occurrence, a reality of soldiering, that did not emotionally affect them; below the surface, they struggled with the anguish that came from witnessing the shocking human consequences of war—consequences that they, with their own hands, had caused.[27]

But Oates's response to hard war involved more than just seasoning. The exigencies of total war, as it began to take hold of Americans living north and south of the Mason-Dixon line, required adapting oneself to the changes wrought by a conflict that channeled every resource, human and materiel, into the cause of victory. In Oates's case, and for other Confederate officers, the intensifying war emphasized the need for more discipline among the troops, less democracy within the ranks, and more authoritarian leadership. Lives, quite simply, depended on men obeying orders, marching when they were told, and attacking an enemy position without questioning the tactical wisdom behind it.

Commanding the 15th Alabama after Gettysburg, Oates found himself pondering survival—his own, his men's—more than he had before as the conflict continued to churn up and as each battle became more and more bloody. After Gettysburg, Lee's first great defeat, the Army of Northern Virginia experienced weakening morale among its soldiers, greater shortages in supplies, and a steady depletion in its strength that would continue until the final days of the war. With no end to the conflict in sight, with no sign that the war would be over soon, Oates and his fellow officers worked to keep their commands together, strong and disciplined, and fighting—no matter how bad the apparent odds—toward the goal of victory. To do so, Oates learned that he could not effectively lead his men if he appeared only to be their friend. In distancing himself from his troops, as every good officer must, Oates also helped to create an emotional chasm that would potentially ease his suffering if any more of his cherished comrades fell in the flames of battle.

His troops took his hardness in stride, knowing at the same time that the war was making them into different men than they had been before this cruel war ripped their world apart and turned them into remarkably efficient and deadly soldiers. For all his toughness as a regimental commander, Oates was admired by his men. Most of them seemed to like him and trust him. And he liked them back. "There was no better regiment in the Confederate Army than the Fifteenth Alabama," he wrote many years later, looking back on the war and the men he had commanded. In his estimation, no finer fighting force could be found in all the South.[28]

In the late summer of 1863, Oates continued to struggle with his depression. Civil War soldiers more commonly referred to Oates's condition with a variety of descriptive terms, including having "the blues," "nostalgia," "melancholy," or being "played out," "demoralized," and "downhearted." After receiving a letter from one of the 15th Alabama's wounded men left behind in Gettysburg, he learned for certain that Bud Cody and his brother John had both died. He wrote to the Reverend Edmund Cody, Bud's father, to inform him of his son's death—not an easy task, by any means. In the letter, Oates admitted that he was depressed. Of Bud, his young friend, he wrote poignantly: "I loved him with the tenderness of feeling I have for my Brother. Noble and manly in bearing, brave, honest, reliable and true[,] he challenged the admiration of all who knew him. Strict in discipline, accurate in drill and obedient and respectful to superiors[,] he was unsurpassed as an officer by any in the Confederate army of his age. Poor Boy[,] he has gone to a better world. Nobly did he fall in the discharge of his duty."

He probably also wrote to his parents about John, confirming what Sarah Oates had already sensed. And he must have written similar letters to the relatives of other soldiers in the regiment who had fallen at Gettysburg. As commander of the regiment, it was his job to communicate such sad news to family members back home. Oates appears to have been diligent in doing so, but it must have required a herculean effort to compose these letters without falling apart. The regiment was a community unto itself. He knew the men who marched in the unit—some better than others—at least by name and by face. So many of them had been lost at Gettysburg. So many of them had been his friends. As he told Cody's father, "Sadly do I feel my own bereavement."[29]

Other men in the camp were also crestfallen. The discouragement that came with defeat—particularly the withdrawal of Lee's army from Pennsylvania and the fall of Vicksburg—produced feelings of loneliness, homesickness, and self-pity among Lee's soldiers. In the Alabama camps, everyone talked about furloughs and longed to be given leave so that they could go home. They realized, though, that only a small number of men in the army would be allowed to leave it that summer, what with Meade's army just a stone's throw across the Rappahannock. Toward the end of August, Lee issued an order allowing one man from each company to be given a furlough of thirty days. Two names from each company were submitted by the company commander to the regimental commander, so that Oates was burdened with the job of deciding who should go and who should stay. Oates understood what his men were going through. In later years, he observed: "The most terrible ordeal through which our soldiers passed was that of being separated for years—as many of them were—from a loving wife and dear little children who were at home hoping, praying, and sighing for the safe and speedy return of the husband and father." He noted sadly that in too many cases the men returned to their homes as corpses.[30]

Disillusionment with the war and the small number of available furloughs led more men than ever before to desert from the Army of Northern Virginia that summer. During early September, Lee went to Richmond to discuss strategy and the growing problem of desertion with President Davis. Oates rarely condemned deserters for abandoning their posts, for he knew that men often left the army in order to care for their destitute families back home. And though he believed that deserters deserved no honor, and though he felt that they had less of an excuse in the summer of 1863 than they did later on in the war, when the Confederacy became a "hopeless cause," he nevertheless took a realistic view of the problem and refused to think of deserters as traitors or devils.

As he declared in 1905: "If ever good men were excusable for desertion, it was in the case of the Confederate soldiers. They had suffered all the privations and hardships that men ever did and then saw no hope of success." On July 30, Private William R. Hendley of Company H, 15th Alabama, deserted the regiment. Years later, all Oates had to say about Hendley was this: "It was reported that he joined a cavalry regiment and served in that capacity, but I do not know as to the truth of this." He said similar things about other deserters, condemning very few of them for their decisions and their actions. Hard war did not soften him, but it did effect a fundamental change in Oates's sense of honor. In both armies, Union and Confederate, the rank and file regarded deserters as dishonorable soldiers—cowards who fled from the manly arena of combat. But opinions changed, including Oates's attitude toward deserters, as the war ground the armies down, particularly the Southern armies that could not replenish their resources. Confederate soldiers often left the

ranks for good reasons—they were needed at home, there was no one else to
care for their families, they were too worn out to keep up the fight. Some
deserters, of course, did not leave the war for any of these reasons, apart from
the fact that the hard war was becoming even harder to bear, and Oates did
not spare his criticism of these shirkers.

For the most part, though, he tried to be kind and understanding to deserters, and he did not portray them as dishonorable or worthless men. A man
could leave the war and still be a man. Even a good soldier could come to the
conclusion that the hard war, with all its perils and its accelerating violence,
was simply not worth giving up one's life for. Deserting, then, was one means—
for some men the *only* means, short of dying on the battlefield, by which
soldiers might escape the hard war, the escalating war, that had become so
grim and so terrifying. Beneath the surface of Oates's fair judgment of deserters and their motives, one detects not only a shift in his own definition of
manly honor, but a hint that he must have contemplated, probably on more
than one occasion, how good it would have felt to leave this cruel war far
behind.[31]

While Oates and the 15th Alabama refitted that August near the banks of the
Rappahannock, they shared in a new and widespread realization about the
hardness of war. Quite simply, the war had become something quite different
than the one they thought they were fighting. Without anyone understanding it or seeing it clearly, the war had been transformed since the first guns
were sounded in 1861; what had seemed at one time to be a courtly contest
between the knights of opposing realms had with every battle turned brutal,
vicious, monstrous. Knowing the terrible realities of Gettysburg and
Vicksburg, hardly anyone could pretend anymore that the war was a
gentleman's tournament fought according to acknowledged rules and with
honorable intentions. The rules—if ever there had been any—were gone now.
Without comprehending that the summer of 1863 was any kind of significant
turning point in the war, for no one yet could measure the real importance of
the Union victories that July, Northerners and Southerners at least could
begin to sense that the struggle between the sections was not about to be
concluded anytime soon; instead, the hostilities were expanding and intensifying. It had become a fight to the finish, a conflict without limits, a war of
utter destruction.

It was not simply the appalling casualties and the daunting destruction of
that summer that marked a change in the war. Something else was different.
The North had finally gotten a taste of the real war, something the inhabitants of Virginia had been experiencing ever since the first shots had been
fired at Manassas. But the escalating desolation of the armies and the mount-
ing deaths on the battlefield and the bitter cries of suffering civilians caught

in the throes of war were parts of the transformation that was taking place. The new war was now a hard war largely because of Lincoln's Emancipation Proclamation, issued the winter before. Here was an edict that ensured that Southern property—specifically Confederate *slave* property—would henceforth be a target for destruction by the Union armies. With Lincoln's proclamation, the elimination of slavery as a war measure would blur the distinction between combatants and noncombatants, between soldiers and civilians, as the Northern armies set about doing everything they could to destroy the economic resources that enabled the Confederacy to sustain itself and keep fighting. The proclamation, put forth as a war measure by Lincoln, would now raise black troops to fight their own war of freedom against the Southern foe; in that war, all the prevailing notions of a racial hierarchy in the South would be under attack and would turn the war into a revolutionary struggle for freedom and civil rights. Lincoln's document accomplished something else as well: It replaced the Confiscation Act of 1862, which had allowed for the military seizure of Confederate property and for slaves who came into the Union lines to be "forever free," with a new military policy that came from the president, the commander in chief, himself—everywhere, in eastern and western theaters alike, the Union army would henceforth officially serve as a great legion of liberation. As of the late summer of 1863, the kind of total war that would be waged by Grant, Sherman, and Sheridan to great effect by directly targeting Southern resources and morale had not yet come to pass, but such a war was only around the corner.[32]

In both North and South, the progress of the war through the first half of 1863 brought unrest and despair to the sections as people tried unsuccessfully to cope with the awakening realization that the conflict seemed to have no end, that the body count was getting higher and higher, and that the means for bringing the struggle to a successful conclusion seemed not to exist. Southern newspapers that, at first, had dismissed Lee's retreat at Gettysburg as a "retrograde" movement compelled by strategic necessity now bemoaned the entire campaign as a blunder. "Yesterday we rode on the pinnacle of success; today absolute ruin seems to be our portion," wrote Josiah Gorgas, Confederate chief of ordnance. "The Confederacy," he predicted gravely, "totters to its destruction."[33]

To many Confederates, it seemed as if God had turned his back on the South. For two years, Southerners had assumed that the Almighty was on their side, that the Confederacy had become God's chosen nation. The fact that both sides, North and South, worshipped the same God and equally enlisted his celestial assistance in their respective causes—as Abraham Lincoln later eloquently pointed out—didn't seem to matter much. Confederates believed they were fighting a holy war against Northern sin, evil, and corruption. The preamble of the Confederate Constitution invoked "the favor and guidance of Almighty God." Ministers preached to civilians and soldiers the gospel of the South's righteous cause. The demonstrative piety of Robert E. Lee and Stonewall Jackson only helped to convince Southern soldiers that they had joined a divine crusade and marched to direct orders from God.[34]

But after Antietam, when the first religious revivals in the Army of Northern Virginia began, the circumstances seemed less than certain about God's blessings on the South. Stalemate at Sharpsburg, and the retreat of Lee's invading force back to the Virginia side of the Potomac, did not appear to be signs of God's pleasure and grace. The revivals, after a winter hiatus, resumed in the spring of 1863, an event that Oates and the 15th Alabama appear to have missed while they dodged Union bullets in the entrenchments outside of Suffolk that April. But those religious meetings were soon interrupted by Chancellorsville and the commencement of the Gettysburg campaign. Now, after the defeat in Pennsylvania, when the Army of Northern Virginia was suffering from low morale and depleted manpower, the religious revivals in Lee's camps erupted again, this time with more fervor than ever. A tidal wave of evangelical Protestantism burst forth among the Southern soldiers after Lee's army crossed the Rapidan and settled into camps below Fredericksburg.[35]

Disquieted by the war's deep and rapid changes, Confederates turned once more to religion to find the means of restoring God's favor on the South and its armies, to rekindle optimism out of the fading sparks of defeatism, and to come to terms with the uncertainties and instabilities in their own lives. Some believed that the defeats of the summer of 1863 demonstrated that God was punishing the South for its sins or testing the spiritual resolve of the Confederate people to find true redemption through the trials of war. Even General Lee took up this refrain that August. "Soldiers! we have sinned against Almighty God," Lee declared in orders for the observance of a presidential day of prayer and fasting. "We have forgotten his signal mercies, and have cultivated a revengeful, haughty and boastful spirit. . . . God is our only refuge and our strength. Let us humble ourselves before him. Let us confess our many sins, and beseech him to give us a higher courage, a purer patriotism and more determined will."[36]

Throughout the Confederacy, there was a critical disjunction in the public's understanding of what the war meant and what the future held for the South. The promises of Confederate political leaders like Jefferson Davis, who tried to reassure the people that defeats were simply temporary setbacks and that the Southern cause was not hopeless, no longer seemed to fit the reality of the situation. In the army, the disparity between hope and reality seemed all the greater, if only because the losses of Lee's forces at Gettysburg had been so enormous. Among a large number of the soldiers (although their actual numbers are not known), this disorientation led to profound doubts— doubts about the Confederacy, about the war, and about themselves. Having lost their bearings, they sought to achieve a sense of security, a feeling of belonging, and a newfound faith in old beliefs. To help refocus their sights on God's kingdom, they became reborn in their commitment to the Almighty. They wanted to find answers they could not find on the battlefield.

Many Confederates believed that God's disfavor had resulted from the South's failure to adhere to Protestant doctrine, to cast out sin (conveniently, however, the sin of slavery was not among the catalogued items of transgressions), and to accept God's immanence. To remedy these spiritual shortcomings, the soldiers of Lee's army attended religious meetings, proclaimed their faith in God, went through the emotional transformation of conversion experiences (becoming "born again"), and looked at old truths with a new perspective that would enable them to keep on fighting in what they wanted to believe was a struggle between the forces of good and light and the forces of evil and darkness.

Civilian ministers, military chaplains, and religious newspapers aimed primarily at readers in the army worked together to create what would later become known as the "Great Revival" in the Army of Northern Virginia. While religious sentiment exploded through the ranks of other Confederate armies at about the same time, it was in Lee's army that the largest outpouring of revivalism took place. Caught up in the religious enthusiasm that swept through the army, the *Richmond Christian Advocate* reported, with some exaggeration: "Not for years has such a revival prevailed in the Confederate States. . . . Its progress in the army is a spectacle of moral sublimity over which men and angels can rejoice. Such camp meetings were never seen before in America. The bivouac of the soldier never witnessed such nights of glory and days of splendor. The Pentecostal fire lights the camp, and the hosts of armed men sleep beneath the wings of angels rejoicing over many sinners that have repented."[37]

The principal revival meetings held for Law's brigade were conducted by the Reverend W. H. Carroll, an agent of the Domestic Missionary Board of the Southern Baptist Convention. Carroll's purpose was to proselytize the Alabamians and to win as many converts as he could from their number. He began preaching on July 19 at Bunker Hill, Virginia, continued his meetings at Culpeper, and held numerous services and meetings at the encampments near Fredericksburg and Port Royal. Although many of the Alabama brigade's chaplains had been killed or wounded during the Gettysburg campaign, Carroll did find help from lay clergy in the brigade, including Private Samuel B. McJunkin of the 15th Alabama, a Presbyterian and a school teacher by profession who had been discharged from the army after having been wounded at Second Manassas, but who voluntarily returned to the brigade's camp to spread the Gospel. Carroll and McJunkin discovered that their work would not be easily accomplished among the Alabamians. Even the soldiers who claimed to be Christian, wrote Carroll in a report to the missionary board, "were in a cold backslidden condition, and some had become outbreaking," by which he meant that they were Christian in name only.[38] Oates stood as a

good example of such an "outbreaking" Christian. Since Gettysburg, his nomi-
nal Christianity had worn paper thin, and he refused to believe that providence had anything to do with the course of war, good or bad. But most of his
anger at God, and his lack of faith in anything beyond the earthly and the
tangible, derived from John's fate at Gettysburg—something that Oates believed could not have been ordained or condoned by a providential God.

Throughout August, the camp meetings became more intense and more
frequent. One soldier from the 4th Alabama rejoined his regiment after an
extended leave to find, much to his surprise, that most of his formerly "wicked"
comrades had not only become "members of the Church of the living God,
but professors of religion." This great transformation, wrote the soldier, "is
not limited to my company, but it extends throughout the entire regiment,
and I might say the whole brigade. God grant that this good work may continue to flourish throughout the entire army." By the end of the month, Brother
Carroll was conducting three meetings a day. The men spent their hard-earned
money by contributing generous subscriptions to pay Carroll for his preaching. Thirty-two soldiers in Company F, 15th Alabama, donated at least a
dollar each for Carroll's "ministerial services." By the beginning of September, according to Brother Carroll's later report, thirty-nine Alabamians had
been baptized, twenty-five had converted to Methodism, and more than one
hundred soldiers had found God during the revival.[39]

Surprisingly, William Oates was one of them. Having been raised as a
Christian by a pious Baptist mother (even his father, by this time, had sworn
off liquor and had joined the Baptist church), he had never been an unbe-
liever. Even still, he had never demonstrated much interest in organized religion and previously put little stock in the preachings of evangelical ministers,
whom had been the objects of his pantomimes during his youth. Although
the records are annoyingly sparse, Oates later maintained that he had experienced a "conversion" sometime prior to November 1863, with the likelihood
being that he participated in the revivals along the Rappahannock three months
earlier.

His grief for his brother made him long for consolation, and the comfort
that religion brought—besides its binding force to a larger community of
true believers and to God and Christ—must have given him great solace in
his hour of need. Firmly believing in God and in the power of prayer, Oates
seems to have embraced his conversion—his new birth of faith—with serious
intent and heartfelt sincerity, even to the point of promising himself not to
swear or take the Lord's name in vain. His conversion that summer, however,
does not appear to have changed him into a full-fledged evangelical. Unlike
the Reverend Carroll and the evangelical ministers who preached to Lee's
army that summer, Oates had a decidedly different understanding of God
and his workings on earth. The evangelicals and those who followed them
discarded the Calvinistic doctrine of predestination and its view of mankind

as depraved and untrustworthy, replacing it with a more optimistic belief that all men, whatever their spiritual condition, could experience a "new birth" and could achieve salvation. This, in its essence, was the religion of Oates's mother, a Baptist evangelical pietism that emphasized the dynamics of a personal union with God. But the kingdom of God could only arrive on earth after man renounced sin, readmitted God and Christ in his daily life, embraced God's word and a fervent piety, and recognized that God's hand could be seen as operating in every event—no matter how big or small—on earth.

Characteristically, Oates underwent a spiritual rebirth that did not strictly adhere to the conversion experience or the religious principles that led others to achieve an assurance of salvation. Focusing on the elements of individualism that ran as a strain through Southern evangelicalism, his personal great awakening stressed the positive qualities—and somewhat secular attributes—of free will, reason, and the moral benefits of hard work and honest living.[40] His idiosyncratic piety creatively combined selected principles from old Calvinism (a vengeful, sovereign God), deism (a rational God), and evangelical Protestantism (a forgiving God). In his syncretic belief system, which contained more than its share of inner contradictions, Oates tried to find consolation and escape from the hard war that was reshaping the world around him.

Mostly, though, he held a deistic view of God's workings in the universe. "Under His laws, which are perfect and ample for the government of the world," wrote Oates, "it was given unto men to originate, formulate and regulate their governmental affairs in their own way, being responsible under those laws for individual acts as in every department of life." He seems not to have believed that God was punishing the Confederacy for its sins (although he appears, at times, to have wondered if God was punishing *him* alone for failing to be his brother's keeper and for causing John's death at Gettysburg). Yet, he held forth that "[God] never diverted a bullet from one man, or caused it to hit another, nor directed who should fall or who should escape." The Creator, in Oates's opinion, also never directed how a battle "should terminate." If not God, then men—Oates and his comrades and everyone fighting this hideous war—were the fiendish agents turning this conflict into a Gehenna.

Man's depravity and his wicked passions had brought about this war and had transformed it into a nightmare. Like other evangelicals, Oates believed as much in the agency of free will as he did in God the Great Creator. The war and its horrors were the outgrowth of man's will. But it was upon the operation of free will that one's personal salvation depended. All of these theological opinions, whenever Oates discussed his religious beliefs, became a mish-mash. On one hand, he tended to express his religious ideas with the rhetoric of deism, despite his broader belief in God's immanence and in the possibility of human redemption, which could hardly have been facilitated by an absentee Creator. Late in life, for example, he stated with great certainty and passion, using words that made him sound like Thomas Jefferson or Benjamin Franklin: "I am an unwavering believer in God as the Creator of all things." Yet his deism was limited in scope and largely conditional, based on his understanding of God as the prime mover of the universe and, to some degree, on his own inability to express his various beliefs as perfectly—as syncretically—as he actually held them in his heart. On the other hand, the evangelical side of his new-found faith emphasized a thorough conviction in man's sinfulness and his need for salvation. Yet, strangely, Oates never brought Christ into the picture. Finding rebirth in Christ was the usual source of an evangelical's personal awakening. But Oates's piety rested on his relationship with God the Father and not on a spiritual connection with Christ or even a belief in the Trinity. In this regard, Oates superficially embraced doctrines resembling those of Northern Unitarians and Universalists—the abhorrent abolitionists, those evil descendants of the Puritan Roundheads whom he so thoroughly despised.

Only by admitting one's sins did Oates believe he and his fellow converts could take control of their spiritual destinies and achieve redemption. Only by reaching for a heaven on earth could they possibly escape the hell of a war they had created, a hard war they kept making harder, a war that brought death and meeting the Almighty face-to-face closer to reality. Given all that had occurred in this war so far, given all the ways in which it now grew more out of control and more deadly with every passing day, it behooved a sinner like Oates to seek out his God before a bullet randomly sought him out first.[41]

On August 30, as the prayer meetings continued day and night at high pitch, a committee of soldiers from Company G, 15th Alabama, wrote a resolution expressing their grief over the loss of Captain Henry Brainard, Lieutenant John Oates, and Lieutenant Bud Cody at Gettysburg. Whereas God in his infinite wisdom had seen fit to remove these beloved men "from our midst," Company G wished to honor them by mourning their deaths "as a sad and heavy loss to their Country and their Company." The men of Company G wanted to go on record as mourning these three lost friends and officers and acknowledging their deaths "as a dispensation of God's allwise providence," trusting that "what is our loss may be their eternal gain." Their memories would be forever "embalmed in the hearts of the mourning comrades in arms whom they so faithfully served." Colonel Oates sent copies of the resolution to the surviving relatives of the three slain officers.[42]

A few days later, a Federal courier arrived under a flag of truce at the camp of the 15th Alabama. The messenger was escorted to the regiment's headquarters tent, where he presented Colonel William Oates with a small package, compliments of J. A. E. Reed, the surgeon who had ministered to John and Bud Cody in the Fifth Corps hospital at Gettysburg. Inside the package, Oates found a note from Dr. Reed and a few items that constituted the personal effects of his late brother, John. There was an old gold watch, a little Confederate money, and a small book of poetry that John had used as a notebook, inscribing the blank pages from time to time with his thoughts. The book was an antebellum edition of *The Poetical Works of Mrs. Felicia Hemans*, a Romantic poet of great renown in England and America. It was stained red with John's blood. One of the poems in the book was entitled "The Effigies." The first two stanzas read:

> Warrior! whose image on thy tomb,
>
> > With shield and crested head,
> > Sleeps proudly in the purple gloom
> > By the stain'd window shed;
>
> > The records of thy name and race
> > Have faded from the stone,
> > Yet, through a cloud of years I trace
> > What thou hast been and done.

Years later, before he could return to Gettysburg for a visit to the battlefield, William Oates learned that the headboard Dr. Reed had so carefully placed over his brother's grave had disappeared, making it impossible for anyone to distinguish John Oates's remains from those of at least twelve other Confederate soldiers buried in the field overlooking the clear stream on Fiscel's farm.[43] Now his brother, in every conceivable way, was lost forever.

7

GONE TO FLICKERING

In the hidden recesses of his soul, William Oates knew—although he never explicitly admitted it to anyone—that Gettysburg was the great turning point in his life. He did refer to it as the Civil War's most pivotal battle, the high tide of the Confederacy, the event that spelled an end to any hope for Southern independence. But, like countless veterans—and numerous historians—have done down through the decades, deep inside, he realized that the battle had a greater significance, a more personal meaning. Nothing, in his past or in his future, would ever change his life as thoroughly or as dramatically as Gettysburg had done. Nothing would ever bring him a greater sadness, a deeper emptiness, than Gettysburg. Nothing could ever heal the deep personal wounds buried inside him that he had suffered at Gettysburg.

Something in him was missing after the battle, a vital flame, an air of wild indifference, the special gleam in his dark eyes. To be sure, he was still a brave and fierce warrior. Pugnacious to a fault, he continued to show aggressiveness in his leadership of the 15th Alabama and his behavior on the battlefield. But his disillusionment with the Confederate cause after the defeats of the summer of 1863, and his own inability to pull out of the depression caused by the death of his brother and so many close friends at Gettysburg, left him morose, argumentative, and righteously indignant. Behind his annoyance at the world, however, there seemed no real passion. To others, he appeared increasingly like a fire with heat but no light.

Depression can often cause errors in perception and judgment, and in Oates's case it seems to have affected his conduct on the battlefield in the months following Gettysburg. Whether or not his despondency was the sole cause of his poor performance in battle cannot be determined with any precision, but the fact is that Oates did not function in combat as he had in the past and his mistakes kept piling up.

His string of blunders began at Chickamauga in late September 1863. Earlier that month two of Longstreet's divisions—McLaws's and Hood's—had been transferred from Virginia under Longstreet's personal command to reinforce General Braxton Bragg's Army of Tennessee and to halt the Union advance on Chattanooga of Major General William S. Rosecrans's Army of the Cumberland. Outflanked by the Federals before Longstreet could arrive, Bragg had withdrawn his army to northern Georgia, south of Chattanooga, where he concentrated his forces and made plans to hit separate columns of Rosecrans's army piecemeal.[1]

Without baggage, tents, artillery, or ambulances, Law's brigade arrived in Atlanta on the morning of September 15, having survived the arduous rail journey south. After waiting more than a day for adequate rolling stock to carry them north to Bragg's army, Longstreet's reinforcements—including Oates and his regiment—were transported to Ringgold, where they took to the dry roads to complete their rendezvous with Bragg. Meanwhile, having failed to defeat Rosecrans's separate columns as he had planned, Bragg had learned that the Union general was bringing his forces together again north of the Chickamauga. On September 18, Bragg ordered his army to secure the crossings at Chickamauga Creek, a dullish stream with an ominous name, meaning, as some said, "River of Death" in Cherokee, located a little more than ten miles south of Chattanooga.[2]

With the timely arrival of Longstreet and his divisions, Bragg enjoyed an advantage over Rosecrans that few Confederate generals ever had during the entire war: He outnumbered his adversary, 62,000 effectives to 58,000. Yet his superiority in numbers did not result in the kind of decisive victory that Bragg—probably the most incompetent Confederate general in the war—wanted or needed. The battle began on the morning of September 19, when Union infantry accidentally ran into Confederate cavalry at Jay's Mill on the west side of the Chickamauga. As the fighting heated up, each side began throwing in more and more reinforcements. The thick woodlands and dense battle smoke turned the engagement into a blind fracas, with officers and enlisted men completely unaware of what lay in front of them.[3]

At about 10:00 that morning, Oates and the 15th Alabama crossed the Chickamauga and went into battle line without breakfast, their rations having been depleted the day before. In the afternoon, when orders came up to advance, Law's brigade stood covering a gap in the line, with the former brigade of Brigadier General Bushrod R. Johnson (who had been promoted to division command) on the left of Oates's 15th Alabama. Around 3:00 or 3:30 P.M., when Colonel James L. Sheffield, in command of Law's brigade, led the Ala-

bamians forward, the Confederates encountered brisk artillery fire and light
musket fire as they stepped off for the assault. Without warning, the brigade
was hit by a bristling enemy volley out of nowhere. In the resulting melee,
Perry's 44th Alabama became detached from the rest of the brigade and it
advanced toward the source of the Federal musket fire. Perry could not keep
up with the 44th, which eventually was repulsed by Union artillery fire, and
General Law mistakenly came to believe that Perry had led the rush of his
regiment to the rear.[4]

In the meantime, the rest of the brigade drove ahead, but an artillery
shell exploded near Sheffield's horse, which threw him to the ground. Badly
injured and unable to resume command, Sheffield had no way of informing
Oates that leadership of the brigade had fallen to him, since Perry, the only
other brigade officer who outranked Oates, could not be located. Oates soon
learned that he was in command when one of Law's aides found him on the
battlefield. He took over the brigade, led it through the tangled woods to the
west, and came out of the trees to the south of the Brotherton house, where
he halted the Alabamians in a field on the La Fayette Road. Oates could not
see any Federals to the west, where he expected to, but rifle fire to his left,
where Johnson's old brigade (now under the command of Colonel John S.
Fulton) was taking heavy fire from the enemy, warned him that the serious
threat was on his flank, not on his front. Soon Fulton's men retreated back
across the road, and Oates immediately—but a little too impetuously, as it
turned out—ordered his men to about face and pour enfilading fire down on
the Federals.

He had failed to act quickly enough, however, and the shout of his order
attracted the attention of the rolling Federal line, which fired a deadly volley
into the ranks of the Alabamians. Attempting to get his men out of this inferno, Oates withdrew the brigade to the road, but the blazing Federal volleys
were too much for them and they panicked. In the heat of the moment, he
instructed his officers "to draw their pistols and shoot any man" who crossed
the road "without orders." Luckily the men halted without being fired on by
their own officers, and Oates restored order in the ranks, maneuvered the
brigade into a new battle line, and managed, despite all the chaos, to throw
out skirmishers and effectively beat back the flanking Federals. Oates later
led the brigade to the safety of the woods, where the Alabamians spent the
night sleeping on their arms.[5]

The men were hungry. After dark, Oates managed to get rations for his
regiment from the quartermaster's stores. "I was in as bad a condition in this
respect as any of the men," he explained, for none of them had eaten anything
over the past twenty-four hours. "If anything will make a man hungry," Oates
observed, "it is hard fighting." Around midnight, Colonel Perry came forth
out of the utter blackness of the night, and Oates gratefully turned command

of the brigade over to him. In the morning, said Oates, the men of the 15th Alabama "were as game as ever and ready for the fray."[6]

There was no doubt the battle would be continued on the new day, Sunday, September 20. When General Law learned that Perry had assumed command of the Alabama brigade, he insisted that Oates should lead the brigade, for he still believed that Perry had acted dishonorably during the previous day's battle. But Oates had his own honor to uphold. He could not assume command of the brigade—or so he wanted posterity to believe—if it would make him appear personally ambitious or if it would serve only to dishonor Perry, whom he considered a fine soldier. Fully convinced that Law was in the wrong, Oates—ever the courtroom attorney—went to the general and argued Perry's case. He persuaded Law to let Perry retain command that morning, but Law instructed Oates to keep on eye on Perry, "and if he goes to flickering today, you assume command of the brigade at once." It was a mark of Oates's strong character, and his steady moral compass, that he felt compelled to do the right thing and demonstrate to Law that Perry deserved to lead the brigade, even if he later painted the episode in colors that made him look totally heroic and completely self-effacing. Yet even during the continuing crisis of his own deep depression, which clouded his thinking and periodically knocked him off balance, Oates kept a clear head when it came to speaking up for a fellow officer. Ironically, and sadly, the unfolding events that day on the battlefield would cause Law and others to think that Oates, and not Perry, was the one who had gone to flickering.[7]

A blanket of cold fog covered the thick woods and brambled fields near the Chickamauga that morning. Oates and his Alabamians expected to attack sometime after dawn, but the morning hours dwindled away before they heard the echoes of rifle fire piercing through the mist from on their right. Shortly after 11:00 A.M., Longstreet moved his divisions forward. As luck would have it, the Confederates struck a portion of the Union line where practically no Federal troops were in position. Rosecrans had mistakenly moved one of his divisions to plug a gap in his line that didn't exist; in so doing, the removal of the division had created a very real gap, a quarter-mile wide.

Back toward the rear of the deep Confederate lines, Oates and his 15th Alabama waited for their turn to rush forward in the advance. Up ahead of them, the fighting was heavy and deadly. By the time Oates and his men crossed the La Fayette Road at the double-quick, so much dust had been raised by Longstreet's attacking Confederates and so much battle smoke clung to the ground that Oates could not see the other regiments of the Alabama brigade to his right or anything of what lay ahead of them in the dark woods. "I soon discovered," he wrote after the war, "that my regiment was not connected, right or left, with any other command." Such a realization would have unnerved a lesser man, but Oates always remained cool in a crisis. From the time of his youth, he had often manifested hard courage and nerves of steel. The battlefield enabled him to rely on these traits when he most needed them. He never faltered when the circumstances called on him to be strong or decisive. A pronounced streak of independence, which he shared in general with Confederate soldiers of the rank and file, reinforced his personal bravery and made him sure of himself, even when he discovered—as he did at this moment near the La Fayette Road—that he must rely on his own wits and his own tenacity to avoid disaster. Yet it was that same independent streak, that inner self-confidence and iron fortitude, that sometimes got him into trouble. As he had learned at Gettysburg, it was not always an advantage for a military officer to be so independently minded.[8]

So he surveyed the situation as soon as he comprehended that he and his men were connected to their advancing brigade. Off toward his left and front, though, he could see some fighting going on, where the 19th Alabama, under the command of Colonel Samuel K. McSpadden, was hotly engaged with the enemy. Realizing that he and his regiment were now fully cut off from their own brigade, Oates decided without orders to advance toward the "hard fight" in which he thought "the Federal troops seemed to be getting the better of it." Enemy artillery fire caught Oates and his regiment full force as they advanced. Suddenly a shell exploded near him and he fell to the ground, struck in the left hip by a huge piece of shrapnel that had cut a hole in his coat as large as his hand. His leg went numb, but he limped along with his men anyway and called out: "Don't fire, Fifteenth, until you are ordered!" In reply, the men raised a shout. He wanted his regiment to pass beyond McSpadden's 19th Alabama and then take up a position to the front of the 19th, thus essentially relieving McSpadden's regiment and taking over the fight with the Federals. But no one—including his own officers, his men, or, for that matter, Colonel McSpadden—knew what he intended to do. Trying to keep up with his men as they drove quickly toward their destination did not help the situation or Oates's control over his advancing regiment. Wounded men fell from the ranks and, as the enemy fire became increasingly effective, the remaining soldiers in the 15th Alabama grew impatient, readying their muskets to fire; seeing this, Oates sternly warned them again to hold their fire.[9]

No one will ever really know what happened next. Oates later maintained that his regiment did not open fire until they had moved beyond the 19th Alabama to its left and had advanced to within eighty yards of the enemy. But Colonel McSpadden told a different story and accused the 15th Alabama of firing into his lines. In his official report, which revealed how spitting mad he was over this incident, McSpadden declared that Oates's men had opened fire on his regiment from the rear. When, said McSpadden, he had realized that the 15th Alabama was enfilading his lines, he ordered his colors "back to the edge of the open field, and waving them, discovered to the Fifteenth Alabama their error, upon which they came up by a left oblique march in fine order" and linked with McSpadden's lines for the assault on the enemy's guns. Oates vehemently denied that his men had fired on friendly forces, stating that McSpadden's regiment was actually prone in the grass on the hillside, trying to take cover from the Federal fire, when the 15th Alabama approached from the rear. Just about anything, of course, had been possible in the dust and smoke that covered the field. After being left behind by his regiment, Oates could hardly tell what his front line was doing, as he hopped along trying to catch up with his men. It is likely, given the strength of McSpadden's account, that some of the 15th Alabama's front ranks let off a few shots before Oates could order them to hold their fire. For his part, Oates seems to have been completely unaware of the incident until he learned that the 15th had been accused of friendly fire in McSpadden's battle report.[10]

As the 15th moved up, the entire Confederate line rushed forward and drove the Federals from their position up the slope of what later became known as Lytle Hill, named for Union Brigadier General William H. Lytle, who fell mortally wounded as his command abandoned the hill to the wave of Alabamians who swept over it. With his hip aching, Oates found it difficult to keep up with his regiment, which had succeeded in capturing a Federal gun and turning it on the retreating enemy, so he tried to mount a horse standing near the dying form of General Lytle. Seeing that the horse was badly wounded, Oates left it behind, but he went to the Union general and—in an act of kindness that expressed his sense of honor as a soldier—dragged him out of the blazing sun and into some shade. It was like countless other acts of kindness shown by soldiers on both sides in this strange war—a war that brought out the worst and best in men. If Oates could have done more for Lytle, he would have. But the general was at the end of his road.[11]

Still limping, Oates hobbled along trying to catch up with his regiment, which had been carried along with the Confederate tide of Longstreet's legions as they crumbled the Union right and drove the fleeing Federals toward Snodgrass Hill, to the northwest. He finally found his men on a hillside, resting and "panting like dogs tired out in the chase." Despite his bruised hip, he ordered the men to fall in and led them back to where they had started their assault. He then spied General Bushrod Johnson, who had been separated from his division but who ordered Oates and the 15th to march northward through an old field, where there had been hard fighting that morning.

Eventually the Alabamians came upon Brigadier General Joseph B. Kershaw's South Carolina brigade halfway up the slope of Snodgrass Hill, and Oates led them into position to fill a gap between the 7th and 3rd South Carolina regiments. In doing so, his independent streak took hold of him again and he neglected to inform Kershaw of his actions. Dauntless and impetuously brave, Oates nevertheless suffered from a major shortcoming as a combat commander. He rarely could see the big picture on the battlefield. As a brawler in frontier Alabama or in Texas as a young man, he had never had to comprehend more than the trouble that stared him in the face. As a Confederate regimental commander, though, he repeatedly encountered situations that could not be instantaneously understood in all their particulars, for the fog of war restricted everyone's comprehension, everyone's line of sight. Oates knew well about the fog of war and about unseen dangers on a battlefield, but his instincts—his natural tendency to act or to use violence when a situation seemed threatening—always got the better of him and propelled him into motion, even when all the signs pointed to the need for contemplation rather than action. At Chickamauga, even his instincts weren't what they normally were. His deep depression continued to dull his responses, hamper his powers of observation, and muddle his judgments.

On Snodgass Hill, Oates compounded the problem of moving into Kershaw's lines without authority when he noticed three Federal regiments advancing toward the position held by the South Carolinians. Immediately Oates found the commander of the 3rd South Carolina and asked him to move his troops forward to connect with Oates's left flank. When the South Carolinian refused to do so, Oates ordered him to redeploy his regiment, but the stalwart colonel refused to obey any order from an unknown Alabama officer. "I bestowed upon him a few encomiums," Oates recalled years later, "and returned to my regiment and extended my line by placing the men in one rank."

Realizing that his flanks were exposed, however, Oates went to the 7th South Carolina, found a captain in command, and ordered it to move up a ridge to Oates's right, which the captain refused to do without General Kershaw's approval. Frustrated and angry, Oates mounted a log and, speaking directly to the South Carolinians in the ranks, "made an appeal to the State pride of the regiment, and asked the men not to go where I directed merely, but to follow me." A solitary captain stepped forward and said: "Colonel, I will follow you with my company." With that, the entire 7th South Carolina moved with the 15th Alabama to the advance, but as soon as the enemy opened fire, the South Carolinians "fled ingloriously," or so Oates claimed. Nevertheless, the captain who had volunteered his company and himself stayed on through the fight.[12]

Laying down a devastating enfilade volley, the Federals succeeded in turning Oates's flank. The Alabamians could no longer take the pounding and broke their ranks for the rear. Oates ran among the panic-stricken men, yelling: "Halt, halt, men! About face and return to your position! Is there no officer who will set the example?" A lieutenant from Company I sprang forward and the men began to rally. The Alabamians attacked the hill once more and this time they surprised the Federals and raked them with rolling volleys. Overwhelmed by this counterattack, the Union troops fell back, crumbled, and ran in confusion. With his ammunition running low, Oates kept his regiment in a ravine, which afforded protection from the Federal fire that poured down on them from farther up the slope of Snodgrass Hill. Oates held this position for some time, stretching out his ranks into a single line once again so his flank would not be unprotected.[13]

As the Alabamians exchanged sporadic musket fire with the Federals on Snodgrass Hill, Oates walked up and down his line trying to keep spirits up and strengthen his defenses. He passed by sixteen-year-old Tom Wright, a cross-eyed youngster whose face was black with grime and powder. The boy was firing steadily and taking aim with each shot. Oates slapped him on the shoulder and said: "Give it to them, Tommie, my boy; I will remember you." Wright looked up, smiled, and replied: "All right, Colonel." Oates continued down the line, and when he returned less than two minutes later Wright lay dead on the ground, a bullet in his head. "I could not repress my tears," Oates remembered, "and in the heat of battle I shed a few in passing as a tribute to the sublime courage of that child." No doubt the sight of the dead boy brought back all the pain and sorrow of his brother John's death.[14]

By late afternoon, Oates and his men were practically out of ammunition, and he breathed a sigh of relief when Law's adjutant, Leigh Terrell, rode up and ordered the 15th Alabama to rejoin the brigade in the woods next to Dyer field. Just as Oates brought his men up, Law's brigade moved forward in an assault on the Federal line, but it became obvious rather quickly that there was no enemy to attack—the Union troops had withdrawn. The Battle of Chickamauga was over. Assessing the day's damage, Oates learned that his regiment had lost heavily at Chickamauga: 11 killed and 121 wounded, out of approximately 450 men who went into the action.[15]

Although he was pleased with himself for his conduct at Chickamauga, he found out later that others did not hold his actions in such high regard. For one thing, he had earned the enmity of Colonel Samuel McFadden for firing into the rear of the 19th Alabama. For another, Brigadier General Joseph Kershaw was furious with Oates for having led an assault without authorization. In his official report, written after the battle, Kershaw icily denounced Oates for having pushed his way into the affairs of the South Carolina regiments and for having taken it upon himself to direct an attack on the enemy's works.[16]

On the battlefield, Oates was becoming too impetuous, too unpredictable, too imprudent. In his youth, he always fought best alone, one-on-one in a match with his opponent. As his emotional stamina seeped away in the months following Gettysburg, he reverted to his instincts as a brawler, fighting his own fight on the battlefield in his own way, rather than as a military officer cognizant of his responsibility for the lives of the men who must follow him into battle. Something more than frontier self-sufficiency, though, worked to stimulate Oates's autonomous—and sometimes reckless—behavior on the battlefield. After so many battles, so many engagements in this hard war, his personal and military life had forged together. Oates the man could not be separated from Oates the warrior. Yet before Gettysburg he had always gone into battle with his brother beside him, fighting the enemy together as a team, usually in sight of one another, always mindful of the other. It was like when they had been boys in the wiregrass country, constantly together, as if in harness, imitating camp meetings, tormenting their teachers, avoiding their father's switch, or laughing in unison at the loafers who told wild tales and drank themselves into a stupor at Oates's Crossroads. Then came Gettysburg, the turning point. John was now gone, forever gone, and Oates was all alone. John had always kept him steady. All his life, William had thought his job was to care for John, keep him safe, protect him from all the dangers in the world, seen and unseen. But it had actually been the other way around. It was John who had brought William home from Texas, John who had enlisted first in the Confederate army, John who had insisted that the attack on Little Round Top simply had to be made, no matter what. John had been the leader, the guide. Now William Oates had lost the one person in his life who had served as his counterbalance, who had kept him from losing his equilibrium, who had always, in more ways than one, brought him home from the chaos of Texas.

So now, in the dark and unfamiliar Georgia woods, he confronted an empty and lonely world without John. And in the confusion of battle, when the need for balance and steadiness was so great, William Oates could only depend on his instincts for guidance and follow their lead. Without his brother, he must always face the whistling bullets and all the terrible perils of war alone.

With the fighting over, Bragg's army possessed the battlefield, while Rosecrans and his battered brigades took refuge in Chattanooga. Over the next few days, Longstreet moved his wing of the Confederate army closer to Chattanooga and took up a position along the siege line south of the city. Oates and his men occupied the line with the rest of Law's brigade between Chattanooga Creek and Lookout Mountain. Apart from fighting a heated skirmish over the possession of a corn field and its harvest, the 15th Alabama spent a relatively quiet time on the picket lines trying to stave off the boredom that comes with excessive inactivity.[17]

The investment of Chattanooga kept Oates busy, but in his darker moments his thoughts turned to his brother John and the cruel fate he had met at Gettysburg. But his contemplative moments were not only filled with the past. He also gave some serious consideration to his own professional future, both in and out of the army, and he took steps to put himself in the best possible situation. He was particularly concerned that his rival, Major Alexander Lowther, now back with the regiment, was attempting to displace him as colonel by claiming seniority, despite Lowther's frequent absences from active service. Oates was right to be concerned; his thoughts about his future involved more than ambition or a petty rivalry with Lowther. For his part, Lowther was attempting to win command of the 15th Alabama, which he regarded as his own. Probably no officer in the Confederate military deserved a command less than Lowther did. Oates's personal dislike for Lowther was one thing, but he was right to regard Lowther's campaign as a serious threat to the welfare of the regiment. For all of Oates's faults, he had proved himself to his men, in and out of battle. He always tried to put the regiment first, even when it meant saving his men and leaving his brother behind with a mortal wound on a hillside in Pennsylvania. Lowther had proven himself skillful in avoiding combat and complaining about his various illnesses. Probably if anyone had chosen to ask the men of the 15th Alabama which commander they preferred, the soldiers undoubtedly would have cast their ballots for Oates.

Realizing that Lowther was a formidable opponent, Oates knew he had to protect himself, front and rear. In late September, he persuaded General Law to submit a statement in his behalf to the War Department that dismissed Lowther's claims and endorsed Oates's commission as colonel and commander of the 15th Alabama, something the general was more than willing to do. Law's affidavit seems to have received little notice in Richmond, and Lowther's endeavor to assume command of the regiment continued to threaten Oates. He faced the very real possibility that he might lose his command, and not gain another, if Lowther succeeded in finding political support in the Davis administration and in the Confederate Congress. If Lowther took over the 15th Alabama, Oates could easily be out of the war. Being a warrior with no war to fight was a proposition he did not relish.

But what if he were forced to return to Alabama and take up life again as a civilian? He could resume his law practice, but doing so without John as a partner probably had little appeal for him. In weighing his opportunities, he wrote to influential friends in Alabama and declared himself a candidate for solicitor of the Eighth Circuit Court, a position that would require his election by the state legislature. The solicitor's job, he explained in a letter to a fellow attorney back home, would involve little work while the war lasted, so, if elected, he could hire someone to do the work while he attempted to get back into the army, thereby fulfilling what he considered to be "the most paramount duties a freeman owes to his native land." After the war ended, he said, he would then have "a fine position—an office in the line of my profession, well suited to my tastes and which I feel that I could fill with credit to myself and my native State."[18]

All of this sounded terribly self-serving and opportunistic. But Oates's depression was also making him feel less than confident about the future. Lowther's bid for command of the 15th Alabama made things worse. Fearful that he would lose his regiment, Oates probably felt besieged and lacking the resources—including the personal stamina, physical energy, and lucid concentration—necessary to wage battle against Lowther and win. He was

more than a little panicked. Nothing had been going right since the beginning of the year, when the 15th Alabama had been taken away from Jackson
and given to Longstreet. One disaster had followed on the heels of another.
Even his hope for an easy job in Alabama, should he need it, did not pan out.
He was not elected to the solicitor's office by the Alabama legislature.

Nevertheless, Oates did receive an official certificate, signed by Secretary
of War James A. Seddon and dated October 8, 1863, documenting his promotion to colonel and verifying that his appointment had been made by President Davis.[19] The Confederate Congress, however, still had not confirmed
his commission as colonel, and without that confirmation Oates technically
remained a captain on the books (although some rosters listed him, incorrectly, as a major, probably based on the short time he served as acting major
of the 15th Alabama in the summer of 1862). He seemed unable to get the
confirmation from the Confederate legislature, and the lack of action by Congress both puzzled and frustrated him.

In an honorable war, such inequities were not supposed to happen. In
this war, Oates began to feel slighted, unappreciated, and neglected. There
was no earthly reason why the Confederate Congress had not acted on his
colonel's commission. Nothing indicates that he had made any particular enemies among the politicians in Richmond or even among his superior and
fellow officers in the Confederate Army. Some politicians and officers liked
him, others didn't. That seemed to be the case for most field officers in the
Confederate army, if they had distinguished themselves on the battlefield at
all. Behind the scenes, Lowther may have been working against Oates and his
commission, but there is no evidence to say that he was or wasn't. It seems
more likely that Lowther was busy advancing his own interests than conspir-
ing to hold Oates back. In the end, the Confederate Congress never got around
to confirming Oates's commission before the war ended. No reason ever presented itself; no historical record even hints at a reason. In all likelihood,
Oates had slipped through a bureaucratic crack in Richmond. The ineptitude
of the War Department or of some minor clerk in the Confederate Congress
probably was the frivolous cause of Oates's unconfirmed commission.

As the foliage atop the broad crest of Missionary Ridge and the towering peak
of Lookout Mountain changed from lush green to dull crimson, making the
high ground above the city of Chattanooga seem to be strangely awash in a
sanguinary display of nature, Oates nursed his bruised hip and his bruised
pride during the weeks following the fight at Chickamauga. His pride seemed
more injured than his hip. Failure to get his commission confirmed by the
Confederate Congress or to be elected solicitor of the Eighth Circuit Court
by the Alabama legislature sent his spirits plummeting. And things were about
to get worse.

To keep the Union army bottled up in Chattanooga, the 15th Alabama was moved on October 9 to Lookout Valley, a small strip of land between Lookout Mountain and Raccoon Mountain, where the Tennessee River takes one of its many hairpin turns. Getting there required Oates and his men to drag a battery of cannon over Lookout Mountain during the night, a difficult enough feat for anyone, but the Alabamians were told to make as little noise as possible so the Federals would not detect the arrival of artillery.[20]

Once in the valley, the 15th Alabama took up a position along the muddy banks of the Tennessee from Raccoon Mountain to Brown's Ferry. There Oates put five of his hardened companies forward as pickets to watch the river crossings, while the 4th Alabama was deployed to their right in the direction of Lookout Mountain. In the shaded valley, about a mile behind the pickets, Oates established his headquarters. Under orders from Law, Oates led an amphibious scouting party across to Williams Island to see what the Federals were up to, but the reconnaissance effort was cut short when the Alabamians ran directly into some Union sentinels who forced them back across the river. One bullet zipped through the gunwale of Oates's boat and passed between his legs. Luckily he got his men out of the ambush without suffering any casualties.[21]

Meanwhile, despite concerns over the weakness of the Confederate lines guarding the ferry and Lookout Valley (Oates's men were stretched three to five men at a post, with 200 to 400 yards between the posts), General Law requested a short leave of absence to visit the wounded General Hood, who had lost his right leg in the Battle of Chickamauga. That left Oates in command of the Alabamians in the valley, even though he was given no instructions, no notification of Law's departure, and no hint that he held temporary command. Law returned on the evening of October 26, but the comings and goings of Longstreet's high ranking officers—including Brigadier General Micah Jenkins, whom Longstreet had placed in command of Hood's division, passing over Evander Law—left the command situation in Lookout Valley unnecessarily confused and uncertain. At one point, Oates reported to General Jenkins, probably because he had discovered Law's absence and did not know who was serving as his temporary superior officer, but he later admitted that his communication should have gone to Law, who apparently had returned to his post in the same manner as he had briefly vacated it—without informing Oates one way or the other of his actual whereabouts.

After Lincoln appointed Ulysses S. Grant to take command of all the Union forces between the Appalachians and the Mississippi, Rosecrans's days as commander of the Army of the Cumberland became numbered. In short order, Grant replaced Rosecrans with Brigadier General George H. Thomas and, on October 23, arrived in Chattanooga to oversee personally the breaking of Bragg's siege. The next day Grant approved plans for opening a supply line by breaching the Confederate blockade at Brown's Ferry.

On October 26, Oates watched nervously as the Federals began to build up their forces across the river throughout the day. He also discovered evidence that a deserter had probably carried intelligence to the Federals, thus informing the enemy of precisely how weak the Confederate lines were at the ferry. Later that evening, he learned that a large enemy force under General Joseph Hooker was crossing the river at Bridgeport, south of Raccoon Mountain, threatening his rear. Uncharacteristically, but perhaps due to his depression, he became painfully indecisive, wondering if he should send word of these developments to Law or Jenkins or to both. Finally he settled on sending a note to Longstreet that a Union attack was about to take place and that he desperately needed reinforcements. He received no reply. There was nothing else he could do. As the darkness deepened, he drifted off into a doze, anxiously expecting to hear gunshots echoing up from the river edge at any moment.[22]

The echoes came just before daybreak on October 27. Oates was stirred from his sleep by the sound of musket fire rolling in from the direction of the river. Within minutes, he was approached by a courier, William Jordan, a private in Company B, who had been on picket duty at the ferry when the Federals crossed the river and drove in the 15th Alabama's guard posts. Oates ordered the "long roll" beaten, mounted his horse, and led the regiment's reserve companies—about 150 men— toward Brown's Ferry at the river. A dense fog enveloped everything in a dim gray light as dawn struggled to push out the darkness. The poor visibility did not stop Oates, who instructed his men "to walk right up to the foe, and for every man to place the muzzle of his rifle against the body of a Yankee when he fired." Oates kept putting in his companies, one by one, hoping to overpower the Federals, but the might of the enemy's fire ripped through the 15th Alabama with devastating results. Oates's horse was shot from under him and he saw a bullet pass through his coat sleeve. After Captain Terrell arrived on the scene, Oates finally began to pull his companies back to consolidate his command into a massed force.[23] Again his judgment had been less than sound, and more men had died as a result.

As the fog lifted and morning light spread through the woods, Oates jumped in among his men and led them in an attack on the Federal works. They were only about thirty steps away when Oates was shot through the right hip and thigh, the ball striking the thigh bone about an inch below the hip joint. The bullet fractured the hip, ringing itself around the bone, and passed through eight inches of flesh. To Oates, it felt like "a brick had been hurled against me," and he was in such pain as he fell that he began to let out a curse, "God d—," but thought better of it in case his wound was mortal; instantaneously he shortened his oath to a simple "d—" and did not finish the sentence.

One of his childhood playmates, M. E. Meredith, came forward and raised him up into a sitting position. Through blurry eyes, Oates looked around and saw another boyhood friend, Jefferson E. Hussey, sitting behind a stump. Both of the men must have been reminders of better times, when they were all young and innocent, with John Oates among them, playing in the woods around Oates's Crossroads. With his arms around the shoulders of Meredith and Hussey, Oates limped on his left leg toward the rear, as the 15th Alabama retreated from its forward deployment in the valley. His men took him to a small house, where many of the wounded Alabamians had been brought and laid out in the yard. Two ladies still occupied the house, and Oates, whose wound was bleeding badly, asked them for water. One of the ladies bravely attempted to bring a dipper full of water out to the yard, but the unslackening musket fire from the Federal lines made her flee back into the relative safety of the house. Oates decided that he would have to crawl to the house for his drink, and so he dragged himself across the yard and to the doorjamb, where the ladies pulled him inside and gave him water. "God bless them," he said in telling the story years later. "Never," he wrote, "did water taste sweeter."[24]

As the Alabamians retreated from the vicinity of Brown's Ferry, an orderly brought Oates's spare horse to him. The colonel was helped onto his mount and led away from the house, thanking the two ladies as he rode painfully out of their yard. At that moment Private Jordan reappeared with eleven Union prisoners, which Oates took into his own custody. With prisoners in front, and his orderly leading his horse, Oates continued to make his way toward Lookout Creek, about four miles away. He felt faint from loss of blood and thought more than once that he would topple from the saddle. They came upon the brigade surgeon, Dr. William O. Hudson, who ordered the prisoners to carry Oates into a house near Lookout Creek, despite the protestations of the owner, a "stout-looking woman" with Unionist sympathies.

Dr. Hudson successfully staunched the bleeding. General Laws, who had arrived at Lookout Creek with the other three regiments of the Alabama Brigade and with the Texas Brigade, ordered eight men to carry Oates in a litter over Lookout Mountain, a treacherous journey over rough ground made all the worse by the artillery shells that kept exploding all around them. Just before night on October 28, Oates arrived at the brigade's field hospital, where he was treated by the 15th Alabama's own surgeon. He later learned that his regiment had retreated to safety, but that the men had lost most of their blankets, clothing, and other supplies. Out of about 240 men, the 15th had lost 6 killed and 14 wounded, including Oates. Despite a counterattack by Law's command on the night of October 28, when the 15th Alabama lost another 5 wounded and 11 missing, the Confederates had been unable to dislodge the Federals from either Brown's Ferry or the Wauhatchie Valley along the western base of Lookout Mountain. Grant's "cracker line" of supply was now firmly established. After the fighting was over, Major Alexander Lowther showed up to take command of the 15th Alabama.[25]

Oates's wound was serious, and he knew it. He realized there was a good chance he would lose his right leg. Luck was with him this time. He kept his leg, and on October 30 the doctor sent him—accompanied by Jimmie Newberry, one of the 15th's drummer boys—to Atlanta. In the city, he was taken to a military hospital, where the doctors dressed his wound for the first time and kept him comfortable, despite the agonizing pain. From there he managed to get as far as Griffin, Georgia, where he boarded a train for Eufaula.

His wound had not been dressed for two days, and this, with the failure of suppuration, threw him into a high fever and delirium. In Eufaula, he received good treatment either from friends or from doctors he had known before the war, but "for two or three days," he wrote in later life, "I did not know day from night." During this time, someone stole more than nine hundred dollars in Confederate currency and five dollars in gold from him—an incredibly large sum of money that he, inexplicably, was carrying around with him.

While he recovered and regained his strength in Eufaula, he was visited by Colonel Washington Toney and his wife, Sarah Bass Toney, who lived at Roseland, a prosperous plantation in the country, about seven miles north of Eufaula. Their son, William Toney, had served as a sergeant in Company K of the 15th Alabama and had died in June 1862, after receiving a mortal wound at the battle of Cross Keys. Before his death, Sergeant Toney had written home to his parents and had praised Oates's leadership and his unusual compassion for the men. The Toneys now wanted to thank Oates for his special kindnesses to their son. They invited him to convalesce at Roseland, and he gladly accepted the offer.[26]

Oates must have thought he had arrived in paradise. Roseland gave him a taste of life he had never known before, a sample of how the aristocracy of the South lived. The manor house and plantation had been established before 1840 by General Thomas Flournoy, a veteran of the War of 1812. After the government had forcibly removed the Creek Indians from the area, he acquired an immense tract of land that stretched from the River Road to the Chattahoochee River. The plantation became well known for its bountiful cotton crops, its herds of fine horses and cattle, and its plentiful slaves, including "cooks, house servants, blacksmiths, carpenters, hostlers, and good plantation hands." Streams flowing across the estate out of Cowikee Creek provided water power for saw and grist mills and even a hydro-powered cotton gin. A sturdy wharf extended out into the Chattahoochee, a private landing for Roseland and the Flournoy family.

After the general died in 1858, the plantation was sold at auction to pay Flournoy's considerable debts. William Toney, Washington Toney's father, bought and then gave the estate—which consisted of more than 1,200 acres and included the manor house, furnishings, dependencies, horses and cattle, and slaves—to his son. Washington Toney, a native of South Carolina, had graduated from South Carolina College in Columbia in 1832 and read law in Columbus, Georgia. He had distinguished himself in the Creek War of 1836 by rising quickly from the rank of private to colonel. As master of Roseland, he traveled frequently by coach over the River Road to the bustling market town of Columbus, Georgia, where he sold his cotton to the highest bidders.

He married Sarah Bass in 1840 and moved to Henry County, Alabama five years later. William, their eldest son, was born about that time, the first of nine children—three sons and six daughters—who survived past their child-hoods. Washington Toney was a firm supporter of the Confederate cause and denounced "Lincoln's Military Despotism" with stern words and grave determination. He liked to discuss politics with the Reverend Edmund Cody, Bud Cody's father, who owned the plantation adjacent to Roseland. Toney was known as a charitable man, and Oates was not the first wounded soldier he had taken into his household.[27]

Toney and his wife loved to spend money. Throughout southeastern Ala-bama, they were known for their lavish parties at the Roseland manor house, a splendid two-storied, Corinthian-columned mansion, facing due west, that sat in a grove of oak trees down a short drive of white sand that passed through a wide gateway of stone buttresses before circling gracefully in front of the house. A few hundred yards behind the house stood the overseer's residence and the slave quarters. A horse stable was located near the front of the house, in close proximity to the driveway. The manor house was not lavish, at least not when measured against far more luxurious properties owned by planters in Georgia and South Carolina, but Roseland displayed a subdued elegance all its own. The Toneys could be counted among Eufaula's privileged elite. Sarah Toney was said to know Jefferson Davis personally, and Davis may even have stayed as a guest at the plantation.

Inside the house were wide hallways and spacious rooms with ceilings sixteen feet high. A grand stairway with a carved newel post of mahogany led from the grand hall to the second floor. At the back of the house was a huge dining room with fireplaces on either end; the great room was where guests would dance for hours and hours to the music of slave fiddlers. One later account asserted that "the hospitality of the family [was] proverbial." It was easy, said this writer, to lose oneself at Roseland because its resources were "unlimited."[28]

One luxurious party was held on Christmas Eve, 1863, while Oates was still recovering from his wound. Among the guests were several other Con-federate officers and soldiers and numerous ladies from around the nearby countryside. Oates, still on crutches, watched enviously as the soldiers danced around the great room with their pretty ladies swirling all about. He must have felt worlds apart from the country dances he had enjoyed during his youth. A woman who attended the Toney party noted in her diary that "one would not dream that a terrible war was raging," for there had been numerous soirées around Eufaula all week, and the Toneys' ball was simply one in a string of extravagant levees.[29]

Oates relished the aristocratic snobbery, the high living, and the patrician exclusivity that he found at Roseland. Highly opinionated and independent in his own thought and spirit, Oates identified with the Toneys and with the elite planter class, even though he could never claim to be one of them. Yet he did share some things in common. In the first place, he had already aligned himself before the war with the Eufaula Regency, that group of Democrats who revolved around the Shorter clan and who wielded great political power in southeastern Alabama. The Toneys supported the regency, although Colonel Toney did not hold any public offices. In the second place, he shared their likes and dislikes, their values and their assumptions, including their distrust of the masses, their views on the economic necessity of slavery (despite its many evils, which many slaveowners ritualistically conceded), and their utter faith in the supremacy of whites over blacks. And in the third place, he admired their ambition and entrepreneurial aggressiveness. Many of the cotton lords were self-made men, just as he was.

When he wasn't attending opulent parties at Roseland, he spent his time getting the rest and exercise he needed to become well again. Often he could be seen perambulating on his crutches through the grand house and around the unlandscaped grounds, under the bowers of Cherokee roses and the arbor of scuppernong grapes. When he needed rest, he could sit for hours on the spacious porch that ran along three sides of the house. The children of the house delighted him and kept him entertained. He especially enjoyed holding and pampering the youngest member of the household, little fifteen-month-old Sarah, called Sallie, whose wide-eyed beauty, even in infancy, caught his attention. She had been born on September 28, 1862, just eleven days after the battle of Sharpsburg. A family story maintains that once, while Oates was cradling the baby in his arms, Mrs. Toney remarked offhandedly: "Who knows but that you are holding in your arms—your future wife."[30] If Oates thought her remark odd, for he was thirty years old as he gazed down at the infant, he did not mention it, then or later. He may have thought nothing of it, but Mrs. Toney never forgot the moment.

Oates spent more than three months at Roseland, living with the Toneys, gaining an intimate knowledge of the family, solidifying his political connections to the Eufaula Regency, and marveling at the care and love he received from Colonel and Mrs. Toney, whom, he said in his memoirs, treated him like a son. By early March 1864, he walked well enough to abandon his crutches and get about with only a cane. He was feeling strong and healthy. It was time to rejoin his regiment and get back into the war.[31]

8

THE END OF CHIVALRY

Under the silver skies of March, William Oates—accompanied by a slave named William, probably loaned to him by the Toney family—returned to a war that had grown in intensity and that hammered away relentlessly at the South's meager resources. Clear signs in the army revealed that the Confederacy was beginning to unravel. At Bull's Gap in Tennessee, up in the northeastern corner of the state below the western slopes of the Appalachians, Oates found his regiment in a desolate defile along the East Tennessee and Virginia Railroad, not far from where Longstreet's corps had camped for the winter. The 15th Alabama was in a sorry state. It was all tattered, hungry, and racked by poor leadership and practically no discipline. No one seemed to be in command. Major Lowther was, as usual, absent and on leave at home in Alabama. Many of the regiment's best soldiers had been killed or wounded in the engagements around Chattanooga in November and during Longstreet's unsuccessful attempt to break the Union army's iron grip on Knoxville over the winter months.[1]

Since December Longstreet had slipped into a funk and was taking his frustrations out on his division and brigade commanders, namely Lafayette McLaws, Jerome Robertson, and Evander Law. His quarrels with subordinate officers not only demonstrated his inability to control his formidable temper or to put petty concerns aside, but revealed the way growing pressure from an increasingly effective Union army and dwindling Southern resources were working to unhinge the Confederate military. Longstreet, said Oates, was at this time "brim full of malice." Law wanted Oates to serve as his attorney when his dispute with Longstreet came before a court martial, but President Davis refused to appoint a court to hear Law's case. Finally the dispute was settled when the War Department gave Major General Charles W. Field command of Jenkins's division. As a result of a specific request made by Lee, the Alabama Brigade was ordered in April 1864 to rejoin Longstreet's corps and the entire Army of Northern Virginia.[2]

On May 4, the Alabama Brigade with the rest of Longstreet's corps moved north to counter the crossing of the Rapidan River by Union infantry and cavalry. The Army of the Potomac—still under the command of Meade, but now also under the supreme command of Ulysses S. Grant, whom Lincoln had named lieutenant general and commander of all Union armies—was attempting to turn Lee's right flank while other Federal forces moved on Richmond up the James River and up the Shenandoah Valley. That night the Union troops bivouacked near Wilderness Tavern, not far from where the fighting had raged around Chancellorsville a year ago. On the morning of May 5, Lee had advanced close enough to the Wilderness to launch a surprise attack, which came with the first light of day. Remarkably, Lee's outnumbered force, dangerously divided into two assault lines, was able to hold off three Union army corps that day along the Orange Turnpike and the Orange Plank Road, buying time for Longstreet's corps to move up.[3]

But Longstreet was suffering from the slows. The next day, May 6, a Union attack drove up the plank road before Longstreet's corps arrived on the battlefield, and the Confederate lines broke into pieces as the blue tide plunged forward. Out of nowhere, Longstreet's gray lines appeared in the pale light of the morning, and Lee—buoyant with enthusiasm—began to move forward as the counterattack got underway. The Texans in Longstreet's vanguard, however, refused to advance until Lee removed himself to safety in the rear; then, with the fury of demons, Longstreet's corps hit the Federal battle lines with full force.[4]

Now under the command of Colonel William F. Perry, the Alabama Brigade took up a position north of the Orange Plank Road, and as it did, the men noticed Lee among a group of horsemen watching the progress of the battle. They could see him clearly, as distinctly as when he had trotted past during the recent review, and now they noticed that his face was flushed and full of animation. "I thought him at that moment," wrote Oates years later, "the grandest specimen of manhood I ever beheld." When Lee noticed the brigade moving up, he called out: "God bless the Alabamians!" The men whooped and went on line.[5]

The Almighty seemed to be listening. As the shriek of the Rebel Yell cascaded over the fields, the Alabama brigade struck the Federals with a hammer blow. Down a steep slope and across a stream, the brigade advanced as the enemy, surprised by the onslaught, wavered and then broke its lines. Toward his left, Perry became aware of Federal troops about to enfilade his lines, and he ordered Oates and the 15th Alabama to wheel about and attack. Oates responded with alacrity and clearheadedness, leading his men around through open ground and then into thick woods in a thunderous charge that successfully removed the threat to Perry's flank. Years afterward, Perry called the assault "one of the most brilliant movements I have ever seen on a battle-field." The 15th Alabama lost only two men killed and eleven men wounded in the charge.[6]

Seeing that his flank was now safe, Perry ordered Oates and his regiment back into the main line. As the brigade became stalled in the face of galling enemy fire, which kept the Alabamians from pushing up the slope from the stream to the crest of the ridge, Oates saw an opportunity to strike the enemy's right by pushing beyond the Federal battle lines, where no Union troops had been positioned. He got his men from column into battle line under fire, led them in an arc through the woods to the left, overlapped the Union right, and poured a perfect volley down the enemy line. Almost at once, the Federal line was shattered and the bluecoats vanished into the dense woods.[7]

It was only about ten in the morning, and the worse fighting was yet to come. For about an hour, the Alabama brigade rested inside the line of breast-works they had just captured from the Federals. In the meantime, Longstreet determined that the Federal left was vulnerable to a flank attack, and at about 11:00 A.M. he sent four brigades to roll up the Union flank, while Field's division—including the 15th Alabama, still formed on the Alabama brigade's left—moved forward to press the Confederate advantage. While the assault was about to reach a crescendo, word arrived that Longstreet had been seriously wounded and General Micah Jenkins had been killed, both of them struck down by Confederate fire just as Stonewall Jackson had been a year earlier. Without Longstreet, the attack along the Orange Plank Road became confused and soon fizzled out.[8]

Around noontime, another lull let the Alabamians relax for a while along the plank road. In the early afternoon, the Confederates soon suspected— correctly, as it turned out—that the Federals were moving toward their left. To protect the flank, Colonel Perry put Oates in command of the 48th Alabama, besides the 15th, and sent him to feel for the enemy out beyond the left; meanwhile, General Edward A. Perry, in command of three Florida regiments, would move off in echelon in lead of the probe. Oates, worried about his own uncovered left and convinced the enemy was not far away, put out skirmishers and soon heard the crackle of musket fire as his men ran into Federal troops. As Oates came around a hill, his command was swept by enemy fire, and he quickly ordered the Alabamians to throw up breastworks and take cover. In dismay, Oates watched as long lines of bluecoats smashed forward, catching General Perry's Floridians and Colonel Perry's Alabamians in an enfilade, which sent the Confederates scurrying for the rear.

Oates's blood was up and he tried to charge the Federals, but the deter-mined blue wave was unstoppable. Enveloped on both flanks, and short of ammunition, Oates wisely ordered a retreat and, as he recalled years later, "we had a lively run for three or four hundred yards." The whole Alabama brigade, and General Perry's Floridians with it, broke and ran. It was the only time during the entire war that Law's brigade was driven from the field. Ma-jor General Henry Heth's division came up to relieve the Alabamians and successfully drove the Federals back.

Despite the inglorious retreat of the 15th Alabama, Oates could take pride in his regiment and in his own actions that day in the Wilderness. His bad luck on the battlefield was over, and he had demonstrated expert skill as an officer along the Orange Plank Road, even, as Colonel Perry noted, perform-ing brilliantly under fire. Oates and his men had won back their laurels at the Wilderness. That night they all slept soundly on their arms.[9]

William Oates and his men—and every American living in the North and South—awoke the next morning to a war vastly different from the one they had known before. The Confederate victory at the Wilderness, such as it was, had cost Lee some 11,000 casualties and had badly depleted his army, for there was a diminishing number of new recruits in the South who could take their place. Yet, at the same time, the war was becoming more relentless, as well as more bloody. Lee's adversary, the tenacious Grant would not, like other Union generals in the wake of previous battles and earlier defeats, with-draw to lick his wounds, ask for reinforcements, and waste time in camp try-ing to reorganize his army. He chose purposely to press on, to keep the pressure on Lee as much as possible, and to maneuver around the Army of Northern Virginia's right, hoping to catch the Confederates off guard or lure Lee out of the defensive works that surrounded Richmond.

Yet there was another new element in this war that greeted both sides that spring morning in America, an element that surprised few of the battle-hardened veterans who had come to expect horror and savagery as a matter of course in their bloody encounters with the enemy, but that terrified the new-est recruits in the two armies and shocked them into a dull, incredulous stu-por. Out of the three years of war that had caused so much death and destruction and loss across the land came a new brutality, a raw murderous purpose, an intensified viciousness and bloodlust that would define how the final year of the conflict would be fought—and how, in the end, it would be won and lost.

The days of chivalry were finished. Gone were the shiny armor and the glistening swords. The face of battle wore a new, gruesome mask. The Union and the Confederacy now held each other by the throat, in a death struggle that only one side could possibly win. Casualties multiplied, the Southern landscape became a wasteland, despair and confusion reigned supreme on both sides of the Mason-Dixon line, and still no armistice seemed near at hand. The war had been transformed into a macabre and ugly contest, a deadly game, a mortal tournament without honor or glory or prestige. Quite simply it had become—as Union Captain Charles Francis Adams, Jr., put it so aptly— a "Carnival of Death."[10]

In Virginia that spring, the two armies took hold of one another in a death grip and would not let go. On May 8, as Lee attempted to check Grant's movement around the Confederate right flank, the armies collided briefly at Laurel Hill, west of Spotsylvania Court House, where Oates—once again in temporary command of both the 15th and 48th Alabama—led his men in a hot firefight in support of Kershaw's division. Overwhelmed by the enemy, Oates and his regiments retired, but as they did friendly fire from Confederate troops caught them from behind. The Alabamians survived the confusion and went into battle line behind some hastily constructed log breastworks. Sharp firing between the opposing lines continued through the evening and over the next two days.[11]

As part of a grand assault by Grant against Lee's fortified lines near Spotsylvania, the Federals tried on May 10 to take the Confederate breastworks along the Alabamians' front in two separate attacks, but Law's brigade— feeling particularly secure behind their defenses—easily repelled the charges.[12] Two days later, Grant attempted to break through Lee's lines along the Confederate right, at the salient known as the "mule shoe." The fighting there was fierce and deadly, both sides battling like fiends, and the heightened savagery of this war displayed itself that day in frightening dimensions. "It was a literal saturnalia of blood," said one Pennsylvania soldier.[13] Although the Union forces shattered the Confederate line at the "Bloody Angle," the bluecoats were unable to hold on to their advantage in the maelstrom of bullets and shells that thundered all around them. On the Confederate left, where Oates and his Alabamians stood in relative safety behind their sturdy defenses, the Federals made one last effort to breach the Southern breastworks and failed. "Our fire [was] so destructive," wrote Oates after the war, "that the enemy could not face it long."[14]

In the days that followed, while blossoms filled the woods with pastel colors and green grass returned to the fields and meadows of Virginia, the two armies fought incessantly. Sometimes the engagements were brief and inconsequential; on other occasions, the clashes were stubborn and deadly. All the while, Grant kept moving his army to the left, toward the North Anna River, where he hoped to catch Lee away from his entrenchments. The 15th Alabama had a pretty easy time of it, avoiding any major confrontation with the enemy, until the last day of May. Ordered to hold an abandoned trench, Oates and his men drove off an annoying party of Union sharpshooters, but later in the day they faced a large enemy force bearing down on them. In the nick of time, General John B. Gordon arrived with his Georgia brigade to reinforce the Alabamians. Oates gratefully withdrew his regiment from the entrenchments "as quickly as I could" and before dark caught up with the Alabama brigade, which was once more under the personal command of Evander Law.[15]

On June 3, the 15th Alabama occupied a section on the left of Lee's defensive line near Cold Harbor, between the Pamunkey and Chickahominy rivers, not far from the Gaines Mill battlefield, where the regiment had fought in June 1862. Frustrated in his efforts to force Lee out of his trenches for a fight in the open, Grant decided to launch a frontal attack on the Army of Northern Virginia and use the overwhelming might of the Union army to crush Lee once and for all. He mistakenly believed that Lee's army was on its last legs and that a straight assault would be successful, even though he and his fellow generals, most of whom he barely knew, could claim no firm knowledge of the terrain or the extent of Lee's intricate earthworks.[16]

The result of Grant's decision at Cold Harbor has become legendary in the annals of Civil War history, for the attack made by the Army of the Potomac against Lee's lines proved to be one of the bloodiest events in the entire war. Most of the hardest fighting took place along Lee's right, where the Union Second, Sixth, and Eighteenth Corps threw wave after wave of bluecoated troops against the formidable Confederate works. In short order, the Federal onslaught faltered and failed, not only because of Lee's strong defensive position, but also because the Union generals could not properly coordinate their attacks.

At the same time, toward Lee's left, Oates and the 15th Alabama—tired almost to the point of complete exhaustion—waited in the morning darkness for the enemy to strike. Inexplicably, Oates had failed to order his men to load their weapons, so that all was nearly chaos when the perfectly ordered Federal lines approached the Confederate earthen works and the Alabamians rapidly bit into cartridges and slammed ramrods down the barrels of their muskets. As an indication of how brutal this war had become, Oates told his officers to arm themselves with axes in case the Federals broke through the regiment's lines. When the 15th finally opened fire the enemy was only about thirty steps away. A Napoleon cannon in a barbette nearby raked the Federal ranks with fiercesome effectiveness. The Union troops could stand it only for a few minutes. They retreated in haste, leaving their dead and moaning wounded behind.

About half an hour later the Federals tried again with another charge and dashed in column toward the 4th Alabama on Oates's right. The Union troops, all perfectly formed, looked like they were on parade. Within seconds, a frontal and flank fire from the Confederate line hit them simultaneously, and the blue ranks fell in heaps. Oates remembered years later that he could see "the dust fog out of a man's clothing in two or three places at once where as many balls would strike him at the same moment." In two minutes, said Oates, "not a man of them was standing." The Federal casualties were piled up five and six deep. Some of the Alabamians were appalled by the outright slaughter. "We really mowed them down," wrote one man in the 44th Alabama. But the grim reality of the carnage became even more apparent when the stench of the dead and wounded, who lay untended between the lines for four days, swept over the Confederate lines, making men sick with nausea.[17]

The Confederates, including Oates and his men, experienced the double-edged horror of war at its worst. On one hand, these soldiers felt the horror of knowing they might be struck down at any moment by an enemy ball or a flying piece of shrapnel. On the other, they witnessed the horror of striking down the enemy in such profusion that the sight of it sickened them. The war brought decimation to both sides, but it also brought the realization of how dehumanizing, how utterly abominable, this new destructive war was and would continue to be until one side or the other was forced to its knees. After Cold Harbor, a Confederate officer told a New Hampshire soldier: "It seemed almost like murder to fire upon you." Grant himself recognized this when, years later, in troubled retrospection, he admitted that "I have always regretted that the last assault at Cold Harbor was ever made."[18] But what the Confederates underwent at Cold Harbor as they retched at the sight of Union soldiers being mowed down by their merciless volleys was something that went beyond sadness, guilt, or even remorse. They saw, and felt, with the kind of profound human understanding that comes in an epiphany, that the hard hand of war could bring misery—and a great deal of anguish—not only to those who fell under the sword of destruction, but to those who wielded it as well.

As if to confirm this grotesque revelation, the combat at Cold Harbor sparked and sputtered, continuing to take lives and maim men without any apparent purpose. Over the next week, the fighting flared without stop between the armies, mostly sniper fire and sharpshooting that caused few casualties, but was spirited enough to wear down the men on both sides. From the start of the Cold Harbor campaign until its end on June 12, the 15th Alabama lost six men killed and sixteen wounded. One of the injured was Major Alexander Lowther, Oates's rival, who went to Richmond to recuperate despite the superficiality of his wound.[19]

Every man in the Union and Confederate armies was tired, dead tired. It was a fatigue of the body, of the mind, and of the spirit. "None of us had slept any," explained Oates.[20] But there was more to it than that. The war was spinning out of control, and no one could stop it.

Since the guns had sounded in early May, opening the spring campaign, the fighting had gone on without pause, rising and falling like the tides at sea, and seeming just as vast and endless. The men were nearly worn out from it all, pummelled senseless like a boxer in his final round. Morale among the Confederates was high, with most of Lee's troops seeing their recent victories as a sure sign that Grant would soon withdraw toward Washington. Nevertheless, even with such hopes, the men—including Oates and his regiment—were exhausted and drained. And each side kept wearing out the other. Every time one army would open fire in the middle of the night to rattle the enemy and prevent its foes from getting sleep, it also interrupted the precious rest of its own men.

The drums of war kept beating and would not stop. On June 13, Law's brigade marched out of the trenches at Cold Harbor and crossed the Chickahominy along with the rest of Longstreet's corps, under the command of Anderson. A few days later, the Alabama and Texas brigades supported Major General George E. Pickett's Division in an assault on the Federal works near Chester Station, and, according to Oates, the Texans carried the enemy trenches and deserved the sole honor for "capturing that line." Law's brigade then took its place in the trenches around Petersburg, where Lee was now establishing a solid defensive position to block Grant from moving on Richmond from the south. Oates and his men spent nearly the entire month of July working on the earthworks and trying to keep their heads down as enemy sharpshooters trained their rifles expertly on the Confederate trenches and found any target that foolishly presented itself above the rim of the muddy ditches.[21]

On June 21, Alexander Lowther returned from Richmond and the leave he had taken for a minor wound at Cold Harbor. His days in the Confederate capital had not been entirely wasted in hospital, however. After spending months lobbying strenuously with President Davis, Secretary of War Seddon, and the War Department and presenting them with extensive documentation showing his right to command the 15th Alabama, he had been commissioned a colonel and given command of the regiment on June 9, although his commission was awarded retroactively to April 28, 1863. Despite this amazing political victory, Lowther stayed another two weeks in hospital before getting back to the field. He apparently suffered not only from his minor combat wound, but also from severe dyspepsia and diarrhea, which in turn resulted in extreme intestinal pain.[22] Word of Lowther's promotion reached Oates, however, before the new colonel rejoined the 15th Alabama on June 21.

When Lowther arrived in the regiment's encampment, he also carried with him commissions, all confirmed by Congress, for Isaac Feagin, who was promoted to lieutenant colonel, and for Oates, who was made major of the regiment. Oates was furious at not receiving a command, and, after recovering from the initial shock, he set about gaining support for his case from politicians and his superior officers, including Confederate Congressman James L. Pugh, generals Hood and Field, and Colonel Perry. Pugh wrote President Davis that "a great wrong has been done a constituent of mine and I appeal to

you for his relief." Both Field and Perry attested to Oates's courage, his ability as a commander, and his superior qualities as an officer when compared
to Lowther. Of Oates, Hood wrote: "I have always regarded him as one of
my best colonels in my division and I know of no officer more worthy of
promotion."[23]

But these testimonials did no good. In desperation, Oates went to see
Lee, and all the commanding general could do was recommend that Oates
take his appeal to President Davis. Oates met with Davis, who received him
cordially and expressed sympathy with his plight. But after consulting with
Samuel Cooper, the Adjutant General and Inspector General of the armies,
Davis told Oates that the congressional confirmation of Lowther's commission had effectively tied his hands. "I am sorry to say, sir, that he [Lowther] is
beyond my reach," Davis said to Oates, "[and] I have no power over the matter." Davis did, however, offer Oates the possibility of assuming command of
another regiment. The president also commended Oates for his "faithful-
ness" to the Confederate cause and his service to his country. With that, said
Oates in his memoirs, "my only interview with Jefferson Davis closed."[24]

In a memorandum from Cooper, Oates learned that his own previous
appointment as colonel, made by Law and issued by the War Department in
October 1863 (with an effective date of April 1863), had been declared illegal
and thus had been revoked. On the basis of Cantey's organization of the regiment at Fort Mitchell in July 1861, when Lowther had been given command
of company A of the 15th Alabama, the War Department regarded Lowther
as the senior officer, despite his frequent absences, poor health, and lack of
experience in combat. Incredibly, no one in the War Department seems to
have taken notice of the fact that Lowther had officially resigned his commission as major of the 15th Alabama on July 12, 1862, for reasons of poor health
and fatigue. Lowther said at that time he did not think "it just and right either
to the Service or other Officers for me to hold a position in name and not be
able to stay at my post without having to ask for sick leaves so often." According to the docket on his letter, his resignation was approved by Stonewall
Jackson and Robert E. Lee and forwarded to the War Department, which
issued its approval on July 21. He must have retracted his resignation orally,
and an unknown hand later wrote the word "revoked" on the docket.[25]

Both Field and Perry petitioned the War Department to find a colonel's
place for Oates in a regiment where a vacancy existed, but no such regiment
could be immediately found. Perry subsequently asked Cooper to promote
Oates to a colonelcy in the Provisional Army of the Confederate States "on
account of special skill and gallantry." He suggested that Oates could be appointed to temporary command of the 48th Alabama, which lacked a field
officer. But there was no law that would allow such a promotion. The only
thing that could be done was to transfer Oates as a major to temporary command of the 48th. Oates, understandably, was reluctant to accept temporary

command, after having spent more than a year as a colonel in what he believed to be permanent command of the 15th Alabama. He also did not want to stand in the way of any qualified officers in the 48th Alabama who might be deserving of promotion. In the end, however, he had little choice. He would either have to serve under Lowther in the 15th or accept a new temporary command as a major in a different regiment. On July 1, 1864, he assumed command of the 48th Alabama.[26]

Oates's failure to retain his command of the 15th Alabama hit him hard. "My regret," he wrote after the war, "was to part with the men with whom I had served all through the war." On the day after his interview with Davis, Oates located the 48th Alabama in its camp with the rest of Law's brigade on the north side of the James River, near one of its hairpin turns along a stretch of lowland called Deep Bottom. At Camp Holly, where George Washington and his troops had bivouacked after the surrender at Yorktown, the Alabamians enjoyed a spectacular view of the James and of the Federal gunboats that slipped silently through its waters. Oates quickly took charge of the 48th Alabama and made sure that the regiment had what it needed in the way of supplies, uniforms, and rations, even to the point of paying himself for some wagon loads of watermelons as a treat for the men. He also reinstituted regular drills and stern discipline. After the war, he proudly remembered that he "soon had the good will and confidence of every officer and man in the Forty-eighth, more completely, if possible, than I ever had of the Fifteenth." One doubts if the hearts and minds of the men in the 48th were won as easily as Oates recalled, but he does seem to have been well received by the rank and file.[27]

The men of the 48th were not pushovers whose affections could be won merely with gifts of clothing and melons. These men were hardened veterans of Law's brigade who had experienced the same perils, had fought in the same battles, and had endured the victories and defeats of Lee's Army of Northern Virginia. The regiment had been mustered in just before the Peninsula Campaign in the spring of 1862 and had seen its first action at the Battle of Cedar Mountain on August 9. Since that time, the regiment had accompanied Law's brigade during all its campaigns, driving north to invade the enemy's territory twice, serving with distinction at Chickamauga and Chattanooga, surviving the catastrophic Knoxville campaign, and engaging the enemy with considerable losses at the Wilderness and Spotsylvania. Oates was known to the men of the 48th, for the regiment had been placed under his temporary command during the tough fighting at the Wilderness and Spotsylvania, where he had performed admirably under tense circumstances.[28]

Oates and the 48th, along with his old regiment, the 15th, were ordered on August 13 to occupy some works at New Market Heights, a high bluff about two miles below Drewry's Bluff on the James. All through the next two days, the Alabamians took a beating from a Federal gunboat on the river. The enemy shells, said Oates, crashed right through the earthworks and exploded in the ground, throwing dirt and stones and shrapnel in every direction. The Federals tried to push their infantry up to the heights, but failed in the attempt.

On the morning of August 16, the enemy, under the command of Major General Winfield Scott Hancock, who hoped to smash Lee's defenses and open the way to Richmond, made an assault on the Confederate works near Fussell's Mill on the Darbytown Road. The Federals quickly broke through the Confederate lines and sent the graybacks reeling. Oates and his men of the 48th moved forward to check the Union advance, and as they did Colonel Lowther and the 15th Alabama went with them. About fifty steps from the enemy, both battle lines—Confederate and Union—opened up with a blinding blaze of musket fire. Lowther fell wounded and then retired to the rear, while Oates—impervious to the hail of bullets around him—led his men in an impulsive advance over an old rail fence. The 48th successfully pushed back the Federals, but at a dear cost in lives. Reaching a farm irrigation trench, Oates had his men take cover and fire at the enemy from their relatively protected position. But his men—who probably only numbered about 150—kept falling, and there seemed no end to the fighting in sight. "Every officer in the five left companies," reported Oates, "had been killed or disabled." Among the remnants of the two Alabama regiments, Oates was now the senior officer on the field.[29]

Just then, as Oates stood in the ditch behind his men, a bullet passed between his left arm and his body. His men called for him to get down, but Oates remained where he was, gesturing with his sword toward the enemy lines. In another moment, a minie ball struck him in the right arm, midway between the elbow and shoulder, shattering and splintering the bone. "I caught a good long furlough," Oates dryly remarked in his memoirs, but at the time he knew perfectly well that he had been seriously wounded. He leaned against a little apple tree; the pain in his arm was excruciating. "One of those large Minie-balls," he said matter of factly, "strikes a hard blow."

He relinquished command to a captain (who within minutes fell wounded on the field) and watched as his new regiment swept toward the Federals in a spirited charge. Overpowered and outgunned, the Alabamians fell back, but Oates had nothing but praise for his command. He later declared: "No men, in any battle of the world, ever fought more heroically, on any field, than did the officers and men of that regiment near Darbytown Road." The *Richmond Enquirer* seemed to agree. The 48th Alabama, said the newspaper, had advanced against the enemy "with an impetuosity that was almost irresistible." In the end, Oates's attack did help to halt Hancock's advance on Richmond.[30]

Oates walked out of the woods on shaky legs with bullets still hissing all around him and fearful that he might be shot in the back. Staggering along, he came upon Major General Richard Anderson, who ordered a courier to dismount and give his horse to Oates. Grateful for the favor, Oates discovered the pain was too great as he rode toward the rear, so he dismounted and found a cool place to rest in the shade. He continued walking after a while, met Major General Charles Field, and gave a brief report on what was happening on the battle front. Now he was growing weak from fatigue and loss of blood, and a surgeon from a Georgia regiment luckily happened by and administered morphine to Oates to dull the pain. But as the doctor was binding Oates's arm, a shell fell close to them, and the surgeon ran for his life, leaving Oates alone again. Eventually he was helped by two ambulance corpsmen from the 15th Alabama. Using a blanket from a captured Yankee, the corpsmen made a makeshift litter upon which to carry Oates off the field.[31]

Finally Oates and his litter-bearers found an ambulance, and he was transported to a field infirmary, where, as he later remembered, "about an acre of ground was covered with the wounded and dying" from the 48th and 15th regiments. The doctors gave him chloroform as an anesthetic, but he clearly "knew what was being done to me when they sawed the bone." He awoke around sunset, lying beneath a tree; one of his men from the 15th Alabama sat beside him, crying his eyes out, for he believed the brave Oates was dying. After getting more whiskey, Oates dictated a letter informing his father and mother of the amputation of his right arm. He instructed a man to bury his severed arm, which the fellow did by digging a hole near Oates's tree. Through the night, Oates slept fitfully, waking occasionally to the sounds of moans and lamentations from the wounded around him.

The next day, he and hundreds of other wounded Alabamians were transported to the Confederate hospital at Howard's Grove in Richmond. There Oates received effective treatment from an Alabama doctor, J. B. Gaston of Montgomery, who used a compress on the arm to stop the incessant bleeding and watched over his patient until the arm began to heal. Oates was placed in the same ward with Captain William Strickland of the 15th Alabama, who had been wounded in the hand at Fussell's Mill. Strickland was described by Oates as "mischievous, mirthful, and companionable," and he was exactly what Oates needed to keep his mind off his lost arm. As Oates explained, "I was a young man of fine physical strength and activity, and to be so impaired by the loss of my right arm made me despondent and at times to feel a regret that I had not been killed." Strickland dispelled his gloom by wooing the nurses to get extra allowances of whiskey out of them. The captain also teased some of the other wounded, sometimes hounding them so badly that they requested transfers out of the ward. Together Oates and Strickland ate at a table between their beds, each man assisting the other as required. Once, when Oates was served a rotten boiled egg for breakfast, he let out an oath about his ruined meal, and Strickland—who saw the humor in almost every situation—

shouted for all to hear: "Lost your religion, Colonel, at the first fire." Oates replied, "Well, I don't care, it was a d——d poor breakfast anyway."

Every few days, his comrades who were wounded or sick would visit him in the hospital. Some of the visits brought sadness when he learned of men from his regiments in the hospital with fatal wounds. In a few instances, Oates took responsibility for notifying the families of the deceased or arranging to have their remains shipped home. His brother-in-law, James B. Long, was admitted to the hospital with typhoid fever. Long was dying, and Oates tried to comfort him as he slipped away. Oates sat by Long's bed, held his hand, and heard the man faintly say, "Don't let my wife and children suffer." Promising to do everything in his power for Long's family, Oates watched as his friend and relative sank rapidly. Long died in the hospital as Oates stayed by his side.

Oates remained in the Richmond hospital until November, when the doctors decided he was well enough to travel home. A man named Coleman, a Polish Jew who had been the sutler to the 15th Alabama when Oates was in command, offered to escort him to Alabama. "He was," said Oates, "one of the most liberal, big-hearted men I ever knew." He and Coleman became staunch friends. The journey, however, was not easy. The trip exhausted Oates, and he had to stop to rest for two days in Kingsville, South Carolina. Elijah W. Lingo, a veteran of Oates's old Company G, was traveling home on furlough and accompanied Oates and Coleman south from Kingsville. For the rest of the journey, Oates suffered little pain or discomfort. His friends took him to Eufaula, and from there they went by coach down the dusty southern road to Abbeville.[32]

Finally at home, he recuperated in his small house and took comfort from the ministrations of a black nurse, Sarah (Sallie) Vandalia, a thirty-one-year-old slave who was his domestic servant. As he regained his strength and got back on his feet, he took advantage of Sallie's proximity and tenderness toward him and became intimately involved with her. Virtually nothing is known about her or about the details of her relationship with Oates, other than the fact that he later acknowledged having a sexual liaison with her. In his youth, he had expressed his own attraction to women of color, and it seems likely that Sallie Vandalia was not the first black woman he had ever taken to his bed.[33] Perhaps Vandalia consented. But, just as likely, she was the victim of Oates's coercion.

Surviving evidence does not reveal whether Oates owned her or rented her. It is possible that Sallie belonged to the Toney family and that she had been loaned to assist Oates in his recovery. Although his convalescence began in Abbeville, it continued mostly at Roseland Plantation, about thirty miles to the north, where, it seems likely, Sallie continued to tend to his needs, both medical and sexual. As the chill of winter set in, he spent long hours in the plantation house and took short walks around the grounds. His shoulder healed slowly, but his soul was in despair. Religion provided little comfort to him; besides, he had been unable to maintain the discipline and the faith required of an evangelical Christian. One sign of this was the frequency of his oaths and cusses, which he no longer desired to curb. It was the war that had dissipated his spiritual resolve, the war that had shown him too many miseries, too many defeats, too many heartaches.[34]

His relationship with Sallie Vandalia could not have helped his state of mind, no matter how much he enjoyed her company. In Southern society, white masters often took unfair sexual advantage of young female slaves, sometimes by raping them, treating them as concubines, or even entering into caring relationships with them. Sexual relations between white males and black female slaves occurred frequently throughout the slave South, even though such practices were frowned on and considered taboo, especially by white women, who served as the region's moral conscience. Yet men, like Oates, seemed unable to stop themselves and their urges. Female slaves were often blamed as temptresses, but the fact was that white males used their omnipotent power as members of the master class to get what they wanted in the slave quarters—or, in Oates's case, in his recovery room.

Even with Sallie's help, Oates's recovery was not easy. He worked hard to handle things on his own, without any assistance from his nurse or from the Toneys, but he found his efforts often exhausting and frustrating. As he recalled years later: "Several times when trying to dress myself or write, and a time or two when I got a fall by not being able to balance properly, I had felt a regret that I had not been killed instead of maimed." The Toneys sought to boost his spirits through these dismal times and remind him of his worth. In the sanctuary of Roseland, where the war seemed very far away, he shook off his despair and tried to cope with his physical limitations. No doubt his sexual relations with Sallie Vandalia showed him that a one-armed man could also be a virile man.

That winter, in the placid surroundings of the Toney plantation, he took particular delight in watching the playfulness of little Sarah Toney, nicknamed Sallie, the baby he had held in his arms during his convalescence after Brown's Ferry. Sallie was now a toddler and her antics around the house made him laugh out loud. His pet name for the little girl became "T," which stood for Toney and helped to distinguish her from all the Sarahs and Sallies in his life, including Mrs. Toney, his mother and sister, and his slave lover. The kindness of the Toney family, he confessed as an older man, gave him the desire to live, "and thereupon I made a virtue of necessity and undertook to learn to do nearly everything that a man with two hands could." He became, he said, "like the sailor who fell from the masthead of the ship and broke his leg—he thanked God it was not his neck."[35]

Yet even as he regained his strength and his health, and as "T" and the Toneys successfully pulled him out of his deep depression, Oates neverthe-less became morose about the fate of the Confederacy and the blunders that were contributing to its demise. He tried not to become too gloomy, but he could see all the signs of a dying nation around him. "The entire Southern country," he recalled, "had been drained of its war material and there were no more men or boys capable of being sent to the front as soldiers." The home guards, called "Buttermilk Rangers," were few in number and outnumbered by Confederate deserters who had formed themselves into marauding bands of outlaws bent on terrorizing southeastern Alabama. Desertions from the Confederate army were indeed a problem, although Oates did not blame any-one for leaving the military in the war's final months: "Brave men who had fought heroically for years, after the summer of 1864 had passed, had the intelligence to see and to know that to continue the fight was a hopeless struggle, and many deserted for that reason. An enlisted man could not re-sign, as an officer was permitted to do; his only way to escape the further risk of his life in a hopeless cause was to desert."[36]

After spending another Christmas with the Toneys, Oates decided he could not stay out of the war. In January 1865, he left Roseland and traveled north to rejoin Lee's Army of Northern Virginia in its defenses around Pe-tersburg. After a tedious journey, he finally found Law's brigade in the trenches and saw that the Alabama regiments had become decimated by siege warfare, disease, and desertions. The 48th Alabama could muster fewer than 100 men and officers. And the 15th Alabama consisted of no more than 200 men. Oates stayed with the brigade for three or four days, but when his right shoulder swelled and began aching, he went to Richmond and rested for two weeks. He reported for duty to Adjutant General Samuel Cooper at the War De-partment when he felt better, and he was offered several desk jobs in Rich-mond, which, typically, he declined because he wanted to be on the frontlines.[37]

He soon realized, however, that his weakened condition would not allow him to lead men in battle, so he petitioned President Davis and the War Department for an appointment as a judge in the military court attached to Major General Joseph Wheeler's cavalry. His application was supported by Congressman Pugh, who wrote to Davis twice on Oates's behalf. As a result of these requests, Oates not only won appointment to the military court, but he also received a promotion to lieutenant colonel because Isaac Feagin, whose wounds had kept him in poor health, resigned his commission from the 15th Alabama around the same time. So, somewhat miraculously, Oates became lieutenant colonel of the 15th Alabama on detached service to Wheeler's cav-alry. By the end of February, his commission was confirmed by John C. Breckinridge, the Confederacy's new secretary of war.[38]

But he never reported for duty to the military court. His shoulder contin-ued to bother him, enough that he found it necessary to go home on furlough.

Oates returned to Abbeville and fixed up his living quarters in the small, white clapboarded structure at the corner of Kirkland and West Washington streets that had served as his law office before the war. Apparently Sallie Vandalia lived under his roof as a maid and as his lover. She was now five months pregnant with his baby. How Oates took this news is not known, but apparently he was resolved—despite the customs of his time and place—to care for Sallie and the child. His actions suggest that he may have felt more for Sallie than conventions condoned or permitted, although years later he described her as a mean-spirited shrew and someone completely unworthy of his attentions. It is likely that he felt more for her than he let on, perhaps even to himself, for his later contempt for her seemed to mask a deep attachment to her that, years later, he could only express through anger and derision.

Hoping to get back into the war, he waited patiently for orders from General Joseph Johnston to report to Wheeler's cavalry, but the orders never came. All he could do was watch from afar as the Confederacy seemed to melt away in the winter and early spring of 1865. He still hoped the South's slaves could be enlisted into the army, but when the Confederate Congress passed a bill on March 13 to allow the enlistment of slaves into the military, without any provision for granting freedom to those slaves who served and fought for the Confederacy, Oates knew the effort was too little, too late to matter. By that time, the end of the war was in sight, and while the Confederacy was about to lose the war on the field of battle, Oates nevertheless blamed the incompetent politicians and War Department officials in Richmond for its demise. Praising the Confederacy's brave soldiers, he wrote after the war: "Had all others—President, Congress, generals, colonels, and officials generally—performed their respective parts near so well as the men in the ranks, the Confederate Government would have been a veritable reality today."[39]

Oates was in Abbeville when word reached him of Lee's surrender at Appomattox. He later learned that the 15th Alabama had stacked 170 guns, although its battle flag was hidden by one of the regiment's loyal soldiers in his shirt, and the same man was buried with that flag years after the war had ended. Colonel Lowther, who had been absent from the regiment for more time than he ever spent with it in the field, was present at Appomattox for the laying down of arms on the morning of April 12.[40] But it was Oates who seemed to feel the regiment's greatest pain. "There was no better regiment in the Confederate Army than the Fifteenth Alabama," Oates wrote years later. Of the men who served in its ranks, he said: "Too much praise cannot be bestowed upon them." For him, the bonds he forged in battle and through four years of war with the men of the 15th were ironclad. "They are my brothers," he said solemnly.[41]

For Oates, as for many Civil War soldiers, his strongest loyalty was to the men with whom he had served, not to the politicians or generals who, in his estimation, had led the Confederacy to defeat. The 15th Alabama and, to a lesser degree, the 48th Alabama became the objects of Oates's greatest affection and devotion—far more so than his fidelity and emotional attachment to country, state, army, corps, or brigade. Unit cohesion in the regiments had transformed them into surrogate families for men who served far from home and loved ones. Camaraderie reinforced the bonds that tied the regiments' rank and file together, and military successes—like the ones enjoyed by the 15th Alabama in Lee's Army of Northern Virginia—promoted the regiments' reputation and honor. Sacrifice, loss, and shared experiences, including the elation of victory, the sorrow of defeat, and the boredom of soldier life between the battles, all worked to increase a sense of pride among the surviving soldiers of a regiment. When Oates boasted of the achievements of the 15th Alabama, he simply echoed the sentiments held by nearly every Civil War soldier, Union and Confederate, who believed in his heart of hearts that his regiment, and his regiment alone, was the bravest, fiercest, and most effective fighting unit in all the armies. Oates's high regard and deep emotional attachment for the 15th Alabama would endure for the rest of his life.[42]

But his life as a soldier was over. At age thirty-one, now fully in his prime, he had lost a right arm, a brother, bosom friends, cherished comrades, and four years of his adulthood. He had been wounded six times in combat, and while he rose no higher in rank, technically speaking, than lieutenant colonel, he would insist for the rest of his life that he had been properly commissioned a full colonel in the spring of 1863. But the winds of war and the incidentals of military life were finished for him and for everyone in the South. The future lay before him, but the paths he would follow were uncertain ones. Just as he had done when he returned from Texas in his youth, when nothing seemed sure or clear in his life and his prospects appeared particularly dim, he would have to make his own way.

9

BEFORE THE BAR

E ven before the last shots had been fired in the Civil War, Oates was busy in Abbeville trying to make a new life for himself. The surrender at Appomattox left him sad and bitter, especially toward the Confederacy's inept political leadership, but he felt no melancholia about the South's defeat and the end of slavery. His commitment to the romanticism of the "Lost Cause" would come later. For now, like most other Southerners, he accepted the North's victory, expressed deep sorrow over Lincoln's assassination, and quickly turned his attention to his own private affairs.[1] He badly needed an income, and in pure Oates fashion he went about earning a living with consummate determination and characteristic diligence.

Venturing forth to make a success of himself meant that Oates would have to confront a South that differed considerably from the one he had left behind when he marched off to war with the 15th Alabama. Not only did the South's lack of resources in the wake of the war—the destruction that had ruined towns and homes and businesses and farms—leave much of the region a wasteland, but the removal of slavery had transformed the work force throughout the former Confederate states from one of involuntary servitude to labor paid in wages or goods. A new economy tried to establish itself in the postwar years—a turbulent economy that sought to mirror its functions on the old forms while incorporating innovations required by necessity. Into this setting, Oates tried to make something of himself. Like other Southerners, white and black, he did not exactly know what he was doing. What he did not lack, however, was a sense of the marketplace, the instincts of a good capitalist and entrepreneur, a fierce desire to make money, and the energy to do so. His ambition, such as it was, seemed no different than what it had been before the Civil War. Even then, before the first shots had been fired, he had worked hard and had immersed himself in the commercial culture of growing Abbeville and the rising prosperity of Henry County. After the war, he attempted to pick up where he had left off, although the opportunities for an attorney in an economically depressed region were not abundant. So Oates did what all good capitalists usually do. He created his own opportunities, got involved in new activities that never occurred to him before the war, and expanded his economic and financial base beyond the confines of his law practice, while keeping the business of his law office a going concern.

The first step was to rebuild his practice, which had suffered during the war years; there are hints, though, that he had kept his law office open and running throughout most the conflict, even while he was marching along endless roads and fighting in equally endless battles hundreds of miles from home. How he accomplished this feat is not known, but he may have taken care of business when he was on furlough or worked on cases from afar, perhaps with the assistance of other attorneys in Abbeville and Eufaula. When he returned to Abbeville for good in February 1865, he went about finding clients and arguing cases as if he were going into combat. He was aggressive inside and outside the court room, and he performed in the court room with the same fierce resoluteness and the same glint in his eye that had gotten him around the Union flank in the Wilderness.[2]

For the most part, he did not represent elite clients—the planters and manufacturing leaders who were becoming the new political barons of the South. Oates's clients were ordinary people with small claims or desperate defenses. Mostly his cases involved rather mundane points of the law. To the greatest degree, he handled most of the usual everyday cases that were the bread and butter of small-town attorneys: probate and other inheritance actions, title disputes, debt collecting, defense against creditors, and bankruptcy proceedings. Some of these cases were heard by justices of the peace; others by judges in the local probate, criminal, common law, and chancery courts. He also argued a significant number of cases before the Alabama Supreme Court—169 in all from 1866 to 1910. Sometimes he was joined in representing clients by other attorneys, law firms, or partners. For most of his clients, he argued their cases personally and without assistance. His clients generally came from Henry County, although he also represented individuals from other counties and argued cases in several different counties, including Pike, Bullock, Russell, Lowndes, Houston, Barbour, Dale, Coffee, and Talladega. Frequently he represented clients in the city courts of Eufaula and Montgomery. He also argued a few cases before the U.S. Fifth Circuit Court for the Middle District of Alabama and at least one case, in which he was both the appellant and represented himself as the attorney for the plaintiff in error (joined by W. Hallett Phillips) before the U.S. Supreme Court.

He maintained his law office in his house at Kirkland and West Washington streets in Abbeville. His quarters were plain, befitting a local attorney in a rural community. Like other attorneys, he regularly performed a variety of nonlitigious services for his clients, such as giving legal advice and preparing wills, land conveyances, and other legal documents. He also registered land instruments at local court houses, including the ones in Abbeville and Eufaula. Mostly his clients were individuals, many of them poor farmers and impoverished widows down on the their luck. Sometimes he did take on more noteworthy clients, including small businesses, some manufacturing concerns, and even some railroad companies; but his practice seemed dominated by ordinary folks who had become entangled in legal difficulties and who wanted nothing more than to reach the easiest—and least expensive—settlement of their problems in short order, preferably without having to go to court. Oates rarely handled criminal cases, but when he did, he earned a fee of $37.50 per client, according to the Revised Code of 1867. On several occasions, he succeeded in getting convictions reversed on appeal for his criminal clients—not on technicalities, but on points of evidence and by proving reasonable doubt.[3]

He seems to have prospered in his practice by taking as many clients as he could humanly handle at any one time, which was often more than he could possibly give adequate attention to. As a result, his fees streamed in with a good flow, sometimes in barter, less often in cash, and occasionally in land conveyed to him in exchange for his services. In this way, his personal income grew steadily over the years, and he wisely began to invest a portion of his cash income in stocks and bonds at an early date. Oates was a competent lawyer and a very good businessman; he must have been, or else he could not have kept up his practice and have earned such a lucrative income, as he apparently did. By no means, though, did he win every case he took on. Of the 169 cases he argued before the Alabama Supreme Court between 1866 and 1910 (sometimes as counsel for the appellant, and on other occasions as counsel for the appellee), he won 83 and lost 85; in one case, the court affirmed one part and reversed another part of the lower court's decision. Oates represented the appellant in 50.3 percent of those cases. His only appearance before the U.S. Supreme Court in 1879 ended in utter failure; the stakes were higher than usual in that particular case: He was both the appellant and the appellant's counsel.[4]

Even in his law practice, Oates could not escape the Civil War or its legacy and meaning. Indeed, the Alabama legal minds could not detach themselves from the war and its enormous effects. Memories of the Civil War— and the myth of the Lost Cause—molded Alabama legal thought and solidified the attitudes that enabled white Alabamians to treat freed slaves according to prevailing racial assumptions rather than the rule of law. Nevertheless, the law proved to be particularly malleable during the postwar years in the South. The Alabama Supreme Court, for example, revealed no ironclad ideology in its decisions over the two decades following the Civil War. Presiding justices used their own personal understandings of the war to shape their interpretation of laws involving contract and property disputes, the identity and legal standing of former slaves, marriage and antimiscegenation laws, and issues directly concerning equal protection. Some of these decisions, especially during the Reconstruction years, seemed to challenge the emerging consensus behind the Lost Cause ideology. Soon after the Alabama legislature passed a series of laws in 1866 that would become collectively known as the state's "black code," the Supreme Court, in several decisions written by Justice Thomas Minott Peters, who had been elected during the brief period when Republicans controlled the state government between 1868 and 1874, declared that the Confederate government was illegal, that its courts "were as much a part of the machinery of the rebellion as any other department of the insurrectionary administration," that slave marriages were valid under common law, and that slavery was an unqualified "wrong." Even Chief Justice E. Wolsey Peck, who tended to be more of a Southern apologist, boldly held that the Confederate state governments, including that of Alabama, had been "rebel governments, and nothing more—governments in hostility to, and not parts of, the government of the United States."[5] Later, once the Redemption Democrats took back political control of the state, many of these rulings were reversed, including the one that held slave marriages to be legal. In 1877, the court upheld laws prohibiting miscegenation and interracial marriages. By the turn of the century, the justices of the Alabama Supreme Court were true believers in the Lost Cause mythology, and they liberally applied its rationale to their decisions, especially those regarding black civil rights and equal protection.[6]

Oates, like the Supreme Court justices before whom he argued so many of his cases on appeal, also discovered that the Civil War played a huge role—and left something of a confused legacy—in his own legal thinking and the clients he represented in the decades after Appomattox. The war repeatedly cast its shadow across his law practice: when he represented a former Confederate cheated out his rightful share of a father's estate while the young soldier was away from home fighting, when he defended a client's payment of a war debt at the face value of Confederate currency, and when, in stark contrast to antebellum racial and legal protocols, he filed and won an appeal for an African American church group that had been denied a bequest contained in a parishioner's will.[7]

While arguing the war debt case appeal in 1870, Oates—with help from his old mentor, James L. Pugh, as co-attorney—led the Alabama Supreme Court into one of its most important decisions during the postwar era: a judgment that further reflected the court's ambivalence about the war and its memory. In *Roach, Administrator, v. Gunter et al.*, Justice Benjamin Franklin Saffold—following a line of argument supplied by Oates and Pugh in their brief—declared "null and void" and unconstitutional an ordinance passed by the 1867 Alabama Constitutional Convention that invalidated contracts based on payment in Confederate notes and bonds. The ordinance, asserted Saffold, impaired "the obligation of contracts." His ruling, which had a profound impact on contract litigation over the next several decades in Alabama, upheld the principle that all contractual agreements had to be respected under the law, even those formed during the war and fulfilled with payments in Confederate currency, the only means of payment that Alabamians had in hand during the conflict.[8]

In another noteworthy case, which also took place in the early 1870s, Oates represented the widow of William F. Gunter, a former Confederate soldier and a planter in Dale County who had been murdered by one Turner Riley, a known "outlaw." Although the case did not hinge directly on any legal issues connected to the Civil War, it did reveal how the war had helped forge a new world of confusion, disorder, and unchecked violence in the South. The murdered man, Gunter, had gotten into a private dispute with Riley during the summer of 1869, and the two men had exchanged gunshots at each other, Riley actually wounding Gunter in the arm. Later, Riley waited in ambush for Gunter and killed him with a "load of large shot" from a shotgun. The authorities caught up with Riley in Corinth, Mississippi, where he was arrested and brought back to Dale County for trial. Riley acknowledged, while under arrest and manacled, that he had killed Gunter, and he said that "if he was carried back to Dale county and convicted and hung for killing Gunter, he would go to hell and fight Gunter there as long as the devil would allow him to do it." In the Dale County Circuit Court, Oates filed a petition for Gunter's widow and asked the county to pay her $5,000 in damages for her husband's death. Under a recently passed law, next-of-kin could collect damages for anyone assassinated or murdered by an "outlaw, or person or persons in disguise, or mob, or for past or present party affiliation or political opinion." Among his friends and neighbors, Gunter was known for having blatantly refused to take "any oath of allegiance to the United States government since the war." Presumably Riley had quarreled with Gunter over their differing political opinions. On this point, Oates waxed eloquent before the bar. He told the court: "Every one in Alabama, or within the American Union, is entitled to the protection of the law, for his life, liberty, and property."

When the circuit court rejected the petition, though, Oates appealed to the Alabama Supreme Court and succeeded in winning a decision that reversed the lower court's ruling and remanded the case for retrial. Yet Oates fared no better a second time around. Even though the circuit court now ruled in favor of Gunter's widow, the court's decision was appealed by Dale County; this time, the Alabama Supreme Court issued a strongly worded opinion in the county's favor and rejected the grounds on which the widow had sought damages, pointing out that it was not at all certain whether Gunter had been murdered for his political opinions. From the looks of it, Oates realized that the case was unwinnable. During the second appeal, he didn't even bother to file a brief in the case, although he did make a spirited oral argument that left the court unimpressed. At the close of the case, he must have been left wondering whether everyone's life, liberty, and property was as fully protected as he had asserted. No doubt Oates stewed over the fact that a former soldier had been killed—at least so far as he believed or could tell— for voicing an undying allegiance to the Confederacy, a noble sentiment that Oates himself still held dear. For the remainder of his life, Oates would remain an unreconstructed and unapologetic Southerner. He and Gunter, although not precisely of the same mind, had a lot in common.[9]

Nevertheless, Oates's law practice also revealed how far he had come in a very short time toward accepting some of the most obvious—and even revolutionary—consequences of the war and of the Confederate defeat. Despite all the turmoil over race caused by the war's outcome and by the ratification of the three "Civil War amendments"—the Thirteenth, Fourteenth, and Fifteenth Amendments to the U.S. Constitution—Oates seemed to relish the opportunity to acknowledge freed slaves as citizens and take them on as clients. He represented free blacks and former slaves without flinching or doubting their legal status as citizens under the law.

In 1867, he defended an African American, George Montgomery, who had been charged with stealing two mules. On appeal, though, Oates failed to win a reversal of the Montgomery conviction. He was more successful three years later, as counsel for a black man named Crawford who had been convicted of burglary and sentenced to three years in prison. Arguing the appeal before the Alabama Supreme Court, Oates presented a convincing case that the evidence used in the conviction was only prima facie, which should have left plenty of room for reasonable doubt. Chief Justice Peters agreed, noting that there was no direct evidence of any breaking and entering, and ruled that the charge to the jury, which decided the case in the Henry County Circuit Court, was erroneous. Peters reversed the judgment of the lower court. In a second opinion involving the same case, Peters also struck down the indictment that had led to Crawford's arrest in the first place, and he remanded the prisoner for a new trial—one in which, presumably, the prosecution avoided procedural mistakes and prima facie evidence and obtained a conviction of Crawford that contained no grounds for further appeal.[10]

Like many small-town lawyers, he took practically every case that came his way, but mostly he handled the usual cases of surety and equity, property claims and damages, wills and petitions, small debts, petty suits, and divorces. In his small office on the court house square in Abbeville, he kept a basic library of law books and legal opinions for looking up precedents whenever he needed to.[11] Otherwise, he relied on a good knowledge of the law, common law, and an ample supply of his own common sense. Long afterward, he was praised for knowing "the frame-work, the anatomy, the foundation of law" and for being familiar "with the great streams and currents and tides of authority." He was an attorney who "had breadth and scope, resource, learning, logic[,] and above all a sense of justice."[12]

He must have been constantly working, although his shoulder still pained him from time to time and he still had not fully recovered his strength. Yet his stamina was enormous, and he accepted every case willingly and without worrying about the load. As his later account and record books show, he was a indefatigable worker and, in the practice of law, he knew what he was doing and he was very good at it. Oates had good cause to throw himself into his work after the war, not only for his own sake and for his future prospects, but also because he had taken on the added responsibility of caring for his infant son and Sallie Vandalia, who, now that the war was over, could no longer be legally treated as a slave. The child was born on June 18, 1865, and they named him Claudius, although over the years his given name became shortened to simply Claude. Oates provided financial support for both mother and infant by giving them a roof over their heads and putting food on their table. He also managed to earn enough to save some money for himself and invest part of his income in real estate.[13]

Oates recognized that land—and not his law practice—was the key to his financial well-being, although occasionally his work as an attorney afforded him opportunities to acquire valuable land that he otherwise might not have known about. In some instances, he purchased acreage from clients, at tax sales, or when landowners were unable to keep up their mortgages. On at least one occasion, he was accused of swindling his clients out of land, but the facts in the case are cloudy. He seems, rather, to have been particularly adept at accepting land as payment from his clients for his legal services; an astounding number of U.S. and Alabama land-grant deeds—most of them dating from the antebellum period—in his possession suggest that his clients paid him with real estate by simply handing over their land-grant certificates.[14] However he managed it, he succeeded in acquiring thousands, if not tens of thousands, of acres in several different counties in southeastern Alabama, although his primary holdings were located in Henry County, where he resided. For the remainder of his life, he was praised for having accumulated an immense fortune in the decades following the war, although no one—including himself—ever publicly revealed precisely how he had done it.[15]

For a man who claimed—with obvious exaggeration—to have owned nothing more after Appomattox than a one-eyed horse he had captured from a Yankee, he did exceptionally well for himself. Some folks said that he earned as much as $500,000 in the years between 1865 and 1880, when he was elected to Congress. If he did make that much money in the poverty-stricken South,

he must have become an extremely successful landlord who demanded hard
work and large shares of the crops raised by the tenant farmers, mostly former
slaves, who worked his land. While the records reveal few details, he seems to
have shamelessly exploited his sharecropping tenants as most white land owners
did and put them to work raising as much cotton as possible, the staple crop
that produced more dollars per acre that any other crop in the postwar South.
He probably also turned a profit selling cotton seed. Although blacks hoped
to rent if not own their own land, they acceded to the sharecropping system
because it required contracts between the landowner and the laborer (which
usually included the laborer's family as well) and allowed African Americans
to escape from the gang labor they associated with slavery. But the arrangement always worked in the landowner's greatest interest, fostering the economic oppression and debt peonage of blacks.

How Oates managed his property and the blacks in his employ is not
evident. Most likely, he relied on local white overseers to conduct his business, although records for such arrangements do not survive. There is no
indication that Oates took over any huge estates or plantations and established new residences on his lands. As an absentee landlord, it is a mystery
how he was able to earn such huge profits from his land at a time when Southern agriculture was not necessarily thriving and the Alabama economy had
practically bottomed out. But make money he did, and it seems that he did so
on the backs of former slaves and perhaps poor whites. Besides his land and
sharecropping interests, which transformed him into a parvenu cotton planter,
he put his vast timbered acreage in southeastern Alabama to good use by
leasing it out to logging firms and providing raw materials for the manufac-
ture of turpentine. It is possible that Oates made more money from his timber interests than he did from cotton, but it seems certain that land—however
he used it—was the commodity that made him wealthy.[16]

Obviously Oates had a good head for business, but his success in the
postwar years seems all the more remarkable when one considers the economic ruin and social turmoil that plagued Alabama at the time. The war and
emancipation had changed everything. The end of slavery transformed the
economic and social foundations of the South in a single stroke. Plantations
stood in ruins, with no labor sources to keep them going, and the planter class
fell from power and from favor. White farmers, who had always struggled
hard to survive in good times and bad, now found themselves impoverished
and in debt. The war had also destroyed state and local government institutions; in fact, there was no government in Alabama after the Confederacy
collapsed. Sectional sentiments rose in the bitterness that whites felt in the
wake of defeat, and white Alabamians found themselves fiercely divided over
issues of politics, economy, and race.[17]

The fruits of emancipation in Alabama and throughout the defeated South
would depend on how the federal government went about reconstructing the

former Confederate states and ensuring the rights and welfare of black people. Before the war ended, Lincoln had experimented with a reconstruction scheme outlined in his Proclamation of Amnesty and Reconstruction, issued in December 1863, by which the Southern states in rebellion could reenter the Union if a minimum 10 percent of the qualified voters from 1860 in each state took a loyalty oath, framed a new state constitution, agreed to abolish slavery, and provided some means for black education. The Radical Republicans thought this plan—which was tested in Louisiana, Tennessee, and Arkansas—far too lenient, and they asserted that only Congress had the authority to determine the terms for admitting (or readmitting) states into the Union. Lincoln's approach to Reconstruction let the former Confederate states down easy and it contained no provisions for guaranteeing black suffrage or punishing Confederate officials and barring them from holding office.

Oates and many other Southerners believed that Lincoln would have been generous with his pardons and would have carried out his lenient Reconstruction policy had he lived. Lincoln, said Oates, "would have extended his kind offices to reconciliation, aiding the Southern people to rebuild their ruined homes and resurrect their States, rather than to have adopted a narrow, spiteful policy."[18] Yet Lincoln seems to have realized, in the weeks before his death, that political necessity would require him to make concessions not only to the Radicals in Congress, but to the more influential and powerful moderate Republicans whose votes would ultimately determine the path that Reconstruction would take, and that he as president would be unable to implement any policy without the assistance and support of Congress. At the time of his assassination, Lincoln appeared to be leaning toward more rigorous measures in devising Reconstruction plans for each of the different Confederate states.[19]

When Andrew Johnson became president, he naively believed—as Lincoln once had—that a simple executive policy, formulated and implemented without the help of Congress, would be sufficient for the readmission of the states. Under Johnson's plan, the Southern states, including Alabama, would be reconstituted beginning with the appointment of a provisional governor, which for Alabama came when Johnson named Lewis E. Parsons of Talladega on June 21, 1865, and with the establishment of a "loyal" electorate willing to take an oath to support, protect, and defend the Constitution of the United States. The following August these electors chose delegates to a state constitutional convention, which ultimately put together a document that restored the planter elite and supporters of the former Confederacy to power, denied blacks their full political rights, and set apportionment of state legislators on the basis of white population alone. In November 1865, with the state divided along similar lines that left Alabama's Unionists out in the cold, the white voters elected new state officers, legislators, and delegates to the U.S. Congress. To comply with President Johnson's requirements for readmission, the Alabama legislature promptly ratified the Thirteenth Amendment abolishing slavery. Oates enthusiastically supported these measures, for they showed Alabama's willingness to accede to Johnson's reconstruction plan in all its particulars and handily revived a white man's government in the state, without forcing any onerous penalties onto former Confederates like himself.[20]

But these carefully considered steps by the white power brokers in Alabama did not bring the state back into the Union. Congress refused to seat the congressmen and senators from the states reconstituted under Johnson's plan, claiming that too many of those elected representatives were the same people who had held office in those states before the war or were former high officials of the Confederacy. Under a strong coalition of moderates and Radical Republicans, Congress rejected the president's plan for reconstruction as being too lenient toward the South and paying too little attention to black civil rights, which had been effectively circumscribed in the former Confederate states by the enactment of "black codes."

Congress asserted its own Reconstruction policy by extending the life of the Freedmen's Bureau—which had been created in March 1865 to provide emergency food, clothing, and medical care for the freed slaves—and expanding its duties to include the establishment of special courts and schools for Southern blacks. It also passed civil rights legislation (over Johnson's veto), drafted the Fourteenth Amendment and sent it to the states for ratification, campaigned vigorously and successfully against Johnson's program in the 1866 election (which gave the Republicans a two-thirds majority in both houses of Congress), and also passed reconstruction legislation (also over Johnson's veto) that divided the eleven former Confederate states into five military districts, provided for the registration of black voters, framed the terms under which states could call constitutional conventions, limited the involvement of former Confederates in the political process, and gave Congress the right to approve the new state constitutions before permitting the election of any new federal representatives and senators from the Southern states.[21]

Whites in the South, including Oates, were outraged by the provisions of congressional reconstruction, and many Southerners bewailed the burdens of Federal military occupation, the elevation of blacks politically and socially, and the economic forces—identified as Northern and Republican—that seemed to be working against any chance of renewed prosperity in the South. Throughout the region, whites reacted with anxiety to the chaos that churned around them—displaced blacks roaming city streets and country lanes, Union soldiers stationed on every street corner in every town, *black* Union soldiers enforcing laws and compelling white people to obey them, impoverished whites being left to their own devices, rumors circulating in whispers about planned rebellions by blacks seeking revenge.

In Alabama, the maelstrom of disorder and uncertainty erupted into violence as Unionists and former Confederates took up arms against each other in the northern part of the state. Whites in the state also resorted to violence against blacks who held political meetings or who gathered to hear speeches by white politicians from the North. The Ku Klux Klan, which had been founded in Tennessee in 1866, extended its reach into Alabama, and soon the Klan's campaign of violence and intimidation against blacks, scalawags, and carpetbaggers spread throughout the state. For the most part, Klan members were Democrats and former Confederate soldiers and officers. Despite the Klan's effective tactics and the howlings of white Democrats, Alabama established a new constitution, elected a new state legislature and congressional delegation, and qualified (under the Fourth Reconstruction Act of 1868) for readmission into the Union. Alabama reentered the United States on June 25, 1869.[22]

Ignoring the fact that it was the war, and not Reconstruction, that brought severe hardships to Alabama and the South, Oates condemned congressional reconstruction as the "dark period" and the cause of every problem in his state and region. In Abbeville, Federal soldiers walked the dusty streets and the Freedmen's Bureau set up shop to assist local blacks and their families. Although Abbeville had escaped the direct ravages of war, the condition of the town during the late 1860s made it appear weary and worn. Public buildings and houses were badly in need of repair, fences were down or missing rails, fields were overgrown from lack of cultivation, roads were rutted and rocky, and schools were closed. Townspeople worked at any job they could find for wages or food, and poor crops in the postwar years left farmers in Henry County hungry and without hope. Efforts to rebuild the town began in 1866, when the county authorized some public works—including the repair of bridges and roads and the founding of a "poor farm"—that employed local laborers and helped to boost the local economy. The Masons, who revived the Abbeville lodge and elected new officers in 1866, were instrumental in getting the town back on its feet. Oates, who had joined the order before the war, was initiated as a Master Mason in June 1866.

As part of the rebuilding in Abbeville, Oates began construction around this time of a simple one-and-a-half-story frame house on West Washington Street, not far from his office, that would become his home for the next decade and a half. Construction was probably completed before 1868. Over the years, rooms and hallways were added onto the house when the demands for space grew greater. For now, Oates seemed to be content living in his new house with Sallie Vandalia, who probably still served as his housekeeper, and with his infant son, Claude.[23]

But Oates soon found himself in somewhat bigger trouble than he had experienced before. In the spring of 1867, and perhaps earlier than that, he became sexually involved with a young fourteen-year-old white girl, Lucy

Hickman. She was probably the cousin of Robert H. Hickman, a farmer who had married Oates's younger sister, Melissa, in 1858. Lucy (called Lou by family and friends) lived with her mother and younger brother in Abbeville. Although Oates and Lucy Hickman were not related by blood, they were distantly related by marriage; dallying with the sister of one's brother-in-law was not incestuous, but it was—at the very least—exploitative and predatory. The girl was less than half his age. By nineteenth-century conventions, she was a member of the family (although not a relative per se), which was how Oates came to know her in an intimate setting. Even in an age in which first cousins married one another (such as twenty-seven-year-old Edgar Allan Poe and his first cousin, thirteen-year-old Virginia Clemm), an illicit sexual relationship between a man twenty years older than his teenage partner was not considered appropriate. One can only imagine what Melissa and Robert Hickman—not to mention the entire community of Abbeville—thought when they learned that spring that Lou was pregnant with Oates's baby. On December 13, 1867, at the age of fifteen, she gave birth to a son named Joshua Cornillus Oates. William Oates now had two illegitimate sons to support.[24]

Surely the community of Abbeville buzzed with gossip as the scandalous and scurrilous tale became known, which surely it did. Oates never hid the fact that he had fathered two sons out of wedlock, and the births of the boys were recorded in the family Bible along with the birth dates of other family members.[25] On the face of it, no one can know how the good citizens of Abbeville reacted to the titillating news or how quickly the gossip spread from one end of the town to the next and spilled over into the countryside of Henry County. Apparently Lou Hickman's mother did not accuse Oates of rape. The lack of any apparent legal complaint against Oates does not mean that he was free of any wrongdoing. To accuse him of rape would have been an unusual occurrence in a small community like Abbeville. For one thing, Lou Hickman was above the age of consent, which, under Alabama law, was ten years old.[26] Even if Oates did rape the girl, and there is no evidence at all to suggest that he did, it is unlikely that legal action would have been taken against him. Most rapes in the nineteenth century went unreported; those that did come to the attention of the authorities were often not prosecuted for lack of evidence. Prosecutions often resulted in questions being raised about the moral fiber of the victim rather than the violent actions of the male perpetrator. Sometimes raped women were regarded as "fallen" rather than as victimized. If the victim was poor, especially in the South, the women's credibility was particularly challenged. Southern judges believed that the testimony of poor women could not be trusted. Moreover, these jurists often found it difficult to determine what constituted force. Poor women were assumed to be promiscuous. In 1860, an Alabama court held that "indecent advance, or importunity, however revolting" was not necessarily an assault made with the intention to rape.[27]

The court system worked against raped women in other ways, despite the assumption of most jurists that rape laws adequately protected women and girls from sexual predators. For many victims, the airing of rape accusations brought humiliation, social disapproval, and ostracism that could last for years. Rape victims did not relish the prospect of having their personal lives unveiled in public or reliving the ordeal of the assault. Many women felt intimidated by the necessity of convincing all-male juries that they had been raped or that intercourse had occurred against their will. Victims of rape who wanted to file criminal charges against their attackers often had to rely on male family members to assist them in taking the case through the courts and standing by them when the community reacted against them. Lou Hickman's mother lived alone as a single parent. The only male in the immediate family was Lucy's younger brother, Edward, age six. Without male providers and protectors, Southern women found it difficult to maintain their households and support their families. Lucy's mother worked as a domestic servant, which probably meant she spent a good deal of time away from home. There were no adult males, other than Robert Hickman, Oates's brother-in-law, to turn to. Under the circumstances, Robert Hickman was not likely to wage an effective legal campaign against his sister's brother, who just happened to be a lawyer and the richest man in Abbeville.[28]

But it cannot be determined if Lou Hickman's sexual intercourse with Oates was consensual or if he forced himself on the girl. No matter the specific circumstances, the liaison between Oates and Lou Hickman was conspicuously peculiar—a rather shocking incident that reveals a huge fissure in Oates's moral character, more so than does his relationship with Sallie Vandalia. His relationship with young Lou raises crucial, but unanswerable, questions about his attitude toward women and his fondness for young women, for this girl would not be the last teenager to attract his sexual attention. How did he approach her? Why did he chose her as a partner, when Sallie Vandalia was at that moment living under his own roof and, presumably, was an available—although not necessarily an entirely willing—sexual partner? What did he see in the very young Lou Hickman, who could not have had much in common with him and his adult world?

The answers to these questions are not known and may be unknowable. But Lou Hickman did succumb to Oates's sexual advances, and it remains quite possible that she did so under duress and not completely of her own free will. That possibility throws a different shadow over Oates and raises new questions about the man, his identity, and his desire for control and power. While it would be inept blindly to accuse Oates of committing intimate violence against the Hickman girl, he must have known that, as the adult, he held the reins, most of the real power, in their relationship and would be the one to guide it wherever he wanted it to go. Power, however, was something

that Oates could not always keep within safe bounds. He had already demonstrated to a considerable degree his own yearning for power, authority, and
control in his private and professional life—particularly for mastery over others or over himself. In obtaining sexual favors from Lou Hickman, he asserted his manly dominance over her, if only to persuade her—willingly or
not—to have intercourse with him. In so doing, he used a manner of either
direct or indirect coercion—coercion, either in the form of guile and seduc-
tion or of physical bullying—to fulfill his sexual desires. He did not have to
hold her down against her will to commit sexual violence against her. Violence and brutality were inherent in the act of a thirty-four-year-old man
taking sexual advantage of a fourteen-year-old girl. For Oates, such sexual
coercion was an expression—a distinctive and explicit extension—of his violent streak, which more often revealed itself in his brawls with adversaries or
in his deadly determination to kill and defeat the Confederacy's enemies in
combat. In this case, his sexual coercion received approbation—or, at the very
least, subtle encouragement—from the mores of his times and from Southern
male attitudes. Oates could express his sense of mastery in his sexual relations
with women (and girls) without much fear of condemnation because nineteenth-
century society, particularly Southern society, accepted and tolerated a modi-
cum of violence and coercion in the male's quest for sexual satisfaction. Any
assertion of sexual dominance over women was mostly perceived as a natural
manifestation of manliness. Prevailing male attitudes toward rape, including
the rape of slaves and former slaves, revealed a pervasive and insidious misogyny. On the surface, Oates enjoyed women, liked their company, relished
their conversation, and prided himself in his ability to make them swoon or
otherwise to conquer them completely. But he greatly feared them, too, which
became specifically demonstrated in his tendency to seek out sexual satisfaction with girls like Lou Hickman rather than with mature women.[29]

Sometimes men show their frailties, their excruciating anxieties, through
action rather than words and in a manner that they themselves cannot perceive or comprehend as revealing of their inner selves. So much of Oates was
locked up inside himself that he believed his private self was safe from view
and well defended against any outside penetration. Yet actions often do speak
louder than words. Oates's sexual behavior after the war, for example, disclosed a matrix of inner fears and doubts that challenged his identity and
threatened his masculinity. Having lost his arm in the summer of 1864, a
wound that meant he would never again return to the battlefield or assume
combat command, he must have wondered if he had lost his manhood as well.
Soldiers who lose a limb in combat often suffer from severe psychological
effects, including phantom pain, stress, depression, loss of control, and grief.
Typically for Oates, he hid his reactions and never admitted to any negative
feelings after losing his arm, except for the discomfort and pain that occurred
during his early recovery. But even that he minimized and barely discussed in

his letters and memoirs. Despite his ability to mask any distress he may have felt, he undoubtedly had to adjust to the loss of his limb beyond the practical aspects of learning how to use his left hand to dress himself, hold eating utensils, and write. Like other amputees, he probably experienced some difficulty adjusting his self-image, his conception of himself, to the new reality of life without his right arm. To his credit, he seems to have developed a new sense of strength and achievement during his recovery and his adjustment. But his sexual behavior, with Sallie Vandalia and Lou Hickman, suggests that he worried about his attractiveness—his body image—to the opposite sex and, even more basically, about his ability to continue performing sexually as he had done before the amputation. Being a single male did not improve his concern. Oates lived in a society that promoted marriage and that assumed adult males would marry. As a single male, Oates's sexual opportunities were presumably limited; more to the point, he could not always know what the response of his partner would be to his missing arm.[30]

War does strange things to people, and the Civil War had changed Oates to such an extent—physically and emotionally—that he could no longer know with certainty who he was and why his life mattered. The war had not made more of a man out of him; it had, by taking away one of his limbs, made him into something less than a whole man, at least physically. It had not instilled fortitude or courage in him, although during the war itself he had displayed those traits amply. In the end, the cost of the war for him had been high—the cause he had so fully and fervently believed in had been lost, the war's brutality had scarred him as it had hundreds of thousands of other veterans, his brother had been left in enemy hands to die, and he had suffered his own combat wounds, six of them in all, finally losing an arm. His brother's death at Gettysburg had left him bereft and, now with the war over, profoundly lonely. He wanted his soul back. But he did not know how to retrieve it.

He carried in his heart a double burden: He had abandoned his younger brother—a brother who had looked up to him and adored him and depended on him for so many things—on the slopes of Little Round Top because he had had no choice. William Oates would live with that formidable burden forever. That was not all. Added to it, down into his inner recesses where burden merged with guilt, he also could not understand why he had survived and John had not. Why had he deserved to live? Why had the war, which had taken so many countless young men in their prime, not taken him instead of John? It almost had. The minie ball that shattered his arm almost killed him. But it had not. He was alive and John was gone, buried in an unknown grave in some faraway field in Pennsylvania, lost, anonymous, forsaken, and it had all been his fault. So he hauled about the twin burdens of failure and guilt and bore them like sackcloth and ashes. They were not always visible, and he tried as much as possible to repress them and to smother their accompanying emotions. Yet they remained in place nonetheless. They would sustain themselves for the rest of his life, for he would never find repentance. No matter how coarse the sackcloth or how hot and sooty the ashes, there was no one to forgive him and he could not forgive himself.

Tied to these burdens and to his physical disfigurement was his need to prove his manhood, to overcome the war's deepest wounds. One path to winning back his soul and experiencing life's vitality, while also reasserting his virility, was to find some means of satisfying himself sexually. In the case of Sallie Vandalia, he had become caught up in—or had actively fostered—an intimate relationship, so much so that she and his illegitimate son now lived with him in the Abbeville house. With Lou Hickman, he probably went looking for a partner with whom he could avoid such binding intimacy and, one assumes, pregnancy. Yet like other men of his time, particularly veterans who had experienced four years of despair and hate and death, Oates encountered a new world in which true intimacy seemed remote and practically unattainable, given what the war had done to personal relationships and to civility; sexuality seemed more than beyond reach, given his broken body and the dictates of Victorian society; and male identity seemed distorted by the deep chasm that existed between the genders, which became even more gaping by the transformation in customary male and female roles wrought by the war.[31] He sought clarity and fulfillment—and a chance to reclaim his masculinity— by conquering women who otherwise might be considered unattainable or whom he felt he could control: a woman of a different race and a girl who had barely entered pubescence. Establishing a sexual relationship with Sallie Vandalia made him feel powerful and masterly as all white men did when they took sexual advantage of slave and freed black women; his erotic involvement with Lou Hickman, on the other hand, made him feel like he was young again, thrusting him back to the days when he roamed the gulf states looking for manly adventure and carefree escapades with women—that time in his life when he was rakish, full of himself, and whole.

Another way of demonstrating his manliness—to himself and to others— was to sire sons, something he succeeded in doing probably beyond his expectation and no doubt to his great surprise in the two years following the end of the Civil War. Surprised or not, he seems not to have been chagrined by the arrival of his illegitimate children. Oates forthrightly and without hesitation acknowledged Claudius and Joshua as his own and, according to family legend, provided for them until they reached adulthood. Yet Oates never could see, and it's doubtful that he ever really tried to perceive, how his sexual involvement with Lou Hickman had altered her life forever, not only by bringing a baby into the world who required care and nurturing, but also by robbing the young girl of her adolescence and propelling her into womanhood. Society did not demand that Oates reach such a reckoning or atone for his actions. Nor did he ever show any inclination toward personally recognizing, by means of his own insight, the injustice he had committed by taking advantage of her or the inherent coercion that he might have brought to bear when he decided—with her consent or not—to have intercourse with her.

Rarely can individuals see with deep discernment that their deeds flow out of something larger than themselves, something beyond their own specific choices and desires, something having to do with their place and time and their social circumstances. Oates, who tended not to be overly introspective or even curious about his hidden motivations, never seemed to ask himself why he found Lou Hickman so sexually appealing. Perhaps she was physically and coquettishly attractive beyond what her years suggest. But Oates, even if he had wondered why he had become involved with a teenager, could not have known that his attraction to young girls was not simply an individual trait or the result of a lustful and solitary indiscretion. A pedophilic dynamic was something that other notable Southern white men of his time manifested in their sexual and marital preferences, and it seems likely that this particular sexual proclivity was linked to gender and racial tensions, made all the more pronounced by the upheaval and displacements of the Civil War.[32] These Southern males, though, were probably few in number, and they were not necessarily sexual monsters out stalking or abducting teenage girls; nor would it be fair, given the different world in which they lived and the distance that separates our time from theirs, to accuse them of pedophilia, as it has come to be defined in our modern era, or even of psychosis. But Oates's sexual peculiarities were distinctive enough and unusual enough to set him apart from most Southern males, especially men in their mid-thirties, the greatest number of whom did not become erotically involved with young teenagers or take them as their wives. Typically Southern men and women married in their twenties to spouses who were approximately their own age.[33] Like other aspects of his character, Oates's sexual preferences set him apart from the accepted standards of how Southern white men—particularly men of his wealth and community standing—should think and behave. In choosing to have sexual relations with a young girl, Oates revealed an erotic idiosyncrasy that would later repeat itself in his choice of a wife: a fondness and a passion for teenage girls.

He also unwittingly revealed his inability to keep his sexual urges, whatever they might be, under control. The struggle for self-mastery, which was so vital to Southern manhood, held that sexual impulses were natural in men, but that unbridled passions and unrestrained erotic compulsions—particularly animalistic lusts and prurient desires—had to be kept in check for men to remain basically good and noble. But Oates found it difficult to live up to the cavalier virtues, not only in his sexual behavior but in many other aspects of his life. The dominant codes of moral virtue (what some Southern whites referred to as "manners") called on males to value reputation and honor above all other things, while also requiring them to attain mastery over one's environment, one's dependants, and one's self. Yet Oates was a flawed man living in a very flawed society. Trapped by his own and his culture's definition of manhood, Oates—and a good number of his male contemporaries who had survived the war—found it nearly impossible to live their lives in strict adherence to the prevailing standards of manhood in the postwar South. Like many other Southern men, Oates felt ill at ease in the new world that the war had forged: a world where the planter elite no longer could be trusted to wield power for the good of all, where old values seemed to have gone down in defeat with each of the Confederate armies, where patriarchal authority was challenged by gender and racial turmoil, where the impersonal marketplace could ruin the unwary and the unwise, where manhood no longer had a stability or comprehensible definition.[34] To a great extent, it was the pull of the market economy throughout the South, and not just Oates's personal shortcomings, that made it virtually impossible for anyone—other than great public models such as Robert E. Lee—to live up to the ideals.[35]

Parvenus like Oates—who stood outside looking in and worked to replace the old planter elite—had a much harder time, and accumulated more failures, trying to live up to the standards of the Old South than patricians did, if only because Oates and his fellow newcomers had to start from scratch without relying on all the advantages of name, money, prestige, and position. Nevertheless, the South after the Civil War was a place that bred confusion, uneasiness, and uncertainty. Oates's competitive individualism and his comfortable ability to challenge authority, including patrician authority, led him away from the cavalier virtues even as he attempted to mimic them. But as a man on the make, as Oates most certainly was in his feverish desire for wealth and sexual satisfaction, he could never become—no matter how hard he tried or how much money he made or how well he could imitate the cavalier code—a true man of manners.

One could even see this unalterable fact in the women he chose as his lovers. There was a kind of odd—yet significant—equality in Oates's promiscuous behavior, for he chose his sexual partners apparently without regard to their skin color. His sexual choices did not, of course, mean that he was an egalitarian; nor, certainly, was he the first white Southerner to show unconcern over the matter of race in his love making. But it was true, nonetheless, that one of his lovers was black, one was white. The children who resulted from those sexual relationships later received—if family stories can be believed—his equal financial support and caring attention: Both sons were provided for, both were given educations, both later became professional men, including Claude, whose status as a mulatto apparently did not impede his professional pursuits. Their mothers, unfortunately, fared less well when it came to Oates's concern for their welfare; from all appearances, Oates cast them aside and acknowledged no responsibility for having dramatically transformed their lives. To him, Sallie Vandalia and Lou Hickman were disposable commodities. And he did not hesitate to wash his hands of them when the opportunity presented itself.

Not surprisingly, sometime after learning about Oates's involvement with Lou Hickman and the birth of Joshua, Sallie Vandalia left him and his household—or he somehow managed to force her out. However, she may have taken about as much from him as she could stand. It would appear that she refused to leave Claude behind. Apparently Oates provided financial support for the child from afar. Later she married a man named Knight, or assumed his name, and moved with him (and Claude) to Texas, where she began a new family and a new life.[36]

Even with Sallie Vandalia's departure, Lou Hickman and her baby did not move into Oates's house. Perhaps he didn't invite her. Perhaps she didn't want to reside there. Either way, she set up housekeeping in Abbeville, where she lived as a single mother, but she seems not to have been gainfully employed. She remained in Abbeville until sometime after 1880, when she moved to Dale County, Alabama. No evidence exists about how involved Oates was in Josh's life. Family stories tell of him sending Josh to school and to college, although the surviving traditions claim that one of Oates's sons attended Vanderbilt University, which the extant university records can neither confirm nor deny. The names of both sons are to be found in the Oates family Bible, where they were carefully inscribed in the senior Oates's own handwriting. If nothing else, Oates never publicly denied that he had sired two illegitimate sons.[37]

Characteristically, Oates turned away from these personal dramas as quickly as he could and focused his professional attention on state and national politics, where he hoped to find the right opportunity to run for office. He became a strong force behind the conservative leadership in the county, primarily white Democrats who opposed the Reconstruction policies imposed by Congress. In 1867, Oates had campaigned for election as Abbeville's delegate to the state constitutional convention, but he came in third. After the convention had completed its work, Oates helped unite Henry County conservatives into a political faction of white Democrats who sought to defeat, in Oates's words, "the constitution recently adopted by the late Convention in Montgomery."

Early in 1868, he was elected president of the Control Conservative Club of Henry County, an organization that—despite its extralegal status—managed to form a tight partnership with the local Board of Registration, which worked to limit black suffrage in the country as much as possible. To Oates, and to many other of his white "conservative" compatriots, the "greatest affliction that has ever befallen the people of the United States . . . has been the presence in their midst of the African race." This belief would govern his personal and political behavior over the next three decades.

But declaring blacks to be an affliction was something Oates could say only by blatantly ignoring his own reality. At home, he had lived with an African American woman, had allowed himself to have sexual relations with her, and had fathered a mulatto son. With Sallie's departure, and with Claude's very apparent light skin, perhaps Oates felt less trepidation about letting his personal life fuse with his political one in such a way that he could openly condemn blacks without remorse. Yet Claude would always be a reminder to him of his own indiscretion, his own weakness, his own acquiescence to carnal desire with a woman whom he otherwise regarded as a member of an inferior race—a race that he believed had caused America nothing but trouble and woe.

One wonders if he was even aware of his own hypocrisy, which seems very unlikely. To have recognized the depths of his hypocrisy, he would have had to admit to some degree of self-hate and self-embarrassment over fathering a child with an African American woman. Oates thought too highly of himself for such recriminations and any dosage of self-doubt. So he became carried away with a personal endorsement of white supremacy and the prevailing Southern politics of race. The threat of black civil rights, black suffrage, and black equality made him view Reconstruction as a time "most cruel and relentless" that threatened racial amalgamation, even though he had played a personal role in helping to mingle the races and bring about the doom of civilization.[38] Not surprisingly, he wanted to see that period ended as soon as possible. But he also knew that even if he hid the reality of Claude's mixed blood from others, he could never remove the reality of Claude's existence from his conscience. In the meantime, he satisfied himself with pursuing victories in local politics and using race to further his own ends. And, as he did so, he continued his own meandering search for his soul.

10

THE ONE-ARMED HERO
OF HENRY COUNTY

U nwilling to assume a posture of defeat in the aftermath of war, William C. Oates took up politics to fight back against what he considered to be the injustices imposed on the South—and particularly on Alabama—by the Radical Republicans in Congress who sought only vengeance against the former Confederate states and their loyal citizens. Although Reconstruction was far less horrendous in its treatment of whites in Alabama than Oates supposed, it provided a cause celebre for his participation in state, and later national, politics. Oates recognized that his own future, and the future of his state, rested in the hands of the Democratic Party.

As in war and law, Oates practiced politics as if he were fighting to the death. Politics for him was, as those who knew him recognized, "the battlefield of peace." Whether on the stump or dealing with the challenges of elected office, he called on the "same courage," his friends said, that had motivated him in war. In fact, it was the survivors of the 15th Alabama—and other Confederate veterans—from Henry County who encouraged him to enter politics, supported his political leadership, and kept him in the public arena. In running for election, he made a great deal of his humble origins, his independence of thought and action, his courage and honesty, his belief in the sanctity of "a white man's government," and his war record for the cause of the Confederacy. On the campaign trail, he became known as "the one-armed hero of Henry County."[1]

With the support of the Conservative Club and local veterans, Oates was elected to represent Henry County at the National Democratic Convention held in New York in July 1868. It was Oates's first successful bid for an elected office, and it was also his first visit to Manhattan. The Democrats held their convention at Tammany Hall on East 14th Street, near Union Square. The Alabama delegation arrived with its votes pledged to Andrew Johnson, despite the president's loss of popularity during his impeachment and acquittal earlier that year, but eventually Oates and his fellow delegates joined the bandwagon for the former governor of New York, Horatio Seymour, a die-hard supporter of states' rights and white supremacy, who was nominated on the twenty-second ballot.[2]

After returning to Alabama, Oates and his white supporters denounced the Republicans and their Reconstruction policies, despite the fact that Alabama already had been accepted back into the Union. It was the military and racial aspects of Reconstruction that Oates and his allies detested, and they worked avidly to convince whites in the South—and throughout the nation— that Republican rule in the White House and in Congress was too harsh and should be curtailed. Throughout southeastern Alabama, he became known as a man who stood for "common sense" and who expressed his political opinions with "combativeness."[3]

In 1870, he was elected to the Alabama General Assembly as a representative and served a two-year term. Throughout the state, the Klan tried to ensure the outcome of the election by terrorizing and even murdering white and black Republicans. Its tactics were largely successful, and Alabamians voted overwhelmingly for a Democratic governor and legislature. Nevertheless, some blacks were elected to the General Assembly, and one African American, James T. Rapier, was nominated for secretary of state. The legislature at this time was composed of whites and blacks, and while Oates still argued against black participation in politics and government, he worked beside his fellow representatives of both colors without incident or complaint. On one occasion, during the 1871 session of the assembly, he watched while a fight broke out between a "leading carpetbagger" from Montgomery and a black employed by the House of Representatives, probably as a steward. "I stood over them myself," said Oates, "and kept anybody from interfering until the Negro gave him a good beating which he deserved, and I never incurred the disapproval of a single one of the Democratic members of the House." When asked how he could do such a thing, Oates said the carpetbagger was in favor of "social equity," and "the Negro was a long ways the better man of the two, and everybody will testify to that, who knew both of them." His response reflected a Jacksonian mentality that he often articulated. Like so many Jacksonian Democrats before him, Oates was not so much against blacks bettering themselves— although he could never quite bring himself to admit that any black could rise above his biological inferiority—as he was against the idea of government engineering laws and programs toward that end. His idea of equality also stemmed from some simple Jacksonian assumptions. For him, equality was something earned, not something granted from on high. It was easy for him to think this way because he didn't yearn for equality in the same way that those who lacked it—including blacks, poor whites, and women of both races—were forced to admire it from afar.[4]

For his entire term, he served as chairman of the House Ways and Means Committee, which gave him valuable experience dealing with public finance at a time when the state was teetering on the brink of economic ruin. But his service as chairman also indicated how quickly he was rising in Democratic state politics, since the chairmanship of the Ways and Means Committee was a plum appointment and provided him with a great deal of political influence by doling out patronage jobs. Feeling particularly pleased with himself and his political accomplishments, he over-reached himself in 1872 and hoped to be nominated as the Democratic candidate for governor. He wasn't. Later that year, he ran in his first race for national office as a candidate for Congress from his home district in southeastern Alabama, but he lost that election to a Republican and blamed his defeat on the decisive black vote against him.[5]

At home, while he mapped out his political future, Oates took on more responsibility as a caretaker. In August 1871, his father died at Oates's Crossroads. He was seventy-four years old. For the last sixteen years of his life, he had become a faithful parishioner of the Missionary Baptist Church, which he helped to build not far from his cabin near the crossroads. For all the abuse that Oates during his youth had suffered at his father's hands, and for all the ways that he molded his adult life so it would not resemble his father's, he recognized nevertheless that his father possessed some good in him as well as bad. About him, Oates wrote in his unpublished autobiography: "He . . . loved his wife and children and was esteemed by his neighbors as an honest man. He lived fairly well for that time and country, but never accumulated much property. He was always a poor man. He could not be said to be a money maker. . . . All he ever made was by honest toil and personal industry."[6]

Rather than have his mother and his youngest brother, James Wyatt Oates, live alone in Pike County, Oates moved them both into his house on Washington Street in Abbeville. About a year later, he kept his promise to his dead brother-in-law, James B. Long, the husband of his sister Mary, and took in the widow and her four children, providing for them out of his own pocket. Years later, Oates wrote of them in his memoirs: "They are the best of people, and the satisfaction of having performed more than the full measure of my promise and their gratitude are ample rewards to me. Such is my religion." A total of eight people lived in his house, and all were dependent on Oates's good will and income. Like a true patriarch, Oates ruled over the dependents who lived in his house and who comprised both his domain and his family. But he did so only for a relatively short period of time. By 1873, he was living in Eufaula, either in a residence of his own or at Roseland, the Toney family plantation.[7]

Whether he lived at Roseland or not, he could be found there fairly regularly. The number of people in the household exceeded even those that he had moved into his house in Abbeville. One frequent visitor to Roseland remembered at least sixteen people sitting down at the dinner table on most evenings. Still, life was not what it had been at the plantation. With the slaves gone, the opulence and grandeur that the Toneys had enjoyed could not be sustained. Some of the former slaves remained on the plantation to work as laborers, but cotton production was down and so were market prices. The war had not ruined Colonel Washington Toney and his family, but plantation life as they had known it was now just a memory.

For Oates, though, Roseland was the perfect getaway. Even as the glitter began to rub off the plantation, he could still feel like he was part of the South's elite, for the Toneys accepted him as one of their own. He took pleasure in the political and legal discussions with Colonel Toney, Allan Bass (the older brother of Mrs. Toney), Sterling Toney (the Toneys' eldest son), and old Judge John Cochran (the husband of the Toneys' eldest daughter, Caroline). But he found particular delight in spending time with young, precocious T, Sallie Toney, the family's youngest and startlingly attractive daughter, who was now eleven years old. As with Lou Hickman, Oates found satisfaction in the company of this young girl who entertained and amused him with her playful banter.

At age ten, T had begun reading Macaulay's *Essays*, writing Gothic short stories and novellas, and composing sentimental poetry about raindrops, streams, and babies. Many of her poems were published in the Eufaula newspapers. Her artistic skills were more limited, but she drew pencil and ink sketches fairly well. She liked to read, and her mother gave her volumes of Mrs. Heman's poems (a collection similar to the volume of poems John A. Oates had carried with him into the battle of Gettysburg) and Tennyson's verse. T acted much older than her age, and Oates discovered he could converse as intelligently with her on a range of intellectual subjects as he could with most adults. In the Toney household, where the daughter Caroline had already married a man more than twice her age, Mrs. Toney's earlier prediction about his marriage to T had become a standing chestnut at Roseland, told often in his presence and within the child's earshot.[8] Suffice it to say that Mrs. Toney, who had set her sights on Oates for her daughter, either knew nothing about Claude and Joshua Oates, or, like so many other Southern white women whose husbands and fathers and sons had sired illegitimate children, denied to herself the existence of Oates's children and his earlier relationships with Sallie Vandalia and Lou Hickman.

One day, in the shadow of the Alabama State Capitol in Montgomery, Oates met Colonel Willis Brewer and his youngest daughter, Miriam, on the street. As Colonel Brewer puffed on his pipe, and he and Oates shared memories of the late war, the little girl became intrigued by Oates's dark eyes and his empty sleeve, which was pinned to his jacket. She asked shyly if she could touch the sleeve, and Oates smiled and said she could, adding that he knew her loyal Confederate background and understood that any sacrifice made for the cause "had a deep spiritual value for her." Brewer silently stood by, still puffing on his pipe, and nodded three times. The girl reverently touched the sleeve and pulled her hand back. She would remember the event for the rest of her days, even though she had grown bored as the two old Confederates continued to talk endlessly about the war and their glory days.[9]

Oates was indeed an impressive figure. He stood two inches over six feet tall, had thick dark hair combed back off his handsome face, and a brawny build that, unfortunately, would leave him barrel-chested and a little too wide around the waist in the years to come. Now in his forties, he wore a full, dark beard and moustache, which gave his youthful-looking face a more mature appearance than the wispy whiskers he had worn throughout most of the war. His dark shining eyes were his most memorable and beguiling feature, especially to young girls like Miriam Brewer and T Toney. There was a hint of daredevil and rapscallion in those eyes, and the black pools, like the sea at night, divulged both the gentleness and the violence that coexisted in the man. Despite his empty sleeve, he looked physically overpowering in build and stature, and when he walked down the street—whether in Montgomery or in Abbeville—people could not avoid noticing him as he strode by with an air of potency and supreme confidence.

It helped that he was a Confederate hero. His war record had become his credential for high status among his contemporaries, and his newly acquired wealth a ticket for social prestige. Moving within the political circle of the Eufaula Regency, and especially among the influential Shorter family— including John Gill Shorter, who had served as the Confederate governor of Alabama from 1861 to 1863—and their closest friends, also gave him an upper hand in his quest for elective office and public recognition. Although the Shorters could claim a true heritage from old Alabama money, much like the Toneys could, Oates would never fully be accepted into the ranks of the Old South's aristocracy. His roots were much too plain, far too humble, and he would always remain just a little too rough around the edges for the elite's finer tastes. And his money was too new to be acknowledged by the blue bloods as real wealth. But Oates had certainly come a long way in a relatively short period of time, and whether he really wanted to be exclusively identified with the South's declining aristocracy is open to doubt. He was too proud of his own success, of all the hard work and the relentless effort that had brought him up in the world, for him to disown his humble origins entirely. Oates was a man on the make, and he was never embarrassed to admit it.

Any sting Oates might have felt because of his exclusion from the old aristocracy was salved by the reputation he enjoyed as a Confederate hero, which meant far more to him than a means by which he might win votes. His experiences in the war—including the personal loss of his brother John— became an integral part of how he defined himself. In his public persona, he was "The One-Armed Hero of Henry County," but deep inside himself he also valued his accomplishments and sacrifices as a soldier. Likewise, the Civil War had forged the society in which he lived, had shaped the world around him, so much so that he became ever conscious of the South's tragic defeat and the Lost Cause. For Oates, the Lost Cause was not simply an ideology that explained how and why the South had failed to win its independence from the North; it was also a mind set, a world view, by which he and other Southerners found a semblance of order in the midst of social turmoil and upheaval.

It was comforting to Oates and other believers in the Lost Cause to think that the South had not truly been defeated, that it had merely been over-whelmed by the North's superior numbers and resources. Such a rationale also enabled Southerners, including Oates, to hope that the cause ultimately had not been entirely lost. He wrote to Edward Porter Alexander, Longstreet's former artillery chief, in August 1868 to say that the South might rise again and triumph, although perhaps in a different form. "It may be clad in new habitments," he wrote, "but the principles . . .will be triumphant in the end." Those "principles," of course, were white supremacy and states' rights. Whereas the South had fought the war to obtain its independence, now South-erners must labor within the Union for the same ends, including what Oates called "constitutional liberty" as it had been handed down by the Founding Fathers to the Civil War generation.[10]

In defending the Confederate cause—including the constitutional right of secession, which many other white Southerners abandoned in the after-math of Appomattox—Oates joined the ranks of other politicians and leaders in the South who, using the rhetoric of the Lost Cause, consistently praised the heroism of Confederate soldiers who had fought for what they had be-lieved in and had done the best they could on the battlefield, given the over-whelming odds against them. In the 1870s, Jubal Early and the other members of the Southern Historical Society in Virginia preached this gospel of the Lost Cause, and Oates took up their banner by writing an article for the society's journal, the *Southern Historical Society Papers*, in which he sought—as Early himself had done—to blame Longstreet for the defeat at Gettysburg. Much of Oates's article, which was published in 1874, actually dealt more with his own eyewitness report of what had taken place during the 15th Alabama's encounter with the 20th Maine on Little Round Top on the afternoon of July 2 than it did with Longstreet's failures leading up to the combat that day. The article became more autobiographical than Oates may have intended, but it did pointedly accuse the First Corps commander of what Oates called "the *want of generalship*."[11]

Oates's article was a minor contribution to the controversy over Longstreet's responsibility for the defeat at Gettysburg and ultimate Union victory in the war. It was more important as a demonstration that Oates could be counted among those Southerners who unquestioningly accepted the tenets of the Lost Cause and who politically supported the rising tide of the Redeemers, the Southern conservative Democrats who were steadily reversing the outcome of the war by winning elections in their states and casting out of power the carpetbaggers, scalawags, and blacks.

The Redeemers gained their greatest advantage by using violence against black and white Republicans. In the 1874 election, white terrorists—either former members of the Ku Klux Klan (which ostensibly had been disbanded in the wake of Federal investigations conducted during the early 1870s) or the White League (which simply carried on the Klan program of violence and intimidation under a different name)—fired into a crowd of African American voters in Eufaula, killing seven or eight and wounding as many as seventy others. Blacks waiting in line to vote fled for their lives, and the whites, who had been assisted by two organized militia companies, threw their hats in the air and gave a victory cheer. Amidst the Rebel Yells, someone cried out: "Let the Yankees come. We are ready for them."[12]

There is no evidence that Oates was a member of either the Klan or the White League, and like other conservatives he may have actually denounced these groups for their antidemocratic ideology, but he made no secret of the fact that he approved of their violent methods to keep blacks, scalawags, and carpetbaggers from defeating Democratic candidates at the polls. As far as Oates was concerned, black voters constituted a "vast mass of ignorance" and could cast ballots only because Congress had usurped the right of the states with "bayonet rule." In his estimation, even education could not supply blacks with "the capacity to govern." Such a capacity, he said, "depends more upon natural gifts, than culture."[13]

Throughout Alabama similar tactics to the ones used in Eufaula—including violence, fraud, and even the destruction of ballot boxes—ensured a Democratic victory in the election of 1874, and with that victory came the end of Reconstruction in the state. In no time, the Democrats proclaimed the redemption of the state and began to abolish Republican policies and laws, although when it came to accepting bribes from railroad concerns, the Democrats proved as adept as their Republican predecessors. This was the beginning of a long political regime controlled exclusively by the Redeemers, conservative Democrats who came to be known pejoratively as "Bourbons," after the House of Bourbon that was restored in France following the defeat of Napoleon.[14]

Riding the crest of the Democratic wave was William C. Oates. Although he did not run for office in the election of 1874, the Democratic victory that year ensured that he would soon reenter the political arena. In 1875, after the Democrats called for a constitutional convention that would solidify the "redemption" of the state, Oates ran for election as a delegate and won handily. The convention met in Montgomery in September, and Oates took his seat in the company of many current political friends and former Confederate comrades from around the state. As a reward for his party loyalty and as a result of his rising political influence, Oates was appointed chairman of the convention's judiciary committee.[15]

The convention met for only a month, adjourning on October 2, 1875, but that was all the time the delegates needed to reverse the strides made by the Republicans since 1868 and to advance agrarian over commercial interests in the state's fundamental law. On the surface, there was nothing in the new constitution that overtly violated Federal statutes or the law of the land. The delegates, for example, carefully ensured that the 15th Amendment, finally ratified in 1870, was included in the new document. But beneath the surface, the men who drafted the state constitution—Oates and his fellow conservative Democrats—knew that violence and intimidation were enough to keep black and Republican votes to a minimum in most elections, no matter what the Federal and Alabama constitutions proclaimed about the suffrage rights of all citizens.

As for Oates's judiciary committee, it recommended the popular election of judges for six-year terms and the election of solicitors by the legislature for three-year terms. The convention actually opposed the popular election of judges, as did Oates himself, but the delegates realized that ratification of the constitution could well hinge on this issue. Oates's committee also restricted the number of judicial circuits in the state and specified in detail how judges and justices could be removed from office, but Oates failed to win approval of his own proposal to abolish chancery courts and assign all cases in equity to the circuit courts. Besides limiting taxes and abolishing the state Board of Education, the constitution provided for segregation of the races in all schools. On November 16, Alabamians ratified the new constitution by almost a three to one vote. Such an overwhelming majority meant that the Democratic Party was firmly holding the reins of power in Alabama, and there was no force that could take those reins away.[16]

After the constitutional convention adjourned, Oates returned to Abbeville and his law practice. Most of his time was taken up with land cases, with his own purchase of lands and plantations, and with his loaning money as mortgages to his neighbors. But he also took on civil and criminal cases of various kinds. One of the most dramatic criminal cases involved his younger brother, James Wyatt Oates (whom the family called Wyatt), who had left home at an early age and who, in a fit of anger at the age of sixteen, had killed a man for insulting his youngest sister, Amanda. Wyatt turned to William for protection and advice, and his older brother sent him off to an uncle's home in South Carolina, where the local authorities could not reach him. If all of this sounded more than familiar to the Oates family, it should have, for Wyatt seemed to be repeating William's own brush with the law and flight from justice at about the same age. Wyatt stayed with his Carolina relatives for a while and then, with William footing the bill, went off to Emory and Henry College in Virginia, where he earned a bachelor's degree.

Returning to Alabama after college, Wyatt looked to William to handle the problem of the capital offense still hanging over his head. William surrendered him to the authorities, got him released on $10,000 bail, and changed the venue to Barbour County, where the Oateses had numerous friends. Unfortunately for William and Wyatt, the father of the murdered man ended up prosecuting the case, so William was forced to reach a "compromise" with him by which the jury was persuaded to submit a verdict of not guilty. "It cost me a considerable sum of money," William Oates later admitted. He also acknowledged that without the bribe, Wyatt would have been convicted, even though the jury seemed to be in sympathy with him. After that, Wyatt read law in William's office, passed the bar, practiced with his older brother for about four or five years, and then moved to California, where he had a prosperous career as an attorney and a judge.[17]

Whether handling clients with his younger brother, who, despite his proficiency in the law, could not suppress William's memories of when he and his other brother, John, had practiced law together or diminish his longing for his lost brother, Oates's law business continued to provide him with a sizable income and with the social prestige that came from having money. He also tackled some significant cases. In 1874, he (along with two other attorneys) filed and won an appeal in the Alabama Supreme Court in a case that involved a family named Raines. A mother and her children as slaves had been promised freedom to live in Alabama or in a free state in the will of their owner, who had died in 1859. Further provisions in the will provided a trust for the care and welfare of the former slaves and money to provide for the children's education. But the executors of the estate failed to provide for the freedom of the slaves or for their transportation to a free state. Their freedom came, instead, when the war resulted in the end of slavery. When the executors disposed of the estate, they divided its remaining assets—$25,000 in cash—among themselves, ignoring the bequest made to the Raines family. Oates and his partners in the case took up the cause of the Raines family and argued that the actions of the executors were illegal under Alabama law. The Barbour

County Chancery Court found in favor of the executors, but Oates and his partners appealed the case to the state Supreme Court. Justice Benjamin Franklin Saffold ruled for the court that the executors had improperly mixed whatever allotments were due them for their services in settling the will with funds from the trust, and he reversed the decision of the chancery court and remanded the case for a new adjudication. Oates and his colleagues had won a victory for the Raines family, although it is unlikely that the mother and her children ever saw any of the money that had been promised them.[18]

Several of his cases in the mid-1870s involved the complicated issue of debts paid off in Confederate currency—another of the many legacies of the Civil War that kept the war fresh in everyone's mind and memory. In *McElvain v. Mudd*, decided by the Alabama Supreme Court in 1870, Chief Justice E. Wolsey Peck held that a contract for the sale of slaves created in 1864 was not adversely affected by the Emancipation Proclamation, since no Union soldiers had conquered the state militarily by that time. Then Peck went a step farther and looked to the earlier precedent set by *Roach, Administrator, v. Gunter et al.*—an appeal that Oates had argued before the court and had won for his client—and reaffirmed the court's position that an 1867 ordinance invalidating contracts relying on Confederate money was unconstitutional because it "impaired the obligation of contracts." In another appeal involving Confederate currency, Oates attempted to repeat his earlier success in *Roach*, but in this case the court balked when he tried to show that his client had accepted Confederate money reluctantly in payment for the sale of land. Unfortunately for Oates, the court refused to accept the appellant's testimony and could find no error upon which to reverse the lower court's ruling. Other cases involved Confederate currency more tangentially, but the issue of debt payment in Confederate notes and bonds came up repeatedly in contract litigation throughout the South and, more particularly, in Oates's law practice.[19]

But the case that Oates regarded as his most important of the 1870s was the only one that he ever argued before the U.S. Supreme Court. The case had other significance for Oates, too, since he served as both appellant and appellant's attorney before the bar. Unsure of himself in handling the case on his own, he turned to W. Hallett Phillips, an experienced and well-connected Washington attorney, for assistance. The Supreme Court heard and decided the case in December 1879. For Oates, a great deal rested on the outcome of the appeal, including a huge financial obligation if the court did not reverse the judgment of the federal Circuit Court of the United States for the Middle District of Alabama. But more than money was at stake. Oates hoped to reveal his prowess as a lawyer in arguing his first case before the U.S. Supreme Court. His hopes, however, were dashed. In *Oates v. National Bank*, William Oates the attorney enjoyed both his highest achievement and his lowest defeat.

The facts in the case began in July 1873, when Oates signed a promissory note for $5,200 made payable to B. H. Micow, president of the Tallassee

Manufacturing Company of Montgomery. By the terms of the note, Oates promised to pay Micow (or, perhaps, the Tallassee Manufacturing Company, it was never quite clear which) the full amount on December 1, 1873. In return, Oates received at the time of the note's execution fifty shares of the capital stock in the company in the form of a stock certificate for that amount. He also received an option from the company that when the note matured on December 1, he could either pay the amount owed or surrender the stock certificate and have the note duly cancelled. He claimed to have been induced to buy the stock upon statement made by a company special agent who vouched for the company's stable financial condition. What Oates did not know at the time was that the agent was lying. The Tallassee Manufacturing Company was in dire financial straights.

In November 1873, Micow applied to the First National Bank of Montgomery (where Oates served on the board of directors) for an extension of time to pay off Tallassee company loans amounting to $40,000, all of which were about to mature that month or soon thereafter. The bank had previously extended the company's indebtedness several times at usurious rates of interest, and the company had duly paid off these extensions in advance of their due dates. The bank signified its willingness to give extensions once again for 30, 60, 90, and 120 days, but this time the bank insisted that the company offer collateral security besides paying off the interest on the loans—at a rate of 1¼ percent of the principle per month—in advance. Micow and the company agreed to these terms, and the bank granted the necessary extensions. Among the collateral security turned over by the company to the bank was the promissory note from Oates.

Later testimony failed to corroborate whether or not Oates informed the bank's officers about his special option. Micow maintained that the note was in return for the outright purchase of stock. When the bank accepted the company's collateral security, its officers apparently knew of no defect in the note or any possible circumstances that would result in Oates's failure to pay the note in cash upon its expiration. At the very least, the bank was not aware of the separate written obligation between Oates and the manufacturing company about the possible return of the stock certificate as an option in the transaction.

On November 24, the bank sent Oates written notice that it held his note as collateral security for the indebtedness of the Tallassee Manufacturing Company. A few days later he gave the bank a copy of his agreement with Micow and informed the bank's officers that he had, by the same mail, returned his stock certificate to the company, which would result in the cancellation of his note. Replying to this notification from Oates, the bank stated that it had purchased in good faith the note as negotiable paper for a valuable consideration, without any notice of a private understanding between Oates and the company, its officers or agents. As a result, the bank took Oates to court to receive payment from him for the promissory note of $5,200. The case was heard by the Circuit Court of the United States for the Middle District of Alabama, since the litigation involved a bank chartered under the National Banking Act of 1864. After weighing the evidence, the court found Oates's arguments inadmissible and ordered him to pay the amount of the note to the First National Bank of Montgomery. Oates appealed the decision to the U.S. Supreme Court, apparently on the grounds that the lower court had upheld a denial of a right arising out of the U.S. Constitution or federal law. On that basis, the Supreme Court agreed to consider the case.

Together Phillips and Oates presented his argument, although it is likely that Phillips took the lead in making any oral arguments before the bench. They contended that by the terms of the contract under which Oates had purchased the stock and given his promissory note—terms that proved to be false and fraudulent by virtue of the assurances that the company's agent had given Oates about the manufacturing interest's financial health—he was entitled, as of absolute right, to surrender the certificate of stock to the bank and have his note returned or cancelled. In Oates's estimation, Alabama laws in force at the time when he executed the promissory note gave authority to his construction of his entitlement. But Associate Justice John Marshall Harlan, who wrote the opinion for the court, disagreed. Harlan pointed out that the section of the Alabama Revised Code on which Oates had based his argument had been repealed in April 1873 by statute.

This did not take Oates by surprise. He was aware of this change in the statute, and the repeal of the section in question, but he attempted anyway to persuade the court that despite the explicit wording of the new law, by which "bills and notes payable in money at a certain place of payment, therein designated" were negotiable instruments to be governed by the commercial law, such bills and notes were still nonetheless "subject to all payments, set-offs, and discounts had or possessed against the same, previous to notice of the assignment or transfer." Harlan took issue with Oates's construction. "We concur," he declared, "with the court below in holding that construction to be wholly inadmissible." Upon this precise point, said Harlan, there had been no direct adjudication by the Alabama Supreme Court, to which the real responsibility belonged for giving an authoritative interpretation of this law and the other statutes of that state.

It was the 1873 revision of the earlier state law that gave Oates no legal footing in Harlan's estimation. Given the fact that the bank had accepted the note without knowing that it had any additional stipulations to it, the court could not fault the bank for any error. As Harlan observed, the bank officers "rightfully supposed, as the face of the note imported, that he [Oates] had undertaken absolutely to pay the amount specified at the time and place designated." As a result, the bank officers justly assumed that there was no circumstance attending the sale of the stock that could lessen the obligation of

Oates to pay the note "according to its tenor and effect." The Supreme Court ruled that it was of the opinion "that no error of law was committed by the court below."[20]

For Oates, this defeat meant more than the fact he now had to pay the First National Bank of Montgomery a sizable sum for stock in a company that had since gone out of business. It was also a deep personal defeat, not unlike his day at Gettysburg. Priding himself on his knowledge of Alabama law, he had been humbled by the decision of the U.S. Supreme Court against him— a decision that informed him that he had misread and misunderstood a key state statute and its provisions. Oates always preferred victory over defeat. He never liked being told he was wrong. But Justice Harlan, in language that stung despite its neutral tone, reminded Oates that victory could be as elusive in the courtroom as it had been on the battlefield.

Oates did not rest very often from his labors, but when he did he usually wound up at Roseland with the Toney family. Colonel Washington Toney had died in June 1875, leaving his wife Sarah to carry on alone at the plantation. Since the war, cash had been in short supply at Roseland, and now with the colonel dead, and most of the black laborers gone, the place fell on even harder times than it had endured during Reconstruction. Although the available records only hint at the possibility, it would appear that Oates helped the family through its financial woes by either giving the widowed Sarah Toney cash to live on or loaning her money at terms far more agreeable than he offered to others. At the plantation, he spent most of his time with little T, Sallie Toney, who was now a young teenager and an industrious author of poems, short stories, and novellas. Her head was filled with romantic dreams of Scotland, brave cavaliers, damsels in distress, and a plantation South that no longer really existed—if ever it had existed at all except in the fantasies of little girls, aging matrons, and men who had come to believe in the myth of the Lost Cause, as Oates had done.[21] In 1876, at the age of fourteen, she composed the following poem to her living hero, Colonel Oates:

> May the sunlight of happiness ever attend
> With its genial rays the life of my Friend
> May bright smiling pleasure, his pathway bestrew
> With flowers of fairest and loveliest hue:
> May no cloud of sorrow e'er darken his sky,
> Or cause him to breathe e'er one troubled sigh.

Between the folded sheet of paper on which she had written the poem, she inserted some pressed wildflowers picked for her "Friend" in the fields of Roseland.[22] With all her innocence, intelligence, and romantic way with words,

T was unlike most of the girls Oates had known in his life, but it was her youth that he probably found most appealing. This young women, though, was obviously far more accomplished in her education and her manners—and far more clever in her conversation—than Sallie Vandalia or Lou Hickman. Her eyes, dark and luminous, sparkled like moonlight on the Chattahoochee and hid the deep mysteries of her curious mind. Most days Oates spent his time in his law office or in the court room, dealing with quarrelsome people and gnarly legal cases; but in his visits to Roseland, during the time he spent with T, he lost himself in her youth and charm. If he lusted for her, he seems to have succeeded in hiding his passion. If he and T shared more than a platonic and budding romantic relationship, they kept those attachments private and to themselves. In her girlish way, T had fallen in love with Oates. He, in turn, was completely infatuated with her. She was thirteen; he was forty-two.

For all his happiness at Roseland and with the time he spent with T, for all his success as a lawyer and as a rising capitalist, Oates still was plagued by his memories of the war and by the absence of his younger brother, John. Nothing could make him forget the war and the tragic fate of his brother at Gettysburg. The emptiness he felt was sometimes unbearable. In later life, he admitted that after the summer of 1863, he was haunted each year by two anniversaries and the memories they brought to mind: December 24, his brother's birthday, and July 2, one of the worst days of the Civil War and the worst day of his life.[23]

He did find one outlet for his profound sadness and for his haunting memories. By the mid-1870s, he had also become interested in veteran affairs and with practically anything having to do with the war and its remembrance. He followed with particular interest the efforts in Gettysburg, led by the Gettysburg Battlefield Memorial Association and its historian, John B. Bachelder, to preserve portions of the field for posterity and to demark the lines of battle and the positions of troops over the ground. Since 1869, Bachelder, a portly man with a noble face framed by great mutton-chop whiskers, had organized reunions of Union and Confederate veterans at Gettysburg for the purpose of collecting information about the battle from them and walking the field so they could point out where the most crucial events had taken place. Oates longed to attend these reunions, although he was unable to find the time to make the trip to Gettysburg while he immersed himself in his law practice and politics in Alabama.[24]

In March 1876, he wrote the first of several long letters to Bachelder in which he described—in detail similar to the narrative he had published two years earlier in the *Southern Historical Society Papers*—his experiences in command of the 15th Alabama in July 1863. Answering a query from Bachelder for information about the battle, Oates said that he was happy to comply, seeing as Bachelder seemed "anxious to do both sides justice." At the end of the letter, he told Bachelder that he regarded Gettysburg as "the great battle, the turning point of the war." About a year later, Oates attended a reunion of the 15th Alabama held in Barbour County, the first of many regimental reunions that took place after the war. In 1879, he helped organize another gathering of the 15th Alabama's survivors held in Blue Springs.[25]

Encouraged by supporters in Henry and Barbour counties, Oates ran for his party's nomination in a bid for a congressional seat from Alabama's Third District in 1876 and 1878, but he withdrew from the race both times when he learned that the incumbent intended to seek reelection. After these unsuccessful attempts to win an elective office, he took a long journey in June 1879 through the state of Texas, where he purchased sizeable land parcels in eight different counties in the Panhandle, including several different tracts in Plainview, Hale County, about eighty-five miles south of Amarillo.[26]

Back in Alabama, he continued to forge a vast political network of friends, relatives, and soldiers who had formerly served under him during the war.[27] He finally got his golden opportunity for political advancement in 1880, when the boundaries of Alabama's Third Congressional District were redrawn and Oates could win a Democratic nomination, which he did easily, without having to challenge an incumbent Democrat.[28] Yet his election in November required considerably more effort and entailed far more worry than he would have liked, even after the votes had been counted.

In the presidential race, Republican James A. Garfield, a former Union general, defeated Democrat Winfield Scott Hancock, another former Union general and a hero of Gettysburg, by winning key states in the North and West. But in Alabama, where the Democratic Party was as solid as iron (even in casting its electoral votes for the man who had turned back Pickett's Charge), Oates won his race for the Third District seat by a wide margin over his Republican opponent, Algernon A. Mabson. Realistically speaking, the margin may have been a little too wide, for Mabson immediately filed a formal protest challenging the election results and accusing the Democrats of fraud at the polls.

For the rest of his political career, Oates would claim that he never won an election as a result of fraud or deceit, although the truth of the matter was that he knew full well that his supporters used underhanded means to win him votes and get him elected. Tacitly he condoned corrupt tactics at the polls even while he condemned them in his public statements. More often than not, Oates's election victories were always the result of one kind of underhanded tactic or another. Like many politicians, then and now, he came to believe that the crimes and lies that got him into office were done for the good of the people, for the good of the state, for the good of his region, and for the good of the country. When his opponents tried to use similar fraudulent tactics at the polls, Oates bellowed out his protests with righteous indignation. But when Democrats rigged an election, as they so often did in his behalf, he claimed to know nothing of what had been done to falsify returns or to bribe election officials. In politics as in war, Oates strongly held that the ends justified the means, and he was willing to do whatever it might take to win the final victory.

To win his seat in Congress, Oates personally took up the case of answering Mabson's charges and of proving that no fraud had occurred in the 1880 race. It required some rather fancy footwork to do so. Almost immediately after the election, Mabson filed suit in the United States Circuit Court, accusing the Democrats of having fraudulently appointed election precinct inspectors throughout the state who miscounted votes in Oates's favor (occasionally exceeding the number of registered voters in the precinct), threatened voters with violence or criminal prosecution if they did not vote for Oates, failed to open some polls on time or others not at all, discarded and rejected ballots that would have favored Mabson, and estimated votes for some precincts instead of tallying actual returns. Oates denied these charges in full. Ultimately, Oates turned the tables on Mabson by producing a witness who claimed that Mabson had planned all along to challenge the election because there was money in it for him—thus accusing Mabson of taking a bribe in return for challenging the election. For that reason alone, the witness claimed, Mabson had filed suit against Oates. On the basis of this testimony, despite its hearsay nature, the judge dismissed the suit, and Oates held on to his congressional seat. It is impossible to tell who was outcheating whom in this contested election, and it is quite possible that it was Oates's witness who took the bribe, not Mabson.[29]

During the year between his election and the convening of the 47th Congress in Washington, Oates spent his time fighting the legal battle against Mabson, attending to his own law practice, keeping up his correspondence with political friends and contacts, and passing more and more of his leisure hours in the company of Sallie Toney. Despite her youth, he found her to be surprisingly mature. He enjoyed talking to her about their shared intellectual interests, and he often gave her books to read, including a two-volume edition of the writings of Sir Francis Bacon. Around the same time, he decided to begin a writing project of his own—a history of the 15th Alabama regiment with as complete a roster of its members as he could reconstruct. Oates's history, which also served as his personal memoir of the war, was a huge project, one that would take him nearly the rest of his life to complete.[30]

Like other veterans, Oates probably waited until the 1880s to begin his history of the war, if only to allow the trauma to fade just a little, and let the past become a bit more misty and rosy. For Oates, the emotional wounds of the war would never completely heal, for he could never erase the anguish of having left his brother to die at Gettysburg, but with time even that agony could be subsumed under other memories of comradery, bravery, and glory. In the decade of the 1880s, a floodtide of publications came forth—including the first volumes of the massive series compiled by the U.S. War Department, *The War of the Rebellion: A Compilation of the Official Records of the Union and Confederate Armies*, which came to be commonly known as simply the *Official Records*, and the eyewitness accounts of combat published by the Century Magazine Company as *Battles and Leaders of the Civil War*. The decade also saw the publication in book form of individual memoirs and battle accounts written by former soldiers, Northern and Southern, famous and otherwise. Increasingly, participation in the war became a badge of merit and a mark of valor. Oates began his project to tell his war story just as other veterans began to learn that they could enhance their reputations, increase their chances in politics, and gain status in their communities by letting the public know that they had seen the war and had survived to tell the tale.[31]

Although his future as a congressman lay ahead of him, it was the past that seemed to lay claim to his head and heart. For Oates, the war especially remained a component of his present, a defining force in his life. It was something more than just old and torn memories of the battles he had fought, the regiment he had marched with, and the men who had lived and died beside him. It went beyond memories. The war so firmly held him in its grasp that it would shape his political thoughts and actions for the rest of his life. His course was being determined by the roads that lay behind, not by the ones that lay ahead and wound their way north to the pontifical marble metropolis of Washington, D.C.

In Abbeville, he said goodbye to the bulging household of relatives he had taken under his wing. Oates would never make the Abbeville house his permanent residence again, although he continued financially to support his kin who remained there. He also left behind Lou Hickman, the mother of his son Josh; he never mentioned either of them in his letters or papers. Nevertheless, he would soon help his two illegitimate sons acquire a formal education. In 1883, he sent Claude Oates to the University of Alabama, where the boy apparently finished his undergraduate degree and possibly took a law degree from the same institution. Josh may have attended the Medical College of Alabama in Mobile, for in 1900 he was a practicing physician in Dale County. Student records for both institutions say little about the Oates sons, but family tradition suggests that both did well at school and entered professional life because of their father's assistance. How Claude, of mixed race, managed to matriculate at the University of Alabama is a puzzle, but he must have been light-skinned enough to pass for white. Having provided for his sons financially and seen to their needs by doing what he must have regarded as the right thing, Oates paid them scant attention as the years went on. Once he had done his duty as a father, he let them slip out of his life, probably much relieved that he no longer had to take responsibility for them or show concern for their well being.[32]

Politics began to consume his life. In the nation's capital, he lived for extended periods of time on Pennsylvania Avenue at the Metropolitan or National hotels, both of which he enjoyed about the same. He probably took few of his own possessions to Washington and, while there, lived a spartan life. His living arrangements were like those of other senators and representatives, especially bachelors, who tried to maintain as small a household as possible, given the high expense of residing in the District of Columbia. Staying in the Metropolitan and the National also enabled him to be close to colleagues who had also taken rooms there and to conduct politics in the smoke-filled rooms of these hotels and others—including the famous Willard—where the real work of Congress was conducted.

The first session of the Forty-Seventh Congress convened on Monday, December 5, 1881. His first few months as a freshman congressman must have been exhilarating, for Washington pulsated with the drama of politics in a way that Montgomery never did. Although Garfield's assassination the previous July had stunned and saddened the nation, the House of Representatives seemed unaffected by the succession of Chester A. Arthur to the presidency and plunged ahead with its usual amount of chaos on the floor and disorder in its committee rooms.[33] Being a congressman, Oates learned, resembled nothing he had ever done before, except perhaps in the atmosphere of confusion that prevailed around him during speeches and debates on the House floor, when the deep discordance of the members' voices sounded not unlike the growls and groans of men under fire on a battlefield.

He introduced his first bill—proposing a reduction in the length of time one could reside on lands before claiming them under the Homestead Act—onto the floor only a week into his first term. Samuel J. Randall of Pennsylvania, the Speaker of the House, appointed him to the Committee on Claims. He put forward more bills, made reports on bills considered in the Committee on Claims, and, on February 14, 1882, found the courage to utter his first halting sentences to the assembled House.[34]

On March 7, he requested a twenty day leave from the House "on account of important business." The business was important, indeed. Pink and yellow primroses covered the broad fields around the plantation house at Roseland when, on March 28, he and T were married in a lavish wedding ceremony that spared no expense. He was forty-eight years old; she was nineteen. He had won his child bride. The Reverend De Bernie Waddell—who had served as a captain in Company G of the 15th Alabama, had found God in the winter of 1863-1864, and had later been ordained an Episcopalian minister—officiated at the ceremony. A local newspaper bubbled over with enthusiasm for the match between Oates and the fair maiden of Roseland. Of Oates, the paper declared: "In war as in peace we have watched his plume and always found it in the road to victory. . . . By the dint of intellect and character he has risen to the civil distinction through both houses of the Alabama legislature. He was narrowly defeated for Governor, and now occupies a seat in Congress as the choice of this Congressional district."

The writer's praise for T was even more effusive: "The charming bride is the pride of this community. Her literary accomplishments have ripened into gems of poetry and won for her a wide circle of admirers. . . . Her gifts as a scholar are not, however, her chief attractions. Beauty, grace and loveliness are so bewitchingly blended in her person and character that one hesitates which to admire the most." To both bride and groom, the newspaper offered its hope that "blessings [would] strew their path through life."[35] After the wedding, Oates and T spent a short honeymoon in New York City. During the first week of April (Oates had requested and received a ten-day extension of his leave), they returned together to Washington and began their new life in the hotel rooms that had served as Oates's bachelor quarters. The nation's capital would be their home for the next thirteen years.[36]

It is not evident whether Oates told T about his sons, Claude and Josh, whom he had removed from his life. He might have confessed their existence to her, for it would have been difficult to keep this secret for the rest of their lives together, but, if so, T maintained a wall of silence about it, which Southern women did repeatedly when confronted with their husbands' sexual indiscretions, particularly when they involved black partners. Even if they did not discuss Oates's past and his illegitimate children openly, T must have become aware of something lingering in the shadows of her husband's background. No doubt she was raised as other Southern women were. One simply did not speak about the unpleasantries that took place between white men and black women. In this way, T found a way to live her life in the moment, unencumbered by the complexities of the past.

Yet there was something peculiar—something strained and incongruous— about the relationship between Oates and T that may have sprung from her trying to convince herself that her husband's children had "drop[ped] from the clouds," as Mary Chesnut, the famous Southern diarist, put it so strikingly about the South's mulatto children in general. Or it might have derived as well from their huge age difference, which, even given the times, when the marriage of a younger woman to an older man did not seem unusual or improper, could not have escaped notice. It is doubtful that anyone made a comparison between T and Lou Hickman; if they did, they kept their thoughts a secret. While some young brides might marry a man ten or even twenty years older than themselves, it was not a commonplace to find teenage brides becoming wed to grooms two-and-a-half times their own age. Marrying someone nearly three decades older was something quite out of the ordinary. All things considered, the marriage of Oates and his very young bride is rather mystifying, unless one takes into account his earlier relationship with Lou Hickman. Oates, quite frankly, wanted his women to be adoring and young.[37]

There is no doubt that T was in love with Oates. Her feelings for him developed as her own sense of identity, her own definition of self, came into being. Oates may have been the only man, other than her father and other relatives, to have paid much attention to her. He may also have been the only man—*including* her father—to take her emotions and individual talents seriously. No doubt her own understanding of her emotions was influenced by her romantic fantasies, which found graceful expression in her stylized poems of nature and sentiment and in her novelettes of love and chivalry that purposely mimicked the Waverly novels by Sir Walter Scott. When she married Oates, she was a young woman who still held onto the girlish dreams of ladies and knights, damsels and their courageous defenders, true love and eternal happiness. At nineteen, she was profoundly unfinished as a person. Prevailing ideas about the separate spheres of men and women shaped her understanding, her hopes, her anticipation of what marriage would be like and how a companionate relationship would grow out of her relationship with her husband. Nevertheless, her expectations also would have been governed by her own Southern comprehension of the patriarchal nature of marriage, her husband's domain over their life together, and her sense of duty as a wife who must be loving and obeying—lessons she would have learned firsthand by observing the relationship between her father and mother.

T would soon be caught, as many Victorian women ultimately were, between the contradictions of her romantic love for Oates and the prescribed gender roles, mandated by society, that husbands and wives felt compelled to perform. Even while married Victorian couples often succeeded in blurring their separate spheres, T and Oates found themselves trapped in the realm of an antiquated patriarchy that survived in the South, despite the defeat of the Confederacy, the obliteration of the Old South, and the steady decline of the old planter elite. During the last quarter of the nineteenth century, middle-class white women in the South turned increasingly to the ideal of domesticity in an effort to reassert their racial and class identities; in some respects, this Southern cult of domesticity, which stressed women's role as guardians of morality and benevolence in the household, resembled the paragon of "true womanhood" that pervaded middle-class life throughout the antebellum decades. T learned the proper lessons in domesticity and the boundaries of her definition of womanhood from her mother, sisters, aunts, cousins, and nieces—a large network of female relations who knew how a Southern lady should always behave.[38]

Raised as a Southern belle, who mostly escaped the deleterious effects of the war in southeastern Alabama, T probably saw in Oates many of the same qualities she identified in her father, who had died when she was thirteen.

When she married Oates, her husband was only a year younger than the age of her father at the time of his death. She would have easily been attracted to Oates's maturity, paternalistic demeanor, his success in politics, his heroism during the war, and his confident manliness. Her options may also have been severely limited. Eligible men of her own age may have been in relatively short supply in the vicinity of Eufaula. More to the point, any potential suitor in his twenties would have lacked Oates's war record, his success as an attorney and politician, his standing in the wiregrass region and in the state, and his financial portfolio. She must have known that Oates, at the very least, would devote himself to taking care of her. She may have also had the fate of Roseland and her widowed mother in mind when she weighed Oates's attributes, including his future potential as a provider, and the shortcomings of his age.

Yet even as she deftly assumed a submissive role in their marriage, willingly taking on the burden of moral virtue in the household and carrying the mantle of purity that had been so long bestowed by Southern white men on their women, she also began to assert herself and to challenge Oates's authority, reflecting in part the rise of "the new woman" among the elite whites in the region. Although she must have been active in women's organizations, as any good wife of a politician must be, including, one assumes, the United Daughters of the Confederacy or the Women's Christian Temperance Union and other civic leagues and voluntary associations, there is no specific record of her having joined any groups devoted to women's suffrage or other political and social reforms in the South. Yet her assertiveness, her reaching for a greater amount of freedom in her marriage and individual autonomy for herself, reveals how much she shared in her generation's growing sense of independence and its desire to throw off some of the shackles of female dependency on husbands. She was forced to struggle against Oates's patriarchal dominance, which he wielded relentlessly, and the continuing values of a society that honored male authority, even as it underwent transitions in gender roles and family relations. As an unwitting proponent of what some scholars have called "the new domesticity" that swept through the South in the postwar decades, she held onto old values while also trying to achieve a mastery over her self and her identity. Often she voluntarily occupied the pedestal where Oates and other Southern white men thought their women belonged.

T, however, was not entirely a new Southern woman—not a radical or an activist or a feminist. She never challenged the prevailing racial assumptions of her time; in that regard, she and her husband held much the same ground, although he actually tended to be less doctrinaire in his views toward blacks. Her acceptance of Oates's overall authority over household and family indirectly served the greater purpose of reinforcing the white male patriarchy while relegating blacks to the political and social margins. But like other new women of her age, T possessed an outstanding education (although she seems to have been schooled on her father's plantation rather than at a girls' academy) and a sharp intellect. In these traits, she even outshone her husband, whose learning was always limited to more practical concerns (despite his fondness for Shakespeare).[39]

Her feelings for Oates were returned, though not precisely in kind. Surely he loved her, as he often told her and reassured her; he may have even loved her more than he did any other person in his life. But for him "love" and the burdens of marriage took on an entirely different meaning than they did for her. Like other Victorian husbands, Oates expected his marriage—and his wife—to be quiet, calm, and stable. His own identity, the source of his manhood, was constructed on the foundation of his memories of heroic and significant accomplishments—those achievements that comprised the core of his unpublished autobiography and his memoir of his military service—and of his lucrative work as an attorney and a politician. He never thought of defining himself in terms of his emotions for another person, including his wife. His outward activities, not his inner consciousness, defined who he was. Within the culture of his times, he understood and accepted his role as a provider, for himself, for T, for his children, and for relatives to whom he felt a special obligation. Like other men, Oates believed that he was fulfilling his ambition by working hard to provide not only for himself, but for the ones he loved. In so doing, he separated himself from the domesticity of family and from the household as much as he possibly could, as if he stood on a mountain top and rained blessings down on his dependents in the valley below.[40]

Like other Southern husbands of his time, Oates managed to perpetuate an old-fashioned hierarchical relationship with T that was, to a great degree, an anachronism, even in the powerfully patriarchal South of the postwar era. Their age difference enabled him to do so, for he gained authority not only by virtue of his maleness, but also by the might of his maturity, seniority, breadwinning, and vast experience in the ways of the world. Even in marriage, Oates treated T as a child, perhaps because she had been a child for most of the years he had known her. From the start, and more so than in most marriages of the period, Oates tightly held the reins of power in his relationship with T and disliked ever having to loosen his grip. The difference between their ages also accentuated their clashing natures. Theirs was truly a union of opposites: T was submissive, intellectual, emotional, and fragile; Oates was aggressive, pragmatic, reserved, and strong. He turned to her to make him whole, and in many respects she succeeded. She looked to him for support and comfort, and while he gave her those things readily, they did come with a price. In Oates's search for control and power in his marital relationship, he was almost always victorious.[41]

What came into conflict repeatedly was T's working ideas of companionate marriage and Oates's sustaining belief in a hierarchical relationship. The ideal of a companionate marriage rested on the foundation of a bond of intimacy between husband and wife. Although their roles might be very un-equal, with the husband continuing to assume the duties of head of the house-hold and to make most of the important decisions, the husband and wife in a companionate marriage came together in a true union of two persons, two kindred spirits, two souls into one. Oates had great difficulty expressing af-fection and feeling intimate. He could never fully open up to T. He kept his business matters private and the secrets of his heart to himself. No love let-ters from him to T survive; only a scarce number of letters, from a later time in their marriage, remain from her to him. But even without direct evidence, it seems unlikely that he ever wrote her any letters that departed from his usual businesslike manner of addressing her. His lack of candor with her re-flected his inability—and possibly his lack of desire—to achieve intimacy with her. During twenty-eight years as her husband, Oates never reached a point of mutual identification with T—that point in a romance or a relationship when one realizes that wholeness comes from one's love for another. Oates often retreated from the marriage into silence; T suffered a great deal from loneliness.[42]

And yet the two remained married for a very long time. Obviously each of them received some higher reward, some positive benefit, out of their union. Maybe Oates married T hoping to reclaim his lost youth, as many older men try to do in pursuing May-December romances and as he had probably at-tempted to do in his relationship with the young Lucy Hickman. Maybe T hoped that Oates would replace her lost father. Or perhaps it was enough that their relationship validated their individual expectations: Oates played the role of a successful provider, T excelled in her part as an acquiescent Southern belle and a hostess par excellence. No one (including the Washing-ton gossips) ever expressed any doubt that they were the perfect couple. The fact that T accompanied Oates to Washington, and was not exiled to Mont-gomery while Congress was in session, speaks to the fact that they enjoyed a genuine companionship. For Oates and T, their marriage was not dismal or loveless. Together they found a happiness that was private and not always visible on the surface. Somewhere deep inside themselves, they could define what love meant for each of them and they could not, in the end, conceive of their lives without the other one being there for better or for worse. But this affection still could not make the rough spots in the marriage completely go away. Ahead of them lay some troubles that would drive a wedge between them, no matter how much they really wanted to love one another.

It was a cold spring in Washington. While Oates learned the ins and outs of the House of Representatives, he doggedly stood with other Southern Demo-crats in fighting to reduce the tariff, the Federal customs tax that had been a controversial political issue ever since the early days of the republic and that, before the war, had kept the North and South at loggerheads. After the War of 1812, the North favored a high protective tariff to aid American manufacturers; the South supported a low tariff to keep prices down on the commodities it purchased from abroad and to reduce the chance of foreign countries imposing retaliatory tariffs on American exports, like cotton. The Civil War did not resolve the tariff issue. Steadily the Northern victors increased the tariff as industry grew and spread above the Mason-Dixon line. Oates and his fellow Southern Democrats repeatedly lost the tariff war, a fact made clear by the passage of the Dingley Tariff of 1897, one of the highest in the country's history. Against the rising tide of Republican majority politics in Washington, Oates nevertheless joined with his Southern colleagues to enact legislation that would benefit their region and states, including a refund of the cotton tax imposed on the Southern states and a reduction in the size of the growing federal government. In getting specific legislation passed that helped Alabamians and Southern whites in general, he was not particularly successful, as he admitted several years later, but he took pride in standing up for his state and region. His time in Congress convinced him that it was the Republicans, the victors of the Civil War, who kept trying to keep the South down.[43]

He could not get the pounding memories of the war and the lyrical refrains of the Lost Cause out of his head. In June 1882, he met in person with Ellis Spear—a former officer of the 20th Maine who had fought at Little Round Top—who was on his way home from a veterans' reunion organized by John Bachelder in Gettysburg, and the two men spent hours together reminiscing about the battle and the parts they had played on Little Round Top. The meeting seems to have prompted Oates's decision to attend another Gettysburg reunion the following week, although that gathering was solely intended to bring together only veterans of the first day's battle, which Oates himself had missed. He did not let that fact inhibit him in any way. Returning to the battlefield for the first time since the battle itself, he—and several other former Union and Confederate officers—offered some appropriate remarks to a crowd assembled at the Adams County Court House on the evening of June 13.

The next day, Wednesday, June 14, the entourage went out on the rutted Chambersburg Pike and toured the first day's battlefield, driving wooden stakes to mark the places where Buford's cavalry had deployed on McPherson's Ridge and where John Reynolds had fallen in a clearing within sight of McPherson's old wooden barn. Late in the day, Oates broke away from the organized tour and accompanied former Confederate Colonel William H. Swallow up to the crest of Big Round Top, showing him the perilous route the 15th Alabama had followed on July 2, and then down to the ledges of Little Round Top. There the two men walked the ground, Oates pointing to the places he and his men had tried to win with their blood. He must have showed Swallow the spot where John Oates had fallen and had been hidden behind a boulder during the height of the battle.[44]

The train ride back to Washington on the following afternoon must have been a somber time for Oates. All the memories of the battle, good and bad, had been resurrected in his mind, and to see Gettysburg and the rocks of Little Round Top again must have been unsettling for him. He left no personal account of this first trip back to the battlefield, perhaps because the event was simply too painful for him to put down on paper. He would wait another fourteen years before visiting Gettysburg again, despite his proximity in Washington.

His work in Congress helped him forget his private miseries. So did the social calendar that T kept for him. They had not been long in Washington before T became the toast of the town. She delighted in throwing parties, the bigger the better, and she gained a reputation in Washington as a supreme hostess and a radiant beauty. One newspaper account stated that "Mrs. Oates . . . had the much coveted entre with the diplomatic set and was a favorite with the official people." Her parties reminded Alabamians of the opulent affairs held at Roseland in the antebellum period and during the war, and T seemed proud of the fact that she had gained her knack at organizing dinner parties and other social events from her mother, also an accomplished hostess. The Oates's guests reciprocated by inviting them to parties all over Washington, including many at foreign embassies and the White House.[45]

T Oates was one of the most beautiful women in Washington. She was also one of the youngest hostesses among the congressional social set. At twenty-five, she had an oval face, a flawless complexion, sparkling dark eyes, and a fetching smile. She usually wore her thick, dark hair pulled up and back off her face. A petite woman with a tiny waist, she showed off to advantage her wardrobe of fashionable gowns and party dresses. For all her supposedly wastrel ways and childlike qualities (at least so far as Oates was concerned), she was mature beyond her years and carried herself in social settings with great charm and poise. T had a deep appreciation of art and literature and could converse on these subjects with a felicity that Oates himself could never match. Her intellectualism complemented her charm, and people often sought her out at parties to hear her opinions of the latest books and art exhibitions.

She could be feisty and stubborn, as Oates frequently discovered. Although she held tradition dear, including the elevated place of women in Southern white society, she had a bold independent streak that set her apart from most Southern belles. She was happiest at parties and "jubilees," as she called them, reading at home, or in an art museum or gallery. The hustle and bustle of Washington, D.C., appealed to her cosmopolitan tastes, and she quickly settled in and became accepted among the dazzling denizens of the capital's high society.

But T's fondness for socializing caused friction in her relationship with Oates. He preferred to stay home evenings with his young bride, reading and relaxing, and the crunch of crowds disturbed him and made him feel almost claustrophobic. Oates also disliked spending his hard-earned money on parties and other frivolities. Despite his gregarious public persona, he was a very private person who could relax only by himself or in the company of T or two or three friends, never in the middle of a crowd.[46]

T's parties and high living also caused him political problems. In 1892, she was accused of spending more than $150 a month on carriages in Washington, an expense that voters at home saw as unnecessarily extravagant. Oates defended her publicly and claimed that such accusations of reckless spending were "twaddle" and "ridiculous nonsense," but privately he knew the claims were true and her style of living improvident. He grew to resent T and what he considered to be her only real inheritance from her parents—spendthrift ways and a desire to make life into a series of endless parties. During the first years of the marriage, Oates held his tongue and gave his bride whatever she wanted. But as the years went on their relationship became more and more brittle, largely over the issue of money and social occasions. Convinced she knew absolutely nothing about money, Oates criticized her spending, made her hold to an annual allowance (which she could not do), and terrorized her if she dared to ask for more than he was willing to dole out to her. But she continued to hold her jubilees and overspend her allotment in a direct defiance of Oates's wishes. In many respects, she repeatedly tested him and his affection for her, pushing him as far as he would go to see if his love for her would outweigh whatever other differences divided them. Sometimes he would pass the test; other times he would not. T continued to look for reassurances from him that often never came. He persisted in complaining about her frivolous ways and her lack of concern over money. Neither one seemed to be getting what he or she wanted from the relationship.[47]

Out of these clashes, it became clear that the couple was caught in a dance they could not stop. She looked up to Oates as a father figure and loved him for his courage, confidence, good looks, and knowledge of the world. He, in turn, regarded her as a child and treated her accordingly.[48] When perturbed, he would act the bully by first roaring at her and then withdrawing from her; she would cower, offer her sweet apologies, and promise not to upset him again. They genuinely seemed to miss one another when they were apart. But the years helped to drive a wedge between them, and eventually T spent more of her time in resorts like Asheville, Saratoga, Atlantic City, and Narragansett than she did by Oates's side.[49]

During the first year of their marriage, however, they seemed happy and content with one another. Any frustrations or irritations they mostly kept to themselves, and their life together was pleasant and loving. In September 1882, T learned she was pregnant, and the two of them looked forward to the birth of their baby and the start of their family. This child would be his first in wedlock, and he nearly burst with pride when, on May 20, 1883, T gave birth to a baby boy, whom they named William Calvin Oates, Jr.[50]

Oates was devoted to his son Willie (who, when he began to speak, affectionately called his father "Pofs"—a nickname that stuck for the rest of the elder Oates's life), but his work in Congress often kept him away from T and the child more than he would have liked. Late nights on the floor of the House or in his office or absences while on the campaign trail meant that Oates gave more time to his work and his ambition than he did to his family. Even when he did find time to be at home, he acted the rather stern husband and parent.[51] He believed it necessary to spell out certain rules of life for his son, which he did in a letter to Willie when the boy was eight years old, and he acted rather stiffly and formally around T and Willie, even in the privacy of their rooms at the Metropolitan or the National hotels. T strove to make Oates happy and proud of his family, which he was, but she found that to do so she had to walk on eggshells. Oates's temper could flare at the slightest provocation, and T tried to shield Willie from the vehemence of his father.[52]

Willie became T's true source of happiness. He served as the center of her life, and she discovered that she enjoyed motherhood and parenting, perhaps because raising a child enabled her to fulfill her own—and society's—expectations of her gender role as a nurturer and moral guide. Like other Victorian mothers, T forged a special bond with her son and achieved an emotional attachment that persisted unabated for the rest of her life. Oates occasionally resented the affection that linked T with their son, although later—as Willie grew older—he unfairly used the boy as an intermediary in his dealings with his wife, knowing that the son might be able to influence or persuade the mother. Given the strength of his relationship with his mother, which grew even stronger with each year of his childhood, Willie maintained a steadfast loyalty to T and regarded his father with some wariness. With Oates so frequently occupied with his politics and his war memories, and later with his law practice and his war memories, T assumed the role of primary parent. That tended to increase the chasm between husband and wife.[53]

The Civil War and its legacy also put a great distance between Oates and his family. Like other veterans, Oates believed that no one who had not participated in the war as a soldier could understand what the conflict had been like or what it meant to those who had survived its destruction. "No one but an old soldier who has 'been there,'" he wrote in his memoirs, "knows how . . . we felt."[54] Certainly T, born in 1862, had no memory of the war years, and while the Reconstruction years brought deprivation to the Toneys and their Roseland plantation, their personal losses were hidden behind the house parties and levees that went on as if no war or economic upheaval in the postwar period had ever happened. The Civil War left no particular impression on T, other than adding to her girlish admiration for one of Alabama's prominent

veterans. But when Oates was not away from home for long days and evenings as he attended to his work in the House or took campaign trips to
Alabama and beyond, he was buried in the relentless past as he labored to
write an accurate history of the 15th Alabama and of his own experiences in
the war. The war was not simply a dead memory for him, a pale recollection
of a remote time in his own experience; it was a living event, as real as the
here-and-now, something that would not stop replaying itself in his mind,
over and over again.

There was, for Oates, no escaping the war. Even his political ideology
and the stand he took on issues facing the Congress were shaped by the war
and the things it had left unresolved, including racial injustice, ardent sectionalism, and the peculiar economics of King Cotton. When campaigning
for reelection in 1882 and every two years after that, he blatantly referred to
his empty sleeve as a reminder to his voters of the sacrifices he had made for
them, for Alabama, and for the South in the great war. In Congress, he fought
bitterly to have the cotton tax collected by the federal government during the
early years of Reconstruction returned to the people in the form of a tax
refund. He was strident in his opposition to the tariff, the creation of the
Interstate Commerce Commission, federal flood relief, a tax refund to the
Northern states based on the levies collected after the war had begun, unlimited immigration, civil service reform, and pensions for the widows of Union
generals Sheridan, Hancock, McClellan, Fremont, and others. Actually he
favored any federal bill that aided Alabama and the South or that restricted
the power of the central government. He was a fervent states' rights advocate,
and he gained a reputation in the House as something of a constitutional
expert. By and large, he seemed to be *against* more things than he was *for*.[55]

Yet not all of his political stands consistently reflected his loyalty to the
South or his previous fidelity to the Confederacy. In the winter of 1884, the
question came before Congress as to whether Fitz John Porter, a Union major general who had been found guilty in 1863 of disobeying orders at the
Battle of Second Bull Run, should be exonerated and his commission reinstated. The Porter case had become a political hot potato, and even though
an impartial commission appointed by President Rutherford B. Hayes in 1878
had found Porter not guilty of the original charges brought against him, there
was enough controversy surrounding the case to make politicians especially
wary of expressing an opinion about Porter, pro or con. Oates possessed no
such fear. On February 1, 1884, he rose in the House and delivered a long
oration praising Porter as a formidable former enemy, celebrating the man's
courage and integrity as an officer, and arguing that justice could only be
served by reversing the sentence of the court martial. Given at a crucial moment in history when more and more Southerners were preaching the benefits of reconciliation with the North and were doing so by honoring the

courage of soldiers on both sides, Oates's speech was widely regarded as offering an olive branch to the North.

"No member of the House is in a position to vote on this bill more impartially, more completely emancipated from every bias common to human nature, than those of us who belonged to the confederate army," Oates said. Partisan politics, he argued, should be put aside, including the boiling contentions of those factions that still perceived the Porter case in light of the political squabble that had taken place during the war years between McClellan Democrats and Lincoln Republicans. Based on the evidence, including the facts gathered by Cleveland's board of inquiry, Oates could only conclude that Porter was no traitor to the Union cause, that he was in fact a "brave Union soldier," and that "his punishment has been far greater than his conduct ever merited." As a result, said Oates, it "gives me pleasure to vote for this bill as an act of justice long delayed."[56]

On one hand, his remarks seemed to fit nicely with the growing sentiment in the South that welcomed reconciliation with the North and that celebrated the courage of the soldiers who had fought on both sides. On the other hand, he couldn't quite make up his mind whether he wanted the South to come to terms with the North over the war or personally to rub the conflict and its outcome in the faces of his former enemies. Like other Southern leaders, including Jefferson Davis, Oates continued to defend the right of secession under the Constitution, citing the Ninth and Tenth Amendments, and to buttress his argument he increasingly relied on an article entitled, "A Vindication of Virginia and the South," written by Commodore M. F. Maury and published in 1876, that justified the creation of the Confederacy, portrayed the South as a victim of Northern oppression and regression, and commended the sons of the South "who died in defence of their country, their homes, their rights, and all that makes native land dear to the hearts of men."[57]

11

STRIKING TO HURT

A s the nation entered the modern age of industrialism and urbanism, which ignited political and social conflagrations during the last two decades of the nineteenth century, Oates tried in the halls of Congress to maintain order and his own sense of balance by sticking steadfastly to his archconservative ideas and to his "antilatitudinarianism" philosophy. His defensive xenophobia—which had expressed itself during the war as a sweeping condemnation of all soldiers of Irish ancestry as drunkards, cowards, and rogues—evolved during the postwar years into a bristling attack on immigrants from nearly every part of the world. Years later he would write a vicious denunciation of foreigners who sought refuge in America and call them "trash," oddly placing the embarrassing passage in one of the Gettysburg chapters of his memoirs.[1]

But it was the ugly beast of race and the poor condition of blacks in the South—crucial matters of public policy that the Civil War and Reconstruction had left unresolved—that enabled Oates to practice his rampant conservatism in Congress and to keep hoping that American society, particularly south of the Mason-Dixon line, would not change so markedly as to unseat the iron rule of whites or undermine the potent premises of white supremacy. Back home in Alabama, Oates kept winning his party's nomination and trouncing his opposition in the general elections throughout the last half of the 1880s, largely by appealing to the racial prejudices of the voters and to their old Confederate and Lost Cause sympathies. Having purchased a fine house on Q Street in Washington, D.C., where he and his family now firmly established their home, he spent little time in Alabama or in the Third Congressional District, usually just enough to campaign effectively in person and win reelection every two years.

Out on the campaign trail, Oates spoke to his constituents in prepared speeches that contained elements he knew would appeal to voters. Some observers claimed that he lacked the "graces of oratory," but what they probably meant is that The One-Armed Hero of Henry County dispensed with the form and substance of classical rhetoric in his speeches and instead relied on his natural ear for language and the commonplace vocabulary of the working man to get his messages across. For all his political conservatism and traditional ideas, Oates unwittingly embraced a new American language in his speeches—the vernacular style of expression that would eventually find its way into the short stories of Joel Chandler Harris and the novels of Mark Twain. Relying on colorful figures of speech and a host of Southern idioms, Oates's campaign echoed the revolution in language that his fellow Civil War soldiers had helped bring about during the war years and afterward with their snappy camp talk, coarse popular sayings, and informal military jargon. He took pride in speaking his mind and speaking from his heart, and in so doing he eschewed the formalities of political discourse and communicated with his constituents in a plain, conversational English.

Oates never achieved an exceptional prose style, so his writings—other than his memoirs, written much later in his life—have not been well remembered. His real forte was the spoken word—or, rather, writing out the words he would speak on the floor of Congress or on the stump in Alabama. To enliven his speeches, he kept notebooks filled with anecdotes and humorous stories. Even those who criticized his manner of public speaking had to acknowledge that he was effective on the stump and that his "candor" and "practical sense" rendered him "estimable and popular." His outright supporters considered him an outstanding speaker, "brave and fearless, logical, earnest, intense and picturesque." One tribute described how Oates "filled the stage, satisfying the eye, and the audience was his." His sentences were "measured and rhythmical" and "fell like music on the ears of the enraptured throng." Others, less poetically, thought him a "gifted orator" and "a direct and powerful speaker."[2]

Frequently Oates laced his speeches with downhome anecdotes and racist jokes, often drawn from his notebook collection. Sometimes he told these stories for what he thought would be the benefit of the African Americans who had gathered around the fringes of his audience. But mostly he warned white voters about the dangers of black voters. "Northern men," he told his constituents, using a popular refrain from the Lost Cause, "do not understand the negro question at all." Defending Jim Crow laws and the practice of segregation, he said that nine-tenths of African Americans agreed with the idea that the races should be separate, and so did he. "I believe in separate churches, separate schools, separate [railroad] cars[,] and separate accommodations and entertainments[,] and a prohibition on intermarriage," he declared with all sincerity. Segregation was not discrimination or "an odious distinction," he said. "It is essential to the control and contentment of the negro."[3]

When black voters continued to exercise their franchise in Alabama and in his district, and when they made no sign of disappearing from the political process, Oates—like other Southern conservatives—then tried to convince them that white Democrats understood them best and could serve their interests better than any Republican. He also attempted to persuade them that history was not exactly what it seemed. The Civil War, he told African Americans in his audiences, "was not begun for your freedom on the Union side; nor was it fought on the Southern side to keep you in slavery." When the Northerners and Southerners found themselves in a clinch, he said, "they were so busy fighting each other that in the scuffle the nigger got loose." Slavery lasted for as long as it benefited the Negro race, he asserted. Then, when it no longer served its purpose, God saw fit to remove it from the South.

If African Americans were now to act in their own best interest, he stated, they must vote intelligently for those candidates who knew them, cared about them, and would look out for them—white Southern Democrats like himself or Northern Democrats like Grover Cleveland. "You are under no obligations to those who compose the Republican Party," he told them. "You are here free men and voters in the providence of God; a people having emerged from the trail ordeal of slavery, from the savage state . . . and it behooves you beyond all others to act wisely and . . . to prove yourselves worthy of the blessings which have been bestowed upon you."[4]

In Alabama, where elections were always messy, things got even messier as the decade of the 1880s came to a close. Farmers became convinced that the state and federal governments no longer represented them with a strong voice in the legislative halls. As a result, Alabama farmers began to organize themselves into an alliance that, like their brethren laborers in factories and on the railroads who had joined labor unions, could speak for them in a world that looked more and more as if it favored only the rich and the captains of industry.

After the first Farmers' Alliance was formed in Madison County, Alabama, in 1887, the movement spread throughout the state like a religious revival. By 1890, when Alliance leaders were preaching an economic program aimed at providing relief and educational opportunities to farmers by establishing various businesses, including exchanges, hotels, warehouses, fertilizer manufacturers, banks, and cotton mills, membership in the organization grew to approximately 25,000 members. One of the most effective Alliance advocates was Reuben F. Kolb (pronounced *cob*), the state commissioner of agriculture and a well-to-do planter who was connected to the Eufaula Regency by his kinship to the Shorter family.[5]

At the start, Oates did not oppose the Alliance or regard it as a political threat, but when the Alliance in the early 1890s began to join hands with the Populists and shift their sights from economic relief to political action, he went on the attack against "Alliancemen" and Populists both, warning farmers against trusting in any organization that sought to dismantle the existing political structure in the name of reform and the promise of agrarian prosperity. In principle, Oates was against all trade unions, cooperatives, and associations, for he believed that these groups—"secret political organizations," he called them—made war on capital, industry, and democracy. As for the Alliance, Oates believed that once it had dropped its economic goals in favor of political ends, it had in essence declared war against the Democratic Party.[6]

What troubled Oates so much about the farmers' movement was its potential for dividing an already badly splintered Democratic Party in Alabama. For all the talk of a solid South, the Democrats were at odds with one another in Alabama. The Black Belt section of the states held tenuously on to most of the political power in the party and in the state. As the famous former slave Booker T. Washington, the founder of the Tuskegee Negro Normal Institute, explained, the Black Belt was first named after "the thick, dark, and naturally rich soil" where slaves lived in the largest number and produced profits for their masters, but by the late nineteenth century the term had come to "designate the counties where the black people outnumber the white." Despite the population density of African Americans in the Black Belt, the white Bourbon Democrats jealousy possessed all the political power in the region and refused to share it. Yet challenges did arise, particularly made by disgruntled elements in the northern hill country, small farmers, poor whites, and industrialists, all of whom resented the dominance of the Black Belt leaders and wanted to end their control over state politics. Much of the leadership of the Farmers' Alliance and of the Populists came from former Democrats, like Reuben Kolb, who called themselves Jeffersonian Democrats to make plain their differences with the Bourbons and to emphasize their agrarian concerns.[7]

Inflaming Oates's concern was the Ocala Platform, a manifesto set forth at a national meeting of the Farmers' Alliance in Ocala, Florida, during the month of December 1890. The platform endorsed the subtreasury scheme, a plan that called for government support of agriculture through the construction of warehouses where farmers could store nonperishable products and receive loans, in legal tender notes, for up to 80 percent of the market value of the stored crops. Oates stridently opposed the scheme and its unsound financial corollaries, which favored an increase in the circulation of cheap currency, the abolition of national banks, and the unlimited and free coinage of

silver. The Ocala Platform, warned Oates, would not bring the needed economic relief to farmers that the Alliance had promised, or so Oates claimed.

The silver issue stood as a bitter controversy at the center of American
politics for several decades following the Civil War and particularly after the
Panic of 1873, when the market price of silver fell precipitously. Those who
supported inflation in the economy, including the Greenback party, turned
away from paper money to silver coinage as a means of expanding the money
supply, which the Republicans had consistently sought to contract by withdrawing greenbacks, first issued during the Civil War, from the economy.
Demands for unlimited coinage of free silver resulted in the passage of a compromise measure, the Bland-Allison Act of 1878, that restricted coinage at a
ratio of 16 to 1 with gold; the legislation, however, failed to stop a steady
decline in silver prices or to increase the amount of money in circulation.
Silver Democrats gained some success in 1890 when they enacted the Sherman
Silver Purchase Act, which provided for government purchases of silver. But
that victory was short-lived. These silver advocates, who largely represented
indebted agrarian interests in the South and West, wanted inflation to ease
the impact of falling prices for farm produce. Eastern bankers and lenders
fought to sustain the value of borrowed money by basing the dollar on the
solid reliability—and, in their estimation, the moral soundness—of the gold
standard. Gold Democrats, like Oates, stood with the Republicans on the
issue of free silver: They saw the coinage of anything other than gold as cheating
lenders from receiving an honest repayment of money loaned at a particular
dollar value. As silver proponents gained political strength in the late 1880s
and early 1890s, the political issue became more complicated. With the passage by Congress in July 1890 of the Sherman Silver Purchase Act, another
compromise measure that ordered the government to purchase nearly the
entire output of the country's silver mines each month, and with the rise of
the Farmers' Alliance in Alabama and the promulgation of its Ocala Platform
at the end of that year, Oates discovered that he could not comfortably denounce free silver without losing some support among his agrarian constituents. Having formerly resisted the idea of free coinage of silver, Oates finally
came around to accepting it, but he fought against any proposal that would
allow the circulation of unlimited, irredeemable greenbacks.[8]

To thwart the Jeffersonian Democrats, Oates turned to the tried-and-
true tactics of racial politics. In the 1892 election, he questioned the sincerity
of Alliance candidates who claimed to stand with the Democratic Party on
the question of white supremacy. "If white supremacy be the test and touch-
stone of Democracy and the white Alliancemen by that test are all sound," he
asked in a newspaper interview, "I would like to know what they mean by the
establishment of sixteen hundred negro Alliance lodges within this State?"
Indeed, the Alliance movement gained wide support among African Americans in Alabama, with a membership of about 50,000 in the summer of 1889.

The black Alliances remained separate from the white Farmers' Alliance, but Oates was correct in recognizing the possibility of an amalgamation, especially after the Populists and Jeffersonian Democrats temporarily joined forces by nominating the same congressional candidates and favoring James B. Weaver, who ran for president as a Populist in the 1892 election.[9]

Oates regarded the Alliance supporters as devils incarnate, perhaps because so many of them were turncoat former Democrats like Kolb. He campaigned as vigorously—and as viciously—against the Alliance and the Populists as he had against any Yankee foe during the Civil War. Chaos reigned during the election of 1892 in Alabama. Kolb, who was nominated for governor by the Jeffersonian Democrats, ran against Thomas G. Jones, a Civil War veteran and a Bourbon Democrat. Each side tried to win the African American vote, for both parties realized that black voters could ultimately decide the election. Oates did his share of wooing African Americans by warning them against the Jeffersonian Democrats, but mostly he spoke pointedly to his white audiences, painting the Alliance as an organization that had abandoned white supremacy and had embraced the unthinkable principle of equality between whites and blacks. In the end, the Democrats managed to elect Jones and reelect Oates and other Bourbon stalwarts, but not without having to rig the election in their own favor throughout the Black Belt districts.[10]

Oates was beginning to feel the wear and tear of advancing years and debilitating battles, both in war and politics. As he approached his sixtieth year, he looked strong and robust to any impartial observer. Although tending toward portliness, he carried the extra weight better than most men, mostly because of his height and his excellent posture. He still had a full head of hair, which had turned almost completely white. He had shaved away his beard years ago, so that now he wore only a full white moustache on his rather round and fleshy face. In spite of the vicissitudes of time, there was no change in his eyes, which still flashed with a piercing and chilling gleam of utter determination. But rheumatism, the disease that had stricken his brother John during the war, now slowed Oates down with aches and pains he had never experienced before. At times, his symptoms were so severe he fled for relief to Hot Springs, Arkansas, where he was taking the waters when his son Willie was born.

He felt well enough in the summer of 1889, however, to take a trip to England, Scotland, and a few countries on the Continent. The details of his journey have not been handed down, but it is certain that he was impressed with the shipyards at Glasgow and he stayed long enough in Great Britain to have T and Willie (who was only six at the time) cross the bounding Atlantic and meet him in London. Oates, now joined by his wife and son, toured the countryside of England, visited the battlefield at Waterloo in Belgium, and stayed for a while in Naples.[11]

The war still held Oates captive. In the autumn of 1888, he wrote John Bachelder again, this time in reply to an invitation to attend another reunion in Gettysburg for the purpose of marking troop positions. Fearing that he would not be able to attend the meeting, he spelled out in detail the ground occupied by the 15th Alabama at the foot of Big Round Top on the morning of July 3, the day of Farnsworth's cavalry charge. Oates told of Farnsworth's death that afternoon, making it sound as if he had witnessed the Union general's suicide himself. When Bachelder wrote back insisting that Farnsworth had not killed himself, Oates admitted that he might be wrong and that he should have been more particular in saying that he had not actually witnessed Farnsworth's death himself. In later correspondence with Bachelder, Oates tried to answer the historian's questions as fully as he could about his own experiences during the battle of Gettysburg. Meanwhile, Oates worked on his own history of the 15th Alabama, tracking down and staying in touch with the surviving members of the regiment and researching the history of the war by using a wide array of sources, including the published *Official Records* and other important Civil War publications that seemed to be flying off the national presses in the 1880s.[12]

In May 1892, as Oates kept one eye on House business and the other on the coming campaign and the difficult fight for reelection he would face in the months ahead, his elderly mother died unexpectedly in Abbeville. She was eighty-five years old. Oates and his family returned to Alabama from Washington to make the proper arrangements for his mother's funeral. He buried her in the Baptist cemetery in Abbeville, a simple headstone marking her grave. Oates deeply felt the loss. He had always been emotionally close to his mother, and of his two parents, it was his mother he had followed as a guiding light.

In many respects, Oates believed he resembled his mother, not so much in physical appearance as in temperament and a pronounced intellectual curiosity. He respected her piety, regarded her as a saint, and tried all his life to care for her and live up to her expectations. In Abbeville, he provided a home for her and supported her financially after his father died. Oates never once complained about his obligations toward her. Although he visited her less frequently than he may have wished while he served in Congress, he still felt the close bond that had always tied them together. When she died, he experienced a tangible void in his life.[13]

Back in Washington, Oates turned his attention to the issues of the day and the needs of his constituents. In the House of Representatives, he labored tirelessly to limit the power of Congress, to protect Southern interests, to pass legislation for Alabama and his constituents, to defend the Democratic Party, to fight for the gold standard, and to support Grover Cleveland—the first Democratic president since James Buchanan. During the 50th Congress, he had led the longest filibuster that had ever occurred in the House—eight days and nights—against a bill to refund the direct tax of 1861 to the Union states. His fight against the bill reflected his strong commitment to Southern politics. Like other Southerners, he did not want the federal treasury depleted by giving back to the Union states the tax they had paid to support the war effort in the early days of the conflict. His effort, which required pulling together a strong coalition of representatives, resulted in the defeat of the bill during that session.

As for the legislation he supported, Oates was especially proud of his hard work helping to pass the Nicaragua canal bill, which, long before the construction of the Panama Canal, recognized the strategic and economic importance of a waterway through Central America. During his tenure in the House, he served on important committees, including the Committee on Claims, the Committee on the Revision of the Laws, the Committee on the Tenth Census, the Committee on Immigration and Naturalization, and the Judiciary Committee, of which he became chairman. Although he maintained an uncharacteristic humility during his first terms in the House, he did gain a reputation as a man of high principles and an unreserved advocate for Southern interests.

Despite his fierce party loyalties, he considered himself an independent spirit in Congress, someone who stood up for what was right and never minced his words on any issue. Describing himself in the third person, he wrote less than modestly: "While he is firm and persistent in urging his views and the consideration of measures, he is a conservative man. He never abuses personally those who differ with him in matters of legislation. He does not hesitate to denounce measures which he thinks are wrong, but does not go beyond that boundary. He never indulges in personal denunciations nor says anything intended to give offense, although he is always earnest and outspoken in favor of or in opposition to measures according to his honest beliefs."[14]

Having endured the cataclysm of internecine warfare, the Civil War generation believed that it could ultimately survive just about anything, but the political and social crises of the 1890s raised new and troubling doubts about America's future. At the center of that doubt was an epidemic of violence spreading throughout the land. Labor unrest and strikes around the country nearly paralyzed the nation's industry in 1892, and many of these disputes resulted in bloodshed on the picket lines. At the Homestead Steel Mill on the Monongahela River in Pennsylvania, a strike in July led to a violent confrontation between workers and Pinkerton officers brought in by owner Andrew Carnegie and mill manager Henry Clay Frick. When it seemed like the striking workers would prevail, Frick arranged for the state governor to call out the militia to protect strikebreakers, who took over operations at the mill. Frick was later seriously wounded by an attacking anarchist, and Carnegie, who sat out the crisis in Scotland, lost personal prestige as the strike dragged on and on.

After the strike was ended in November, with most of the mill's regular workers losing their jobs, Oates was named chairman of a congressional committee established to look into the whole affair. Having built his reputation at home as a friend to the poor and downtrodden, Oates nevertheless sided squarely with Frick and the captains of industry against the Homestead strikers. In writing about the strike for the *North American Review*, one of the few times he reached a truly national audience, Oates revealed his own political prejudices against foreign workers ("one-half of the [Homestead] population are of foreign birth and represent various European nationalities"), labor unions ("secret political organizations are inconsistent with our American republican system of government"), the right of workers to organize ("in this country every man is the architect of his own fortune"), federal intervention in labor disputes ("Congress . . . has no power to interfere by legislation in the labor troubles at Homestead . . . or elsewhere"), and the high protective tariff (which "disturbs the laws of trade"). He concluded that Frick's biggest mistake in handling the strike was in not calling for the state militia sooner. In the future, he said, such agitation between labor and capital could be readily averted if Congress repealed "all class legislation" (such as laws to establish an eight-hour work day, pensions for government civil servants, or federal intervention in the workings of commerce) and passed tough laws to restrict foreign immigration. All of these positions revealed how he was far more a Southern Democrat than a national Democrat, for while he worked to exclude immigrants from landing on American shores, the national party was trying to broaden its base of support among those same foreign newcomers. His political views also reflected a strain of the Jacksonian persuasion that was otherwise hard to find among die-hard Democrats at this time. In that sense, Oates was a perfect conservative who wished to protect the country from unnecessary change while keeping the federal government as small—and as weak—as possible.[15]

Yet Congress never passed the restrictive laws or overturned "class legislation" to the extent that Oates wanted it to. Instead, the world kept changing around him in ways that made him uncomfortably aware that it no longer resembled the South he had known before the war or even the society he and other diehard Southern Democrats had tried to create in the Reconstruction era. The Gilded Age had a disquieting effect on Oates, as it had on the nation as a whole, and the new commonwealth that emerged out of America's entry into a new industrial order left Oates baffled and frustrated. The world, as he understood it, no longer seemed to work according to the accepted rules of the game.

So when a severe financial panic struck in 1893, it took Oates—and many other Americans—completely by surprise. He had seen the nation survive earlier depressions, but this one went far deeper into the bedrock of the country's economic well-being and shook its financial institutions to the core. The causes behind the depression were complex, but one of the factors that contributed to the financial plunge (apart from the bankruptcy of the Philadelphia and Reading Railroad and the jittery behavior of British investors) was the depletion of the gold reserves, precipitated mostly by the Sherman Silver Purchase Act of 1890, which Oates—and every other Democrat—voted against in Congress. The act passed Congress and became law. Conservatives, like Oates, firmly believed that the Sherman Silver Purchase Act caused the panic of 1893.

Throughout the postwar period, Oates had wavered on the question of whether the nation's currency should be based on the gold or the silver standard; he personally favored gold, but he could not ignore the wide political support for silver coinage, even among some Southern Democrats and particularly among Jeffersonian Democrats and Populists in his own state, so he declared that he was, in essence, a "bi-metalist." Most Southern agrarians, saddled by debt, favored free coinage of silver as a means of increasing inflation and thus easing their burden in the face of falling produce prices. But the national Democrats stood by Grover Cleveland, a strong supporter of the gold standard. Meanwhile, economic collapse around the country threw at least a third of the labor force out of work and nearly crippled farmers who had been struggling through financially hard times even before banks began to fail, industries shut down, and unemployment lines lengthened.[16]

The depression in Alabama opened the gates for the Jeffersonian Democrats and the Populists to gain ground in their political battles against the Bourbon oligarchy. Outside of the deep South, the financial panic had split the Democratic Party into regional factions, pitting the Northeast against the West and much of the South. But in Alabama the economic collapse gave farmers more reasons to distrust the Democrats and blame their considerable woes on the party in power. The incumbent governor, Thomas G. Jones, one of Oates's Bourbon political allies, became the target of endless criticism, public protests, and political backbiting. Some opponents called boisterously for his resignation, and it appeared at one point that Jones was ready to vacate his office in the dead of night if he had to. At the very least, it became extremely evident that Jones's political days in Alabama were numbered and that the Democrats must find a very strong candidate to run for governor in 1894.[17]

But the issue of free silver, as well as the overall effects of economic collapse, was dividing the Democratic Party in Alabama, and Oates—despite his attempt to stand squarely in the middle of the silver issue—found himself caught once more by changing times and changing politics. In February, the Populists and Jeffersonian Democrats held their conventions in Birmingham, and unsurprisingly the two groups issued a joint platform that called for the free vote, an honest count of ballots, free coinage of silver, a graduated income tax, and better educational opportunities in the state. To the cheers of a tumultuous crowd, Reuben F. Kolb was nominated for governor.[18]

Much to his delight, Oates had been mentioned in Democratic circles as a possible successor to Governor Jones, but he remained coy during the early winter of 1894 as to whether he would give up his congressional seat and run for the governor's chair. No evidence survives to calculate how he weighed the decision in his mind, although it seems certain, based on later events, that he hoped the governor's office—which he felt he would surely win if he agreed to run—would be a springboard to winning a United States Senate seat from Alabama. His decision in early 1894 must have also been influenced by the growing popularity of the reformist parties in the state, namely the Populists and the Jeffersonian Democrats, and by the fact that they had chosen Kolb as their candidate. In Oates's opinion, Kolb was a rogue and knave, and he had already targeted Kolb as a "demagogue" and a "villain" in his political speeches at home.[19]

By late January, Oates decided to resign from Congress and seek his party's nomination as a candidate for governor of Alabama, although he claimed to have reached the decision only after pulling back from it "like a wild mule." It was not the choice T or little Willie would have made. T had grown accustomed to her high station in the society of Washington, and the prospect of moving back to provincial Alabama—if it meant not residing at gracious Roseland—held little appeal. For Willie, who had spent his entire life in Washington, the place was now home and he had no interest in leaving his boyhood friends for a place he hardly knew.[20]

Before he left Congress, Oates voted for legislation close to his heart— bills creating national military parks at Gettysburg and Chickamauga and Chattanooga. Having supported the efforts of John B. Bachelder and the Gettysburg Battlefield Memorial Association to preserve portions of the battlefield and to mark the places where units of the Union and Confederate armies had fought, he enthusiastically endorsed the idea of creating national military parks out of the old Civil War battlefields and putting them under the administration of the War Department. He even recommended William H. Forney, a former brigadier general in the Army of Northern Virginia, to be one of the first commissioners of the Gettysburg National Military Park, along with Bachelder and John P. Nicholson, a Civil War veteran from Pennsylvania. When Forney died shortly after his appointment, Oates applauded his replacement as commissioner, William M. Robbins, who had served as an officer in the 4th Alabama Regiment.[21]

But Oates's eyes were mostly focused on politics in his home state and his election chances. His election to the governorship of Alabama was not a foregone conclusion. Even within his own party, Oates encountered opposition to his candidacy, namely from Joseph F. Johnston, a Birmingham banker who supported free silver and wished to see the Democratic Party reformed from within its own ranks. The struggle with Johnston became even more bitter when John Tyler Morgan, the senior U.S. Senator from Alabama and a prickly critic of Cleveland's policies, supported Oates's opponent and implied that any election with Oates as a candidate would inevitably involve ballot fraud. In the end, Oates won the majority of delegates to the party's convention, despite Morgan's fracturing of the Democratic Party in the state (Morgan later supported Oates's candidacy, but many Alabamians thought that the senator wanted the Populists to win). For Oates, the convention tally was uncomfortably close and the slimness of his victory must have been unsettling to him, for he had become used to winning nominations and elections by wide margins.[22]

He was now about to enter one of the most heated, bitterly contested, mean-spirited campaigns in all of Alabama's history, not to mention the toughest fight of his entire political career. Ever the soldier and proud Confederate veteran, Oates reminded voters of how he had obtained his empty sleeve, but also how his compatriots—the brave Confederates of the Southern armies—had fought on even when defeat was apparent, "showing their devotion until the last hope," when "all was lost save our honor." One of Oates's detractors wrote grudgingly: "Your valiant one-armed hero can work the veteran racket more adroitly and successfully than any follower of the stars and bars who shows a scar or empty sleeve as a passport to office."[23]

The campaign took place in the long shadow of the Civil War. Kolb, too, had been an officer in the Confederate army and had gained the rank of captain by the end of the war. Oates was the more conspicuous hero, partly because of his empty sleeve, but mostly because he wouldn't let the voters forget his personal commitment to the cause of the Confederacy. What's more, he went on the attack as if the election were a military, rather than a political, campaign. Kolb, in Oates's view, was a worse enemy than the Yankees he had fought in the war, if only because he regarded his opponent as a turncoat Democrat.

With years of experience behind him, Oates campaigned across the state with high energy and a strong voice. He promised the electorate that he would serve only one two-year term as governor, which he felt would give him ample time to move the state forward and out of its present economic crisis. The sharp racial divisions in Alabama he turned to his advantage. Although the Populists promised greater freedom and autonomy under the law to African Americans, Oates successfully persuaded blacks that Kolb and his renegade Democrats could not be trusted, especially since they were urging African Americans not to register to vote (a means by which the Jeffersonian Democrats hoped to reduce potential votes for the Bourbons). Casting a ballot for Oates and the Democratic Party, Oates argued, would enable blacks to know for sure who and what they were getting. To predominately white audiences, Oates stuck to his tactic of playing up the Democratic Party's historic adherence to white supremacy. In the end, blacks overwhelmingly gave their votes to Oates and the Democratic Party.[24]

But he did run into some trouble during the campaign. His position on education probably hurt him with rural and urban voters alike. Having long opposed agricultural education in the form of experimental stations funded by federal tax dollars, Oates also helped defeat in Congress the Blair Education bill that sought to overcome illiteracy throughout the country. "It is not the duty, nor is it to the interest of the State," Oates said on the House floor, "to educate its entire population beyond the primaries. Universal experience teaches that if a boy, without regard to his color, be educated beyond this point, he declines ever to work another day in the sun." He was roundly criticized for this view, the Populists accusing him of saying that farmers' children did not deserve a good education. His position on education hurt him so much that he was forced during the 1894 campaign to claim rather feebly that he had meant that a "*classical*" education—training in Latin or Greek—served no useful purpose for the laboring man and was a waste of taxpayers' money.[25]

In no time the campaign became torrid, like the Alabama summer. Kolb, who went looking for endorsements to buttress his campaign, came under fire for soliciting political and financial support from Northern Republicans in exchange for advocating a high protective tariff. Oates particularly enjoyed pointing out that Kolb had never won an election, either for governor or for the Senate, and that he was pretty much a failure as a businessman, too. The popular press, particularly the *Montgomery Advertiser*, wholeheartedly backed Oates and vilified Kolb for abandoning the mainstream Democratic Party. Without mercy, Oates portrayed Kolb as a traitorous Democrat and called the Jeffersonian Democrats "the mule party, because it is without pride of ancestry or the hope of prosperity."[26] At political rallies and other demonstrations, the crowds wore corn cobs on their walking sticks if they supported Kolb and tufts of oats if they favored Colonel Oates. A black school teacher was warned by the Ku Klux Klan against campaigning for Oates, and shots were fired into the school house. Both sides threatened election officials with violence. One old-line Democratic newspaper in Shelby County informed its readers that election day would be "the day for the battle of the ballot." Kolb was described as the leader of a mob; Oates was hailed as the law-and-order candidate. Beneath the surface, tensions between the two sides came close to the boiling point, and violence seemed to be an inevitable outcome of the passions being expressed in the camps of both candidates. In June, a gunfight erupted between the two sides in Birmingham, and the son of the city's former mayor was killed.[27]

The voter turnout that August proved to be less than in the 1892 election, but the outcome was close enough to result in political chaos. Oates won 111,875 votes of the total 195,167 votes cast, giving him a victory over Kolb by 28,583. While Oates only won thirty-two counties to Kolb's thirty-four, he took seventeen of the crucial Black Belt counties; in fact, without those counties, Oates would have lost the election. Kolb immediately contested the results, although Alabama lacked any statute that would allow such a challenge to be waged in the courts. The reformist press accused the Democrats of fraud, and one observer remarked dryly on what had long been the case in the state: "Nobody ever knows anything about the real result of an election in Alabama." On August 8, Kolb, in as desperate a move as any politician has ever made, simply declared himself the winner, claiming that fraud and corruption had prevented his voters from casting their ballots or having them fairly counted.[28]

Kolb and his followers threatened to create a dual government. They kept up their protests until inauguration day, December 1, when Oates delivered his address in the state capitol to the Alabama General Assembly. Like so many of Oates's speeches, his remarks were something less than brilliant. Almost as soon as he had begun speaking, he turned his attention to the charges of election fraud that had been raised by his defeated opponent. He declared, as he had throughout the campaign, that he was in favor of fair elections, a statement that attempted to set him apart from Democrats who had been accused of repeated deception and fraud at the polls. But he also proclaimed, rather disingenuously and with a bit too much self-righteousness, that such unsavory political practices did not exist in Alabama. "I have no knowledge whatever of any [fraud]," he said, "and for the good name of our State regret that such a charge has been made." Besides, he said with assurance, even if every fraudulent vote—presuming there were any at all—were thrown out, he would have still won the election with a large majority.

While Oates was being sworn in, a few blocks from the state capitol Reuben Kolb and his slate of state officers took their own oaths of office, administered by a Montgomery justice of the peace. Then Kolb and about 200 of his followers marched through the streets of the city to the capitol, where units of the state militia stood guard. Despite all predictions, no violence broke out on the lawn of the capitol, and Kolb asked the outgoing Governor Jones if he could be allowed to speak from the capitol steps. Jones refused to grant Kolb permission to hold a public assembly at the capitol, so the reformists left the grounds, crossed the street, and found a wagon that could serve as a speaker's platform for Kolb and his cadre of titular state officers. Almost sedate in his demeanor, Kolb gave a few brief remarks, claiming victory over Oates and raising the old campaign issue of fair elections, and stepped down from the wagon as other speakers took over the spurious proceedings. Kolb the firebrand no longer burned with any intensity. Within a short time, the crowd surrounding the wagon disbanded, the streets became quiet again, and the revolution that many Alabamians had feared would divide their state in two simply failed to ignite on that cold December day.[29]

Somewhat pathetically, Kolb continued to call himself governor, but Oates and his administration paid no attention to the reformer and carried out their duties as if Kolb did not exist. Indeed, there was much business to be done. Oates had stepped into a job that held little promise for success. His predecessor, Thomas Jones, was an ineffective executive whose decisions caused more problems than they had solved. In his first biennial message to the General Assembly, Oates laid out at last an ambitious program of legislation and reform that he envisioned as putting the state back on the right track toward prosperity and modernization. He called on the Assembly and his fellow citizens to support legislation to reform tax assessments, increase the stipends paid to disabled Confederate veterans, revamp the expensive convict labor leasing program, double the number of circuit courts, outlaw concealed weapons, provide for the legal contest of elections in the courts, and increase the governor's salary.

He also urged the Assembly to take all necessary steps to prevent lynchings, which had become "of too frequent occurrence within the State." While endorsing the idea of "race separateness," he pointed out that railroads were not providing truly equal accommodations in their cars to African Americans. "The negroe's dollar," he said, "buys as much in the markets of the country as the white man's, and when he is made to pay as much for a railroad ticket, as a white man, he should be given a seat in as good a coach." Mindful of the Civil War's legacy in his own life and in the lives of his fellow Alabamians, he asked the legislature to approve the erection of monuments on the battlefields at Chickamauga and Gettysburg to the state's Confederate soldiers. "The blood of no troops from any State in the Union flowed more profusely, or freely, than did that of Alabama's in the great battles of Gettysburg and Chickamauga," he told the Assembly.[30]

But hardly any of these proposals were enacted into law during Oates's term. He spent nearly his entire time in office spinning wheels, puffing smoke, and trying to break free of the overwhelming burden of dealing with appointments and with petty requests from constituents. If the surviving official records of his administration are a good measure of his accomplishments in office, then Oates can only be praised as a caretaker Bourbon governor who achieved little of importance. Even in the matter of making appointments, Oates and his personal secretary, Major William J. Vaiden, were less than efficient. His official papers bulge with requests for pardons, the extradition of criminals, and appeals from Confederate veterans for relief or pensions. Amazingly, however, the legislative did pass an election contest law, but it was accomplished largely because of Kolb's persistent pleadings rather than as a result of anything Oates specifically did as governor.[31]

Most of his efforts were spent trying to work through Alabama's financial straits and find the means to obtain more revenue. It was an uphill battle. The gold reserve in the United States continued to dwindle, with the effect of prolonging the economic depression in particularly poor states like Alabama. Oates went to New York and worked out an arrangement to sell Alabama bonds and refund the bonded indebtedness of the state. Down in the shallow canyons of lower Manhattan, where the nation's financial wizards—the "Robber Barons" as Joseph Pulitzer called them—dwelled and worked their magic, he found Yankee bankers more than willing to loan Alabama the money it needed. By the end of his term, he had succeeded in cutting the state deficit almost in half. That in itself was a fairly significant accomplishment, or so it seemed, but he had hoped to do more, especially by getting the state's horrendous finances in order. His negotiated loans from Northern banks provided only stop-gap measures that would one day have to repaid. As a result, Alabama's dire fiscal straits continued for many years after his one term in office.[32]

Oates tried as much as possible to put a good face on Alabama's financial woes. In an article published in the *North American Review* during his first year in office, Oates pointed out that the Panic of 1893 had retarded industrial development in his state and throughout the South. He happily reported, however, that cotton prices were up at last, and higher prices for this staple crop would help bring Southern farmers out of debt. "Every man without regard to his color who is willing to labor finds ready employment at living wages," he proclaimed. Summarizing the growth of mines, foundries, and factories in the South, he attempted to paint a picture of thriving new enterprise throughout the region, although in the end he used his article mostly to argue once more against the free coinage of silver and in favor of the Nicaragua canal.[33]

Although he worked for several reform initiatives during his term as governor, he mostly stood as a steadfast opponent to specific reform movements and proposals. Reformers, for example, had tried ardently to rehabilitate the convict lease system, a cruel and inhumane labor program that seemed to many worse than slavery itself. But the convict lease system brought money into the state, and Oates directed his energies toward reducing the reforms that had been achieved in recent years and supporting the convict labor system without question. Given his reaction to the Homestead strike and his strong belief in the necessity of liberty of contract in the workplace, it came as no surprise to anyone that Oates convinced the legislature to revoke a law that prohibited women and children from working long hours for their employers. He argued that the law kept industry from locating in the state and investors from putting their money into industrial projects and expansion. Having no kind words for Populists of any kind, he viewed reformers as idealists who lacked practical experience in the world—and he publicly ridiculed reformers in the harshest language possible, dismissing their efforts as misguided and fruitless.

Despite his busy schedule as governor and the endless problems he faced daily, he maintained a relatively calm exterior and a cool disposition, both at home and in his executive office in the capitol. But the violent streak that had both plagued him all his life and had made him an intrepid—if not entirely successful—soldier still lay beneath the surface of his relatively placid demeanor. In a birthday letter to Willie when the boy was eight, he set forth several "precepts" by which the boy should live. Like many elders, Oates advised his son to obey his father and mother and never to tell a lie. Strangely, Oates also advised his young son "never [to] get up a quarrel nor begin a fight, but if any one strikes you[,] you strike him back and strike to hurt." If, Oates added, "anyone calls you a liar, thief or other outrageous name[,] you spit in his face and lay hold of a stick or anything and be ready to defend yourself if he strikes you." The father had a more definite rule for the boy to follow and remember: If anyone should ever strike T, the boy should "get a gun and kill him[,] for the first duty is to defend your mother."[34]

Oates still lived by his own violent rules. One day on the steps of the capitol, as Oates was leaving the building, a white man insulted one of the governor's African American friends. Ever the paternalist, Oates was so enraged by the insult that he grabbed the man by the coat, pushed him down onto the marble steps, and while the man was trying to get to his feet, Oates, using his left fist, assailed him with one blow after another until his victim lay there helpless and almost unconscious. No assault charges were filed against the governor.[35]

Although it is impossible to know for sure, Oates was probably more concerned about the implied insult to himself rather than to his black friend when he decided to beat the offender senseless on the steps of the capitol. At the very least, his behavior was what anyone might have expected from Oates who knew him well—a violent act sparked by a pronounced paternalism. The episode revealed, in fact, how deeply Oates's paternalism actually reached.

In other instances, Oates revealed all too clearly that he still believed firmly in the idea of African American racial inferiority and the vital necessity of white supremacy. For example, Oates, like many other Southern whites, supported the work of Booker T. Washington, the black educator and founder of the Tuskegee Institute in Alabama who was well known for his advocacy of racial accommodation. As an invited speaker at the Tuskegee commencement in June 1896, Governor Oates—who seems to have believed that the African American man with whom he was sharing the podium, John C. Dancy, was a militant leader (he was not)—threw his prepared address aside and delivered a tirade against the blacks in the audience. "I want to give you niggers a few words of plain talk and advice," he blurted out in his rage. He told them not to listen to anyone like Dancy, who might urge them to have high hopes and work toward better times. Oates wanted them to know and accept where they stood in society: "You might as well understand that this is a white man's country, as far as the South is concerned, and we are going to make you keep your place. Understand that. I have nothing more to say to you."

The crowd was stunned, Washington—keeping his composure—jumped in to end the program graciously, and the *Montgomery Advertiser*, knowing full well that it could not print Oates's philippic, reported instead that the governor had cautioned the blacks not to get into politics, but to "put the best white men in office." But the speech, no matter how it was reported, seemed terribly out of character even for Oates, who had appeared sincerely to respect Washington and support accommodationist policy as a means of lifting blacks up from their present condition. Sadly, his remarks seem to have been an attempt to pander to the racial prejudices of poor whites—those who had become disaffected with the Populists and tempted to return to the Democratic mainstream—than a direct disparagement intended to offend Washington or his African American audience. If so, he may have been disappointed that his speech was not accurately rendered in newspaper accounts.

On other occasions, Oates fondly, although patronizingly, called Booker T. Washington "the smartest Negro in the world," and he believed in the Tuskegee cause and helped to get financial support for the school from friends in Congress. Five years later, when President Theodore Roosevelt invited Washington to an evening dinner at the White House, T Oates—like so many other conservative white people in the South—expressed great disgust that such a thing could have occurred in the President's Mansion. She blamed it all on Roosevelt's "negro socialism," and Oates presumably agreed with her.[36] In any event, he would soon tell himself that he had every reason in the world to think the worst of anyone who had even a drop of African American blood.

For some reason, the job of speaking in public became somewhat more precarious for Oates during his gubernatorial term, not because he failed to deliver riveting speeches, but because he could never quite tell what was going to happen once he stepped up to the lectern. On one occasion, a heckler interrupted him while he addressed a crowd in Montgomery. As Oates was trying to put his message across, one man in the audience shouted out: "Well, what about all those nigger children you've got in the backyard?" Oates turned his dark eyes on the man and said in an even tone: "What about them? I feed them. I clothe them. I house them and I educate them. What do you do about yours?"[37]

It was a clever and witty response, the sort of thing one might expect from Oates and all his experience on the stump, but the fact was that he had taken care of his two illegitimate sons, who by this time were both in their late twenties. The activities of Oates's younger illegitimate son, Josh, are not known for the decades of the 1880s and the 1890s, but it is possible that by the early 1890s, he had finished studying toward his medical degree or serving an apprenticeship that led him into private practice as a physician in Dale County. The older son, Claude, may have finished law school by this time, perhaps studying at the University of Alabama or at Vanderbilt University in Nashville, successfully passing as white in all his endeavors. Yet Claude Oates had a difficult time finding his way. After finishing his education, with no clear goals or plan for the future, he turned to his father for help.[38]

Oates gave Claude money to move to Polk County in Texas, where the young man could settle down near his mother, who had presumably married again, this time to a man named Allen. Sallie Vandalia Knight Allen, whose household now included several children ranging in age from their early teens to adulthood, owned a millinery shop in the town of Italy, Texas, where the Confederate government had established a hat factory during the war. Eventually, the senior Oates convinced his son to relocate to the Panhandle, but not simply as a fatherly gesture that would enable his son to live closer to his mother. Oates wanted his son to act as his legal agent and purchase land for him in the vicinity of Amarillo, where the senior Oates had previously bought up land parcels in the early 1880s. Apart from a sum of money Oates gave Claude to pay for the move to Polk County and for his services as an agent, he sent his son a working fund of approximately $26,000 in 1890 to purchase tracts of land south of Amarillo in the senior Oates's name as an investment for the future. The arrangement left plenty of room for confusion, since it was probably not clear to Claude how much of his father's money he could reasonably spend on himself and how much was intended solely for the purchase of real estate with William Oates's name alone on the deeds.

But no matter how much ambiguity existed in his dealings with his father, Claude decided he did not want to do his father's bidding and he never acquired all the land he was supposed to buy or that he later assured William Oates that he had indeed bought. Resentful that the senior Oates had sent him to acquire land in the Panhandle (a "God forsaken wilderness" in Claude's words), he purchased only one section for about $6,000 and used the rest of his father's money to invest in schemes that the young man hoped would make him rich. Unfortunately, the Panic of 1893 wiped out all of the young man's investments, and he had nothing to show as a return on the $20,000 he had "borrowed" without his father's knowledge. To cover his debts, he was forced to draw up forged title papers for the one section he had purchased for the senior Oates; with the phony papers, he sold that parcel to an unsuspecting buyer. In turn, Claude sent his father fraudulent deeds intended to prove that he had spent the money as William Oates had expected. As a result, the father thought he had obtained, through Claude's work as his legal agent, land tracts in the Panhandle that, in the end, he discovered that he never really owned at all. The money had actually gone into Claude's pocket and

then into the son's unsuccessful investment schemes. The only land the senior Oates truly owned in Texas were the parcels he himself had purchased in
the 1880s. There was no new land, and now there was no money, either.[39]

The bottom fell out of Claude's scheme when the purchaser discovered
that the deed had been forged and pressed criminal charges. Before the warrant could be served against him, Claude fled to the Texas Gulf coast. When
the senior Oates learned of Claude's actions, and his flight from the authorities (which certainly must have brought back memories of William's own
younger days as a fugitive in the Lone Star state), he hired a lawyer in Texas
to straighten out what had by that time become a tangle of claims and counter-
claims—amidst a profusion of forged deeds and bogus title chains. Another
surprise came when Oates was informed that Claude had magnanimously given
some of his father's land as a gift to his mother, Sallie Allen, the milliner, and
that the woman, through some mysterious but legal means, seemed to hold
true title to the property.[40] Behind the mystery, it seems fairly certain that
Claude and his mother conspired together to defraud William Oates.

Caught up in his own wrath, the senior Oates convinced himself that
Claude's inability or refusal to cut the apron strings to his mother (something
William Oates never demanded of Willie in his relationship with T) meant
that race—and no other reason—had propelled the two of them to swindle
him. It would never have occurred to Oates that Sallie may have harbored a
deep resentment, or even a fiery rage, against him for having taken sexual
liberties with her thirty years before. Nor would he have been able to understand Claude's feelings of powerlessness in being an illegitimate *and* mulatto
son of such a prominent white man. Life could not have been easy for Claude,
caught between two worlds and two very different parents. It was difficult
enough to be the illegitimate son of one of Alabama's most famous politicians, but it was probably more challenging still to sort out his biracial identity. He had been raised by his black mother, but he had chosen to pass for
white, probably when his father offered him the opportunity to attend the
University of Alabama. In making this decision (unlike other mulattos, for
instance, who chose *not* to pass), Claude took on a great deal of psychological
burden and racial discomfiture. The act of passing kept him caught between
two races and wedged between the color quandaries that plagued the South.

The entire incident threw the senior Oates in a paroxysm of familial and
racial malevolence. His enmity tossed him from one malignant thought to
another: Claude had failed him as a son; Claude had stolen from him; Claude
had become more his mother's, than his father's, son; Claude must have embraced dishonesty because of some trait inherited from his mother's race, not
from the white Oates family. But none of this revilement was as simple as he
tried to make it when he later wrote down his account of the episode. Under
the surface, William Oates wrestled with painful realities that he could not
easily trounce. Racial resentment, and probably some self-loathing for having

gotten himself involved with his former black nurse, commingled with parental disappointment and paternal feelings of having been betrayed. All in all, it appears that Oates's jumbled and heated reaction was inextricably linked to the complexity of his feelings about race. For Oates, African Americans, including his mulatto son and his former black paramour, could be managed effectively so long as they behaved in a morally unimpeachable manner, as Booker T. Washington seemed so capable of doing. In that sense, Oates held black people—and certainly his own son—to a higher standard than he did his fellow whites. When whites faltered, they revealed their own individual imperfections as human beings. But when blacks (or anyone with a share of African American blood) stumbled morally or legally, they laid bare all the impurities, vices, and flaws of their race. In Oates's thinking, Claude's wrongdoing was committed not only by William Oates's son, which was unthinkable in itself, but by a mulatto who also happened to be Oates's son. Oates's extreme vehemence toward Claude and Sallie Knight came not just from his outrage at having been swindled by them, but from the utter complexity of his racial attitudes (and, no doubt, from the guilt he may have felt over his own voluntary act in having mixed the two races, white and black, together in the first place).

When Claude's nefarious ways became publicly known, he fled Texas and told his father he had joined the crew of a gulf schooner and would soon be off for South America. Several lawsuits were filed against the young Oates by his creditors, and it appears that William Oates was named as a co-plaintiff in at least one of those actions, but the question of reclaiming his Texas lands came down to negotiating an out-of-court settlement with Claude's mother, Mrs. Allen. Oates, for his part, said that Claude ("one of the worst liars living") and his "trifling mean mother" were actually "closely matched in meanness."[41] What became of Claude cannot be determined. He may have actually ended up in South America, although it is more likely he remained in the states, changed his name, and did the best he could to become his own person—no longer carrying the burden of being William C. Oates's bastard son. But for the rest of his life the reality of being a mulatto could not be cast away or shoved aside. It seems likely that for Claude Oates, who escaped the clutches of his father and of the law, the complex exigency of passing for white became a heavier burden than his illegitimacy ever would be.

For the senior Oates, his tense transactions with Claude threw him into despair. He had always held high hopes for all his children. Claude had not only disappointed him, he had followed a path that Oates himself had rejected as a young man when he turned his back on a rogue's life to follow the straight and narrow. He expected his sons—including the two illegitimate ones—to succeed in life, to do the same as he had done, only in the end to do it better. Oates was determined to make sure that the road Claude had followed, the road that led to deceit and thievery and flight, would never be a route that offered itself to his darling boy, Willie.

12

A SOLDIER IN HIS HEART

For all his success as a politician, an attorney, a land speculator, a cotton planter, and plantation entrepreneur, the past—and particularly the Civil War—remained evermost in William Oates's consciousness and defined his nature and identity as a man, an Alabamian, a Southerner, and an American; he was, in Emerson's phrase, "mortgaged to yesterday."[1] He could not completely leave the war behind and he didn't want to, if only because he regarded the great struggle as his glory days, a time in his youth when he played the part of a great hero on bloody battlefields—the valiant and manly soldier who, in fact, had sacrificed so much for the cause in which he believed and who, with his empty sleeve pinned up, had so impressed a little girl that she had fallen in love with him. As a result, he carried the war with him into all his later years, like an old frayed valise he could not part with—less because he had grown attached to it over time, but rather because it contained so much of what he had once been and could still return to.

He had even come to believe, as only old soldiers can, that his conduct at Chickamauga—probably his worst performance as a field officer—was exceptionally praiseworthy and valorous. So when the commission appointed by the War Department to administer the Chickamauga and Chattanooga National Military Park invited him to attend the dedication ceremonies on September 19 and 20, 1895, in his capacity as governor of Alabama and as one of the "survivors of the armies engaged in the battles," he leaped at the chance, particularly because he was also asked to give an address during the exercises on September 20 honoring the participation of Longstreet's corps from the Army of Northern Virginia in the battles of Chickamauga and Chattanooga.[2]

At 10:00 A.M. on the stifling hot morning of September 20, the ceremonies opened with a short parade of veterans and militia through the business and residential streets of Chattanooga. Along the parade route, the bunting and flags decorated the streets "in great profusion." Fourteen governors, including Oates, rode in the parade as it advanced to Orchard Knob, a little more than a mile southeast of the city, where Grant had made his headquarters in late November 1863. There, beneath a huge canvas tent with a seating capacity for 12,000 people, the Chattanooga battlefields were dedicated with long-winded speeches that spread the goodwill of reconciliation and that told, in excruciating detail, the movements of armies and the struggles that had taken place between Union and Confederate soldiers across this ground.[3]

That evening, as the autumn coolness of night fell on Orchard Knob, the veterans of the Army of Northern Virginia and the Army of the Potomac who had fought at Chickamauga and Chattanooga filled the seats beneath the warm tent and listened to Oates deliver his prepared remarks. Oates's speech, however, proved to be an embarrassment. Ever the die-hard Southern politician, he used the occasion to express his own views on reconciliation between the sections, the Lost Cause, and the meaning of the Civil War. He started out well enough, describing the battle of Chickamauga with hyperbole as one of the "great events of the world." Hoping to ingratiate Northerners in the audience, he declared that "this great occasion is a higher honor to the Union veteran than to the Confederate, because he was a conqueror, and yet he indulges no vain, or offensive boast, over his fallen rival."[4]

But after giving an account of the battle and of the "humble" but "conspicuous" part he played in it, he began to get himself into trouble by digressing into an lengthy exposition on the causes of the war and a spirited apologia for slavery and secession. As he had done in other speeches, he propounded his notion that the North had been settled by Puritan stock and the South inhabited by Cavaliers, an idea that other Southern speakers had voiced earlier in the dedication ceremonies. But while others had used the metaphor of Puritan and Cavalier to draw a cultural distinction between North and South on the eve of Civil War, Oates took the metaphor an insulting step farther to argue that the Southern Cavalier was a vastly superior type of human being. It was, in Oates's estimation, the Puritans and their "aggressive fanaticism" that "caused an ocean of tears to be shed, drenched the land in blood[,] and sacrificed the lives of a million of men and untold millions of treasure."[5]

The audience sat in cold silence as Oates continued to weave his own tapestry of the war's history by maligning Northerners and all that they had fought for. The Union veterans could stand only so much, however, and when Oates denounced Lincoln as an "abolitionist" who had "proclaimed the irrepressible conflict," the angry crowd began to murmur in dissent. Then Oates took a leaf from the Lost Cause manual and asserted that Southerners, in response to Lincoln's election, were "awakened to a common danger—not about slavery alone, but that their ancient and well defined right to govern their own internal affairs in their own way would be denied and destroyed, not directly, but by attrition, under the guise of law and constitutional administration." With this statement, the Northern veterans rose up in protest, shouting Oates down. In reply, Oates said: "I know that some of you Union men do not relish what I am saying, but hear me through; I will tell you the truth and give you nothing but the facts."[6]

In closing, he finally settled on a point that everyone in the audience could agree on. "The earnestness and gallantry of our soldiers on both sides," he said, "will forever command the admiration of the world." Both North and South had now come together and recognized that "the Union and the Constitution are one and inseparable[,] now and forever."[7] Oates had spoken for an hour or more, and he finally sat down to polite applause. But the crowd must have been confused. Used to hearing the rhetoric of reconciliation and apology, the audience heard instead Oates's own brand of harsh finger-pointing and aggressive accusation, which was usually reserved for Southern ears alone, not for mixed groups intent on celebrating the equivalent courage of Union and Confederate soldiers and the joyous bonds of sectional affection. Such blatant laying of blame, particularly on the Northern doorstep, tended to undermine the more complacent language of appeasement favored by reconciliationists like John B. Gordon and Jubal Early, one of the leaders of the Lee Cult.

His remarks offended many who heard them and others who learned about them. "Something of a sensation," reported the *New York Times*, "was created at the meeting." As soon as Oates took his seat, several Northern governors stood up to offer heated responses to his "exceedingly pointed comments." After the ceremonies, Horatio King—a former officer in the Army of the Potomac, a recipient of the Medal of Honor, a competent newspaper editor, and an accomplished lawyer in New York City—sent a fiery report of Oates's speech to John P. Nicholson, commander of the Philadelphia chapter of the Military Order of the Loyal Legion of the United States and chairman of the Gettysburg National Military Park Commission. The "joyful exercises" dedicating the Chickamauga and Chattanooga Military Park "were marred," wrote King, "by the discordant notes of General and Governor Oates of Alabama[,] who . . . declared that their (the Confederate) cause was just and that . . . the peaceable separation of the North and south would have been both wise and desirable." King's damning appraisal of Oates's speech gave Nicholson his first introduction to the man who had fought against Chamberlain and the 20th Maine on Little Round Top.[8]

There was no such criticism of his speech in Alabama, and Oates must have been pleased to receive a request for copies of the address from Thomas M. Owen, who would later gain renown as one of the state's most accomplished historians. Owen also asked about Oates's progress on his history of the 15th Alabama, and while there is no record of Oates's reply, he must have informed Owen that he was continuing to compile information and that his notes were piling up. To facilitate his research, and to satisfy some inner longings, Oates took advantage of an opportunity late in his term as governor to visit Gettysburg for a second time. While T and Willie went on vacation to California, where they visited Wyatt Oates and his family in San Francisco, Oates and a party of eight (including his close friend and political ally, Alabama congressman Ariosto A. Wiley) attended a Confederate reunion in Richmond, toured the capital in Washington, and traveled on by train to Gettysburg, where they walked the battlefield and climbed the slopes of Little Round Top.[9]

Oates was able to find immediately the place where he had left his brother John mortally wounded on the bloody afternoon of July 2. He picked up some minie balls among the rocks and cut a strong hickory pole to use as a walking stick—which he later carried back with him all the way to Montgomery—and tried to shut out the dreadful memories of all that had happened on this hillside more than thirty years earlier. He could not stop remembering. The memories flooded over him, like a surging stream running its banks. He told Emmor B. Cope, the national park's engineer who was serving as Oates's guide that day, and the others in the party all that had happened there—of the multiple attacks up the slope, of the 20th Maine's determined defense of the ground, of his fear that he was being outflanked, and of his men's desperate retreat up the steep and rocky terrain of Big Round Top.

He wished T and Willie could have been there with him, for he wanted to let them see for themselves where the war had been decided—"the great battle of the war," as he called it, "the turning point." More than anything, he hoped Willie could see the battlefield with him some day. "And then," he later wrote to his son, "I can show you how it was fought."[10]

For the first time, Oates saw the granite monument and stone flank markers of the 20th Maine on Little Round Top. The monument had been dedicated in 1889 by Joshua Chamberlain and the surviving veterans of the Maine regiment, and the memorial itself sat high on an outcropping of rocks and dominated the southern slope of the hill. In the sunlight, the monument looked all white and bright on the rocky ledge, like a turret on an ancient castle wall. If Oates felt that the Maine memorial unfairly commanded the attention of sightseers to Little Round Top, he did not say so. But the seeds of wanting to erect a monument to his own regiment may well have been planted during this summer visit to Gettysburg in 1896.[11]

After he returned to Montgomery and resumed his duties as governor, the Gettysburg trip lingered in his mind and he could not shake off his melancholy. With T and Willie still in California, the Oates house on South Court Street was quiet and empty, except for a few black servants who prepared the meals and looked to the other household chores. Throughout Oates's term as governor, his house near the capitol bustled with people and noise—more so than Oates ever preferred. T had become the toast of Montgomery, just as she had in the nation's capital, and her weekly "open house" parties every Thursday were the talk of the town. Assisted by the wives of other state officials, T greeted her guests with a warmth and charm that made everyone feel right at home. When T wasn't throwing soirees in Montgomery, she was gathering family members around her at Roseland for "house parties" that lasted two weeks or more. Sometimes as many as thirty people—including Toney relatives and T's society friends from Washington (but no Oates family members from Abbeville, a few miles away)—would occupy the mansion house at the old plantation, which by this time had mostly gone to seed. T needed these parties in her life more than Oates could understand. Like other Southern women, she had been raised to define herself as a member of a larger network of women relatives, mostly consisting of her mother, aunts, cousins, and nieces, but also extending to friends and other women of the same social class; that network and the context it supplied to her life was crucial to sustaining her own image of herself. Her parties went beyond mere social events: They reinforced her own understanding of who she was and gave her reassurance of her distinctive place among family, acquaintances, and community.[12]

But the gaiety and frivolity ended in late 1895 when T—who was in the prime of her life at age thirty-three—became seriously ill. Outwardly she seemed mostly fine, except that she occasionally left out words when she spoke and could not comprehend some words when she silently read to herself. She also complained of noises in her head. She was diagnosed as suffering from aphasia, a disturbance of the language function usually caused by damage to the left motor area of the brain; in T's case, she may have had a mild stroke that brought on the affliction. In January 1896, Oates took her to Philadelphia, where she received treatment in the form of neck messages and electrotherapy. Oates could not stay for her extended treatment, so he returned to Montgomery.[13]

She remained in Philadelphia for several months, writing as often as she could to Willie back home and waiting patiently for letters to reach her from Alabama. She did not have an easy time of it. The electrotherapy was painful and probably did not help very much. With the coaching of a sympathetic nurse, she was able to learn how to speak and write again, although she became terribly frustrated whenever she made a mistake in grammar or word choice. Soon she reacquired the ability to read to herself without difficulty.[14]

But her recovery was not speedy. By the summer of 1896, while Oates began to ponder the upcoming state elections and he and Willie went to the

New Jersey shore for a vacation, T was recuperating at their house on Q Street in Washington, still under the care of doctors and nurses, although steadily making progress in her recovery. She would never quite feel herself again. To be sure, T's condition steadily improved as the months went on, but for the rest of her life she spoke slowly and hesitantly—a sign of how hard it was for her to speak coherently at all. She found great comfort in her reading, which continued to be wide-ranging among different authors and across diverse subject lines.[15]

Meanwhile, Oates decided to run for the U. S. Senate, a plan that had been in the making even before he had left Congress. But he encountered strong opposition among Democrats. Several leading member of the state party—including H. C. Tomkins and Edmund W. Pettus—vied for the nomination, which Pettus won in the August primary. Division in the party also surfaced in the presidential race that year. When the Democratic Party nominated the free silver candidate, William Jennings Bryan, after his stirring "cross of gold" speech at the national convention, gold Democrats, including Oates, refused to support the ticket and swung their votes to John L. Palmer of Illinois and former Confederate general Simon B. Buckner, who ran for president and vice president respectively on the National Democratic ticket. Most old Cleveland gold Democrats understood that Palmer and Buckner had little chance of winning in a race dominated by the mainstream candidates. On election day, William McKinley roundly defeated Bryan (and the Palmer ticket came in a weak third); McKinley won the White House partly because gold Democrats like Oates had deprived Bryan of crucial support.

Oates's decision to stand by the Cleveland Democrats, while the party embraced the free silver Populism of Bryan, probably hurt him in his bid for the Senate. To Alabama voters, the silver standard was becoming an acceptable alternative to gold, even though the Farmers' Alliance suffered from a weakened political base throughout the state. When the Alabama legislature met in December 1896 to elect a senator to the seat vacated by Oates's law mentor, James L. Pugh, it was Pettus they chose and not Oates. Wanting Pugh's old seat more than anything he had desired in his political career, Oates had hoped that being governor would increase his popularity in the state; instead, it had done just the opposite. Despite several worthy reforms that he proposed in the second year of his term, Oates could not actually claim many solid records of accomplishment, short of having reduced the state's sizeable deficit. Political divisions in the state also worked against him. But what must have hurt Oates as well in his popular standing was his championing of an undistinguished ticket of renegade Democrats in the recent presidential race—a ticket that drew votes away from Bryan and made Oates appear to be more of a goldbug, and less of a "bi-metalist," than he had previously claimed.[16]

He spent his last day as governor on his sixty-third birthday, November 30. The next day, his successor—Joseph F. Johnston, a free silver man who opposed a new state constitution and who embraced many of the reforms espoused by the Populists—was sworn in as Alabama's new governor. Democratic newspapers across the state lauded Oates for his many accomplishments and for having been "a faithful and earnest worker." And despite his political differences with Johnston, he worked with the governor to straighten out the confusing tangle of loans that the state had acquired from banks in Selma and Mobile toward the end of Oates's administration.[17]

Oates's return to private life was uneventful, but it must have been hard on the man. For sixteen years, he had been an elected official, and he had grown used to the pungent aroma of smoke-filled rooms and the incessant chatter about politics that always surrounded him. Now he had ample time to devote to his law practice and his land holdings, neither of which he had totally neglected while in office but neither of which ignited in him the same kind of passion that war and politics had done. He moved the family to a larger house, a spectacular Victorian dwelling with huge rooms and high ceilings, located on North Ripley Street directly behind the Capitol. Separate servants' quarters were housed in a backyard structure. Although he sometimes complained of financial losses while serving the public, his fortune had grown over the years and he remained—despite economic panics and occasional bad investments—a very wealthy man.[18]

With more time on his hands than he had had in years, Oates picked up his work on researching and writing a history of the 15th Alabama regiment.[19] His effort at documenting the activities of the regiment and the individual war records of its rank and file always seemed to lead him back to Gettysburg, no matter which battle or soldier he was concentrating on at the moment. Some of his comrades had been killed or wounded in the battle; others had been captured. Gettysburg came to represent a milestone in the service of every soldier: What happened to each man there marked either an end to life or the beginning of a new chapter in their lives that seemed unconnected to what had come before the battle. For Oates and other survivors of Gettysburg, the battle became a turning point not only because they could see with the benefit of hindsight that the high tide of the Confederacy had been reached there in the summer of 1863, but also—and more significantly—because their own lives, their very fates, had been radically altered over the course of three days in a battle that had no equal in the annals of North America.

His personal reasons for thinking of Gettysburg as a turning point were reinforced in November 1896, when he received an unexpected letter from Dr. J. A. E. Reed, the physician who had served during the war as the surgeon

of the 155th Pennsylvania and who had treated John Oates's wounds following the battle of Gettysburg. William Oates had been trying for years to determine Reed's identity, but his efforts had failed to turn up the doctor's name.
It is not clear if Oates finally succeeded in tracking the doctor down or if
Reed wrote Oates on his own, perhaps realizing that the governor of Alabama
was the brother of the man he had tended. In any event, Reed described John
Oates's last days in detail and assured the governor that his kin had been
treated kindly and professionally on his death bed. "Many little favors, in the
shape of such delicacies as could be procured in our camp or hospital," wrote
Reed, "were given to your brother and his friend [Bud Cody], thereby ce-
menting a friendship so strangely begun." When the end came, the doctor
arranged for John to be buried in a field close to the hospital and erected a
wooden marker over the grave with his name and rank on it. Reed told the
governor that he feared the marker had long since disappeared.[20]

After traveling to Washington to attend President William McKinley's
inauguration on March 4, 1897, Oates received a letter from Joshua L.
Chamberlain of Maine, his old Gettysburg adversary. The two men had never
corresponded with one another, nor had they ever met in person over the
years. Politely pointing out that he was engaged in some controversy with
"the 'Gettysburg Commission' of this State," by which he meant the compil-
ers of a forthcoming official publication on Maine's role in the battle, Chamberlain wanted Oates to clarify whether or not he and his Alabamians actually
crossed over the summit of Big Round Top or a lower spur before assaulting
the 20th Maine on July 2. The commission, he said, thought it impossible for
Oates to have come over the hill's highest point.[21] Oates replied at length
with a full account of the events that had occurred on the afternoon of July 2,
beginning with Oates's promotion to colonel of the 15th Alabama before the
battle. He made it clear to Chamberlain that he felt no rancor. "I have great
respect and kindly feeling for a good soldier without regard to the side on
which he fought," Oates wrote. He did insist, however, that it was not
Chamberlain's bayonet assault that had compelled the 15th Alabama to withdraw. "My regiment was not driven out by a charge," he wrote, "but went by
my order when I had lost one half of them."[22]

Later that same month, Oates corresponded with Dr. F. A. Dearborn of
Nashua, New Hampshire, who was compiling firsthand accounts of the fight
for Little Round Top (and who later asked Chamberlain to supply information about the 20th Maine's role at Gettysburg). Oates supplied yet another
complete account of the events he and his regiment had experienced on July
2, 1863—once more replaying in his mind and putting down on paper what
had happened to him at Gettysburg. This time he corrected several mistakes
he had made in earlier writings about the battle, including casualty figures
that he had published in his article in the *Southern Historical Society Papers*.[23]

More than 850 miles lay between Montgomery and Gettysburg. But in his heart William C. Oates never felt very far away from the Pennsylvania battlefield where he had lost so much and where his life had been forever altered. When it came to recounting what had happened at Gettysburg, he wanted to get the details as straight as possible, but in the end it was not the small particulars that really mattered much to him. Even so, no matter how many times he discussed the battle—with fellow veterans, John B. Bachelder, Joshua Lawrence Chamberlain, or interested individuals like F. A. Dearborn—the verdict of history always turned out to be the same: The 15th Alabama was repulsed at Little Round Top, Lee was defeated at Gettysburg, and Oates left his wounded brother to die in Pennsylvania. Oates repeatedly encountered the ineluctable truth of history, and he never could quite figure out how to cope emotionally with what could not be changed, what could not be undone.

Thoughts of war—past and present—filled Oates's head in the spring of 1898, and he pondered little else as the United States moved closer and closer to armed conflict with Spain. In the aftermath of the *Maine* explosion, public opinion, egged on by the yellow journalism of William Randolph Hearst and Joseph Pulitzer, had swelled into a hysteria against Spain and its policies in Cuba. Finally President McKinley and Congress could resist no longer the public clamor for war. On April 25, the United States declared war against Spain, and from that moment Oates hankered to get into the fray. He was, as one contemporary described him, "a soldier at all times in his heart," and he did not want to miss this war.[24] His desire to enlist combined sincere patriotism, Southern hubris, his old violent streak, and Lost Cause reconciliation sentiment (former Confederates could now prove their loyalty to the United States by fighting alongside their former enemies against an evil enemy) into an emotionally powerful yearning to go to war once more.

In May 1898, he wrote to President McKinley, whom he had known for some time, and asked for a brigadier general's commission in the United States Army. With pride, he pointed out that he had received his military education in the field under the tutelage of Stonewall Jackson—something of an exaggeration, of course, but true in the most general of meanings. "I am in good health," he wrote, "and though sixty years old [actually sixty-four] I am quite active and able to perform acceptably all the duties incident to the position." At the same time, the officers of the 2nd Alabama volunteers, stationed at Mobile, had petitioned Oates and asked to be placed in his brigade, should his commission go through.[25]

McKinley, who saw the value of fostering reconciliation with the South by bringing former Confederate officers into the army he was recruiting for the fight with Spain, speedily approved Oates's request, and Oates received his commission on June 2. The president also commissioned as generals several other Confederate notables, including Fitzhugh Lee, Joseph Wheeler, Matthew C. Butler, and Thomas L. Rosser. The number of Union veterans given general's commissions was even more plentiful. In some respects, then, the Spanish war was a peculiar extension of the Civil War to foreign isles and waters, this time with Northerners and Southerners fighting on the same side against a demonic enemy. Strategy and tactics for land warfare rather slavishly followed the accepted tenets of the Civil War—close order drill, artillery barrages, and massed frontal assaults—with little innovation. The recruitment of soldiers by states resembled the organization of fighting forces on both sides during the Civil War, and although modern smokeless rifles were issued to army regulars, volunteers in this War with Spain often received old black-powder muskets left over from the 1860s.[26]

Oates pleaded with Secretary of War Russell A. Alger, also a Civil War veteran, to be given command of the 1st and 2nd Alabama regiments. But he later found out that corps and brigade assignments in this war were not permanent, an organizational flaw he blamed on Republican policy and their "nationalizing" preferences. It all came down to sectional issues in his mind. He wanted to command Alabamians because he felt state pride, "which springs from love of home, the foundation of true Democracy," and which Northerners apparently lacked or, at least, could not comprehend.

After going to Washington and receiving assurances from McKinley and Adjutant General Henry Clark Corbin that he would be placed in command of the Alabama brigade, Oates went without written orders by train to Mobile, where he learned that his brigade had been given to another officer. Traveling with him was Willie, whom he later said "insisted on going to the war with me," but who probably had little say in the matter. Oates and his son returned to Montgomery to wait for orders that never arrived. Frustrated by the War Department's lack of responsiveness to his situation, Oates went to Tampa to see Major General John J. Coppinger, commander of the Fourth Army Corps and a former colonel in the Union army. He had a low opinion of Coppinger—an Irish Catholic—right from the start. He told Coppinger that the secretary of war had assigned him to command of the brigade composed of the 1st Alabama and the 1st and 2nd Texas regiments. Coppinger wanted to see the orders in writing, but Oates carefully explained the circumstances that had left him without any orders on paper. "I will not obey it if not in writing," Coppinger declared. And that was that.[27]

Coppinger did offer Oates command of a brigade made up of the 1st Ohio, 2nd Georgia, and 69th New York, which would be sailing for Cuba at once. Oates said he would take it, but he wanted permission to return to Montgomery to get his two horses, uniforms, and equipment. What Oates did not tell Coppinger was that he was also worried about T's health, for she seems that summer to have suffered a relapse of her aphasia. In any event,

Coppinger refused to let Oates go home, even for two days, saying that the troops were about to move out. "I saw," Oates wrote after the war, "that he was not disposed to treat me as a gentleman, and I told him plainly that I would not enter on duty instantly—that my health, comfort, and life were worth something to me." So Oates went home to Montgomery and sent a stinging telegraph off to Adjutant-General Corbin asking to be given command of the 1st Alabama and the two Texas regiments, which had by now been transferred to the Seventh Corps. When no answer came from Corbin, Oates wrote a lengthy plea to President McKinley that told the whole story of his luckless adventures trying to obtain a brigade command. "Give me a chance," he begged the president, "and no troops, either volunteers or regulars, will be better soldiers—or carry the enemy's works more successfully than will the Alabamians under my command."[28]

By now the authorities in Washington must have thought him a crank. Corbin summoned Oates to Washington one more time for meetings and interviews. Alger and Corbin assured him that he would soon receive a brigade command.[29] Yet even as he traveled to Washington and home again to Alabama, the war was flashing toward a rapid conclusion in Cuba. On July 1, American troops overran Spanish works at El Caney and San Juan Hill; two days later the Spanish fleet was utterly destroyed in Santiago harbor. A week later, Santiago surrendered to American forces under the command of Major General William R. Shafter, a Union army veteran. By the end of July, President McKinley spelled out peace terms to the Spanish, and John Hay's "splendid little war" was, for the most part, over in Cuba, except for an insurgent rebellion that would annoy the American occupiers of the island and an even fiercer revolt in the Philippines that would bog down the United States in its first military disaster in southeast Asia.[30]

When Oates arrived in Montgomery, he was distressed to find that while T's health had improved during his absence, Willie had contracted a severe case of typhoid fever and was failing rapidly. T was nearly beside herself in anguish over Willie's infirmity. Within a few days after returning home from his trip to Washington, Oates received orders to assume command of a brigade in the Second Army Corps, then stationed in Falls Church, Virginia. But instead he informed his superiors that he could not leave his son and asked for a leave of absence. His request was granted.[31]

Willie's typhoid did not subside until late August, keeping his father in Montgomery much longer than he had expected. Day after day, Oates watched his son's recuperation, while the war with Spain in the Philippines ended with the surrender of Manila on August 13. After spending fifty-five days at the sick boy's bedside, Oates wrote to Adjutant-General Corbin and to President McKinley specifically asking for a combat assignment in Cuba. In the meantime, he left T, who had recovered from the relapse of her aphasia and

from her nervous distress, and Willie, who was slowly mending, despite lingering complications from the typhoid, and reported for duty to the Second
Army Corps at Middletown, Pennsylvania, a small industrial town of stone
and brick located about six miles southeast of Harrisburg. There, at Camp
Meade, he was given command of the Second Brigade of the First Division of
the Second Army Corps, consisting of the 14th Pennsylvania, 3rd Connecti-
cut, and 202nd New York.[32]

There was not much to do at Camp Meade. As in most army camps of the
time, disease spread rapidly among the men, and typhoid especially reached
epidemic proportions during the late summer. Oates spent some of his off-
duty hours riding through the countryside on Sunday evenings with his commanding officer, Major General James D. Graham, a crusty old veteran of the
Regular Army who also happened to be George Gordon Meade's brother-in-
law. Most of the time, though, Oates was bored and lonely.[33]

By mid-October, as the weather turned cold and the green of the woods
surrounding Camp Meade became mixed with bright reds and somber yel-
lows, Willie—whose health had much improved—arrived from Alabama to
keep Oates company and to serve once more as his father's volunteer aide-de-
camp. T, who was also feeling better, traveled with Willie and stayed at Camp
Meade for a short time. Oates was glad to have his family with him at last. He
was especially proud of his son, who "learned to perform the duties of aide
very efficiently, and received the praise of nearly all the field officers in the
brigade."

Around this time, while peace negotiations began between Spain and the
United States in Paris, Oates and Willie requested a short leave and went
with T to Gettysburg, about forty miles from Camp Meade.[34] The details of
the trip are not known. It is safe to assume that Oates showed his wife and son
around the battlefield on a grand tour, pointing out all the famous landmarks
and telling his family the story of the battle and its thrilling episodes in vivid
detail. The park had become even more accessible and more scenic since
Oates's most recent visit, two years before. The Gettysburg National Battlefield Park Commission had been working hard to improve roads, erect iron
observation towers, and place markers with narrative descriptions of the battle
around the field.[35] At Little Round Top, Oates and his family surely spent a
great deal of time walking the ground where he had fought so desperately
against men in blue uniforms—similar to the blue ones he and Willie now
wore—and pointing out the place where the boy's uncle had been cut down
in the prime of life, only a few years older than Willie was now. Taking his wife
and son to Gettysburg was a dream come true for Oates. To have his family see
this ground was a very necessary rite of passage for the aging William Oates.

The visit also drove home for him what he may have concluded on a
previous trip to the battlefield. The shining presence of the 20th Maine monu-

ment on Little Round Top only underscored the rather apparent absence of any memorial to the 15th Alabama. No doubt it considerably bothered Oates to show his wife and son the Maine monument, when, at the same time, there was nothing on the hill to mark the valor of his Alabama men. On a more personal note, Oates also wished that he could memorialize his brother and others in the old regiment who had fallen on this ground. His own desires coincided with a campaign being waged by William M. Robbins, the only former Confederate serving on the Gettysburg park commission, who hoped to persuade the former Confederate states to appropriate money for monuments in remembrance of the units that had fought in Lee's army at Gettysburg. Whether Oates spoke to Robbins during his visit to the battlefield with T and Willie is not recorded, but he certainly must have read the circular that Robbins sent that fall to nearly every important Southern newspaper pleading for memorials that would honor the Confederate forces that participated in the battle.[36]

After Oates returned to Camp Meade from his short vacation in Gettysburg, and T had returned to Montgomery, he learned that the army had decided to reorganize its corps and brigades, and, as a result, the 202nd New York regiment was removed from Oates's brigade and replaced by the 9th Ohio Colored Battalion. Oates was furious. With his Southern racial prejudices bristling, Oates sought out General Graham and refused to accept the 9th Ohio under his command. Graham bucked the problem up the chain of command, and Oates wrote a strident letter to Major General Samuel B. M. Young, the corps commander, complaining bitterly about the black battalion. He admitted that the 9th Ohio contained well-trained troops in its ranks who showed good discipline in camp and during drill, but he argued that his political career would be finished in Alabama if he should be forced to submit to the assignment of black troops under his command.[37]

In Washington, the War Department responded to Oates's request by sending him on a special detail away from Camp Meade in search of a suitable place for the Second Corps' winter encampment in South Carolina. Oates and Willie, and a small staff of officers, went to Summerville, about twenty miles north of Charleston, to inspect the area and to determine the best site for a military camp. While he was away, the War Department reassigned his entire brigade—including the 9th Ohio—to Brigadier General Adelbert Ames of Maine and Massachusetts, the officer who had led the 20th Maine regiment in the Civil War before Joshua L. Chamberlain had assumed command and who had had a distinguished career in the regular army.[38]

At the end of October, Oates returned to Camp Meade, where General Graham gave him a new assignment in command of the First Brigade of the Second Division of the Second Corps, composed of the 4th New Jersey, 2nd West Virginia, and 15th Pennsylvania—all Unionists, in Oates's estimation. On October 27, Oates led his men in a parade of more than 25,000 troops at the Peace Jubilee in Philadelphia. The parade followed a seven-mile route and passed by Independence Hall, where the Declaration of Independence had been signed by the Founding Fathers. He delighted in the crowds that cheered him as he rode leading his men down Philadelphia's wide streets. "The sight of an old maimed Confederate soldier commanding Union troops raised in the Northern States was such an evidence of a reunited country that it produced applause from one end of the line of march to the other," he wrote with elation.[39]

When Oates got back to Middletown, Pennsylvania, he was reassigned once more, this time to command the First Brigade of the Third Division of the Second Corps, consisting of the 15th Pennsylvania, the 3rd New Jersey, and the 202nd New York regiments. The brigade was soon transferred to Georgia. In early November, Oates and his troops went by train to Camp Haskell, outside Athens, Georgia, where they arrived in a torrential and dis-heartening downpour. The rain continued for days, turning the Georgia clay to a sea of red mud and making it impossible for the regiments of Oates's brigade to erect their tents or find any comfortable shelter. Finally, with much difficulty, the tents were raised, staked, and floored. Everyone—including Oates and poor Willie—was wet, tired, and disagreeable.

In Athens, which he described as "a center of learning and refinement," Oates felt at home. In the genteel surroundings of Southern hospitality, he rather fancied the "handsome and attractive" ladies who "visited the camp nearly every evening to witness the dress parade, and their presence stimu-lated the pride of the officers and men to do their best on such occasions." Late in November, T arrived at Camp Haskell, and Oates was very pleased to have her there to partake "of camp fare with myself and staff officers, who messed together." She stayed at the camp for three weeks. On December 13, three days after the Treaty of Paris had been signed by the United States and Spain, the officers of Oates's brigade held a grand ball and invited the resi-dents of Athens to attend as an expression of the army's gratitude for the community's generosity. T was the belle of the ball. The officers chose her "to preside, direct the ceremonial, and receive the guests." Two days later, Oates went with his brigade to Atlanta and marched in the Peace Jubilee there. The parade was reviewed by President McKinley and members of his cabinet.[40]

After receiving another reassignment and learning that his troops would not be sent out of the country as occupation forces, Oates could no longer contain his anger. He said later that he would never have accepted his com-mission as a brigadier if he had known then that he would never be permitted to command Alabama troops. Yet, for all his complaints about his military service in the U.S. Army and his intimations of mistreatment by the War Department's highest officials, he declared with glee: "I am now a Yankee

General, formerly a Rebel Colonel, and right each time!" He delighted in repeating that statement often after the war.[41]

His military service in the U.S. Army ended as inauspiciously as it had begun. During the chilly first week of January 1899, while he and his son remained at Camp Haskell in Athens with virtually nothing to do while his idle troops yawned their days away or fell victim to illness, Oates submitted his letter of resignation to President McKinley. On January 11, 1899, he received his honorable discharge from the War Department, a crisply worded order that confirmed what he already knew: his services were no longer required. Four days later he issued a farewell to his troops, thanking them for obeying his orders and treating him "with courtesy and respect."[42]

Like other Civil War veterans who served in the War with Spain, Oates believed that it never really measured up to the great conflict fought between North and South. It was a piddling affair, made more so by the fact that he had not seen combat and could not relive the exhilaration of leading his men into battle. Throughout the new war, he never seemed to grasp that it involved issues different than the Civil War or that it represented a determined effort by the United States to extend its empire around the globe. Imperialism and the clash of titan nations did not interest him. Oates, like other Civil War veterans, wanted to fight the great war over again. This little war was to them a great disappointment. So Oates went home. His military days were finally over.

By the beginning of February, Oates had shed his blue uniform and returned to practicing law. He was glad to be home in Montgomery; in fact, he said a few months later that he'd rather be home with T and Willie than be "anywhere on earth." His health was good, his law practice seemed not to have suffered much from his absence in the army, and he felt more energetic than he had in several years. He traveled to Washington in the spring on undisclosed business, visited with President McKinley in the White House, and returned to Alabama in high spirits.[43] What he may have discussed with the Republican president cannot be determined. There are no hints to the nature of the conversation, although he may have been trying to get a presidential appointment for Willie to the U.S. Military Academy—an interesting choice for his only son, since it emphasized Oates's latent nationalism and excluded the Southern military academies, such as the Citadel or the Virginia Military Institute. Or his visit to McKinley may have been a simple courtesy call to thank the president for giving him his commission or, even more likely, to tell the man in charge a thing or two about the inefficiency of the War Department and how he had been badly treated during the war. Whatever his purpose, whatever the substance of his discussion with McKinley, Oates probably took the opportunity to advance himself, or maybe his son, in some manner.

One doesn't visit the president for no good reason. And, ultimately, Oates's reasons always came down to politics—*his* politics.

He hoped, now that his war service had been completed, to get back into the political arena. Six months later, he announced his intentions publicly. On November 1, he spoke for two hours at the Abbeville Court House and declared his candidacy for the U. S. Senate. Knowing that the silver issue still ruled in Alabama politics, he tried desperately in his speech to divorce himself from his earlier opposition to free silver, but his effort came off as weak and unconvincing. He threw his support behind William Jennings Bryan for president in 1900, brought up his old cause of forcing the federal government to refund the cotton tax to the Southern states, favored the Nicaraguan canal, and wanted the war against the Filipino rebels to be vigorously waged and won.

Political observers thought that Oates intended to challenge Edmund W. Pettus, who had won election to the Senate in 1897, and win that seat for himself, but it soon became clear that Oates actually hoped to unseat Senator John T. Morgan, whose term would expire in March 1901. In taking on Morgan, Oates had decided to run against an entrenched giant in Alabama politics. "I trust," wrote Oates in a newspaper statement, "that it will not be considered presumptuous in another old soldier in the army of the Confederacy and the ranks of Democracy to assume that the senator be relieved from his responsible and burdensome duties." But many Democrats saw only ambition in Oates's quest to unseat Morgan, and they dismissed his candidacy as lacking serious political motives and purpose.[44]

Meanwhile, Oates found his political ambition compromised by personal desire. Having possibly discussed an appointment for Willie to West Point, he must have known that McKinley—who owed most of his political debts to Republicans, not out-of-office Alabamian Democrats—would not oblige him with a presidential favor, particularly since Oates had thrown his support, for the time being at least, to Bryan. The only other way for Willie, who was then only sixteen, to win an appointment would be if one of Alabama's two senators, Morgan or Edmund Pettus, agreed to give one of their available appointments to Oates's son. Pettus, who had been opposed by Oates in the 1897 election, apparently refused to do so. In the end, Morgan graciously decided to give Willie the appointment. Oates, grateful beyond words and humbled by the senator's generosity and lack of political rancor, seems to have decided at that moment to take himself out of the race for U.S. Senator. The arrangement—Willie's appointment in return for Oates's withdrawal— appears to have been the result of a deal struck between Oates and Morgan.[45] His political ambition would have to wait for another opportunity, although he could not be sure if such an opportunity would ever again present itself. Oates went back to practicing law, watching and waiting for his next chance.

On the warm, quiet evening of Saturday, June 9, 1900, he and T were enter-taining several guests at their home on North Ripley Street. After dinner, the party went out onto the front veranda to enjoy whatever coolness could be found in the evening air. Sometime after 8:00 P.M., while twilight still lin-gered, the house butler, a black man named Fred Houghton, approached Oates on the porch and whispered discreetly but earnestly to him that a man had attacked and was beating the family's cook, Loula McElhaney, also black, in the cook's room behind the stable in the backyard. Oates and Houghton went through the house to the back door, where Oates could distinctly hear Loula moaning and begging her assailant not to hurt her anymore. Apparently Oates determined that the attacker was armed. With that, Oates ordered Houghton to stay where he was, and he went to his room, a parlor near the front of the house, to get his pistol. While he was there, he heard two shots ring out; quickly, he grabbed his .48 caliber British Lion revolver, hurried back to Houghton, and flew out the back door of the residence.

At the doorway to the cook's quarters, Oates could hear nothing. He motioned to Houghton to swing the door open, for Oates was holding the British Lion pistol in his only hand. When the door creaked open, Loula McElhaney's body toppled forward, and it was obvious to Oates that the woman was dead. He called inside for the man to lay down on the floor or else he would open fire. Slowly he stepped inside the room, and he could see the woman's assailant, a black man, in a crouching position ahead of him. He repeated the warning three times to the man, but instead the assailant reached into his hip pocket and moved forward in Oates's direction. The man took one step, Oates pulled the trigger of his revolver, a single shot boomed in the small room, and the black man fell dead to the floor, a bullet in his brain.

The dead man was later identified as Aaron Parker, a drayman, who had no known connection to Loula McElhaney and no apparent motive to mur-der her. In his hip pocket was a .35 caliber Smith and Wesson pistol with two unexpended cartridges in the chamber. Oates suspected the whole affair was a robbery attempt gone bad. "I should not have gone about the room," Oates later told a Montgomery reporter, "but I could not stand the idea of having a servant murdered right on my own premises." Newspapers described the murder scene as "a horrible sight." Blood was everywhere. Police and the coro-ner came quickly to Oates's house, and the coroner impaneled a jury almost immediately. The jury decided to issue no warrant for Oates's arrest, agreeing unanimously that the former governor had killed Parker in self-defense.

That night word of the killings spread quickly around town, and African Americans came out of their neighborhoods to see what had happened. Soon they were congregating outside Oates's house "by the hundreds." The threat of a riot was in the air. Oates's killing of an African American, whether in self-defense or not, was regarded by some blacks in Montgomery as a step over the line. Perhaps they wondered why Oates had gone to arm himself and had deserted McElhaney in her true moment of need. Meanwhile, Oates's white friends rushed to his house, and soon their numbers either equaled or exceeded the size of the black crowd that murmured irritably and milled about in the streets. Eventually everything cooled down, including the night air; the black mob melted away into the darkness, still muttering as they went, Oates's friends returned to their homes, and Oates—ever calm and poised—tried to calm T down and get her to sleep.[46]

From Oates's butler, Fred, the local police and reporters learned how courageously—and how rashly—Oates had inched into the cook's room, knowing that the woman's murderer was in there and could open fire at any moment. Apparently Oates did not even think about the risks he was taking. He simply would not have someone murdering his help and getting away with it. The fact that his aim was steady and true, even while gripping and firing his British Lion pistol in his left hand, his only hand, revealed just how cool he could be in the face of danger. During the Civil War, no one ever dared to question Oates's bravery. Off the field of battle, it was also quite evident that Oates had nerves of steel. Apparently his butler did not seem to think that Oates had failed McElhaney. But, if he did think such a thing, he would not have said so to the newspapers.

There were no legal ramifications from the killings that took place on Oates's property that night. No charges were pressed, no investigation ever determined the reason why Parker had assaulted Loula McElhaney and killed her. Oates never mentioned killing Parker in his correspondence or journals. Although the story should have been the stuff of legends, the incident was largely forgotten in Montgomery. Probably that's what Oates himself hoped for and preferred. He was a hero who could, at times, be remarkably modest and quietly valiant. And in a moment of crisis, he could be cool, calm, and composed. Going to get his pistol did stop the assailant; but it did not save Loula McElhaney. His response displayed prudence and his confrontation with the woman's attacker showed true courage. But his handling of the situation may have cost the woman her life. Perhaps for that reason, if for no other, Oates preferred not to trumpet the tale. At any rate, Oates had proved once more—though it hardly needed confirmation—that whenever he struck, he always made sure it hurt.

13

STUMBLING TOWARD
EQUALITY

L ife refused to slow down for William Oates. As he approached his
seventieth year, he found himself more busy than ever practicing law,
writing his Civil War book, pushing forward his plans for a monument at Gettysburg, and providing encouragement to young Willie, who had
begun his studies at West Point. His health, while generally good, began to
bother him more and more. With each advancing year, his rheumatism became a painful reminder of age and weariness. For Oates, all life still seemed
like a great battle, and surviving that battle required all the physical strength
and moral courage he could muster.

At least his dream for a monument to the 15th Alabama on the slopes of
Little Round Top appeared to be coming true. Despite some early reluctance
by William Robbins, the "Southern" commissioner, to allow Oates to memorialize the 15th Alabama (with no mention of the other Alabama regiments in
Law's brigade and the part they played in the assault against the Union left at
Gettysburg), Robbins seems to have put aside his objections and the commissioners as a whole apparently decided to overlook a standing rule, first promulgated by the Gettysburg Battlefield Memorial Association, to the effect
that all monuments must be located along a unit's position in line of battle
(where they had been deployed to begin fighting), as opposed to its position
when it became engaged in combat (where the opposing forces actually met on
the field). By rights, that meant that Oates's monument would have to be erected
on Confederate Avenue, which ran along the crestline of Seminary Ridge and
Warfield Ridge, about a mile to the southwest of Little Round Top.

But by the summer of 1900, Robbins and John P. Nicholson, the commission's chairman, told Oates that they would support his idea for a monument, if he would drop his proposal for erecting flank markers on Little Round Top—small stone stumps that would indicate where the left and right flanks of the 15th Alabama had stood on July 2, 1863. Robbins even went to a local stonecutter in Gettysburg, got cost estimates and some diagrams for a monument, and put the drawings and cost figures in his files while mailing copies of them back to Oates. In mid-September, Robbins sent Oates a proposed drawing of the monument and how it would be positioned "at the southern end of 'Vincent's Spur.'"[1] Oates must have been thrilled by this progress.

Less exhilarating were the reports Oates received from Willie at West Point. The young man, now seventeen and among the youngest cadets ever to enter the Military Academy, found the regimentation onerous and the academic demands staggering during his first months on the high plain overlooking the Hudson. The senior Oates tried to reassure his son that all would be well: "I know that if you missed this chance you might never get another[,] and by entering now you may graduate by the time you are 21 and be early prepared for the responsibilities of life." Oates wrote Willie at least once a week, on Sundays, but often broke this pattern by writing lengthy letters during the week in which he discussed the young man's future and the latest world and national events. Willie, when he could, wrote short notes of reply to Oates and T, but in the letters to his mother he was far more frank about how utterly overwhelmed he was by everything he had been encountering at West Point.[2]

The boy dug in his heels and tried to hold on. But his grades remained low and his demerits multiplied. To celebrate T's birthday, Willie left his post without leave to visit his mother in Kentucky, at her brother's home in Louisville. Oates was furious with his son, yet he delivered his scolding with more words of encouragement and with expressions of his deep affection. Even as he went through surgery to have a tumor removed from his arm, Oates kept urging Willie to stay the course at West Point and keep fighting. But for Willie, it was an uphill battle all the way.[3]

On Christmas Eve, he wrote to Willie at West Point while "gayety and mirth" rippled through the Oates house during one of T's famous holiday parties. His wife, caught up in the revelry, seemed unaware that Oates had slipped away upstairs or that he never felt like celebrating on December 24. Actually the cause of Oates's despondency was no secret. "The night recalls to me," he told his son, "the fact that one whom you never saw but who was dear to me was born on Christmas eve night." It was his brother John, Willie's uncle, who came to mind every Christmas Eve since Gettysburg. Oates described to Willie how he had attempted to excuse John from duty on the afternoon of July 2 before the attack on Little Round Top, but his brother—despite his illness—had insisted on advancing with the regiment. Every December 24 and every July 2, Oates said, he would remember his brother's final words to him—his desire to go into battle—and he would "feel sad over his fate." "Had he been killed outright," Oates explained, "it would not have been so sad[,] but he fell into the hands of the enemy and died a prisoner of war." Entrapped by his wrenching memories of his lost brother, Oates concluded by saying: "He was a noble young man and died for his country and in a just cause as he and I both saw it."[4]

The new year of 1901 brought a festering political issue in Alabama to its conclusion. During his term as governor, Oates had supported the call for a constitutional convention to abolish frequent and unnecessary elections, reform the suffrage, allow additional municipal taxation powers, reform the judiciary, and expand the terms of office for governor and legislators from two to four years. But the Democratic Party opposed such a convention, mostly because it feared having to change the state constitution to suit federal election laws giving African Americans suffrage rights; finally in 1898, after a great deal of political infighting, a convention bill passed the legislature and was signed into law by the governor. Nevertheless, opposition by poor whites and the introduction of the silver issue into the convention campaign stalled the movement until the following year, when the Democratic Party nominated Oates and other gold Democrats as delegates to the convention. Oates and his allies fought hard for the convention, even to the point of battling against fellow Democrats, like Governor Joseph Johnston, who wanted to repeal the enabling legislation and kill the convention outright. Despite the efforts of Oates and other like-minded Democrats, a special session of the legislature succeeded in repealing the enabling act in the spring of 1899.[5]

Disfranchisement stood at the center of the political battle over a new constitution, just as it had in other Southern states during the last two decades of the nineteenth century. The issue produced heated debate and wide cleavages among white politicians. Like other fiery political controversies in the South, the question of who should be granted suffrage rights was knotty and complicated. In 1890, Mississippi ratified a new state constitution that paved the way for other Southern states to deprive African Americans of their voting rights under the Fifteenth Amendment to the U.S. Constitution by using a poll tax and a literacy test as prerequisites for suffrage. But disfranchisement in other Southern states became entangled with the effort by Democrats to deprive poor whites, as well as blacks, of the vote—a move aimed at eviscerating the Farmers' Alliances that challenged the predominance of the Democratic Party throughout the South. In each state, white power brokers wanted to keep blacks and some whites from voting for different reasons, although on the surface it appeared that Democrats feared the possibility that their political opponents might attempt to win at the polls by wooing black

votes. Beneath the surface, though, the rationale for disfranchisement differed according to the unique political circumstances found in each of the
Southern states in the twenty years leading up to 1900.[6]

Southern Democrats, like Oates, wished to preserve their firm grasp of the
political reins in their states, but they contended not only with political opposition from Republicans, Populists, and blacks. Divisions between regions—in
Alabama, mostly between the so-called black belt and northern hill regions—
also created severe rents in the ranks of the Democratic party, since the politicians in power generally came from the Black Belt counties and did not
want to share the reins with whites from the hill counties. Whites outside the
Black Belt districts, who complained about being underrepresented in the
state legislature, resented the fact that politicians usually won election by fraud,
including the manipulation of black votes, either by currying favor with blacks
and persuading them to cast their ballots for the incumbents, by miscounting
black and white votes to ensure their reelection, or by keeping blacks from
casting any ballots at all. Political divisions also emerged between urban and
rural interests, agrarian and industrial concerns, and the old leadership and rising
newcomers in the Democratic Party. Dissenters and reformers could also be
found in the growing ranks of urbanites and industrialists who espoused a
Southern brand of Progressivism. In Alabama, as in the lower South in general,
the Democratic Party was not as solid as the old planters, the Redeemers, and
the powerful elites—the ruling class—wanted to believe.[7]

By 1900, the Democrats in Alabama—including an enthusiastic William
Oates—had finally united around the issue of a new constitution, and the
only opposition was voiced by a weak cadre of Populists and Republicans.
After the legislature passed a new enabling bill, the Democratic Party met in
January 1901 and endorsed the call for a convention. Oates hit the campaign
trail again, giving countless speeches around the state in favor of a new constitution and promoting his election as an at-large delegate to the convention. Many vocal supporters of the convention wanted the new constitution
to disfranchise African Americans as a way of ensuring white supremacy and
reassuring poor whites that their own votes would be protected. Disfranchising conventions had been enormously successful in Mississippi, South Carolina, and Louisiana.[8]

The white power-brokers of the South wanted to limit suffrage in their
states as much as possible, not only to keep blacks from voting, but to prevent
large numbers of poor white farmers, who had previously supported the Farmers' Alliance in Alabama and the Populists throughout the region, from using
their political power, as they had almost successfully done in the 1890s, to
topple the established regime of the Black Belt politicians and the Bourbon
Democrats. Limiting the suffrage of disgruntled—or potentially disaffected—
whites became as important to the reigning Democrats as prohibiting African
American males from exercising the franchise. Unhappy farmers, whom the

white elites regarded as politically ignorant, even to the point of possibly allying with blacks against the Democratic party and its powerful leaders, might even turn their backs on policies of white supremacy if they found common ground with African Americans on other political issues. To prevent such a thing from happening, the established white politicos kept racial controversy at the forefront of Southern politics; they aroused anti-black sentiments that, in some cases, might even have led to the lynching and terrorism of blacks, waved the banner of white supremacy to remind all white Southerners about their duty to maintain the region as a white man's country, and curtailed or prohibited outright suffrage to any—including African Americans *and* whites—who might attempt to challenge or even unseat the white men in power. Many white Southerners learned that a voting test made permanent in the fundamental law of the state could be an effective device for restricting suffrage to only the most worthy white males.

Knowing the high stakes, and supporting the incorporation of voting tests into any new Alabama constitution that became ratified, Oates asserted that any kind of voting test put into effect, whether based on literacy or property, should be applied to all voters equally. This made him sound wonderfully egalitarian, but his real concern, which he shared with many other white Democrats, was that blacks had often voted for Democratic candidates, preferring, in a sense, to vote for the evil they knew rather than for one they did not know, while some white voters had cast their ballots for opposition candidates, such as those from the Farmers' Alliance or malcontented fusionist Democrats. Oates made plain his own preference for preventing undesirable and unworthy men—white or black—from voting. He purposely kept his definitions of these terms vague, since anyone who voted for him or his political allies was, in his estimation, a worthy voter, while anyone who voted for the opposition was not, but he referred to those who should be kept from voting as "the ignorant, incompetent, and vicious" of both races.

Disfranchisement, however, was not all that created a need for a constitutional convention or for a new constitution to replace the 1875 document. Based on his experience as governor, Oates also saw great need for constitutional reform beyond the question of suffrage, including the possibility of increasing the constitutional limit on the rate of taxation, of adding provisions for the levying of local taxes for education, and of reorganizing the state's judicial system.[9] Across the state, Oates made his case in favor of a constitutional convention and a new constitution. He not only believed fervently in the cause; he also wanted to be elected to public office again. His dream of a seat in the U.S. Senate had not faded, even though his chances for election to such a high office now seemed remote at best. As a delegate to the convention, however, he hoped to launch his political comeback.

On April 23, 1901, as warm and steady spring winds blew over the state from the Gulf, the voters of Alabama went to the polls and overwhelmingly approved the convening of a convention to revise the state's constitution. That same day, Oates was elected one of four at-large delegates (other delegates represented congressional or senatorial districts or counties) to the convention. On May 21, Oates and all the other 154 delegates met in Montgomery and opened the proceedings of Alabama's sixth constitutional convention.[10] Four factions, reflecting the political divisions in Alabama, worked competitively to determine the outcome of the convention. The old ruling class, comprised of Democrats like Oates and his allies, held the majority of delegate seats, although these powerful men did not always see eye to eye. With sixty delegates, the "Big Mules"—wealthy politicians who were mostly large-scale planters or rising industrialists—wielded influence beyond their numbers in the convention, often aligning themselves with the Democratic regulars. Thirty-two Progressives attended the convention and represented the rising urban elite who supported civic reform, religious moralism, and an activist state government. They also wanted to clean up corruption, regulate railroads and their rates, eliminate the convict lease system, promote education through higher taxes, and eradicate the epidemic of lynching that had erupted throughout Alabama and the region. Although Oates considered himself a mainstream Democrat who worked strenuously to maintain the status quo and block reform, his position on several issues raised during the convention revealed that he was drifting toward Progressive attitudes and embracing reform ideas without being entirely conscious of his ascending heterodoxy. Least effective in the convention was a small block of Populists—delegates representing the Farmers' Alliance or the Jeffersonian Democrats. These agrarian reformers were simply too few in number to influence the course of the convention. There were no black delegates, since African Americans had long since been excluded from holding elective office in the state.[11]

Oates was a strong contender for president of the convention, based on his Confederate service, his congressional record, his participation in the constitutional convention of 1875, and his term as governor. But his stand against "the absurd grandfather clause"—a device used in Alabama and other Southern states to prohibit blacks from voting by allowing only those whose grandfathers had cast ballots prior to 1867 to possess the franchise—put him in a small minority of Democrats at the convention. Meanwhile, the railroad interests in Alabama, which held a tight rein on the majority of delegates, came out against Oates's nomination as convention president, mainly because he had vetoed favorable railroad legislation while serving as governor. Seeing the handwriting on the wall, Oates withdrew his candidacy and threw his support to John B. Knox, a corporation lawyer from Anniston who had the backing of the railroads and the Birmingham industrialists.[12]

There was no doubt in Knox's mind about why this constitutional convention was necessary. "The Negro," he said in his opening address, "was the prominent factor in the issue." Disfranchisement stood as the most important question since secession fever had spread through the South in the winter of 1861–1862. The constitutional convention had been called to do something about blacks who voted against the Democratic Party. "So long as the Negro remains in [a] significant minority, and votes the Republican ticket, our friends in the North tolerate him," Knox reminded the delegates. But the North had succeeded in causing racial conflict by trying to invest African Americans with political rights without, at the same time, giving them any "training or preparation" in how to exercise the rights of citizenship. As a result, said Knox, it was necessary for Southerners—and particularly for the delegates of this convention—"to establish white supremacy in this State" within the limits imposed by the Federal Constitution. "This is our problem," he asserted, "and we should be permitted to deal with it unobstructed by outside influences." Abandoning the assumptions of the past that had necessitated coercion and fraud in so many elections, Knox announced that the time had come to ensure white supremacy under the law.[13]

As the convention got down to business, Knox appointed Oates to the chairmanship of the committee on the legislative department and a member of the committee on suffrage and elections. Ever diligent and efficient, Oates convened his committee within a few days after his appointment, holding the meetings in his law office. Oates played a major role in the convention and came to be regarded as one of its leading figures, even though he was distracted at the time by T's having suffered an eye malady and Willie having decided to resign from West Point with the hope that he would be later reinstated. T went off to Roseland for a month to recuperate, which seems to have given Oates more time to devote to the convention and its deliberations.[14]

The legacy of the Civil War hung over the convention. At least thirty-eight of the delegates were Confederate veterans. But it was the issue of race and suffrage—the dark specter left to roam the land after the war and Reconstruction, despite the ratification of the Fifteenth Amendment—that stalked the convention and extended the shadow of the Civil War over its proceedings. The work of the committee on suffrage and elections was seen as the most important of all the convention committees, for the revision of franchise requirements was the principal reason the convention had been called in the first place.[15]

Something in Oates had changed. No longer did he see all African Americans as racially inferior. No one, he said, could deny the intelligence of Booker T. Washington, several other black leaders in Alabama, "and hundreds of other [African American] citizens" in the state. If their intelligence was obvious, their qualification for exercising their franchise should be equally obvious. "Shall they be excluded [from the franchise] merely because they belong to the colored race?" he asked. "I say no." Either through Booker T. Washington's influence or example, or through his own powers of observation and willingness to revise his own thinking, Oates had momentarily taken a small step from the nineteenth century into the twentieth.[16]

Oates was still a man of his time and still very much a Southern conservative. But he was a conservative who seemed to be struggling with new ideas and with a new picture of the world around him. He had reached an accommodationist understanding of the racial problem in Alabama and the South, an ideological position that enabled him to support paternalistic efforts to raise blacks up from their ignorance and poverty by letting the most talented among them enjoy the benefits of democracy and the fruits of capitalism. Like Edgar Gardner Murphy, the Episcopal minister and social reformer who preached an alternative to extreme white racism in Alabama, Oates espoused political policies of moderation that extended decency and justice to blacks—so long as African Americans comprehended and maintained their subservient place in the society dominated by whites. Blacks, in other words, had to demonstrate their worthiness for kindness by staying in their place, just as they had done—or were supposed to have done—under the institution of slavery. In that respect, Oates's attitudes were an extension of the white paternalism that had shaped the relations between masters and slaves, even though most Southern masters never could live up to the demands of a true paternalism that placed the welfare of their human property above every other concern. Similarly, Oates's sentiments toward blacks at the turn of the century revealed his pronounced paternalism and his expectation that in return for expressing a caring interest in the African Americans of his state, they should maintain their visible subservience to him and every other white man in authority. Such a step forward in his thinking—even with its inherent limitations of allowing only intelligent, self-sufficient blacks to enjoy political rights, and even though his assumptions were almost entirely based on the reciprocity of white paternalism—was a significant mark of progress for him and for other Bourbons, such as Thomas G. Jones, who espoused similar policies.[17]

After much wrangling, in which speakers on the floor of the convention expressed a wide spectrum of ideas and solutions to the problem of disfranchising blacks while ensuring the white vote, the suffrage committee considered fifty-five different proposals—not including those recommended directly by committee members to the chairman—on how to handle the franchise. Throughout the remaining days of May and into the last week of June, the committee debated these propositions in secret, sometimes even absenting itself from the convention proceedings to make progress on the suffrage question. Nearly a month had gone by without a report from the committee, and the convention as a whole grew impatient. Finally on June 26, the suffrage committee issued its majority report—and a minority report signed by Oates and three other members of the committee.[18]

Like the restrictive constitutions framed in the other Southern states, the majority report of the suffrage committee required voters to reside at least two years in the state, to pay all poll taxes, to know how to read and write, to be lawfully employed, and to pay all property taxes on land assessed at $300 or more. The franchise section recommended by the suffrage committee automatically disqualified from registering and voting all insane persons, convicted criminals, convicted vagrants and tramps, and anyone discovered buying or selling a vote. A temporary registration measure, which would expire in January 1903, provided that veterans or the descendants of any veteran would be considered exempt from the franchise restrictions so long as they met the age, residence, and poll tax requirements. Also exempt would be "all those of good character who understand the duties of citizenship in a republican form of government"—in other words, all white voters and very few black ones.[19]

Surprisingly, Oates did not lash out against the majority report in its entirety, even though he would later make it plain to the convention that he did not support its narrow construction of the franchise. Instead, he and the other dissenting minority members opposed the "descendants clause"—which they also referred to as a "grandfather clause"—that attempted, on a temporary basis, to enfranchise as many whites as possible by exempting veterans and their descendants from the other requirements contained in the majority suffrage report. Oates and his allies, including John Tyler Morgan, Thomas G. Jones, and Edmund W. Pettus, strongly believed that this provision was unconstitutional and that it violated the 15th Amendment. Said the minority about the descendants clause: "It undertakes by indirect means to deny or abridge the right to vote to citizens of the United States on account of race, color, or previous condition of servitude. . . . The clause . . . does not erect a standard of qualifications applicable alike to both races, but establishes an arbitrary standard, which considered in connection with the history of the country, confers the right of suffrage upon members of the white race (who are descendants of such soldiers) and denies it to members of the black race, who are not such descendants."[20] Oates was less offended by standards equally applied to blacks and whites, such as literary tests or poll taxes, which, in his estimation, would sufficiently weed out unworthy voters of both races. But he would not stand for the arbitrary grandfather clause, which led him, willingly or not, to defend the 15th Amendment and advocate a principle of equality, however narrowly defined and potentially exclusionary, for conferring suffrage among Alabama's males.

The great debate on the floor of the convention over the suffrage issue began on July 23 and lasted through August 3. Up in the gallery, onlookers stood shoulder-to-shoulder to witness the proceedings, and the air in the room became thick and hot. Supporters of the majority report declared that the Fifteenth Amendment was a dead letter in Alabama anyway and had been for thirty years or more, so it made no difference whether blacks were disfranchised by state fundamental law or by the circumvention of national fundamental law. Other advocates pointedly remarked that the special clauses in the temporary plan would ensure white supremacy and governance, would prevent white conservatives (like Oates) from abusing black votes—and winning elections—by fraudulent means, and would improve the quality of the state electorate.[21]

Into this strident and cacophonous exhortation in support of the disfranchisement of African Americans (and, it should be pointed out, poor whites) walked William C. Oates. On the blistering hot morning of July 24, 1901, Oates rose from his chair in the assembly hall and promised his listeners that he would "say nothing except that which may be considered to some profit." He admitted to being a conservative. He was proud of it. But, he said, "I never will, if I know it, be a party to an injustice to anyone—it matters not what may be called the exigency."

He wanted to talk about blacks. Oates could not have been aware that when he spoke on the subject of African Americans, he was unable to sound fair, just, or reasonable, because he could never shake off the shackles of racism that so limited his thinking and his actions. He began, for instance, by acknowledging that blacks in Africa were savages, and that no black man in the United States could claim any responsibility for becoming enslaved or becoming emancipated. By means of his emancipation he was given the franchise. Who gave it to him? Without saying so explicitly, Oates blamed Yankees—and, by implication, mostly the Radical Republicans—for ratifying the Fourteenth and Fifteenth Amendments as part of the punishment doled out to the conquered whites of the South.[22]

There was no mistaking his conservatism. Slavery, he declared, "had benefited the negroes because it lifted them higher in the sunlight of civilization than anything before." It was, he affirmed, "a blessing to them." Nevertheless, he said, "it was only natural that they should aspire to freedom." When they were freed and given the vote, Oates opposed it. In the hands of the carpetbaggers and the scalawags, he explained, the black franchise was abused and used with malice against Southern white Democrats. The polecat carpetbaggers and scalawags controlling the African American vote made sure that the polls were always crowded with blacks, so that white voters could not reach the ballot box, and that black votes always outnumbered white ones.[23]

The only way to beat this system was to cheat the blacks. "I never changed votes with my one hand," Oates confessed, "but I upheld it [i.e., election fraud] and counselled it in those who did. I am just as guilty as those who did." The problem was, he said, that he and his fellow conservatives could never stop. "We have gone on from bad to worse until it has become a great evil," he said poignantly. So much cheating had taken place that there were no more honest elections. Something had to be done. Yet, he said with a solemnity that must have given pause to his audience, the delegates to the convention—including himself—had sworn an oath to uphold the Constitution of the United States, which included the Fifteenth Amendment, like it or not. Oates was pledged to do so, and so was every other delegate. He had also been elected a delegate by promising the voters that he would "elevate the suffrage" and eliminate "from the right to vote all those who are unfit and unqualified," white or black. Despite his apparent support for democratic suffrage, and what seemed to be a commonsensical belief in preventing unfit persons of any race from voting, there loomed a more sinister motive behind Oates's proposal. The white power brokers in the South wanted to ensure that dissatisfied whites—including poor farmers who had sided with the Populists in the 1890s—would not drift into an alliance with other disaffected elements, namely African Americans. Depriving both unfit whites and blacks of the suffrage effectively kept them from banding together and obtaining the political power to threaten the prevailing power structure of the elite whites, including the increasingly displaced planters and the rising new men of the South. Yet Oates did not stand on the same ground as these power brokers, for while he argued against giving the vote to the unfit, he did not necessarily want to deprive all poor whites or even all African Americans of the franchise. In fact, given a choice, Oates actually seemed to favor limiting the suffrage for unqualified *white* voters rather than black ones, which revealed how shaken he still was in the aftermath of his political battles with Kolb and the Populists. In a statement that must have shocked his fellow delegates, Oates announced: "There are some white men who have no more right and no more business to vote than a negro and not as much as some of them."[24]

It was not as if the world had suddenly turned upside down. Oates had always believed that the best men, the worthy men in society, should be its leaders and voters. To say now that poor whites should not get favorable treatment under the Alabama fundamental law was not a reversal in any way of what he had always advocated in politics and in government—that society's capable white men, like himself, should rule and that they should be placed in power by other men, regardless of race, who recognized the superior talents of those most qualified to govern.

Yet Oates's remarks did shake the pillars of the constitutional convention. For all his racial prejudices, for all his belief in racial stereotypes, for all his deep convictions in the inferiority of African Americans, Oates had reached a startling conclusion about the nature of mankind. The color line between the races could not be starkly drawn, completely dividing one race from the other. Each race, white and black, contained within its ranks good and bad, intelligent and doltish, lazy and productive, honest and deceitful, committed and apathetic. He had not stumbled upon the idea that all men should vote without qualification or restriction. But he had stumbled to the realization

that each race of man contains pretty much the same range of human attributes and shortcomings. The differences between the races and how they
behaved might not be genetically determined after all. In fact, it was beginning to dawn on Oates that biological differences made little difference at all.
It was the human similarities that mattered.

No doubt Oates had mixed motives in supporting black suffrage while, at
the same time, bemoaning election fraud and voicing his doubts about the
fitness of some whites to vote. Beneath the surface of his political stand on
suffrage rights lay his own Machiavellian desires to hinder the political aspi-
rations of whites outside the Black Belt, to procure—that is, to manipulate—
black votes for the existing power brokers (including himself) of the Democratic
party without resorting to fraud, and to keep truly unfit men from qualifying
for the suffrage in the first place. In this way, he believed, Alabama could ensure
that the better sort—men like him or blacks like Booker T. Washington—
would be the ones who got to participate in the political process. Such a conservative conviction that governmental order could only be maintained by
respected and worthy men contributing their talents to the political authority
ran all the way back to the Founding Fathers and the arguments made so
cogently by Alexander Hamilton in *The Federalist*, No. 71. Oates, and Southern Bourbons like him, took this republican plea for only good men in government and wrapped their own distinctions of race and class around it.

But to say this and nothing more does Oates a disservice. While he most
certainly supported voting restrictions in the new Alabama constitution because of his less-than-scrupulous hunger to keep himself and his cronies in
political power and deprive others from gaining any share of that power, he
nevertheless turned a corner in his personal opinions about the suffrage and
who in Alabama should possess it, and in so doing he left his political bedfel-
lows behind. When he argued in favor of black suffrage, when he filed his
minority report, when he took a stand on this principle, he did so because he
had come to believe that he was right and that his opponents were wrong.
More to the point, he had come to see that blacks—some blacks, anyway—
deserved the franchise, even while he hoped that their votes could be exploited in favor of the Democratic black belt power brokers. While there was
more than an ounce of guile in his political position, there was also more than
ounce of sincerity in it, too.

Whether he realized it or not, whether he completely understood the
full import of his words, Oates was reaching—struggling, lurching, groping,
really—toward the principle of equality. It was the same equality, the same
lofty principle, that Jefferson had included in the Declaration of Independence and that Lincoln had invoked in the Gettysburg Address. Oates hadn't
quite grasped it with the same intellectual vigor that Jefferson and Lincoln
had—and had expressed so nobly. His strain was not quite as pure as theirs.
Yet his understanding of equality contained the same ambivalence that had

confounded Americas since the Revolution: On one hand, the doctrine emphasized an equality of opportunity that emphasized social distinctions; on the other hand, it accentuated an equality of condition that obliterated those social distinctions. Rejecting any notion that equality implied social leveling, Oates nevertheless was holding out his hand in front of him, stumbling as though he were a blind man, and yearning to grab an American guidepost—an American creed—that he had never clutched before.[25]

Refusing to admit that a race war was underway between whites and blacks, and rejecting extremist arguments that maintained the two races could never live peacefully together, Oates called on his fellow white Southerners—and particularly on his fellow Confederate veterans—to do the unexpected, to do what others claimed could not be done in the South. So long as whites retained their rule and their supremacy, Oates reasoned, then there should not be any obstacle to letting blacks participate in the government. In a rare instance, Oates appealed to the Bible for support. Whites should not rule like Samson out of brute strength, but rather according to the tenets of Scripture that called on man "to do kindly unto those who are in his power."[26]

Oates turned the question on his audience. Shall we, he asked, exclude blacks from all participation in the government or shall we let some of them take an active role? He favored letting some of them—what he called "the better element"—participate "in the Affairs of our State." How could they be totally excluded? No majority should reasonably assume that such a large minority—Alabama's population at the time stood at 1,000,000 whites and 800,000 blacks—could be kept from having a voice in the affairs of government.

"Why," he pointed out, "some of these people are becoming very intelligent and acquiring property, and gentlemen, it may not occur next year, or the year after, or five years hence, but, if you go along with this and practically none of them having a voice in our affairs, you may live to see the time of outbreaks and troubles not now contemplated." Oates pleaded: "Let them occupy a subordinate position, but do not silence them. Let the better element of them, though of an inferior race, who have won the confidence of their neighbors, won respectability and acquired property—allow all of that class a fair showing, and let them go to the polls and vote."[27]

In Oates's estimation, the issue at hand "was not a racial question." Where would such a racial proposition end? Surely not in the extermination of the blacks or in the transporting of black people back to Africa. Oates found such suggestions ludicrous in the extreme. African Americans, he said, "are citizens not only by our State laws and our State Constitution but they are citizens by the Constitution of the United States." Like other citizens, black people "have the right to go when and where they please." Given the fact that blacks performed most of the hard labor in the South, didn't it make sense to treat the black man fairly and give him the full protection of the law?[28]

Oates was not alone in his opposition to the temporary plan. Newspapers throughout the state overwhelmingly denounced the grandfather and inheritance clauses, and Republicans and Populists joined the Oates faction among the Democrats in supporting universal manhood suffrage rather than the majority report of the convention's suffrage committee. Nevertheless, a majority of the delegates favored the temporary plan and understood, on the basis of what had occurred in other Southern states where a vocal opposition had arisen against grandfather clauses, that once these suffrage exclusions were enacted, the dissent quickly melted away. So it proved to be in the Alabama Constitutional Convention of 1901. After a large majority of the convention voted to table Oates's minority report, the delegates adopted the whole temporary plan in the majority report by a vote of 104 to 14. Later the convention adopted the entire suffrage article by a vote of 95 to 19. Oates voted both times with the minority. As a result of this action in the convention, Alabama gained the dubious distinction of having the most elaborate suffrage requirements ever adopted in the United States.[29]

Having lost that battle, Oates went on to fight other ones in defense of African American rights. Just as he argued on the losing side in the suffrage debate, he also took a minority stand against the injustice of dividing funds from a local school district tax on the basis of how much each race, white and black, paid in taxes. But his finest moment in the convention came during a debate over whether or not the state militia should be restricted to white companies.

In the midst of this debate, Oates pointed out that there were two black militia companies that he organized during his governorship, and he never had any trouble with them (he did not tell the convention, however, that he had refused to command African American troops during the War with Spain). His real point, however, was to express utter dismay over the fact that in the past thirty years a change had occurred in white public opinion toward blacks. To illustrate his meaning, he told the story of how a fellow black representative in the state House during Reconstruction had thrashed a leading carpetbagger just a few feet from where Oates was standing now. The carpetbagger, Oates explained, was in favor of "social equality" and "the negro was a long ways the better man of the two."

The delegates were shocked and outraged by Oates's remark. One of them immediately stood up and declared: "That is Bostonian doctrine."

Oates answered calmly: "Where were you making Bostonian doctrines during the war, when I was at the front, in twenty-seven battles, and have six scars on my body, made by Yankee bullets? I reckon my devotion to the South is as great as that of any other man. No man has ever questioned my loyalty to my people, or my State."

He returned to his point. "While I think the negro should remain in his place, and that place a subordinate one to the white people—for this is a white man's government and always will be and always ought to be—but for that reason is it right, when we have a subordinate race here, not responsible for their being among us, to proscribe them and trample them under foot?" He was against any restriction that would keep blacks out of the militia. But there was something else that he was wrestling with, something that disturbed him about "the change . . . in regard to the status of the negro in our State."[30]

What he struggled with this time, and what he simply could not comprehend, was the extreme violence that whites were committing against blacks in Alabama and throughout the South. Between 1890 and World War I, nearly three thousand African American Southerners lost their lives at the hands of white lynch mobs. During the decade between 1890 and 1900, 177 lynchings took place in Alabama alone—the highest number in any state during that ten-year period. Although violence against blacks had been a perennial problem in the South, Oates could see that vigilante violence had become more prevalent, especially in his home state. About two or three blacks were lynched a week in the South after 1900, based on conservative estimates. Other "legal" executions of blacks—usually involving quick trials and speedy hangings—are not included in the statistics. In the South, black lives had become incredibly cheap. One black Southerner remembered, "In those days, it was 'Kill a mule, buy another. Kill a nigger, hire another.'" By 1900, lynchings, executions, and torture had become public rituals, often attended by huge crowds of young and old whites. Sadism, mutilation, and prolonged torture became distinctive hallmarks of the new lawless violence committed against blacks in the twentieth century.[31]

Most of those acts of violence were committed by whites to enforce deference and submission—in other words, to ensure the white supremacy that Oates and like-minded Southerners valued so highly and without which the world was inconceivable. But Oates—a violent man with a killer instinct and temper, a man who only a year earlier had shot and killed a black man in his own backyard—now found himself appalled at the amount of blood that was being spilled for the sake of racial order and supremacy. Keeping African Americans in their place was one thing. But doing so by violent means fell beyond anything Oates could abide or understand. In what was perhaps his most courageous and humanitarian statement to the constitution convention, Oates asked in total bewilderment: "[W]hen the negro is doing no harm, why [do] people want to kill him and wipe him from the face of the earth?"[32]

No one dared answered him. The question simply floated through the hall of the Alabama House of Representatives like an unnoticed leaf dropping in the autumn. Surely Oates never found a satisfactory answer for himself. His racial views had become remarkably complex, much too complicated for him to sort out on his own. If he had come close to perceiving a new world, and all the possibilities of a new South, he could not identify what he was

seeing or what it really meant. As a result, in the months following the constitutional convention, he lost hold of what he had briefly seen.

After the convention adjourned, Oates admitted that he disliked the document produced by the delegates, but he vowed to support ratification of the
new constitution nonetheless—a document that disenfranchised African
American and poor white men; made segregation legal; reduced the state's
ability to pay for public services, including education; and created a system of
apportionment that ensured the dominance of political reactionaries in the
state legislature for the next seventy years. Publicly he appealed to the voters
of Alabama to ratify the document, despite its many flaws. In the end, the new
constitution was ratified on November 11 by a popular vote of 108,613 to
81,734. Ironically, a sizeable number of those votes must have come from
African American voters, the very voters the new constitution would now
disenfranchise. In any event, the returns probably reflected as much fraud
and corruption—and doctoring of the final returns—as any other typical Alabama election.[33]

In public or in private, Oates never again raised the issues of black suffrage, unjust violence against blacks, or black political equality. His moment
in the sun, such as it was, was over.

In the summer and fall of 1901, as the new Alabama constitution was adopted
by the constitutional convention and sent to the voters for ratification, Oates
learned that T was suffering from cirrhosis of the jawbone. She was in a great
deal of pain. Oates had agreed to send Willie to Paris to study French and
mathematics at the Sorbonne, where it was hoped his skills in those subjects
would improve enough for him to reenter West Point in August 1902 and
receive higher grades there. T was to accompany him to France, but what
began for her as a tooth abscess turned into a much more serious malady. In
New York, T sought treatment, worrying all the while that her affliction—
and any surgery to remedy it—would disfigure her for life. Distressed and
frightened without Oates by her side, she even wrote him to promise that she
would refrain in the future from filling their home with guests.[34]

Her illnesses—first the aphasia and then the cirrhosis—were real and
painful, but it is not difficult to see in her physical distresses a plea for a caring
response from her husband. This time, her distress was not enough to lure
Oates away from Montgomery, and he let her deal with her pain and her fears
on her own, with only Willie to console her. What kept Oates from going to
New York is not evident, except that by this time in their marriage he experienced difficulty in keeping up with a young wife and all her needs. Whatever
distance stood between them because of the difference in their ages, Oates
loved T dearly; but he did not show any evidence of his affection by remaining in Alabama while she dealt with her doctors in New York.

By the middle of September, T had survived her surgery without disfigurement and with hardly any lingering pain. She and Willie made ready to sail for France. The dentist's bill was enormous, and she and Willie feared Oates would be angry about the unexpected expense. Instead, he seemed to take it all in stride, having experienced much anguish over T's condition and her recovery. Within two weeks after setting sail, T and Willie had arrived in Paris and found accommodations on the Rue Chalgrin. Arrangements were made for Willie's instruction, and T sought every means to economize and to do without, if necessary. Religiously, she reported their expenses to Oates and, inevitably, she had to ask him time after time to send her more money. She spent most of her time as productively as possible, and as inexpensively as she could, visiting the many art museums and galleries in Paris. When Oates wrote back, she was pleased to hear that he was considering the possibility of purchasing Roseland, her parents' plantation in Eufaula. Nothing, however, seems to have come of his intention, for the estate later fell into the hands of the Shorter family.[35]

Alone in Montgomery, with little to keep him busy except his law practice, which he seems to have picked up again with glee after the adjournment of the convention, Oates consumed hours of his time working on his Civil War book, writing an autobiography that he hoped would be instructional to Willie, expanding his landed wealth, and complaining to T and Willie that they were spending far too much money in Paris. Having fallen in love with France and doing very well in his studies, Willie begged his father not to insist on his coming home. The young man wanted to make this educational venture work, and he was determined to do well and, in the end, to please his father.

But in mid-November Oates could not avoid sending T and Willie the distressing news that he had lost approximately $51,000 when some bonds he held at the Eufaula National Bank were sold without his permission. T could not understand how such a thing had happened, and it does seem as if Oates was exaggerating his losses, perhaps in another attempt to convince T and Willie to cut down on their spending. The loss was real enough, however, and the fact was even reported in the newspapers. In time, Oates estimated that he might be able to recover 20 percent of his loss, but this financial setback caused him considerable distress and made him despondent. Dealing with this crisis from a distance did not make it any easier on T and Willie, who could only try to keep their own depression at bay and to ask, when they had no choice, for Oates to send them more money. T for a time believed from Oates's letters that they were now penniless, but Oates let her know in December that they were by no means poor and that she and Willie could remain in Paris for their son's schooling.[36]

Oates did what he could to make up for the financial setback, mostly by working harder at his law practice, taking on a bigger case load, and selling some of his real estate investments. "The chief forum of the lawyer," declared an essay in an issue of the *American Lawyer* in 1893, "has been transferred from the court house to the office. Litigation has declined and counsel work has become the leading feature of the practice."[37] For Oates, this statement perfectly described his law business, which still served the rural communities of Abbeville and Eufaula, although he did take on more and more clients in Montgomery as time went on. Although he spent less time in the courtroom, he did argue his usual assortment of cases involved with breach of contract, debt collection, and land disputes.

In 1901, he successfully took sides against a fellow veteran of the 15th Alabama, William "Gus" McClendon, in a case that accused McClendon of improperly signing a statutory bond. A year later, another case brought him before the U.S. Fifth Circuit Court of Appeals, where he sought a reversal for a client convicted of moving distilled spirits in violation of federal law. Arguing that the key testimony of the prosecution witnesses was irrelevant and did not prove guilt, Oates persuaded the court to overturn the judgment of the lower court and order a new trial. He also gave effective assistance to the state's attorney by helping to block an appeal filed for a man convicted of poisoning his wife. His most thrilling moment, though, probably came in May 1906, when he sat as a special judge of the Alabama Supreme Court to adjudicate an appeal of a judgment made against the Atlantic Coast Line Railway for failing to deliver 144 pairs of shoes to the rightful receiver. Always a friend to business, Oates reversed the decision and found in favor of the railroad.[38]

But his law practice and his recent financial setback did not keep him from thinking about the Civil War and his brave Confederate comrades, living and dead. Throughout 1901 he was swept up in plans for a reunion of all the surviving Civil War veterans in Alabama. On November 12 and 13 of that year, nearly one thousand old soldiers attended the reunion, held in Montgomery. The newspapers credited Oates with being the driving force behind the meeting, the first statewide gathering of veterans since the war. At the meeting, he collected more accurate information for his Civil War book and traced the whereabouts of former troops in his regiment.[39]

By spring 1902, Oates decided that his separation from his family had gone on long enough. In April, he made plans to join T and Willie in France and to then travel on with the entire family for a grand tour of Europe—a more extensive trip than they had taken together as a family in 1889. Apparently his financial resources rebounded enough for him to consider the lavish expense of such a holiday.

Before setting sail, however, Oates wrote again to William Robbins at Gettysburg National Military Park and acknowledged his disappointment that he could not get permission to erect flank markers on Little Round Top; he asked Robbins, nevertheless, to arrange for the cutting of a proper stone he could use as a memorial to his late brother John and the other men of the

15th Alabama who had fallen at Gettysburg. He wanted the stone work to cost no more than $100. With that, he told Robbins he would be in Europe until the first of July, when he planned to return to Montgomery. He also included the legend he wished to be inscribed on the monument:

> To the Memory of Lt. John A. Oates
> and his gallant Comrades
> who fell here July 2nd, 1863.

> The 15th Ala. Regt., over 400 strong,
> reached this spot, but for
> lack of support had to retire.
> Lt. Col. Feagin lost a leg
> Capts. Brainard and Ellison
> Lts. Oates and Cody and
> 33 men were killed, 76 wounded
> and 84 captured.

> Erected 39th Anniversary of
> the battle
> By
> Gen. Wm. C. Oates
> who was Colonel of the Regiment.

There is no record of a reply from Robbins, but Oates boarded his ship for France convinced that the matter of the stone and its inscription had been settled and that the work would be completed by the time he returned from Europe.[40]

At midnight on April 15, 1902, Oates stood at the rail of the steamship liner *Vaderland* and watched as the ship slid silently past the impressive Statue of Liberty in New York harbor. He had decided not only to make this journey, but also to keep copious notes of his travels and experiences. Oates liked to travel by ship, as he noted in his journal: "This is the greatest place in the world for people to become acquainted with each other. . . . I did not know any person on the *Vaderland* when we left New York, and when we landed I knew nine-tenths of the first cabin and several second cabin passengers."[41]

The *Vaderland* docked in Flushing, Belgium, at dawn on April 26. Later that evening, he arrived in Paris by train. He was elated to see T and Willie once more. They stayed in Paris for eight days. Military sites, such as the Hotel des Invalides, a soldiers' home, Fort Valerian, and the tomb of Napoleon, captured most of his interest and attention. At Versailles, Oates and his family lunched with a fellow Alabamian and Confederate veteran who accompanied them on a tour of the famous palace.[42]

From Paris, the Oates family went on a whirlwind tour of Europe and stayed several days in a variety of cities, including Venice, Florence (which did not impress Oates at all), Rome, Naples, Athens, and Constantinople. All through the trip, Oates commented on the peculiar customs of foreigners and complained that despite golden fields of corn, one could find not a square of corn bread on the entire continent. Leaving Constantinople, they continued their train travel through Turkey, Romania, Bulgaria, and Serbia. After crossing the Danube—which Oates said was muddy, not blue—into Hungary, they eventually arrived in Budapest, a beautiful and prosperous city by Oates's reckoning.

The family then passed into Austria and stopped in Vienna, where, noted Oates with pleasure, the buildings were "elegant" and "the streets well paved and clean." Oates and his family pushed on to Carlsbad, "the greatest watering place in Europe." Then it was on to Berlin, "a great and progressive city." Most of all, Oates admired Frederick the Great, the man who "laid the foundation for the future greatness of the German people." He was "a statesman and a fine general," said Oates. Visiting the Sans Souci palace, Oates learned more about Frederick then he had known before, and he set down his very favorable impressions of the man in a long section of his travelogue devoted to anecdotes about the king and his character. The next stop was Amsterdam and The Hague. Oates enjoyed the hotel there, for it prohibited the giving of tips to employees. He also approved of the Dutch, whom he called "a patriotic, industrious, and prosperous people."[43]

But it was England that he truly loved. "England," Oates proclaimed, "is the most highly improved country in the world in every way." At Queen Annie's Mansions in Westminster, where Oates found accommodations for his family, he met General Joseph Wheeler, his former comrade in arms in the Confederate and United States armies. Oates was thrilled by the color and the spectacle of London. And, in his mind, there were no finer people than the English: "The English are the most conservative and loyal people on earth." He also believed that their military figures got the respect they deserved. "A man who has been a general is never by the most ignorant called a captain or colonel, as is the case with our people."[44]

On June 28, the Oates family boarded the steamship *St. Louis* at Southampton and set sail for Cherbourg, the last stop before the ship made way across the Atlantic for New York. As they sailed into Cherbourg harbor, Oates recalled that it was off these waters that the Civil War naval battle between the *U.S.S. Kearsage* and the *C.S.S. Alabama* had taken place. Rear Admiral Raphael Semmes, the commander of the *Alabama*, "would not strike his colors, and the [ship] went down with them flying," The voyage home was fast and uneventful. On July 7, the *St. Louis* arrived in New York, and Oates and his family were glad to be back in their own country. Except for the language barrier, which was partly overcome by the ability of both Willie and T to speak fluent French, Oates announced that "the tour to me was indeed a pleasant one."[45]

Later that summer Oates wrote to his son, who—no doubt through his father's considerable political influence—had been allowed to reenter West Point and resume his studies. Oates remarked that he was helping William Jelks in his campaign for governor. "Many express a regret that I am not running for governor," he told Willie. Then, with confidence, he added: "I could have been elected governor to a certainty and without much contest."[46] He was fooling himself. His political career was over, and most of the people of Alabama understood that, if he did not. Although he had campaigned for ratification of the new state constitution, his speeches on the floor of the convention in favor of black suffrage and against racial violence sounded the death knell for his future in politics.

As September drew to a close, Oates wrote again to William Robbins about the Gettysburg monument for the 15th Alabama. He reminded Robbins of his letter in April, and now he wondered what the status of the monument was. "I expected on my return [from Europe] to find a letter from you about it, but I did not and have not up to this time," he wrote. He also invited Robbins to attend a reunion of the 15th Alabama that would be held in Montgomery in November.[47]

Oates's letter seems to have caught Robbins by surprise. Normally an efficient administrator, and a devout and caring man, Robbins apparently had let Oates's request from the previous spring slip through his fingers. Having encouraged Oates in the past about the monument, despite his personal opposition to the idea, Robbins now found himself in a difficult position. He wrote to John Nicholson, the chairman, at his home in Philadelphia and tried to explain the circumstances. Major Charles Richardson of New York, the third commission member, thought that commissioners should not approve special monuments erected to single regiments. Robbins said to Nicholson that "I think I have heard you express the same opinion even more emphatically [than Richardson]." Now letting his true feeling be known, Robbins did not want to be responsible for conspicuously memorializing the 15th Alabama's role in the battle for Little Round Top at the expense of the other regiments in the brigade, including his own, the 4th Alabama. He proposed that he should notify Oates that the commissioners now were no longer in favor of the proposed monument.[48] In writing to Oates, Robbins said the commissioners now believed they must enforce the regulation that called for monuments and tablets to be placed "in the positions where they formed line of battle and began the fight"—and not where a brigade, regiment, or company had actually engaged in combat.

This was the old "battle line" rule that had a few years earlier had flamed into controversy for the commissioners, especially among the former Confederate states and their veteran groups who wanted to raise monuments on the Gettysburg battlefield, but who did not want their memorials consigned to the relative obscurity of Seminary Ridge, where most of the Southern units had formed their lines of battle before engaging with the enemy. Many Southerners believed the park rule favored the placement of the Union monuments, which easily could be erected on the very ground they defended from Confederate assaults. Some Union outfits also protested against the battle line rule, including veterans of the 72nd Pennsylvania who fought bitterly with John B. Bachelder and the Gettysburg Battlefield Monument Association in 1888 over placement of their monument near the High Water Mark on Cemetery Ridge. The case was eventually decided by the Pennsylvania Supreme Court, which found in favor of the veterans' preferred location.[49] There seemed to be a double standard inherent in the battle-line rule: It meant one thing for the placement of Union monuments and quite another for Southern ones.

The letter from Robbins hit Oates like a lightning bolt. In reply, he told Robbins that the battle line rule would "prevent any [monuments] from being erected to the Confederates." He could not understand why his proposal for "a simple inexpensive monument about where the center of my regiment stood at the most advanced spot, and where my brother and other officers were killed" should raise any objections. Oates could see no recourse but to take his case to Congress "and write it up in the newspapers[,] for I consider it a great wrong to our [Confederate] side." The Civil War, in other words, was not over, and there was still a battle to be fought at Gettysburg.[50]

Almost immediately, Oates worked to gain support for his monument from the surviving veterans of the 15th Alabama who were scheduled to meet again at another reunion in Montgomery on November 12. Eighty-nine veterans of the 15th Alabama attended the reunion from all over the state. Galvanized for action, the veterans unanimously approved a resolution (no doubt written by Oates) declaring that "we most heartily commend" Oates's effort to raise a monument on Little Round Top and called on the battlefield commissioners to "grant permission to him to have such stone erected with such inscriptions as are pertinent, to stand as an eternal witness of the earnestness and gallantry displayed by our regiment on the evening of July 2, 1863."[51]

He reopened his correspondence with the Gettysburg commissioners in early December by sending them a formal letter "to apply to you for permission to erect a stone, or marble monument on the part of the Battlefield to which my regiment, the 15th Alabama, advanced on the evening of July 2nd, 1863." He enclosed a copy of the resolution passed by the 15th Alabama veterans at their reunion. Robbins replied and suggested that Oates place his monument along Confederate Avenue with a long inscription as to what the 15th Alabama had accomplished in its assault on Little Round Top. He steadfastly maintained that the "battle line" rule could not be broken for anyone, including Oates.[52]

To be sure, the commissioners had a difficult—if not impossible—job trying to satisfy everyone. Relic hounds plowed the ground on the battlefield looking for souvenirs and the discarded accoutrements of war to sell for profit. Robbins, whose health was not good, spent a good deal of his time showing dignitaries and other visitors around the battlefield, an occupational hazard caused by the fact that Chairman Nicholson spent comparatively little time in Gettysburg and fellow commissioner Richardson hardly ever visited the park at all.

More significantly, the commissioners took up the task for the War Department of condemning land to incorporate into the battlefield's boundaries and fighting the court battles that inevitably resulted from their actions. Meanwhile, the work of improving the park went forward—building roads, cleaning up after storms, policing the grounds and trying to prevent vandalism, planting trees, and erecting iron tablets that documented in incredible detail the entire history of the battle and the movements of the armies. To make matters even more difficult, the commissioners still came under fire in the Southern press from former Confederates other than Oates for their "battle line" rule and for the lack of Confederate monuments on the field.[53]

As the new year approached, Oates was no closer to erecting his monument at Gettysburg than he had been in 1899, when the idea first came to him. Just like in the Civil War, the winter months threatened stagnation of his campaign while the opposing sides took to their respective camps and kept their guns silent. At home, he became concerned once more for Willie's future at West Point; the young man's grades fell dramatically again and he seemed not to possess the will to fight his way through the academy's curriculum. For now, T appeared to be in good health, but Oates's rheumatism continued to bother him and his physical stamina was considerably less than it used to be.[54]

Still, he was tougher than most men his age. What weighed on him, though, and sapped his strength—more than Willie's dismal academic record, more than T's uncertain health and lavish parties, more than the financial losses he had suffered over the past year, more than his own aches and pains— were his memories of Gettysburg, of the death of his young brother, of the ghost-like images of his comrades falling on Little Round Top, and of the lost opportunity that the battle represented for the Confederacy and for him personally. Oates could not escape the vise grip Gettysburg had on him, a grip that prevented him from ever gaining any real peace in his old soldier's soul.

Top Left: T Oates, ca. 1894. Ever lovely, and very much the politician's trophy wife, T never stopped loving Oates for the rest of her life, but their marriage hit troubled waters almost from the start, and their age difference only complicated their inability to communicate effectively with one another. *Oates Family Papers*.

Political Friends and Rivals
Top Right: James L. Pugh. A formidable politician who first helped to mentor Oates when he arrived in Eufaula, Alabama, as a young apprentice with the prestigious law firm of Pugh, Bullock, and Buford, Pugh later served Alabama in the Confederate Congress and then the U.S. Senate, where he sometimes stood as Oates's political ally or foe, depending on the changing circumstances of their long association together. *Alabama Department of Archives and History*.

Bottom Left: Reuben F. Kolb. Kolb, a leader of the Alabama Farmers' Alliance, was defeated by Oates in the controversial—and very dirty—gubernatorial election of 1894. He and Oates remained bitter political enemies for the rest of their lives. *Alabama Department of Archives and History*.

Top Left: Edmund W. Pettus. A lawyer who served in the Mexican War and the Civil War, Pettus won the U.S. Senate seat in 1897 that Oates hoped would be his. Oates, however, found him a valuable political ally during the Alabama Constitutional Convention of 1901. The two men maintained a good working relationship and a cordial, if not close, friendship. *Alabama Department of Archives and History*.

Top Right: John Tyler Morgan. Morgan, like Oates, was a lawyer and a Confederate officer, but he achieved what Oates had wanted the most in his own political career—election to the U.S. Senate. During the Alabama Constitutional Convention, Oates and Morgan saw eye-to-eye on the issue of giving the suffrage to African American males, but their views were resented by a majority of the convention delegates and, ultimately, by the white Alabamians who ratified the state constitution, which effectively deprived blacks of the right to vote and thus openly defied the 15th Amendment to the U.S. Constitution. *Alabama Department of Archives and History*.

Bottom Left: Joseph Forney Johnston. Johnston, one of Oates's political rivals in the Alabama Democratic Party, succeeded Oates as governor in 1896. He opposed the Constitutional Convention of 1901 and the ratification of the state constitution promulgated by that convention, both of which Oates had vigorously supported (despite the Constitution's restrictive suffrage provisions). He, too, later won what Oates could not—a seat in the U.S. Senate. *Alabama Department of Archives and History*.

Left: Willie Oates, fourteen years of age. Tall and handsome like his father, young Willie tried hard to please the elder Oates, but discovered that his father's standards were very high and sometimes unattainable, even for someone as bright and talented as Willie was. *Oates Family Papers*.

Bottom: Booker T. Washington, seated at his desk. Oates respected Washington and praised the black leader's accommodationist views, which fit Oates's own political and racial agendas. Washington remained politically loyal to Oates, despite displays of Oates's own petty racial prejudices and churlishness. *Library of Congress*.

Top Right: President William McKinley. Despite Oates's numerous pleas, McKinley would not give him a combat command in the Spanish-American War. McKinley, who held strong attitudes in favor of reconciliation between the North and South during his presidency, liked the idea of appointing former Confederate officers— including Oates, Fitzhugh Lee, and Joseph Wheeler—to generalships during the War with Spain, but he held on enough to his old resentments as a former Union brevet major of volunteers during the Civil War to let any one of them gain great distinction in his own splendid little war of 1898, as his Secretary of State John Hay called it. *Library of Congress*.

Bottom Right: Brigadier General Oates, 1898. This is one of a series of photographs taken of Oates in his U.S. Army uniform of the Spanish-American War. Oates was sixty-five at the time, and while he considered himself sturdy enough to handle a combat command, the authorities in the War Department—and President McKinley—did not agree. Much to Oates's chagrin, a unit of black troops was placed under his brigade command, and he considered it an insult unworthy of his prestige as a former Confederate officer, a former U.S. Congressman, and a white Southerner. *Oates Family Papers*.

The Last Decade

Right: T in a photograph given to Willie, ca. 1900.
T sent this photograph to Willie when he started
his studies at the U.S. Military Academy at West
Point. T and Willie enjoyed a close, loving
relationship until her death in 1933. The elder
Oates may have resented their close bonds, but he
loved them both deeply. *Oates Family Papers.*

Below: Roseland, the Toney plantation house outside
Eufaula, Ala., ca. 1890. Oates and T were married at
the plantation in 1882. The house, although much
altered over time, still stands (2005). Modern
residents of Eufaula, however, have little memory of
the Toney family or of its connection to William C.
Oates. *Oates Family Papers.*

Left: Chamberlain in later life. As old
men, Oates and Chamberlain refought
the battle of Little Round Top, albeit
with words and not with bullets, when
Chamberlain disputed Oates's account of
what had taken place on the hillside
during the late afternoon and early
twilight of July 2, 1863. Chamberlain's
disagreement with Oates led to the
rejection of Oates's request for a
monument to be placed in honor of the
15th Alabama on Little Round Top at the
Gettysburg National Military Park during
the early 1900s. *Pejepscot Historical Society.*

Far Right: William C. Oates, Jr., in cadet uniform, U.S. Military Academy, ca. 1900. Willie tried desperately to succeed at West Point, but the rigorous demands of the academy kept him from achieving a solid academic record there. He was probably more undone by the pressure placed on him by his father than any real lack of academic ability. He would later excel when he studied French at the Sorbonne, took an undergraduate degree from the University of Alabama, and earned a law degree from the University of Virginia. *Oates Family Papers*.

Above: Elihu Root, Secretary of War. Root, an otherwise brilliant and capable administrator, refused to approve Oates's petition for a monument to the 15th Alabama on Little Round Top. Root later served as Secretary of State under Theodore Roosevelt and a U.S. Senator from the state of New York. In 1912, he won the Nobel Peace Prize for his work on various treaties of arbitration. *Library of Congress*.

Left: Rufus B. Weaver. Weaver helped Oates locate the grave of his brother John at Gettysburg and its probable relocation in Richmond. A Gettysburg native and a graduate of Pennsylvania College (now Gettysburg College), Weaver became a medical doctor with a degree from the Pennsylvania Medical College in 1865. In the early 1870s, he worked to identify, disinter, and ship to Southern cemeteries more than 3,000 Confederate remains found on the former battlefield of Gettysburg. Weaver gained greater fame as a master anatomist who revealed every tiny filament of the human nervous system by carefully dissecting a human cadaver (Harriet Cole, an African American woman) until only the connected filaments and their connections to the spinal cord remained. In 1893, he displayed his Mounted Cerebro Spinal Nervous System at the World's Columbian Exposition in Chicago. *Homépathe International (Sylvain Cazalet)*.

President Theodore Roosevelt in action during a speech delivered in 1906. Despite party differences, TR the Republican appointed Oates the Democrat to be the Federal Commissioner for Locating and Marking Confederate Graves in the North, a post Oates greatly appreciated and held until his death in 1910. *Library of Congress*.

Oates's grave monument, Oakwood Cemetery, Montgomery, Ala. Oates designed and wrote the extensive text for the monument before his death. Will Oates, his son, supervised the statue's sculpting and the high obelisk's construction. The inscription reads, in part: "Born in poverty, reared in adversity, without educational advantages, yet by honest individual effort he obtained a competency and the confidence of his fellow men, while fairly liberal to relatives and the worthy poor." *Author's photograph*.

14

REQUIEM

Throughout the winter of 1903, William Oates wrote to John Nicholson and William Robbins, inquiring about the status of his application for erecting a monument on Little Round Top. To Nicholson Oates pointed out that Robbins seemed "opposed to my scheme." Around the same time, Robbins wrote to Oates and denied that he alone was opposed to the 15th Alabama monument. If Oates could get the approval of the two Northern commissioners and the secretary of war, Robbins said he would not oppose the placement of the memorial on Little Round Top; but, he pointed out, locating the 15th Alabama's monument on the hill "would violate the customary plan of marking troops of both Armies on this Field and also might seem to imply that the other Regiments [and, here, of course, Robbins specifically meant the 4th Alabama] of our Brigade were less gallant and effective."[1]

With Robbins, Oates began a new wave of correspondence in which the two old soldiers debated the relative locations of the 15th Alabama and 4th Alabama during the battle and how far up the slope Oates and his regiment managed to push the 20th Maine before being forced to retreat. Oates claimed that he had extended the 15th to his right and had "turned the left" of Vincent's Brigade. As he had already told Nicholson, he wanted to erect his monument at a spot where the 15th Alabama "was completely separated from the brigade." It was near this place that his brother "and many others who were near and dear to me" fell in battle.[2]

Sometime around February 15, Oates sent Secretary of War Elihu Root—through the auspices of his congressman, Ariosto Appling Wiley, who delivered the document to the War Department—a formal application for a monument on Little Round Top. The application outlined the movements of the 15th Alabama on July 2, 1863, its advanced position in the regiment's assault against three regiments of Vincent's Brigade (the 20th Maine, the 83rd Pennsylvania, and the 44th New York), and made plain the fact that Oates's brother had been "mortally wounded" on the hill "and died a few days thereafter a prisoner." Oates described the place where he wanted the monument as being "about one hundred yards distant" from "the marble slab" marking "where General [Strong] Vincent fell." He appended a copy of the resolution adopted by the survivors of the 15th Alabama. A monument to the Confederates under his command who fell on Little Round Top, he said, "seems reasonable and a contribution to the truth of history."[3]

In the meantime, Nicholson tried to buy some time from the War Department. "I have to ask for a little time for the preparation and presentation to the Honorable Secretary of the details bearing upon the erection of this Monument," he wrote John C. Schofield, the chief clerk of the War Department. "There is a wide difference of opinion in reference to the location of the Monument," he told Schofield, "and I am sure the Secretary will appreciate our desire to do that which is just and equitable, but it is difficult, in view of the threats made in regard to appealing to Congress, to write calmly or deliberately." For good measure, he closed his letter to Schofield by saying: "I feel sure that the Honorable Secretary will appreciate the position [in] which the Commission is placed by the determination upon the part of General Oates not to adhere to the resolutions and rules governing the Monuments and markers upon the Field." At the same time, Nicholson identified Major Robbins as being the principal opponent of Oates's proposed monument.[4]

At that moment, though, Oates's concentration shifted from his hope for a monument to his despair over his son. Willie had been dismissed from the academy for poor grades in mathematics. Although the evidence is sketchy, there is a hint that Willie may have also been involved in a cheating scandal. His departure came suddenly and without warning. On March 11, 1903, Willie had left the school and was writing his mother a letter from Tuscaloosa, where the University of Alabama was located. As sparse as the documentation is, it suggests that he met his father there and both arranged for Willie to enter the university at the start of the fall semester. Whatever the circumstances behind Willie's departure from West Point, Oates—rather amazingly—forgave his son without much fuss, and the family got on with their lives.[5]

In May 1903, Oates sat at his oak partners' desk in the spacious library of his house on North Ripley Street and wrote to Nicholson asking—yet one more time—for a status report on his application. Separately, Secretary Root invited Oates to visit the battlefield, hoping that the commissioners might explain their position to him in person and sort everything out. In reiterating the actions of the 15th Alabama at Gettysburg, Oates claimed that he and his men "turned the Union flank, and drove the right of the 20th Maine back on its left" while also attacking the 83rd Pennsylvania and the 44th New York. "I want to erect a little monument out of Gettysburg Stone to cost only two or three hundred dollars," he wrote to Root, "with no offensive or improper inscriptions upon it, right about the point from which I was turned back, and where the officers and men were killed." Raising the politically hot issues of reconciliation and reunion, Oates further wrote: "Cannot one humble shaft be erected on that field where a so-called Rebel command fought? If not, then, Mr. Secretary, it shows that the bitterness of feeling engendered by the Civil War has not completely subsided."[6]

Concerned that Secretary Root's invitation for Oates to visit Gettysburg might be accepted and might force the commissioners to approve the monument application, Nicholson thought up a tactical ploy that he felt would serve the commission well. If anyone could successfully challenge Oates's narration of events about July 2 for accuracy, Joshua L. Chamberlain—the man who had commanded the 20th Maine at Gettysburg—seemed the logical choice for the job. So Nicholson decided to call in Chamberlain as a kind of expert witness, someone not in the War Department or employed by the Gettysburg commissioners who could give them, for the secretary's benefit, what would be considered an impartial assessment of Oates's case.

In Nicholson's eyes, Chamberlain was an august figure, a hero who deserved respect and admiration. Having risen from the rank of lieutenant colonel to brevet major general during the war, Chamberlain later became governor of Maine for four consecutive one-year terms, president of Bowdoin College for twelve years, and a popular figure on the lecture circuit around New England. Throughout the postwar years, he took on a leading role in the Grand Army of the Republic, the Military Order of the Loyal Legion of the United States, the Society of the Army of the Potomac, and other veterans' organizations. He enjoyed close relationships with Ulysses S. Grant, Rutherford B. Hayes, Gouverneur K. Warren, Alexander S. Webb, and other former Union generals.

Chamberlain certainly looked the part of a hero. Although of average height, his erect posture, slim physique, and self-confident demeanor made him look taller than he actually was. In his later years, he wore the same drooping moustache he had worn throughout the war, only now it was pure white. His eyes were probably his most compelling feature—radiant and "twinkling blue eyes," his secretary later remembered, and "no matter how badly he felt, his eyes were always snapping right out at you." Unlike Oates, Chamberlain had avoided putting on weight as he grew older. Late in life, he was still slim and trim.

At the dedication in 1889 of the 20th Maine's monument, which sat prominently on the same hillside where Oates hoped to place his memorial, Chamberlain delivered a stirring—and oddly irritated—speech about what he and
his men had accomplished there. His annoyance seemed to stem from the fact
that others, and not he, had chosen the precise point at which to place the
monument. He wore a hero's mantle, and he was proud of it. In August 1893,
he was awarded the Congressional Medal of Honor for his bravery and leadership at Little Round Top. Hampered financially by poor investments and a
lack of business acumen, he accepted in 1900 an appointment from President
William McKinley as surveyor of the port in Portland, Maine, a post he retained until his death. By the summer of 1903, when Nicholson first thought
of dragging him into the Oates monument controversy, the severe wounds
Chamberlain had suffered in the war still bothered him and caused him terrible discomfort. That summer he also suffered from a debilitating illness,
which, for a while, he thought he could not possibly survive.[7]

On August 6, Nicholson wrote Chamberlain and sent along a copy of
Oates's June 2 letter to Root. "The Commission is contending," he said to
Chamberlain, "that it should not be placed [away] from the Brigade [line] but
on the Confederate Avenue facing the Union positions." He believed that
"some of the statements [in Oates's petition] are so much at variance with the
records that we thought we would ask your opinion upon the subject." Chamberlain wrote back promptly and said "I should feel no objection to the erection of a monument to the honor of a regiment that had pushed its way so far
around the flank of the Union line and made so gallant an attack." But, said
Chamberlain, "I should expect it to be placed on ground where it [i.e., the
15th Alabama] actually stood at some time during the battle."

Confirming Nicholson's suspicions, Chamberlain wrote: "Some of the
statements of Colonel Oates in his letter to the Secretary of War differ widely
from the well established record of facts in the case, and very materially from
former statements of his in his papers published by him and in personal letters in the course of a correspondence with me." Oates and his men, he said,
could not have driven the right of the 20th Maine back upon its left. The
positions held by the 44th New York and 83rd Pennsylvania on the hillside
prevented the Alabamians from doing so, Chamberlain explained.

Nicholson received with great elation Chamberlain's account of the battle
and his disputation of Oates's command of the facts. "You are entirely right
in your statement in reference to the 20th Maine and the 15th Alabama Regiments," declared Nicholson, as if he had witnessed the engagement himself.
What's more, said Nicholson, "the statement of General Oates is at variance
with the facts." Nicholson later forwarded a copy of Chamberlain's letter to
Secretary Root.[8]

In the autumn of 1903, the United States seemed to be at peace with itself. Reconciliation sentiment in the North and the South swept through the land, like a warm breeze on a clear day, and the twentieth century promised a new era of unity and common purpose between the sections. Memories of the war and its murderous toll in human lives faded as the Civil War veterans grew old and died. Decades of Lost Cause rhetoric and ideology cast a romantic hue over the past, one in which Northerners and Southerners could both share.

Buried beneath the falling leaves that autumn was any clear remembrance of what the Civil War meant or why it had been fought. Within the rising tide of racism, which engulfed South and North alike, a national amnesia wiped away all memory of the bitter sectional disputes over slavery, the fate of the freed slaves, and civil rights. White Americans now looked upon themselves as a virtuous people who had fought and survived a bloody Civil War, but who now embraced each other in harmony and friendship as brothers.

Except, of course, for William C. Oates. Beneath the surface of his excruciating fight to erect a monument on Little Round Top lay hidden the unreconstructed and unreconciled antagonisms of the war itself. Oates fully believed—and, to a certain extent, he was right in his thinking—that the Gettysburg National Military Park commissioners enforced their policies of locating monuments on the battlefield to the advantage of Union units and relegated Confederate markers to the obscurity of the field's fringes. The "battle line" rule was a victor's rule.

In Montgomery, Oates put into motion the next phase of his campaign to win a monument at Gettysburg. On October 9, 1903, the Alabama General Assembly passed a joint resolution—written, of course, by Oates himself—that reminded the United States government of its obligation at Gettysburg "to allow the erection of markers and monuments to those who fell on each side, Confederate as well as Federals." To that end, the resolution requested the Alabama delegation in the U.S. House and Senate to investigate why permission had not been given to Oates for his monument.[9]

At the same time, Oates enlisted the services of Judge William R. Houghton of Birmingham—who had served in the 2nd Georgia during the war and whose brother Mitchell had served in the 15th Alabama—to write and publish a scathing attack on the monument policies of the battlefield commissioners after visiting Gettysburg in the summer of 1903. Houghton, who considered himself an "intense Confederate," couched his criticism of the park and its administration in travelogue pieces printed in a Birmingham newspaper. In a veiled reference to Oates's case, Houghton wrote: "It will forcibly strike every visitor that there was a great mistake made in not having some monuments or tablets to show where a particular command fought at particular points." Eventually Robbins attempted to rebut Houghton's assault in the Southern press, but Judge Houghton—no doubt egged on by Oates—refused to be silenced and continued to publish scathing newspapers pieces about how the Gettysburg National Military Park failed to take the Confederate side of the battle into account.[10]

Oates continued to barrage the commissioners with letters about his monument and push them to make a decision about it. He was almost totally immersed in the war. On November 4, he attended in Birmingham another reunion of the 15th Alabama veterans. He neared the end of writing his Civil War book, finishing a chapter devoted to Lincoln. To his son at the University of Alabama, he wrote about football and commented that he would never have been able to play the game, for the first time an opponent hit him on purpose, he would have killed him "as soon as I got able." Now he decided that he could visit Gettysburg without forfeiting his pride. He wrote Nicholson: "I am ready on one day's notice to come to Gettysburg, go over the ground with your commission[,] & show you the spot."[11]

As winter came on, Oates traveled to New York and Washington, apparently to search for a publisher to print his Civil War book, now nearing completion. In Gettysburg, the snows of December returned to shroud the battlefield in white. The commissioners felt embattled. Southerners complained ceaselessly about the lack of Confederate monuments and markers, despite the commission's best efforts to erect its iron tablets around the field. About the same time, Northerners began to criticize the battlefield for having too many memorials. "The adornment of the Gettysburg battlefield has been overdone," declared one visitor. Others, however, complimented the commissioners and commended the marking of the field. "A great military park," proclaimed a veteran of the Pennsylvania Bucktails, "every foot having a history."[12]

On January 22, 1904, Secretary Root sent a formal reply to Oates's application and to the Alabama resolution (based on a draft prepared by Nicholson and approved by the other commission members.) Skillfully, the commissioners and Root had not denied Oates's petition for a monument. They had simply specified the further steps he must take before they would approve a monument to the 15th Alabama, including the submission of a precise location, "a Blue Print or Drawing" showing the monument design, and a copy of the intended inscription.[13] Although Oates had submitted some of this material two years earlier, the commissioners clearly wanted to make the process as difficult as they could for the old Alabamian.

For the time being, though, Oates appeared less preoccupied with the monument campaign than he had been in a year. As spring burst forth in Montgomery, transforming the city into an urban panorama of whites and pinks, he contented himself with letting Congressman Wiley wrangle with Nicholson over the protocol for getting a monument. His law practice was thriving, and he even took on some criminal cases, defending his clients against charges of rape and murder. And while T seemed to be going back on her promise to hold fewer "jamborees" at their house, she was at least traveling less and at home more often to keep Oates company. He seems to have given up on his autobiography, having taken the story only as far as the eve of the Civil War, but he kept working on his book and put the finishing touches on the last chapters.[14]

Although he had been suffering from colds and other ailments through most of the spring, Oates finally finished writing his book in early May. A labor of love, he had been working on it for more than twenty years. He entitled it *The War Between the Union and the Confederacy and Its Lost Opportunities with a History of the 15th Alabama Regiment and the Forty-Eight Battles in Which It Was Engaged*. He was mostly pleased with what he had written, especially the appendix that listed and described every soldier who had served in the 15th Alabama, including himself. To Willie, he wrote: "I have worked long and hard on it. It is twice yea thrice as hard for a man of deficient scholastic education to write a book or good pamphlet article as it is for a man who is a classical scholar to do it."

It took him a while to find a publisher. Eventually he settled on the Neale Company of New York and Washington, a house that specialized in publishing Confederate regimental histories and memoirs. He sent his huge manuscript off to Walter Neale sometime during the late spring. Like most writers, he seemed a bit out-of-sorts and despondent once the manuscript was on its way. But he did not sit around and mope. He filled his time through May and June with his law cases, giving a speech to dedicate a Confederate statue in Greensboro, Alabama, and hoping that Willie would not get injured playing football.[15]

After so much heat and controversy for more than a year, Oates finally decided in early July 1904 to visit Gettysburg and satisfy the commission's insistence that he designate where he wanted his monument before receiving approval. On the evening of July 11, Oates—in the company of Congressman Wiley and two other friends, Judge and Mrs. R. B. Kyle (who happened to own a stonecutting company in Alabama)—arrived in Gettysburg from Washington by train. The next morning, Oates met Robbins and Richardson in town, with friendly handshakes all around, but he bristled when he heard that Nicholson—through some unexplained "misunderstanding"—would not join them until the afternoon. Hiring an omnibus, Oates and the two commissioners, accompanied by Wiley and Judge Kyle, rode out from the center of town to the battlefield, and after passing along the park's new roads made their way to Little Round Top.

Oates and Robbins walked leisurely up the southern slope of the hill, where the 15th Alabama had fought so bravely. Richardson, rather characteristically for a man who preferred a passive role on the commission, remained in the carriage the whole time. Oates at first could not believe what he saw. Since his last visit in 1899 with T and Willie, the commission had constructed a road—which it named Chamberlain Avenue—in the summer of 1902 that ran from Wright Avenue, along the saddle between Little Round Top and

Big Round Top, in the shape of a semicircle up the hill to intersect with Sykes Avenue near the western crest. Although the commissioners emphatically insisted in their annual reports that all their work sustained the terrain of the battlefield as it had existed in 1863, Oates could see before him that the construction of Chamberlain Avenue had severely altered the landscape along the slopes on which he and his men had fought. Beneath the 20th Maine monument, for instance, the hillside had been chopped away for the roadway, and the contour of the hill had been radically transformed.[16]

Despite the topographical changes, which Oates found dismaying, the two old Confederate veterans strolled up the hillside toward the 20th Maine granite monument, which sat prominently on a rocky precipice that had not existed in 1863. Oates showed Robbins the farthest point where his regiment had advanced, a boulder behind the line of the 20th Maine's left wing—as best as that line could be determined now with the hillside so irrevocably altered. Apparently Robbins listened carefully and respectfully, but he made no promises or commitments to Oates while they walked the ground.

Later that afternoon, at the Eagle Hotel on Chambersburg Street, Oates met with all the commissioners to discuss his plans. Nicholson led the meeting, apologizing at the outset for missing the trek to Little Round Top in the morning. The men talked informally about Oates's proposed monument, and Oates emphasized that he had chosen a general location, which he had shown to Robbins, for the placement of the stone. Everything seemed to be going well, until Nicholson pulled from his pocket a copy of Joshua Chamberlain's letter to him, written in August 1903, and read it out loud. Oates could not have been more surprised. Whether Nicholson read the letter word for word is not evident, but what Oates understood from Chamberlain's communication with the commission was that the former commander of the 20th Maine "objected to my locating a monument any where I had indicated in my application."

Oates left no account of how the meeting in the Eagle Hotel ended, but he seems to have maintained his composure. Robbins later noted that he thought the hotel meeting had gone very well, "its tenor being rather favorable to his [i.e., Oates's] wishes."[17] But Nicholson had introduced a new component into the monument controversy. The battle for a monument to the 15th Alabama now had become a struggle between conflicting memories of what had happened on that day. And, in the opinion of Nicholson, if not of all three of the commissioners, Oates's memory was worth about as much as dead fallen leaves.

Despite the unexpected turn of events at Gettysburg, Oates seems not to have been fully aware of the significance Nicholson placed on Chamberlain's letter. From all appearances, Oates believed that his monument would be approved, despite Chamberlain's letter. He told Robbins, in fact, that "Chamberlain is not accurate in his statements, [and] his memory is at fault in some respects." Oates sensed that Chamberlain, like so many other aging Civil War heroes, wanted to make himself "the big push"—the solitary hero, the only worthy man on the field. But Oates did not feel overly threatened by Chamberlain's conflicting account of their struggle for Little Round Top. "When I get the shaft erected and my book published," he wrote Robbins with much satisfaction, "I will have reached a round up of my war record."[18]

While it looked at first that the commissioners were inclined to approve Oates's monument, Chamberlain's objections kept coming up. Oates wrote to Robbins to emphasize once more that Chamberlain's account was the inaccurate one. He declared emphatically: "Just as sure as your name is Robbins and mine Oates[,] my regiment not only overlapped his left flank but drove the 20th Maine from that position back to where I showed you[,] and his right as well as his left was forced back but not too far. The more I have thought about it and examined the evidences the more fully convinced I am of the correctness of my claim." Nicholson, nevertheless, let Oates know that the commissioners regarded Chamberlain's account to be sound and accurate. "Cannot you make some statement," wrote Nicholson, "and let me submit it to General Chamberlain, because we are especially anxious to avoid any controversy in these matters."[19]

Understandably put off by Nicholson's last letter, Oates delayed before replying to it. In early March, he finally wrote the commission chairman a long letter and told him flatly that he expected never to reach any agreement with Chamberlain over what happened on July 2, 1863. "I have heard and read enough of his statements to know that he and I are not likely to agree on the place or point to which I advanced," Oates said. Sketching out the ground and its landmarks, he enclosed a rough pencil drawing of Little Round Top for Nicholson and the commissioners to see exactly what he meant and precisely where he wanted the monument to go. As an afterthought, he wanted Nicholson to know that he was not trying to pull the wool over anyone's eyes: "I am not vain or boastful enough if I ever was in my old age to perpetuate a falsehood forty-two years after the occurrence by erecting a monument to the memory of my dead comrades on ground they never reached in their assault."[20]

The publisher released Oates's Civil War book in the winter of 1905, and he received several complimentary reviews in the press. But the notices were actually divided about the book, with Northern reviews criticizing it for Oates's unreconstructed attitudes and Southern reviews praising it for the author's Confederate loyalties. One New York reviewer regarded the book "as a human document testifying to the provincials' capacity to hug closely the corpse of an issue long since dead." A Southern reviewer, however, praised Oates for his justification of secession and for asserting that the "Confederacy should have succeeded."[21]

Mostly, though, the reviewers did not know what to make of Oates's book. One Chicago newspaper condemned it as a "discursive, diffuse and disconnected narrative." Oates knew his book would be different from other Civil War memoirs and histories, particularly since he had interwoven several genres—eyewitness account, history, and regimental record—into a single, chronological narrative. In the book's preface, he called it "a new venture in historic production, combining regimental with general history." His own characterization, however, did not adequately describe what he had created. Written on a grand scale, with his own opinions of people and events liberally mixed in with his narration of battles and campaigns, his book was a massive tome—almost 800 printed pages long—composed by a participant who made "no pretense to scholarly attainments" and, as he had earlier explained to his son, who "lacked the advantages of a classical education." But beyond his narrative account of the war from secession to Lincoln's assassination, his appendix that listed the names and gave brief profiles of every soldier who served in the 15th Alabama regiment offered a unique glimpse at the men who made up one of the Army of Northern Virginia's greatest fighting units.[22]

What struck reviewers and other readers the hardest, however, must have been Oates's straightforward manner of articulating himself—his plain, easy, conversational style—and his complete lack of self-consciousness when it came to expressing his candid opinion. Unlike other Civil War authors, most of whom found themselves trapped in the conventions of Victorian America, Oates managed to break free of the stylized customs of his age by vividly describing the horrors of battle, admitting his own personal fears in combat, painting realistic portraits of soldiers and the military life they led, and offering unabashed criticisms of generals who could not command and politicians who could not govern.

Oates recognized that all men in battle could not be equally brave. Commenting on this fact, and demonstrating his sincere concern for men who found themselves frightened in battle, he included in his book an analysis of courage and cowardice. "Much depends," he wrote, "upon the state of the nervous system at the time. I knew one [soldier], in the first battle he was in, to run for five miles before he could halt, and afterwards that same man became one of the bravest and best soldiers in the regiment." But war also produced other strange and remarkable occurrences. He reported the following incident, which took place during the battle of Second Manassas, in a straightforward manner: "It was a man in Company G standing up by the fence firing at the enemy. I took him to be Cicero Kirkland, and called him by that name two or three times and told him to sit down. He did not seem to hear me and I was still looking for him when he fell, as I thought, dead. When the fight was over and we were gathering up our dead and wounded the man proved to be John Sauls, a young man about eighteen years old. He was shot through the head. The ball entered between his left eye and his nose, just under his brow, and came out behind his right ear in the lobe, called the mastoid process. He was insensible. That poor fellow is still alive and lived in Eufaula, Ala., in 1904. He was a bright boy before he was wounded, but afterwards his face was drawn on one side, he had but very little mind, and was blind in one eye."[23]

To soften his account, he used dry humor. Pointing out in his narrative that a pouring rain had fallen the night of September 20, 1862, after an artillery duel between the Union and Confederate armies following the battle of Cedar Run, he remarked that "I have no recollection of any considerable battle having been fought, but that it was almost immediately followed by copious rains. The superstitious have said that it was the intervention of Providence to wash from the earth the human gore, etc., but I don't think that the blood of man is held in such high esteem by the Great Creator of all things as to cause Him to interfere with the uniform and perfect operation of His laws for any such purpose. I prefer to attribute the rain to natural and philosophical causes, and am quite certain that the loud noise—the heavy shocks of the atmosphere produced by the artillery firing—causes the rain. If not too expensive, when the farmers' crops are suffering from drought, it might be well to fire big guns in the neighborhood to bring the rain. I had rather risk it than a prayer-meeting."[24]

Using the book as a bully pulpit to preach the legitimacy of secession, the virtue of slavery, and the constitutional efficacy of the Confederate government and its Lost Cause, Oates wrote a flawed work that occasionally revealed his own erratic brilliance. In his finest moments as a writer, Oates was able to make his readers feel like they were standing beside him, experiencing all he saw, all he endured. His language throughout the book was invariably plain, powerful, and passionate. Like Oates himself, *The War Between the Union and the Confederacy* was—and still is—a pure American original.

He was disappointed by the book's reception—not only the reviews, but the sluggish sales. On the fortieth anniversary of Lee's surrender at Appomattox, Oates told his son that the book was "not selling rapidly" and that he believed the publisher was cheating him out of his proper share of the revenues. Convinced that sales of the book had been higher than Neale reported, Oates concluded that the publisher "was trying to swindle me."

Oates was in a terrible mood. Trying to persuade his son to become an attorney, he wrote Willie a short account of lawyers he had known who had distinguished themselves at the bar and, in some instances, had risen to judgeships. "We want you," wrote Oates, "to have the best opportunities & the best preparation for"—and here he used one of his favorite expressions—"the battle of life."[25]

While Oates watched with interest and dismay the fluctuating sales figures for his book that spring, John P. Nicholson was busy in Gettysburg getting Joshua Chamberlain involved again in the dispute over the proposed
15th Alabama monument. Nicholson sent Chamberlain a notice of Oates's
book and a copy of the former Confederate's most recent letter to the
Gettysburg commissioners. Chamberlain took offense that Oates "seems to
have satisfied himself that I am incorrigible on the point he wishes to establish, and that he can never agree with me." Although Oates thought of
Chamberlain's statements as "conflicting claims," the Medal of Honor winner explained flatly: "I have simply stated the facts; first in my official report
written on the march away from Gettysburg, and since in a more extended
account on the same lines in a lecture, perhaps not accurately reported. I
cannot change the facts, nor any statement of my own about them." Trying
to sound beneficent, Chamberlain assured Nicholson that he was "more than
willing" to have the 15th Alabama monument "placed inside my lines, for
some of these men were doubtless there, and I should feel honored by the
companionship of the monument of so gallant a regiment on that historic
crest." But, he said, "the matter of monuments is in your charge, not mine."[26]

After he received a copy of Chamberlain's letter that Nicholson had forwarded him, Oates decided to take the matter into his own hands and get in
touch with Chamberlain directly. Writing on April 14, 1905, he opened his
letter with an admonition: "General[,] neither of us are as young as we were
when we confronted each other on Little Round Top nearly 42 years ago." In
the natural course of things, he said, memories tend to fade. He thought that
Chamberlain may have unintentionally misrepresented his claim of having
driven back the 20th Maine's right flank. "I . . . did not claim to have turned
your right," Oates explained; he merely said he had pushed Chamberlain's
right wing back. However the misrepresentation occurred, said Oates,
Chamberlain's first letter to Nicholson "did the work and caused my application to be turned down." In the end, Oates argued, it didn't matter much
whether Chamberlain agreed with him or not about the wavering of the 20th
Maine's right flank. They could both agree that Oates had driven back
Chamberlain's *left*, and that's where he wanted to put the monument.

If Chamberlain would write the commissioners "and say you have no
objection" to having the monument erected at the farthest point the 15th
Alabama advanced on the 20th Maine's *left*, then Oates could assure him "that
there will be no inscription upon the shaft derogatory to your command."
Reflecting his own understanding of what modern military analysts call the
"fog of war," he said: "No one man can see all that occurs in a fight[,] even
between two regiments." Then he added, hoping Chamberlain might take
him up on the offer: "If you & I were on the ground together[,] I do not
believe that there would be any very material difference between us about
what occurred & the ground on which it did occur."[27]

It took a while to receive a reply from Chamberlain. In mid-May, Chamberlain finally responded and claimed that he had "made no objection whatever to the erection of a monument by you on the ground attained by the 15th Alabama or any portion of it during the battle." He also asserted, "you will perceive by my personal letters to Col. Nicholson . . . my complete and cordial willingness to have the monument of the 15th Alabama placed within my lines on the slope of Little Round Top." Although Chamberlain probably realized that his contradiction of Oates's description of the battle, particularly regarding how far back the right and left wings of the 20th Maine had been pushed, would be enough for the Gettysburg commissioners to deny Oates's monument application, he tried to placate Oates by affirming his support for the memorial to the 15th Alabama: "It is really my desire to have your monument set up, only let us make sure of our ground for the sake of historical fact." He told Oates he would be willing to meet him "again" at Little Round Top, if the occasion ever presented itself.[28]

Chamberlain forwarded a copy of his letter to Nicholson. "I wish to congratulate you," Nicholson replied, "upon the dignified, manly, soldierly and gentlemanly way in which you have replied to him [i.e., Oates]." As for the monument dispute, Nicholson informed Chamberlain that "it is very clear that General Oates has not the slightest idea of admitting the views of any one in the controversy except himself." Nicholson reported that the commissioners were turning all the documentation relating to the controversy over to the secretary of war and leaving the final decision to him.[29]

William Howard Taft, who was by this time serving as secretary of war under Theodore Roosevelt, never made a decision about the monument. Instead, Oates's application simply became forgotten and ignored. Oates himself corresponded off and on for more than a year with Lunsford L. Lomax, a former major general in the Confederate army from Virginia, who was named to the commission after Robbins died in May 1905. In the spring of 1906, Oates tried yet one last time to get Congressman Wiley to pressure the War Department into deciding the issue, but the Gettysburg commissioners relied on Chamberlain's statements to demonstrate that the monument could not be placed where Oates wanted it to go.[30]

Oates and Chamberlain never met at Little Round Top. In fact, they never met in person at all. In the end, the two men never could have comprehended how their own desires to erect monuments on Little Round Top to their respective regiments sprang from very different motives. Having grieved every day since July 2, 1863, for his younger brother John, Oates wanted the monument to memorialize his personal loss, the greater loss of the other men under his command who had fallen in the battle, and the memory of his regiment's great deeds that day. He also knew a monument placed behind the Union lines would demonstrate the valor of the 15th Alabama and his own heroism—something of a consolation for the defeat he and his fellow Alabamians had suffered at Gettysburg. Chamberlain wanted the bravery of his regiment and his own personal courage to be honored and remembered in stone, without the taint of having to admit that his lines had been bent back into a hairpin rather than the semi-circle he preferred to picture in his mind. In the end, Chamberlain's status as a hero and his victor's pride won the day.

To both men, the memory of the Civil War involved something more than just the erection of monuments or competing recollections of what had taken place on July 2, 1863. Oates's memory of Gettysburg combined his personal and melancholic memories with his Lost Cause and Southern collective memories of the Confederate defeat in Pennsylvania. Oates hoped to soothe his survivor's guilt—the pain he felt from the moment he had to leave his dying brother behind a rock on Little Round Top—by paying homage to his regiment and his dead brother at the place where they had seen their worst fighting. He also hoped, in the spirit of the Lost Cause, to transform battlefield defeat into a moment of public triumph by raising a monument that could be unveiled, dedicated, and admired. In doing so, he might also gain the personal recognition he craved for his part in the war and, at the same time, celebrate what Oliver Wendell Holmes, Jr., called the "soldier's faith" by paying tribute to soldierly honor and manly heroism.

But Chamberlain and the Gettysburg commissioners would not cooperate with him. What they may have recognized without saying so was the degree to which Oates hoped to gain control over the memory of Little Round Top—over how future generations would comprehend the battle, how the legacies of victory and defeat would be remembered, how the past itself might be manipulated for present and future purposes. For his part, Chamberlain did not want to concede any portion of his victory on the hilltop to his enemy. By holding his ground in the debate over the 15th Alabama monument, Chamberlain could remain in possession of the military victory he had won on July 2, 1863, and the moral victory he wanted the North to retain into eternity. Beneath the surface of the dispute between Oates and the Gettysburg commissioners, including the role that Chamberlain played in the affair, were the hatreds that lingered between old foes, North and South. Controlling the past in the present and ensuring how the battle would be known to generations yet to come became almost as important as the outcome of the battle fought forty years earlier. Even in their dotage, Oates and Chamberlain came to see that there were still old scores to settle.[31] Losing a second time to Chamberlain did not sit well with Oates. In his quest to dominate his world and nearly everyone in it, Oates's second defeat at Gettysburg reminded him, as it had before, that his mastery did not extend to all things and that he could not attain the upper hand in every contest.

Until his death, Oates wrapped himself in bitterness over the monument controversy and accused the federal commissioners of being ungracious victors. Chamberlain revealed that he, too, had not stopped fighting the battle of Gettysburg. Even in old age, right up until his death in 1914, he dearly held onto his reputation as the man who had saved Little Round Top for the Union cause. For Chamberlain and Oates, the bloody struggle on Little Round Top was an event that kept the issues of the war alive in their hearts for half a century. For them, the wounds of war never would be fully healed. Perhaps they are battling still in Valhalla. But one thing is for certain. To this day, there is no monument to the 15th Alabama on Little Round Top.

The aches and pains of old age continued to bother Oates, no matter how much he tried to exercise or how many times he visited Hot Springs in Arkansas to find relief. He remained active in his law practice and in expanding his real estate holdings, nevertheless. Acquiring extensive parcels in North Montgomery, he became one of the largest landowners in the city. On Sundays, he went to his law office to get caught up on his personal correspondence and other private business. All too regularly, he attended the funerals of friends and clients, sometimes serving as a pallbearer or delivering a eulogy. T continued inviting house guests, holding parties, and dragging Oates to the theater and other social events, all of which he deplored. He was tired and he longed "for peace & quietude."[32]

Willie graduated from the University of Alabama in the spring of 1905 and the following September entered the University of Virginia Law School to begin following in his father's nonmilitary footsteps. In law school, Willie—who now preferred to be called "Will"—showed more confidence in his studies and encountered fewer difficulties in the classroom than ever before. Oates helped by sending him insights and pointers about the law, and he visited Charlottesville and attended some law lectures with his son.[33]

In the summer of 1906, only a few months away from his seventy-third birthday, Oates announced that he was a candidate for the U.S. Senate, declaring his belief in his own qualifications and publicly asserting that while he had opposed some of the provisions of the Alabama constitution of 1901, he now thought that it had proven "to be better and wiser in its provisions than he then thought it was." But his appeal to the voters did no good. He was defeated in the primary, because, in the opinion of many, "he was out of harmony with reigning ideas, and out of harmony with the odd political times."[34] It was the final episode—the denouement—in Oates's political career.

The Civil War still gripped his thoughts, his memories, and his labors. In December 1907, he was appointed commissioner for locating and marking Confederate graves in the North by President Theodore Roosevelt and Secretary of War William Howard Taft. The appointment must have come as a great surprise to him, for he had not asked for the position. He would be the second commissioner to fill the job, the first—William Elliott, a former Confederate lieutenant colonel and congressman from South Carolina—having died in early December 1907. It is possible that he was given this job to quiet him about the outcome over the Gettysburg monument to the 15th Alabama. If that was the case, the strategy worked. Oates left the idea of the monument behind for good.

He seems not to have been concerned about accepting an appointment from a Republican president. Other Confederate heroes, including Longstreet and John Singleton Mosby, had done so some years earlier. Longstreet had been condemned as a traitor to the South for his political involvement with Republicans; Mosby had let whatever mud was thrown his way just roll off his back. Realizing that he had little to lose politically in Alabama, given his involuntary retirement from public life following the state constitutional convention of 1901, Oates took on the job without stopping to worry about the political ramifications of the appointment. As it turned out, he seems not to have suffered any decline in his community standing as a result of his holding a Republican office while remaining a loyal Democrat.

Reconciliation sentiment lay behind the existence of the federal commission. During the first few years of the twentieth century, Confederate veteran organizations took up the cause of advocating a uniform system of Federal care for all Confederate graves in Northern cemeteries, especially the graves in or near prisoner-of-war camps in the North. In March 1906, a statute was signed into law by the president that provided "for the appropriate marking of the graves of soldiers and sailors of the Confederate Army and Navy who died in Northern prisons and were buried near the prisons where they died."[35]

Although he had been laid low in the winter of 1908 with a bout of pneumonia, Oates took over as commissioner the following spring. He tried to spend as much time in Washington as possible, sometimes traveling there two or three times a year for extended stays and occasionally more often than that if the business of the office demanded it. His capable assistant was L. Frank Nye, the local son of a hardware merchant and a graduate of Georgetown University. A dedicated worker without the fussiness of most bureaucrats, Nye did most of the research, kept all the details and files straight, handled correspondence and other office paperwork, and generally kept the commission moving forward and making progress.

Oates, who was more than happy to have Nye push paper in whatever direction it needed to go, nevertheless developed an amazing command of what was going on, what needed to be done, and the details behind nearly every aspect of the commission and its activities. He must have been glad to see that Nye was not only superbly efficient, but also incredibly honest. The clerk had a talent for monitoring expenses, for making sure the government was not cheated, and for getting bills paid and vouchers submitted on time, and all by following the correct procedures. Oates was fond of Nye and trusted him to do what was needed and what was right.[36]

Despite his advancing age (he was now in his mid-seventies) and his painful rheumatism, he traveled extensively throughout the North to visit cemeteries and examine the work that had been done—or still needed to be done—for the commission. In June 1908, he journeyed to Lexington, Kentucky, and Alton, Illinois; that autumn, he went to Kansas City, Missouri, and Cincinnati and Columbus, Ohio. He and Nye together, in a trip that lasted only a few days in May 1909, visited cemeteries in Baltimore, Frederick, and Point Lookout, Maryland; Philadelphia, Chester, Shohola, and Harrisburg, Pennsylvania; Brooklyn, New York; and Finn's Point (Salem), New Jersey.[37]

There was an advantage to his position that he never could have foreseen. Reading the commission's files, he discovered that Elliott, his predecessor, had visited Gettysburg and had learned that Confederate graves had been mapped and marked by Dr. John W. C. O'Neal of Gettysburg and that two other men from the town, Samuel Weaver and his son Dr. Rufus B. Weaver, had worked with ladies' memorial associations in Georgia, South Carolina, North Carolina, and Virginia in the early 1870s to exhume the Confederate dead on the battlefield and reinter them in cemeteries located in those Southern states. In February 1909, Oates corresponded with O'Neal and Rufus Weaver and told them of his quest to find where his brother John was buried. He soon learned that John had died at the Union army's Fifth Corps hospital set up on Michael Fiscel's farm, which was located east of the Round Tops.[38]

Then, Oates heard from Weaver and learned precisely what he wanted to know about his brother's remains. "It affords me great pleasure," wrote Weaver, "to reply that my records of the removal of the remains of the Confederate dead show that, on Sept. 10th, 1872, the remains of Lt. J. A. Oat[e]s, 15th Alabama Regt., were shipped to Richmond, Va., and there interred in Hollywood Cemetery." Weaver explained that John Oates's remains could not be distinguished from the remains of eleven other Confederates buried at the Fiscel farms, so all twelve bodily remains were shipped together to Richmond in a box labeled with the letter A. Eight of the Confederates were unknown, Weaver said, but the remains of Lieutenant Barnett Cody—Bud Cody, Oates's childhood friend—were also included in Box A.[39]

Oates was elated. After all this time, after so many years of mourning for his brother, it appeared he was about to find him at last. John Oates would be lost no more. Oates had Nye write in March to Bettie Ellyson, the recently installed president of the Ladies' Memorial Association, which was the organization responsible for removing the Confederate dead from Gettysburg and for maintaining the graves in Hollywood Cemetery. In the letter, Nye—writing over Oates's signature—asked for the location of Box A in the cemetery.[40]

By July, Oates had heard nothing from Ellyson. The waiting was excruci-
atingly painful. He wrote again to her, enclosing a copy of his earlier letter
and begging her for a reply. He was "exceedingly anxious for the information
asked for."[41] There was still no answer. As the weeks passed, he repeatedly
queried Nye to learn if he had received anything from Ellyson, any letter at
all from Richmond that might contain a clue as to the whereabouts of Box A
in Hollywood Cemetery. Nye could only tell him that no word had arrived.

It was a difficult time for Oates. He complained about failing eyesight,
and that summer, in a letter to Will, he claimed that he could scarcely see. It
is quite possible he had developed diabetes and began suffering from one of
the disease's worst consequences. He may have had the disease for twenty
years or more without it having been diagnosed. By the end of September, his
eyesight had worsened, although Will told his latest sweetheart—Georgia
Whiting Saffold, whom he would marry in 1911—that he thought his father's
condition was only temporary. Nevertheless, the senior Oates gave all of his
cases to his son, and Will began handling the lion's share of the law firm's
business.[42]

Oates grew more frustrated in his search for his brother's grave. Having
still received no response from Bettie Ellyson in Richmond, he wrote her
again in January 1910, pleading for an answer and for some indication of
where his brother might be buried in Hollywood Cemetery. He instructed
Nye to ask John R. Hooper, the Hollywood superintendent, if he could help
get a reply from Ellyson. The tactic worked, for Ellyson finally wrote to Oates
in mid-February and apologized for having been away from home and not
completely familiar with all the records concerning the removal of the Confederate dead from Gettysburg. Nevertheless, she could tell Oates this much:
"The box marked A is on Gettysburg Hill in Hollywood in [the] Soldiers'
part, near the Monument the Ladies from Philadelphia erected in memory of
our soldiers who were buried up there [i.e., in Gettysburg]." She said that if
Oates wished to visit the cemetery, she would be glad to meet him "and show
you about where your brother is buried."[43]

Once again, Oates's hopes were raised. He sent Ellyson a speedy letter in
reply, thanking her for the information and asking for a clarification about
the location of his brother's grave, which he hoped to narrow down to a single
headstone. In a few days, he heard the disappointing news from Ellyson: The
Gettysburg dead were marked not by individual graves, but only by granite
blocks designating huge sections of the plot.[44]

It is a mystery why Oates simply did not get on a train and go to Richmond to see for himself where John was buried. Despite his eye troubles, he
could have managed the trip with little difficulty. Instead, he sent Nye to the
Hollywood Cemetery. Interestingly enough, Nye—either knowingly or by
accident—made his trip so that he was in Richmond on July 2, 1910, the
forty-seventh anniversary of the 15th Alabama's assault on Little Round Top.

Bettie Ellyson was out of town when Nye appeared at the cemetery, but he was able to find his own way around the burial grounds to the section where Ellyson had said Box A had been interred. Nye later wrote to Ellyson: "While I was not able to report to General Oates the exact location of the grave of his brother, yet I could tell him of the excellent condition in which this section of the cemetery is maintained."[45]

Oates's search for his brother was over. By mid-July, when he finally learned that there was no hope of ever finding his brother's individual gravesite, Oates became seriously ill and bedridden. He improved enough in August to accompany T and Will to Asheville, North Carolina, where his doctors thought the cool mountain air might do him good. But then he was stricken again, put to bed, and by the end of August, the decision was made for Will to take his father back to Montgomery, while T stayed on in Asheville for a while longer.[46]

Oates told Will he wanted to die at home. On September 1, riding in a special Pullman car that Will had arranged to be added to the train, Oates and his son made the slow journey back to Montgomery. At home, he was examined by Dr. J. B. Gaston, the physician who had been in charge of Howard's Grove hospital in Richmond, where Oates had been sent after the amputation of his arm forty-six years earlier. But now there was little the doctor could do, and Oates continued to fail rapidly.

He was put to bed in the blue parlor at the front of the house on North Ripley Street. Will stayed at his side and comforted him as much as he could. T was summoned home, and she came quickly from Asheville, knowing this would be the last she would see of her husband. Together she and Will kept the bedside vigil. On September 7, Will thought his father could not possibly survive the night. But Oates held on for two more days. Then the end finally came. Half an hour past noon on September 9, 1910, he died quietly in his bed.[47]

Will Oates made all the arrangements for his father's funeral. T was overcome with grief and could barely function. When she slept, she dreamed of Oates. In Montgomery, flags were lowered to half-mast, the capitol draped in black, and all government offices closed. Expressions of sympathy and tributes to Oates came pouring in from all over the state, all over the nation. Editorials praised him as "one of Alabama's stalwarts" and "one of the most distinguished citizens of the state" and recapitulated his brilliant career as a soldier and statesman—"The One-Armed Hero of Henry County." A Montgomery newspaper reported: "General Oates made a strong battle for life, but his 74 years told against his once rugged constitution, and he passed quietly to the great beyond."[48]

Oates was laid in state in the front parlor of his home, where he had died. Hundreds, perhaps thousands, came to the house to pay their respects. Inside, all was quiet and solemn. The windows and doors were closed. People walked through the house in silence or spoke only in whispers. State officials, city politicians, military officers, Confederate veterans all came to see Oates. Several chapters of the United Daughters of the Confederacy sent huge floral arrangements or wreaths of evergreens.[49]

At four in the afternoon on Sunday, September 11, the funeral procession—consisting of four National Guard companies and the cortege—formed in front of Oates's house. The casket was carried from the house to a hearse as a crowd of people stood outdoors with bowed heads. Fifty carriages with family, friends, and the pall bearers followed behind the military escort as the procession slowly made its way to St. John's Episcopal Church. At the church, the bells were struck in the steeple, and the military escort assumed formation at the front door and presented arms. The pews were completely filled. When the casket was carried up the center aisle to the altar, only some sobbing broke the hush. The organist played the funeral march as the casket was placed before the chancel. The Reverend E. E. Cobbs led the congregation in prayer. The church service ended with the singing of "Nearer My God to Thee."

Then the casket was carried out of the church, and the solemn procession down Montgomery's streets was begun again. In the distance, an artillery company fired a salute to Oates every minute for half an hour, breaking the stillness of the Sunday evening with the sharp reports of cannon. At Oakwood Cemetery, on the outskirts of Montgomery, one reporter remarked that it seemed like "half the people of the city had gathered" there. When the family plot was reached, the military escort lined up again and presented arms. Over the grave, the Reverend Cobbs read the Episcopalian burial service.

Members of the local chapter of the United Confederate Veterans performed their burial rites and placed a small Confederate battle flag at the head of the casket. Then a bugler sounded taps, and the sad notes reverberated across the broad plain of the cemetery as twilight came on. When the veterans dispersed, a unit of infantry dressed in khakis marched forward and fired three volleys over the grave. Once more in the distance a battery fired its salvos of salute.[50] Night fell over Montgomery and brought a chill to the air, now that the sun was gone.

At his death, Oates left an estimated estate of $200,000—what in those days was considered a small fortune. Will Oates, who served as executor of the estate, made the arrangements for the memorial shaft and statue that his father wanted placed over his grave. In his will, Oates specified small bequests to his sister, Mary Jane Long (he had already turned over the deed to her for the Abbeville house and twenty-six acres of land), to another sister, Melissa Hickman (whose husband was a distant relative of Lucy Hickman, the mother of Oates's youngest illegitimate son), to his youngest sister, Amanda Linton, and to his nieces and nephews (the children of Mary Jane Long, whom he regarded "almost as my own"). To T, he left the bulk of his estate, including the house on North Ripley Street and all its furnishings (except the library), and a sizable amount of bonds and securities, all totaling about $40,000 in value. To Will, he bequeathed all property to be held in a trust for T so "that she may not waste the means I leave her." He also gave Will his gold watch, his land in Texas, and all his law books and office furniture. Will would also inherit the library and all other property not specified as such in Oates's will. No bequest was made to Claude or Josh Oates or to their mothers.[51]

Before the casket was closed the day before the funeral, Will Oates had gently placed a white rose and a bright aster next to his father's head. "They now rest with him under the sod," he had explained to Georgia Saffold, "as a fragrant humble little reminder of those who not only loved him but whom he loved."[52]

Even though he had watched his father die, caring for him until the very end, Will found it difficult to accept that his beloved "Pofs" was gone. The man, the father, had always been so much larger than life. In the coming years, the senior William Oates continued to cast a huge shadow over his son's life and career. Like so many sons, Will discovered that no matter what he did, no matter how much he tried to carve out a niche of his own in Alabama, he would always judge himself—or be judged by others—according to how well he measured up to his father. Yet by the time Will died in 1938, his father's public reputation had dwindled, nearly vanishing from view. In less than a generation, the senior Oates's star had faded, and few Alabamians lauded or even remembered the old hero of Henry County in the decades after World War II.

Few heroes achieve true immortality. William Oates—colonel, congressman, governor, general, attorney—had aspired to prominence, recognition, and respect. He acquired some of those things, but there always seemed to be something missing. Oates never surmounted the guilt he felt over leaving his brother behind at Gettysburg and for surviving without him for forty-seven more years. That relentless guilt and its consuming sadness left a gaping hole in his heart. He always pushed himself to succeed, to do his best, but sometimes he found himself falling short of his goals and settling for less than what he really wanted. In his private life, he never gained the mastery—so vitally important to Southern men—that he yearned for. In his public life, he never attained the fame and the high regard that he so desperately sought. For his entire life, he wrestled with all the great Southern demons—slavery, race, violence, and bigotry. He often lost those matches, giving in to the great power of the South's brutal institutions, its harrowing prejudices, and its very demanding ways of life. He also struggled with the issues of truth and honesty, occasionally compromising his principles more than he should have or

settling for prevarications when he really knew better. But for all his imperfections, for all his very human failings, he could proudly declare—to himself
and to the world—that he had fought the good fight, never shrinking from a
contest just because it might be difficult or unwinnable. He liked his own
maverick persona, which led him more than once to proclaim that in his days
as a soldier he had worn Confederate gray in the Civil War and United States
blue in the Spanish-American War—and had been *right* both times. Being
right was always important to Oates. The trouble was that he rarely thought
himself wrong.

It was a bright and clear spring day in Montgomery on Saturday, April 26,
1930. Plans had been made for the commemoration of Confederate Memorial Day—the Southern version of the holiday, not the day that has become
the national holiday—that would include a ceremony to honor the Confederate fallen who lay peacefully at rest in Oakwood Cemetery, just outside the
city. T and her granddaughter Marion Saffold Oates, the ten-year-old daughter
of Will and Georgia Oates, went together to pay their respects to General
Oates, but they visited the graveyard in the morning, before the crowds descended on the place to decorate the old veterans' huddled monuments.
Oates's grave was located between the long rows of budding trees on a broad
plateau that overlooked the rest of the cemetery. There, in all his glory, stood
William C. Oates, his life-sized bronze statue gazing intently across the
wide, open burial ground. Within a brick border that served as a retaining
wall around Oates's tall monument, a plot of grass had been carved out of
the ground; T knew it was only a matter of time before she would be resting
there beside her husband.

For now, T and Marion got out of the car, holding small Confederate
flags and bunches of flowers in their hands, and walked to the base of Oates's
impressive memorial. T had some trouble walking, for her left leg, which had
been bothering her for years, had gone lame and she could only limp slowly
along. In the sunlight, below the imposing, intimidating figure of the man T
had loved, she and Marion placed the flowers and flags on the monument and
watched them flutter in the gentle spring breeze. Wife and granddaughter
stood there for a while, silent and solemn, as the spring morning grew warmer
and the glare of the sun began reflecting off the marble stones.[53] In only a few
minutes, they would be back in the house on North Ripley Street, sipping tea
or lemonade and reading books and telling tales of the past, which seemed to
Marion to be so much a part of her present.

T died three years later on the seventieth anniversary of the battle of
Little Round Top. Marion felt the loss profoundly, for T had been her boon
companion and a guiding light in her life. Later, when she looked back on the
days she spent with T in Montgomery, she acknowledged that it was her

grandmother, and not her parents, who had really raised her. With T gone, Marion had lost her most tangible link to the past. But as the young girl grew into adulthood and took control of her life, she discovered that the past was precisely what William Faulkner, that most Southern of American writers, had said it was. "The past," he wrote, "is never dead. It's not even past."[54]

The name of Oates is not emblazoned across the Southern skies at night, written in the stars. He lived his life with great gusto, but William Oates left little behind as a tangible legacy. To be sure, he provided well for his heirs. But the South marched forward through the twentieth century without paying him much attention or extolling his achievements. His family never forgot him, though, even if their best memories did become thin over time, losing some of the vital details—but none of the precious luster—that had made his life so remarkable. Mindful of history's importance, as many Southerners so often seem to be, his descendants carefully safeguarded his papers and some of his most treasured possessions.

Some other things have endured, too. At Gettysburg, there is no monument to the 15th Alabama, but Little Round Top stands at the southern edge of the battlefield as a craggy reminder of the greatest and worst moment in Oates's life. In Oakwood Cemetery, just outside Montgomery, Oates rests peacefully with T and Will beside him. There, at last, Oates reposes in silence— no more political bombast, no more legal pleading, no more words as weapons. And every November, when the Leonid meteor showers return to the skies, and the stars fall on Alabama, just as they did on the eve of Oates's birth, one may well ponder how history and memory, all knotted and tangled, are revealed in the cascading light—not fully disclosed, only partially seen, never completely comprehended, always dimly construed, but, like William Oates, beheld nonetheless as a recognizable phenomenon, real in all its virtues, troubling in all its flaws, sad in all its tragedy: a fire that comes streaking out of the blackness of a Southern past that is, after all, never really dead.

ABBREVIATIONS USED

ADAH   Alabama Department of Archives and History,
Montgomery, Ala.

AML   Abbeville Memorial Library, Abbeville, Ala.

BC   Hawthorne-Longfellow Library, Bowdoin College,
Brunswick, Maine

CF   Cemeterial Files, Gettysburg National Military Park
Battlefield Commission, Letters and Reports to the
Secretary of War, 1895–1907, Box 231, Records of the
Office of the Quartermaster General, RG 92, NA

CGC1   Confederate Graves Correspondence 1: Records of the
Office of the Commissioner for Locating and Marking
Confederate Graves, Confederate Correspondence File,
1906–1912, RG92, NA

CGC2   Confederate Graves Correspondence 2: Records of the
Office of the Commissioner for Locating and Marking
Confederate Graves, Confederate Correspondence File,
1908–1916, RG92, NA

CGC3   Confederate Graves Correspondence 3: Records of the
Office of the Commissioner for Locating and Marking
Confederate Graves, Confederate Cemeterial File,
Geographic, Box 5, Gettysburg Folder, RG92, NA

Cong. Rec.   *Congressional Record*

Cope, WCO's Visit	Emmor B. Cope, "Account of William C. Oates's Visit to Gettysburg Battlefield," July 2, 1896, Engineers Department, Record of the Position of Troops on the Battlefield, Volume I, pp. 27–29, GNMP
CSR	Compiled Service Records, RG 109, War Department Collection of Confederate Records, NA
ED	Engineers Department, Gettysburg Battlefield Commission, GNMP
EU	Robert W. Woodruff Library, Emory University, Atlanta, Ga.
GBMA	Gettysburg Battlefield Memorial Association
GNMP	Gettysburg National Military Park
GVF	Governors' Vertical Files, Alabama Department of Archives and History, Montgomery, Ala.
HL	Huntington Library, San Marino, Calif.
JAO	John A. Oates
JBB	John B. Bachelder
JLC	Joshua Lawrence Chamberlain
JPN	John P. Nicholson
JPN Letters	Letters from John P. Nicholson, 1903–1904, Park Archives, GNMP
LC	Library of Congress, Washington, D.C.
LEXIS	LexisNexis Academic Database
MA	*Montgomery Advertiser*
MOLC Interview	Author's interview, Marion Oates Leiter Charles, Washington, D.C., Dec. 7, 1991
NA	National Archives, Washington, D.C.
NYPL	New York Public Library
OA	Oates Autobiography, Oates Family Papers, ADAH
OAF	Oates Administrative Files, Miscellaneous Letters, ADAH
OC	Oates Correspondence, Gettysburg National Military Park, Gettysburg, Pa.
ODF	William C. Oates Document File (War with Spain), Records of the Record and Pension Office, 1794–1917, No. 576559, Box 924, RG 94 (Records of the Adjutant General's Office), NA
OFP	Oates Family Papers, ADAH.

O.R.	U.S. War Department, *The War of the Rebellion: A Compilation of the Official Records of the Union and Confederate Armies*, 70 vols. in 128 parts (Washington, D.C., 1880–1901)
SCWC	Schoff Civil War Collection, William L. Clements Library, UM
SHC	Southern Historical Collection, University of North Carolina, Chapel Hill
SHSP	*Southern Historical Society Papers*
STO	Sarah Toney Oates ("T")
SUL	Sanford University Library, Birmingham, Ala.
UM	University of Michigan
WCO	William Calvin Oates, Sr.
WCO Papers	William C. Oates Papers, ADAH
WCOJR	William Calvin Oates, Jr.
WMR	William M. Robbins
Young Papers	Samuel B. M. Young Papers, U.S. Army Military History Institute, Carlisle Barracks, Pennsylvania

NOTES

Works cited by author and short title in these notes will be found fully cited in the Selected Bibliography.

Introduction

1. *Birmingham Ledger*, Sept. 9, 1910; *MA*, Sept. 10, 1910; *Sacramento Union*, Sept. 10, 1910; *Chicago Post*, Sept. 9, 1910; *New York Tribune*, Sept. 10, 1910. There are no other full-scale biographies of Oates. For brief modern sketches, see Farmer, "William Calvin Oates," in Johnson and Malone, eds., *Dictionary of American Biography*, 7:605; Jones, "William Calvin Oates," 338–348; Krick, "Introduction," unpaginated front matter; LaFantasie, ed., "Introduction," *Gettysburg*, 1–20, 35–47; LaFantasie, "William Calvin Oates," in Garraty and Carnes, eds., *American National Biography*, 16:574–575. In a dual biography of Oates and Joshua Lawrence Chamberlain, writer Mark Perry uses only a handful of sources to tell Oates's story with particularly poor results; his Oates portrait is a combination of misleading statements, incorrect assumptions, factual errors, and even fictional passages. See Perry, *Conceived in Liberty*.
2. For scholarly assessments of the reconciliation process between North and South after the war, see Buck, *Road to Reunion*; Woodward, *Reunion and Reaction*; Appleby, "Reconciliation and the Northern Novelist," 117–129; Stark, "Brothers at/in War," 174–181; Foster, *Ghosts of the Confederacy*; Linderman, *Embattled Courage*, 266–297; Kammen, *Mystic Chords of Memory*; McConnell, *Glorious Contentment*, 166–205; Linenthal, *Sacred Ground*, 87–126; Silber, *Romance of Reunion*; Reardon, *Pickett's Charge*; Kinsel, "American Identity," 5–14; Blight, *Race and Reunion*.
3. Moore, *History of Alabama*, 633.

4. On Southern "mastery" and its inevitable failures, I have been particularly influenced by Faust, *James Henry Hammond*; Berry, *All That Makes A Man*; Johnson, *Soul by Soul*; Smith, *Mastered by the Clock*; McCurry, *Masters of Small Worlds*; Perman, *Struggle for Mastery*; Fellman, *The Making of Robert E. Lee*, and an insightful review essay by Kenneth S. Greenberg, "Why Masters are Slaves," 386–389. For informative discussions of American and Southern masculinities in the nineteenth century, see Faust, *James Henry Hammond*; Pugh, *Sons of Liberty*; Wilkinson, *American Tough*; Filene, "Between a Rock and a Soft Place," 339–355; Mangan and Walvin, eds., *Manliness and Morality*; Carnes and Griffen, eds., *Meanings for Manhood*; Mangan, "Men, Masculinity, and Sexuality," 303–313; Rotundo, *American Manhood*; Adams, "Men in America," 14–19; Bederman, *Manliness and Civilization*; Mayfield, "'The Soul of a Man!'" 477–500; McCurry, *Masters of Small Worlds*; Kimmel, *Manhood in America*; Dorsey, "History of Manhood in America," 19–30; Frank, *Life with Father*; Hoganson, *Fighting for American Manhood*; Braudy, *From Chivalry to Terrorism*; Hoffert, *History of Gender in America*; Berry, *All That Makes a Man*.

5. On Southern honor, see Eaton, "The Role of Honor in Southern Society," 47–58; Onwood, "Impulse and Honor," 31–56; Wyatt-Brown, *Southern Honor*; Wyatt-Brown, *Honor and Violence*; Greenberg, "The Nose, the Lie, and the Duel," 57–74; Greenberg, *Honor and Slavery*; Wyatt-Brown, *Shaping of Southern Culture*. For the "language of honor," which was used by white men without regard to background throughout the South, see particularly, Greenberg, *Honor and Slavery*, 115–146.

6. My understanding of the dynamics of Southern violence—and how violence relates to honor—comes from several key works on the subject: Cash, *Mind of the South*; Franklin, *Militant South*; Parsons, "Violence and Caste in Southern Justice," 455–468; Hackney, "Southern Violence," 906–925; Reed, "To Live—and Die—in Dixie," 429–443; May, "Dixie's Martial Image," 213–234; Roland, "The Ever-Vanishing South," 3–20; Wyatt-Brown, *Southern Honor*; Fede, "Legitimized Violent Slave Abuse," 93–150; Wyatt-Brown, *Honor and Violence*; Ayers, *Vengeance and Justice*; Gorn, "'Gouge and Bite, Pull Hair and Scratch,'" 18–43; Faust, "Southern Violence Revisited," 205–210; Pyron, "Lawlessness and Culture," 741–751.

7. Hofstadter and Wallace, eds., *American Violence*, 7. On war as a "legitimate" form of violence, see Brown, "Historical Patterns of Violence in America," 43–80.

8. Wilde, *The Importance of Being Earnest* (1895), act 2, sc.1: Miss Prism. "Journal of the soul" is borrowed from Richard Schikel, "Connections," *Time*, 123 (Jan. 23, 1984). Historians, as a rule, don't seem to know much about modern scientific understanding of how memory and forgetfulness work in the brain; as a result, Civil War scholars have tended to make the wrong assumptions about memory. Some historians think there is a vast chasm between "memory" and "history," apparently believing that memories are fictions and history is truth. See, for example, Reardon, *Pickett's Charge*. But more fundamentally, historians—and, for the most part, the general public—seem to believe that all memories fade with age. Based on this notion, a good number of scholars have declared that they give preference to primary sources written as soon as possible after an event has taken place over ones written months or years or decades later. These historians, hoping to get closer to what they believe is the "truth" in history and the "accuracy" of memories, discard autobiographies and memoirs as lacking an inherent credibility. See, for instance, Reardon, *Pickett's Charge*; McPherson, *For Cause and*

Comrades; and, Power, *Lee's Miserables*. There is, of course, some validity to the idea that one's memory decreases—or at least *seems* to decrease—with age. But the trouble with that observation is that it fails to take into account the possibility that any memory, from the time of its inception, can be faulty. Criminal investigators have learned that lesson firsthand about eyewitness testimony in countless cases. And scientists now tell us that memories, if conjured up by the right stimulus, can be theoretically sharper twenty years after an event than they might be on the very day of the event—depending, that is, on the nature of the stimulus and the chemical linkages that fire off billions of hippocampal neurons in the cerebral cortex of the brain. Remembering is an act of reconstruction, the blending of reality with perception and suggestion; it is an accretion process, often mixing fact with imagination, and never a picture-perfect reproduction of the past. To say that recent memories are necessarily more truthful or more accurate than memories retrieved after a lapse of time reveals not a truism, but a myth. In fact, both "working" (short-term) memories and long-term memories may be completely and equally spurious. Age does not reduce the human capacity for memory or cause a deterioration of memory; instead, it simply makes memory more inefficient and occasionally slower. What aging makes more difficult in humans is the ability to remember *new* information, not old. The nature of memory and the act of remembering, at least so far as science has discerned the memory process, cannot supply historians with an alternative to weighing the relative credibility of a source—that is, the reliability of a specific memory— and deciding whether or not to use it as evidence. So the credibility of a source rests not in its relative age, but in its relative veracity. For that reason, I have chosen to use Oates's memories of his own experiences when they have seemed to make sense or when they have been corroborated by other sources, whether or not those memories happened to have been recorded soon after an event or much later in his life. Not all of Oates's memories are truthful or accurate, but I have tried to determine to my own satisfaction which ones are and which ones aren't.

9. WCO to WCOJR, Dec. 24, 1900, Oates Family Papers (OFP). I used the Oates Family Papers while they were in the possession of Marion Oates Leiter Charles, Oates's granddaughter. The collection has since been donated to the Alabama Department of Archives and History in Montgomery.

10. The study of historical memory, as Michael Vorenberg ruefully observes, has become "not merely a cottage industry but a boom trade," and the study of Civil War memory in particular "is the cash cow of the business." Vorenberg, "Recovered Memory," 550. David Blight's book, *Race and Reunion*, is by far the most insightful and elegant of all the recent scholarship on Civil War memory. Several works have influenced my interpretation of historical memory, both collective and individual: Halbwachs, *Collective Memory*; Connerton, *How Societies Remember*; Thelen, "Memory and American History," 1117–1129; Kammen, *Mystic Chords of Memory*; Ketchum, "Memory as History," 142–148; Fentress and Wickham, *Social Memory*; Kammen, "Frames of Remembrance," 245–261; Schacter, *Memory Distortion*; Olick and Robbins, "Social Memory Studies," 105–140; Kenny, "A Place for Memory," 420–437; Hutton, "Recent Scholarship on Memory and History," 533–548; Schacter, *Seven Sins of Memory*. On Civil War memory, the list of works is long and ever growing; see, for example, Warren, *Legacy of the Civil War*; Wilson, *Patriotic Gore*; Aaron, *The Unwritten War*; Connelly, *Marble Man*; Connelly and Bellows, *God and General Longstreet*; Foster, *Ghosts of the Confederacy*; Piston,

Lee's Tarnished Lieutenant; Blight, "'For Something Beyond the Battlefield,'" 1156–1178; Gallagher, *Lee and His Generals*; Silber, *Romance of Reunion*; Nolan, *Lee Considered*; Kinsel, "'From These Honored Dead'"; Peterson, *Lincoln in American Memory*; Kaser, *At the Bivouac of Memory*; Pettegrew, "'The Soldier's Faith,'" 49–73; Davis, *The Cause Lost*; Cullen, *Civil War in Popular Culture*; Kinsel, "From Turning Point to Peace Memorial," 203–222; Reardon, *Pickett's Charge*; Savage, *Standing Soldiers*; Gordon, *General George E. Pickett*; Cushman, *Bloody Promenade*; Horwitz, *Confederates in the Attic*; Young, *Disarming the Nation*; Schwartz, *Abraham Lincoln*; Kinsel, "American Identity," 5–14; Brundage, ed., *Where These Memories Grow*; Sizer, *Political Work of Northern Women Writers*; Gallagher and Nolan, eds., *Myth of the Lost Cause*; Blatt, Brown, and Yacovone, eds., *Hope and Glory*; Fahs, *The Imagined Civil War*; Chadwick, *Reel Civil War*; Latschar, "History and Memory," 59–64; Blight, *Beyond the Battlefield*; Goldfield, *Still Fighting the Civil War*; Fahs and Waugh, eds., *Memory of the Civil War*; Samuels, *Facing America*. For a helpful historiographical essay, see Grow, "Shadow of the Civil War," 77–103.

11. Scholars from various disciplines, including historians, are engaged in a heated debate over how the reconstruction of the past is potentially contaminated by "memoropolitics"—i.e., "a power struggle around knowledge, [and] claims of knowledge." See Crews, *Memory Wars*; and Hacking, *Rewriting the Soul*. Despite my belief that memory, and the act of remembering and forgetting, contains inherent power, I hope to steer clear of the debate.

12. WCO, Speech on Confederate Patriotism, n.d.; WCO, Speech on Confederate Soldiers, n.d.—both OFP.

13. For a summary of Oates's Lost Cause views, see WCO, *War*, 25–51, 534–543. The historical literature on the Lost Cause is vast, but rich. See, for example, Pollard, *The Lost Cause*; Woodward, *Origins of the New South*; Osterweis, *Myth of the Lost Cause*; Simpson, "The Cult of the 'Lost Cause,'" 350–361; Connelly, *Marble Man*; Wilson, *Baptized in Blood*; Connelly and Bellows, *God and General Longstreet*; Foster, *Ghosts of the Confederacy*; Piston, *Lee's Tarnished Lieutenant*; Royster, *The Destructive War*; Clinton, *Tara Revisited*; Silber, *Romance of Reunion*; Davis, *The Cause Lost*; Gallagher, *Jubal A. Early*; Cullen, *Civil War in Popular Culture*; Reardon, *Pickett's Charge*; Savage, *Standing Soldiers*; Gordon, *General George E. Pickett*; Horwitz, *Confederates in the Attic*; Kinsel, "American Identity," 5–14; Brundage, ed., *Where These Memories Grow*; Gallagher and Nolan, eds., *Myth of the Lost Cause*; Cox, "Women, the Lost Cause, and the New South"; Poole, "Never Surrender"; Blight, *Race and Reunion*; Blight, *Beyond the Battlefield*; Goldfield, *Still Fighting the Civil War*.

14. Thelen, "Memory and American History," 1122–1123. On the merging of individual and collective memories see Kenny, "A Place for Memory," 420–437; Thelen, "Memory and American History," 1121–1129. For the theater of memory see also Yates, *Art of Memory*; Samuel, *Theaters of Memory*. As for Nathan Bedford Forrest and the Lost Cause, see Court, "Contested Image of Nathan Bedford Forrest," 601–630.

15. WCO to Alexander, Aug. 25, 1868, E. P. Alexander Papers, SHC.

16. On Sherman's sharp ambivalence about the war and warfare, see Royster, *Destructive War*, and Blight, *Race and Reunion*. Oates's book was published in 1905 by the Neale Company. He spent two decades or more working on it piecemeal and publishing portions of it in Montgomery newspapers before pulling its parts together and shaping it into a book manuscript after 1900.

17. For an assessment of Oates's *War*, see Krick, "Introduction," unpaginated front matter; LaFantasie, "The Classic Regimental Bookshelf," 346–350.
18. WCO, *War*, xxiii–xxiv.
19. See WCO to JLC, Mar. 8, 1897, SCWC; WCO to JLC, Apr. 14, 1905, OC.
20. WCO to Alexander, Aug. 25, 1868, E. P. Alexander Papers, SHC. See also LaFantasie, "William C. Oates and the Death of General Elon Farnsworth," 48–55.
21. For a scholarly discourse on the sociological notion of unanticipated consequences, see Merton, "Unanticipated Consequences," 894–904.
22. WCO, Some Thoughts about the Negro Enfranchisement, ca. 1888, OFP. On Hegel's view of the relation between masters and slaves, see Hegel, *Phenomenology of Mind*, 228–240; on the significance of Hegel's ideas in a Southern context, see Greenberg, *Masters and Slaves*, viii, 137–138.
23. On Brooks's caning of Sumner, see Gienapp, "The Crime Against Sumner," 218–245; Sinha, "The Caning of Charles Sumner," 233–262; Greenberg, *Masters and Statesmen*, 144–146. Scholarship on the history of American anger is small but growing. See, for example, Stearns and Stearns, *Anger*; Stearns, "Men, Boys and Anger in American Society, 1860–1940," in Mangan and Walvin, eds., *Manliness and Morality*, 75–91; Grasso, *Artistry of Anger*.
24. Russell, *My Diary*, 116. Sheldon Hackney has written that "a distinctly southern pattern of violence . . . [is] a key to the meaning of being southern." Hackney, "Southern Violence," 908. For the ways in which individual violence transformed itself into collective violence in the South, see Cash, *Mind of the South*, 43–44; Franklin, *Militant South*, 227–250.
25. The fact that Oates and his family never had any "real money" comes from a comment made to me by Virginia Foster Durr, the white civil rights activist. Interview, Virginia Foster Durr, Feb. 10, 1993. Edward Ayers describes the "new men" of the New South as young, roughly in their thirties and forties during the 1890s, and portrays them as the rising rulers of the region who successfully supplanted the old planter elites. Ayers, *Promise of the New South*, 63–65. Oates, of course, was in his sixties in the 1890s, but he had earlier demonstrated his kinship to the younger generation of Southern leaders through his ambition, entrepreneurial determination, and relentless hunger for wealth and status. As I hope to show, Oates never came to be accepted by the planter class, if only because he—and others like him—caused the old plantocracy to lose power and go into decay. My view of the New South, with its rambunctious politics and its unstable economy and its various contests for power, is influenced to a considerable degree by Woodward's classic work, *Origins of the New South*, and Ayers's own agreement with Woodward's major arguments in his synthesis, *Promise of the South*. See also Ayers, "Narrating the New South," 555–566, for an explication of his interpretive intentions in *Promise of the New South*.
26. Edel, "The Figure Under the Carpet," 16–24. From among the enormously extensive literature on the art of biography, I have been particularly inspired by Mumford, "The Task of Modern Biography," 1–9.
27. See Catton, "The Confederate Legend," 9–23.
28. See Klein, *Edward Porter Alexander*; Hassler, *Colonel John Pelham*; Carmichael, *Lee's Young Artillerist*; Siepel, *Rebel*; Ramage, *Gray Ghost*; Davis, *Boy Colonel*.
29. *Birmingham Age-Herald*, Sept. 10, 1910.

Chapter 1: Rough and Tumble Days

1. MOLC interview.
2. OA, Introductory. Oates's autobiography tells his story in a rather jumbled narrative beginning with his ancestry and birth and roughly ending on the eve of the Civil War. Two versions of the autobiography exist, both in typescript: a version that has Oates's own handwritten emendations and a transcription prepared by Georgia Saffold Oates, probably in the 1940s. Although the former rather than the latter is cited throughout this book, I have chosen to cite chapters rather than page numbers because of a peculiar—and confusing—numbering system that exists in the emended version. Besides these two typed manuscripts, some other autobiographical fragments survive as well, including two written in the late 1850s in Oates's own hand. All of these autobiographies are among the Oates Family Papers (OFP), except for one that is to be found in Oates's gubernatorial records at the Alabama Division of Archives and History (ADAH), Montgomery, Ala.
3. Several reference sources published during Oates's lifetime, and to which he presumably supplied information about himself, give the wrong date of his birth. One prominent biographical dictionary listed his birth date as Dec. 1, 1835, an error that crops up regularly in brief biographical accounts of Oates. See Johnson and Brown, eds., *Twentieth Century Biographical Dictionary*, Vol. 8. Another reference source gave his birthday as Nov. 30, 1835. See *National Cyclopedia of American Biography*, 2:244. In the 1880 census, his age was given as 44, suggesting that he had been born in 1835 or 1836. See U.S. Population Census, Henry County, Alabama, 1880. His obituary in a leading Montgomery newspaper gave his birth date as Nov. 30, 1835. See *MA*, Sept. 10, 1910. At least the Oates family bible gets his birthday right. See Oates Family Bible (photocopy), Old Settlers' Records, AML. But a genealogical history of Henry County gives two different dates for his birth: Nov. 30, 1833 *and* Dec. 24, 1835. Scott, *History of Henry County*, 382, 384. (Actually, Oates's brother John was born on Dec. 24, 1835.) The official biography of Oates disseminated by the State of Alabama, via "Alabama History Online," asserts that Oates was born on either Nov. 30 *or* Dec. 1, 1835. See "William Calvin Oates, 1894–1896," http://www.asc.edu/archives.govs_list/g_oatesw.html, accessed July 7, 1995.
4. "The night the stars fell" occurred on Nov. 12–13, 1833, and it was one of the first occasions when what later became known as the Leonid meteor showers was carefully observed not only by whites and slaves in the American South, but also by astronomers, including Yale professor Denison Olmsted, one of the founders of modern meteor science. See Littmann, *Heavens on Fire*, 1–32; Cobbs, "The Night the Stars Fell," 147–157.
5. OA, chap. 1; WCO, "Biographical Sketch of Hon. Wm. C. Oates," typescript, ca. 1892, OFP. For life on the Alabama frontier see Moore, *History of Alabama*, 128–158; Owsley, *Plain Folk*, 34–38; Rogers et al., *Alabama*, 54–66, 78–92.
6. OA, chap. 1; WCO, Untitled Autobiographical Statement (fragment), Aug. 26, 1857, OFP. In later years, the senior William Oates gave up drinking and turned to religion, largely from the persistent prodding of his wife. See OA, chap. 1; *Henry County Register*, Aug. 5, 1871. Interestingly enough, David Crockett's father was also a violent man who drank too much. See Davis, *Three Roads to the Alamo*, 11–22. While such brutal men could be found in abundance on the frontier, there are some hints that Oates consciously modeled his own autobiography

on Crockett's *A Narrative of the Life of David Crockett*, first published in 1834. No doubt Oates's own father was as violent as Oates claimed, but the parallels between his autobiography and Crockett's memoirs are at times striking.

7. On southern frontier violence see Franklin, *Militant South*, chapter 3; Wyatt-Brown, *Southern Honor*, 366–369; Gorn, "'Gouge and Bite, Pull Hair and Scratch,'" 18–43; Davis, *Way Through the Wilderness*, chap. 12.

8. For life on the Alabama frontier see Moore, *History of Alabama*, 128–158; Owsley, *Plain Folk*, 34–38; Rogers et al., *Alabama*, 54–66.

9. OA, chap. 2. On the Creek war that ended predictably with the forcible removal of more than 14,000 Creeks from Alabama, see Valliere, "Creek War of 1836," 463–485. For a convincing look at frontier survival that stresses the cooperative aspects of community life, rather than the disputes that divided its settlers, see Faragher, *Sugar Creek*.

10. OA, chap. 4; WCO, *War*, 674.

11. OA, chap. 2; WCO, Untitled Autobiographical Statement (fragment), Aug. 26, 1857, OFP. On Barnett Cody see WCO, *War*, 675–676; Burnett, ed., "Letters of Barnett Hardeman Cody," 265–299, 362–380.

12. OA, chap. 1. On American Spiritualism, see Braude, *Radical Spirits*; Carroll, *Spiritualism in Antebellum America*; Cox, *Body and Soul*. Gender relations in the antebellum and Civil War South have been examined with great thoroughness by scholars during the past thirty-five years. In exploring Southern women and their lives, the emphasis has been decidedly on plantation mistresses and other elite white women. See, for example, Scott, *Southern Lady*; Clinton, *Plantation Mistress*; Fox-Genovese, *Within the Plantation Household*; Rable, *Civil Wars*; Clinton and Silber, eds., *Divided Houses*; Cashin, *A Family Venture*; Clinton, *Tara Revisited*; Faust, *Mothers of Invention*; Weiner, *Mistresses and Slaves*; Kierner, *Beyond the Household*; Waugh, Greenberg, and Clinton, eds., *Women's War in the South*; Edwards, *Scarlett Doesn't Live Here Anymore*; Blesser and Gordon, eds., *Intimate Strategies*; Delfino and Gillespie, eds., *Neither Lady nor Slave*.

13. His childhood home, Oates's Crossroads, is now called Ebenezer Crossroads, renamed for the clapboarded Baptist church that sits beside the intersection (a parish Oates's father helped to found).

14. OA, chap. 5. In his private papers, Oates left several different versions of the dancing episode that he had written down over the years. See, for instance, Dancing with Polly, n.d., OFP.

15. WCO, Untitled Autobiographical Statement (fragment), Aug. 26, 1857, OFP; OA, chap. 2; "Gov. Oates's Early Education," *MA*, June 1, 1930.

16. OA, chap. 4. Spiritualism gained a significant following in the United States after March 1848, when Margaret and Catherine Fox of Arcadia, New York, claimed that they had heard spirits tapping inside the walls of their house. They became the most famous Spiritualists in antebellum America. In the late 1880s, Margaret Fox admitted that their claims had been fraudulent but she later recanted this confession. On the Fox sisters and the advent of American Spiritualism, see Weisberg, *Talking to the Dead*.

17. OA, chap. 4. On white paternalism in the South, see Stampp, *Peculiar Institution*, 162–163, 322–330; Genovese, *Roll, Jordan, Roll*, 3–25, 133–149, 661–665; Johnson, *Soul by Soul*, 35–38, 107–112. For the complexities inherent in white racial views of African Americans, see Fredrickson, *Black Image in the White Mind*; Oakes, *The Ruling Race*. On the relationship between slavery and race, see Fields,

"Ideology and Race in American History," 143–177; Fields, "Slavery, Race, and Ideology," 95–118.

18. OA, chap. 5. On Travis, see McDonald, *William Barret Travis*, and Davis, *Three Roads to the Alamo*. Davis gives a detailed explanation, based on a rational reading of the evidence, of the reason for Travis's departure from Alabama. See Davis, *Three Roads to the Alamo*, 635–638. Jeff Long calls the Texan settlers of the 1820s and 1830s "shadowy men" and "fringe dwellers who had lost their vision or never had any." See Long, *Duel of Eagles*, 22. On the Alabama exodus to Texas, which began in the 1830s and continued into the 1850s, see Rogers et al., *Alabama*, 151–152.

19. OA, chap. 5. The fullest description of Wyatt Oates is included in WCO, Sketch of Myself, Aug. 4, 1857, OFP.

20. OA, chap. 5. In an official biography, written by Oates himself when he was serving in the U.S. Congress in the early 1890s, he described his youthful sojourn in the simplest of terms: "He [i.e., Oates] worked at mechanical trades in Florida, Louisiana and Texas for two years." See "Biographical Sketch of Hon. Wm. C. Oates," typescript, ca. 1892, OFP. Following his lead, the Oates family for years glossed over his adventures as a young man and his wanderings throughout the southwest. See, for example, the statements made by his son, William C. Oates, Jr., in "Gov. Oates's Early Education," *MA*, June 1, 1930. Later historians also sanitized the reason for Oates's departure from Alabama and made no mention of his rather wild adventures in Louisiana and Texas. See Jones, "William Calvin Oates," 338–348. The existence of Oates's autobiography did not become generally known until the early 1970s. See Krick, "Introduction," unpaginated front matter.

21. On these points, see Berry, *All That Makes a Man*, 86–94, 172–173.

22. OA, chaps. 5, 6; "Biographical Sketch of Hon. Wm. C. Oates," typescript, ca. 1892, OFP; "Personal Data" (WCO/State Constitutional Convention), ca. Oct. 1901, GVF; "Gov. Oates's Early Education," *MA*, June 1, 1930. On the importance of academies in the education of rural Southerners during the antebellum years see Owsley, *Plain Folk*, 148–149.

23. WCO, Untitled Autobiographical Statement (fragment), Aug. 26, 1857, OFP.

24. OA, chap. 6.

25. OA, Introductory.

26. OA, chap. 6; "Personal Data" (WCO/State Constitutional Convention), ca. Oct. 1901, GVF. On Eufaula, see Boyd, *Alabama in the Fifties*, 15–16. For Pugh, see Brewer, *Alabama*, 128–129; Owen, *History of Alabama*, 4:1397–1398.

27. OA, chap. 6. For Bullock, see Brewer, *Alabama*, 130–131; Owen, *History of Alabama*, 3:255.

28. Brewer, *Alabama*, 128, 130, 131–132; Owen, *History of Alabama*, 3:251–252; Dorman, *Party Politics*, 36, 47, 101, 119, 137; Brannen, "John Gill Shorter," 5; Thornton, *Politics and Power*, 250–254; Rogers et al., *Alabama*, 158, 168, 171, 204. Pugh later served as a U.S. congressman, a Confederate congressman, and a U.S. senator. On Southern masculinity as a combination of private and public personae, see Berry, *All That Makes a Man*, 10–12. For Buford's failure in Kansas, see Fleming, "The Buford Expedition to Kansas," 38–48.

29. OA, chap. 6; "Personal Data" (WCO/Governor), ca. May 1, 1901, GVF; WCO, Application to Practice Law, Oct. 19, 1858, OFP. Later Oates also became qualified to practice in the state of Georgia. See License to Practice Law, March 29,

1859, OFP. No copies of the *Abbeville Banner* have been found, despite persistent rumors in Alabama and Georgia that some issues are extant.

30. OA, chap. 6. According to Drew Faust, "white men stood at the apex of a domestic pyramid of power and obligation that represented a microcosm of the southern social order." See Faust, *Mothers of Invention*, 32. On Southern patriarchal society, see also McCurry, *Masters of Small Worlds*; Scott, *Southern Lady*, 4–21; Scott, "Women's Perspective on the Patriarchy," 52–64; Johnson, "Planters and Patriarchy," 45–72.

31. WCO, *War*, 674. For the Oates brothers' partnership, see the document executed in the firm's name among the records of the administration of Thomas Howard's estate, Dec. 29, 1860, OFP.

32. On John Oates, see Pardoe, "No Brothers Loved Each Other Better," http://www.users.globalnet.co.uk/~pardos/JohnOates.html, accessed Mar. 17, 2000. For John Oates's physical attributes, see Descriptive List and Account of Pay and Clothing of Private John A. Oats, Company A, 6th Alabama, Nov. 30, 1861, CSR (JAO).

33. OA, chap. 6; Warren, *Henry*, 73; Dorman, *Party Politics in Alabama*, 155. On secession sentiment in Alabama see Denman, *Secession Movement in Alabama*, 89–92; Bailey, "Disaffection in the Alabama Hill Country," 183–193; Silbey, "Southern National Democrats," 176–190; Long, "Unanimity and Disloyalty in Secessionist Alabama," 257–273; Thornton, *Politics and Power*, 416–417. On the role played by the Breckinridge Democrats in the secession of Alabama, see Barney, *Secessionist Impulse*.

34. OA, chap. 6; Warren, *Henry*, 73–74.

35. WCO, *War*, 26, 28–29, 33–34, 36–39. For Fitzhugh's opinion, see Fitzhugh, "Disunion in the Union," 1–7. On the sectional conflict as an irreconcilable clash between "Cavalier" Southerners and "Puritan" northerners, see Taylor, *Cavalier and Yankee*, 67, 85–86, 97; Dawson, "The Puritan and the Cavalier," 597–614.

36. WCO, *War*, 33–34, 50. On the ways in which virtue, honor, and fear of corruption became interwoven in Southern society, politics, and the secession crisis, see Greenberg, *Masters and Statesmen*, 124–146. On the importance of virtue in Revolutionary republicanism, see Wood, *Creation of the American Republic*, 65–73, 95–103, 415–425; Wood, *Radicalism of the American Revolution*, 104–107, 109, 215–220, 252–258, 264–267, 336–337. Greenberg remarks that "the central problem of political life for antebellum Southerners was how to avoid becoming an enslaver or a slave." For Southerners who sought both republicanism and honor, he says, "it was an insoluble problem." Greenberg, *Masters and Statesmen*, 146.

37. WCO, *War*, 26–27, 50, 55–56. On the dividend of unity that flowed out of secession, see Johnson, *Toward a Patriarchal Republic*, 124–142.

38. WCO, *War*, 52, 55. On the ages of Alabama's secessionists, see Barney, *Secessionist Impulse*, 61–76, 277–285, quote from 278. Southern male ambition is treated sensitively and insightfully in Berry, *All That Makes a Man*, 3–45. For a much older and outdated work on Alabama secessionism, see Denman, *Secession Movement in Alabama*.

39. WCO, *War*, 35–36. In his study of Georgia, Michael Johnson calls secession there a "double revolution," a revolution for home rule (separating Georgia from the federal Union) and a revolution for who should rule at home (a conservative response in Georgia to fears of a rising popular democracy). See Johnson, *Toward a Patriarchal Republic*, xx–xxi, 179–188. In some respects, his argument is similar to the one Thornton makes for Alabama (see *Politics and Power*), although

Johnson's case—with its emphasis on the political ramifications of patriarchy—is more intricate and nuanced.

40. WCO, Some Thoughts on the Negro Enfranchisement, ca. 1888, OFP; U.S. Slave Schedules, Henry County, Alabama, 1860; U.S. Population Census, Henry County, Alabama, 1860; Brewer, *Alabama*, 278, 504; Boyd, *Alabama in the Fifties*, 20–21. The Alabama slave census schedules for Henry County do not list Oates or his brother John as owning any slaves in 1860. William Oates's thoughts on black suffrage, written sometime in 1888, appear to have been prepared as a speech to be given on the floor of the U.S. Congress, although the speech was never made. On the status that came from slave ownership, see Johnson, *Soul by Soul*, 78–88.

41. McCurry, *Masters of Small Worlds*, 5–36, 56–61, 85–90.

42. WCO, Speech on Confederate Patriotism, undated, OFP; WCO, *War*, 498. For the "herrenvolk" thesis, see Fredrickson, *Black Image*, 61–70. That thesis has been challenged by Wayne, "An Old South Morality Play," 838–863; McCurry, *Masters of Small Worlds*, 92–129, 208–238, 240–251. Rightly rejecting interpretations that regard secession as a product of an overbearing slavocracy of aristocratic elites, J. Mills Thornton III argues that secession was instead an expression of white male egalitarianism and an effort by yeomen to protect their white liberties. His study, however, suffers from a flawed working assumption that antebellum Alabama was a herrenvolk society and from his inexplicable failure to consider Barney's earlier important scholarship. See Thornton, *Politics and Power*, 167–168, 226–227, 320–321, 343–461. On the necessity of keeping subordinates in their places, see Johnson, *Toward a Patriarchal Republic*, 46–58; McCurry, *Masters of Small Worlds*, 7–13, 56–62, 76–90.

43. WCO, *War*, 30, 34; WCO, Speech on Confederate Patriotism, undated, OFP; WCO, The Confederate Veteran, undated speech, OFP. Revealing the antidemocratic thrust of proslavery ideology in South Carolina, Manisha Sinha convincingly argues that white Southerners' support of slavery was totally at odds with "the ideals of universal liberty, equality, and democracy that lay at the heart of the antebellum American republic." See Sinha, *The Counterrevolution of Slavery*, 3–33, 88–90, 221–256, quotation at 5. On slavery and the racial attitudes of whites in antebellum Alabama, see Rogers et al., *Alabama*, 93–112. For a provocative and convincing discussion of the paradoxical relationship between liberty and slavery in the South see Morgan, *American Slavery, American Freedom*. See also the insightful essay by James M. McPherson, "Liberty and Power," 131–152. Elsewhere McPherson has pointed out that some Confederates expressed their belief that they were fighting against the North for the sake of liberty *and* slavery. See McPherson, *For Cause and Comrades*, 19–21. For the same point, more briefly stated, see Gallagher, *Confederate War*, 57–58.

Chapter 2: Baptism by Fire

1. WCO, *War*, 54–55, 57, 510–513.

2. WCO, *War*, 674; Records, Company A, 6th Alabama Regiment, Nov. 30, 1861, CSR (JAO); Gordon, *Reminiscences*, 26–27, 38; Davis, *Battle at Bull Run*, 25, 190–191; Pardoe, "No Brothers Loved Each Other Better," http://www.users.globalnet.co.uk/~pardos/JohnOates.html, accessed Mar. 17, 2000.

3. WCO to M. A. Baldwin, Apr. 29, 1861, OFP; WCO, *War*, 68.

4. WCO, *War*, 671–672. Brief sketches of the men who comprised the Henry Pioneers may be found in WCO, *War*, 671–708. On Southern nationalism as a motivation for Confederate soldiers see, for example, Jimerson, *Private Civil War*, 8–26; McPherson, "The Holy Cause of Liberty and Independence," in *What They Fought For*, 9–25; McPherson, *For Cause and Comrades*, 19–22; Gallagher, *Confederate War*, 61–111; Carp, "Nations of American Rebels," 5–33. For salient discussions of motivation among Civil War soldiers, see Catton, *America Goes to War*; Wiley, *Life of Johnny Reb*; Wiley, *Life of Billy Yank*; Linderman, *Embattled Courage*; Hess, *Union Soldier in Battle*; McPherson, *What They Fought For*; and McPherson, *For Cause and Comrades*. See also an incisive historiographical essay by Mark Grimsley, "In Not So Dubious Battle," 175–188. On the crucial question of Southerners fighting to sustain white supremacy, see Mitchell, *Civil War Soldiers*, 6–7; Robertson, *Soldiers*, 3–11; and, most persuasively, Logue, "Who Joined the Confederate Army?" 611–623. Prevailing fears among Southern whites over the loss of patriarchal mastery are convincingly argued in Johnson, "Planters and Patriarchy," 45–72; McCurry, "Two Faces of Republicanism," 1245–1264; McCurry, "Politics of Yeoman Households," 22–38; Sinha, "Revolution or Counterrevolution?" 205–226.

5. McClendon, *Recollections*, 7–13; Barnett H. Cody to Edmund Cody, Aug. 20, 1861, in Burnett, ed., "Letters of Barnett Hardeman Cody," 287. On Cody and McClendon see WCO, *War*, 675–677.

6. WCO, *War*, 68–69; McClendon, *Recollections*, 13–15.

7. McClendon, *Recollections*, 16; WCO, *War*, 68.

8. WCO, *War*, 68–69; McClendon, *Recollections*, 16–19.

9. Chase, "Fort Mitchell"; McClendon, *Recollections*, 16–19; Burnett, ed., "Letters of Barnett Hardeman Cody," 284; Wight, ed., "Sam Lary's 'Scraps,'" 506; WCO, *War*, 74.

10. WCO, *War*, 67–70, 121–122; McClendon, *Recollections*, 19; Laine and Penny, *Law's Alabama Brigade*, 21. On Cantey see Owen, *History of Alabama*, 3:296; Warner, *Generals in Gray*, 43. Several letters written by Cantey during the war are published in Mathis, *In the Land of the Living*.

11. WCO, *War*, 70, 74–75; McClendon, *Recollections*, 20–21, 30–31; Wight, ed., "Sam Lary's 'Scraps,'" 510–511.

12. WCO, *War*, 76; McClendon, *Recollections*, 31–32; James Cantey to Samuel C. Benton, Aug. 24, 1861, in Mathis, *In the Land of the Living*, 15.

13. McClendon, *Recollections*, 29, 32; G. E. Spencer to Joseph Park, Aug. 18, 1861, Park Family Papers, EU; Houghton and Houghton, *Two Boys*, 20, 54; WCO, *War*, 671; Barnett H. Cody to Edmund Cody, Aug. 20, 1861, in Burnett, ed., "Letters of Barnett Hardeman Cody," 288; Cody to Henrietta S. Cody, Sept. 20, 1861, in ibid., 292. The issue of discipline was at the heart of how Southerners both accepted the rigors of army life and resisted its authoritarian dictates. David Donald has observed that because of this ambivalence, "the Southerner made an admirable fighting man but a poor soldier." See Donald, "Confederate as a Fighting Man," 193.

14. WCO, *War*, 76; Wight, ed., "Sam Lary's 'Scraps,'" 514–515; McClendon, *Recollections*, 32–35.

15. WCO, *War*, 77; McClendon, *Recollections*, 32; William A. Edwards to W. R. Painter, Nov. 11, 1915, unidentified news clipping, 15th Alabama Regimental File, ADAH; Wight, ed., Sam Lary's 'Scraps,'" 511–513.

16. WCO, *War*, 79–82; Wight, ed., "Sam Lary's 'Scraps,'" 514, 518; Barnett H. Cody to Henrietta S. Cody, Sept. 20, 1861, in Burnett, ed., "Letters of Barnett Hardeman Cody," 292–293; McClendon, *Recollections*, 36. Oates says that at least 150 soldiers from the 15th Alabama were buried in Haymarket, but a regimental roster that he diligently compiled in the postwar years reveals that the number was actually closer to 200. See WCO, *War*, 81, 571–772, passim. For an alphabetical listing of the roster see "Muster Rolls, 15th Alabama Infantry Regiment," http://www.tarleton.edu/activities/pages/facultypages/jones/#15th, accessed July 15, 1996. On measles as a Civil War killer disease, see Steiner, *Disease in the Civil War*, 12–13, 28–29. On the deaths at Haymarket, see also LaFantasie, "Decimated by Disease," 86–92.

17. WCO, *War*, 83.

18. WCO, *War*, 674; Special Orders No. 551, Nov. 27, 1861, CSR (JAO); List of Officers of Trimble's Brigade for the Month of Nov. 1862, CSR (JAO); Barnett H. Cody to Henrietta Cody Burnett, Jan. 26, 1862, in Burnett, ed., "Letters of Barnett Hardeman Cody," 363. For the ages of the recruits in the Henry Pioneers, see WCO, *War*, 671–708. On the ages of Civil War soldiers, see McPherson, *Ordeal*, 386; Rorabaugh, "Who Fought for the North," 695–701; Vinovskis, "Have Social Historians Lost the Civil War?" 15–16; Logue, "Who Joined the Confederate Army?" 611–623. For the hardening experienced by the young soldiers, see Catton, "Hayfoot, Strawfoot!" 30–37; Catton, *America Goes to War*, 48–86; Mitchell, *Civil War Soldiers*, 56–89; Mitchell, *Vacant Chair*, 3–18; Glatthaar, "Common Soldier," 119–147.

19. On Johnston, see Symonds, *Joseph E. Johnston*.

20. Wight, ed., "Sam Lary's 'Scraps,'" 516, 522; McClendon, *Recollections*, 38–39; Burnett, ed., "Letters of Barnett Hardeman Cody," 297; WCO, *War*, 84. On Crittenden see Warner, *Generals in Gray*, 65–66.

21. WCO, *War*, 84. On Trimble see Warner, *Generals in Gray*, 310–311. For good biographies of Ewell, see Hamlin, *"Old Bald Head,"* and Pfanz, *Richard S. Ewell*.

22. WCO, *War*, 84–85.

23. McClendon, *Recollections*, 40, 42–45; Burnett, ed., "Letters of Barnett Hardeman Cody," 298; WCO, *War*, 85–87.

24. WCO, *War*, 86–88; McClendon, *Recollections*, 40, 42–45; James Cantey to wife, Dec. 23, 1861, in Mathis, *In the Land of the Living*, 18; Laine and Penny, *Law's Alabama Brigade*, 21–23.

25. On the supposedly democratic traits of Southern soldiers and the Confederate forces in general, see Donald, "Confederate as a Fighting Man," 178–193; Donald, "Died of Democracy," in Donald, ed., *Why the North Won the Civil War*, 77–90.

26. WCO, *War*, 88–90; "Casper W. Boyd," 292; McClendon, *Recollections*, 47–50. Rappahannock Station is now the town of Remington, Va.

27. WCO, *War*, 89–90; "Casper W. Boyd," 291–293; McClendon, *Recollections*, 47, 51.

28. WCO, *War*, 90, 92; McClendon, *Recollections*, 52.

29. WCO, *War*, 89–95; "Casper W. Boyd," 291–296; McClendon, *Recollections*, 45–53; Houghton and Houghton, *Two Boys*, 36; Laine and Penny, *Law's Alabama Brigade*, 23. A reliable history of Jackson's Valley Campaign is Tanner, *Stonewall in the Valley*. The best biography of Jackson is Robertson, *Stonewall Jackson*.

30. Houghton and Houghton, *Two Boys*, 36–37; WCO, *War*, 96–99; McClendon, *Recollections*, 54–56; Barnett H. Cody to Henrietta Cody Burnett, June 13, 1862, in Burnett, ed., "Letters of Barnett Hardeman Cody," 364.

31. WCO, *War*, 187.

32. WCO, *War*, 28–29, 98–101; McClendon, *Recollections*, 56–60, 62; Houghton and Houghton, *Two Boys*, 28.

33. W. D. W. [William D. Wood] to the "Spirit of the South," June 13, 1862, unidentified news clipping, OFP; WCO, *War*, 101–102; *O.R.*, Ser. 1, 12, Pt. 1, 795; McClendon, *Recollections*, 64; Tanner, *Stonewall in the Valley*, 280–281; Henderson, *Stonewall Jackson*, 1:368.

34. WCO, *War*, 102–103; W. D. W. [William D. Wood] to the "Spirit of the South," June 13, 1862, unidentified news clipping, OFP; McClendon, *Recollections*, 66–67; Burnett, ed., "Letters of Barnett Hardeman Cody," 364; *O.R.*, Ser. 1, 12, Pt. 1, 795–796. Standard accounts of the Cross Keys battle may be found in Henderson, *Stonewall Jackson*, 1:367–376; Freeman, *Lee's Lieutenants*, 1:444–447; Tanner, *Stonewall in the Valley*, 293–295. Inexplicably, Freeman refers to the 15th Alabama as the 18th Alabama. The most recent—and the most reliable—account is Krick, *Conquering the Valley*, 137–275. For the fate of the Cross Keys battlefield in recent times see Svenson, *Battlefield*.

35. W. D. W. [William D. Wood] to the "Spirit of the South," June 13, 1862, unidentified news clipping, OFP; WCO, *War*, 101–104; *O.R.*, Ser. 1, 12, Pt. 1, 781, 784, 795–796; McClendon, *Recollections*, 64–67; John F. Treutlen to Isaac Trimble, June 14, 1862, in the possession of Jack Anderson, Enterprise, Ala. (1994).

36. WCO, *War*, 102–104; W. D. W. [William D. Wood] to the "Spirit of the South," June 13, 1862, unidentified news clipping, OFP; McClendon, *Recollections*, 66–67; Barnett H. Cody to Henrietta Cody Burnett, June 13, 1862, in Burnett, ed., "Letters of Barnett Hardeman Cody," 364; *O.R.*, Ser. 1, 12, Pt. 1, 781, 784, 795–796; Laine and Penny, *Law's Alabama Brigade*, 23. Colonel Cantey reported slightly higher casualties: nine killed and thirty-six wounded. See Cantey to Parents, June 11–15, 1862, in Mathis, *In the Land of the Living*, 45.

37. *O.R.*, Ser. 1., 12, Pt. 1, 798; WCO, *War*, 104–105. The best secondary account of the battle of Port Republic is Krick, *Conquering the Valley*, 276–503.

38. Henderson, *Stonewall Jackson*, 1:390–391; WCO, *War*, 107; McClendon, *Recollections*, 70.

39. McClendon, *Recollections*, 68–80; WCO, *War*, 68, 107, 114–116; Frank Park to Joseph Park, July 6, 1862, John Park Family Papers, EU; *O.R.*, Ser. 1, 11, Pt. 2, 605–606, 614–616. Oates reprinted in his own book lengthy excerpts from McClendon's account, which he considered to be a definitive statement of the 15th Alabama's role at Gaines Mill. See WCO, *War*, 116–121. For Colonel Cantey's part in the battle, see *O.R.*, Ser. 1, 11, Pt. 2, 857, 864–865. A full account of the battle at Gaines Mills may be found in Sears, *To the Gates of Richmond*, 210–248. On bayonet charges during the Civil War, see Buechler, "'Give 'em the Bayonet,'" 135–140; McWhiney and Jamieson, *Attack and Die*, 76–80.

40. WCO, *War*, 115–116. Forty years after the war, Oates wrote: "When I look back at the scenes and perils through which I passed I feel profoundly grateful that I was spared to enjoy life." WCO, *War*, 383.

Chapter 3: An Unchristian State of Mind

1. WCO, *War*, 121–122, 128; McClendon, *Recollections*, 87–90; Laine and Penny, *Law's Alabama Brigade*, 23.

2. WCO, *War*, 128–130; McClendon, *Recollections*, 94–95; Houghton and Houghton, *Two Boys*, 29–30; *O.R.*, Ser. 1, 12, Part 2, 180–181, 235–236. The official returns

showed that the only casualties suffered by the 15th Alabama at Cedar Mountain were three men wounded. See *O.R.*, Ser. 1, 12, Pt. 2, 180. On the Crittenden women, see Krick, *Stonewall Jackson at Cedar Mountain*, 55–56, 76, 89, 339–340, 394–395.

3. WCO, *War*, 131–137; McClendon, *Recollections*, 98, 100, 103–106; Houghton and Houghton, *Two Boys*, 23–25. For Oates's memory of the fight at Hazel Run, see also WCO to WCOJR, Aug. 22, 1902, OFP. The most complete and authoritative study of the Second Manassas battle is Hennessy, *Return to Bull Run*.

4. WCO, *War*, 134–135, 137–140; McClendon, *Recollections*, 106–108; Houghton and Houghton, *Two Boys*, 24.

5. WCO, *War*, 139–140, 143–146; McClendon, *Recollections*, 108–109, 111–120, 121–122; Houghton and Houghton, *Two Boys*, 24–26; *O.R.*, Ser. 1. 12, Pt. 2, 812.

6. McClendon, *Recollections*, 120, 122–124; WCO, *War*, 149–151.

7. Houghton and Houghton, *Two Boys*, 54. On war as a "positive"—or socially and politically legitimate—form of violence see Richard Maxwell Brown, "Historical Patterns of Violence in America," 43–80. A brilliant exposition on the meaning of violence in the Civil War is Royster, *Destructive War*.

8. WCO, *War*, 151.

9. Fremantle, *Three Months in the Southern States*, 293. See also Donald, "Confederate as a Fighting Man," 178–193; Catton, "Confederate Legend," 9–23.

10. WCO, *War*, 153–154; McClendon, *Recollections*, 127–128; Sears, *Landscape Turned Red*, 84–85; Hartwig, "Robert E. Lee," 334–338.

11. WCO, *War*, 159–160; McClendon, *Recollections*, 134–137; Sears, *Landscape Turned Red*, 94–95, 121–124, 126, 143–144, 152–154; Robertson, *Stonewall Jackson*, 594–606.

12. Sears, "Last Word on the Lost Order," 66–72; Robertson, *Stonewall Jackson*, 606–607.

13. Robertson, *Stonewall Jackson*, 594; McClendon, *Recollections*, 138–139; WCO, *War*, 160.

14. WCO, *War*, 163. There is no record of Oates's "disability," as he called it, among his compiled service papers in the National Archives. Nevertheless, Oates specifically states in his memoirs that he had received "a surgeon's certificate of disability" at the time, almost as if he hoped thereby to prove that he was truly ill and not shirking his duty as so many other Confederates did before and during the Maryland invasion. The identity of the "old Dutchman," in whose house Oates recuperated, is not known.

15. Sears, *Landscape Turned Red*, 295–296; Report of Surgeon Lafayette Guild, n.d., *O.R.*, Ser. 1, 19, Pt. 1, 813; Robertson, *Stonewall Jackson*, 620–622; WCO, *War*, 163–164; McClendon, *Recollections*, 155–156.

16. Robertson, *Soldiers Blue and Gray*, 186–188; Royster, *Destructive War*, 268–269; Faust, "Christian Soldiers," 88–109.

17. Cody to Edmund Cody, Oct. 9, 1862, in Burnett, ed., "Letters of Barnett Hardeman Cody," 366; Robertson, *Stonewall Jackson*, 635.

18. McClendon, *Recollections*, 156–157; WCO, *War*, 164–165.

19. McClendon, *Recollections*, 157–158; Sutherland, *Fredericksburg and Chancellorsville*, 34–36. Oates thought the bombardment took place on December 12. See WCO, *War*, 165.

20. WCO, *War*, 165–166; McClendon, *Recollections*, 158–159.

21. McClendon, *Recollections*, 159.

22. Robert F. Hoke to S. Hale, December 19, 1862, in *O.R.*, Ser. 1, 21, 672; O'Reilly, *"Stonewall Jackson" at Fredericksburg*, 28–29.

23. O'Reilly, *"Stonewall Jackson" at Fredericksburg*, 46–49, 51–53, 64–65; Whan, *Fiasco at Fredericksburg*, 65–66; Sutherland, *Fredericksburg and Chancellorsville*, 47–48.

24. O'Reilly, *"Stonewall Jackson" at Fredericksburg*, 85–88, 96–107; Whan, *Fiasco at Fredericksburg*, 67–68; WCO, *War*, 166.

25. McClendon, *Recollections*, 159–160; WCO, *War*, 166; [Randolph C. Smedley] to Father, Dec. 17, 1862, in *Southern Advertiser* (Troy, Ala.), Jan. 7, 1863.

26. WCO, *War*, 166–167, McClendon, *Recollections*, 160; [Smedley] to Father, Dec. 17, 1862, in *Southern Advertiser* (Troy, Ala.), Jan. 7, 1863; Hoke to Hale, Dec. 19, 1862, in *O.R.*, Ser. 1, 21:672. On Hoke's charge, see also O'Reilly, *"Stonewall Jackson" at Fredericksburg*, 128–131, 135–136; O'Reilly, *Fredericksburg Campaign*, 219–221.

27. Whan, *Fiasco at Fredericksburg*, 77–101; Sutherland, *Fredericksburg and Chancellorsville*, 51–59.

28. WCO, *War*, 167–168; [Smedley] to Father, Dec. 17, 1862, in *Southern Advertiser* (Troy, Ala.), Jan. 7, 1863; McClendon, *Recollections*, 161–163; O'Reilly, *Fredericksburg Campaign*, 441–442.

29. WCO, *War*, 168–172. The official report of killed and wounded listed one killed and thirty-four wounded in the 15th Alabama, but Oates's figures may have included in the "killed" category men who later died from their wounds. See Report of Killed and Wounded in the Battle of Fredericksburg, Jan. 10, 1863, in *O.R.*, Ser. 1, 21, 561.

30. McClendon, *Recollections*, 165; Special Orders 19, Jan. 19, 1863, in *O.R.*, Ser. 1, 21, 1099–1100; WCO, *War*, 174. On Evander Law, see Warner, *Generals in Gray*, 174–175.

31. McClendon, *Recollections*, 167; WCO, *War*, 174; Thomas J. Goree to Sarah Williams Kittrell Goree, Feb. 4, 1863, in Cutrer, ed., *Longstreet's Aide*, 103–104; Polley, *Soldier's Letters*, 102–104; Laine and Penny, *Law's Alabama Brigade*, 38–39.

32. McClendon, *Recollections*, 168; Gallagher, ed., *Fighting for the Confederacy*, 188; Foote, *Civil War: Fredericksburg to Meridian*, 165–166.

33. Mark Grimsley points out that the term "total war," when used in the context of the Civil War, has been defined in two ways: "to indicate a no-holds-barred conflict that targets civilians as readily as soldiers, or to describe a war in which one side or both mobilize their populations and economies to a high degree and conduct large-scale attacks on their opponent's war resources." I agree with his assessment that "the American Civil War fits the second definition but not the first." Grimsley, "Surviving Military Revolution," 75n. See also Grimsley, "Modern War / Total War," 379–389. Other historians implicitly accept Grimsley's second definition as their own. See, for example, McPherson, "From Limited to Total War," 66–86; Sutherland, "Abraham Lincoln," 567–586; Janda, "Shutting the Gates of Mercy," 7–26. Mark Neely insists that the Civil War could not possibly have been a total war, but his argument is based on a slavish adherence to Grimsley's first definition of the term. See Neely, "Was the Civil War a Total War?" 5–28; Neely, "'Civilized Belligerents,'" 3–23.

34. McPherson, *Ordeal By Fire*, 321; Franklin, *Emancipation Proclamation*, 118–119; Vorenberg, *Final Freedom*, 1–2, 27–34; Guelzo, *Lincoln's Emancipation Proclamation*, 178–179.

35. WCO, *War*, 495–504; Fellman, *The Making of Robert E. Lee*, 209–218; Pfanz, *Richard E. Ewell*, 139, 423. Jefferson Davis later denied that Ewell had suggested using slaves as soldiers. But Ewell insisted that he had made his proposal during a conversation with Davis soon after First Manassas, and it is unlikely that Ewell fabricated the story. See Pfanz, *Richard E. Ewell*, 139. Despite Mark Perry's contentions, there is no evidence that the Confederate government prevented Oates from achieving higher rank in the army because he had asked Richmond to consider enlisting slaves. See Perry, *Conceived in Liberty*, 319–322.

36. Durden, *The Gray and the Black*, 53–73, 101–142, 204–267; Beringer et al., *Why the South Lost*, 369–392; Rable, *Confederate Republic*, 287–296.

Chapter 4: Ragged Jacks

1. WCO, *War*, 660, 688–689, 714. On the Civil War as a "brother's war," see McPherson, *Ordeal by Fire*, 167–168, 196. See also Catton, "Brother Against Brother," 4–7, 89–93; Murrell, "Union Father, Rebel Son," 358–391.

2. The data on brothers serving in Company G is taken from Oates's compilation of biographical information published in WCO, *War*, 671–708.

3. On familial dynamics in the Civil War military, including the element of small-unit cohesion, see Mitchell, *Vacant Chair*, 14, 43–44, 51–54, 158, 166; McPherson, *For Cause and Comrades*, 85–89.

4. Register Containing Rosters of Commissioned Officers, Jan. 1, 1863, CSR (JAO); JAO to Pugh, Apr. 22, 1863, CSR (JAO). On John Oates's recruiting mission, see also Barnett H. Cody to Mrs. Fransinia McGarity, Feb. 2, 1863, in Burnett, ed., "Letters of Barnett Hardeman Cody," 367–368.

5. Wert, *General James Longstreet*, 228–234; Laine and Penny, *Law's Alabama Brigade*, 47–48.

6. WCO to Alexander, Aug. 25, 1868, E. P. Alexander Papers, SHC; WCO, *War*, 175–176; McClendon, *Recollections*, 171, 174; Stevens, *Reminiscences*, 97; Vaughan, "Diary of Turner Vaughan," 528; Barnett Cody to Mr. and Mrs. J. M. L. Burnett, Apr. 4 [actually Apr. 14], 1863, in Burnett, ed., "Letters of Barnett Hardeman Cody," 370. On Nat Turner's Rebellion, see Oates, *Fires of Jubilee*.

7. Cody to Mr. and Mrs. J. M. L. Burnett, Apr. 4 [actually Apr. 14], 1863, in Burnett, ed., "Letters of Barnett Hardeman Cody," 370; JAO to James L. Pugh, Apr. 22, 1863, CSR (JAO); Pugh to Secretary of War, Apr. 28, 1863, CSR (JAO). Although rheumatism was the favorite feigned illness among shirkers during the Civil War (see, for example, Catton, *Glory Road*, 105), all evidence points to the fact that John Oates truly suffered from a severe case of the disease.

8. John B. Hood to James Longstreet, June 28, 1875, in *SHSP*, 4 (Oct. 1877), 146–147; Wert, *General James Longstreet*, 238–239; Piston, *Lee's Tarnished Lieutenant*, 38. On the Chancellorsville battle, see Furgurson, *Chancellorsville 1863*, and Sears, *Chancellorsville*. After the war, Longstreet was criticized for his slowness in responding to Lee's call for him to rejoin the Army of Northern Virginia, but the evidence—including Lee's own admission that Longstreet could not have possibly gotten to Chancellorsville in time for the battle—shows that Longstreet pulled out of Suffolk as quickly as he could.

9. WCO, *War*, 178–179; Jordan, *Some Events and Incidents*, 36–38. See also Cormier, *Siege of Suffolk*, 272–283; Laine and Penny, *Law's Alabama Brigade*, 63–65. On the news of Jackson's wounding and death, see McClendon, *Recollections*, 175;

Stocker, ed., *From Huntsville to Appomattox*, 94, 96; Lasswell, ed., *Rags and Hope*, 175; Pierrepont, *Reuben Vaughan Kidd*, 323.

10. WCO, *War*, 121, 179, 369–371, 672–673; Register Containing Rosters of Commissioned Officers, Apr. 28, 1863, CSR (WCO); Register of Appointments, Oct. 21, 1863, CSR (WCO); Roster of the 15th Alabama Regiment, Aug. 10, 1864, CSR (WCO); Laine and Penny, *Law's Alabama Brigade*, 63. Some records, strangely, show Oates as being promoted to major on Apr. 28, 1863, although this was certainly not the case. See, for example, the endorsement on Promotions of A. A. Lowther, I. B. Feagin, and W. C. Oates, Apr. 24, 1864, CSR (WCO).

11. WCO, *War*, 180–181; Simpson, *Hood's Texas Brigade*, 242–243; Laine and Penny, *Law's Alabama Brigade*, 66.

12. Freeman, *Lee's Lieutenants*, 3:2–4; WCO, *War*, 189–190; West, *Texan*, 58, 72; Vaughan, "Diary of Turner Vaughan," 584; Thomas, *Bold Dragoon*, 217–218. On Watts, who later became governor of Alabama, see Brewer, *Alabama*, 460–461. Oates mistakenly thought that General Lee watched Stuart's legions from the reviewing stand on June 5. See WCO, *War*, 190. Although invited, Lee was not present on the fifth; he did attend another cavalry review put on by Stuart on June 8. These two separate cavalry reviews within three days of one another have caused endless confusion among historians. Some writers place Hood's division at the review on June 5, others at the one on June 8, and at least one historian says that Hood and his men attended both reviews (an unlikely occurrence). McMurry, *John Bell Hood*, 73–74; Freeman, *Lee's Lieutenants*, 3:3–4; Thomas, *Bold Dragoon*, 220; Nye, *Here Come the Rebels*, 49–50. Despite the vast confusion, it appears certain that Hood and his troops witnessed the June 5 cavalry review and no other.

13. Freeman, *Lee's Lieutenants*, 3:3–5; Vaughan, "Diary of Turner Vaughan," 584; WCO, *War*, 190; West, *Texan*, 59, 74; von Borcke and Scheibert, *Great Cavalry Battle*, 71. For full accounts of the battle of Brandy Station, see Freeman, *Lee's Lieutenants*, 3:6–19; Thomas, *Bold Dragoon*, 221–231; and Coddington, *Gettysburg Campaign*, 47–72.

14. WCO, "Gettysburg—The Battle on the Right," 178. On Lee's reorganization of the Army of Northern Virginia, see Freeman, *Lee's Lieutenants*, 2:683–714; Coddington, *Gettysburg Campaign*, 11–18.

15. WCO, *War*, 195; Vaughan, "Diary of Turner Vaughan," 585; Jordan, *Some Events and Incidents*, 39; West, *Texan*, 74–76; Stocker, ed., *From Huntsville to Appomattox*, 100; M. W. Henry to J. B. Walton, Aug. 23, 1863, in *O.R.*, Ser. 1, Pt. 2, 427–428; Barziza, *Adventures*, 38–39; Penny and Laine, *Struggle*, 8.

16. Barziza, *Adventures*, 39; Youngblood, "Unwritten History," 312–313; Stevens, *Reminiscences*, 103; Vaughan, "Diary of Turner Vaughan," 586; Stocker, ed., *From Huntsville to Appomattox*, 100–101; West, *Texan*, 76–77; Polley, *Hood's Texas Brigade*, 146; Penny and Laine, *Struggle*, 10.

17. Stocker, ed., *From Huntsville to Appomattox*, 101; Vaughan, "Diary of Turner Vaughan," 586; Penny and Laine, *Struggle*, 10–11.

18. Stevens, *Reminiscences*, 104.

19. Vaughan, "Diary of Turner Vaughan," 587; Jordan, *Some Events and Incidents*, 40; Hood, *Advance and Retreat*, 54; Houghton and Houghton, *Two Boys*, 31–32; Stocker, ed., *From Huntsville to Appomattox*, 102. Oates mistakenly thought that Longstreet's Corps and the 15th Alabama had crossed the Potomac on June 23. See WCO, *War*, 195.

20. WCO, *War*, 198; Jordan, *Some Events and Incidents*, 40; Vaughan, "Diary of Turner Vaughan," 587; Stocker, ed., *From Huntsville to Appomattox*, 102; Stevens, *Reminiscences*, 105–106; Simpson, *Hood's Texas Brigade*, 252.

21. WCO, *War*, 198–199. Oates even condemned foreigners who served in the 15th Alabama, including some thirty Irishmen and one Frenchman. All except four or five of them ended up deserting, he said. See ibid., 200.

22. For Oates's ambivalent comments on Irish soldiers in the 15th Alabama, see WCO, *War*, 200. On American nativism and Anglo-Saxon ethnicity, see Kaufmann, "American Exceptionalism Reconsidered," 437–457. For American nativism in general, see Higham, *Strangers in the Land*; Anbinder, *Nativism and Slavery*; Knobel, *"America for the Americans"*. Among a growing number of important works on white racial identity as a social fabrication, see Roediger, *The Wages of Whiteness*; Roediger, *Towards the Abolition of Whiteness*; Allen, *Invention of the White Race*, vols. 1 and 2; Jacobson, *Whiteness of a Different Color*; Hale, *Making Whiteness*.

23. WCO, *War*, 200; Ward, "Incidents and Personal Experiences," 345; Polk, *North and South American Review*, 26–27; Fremantle, *Three Months in the Southern States*, 239; Simpson, *Hood's Texas Brigade*, 257; Hoke, *Great Invasion*, 210–211.

24. WCO, *War*, 200; Stocker, ed., *From Huntsville to Appomattox*, 102–103; Vaughan, "Diary of Turner Vaughan," 587–588; Ward, "Incidents and Experiences," 346; Houghton and Houghton, *Two Boys*, 38.

25. WCO, *War*, 206; Jordan, *Some Events and Incidents*, 40; Vaughan, "Diary of Turner Vaughan," 588; Stocker, ed., *From Huntsville to Appomattox*, 103; Ward, "Incidents and Experiences," 346; William A. Edwards to W. R. Painter, Nov. 11, 1915, unidentified news clipping, 15th Alabama Regimental File, ADAH; Penny and Laine, *Struggle*, 21–22; Elmore, "Meteorological and Astronomical Chronology," 10.

26. WCO, *War*, 140.

27. WCO, *War*, 206; Powell, "With Hood at Gettysburg," *Philadelphia Weekly Times*, Dec. 13, 1884; Jordan, *Some Events and Incidents*, 41.

28. WCO, *War*, 206; Hoke, *Great Invasion*, 170–171; Coddington, *Gettysburg Campaign*, 166.

29. WCO, *War*, 206, 684–685, 704, 750.

30. WCO, *War*, 226, 674.

31. WCO, *War*, 206; Stocker, ed., *From Huntsville to Appomattox*, 103.

32. Law, "Struggle for 'Round Top,'" 320; Penny and Laine, *Struggle for the Round Tops*, 24; Longstreet, *From Manassas to Appomattox*, 365; WCO, *War*, 206; LaFantasie, ed., "William C. Oates Remembers Little Round Top," 59. Water was particularly scarce because of a dry spring and summer that year. See Early, "A Southern Boy at Gettysburg," 40.

33. WCO, *War*, 206; Ward, "Incidents and Personal Experiences," 346. On Longstreet's countermarch, see the full accounts in Coddington, *Gettysburg Campaign*, 377–381; Pfanz, *Gettysburg—The Second Day*, 104–123.

34. WCO, *War*, 206–207; Law, "Struggle for 'Round Top,'" 320.

35. Coddington, *Gettysburg Campaign*, 341–356, 380–384; Pfanz, *Gettysburg—The Second Day*, 124–158.

36. Alexander, *Memoirs*, 394; Hood to Longstreet, June 28, 1875, in *SHSP*, 4 (1877), 148–150. Evander Law later maintained that he, based on the reports of scouts, first noticed the importance of Big Round Top and entered a protest to Hood, who, in turn, endorsed Law's protest and forwarded it to Longstreet. See Law,

"Struggle for 'Round Top,'" 320–322. Hood does not mention Law's role in his account.

37. WCO, *War*, 207; Ward, "Incidents and Personal Experiences," 347; Barziza, *Adventures*, 48.

38. WCO, *War*, 226. In all, Oates recorded three different versions of the words his brother spoke on Warfield Ridge; two of the versions appeared in *War* at pp. 226 and 674. The other version may be found in a letter from WCO to his son, WCOJR, dated Dec. 24, 1900, OFP. The three versions, while entirely different in wordage, consistently articulate a message of courage, duty, and sacrifice.

39. WCO, *War*, 212; LaFantasie, ed., "William C. Oates Remembers Little Round Top," 59. In the latter account, Oates claimed he sent off twenty-five or more men in the water detail, but it seems more likely that the number was actually twenty-two. Probably Oates sent the men to fill the canteens in the well near the Alexander Currens house on the Emmitsburg Road.

40. WCO, *War*, 207, 212; Stocker, ed., *From Huntsville to Appomattox*, 104; Jordan, *Some Events and Incidents*, 42; West, *Texan*, 94; Law, "Struggle for 'Round Top,'" 323–324; Ward, "Incidents and Personal Experiences," 347; Barzizo, *Adventures*, 45; Polk, *North and South American Review*, 28.

41. WCO, *War*, 207–208, 210, 224, 584; White, ed., *Civil War Diary of Wyman S. White*, 163–165; Stevens, *Berdan's United States Sharpshooters*, 325–326; WMR to A. H. Belo, Jan. 10, 1900, in Belo, "Battle of Gettysburg," 168; Stocker, ed., *From Huntsville to Appomattox*, 104.

42. WCO, *War*, 207; Stevens, *Reminiscences of the Civil War*, 114; Penny and Laine, *Struggle for the Round Tops*, 42–43.

Chapter 5: Boulders Like Gravestones

1. Penny and Laine, *Struggle for the Round Tops*, 1–3; Oates, *War*, 261. For an uncomplimentary comment on Law by one of his soldiers, see Pierrepont, *Reuben Vaughan Kidd*, 330.

2. Law, "Struggle for 'Round Top,'" 323–325; Alexander, *Memoirs*, 395–396; WCO to B. O. Peterson, Aug. 8, 1863, *O.R.*, Ser. 1, 27, Pt. 2, 392; WCO, *War*, 210; WCO to Homer R. Stoughton, Nov. 22, 1888, in *Gettysburg, July 2, 1863*, [p. 1]; WCO to JLC, Mar. 8, 1897, Clements Library, UM; WCO to WMR, Feb. 14, 1903, OC; Penny and Laine, *Struggle for the Round Tops*, 42–44, 48–51. Although many historians doubt that Law placed the 47th Alabama under Oates's command, Oates claimed to have received confirmation of that order in a letter from Law long after the war. See WCO to JPN, Nov. 13, 1903, OC.

3. WCO to Peterson, Aug. 8, 1863, *O.R.*, Ser. 1, 27, Pt. 2, 392. For Bulger's apparently different orders from Law, see Penny and Laine, *Struggle for the Round Tops*, 51.

4. WCO to Peterson, Aug. 8, 1863, *O.R.*, Ser. 1, 27, Pt. 2, 392; WCO, "Gettysburg—The Battle on the Right," 174; WCO, *War*, 210–211; WCO to WMR, Feb. 14, 1903, OC.

5. WCO to Peterson, Aug. 8, 1863, *O.R.*, Ser. 1, 27, Pt. 2, 392; Oates, *War*, 210–211; WCO to WMR, Feb. 14, 1903, OC. As a result of his wound, Feagin later lost his right leg.

6. WCO, *War*, 210–211; WCO to Stoughton, Nov. 22, 1888, in *Gettysburg, July 2, 1863*, [p. 1]; WCO to JPN, Feb. 11, 1903, OC.

7. WCO to Stoughton, Nov. 22, 1888, in *Gettysburg, July 2, 1863*, [p. 1]; WCO, "Gettysburg—The Battle on the Right," 174–175; WCO, *War*, 211, 687; WCO to Peterson, Aug. 8, 1863, *O.R.*, Ser. 1, 27, Pt. 2, 392; Homer R. Stoughton to John M. Cooney, July 27, 1863, in ibid., Ser. 1, 27, Pt. 1, 518–519.

8. WCO, *War*, 211. Oates never satisfactorily explained why he continued to lead his men up to the summit of Big Round Top rather than return to his appointed place in the brigade line.

9. WCO, *War*, 211. Ten years later, John Bachelder described the superb view from Big Round Top in his guidebook. See Bachelder, *Gettysburg*, 84.

10. WCO, *War*, 211–213; WCO, "Gettysburg—The Battle on the Right," 175. On Terrell, who settled his differences with his opponent without facing him on the field of honor, see Cormier, *Siege of Suffolk*, 162–164.

11. WCO, *War*, 211–213; WCO, "Gettysburg—The Battle on the Right," 175. As it turned out, Terrell never communicated Oates's message to Law that day because the aide was unable to find the general until the close of the battle. See WCO, *War*, 213.

12. WCO, "Gettysburg—The Battle on the Right," 175–176; WCO, *War*, 213.

13. WCO, "Gettysburg—The Battle on the Right," 176; WCO, *War*, 214, 221, 586; Alleman, *At Gettysburg*, 52, 57–58; Washington Roebling to Oliver W. Norton, July 13, 1915, Clements Library, UM.

14. "General M. J. Bulger: An Alabama Hero," *MA*, Oct. 2, 1898. This source, unfortunately, contains numerous inaccuracies—and some downright fabrications—about the role played by the 47th Alabama in the attack on Little Round Top. For example, Bulger and his men did not capture a cannon on the slopes of the hill, as the article maintains. Nevertheless, it is one of the very few extant sources that provides any detail about Bulger and his regiment during the battle. For biographical information on Bulger, see also *Memorial Record of Alabama*, 2:997–998; Penny and Laine, *Struggle for Little Round Top*, 48–49. For a more detailed account of the 20th Maine's defense of Little Round Top, see Desjardin, *Stand Firm Ye Boys From Maine*, esp. 33–78.

15. WCO to JBB, Mar. 29, 1876, in Ladd and Ladd, eds., *Bachelder Papers*, 1:465; WCO, *War*, 214.

16. WCO, *War*, 214.

17. McClendon reported that Company G "was between K and B, on the left wing of the regiment, a position we occupied all during the war." McClendon, *Recollections*, 19.

18. WCO to Peterson, Aug. 8, 1863, *O.R.*, Ser. 1, 27, Pt. 2, 392; LaFantasie, ed., "William C. Oates Remembers Little Round Top," 62; WCO to WMR, Feb. 14, 1903, OC; WCO, *War*, 214, 219.

19. WCO to Peterson, Aug. 8, 1863, *O.R.*, Ser. 1, 27, Pt. 2, 392–393; WCO to JBB, Mar. 29, 1876, in Ladd and Ladd, eds., *Bachelder Papers*, 1:465; LaFantasie, ed., "William C. Oates Remembers Little Round Top," 62; WCO, *War*, 214, 227, 612–613; Jordan, *Some Events and Incidents*, 43.

20. "General M. J. Bulger: An Alabama Hero," *MA*, Oct. 2, 1898; WCO, *War*, 217; WCO to JLC, Mar. 8, 1897, Clements Library, UM; WCO to WMR, Feb. 14, 1903, OC. Survivors of the 47th Alabama never mentioned this rout in their writings, which is curious. There is no doubt that the regiment retreated and fled, but that fact is not mentioned in any extant official reports or soldiers' letters and memoirs. See, for example, Soldier to Editor, *Montgomery Daily Mail*, July 7, 1863 (in which the 47th Alabama captures Little Round Top); J. W. Jack-

son to Wife, July 7, 1863 (in which the 47th Alabama makes four assaults on Little Round Top before it falls back); James M. Campbell to [?], Aug. 7, 1863, *O.R.*, Ser. 1, 27, Pt. 2, 395 (in which the 47th retires during "the first repulse of the brigade"; Botsford, *Boy in the Civil War*, 9 (in which hardly any mention is made of the attack on Little Round Top).

21. WCO to JBB, Mar. 29, 1876, in Ladd and Ladd, eds., *Bachelder Papers*, 1:465; WCO to JLC, Mar. 8, 1897, Clements Library, UM; WCO, *War*, 217–218; WCO to Elihu Root, June 2, 1903, OC; WCO to WMR, Sept. 4, 1904, OC; WCO to JPN, Mar. 1, 1905, OC; WCO to JLC, Apr. 14, 1905, OC; Pfanz, *Gettysburg—The Second Day*, 232.

22. WCO to Peterson, Aug. 8, 1863, *O.R.*, Ser. 1, 27, Pt. 2, 393; Record of the Positions of Troops on the Battlefield, Vol. I, July 2, 1896, pp. 27–28, ED; WCO, *War*, 218.

23. Lincoln, Annual Message to Congress, Dec. 3, 1861, in Basler, ed., *Collected Works*, 5:49. See also Royster, *Destructive War*, 250–256; Grimsley, "Surviving Military Revolution," 75, 90–91.

24. WCO to Stoughton, Nov. 22, 1888, in *Gettysburg, July 2, 1863*, [p. 2]; WCO to JLC, Mar. 8, 1897, Clements Library, UM. For the actions of Chamberlain and his 20th Maine regiment, see Desjardin, *Stand Firm Ye Boys From Maine*, esp. 33–78, and LaFantasie, *Twilight at Little Round Top*, 160–192.

25. WCO, *War*, 218, 688; Record of the Positions of Troops on the Battlefield, Vol. I, July 2, 1896, p. 28, ED; William A. Edwards to W. R. Painter, Nov. 11, 1915, unidentified news clipping, 15th Alabama Regimental File, ADHA.

26. See Linderman, *Embattled Courage*, 21–22; Oates, *War*, 688. See also McPherson, *For Cause and Comrades*, 58–60. On the "glaze of war," see Perkins, "Impressions of Wartime," 566–567. This phenomena has also been called "combat narcosis." See Frank and Reaves, *"Seeing the Elephant,"* 118.

27. WCO, *War*, 218, 226, 674; Register of Sick and Wounded Confederates, July 25, 1863, CSR (JAO).

28. WCO, *War*, 226; Register of Sick and Wounded Confederates, July 25, 1863, CSR (JAO); Record of the Positions of Troops on the Battlefield, Vol. 1, July 2, 1896, p. 28, ED.

29. WCO, *War*, 218–219; WCO to JPN, Mar. 1, 1905, OC. The location of the boulder is not definitely known, although Oates drew a crude map indicating its whereabouts and appended it to a letter he wrote to the Gettysburg Battlefield Park Commissioners in 1905. See WCO to JPN, Mar. 1, 1905, OC. Unfortunately, the construction of a park road and its later removal below the 20th Maine monument destroyed the slope of the hill and the physical appearance of the ledges enough to make impossible any attempt today to pinpoint the location of the actual boulder.

30. WCO, *War*, 221.

31. LaFantasie, ed., "William C. Oates Remembers Little Round Top," 61; WCO to WMR, Feb. 14, 1903, OC; WCO, *War*, 219–220. Historians have doubted Oates's claim that dismounted Federal cavalry troopers were in the area or that the 15th Alabama later captured some of the horse soldiers, but at least one primary source indicates that the 6th New York Cavalry was indeed engaged in dislodging Confederates from Little Round Top on July 2. See Clarke, "Sixth New York Cavalry," 413–414.

32. WCO, *War*, 220; WCO to JBB, Mar. 29, 1876, in Ladd and Ladd, eds., *Bachelder Papers*, 1:465.

33. On Civil War honor, see Linderman, *Embattled Courage*, 11–16; McPherson, *For Cause and Comrades*, 76–84.

34. WCO to Peterson, Aug. 8, 1863, *O.R.*, Ser. 1, 27, Pt. 2, 393; WCO to JBB, Mar. 29, 1876, in Ladd and Ladd, eds., *Bachelder Papers*, 1:465–466; WCO to Stoughton, Nov. 22, 1888, in *Gettysburg, July 2, 1863*, [p. 2]; WCO, *War*, 220; Wright, "Time on Little Round Top," 53–54. In some accounts written after the war, Oates claimed that he ordered his retreat *after* repelling the 20th Maine's fifth counterattack against the Alabamians. See WCO to JLC, Mar. 8, 1897, Clements Library, UM; WCO, *War*, 220. But it seems more likely that he gave his order to withdraw at about the same time that Chamberlain's last—and most famous—advance down the hill took place.

35. WCO, *War*, 220–221; Jordan, *Some Events and Incidents*, 43–44; WCO to JBB, Mar. 29, 1876, in Ladd and Ladd, eds., *Bachelder Papers*, 1:465; WCO to JLC, Mar. 8, 1897, Clements Library, UM; WCO to JLC, Apr. 14, 1905, OC. The man who ran by Oates's side, Private John Keils (or Keels) of Company H, later died in a field hospital. See WCO, *War*, 221. Oates's claim to have captured three dismounted Federal cavalrymen in his rear has been disputed by historians, although it remains possible that a line of vedettes, perhaps from the 6th New York Cavalry, had found its way into the saddle of land between the two Round Tops. See footnote 31, above. One historian, however, cites evidence that Oates actually captured three infantrymen from Company B of the 20th Maine. See Desjardin, *Stand Firm Ye Boys From Maine*, 217. Interestingly enough, General Law thought it unlikely that any Federal cavalry was in the vicinity of the Round Tops: "But if there *was* a division, or even a single picket-post of cavalry, either Federal or Confederate, on our right flank, at any time on the 2d of July, it was kept most persistently out of sight, as my scouts, who were sent out in all directions, failed to find it." Law, "Struggle for 'Round Top,'" 323.

36. WCO, *War*, 221; LaFantasie, ed., "William C. Oates Remembers Little Round Top," 59. Captain Shaaf later told Oates that he had been unable to capture the Federal ordnance train near the Taneytown Road because there were enemy troops in the woods and he feared capture if he tried to approach the wagons. Instead, he remained hidden in the woods with his company, about 300 yards east of where Oates and the rest of the regiment were trying to take Little Round Top. Oates, who believed that Shaaf should have speedily rejoined the regiment after deciding not to capture the wagons, never forgave him for this dereliction of duty. See WCO, *War*, 221, 586.

37. WCO to Peterson, Aug. 8, 1863, *O.R.*, Ser. 1, 27, Pt. 2, 393; WCO, *War*, 222, 225; LaFantasie, ed., "William C. Oates Remembers Little Round Top," 59–61; Jordan, *Some Events and Incidents*, 44–45.

38. WCO, *War*, 216; LaFantasie, ed., "William C. Oates Remembers Little Round Top," 63.

39. WCO to JLC, Mar. 8, 1897, Clements Library, UM; WCO to Stoughton, Nov. 22, 1888, in *Gettysburg, July 2, 1863*, [p. 2]; Record of the Positions of Troops on the Battlefield, Vol. I, July 2, 1896, pp. 28, ED.

40. WCO, *War*, 217–218, 226. Bulger survived his wounds and the war. See "General M. J. Bulger: An Alabama Hero," *MA*, Oct. 2, 1898. Based on what Bulger told him after the war, Oates believed that Bulger had surrendered to Colonel James C. Rice of the 44th New York, who took over command of Vincent's Brigade at Gettysburg after Vincent was mortally wounded. In so doing, Oates

disputed the fact that Bulger surrendered to Joshua Chamberlain, as Chamberlain himself had claimed long after the battle. See WCO, *War*, 217.

41. WCO, *War*, 225; LaFantasie, ed., "William C. Oates Remembers Little Round Top," 61. Oates never really knew how many men he went into battle with. In 1878, he gave his effective strength as 644, an error he later acknowledged. WCO, "Gettysburg—The Battle on the Right," 178; WCO, *War*, 222; LaFantasie, ed., "William C. Oates Remembers Little Round Top," 59. But he could never quite settle on a precise number, preferring instead to refer to the regiment's strength as "below 400" or "above 400." The regiment probably had about 380 or 390 men fighting on the second of July. As for casualties, Oates said in his official report that the 15th had lost 17 killed, 54 wounded "and brought off the field," and 90 missing. See WCO to Peterson, Aug. 8, 1863, *O.R.*, Ser. 1, 27, Pt. 2, 393. Almost forty years after the battle, after he had spent years compiling information about the battle, he listed his casualties as 33 killed, 76 wounded, and 84 captured. See WCO to WMR, Apr. 1, 1902, OC. Actually his casualties seem to have been: 21 killed, 57 wounded, 22 wounded and then captured, 10 mortally wounded, 89 captured and not wounded. For an intelligent discussion of the 15th Alabama's effective strength—and the number of its casualties—at Gettysburg, see Desjardin, *Stand Firm Ye Boys From Maine*, 183–184, 195–202.
42. Jordan, *Some Events and Incidents*, 45; Law, "Struggle for 'Round Top,'" 326.
43. WCO, *War*, 225–226, 674.
44. On Civil War deaths, see LaFantasie, *Twilight at Little Round Top*, 209–227; Faust, "Civil War Soldier," 3–38; Faust, "*A Riddle of Death*"; Fahs, *Imagined Civil War*, 93–119; Hess, *Union Soldier*, 138–142; Mitchell, *Civil War Soldiers*, 60–64; Royster, *Destructive War*, 250–253. For the lyrics of "Somebody's Darling," which were written by Marie Ravenal de la Coste, see a copy of the original sheet music online at "Historic American Sheet Music, 1860–1869," Rare Book, Manuscript, and Special Collections Library, Duke University, http://scriptorium.lib.duke.edu/sheetmusic/conf/conf03/conf0370/.
45. Elmore, "Meteorological and Astronomical Chronology," 19–20; Lasswell, ed., *Rags and Hope*, 181.

Chapter 6: In the Purple Gloom

1. For the Bagwell brothers, see WCO, *War*, 680. On the morphology of condolence letters during the Civil War, see Faust, "Civil War Soldier," 3–38; Barton, "Painful Duties," 123–134; Schultz, "Healing the Nation," 33–41. At least one condolence letter written by Oates has survived. See Oates to Edmund Cody, Aug. 30, 1863, in Burnett, ed., "Letters of Barnett Hardeman Cody," 372–373.
2. Law, "Struggle for 'Round Top,'" 326–327; Evander M. Law to JBB, June 13, 1876, in Ladd and Ladd, eds., *Bachelder Papers*, 1:495; WCO, "Gettysburg—The Battle on the Right," 182; WCO, *War*, 235; WCO to JBB, Sept. 16, 1888, in Ladd and Ladd, eds., *Bachelder Papers*, 3:1556–1557; Benedict, *Vermont in the Civil War*, 2:597.
3. Coddington, *Gettysburg Campaign*, 523–524; Kross, "Farnsworth Charge," 45; Law, "Struggle for 'Round Top,'" 327; Benedict, *Vermont in the Civil War*, 2:596–598.
4. Law to JBB, June 13, 1876, in Ladd and Ladd, eds., *Bachelder Papers*, 1:496; Law, "Struggle for 'Round Top,'" 328–329; Parsons, "Farnsworth's Charge and Death," 393–395; Benedict, *Vermont in the Civil War*, 2:598–600; Coddington, *Gettysburg*

Campaign, 524–525; WCO, *War*, 236; Bachelder, "General Farnsworth's Death," *Philadelphia Weekly Times*, Dec. 30, 1882; Law to JBB, June 13, 1876, in Ladd and Ladd, eds., *Bachelder Papers*, 1:496; Stocker, ed., *From Huntsville to Appomattox*, 110–112. According to several sources, sometime into the afternoon, Texas and Alabama skirmishers along the most advanced of the picket lines overheard a peculiar conversation between Kilpatrick and Farnsworth. Although accounts differ, the two generals were arguing fiercely over whether a cavalry charge should be made against the Confederates, Kilpatrick in favor of the charge, Farnsworth against it. Kilpatrick, who had learned that the Union center had held against Longstreet's onslaught on Cemetery Ridge, wanted to hit the Confederates hard and take advantage of the victory just won about a mile to the north. Farnsworth, who had sized up the situation carefully, feared that an attack would be suicide. Furious with his subordinate, Kilpatrick screamed at him: "By God, if you are afraid to go, I will lead the charge myself!" Thus challenged, Farnsworth agreed to lead his men into battle, so long as Kilpatrick accepted responsibility for the decision to attack, but judging from the outcome of the engagement that followed that afternoon, which proved to be one of the most ludicrous cavalry actions of the entire war, it would have been better for Farnsworth to have stood his ground. See Parsons, "Farnsworth's Charge and Death," 394; Bachelder, "General Farnsworth's Death," *Philadelphia Weekly Times*, Dec. 30, 1882; WCO, *War*, 235–236; Stocker, ed., *From Huntsville to Appomattox*, 109–110; Coddington, *Gettysburg Campaign*, 524–525. Some historians have challenged whether such a conversation ever took place. See, for example, Custer, "Kilpatrick-Farnsworth Argument," 100–116.

5. WCO, *War*, 236; Law to JBB, June 13, 1876, in Ladd and Ladd, eds., *Bachelder Papers*, 1:496; WCO to JBB, Sept. 22, 1888, in ibid., 3:1558–1559; Law, "Struggle for 'Round Top,'" 329; Benedict, *Vermont in the Civil War*, 2:600; Parsons, "Farnsworth Charge and Death," 395. Adrian was a lieutenant in the 44th Alabama; he had joined the 15th Alabama skirmish line hoping to capture a Federal horse for himself. See WCO, *War*, 237.

6. WCO, *War*, 236–237; WCO to E. P. Alexander, Aug. 25, 1868, E. P. Alexander Papers, SHC; WCO to JBB, Mar. 29, 1876, in Ladd and Ladd, eds., *Bachelder Papers*, 1:466; WCO to JBB, Sept. 16, 1888, ibid., 3:1557; WCO to JBB, Sept. 22, 1888, ibid., 3:1558–1560. For other accounts of Farnsworth's death, see Stocker, ed., *From Huntsville to Appomattox*, 112; Botsford, *Boy in the Civil War*, 9; WMR to A. H. Belo, Jan. 10, 1900, reprinted in *Dallas Morning News*, Feb. 25, 1900; Parsons, "Farnsworth's Charge and Death," 396; Benedict, *Vermont in the Civil War*, 2:602–603; Bachelder, "General Farnsworth's Death," *Philadelphia Weekly Times*, Dec. 30, 1882. In earlier accounts, Oates implied that he himself had removed the shoulder straps and several letters from Farnsworth's body. Apparently he possessed the shoulder straps as late as 1866, but ten years later could no longer find them. See WCO to Alexander, Aug. 25, 1868, E. P. Alexander Papers, SHC; WCO to JBB, Mar. 29, 1876, in Ladd and Ladd, eds., *Bachelder Papers*, 1:466. Oddly enough, John B. Bachelder said that he had first heard the story of Farnsworth's suicide a few days after the battle from John A. Oates while he was being treated for his wounds in a Union hospital. The young Oates not only described Farnsworth's death, but told Bachelder that his brother—the colonel of the 15th Alabama—had removed Farnsworth's shoulder straps from his uniform. How John Oates, mortally wounded the day before on the slopes of

Little Round Top, could have known these details of Farnsworth's demise is, quite frankly, a complete mystery. It is within the realm of possibility that someone from the 15th Alabama, later captured and allowed to visit the dying Oates, told the young lieutenant of the events that had transpired on the evening of July 3. See Bachelder, "General Farnsworth's Death," *Philadelphia Weekly Times*, Dec. 30, 1882. For historians' assessments of Farnsworth's alleged suicide, see, for example, Longacre, *Cavalry at Gettysburg*, 243; Penny and Laine, *Struggle for the Round Tops*, 151–153; Kross, "Farnsworth's Charge," 52–53. For a fuller treatment of the Farnsworth incident, see also LaFantasie, "William C. Oates and the Death of General Elon Farnsworth," 48–55.

7. For Civil War military suicides in general, see Hess, *Union Soldier*, 90–92; Dean, *Shook over Hell*, 151–160. Hess observes that it is impossible accurately "to . . . gauge the number of Northern soldiers who refused to obey orders on the battlefield, ran away from battle never to return to duty, or committed suicide rather than face a horrible wound." Hess, *Union Soldier*, 91. On Cocke's suicide, see *Charleston Mercury*, Dec. 31, 1861; *New York Herald*, Jan. 4, 1862; *New York Times*, Jan. 10, 1862. Two articles that discuss cases of *attempted* suicide by Northern soldiers are Glenn, "Political Intrigue," 41–56; Beaudot, "A Civil War Madness," 58–69. On the historical context of suicide in America, see Kushner, "Suicide of Meriwether Lewis," 464–481; Kushner, *Self-Destruction in the Promised Land*. See also Riemer, "Durkheim's 'Heroic Suicide' in Military Combat," 103–120.

8. *New York Times*, Aug. 24, 1861; *New York Herald*, July 8, 1862; *New York Times*, Sept. 19, 1861.

9. *New York Times*, Oct. 10, 1861

10. WCO, *War*, 237–239; WCO to JBB, Mar. 29, 1876, in Ladd and Ladd, eds., *Bachelder Papers*, 1:467; WCO to JBB, Sept. 16, 1888, ibid., 3:1557–1558; Record of the Positions of Troops on the Battlefield, Vol. I, July 2, 1896, pp. 29, ED; Jordan, *Some Events and Incidents*, 45.

11. WCO, *War*, 239; Law, "Struggle for 'Round Top,'" 330; "The Battle Field at Gettysburg," *Berks and Schuylkill Journal*, July 18, 1863; Jordan, *Some Events and Incidents*, 45–46. Alexander Currens was told by a Confederate soldier that his stone house on the Emmitsburg Road was set on fire by Union artillery shells. See Coco, *Strange and Blighted Land*, 362.

12. WCO, *War*, 225; WCO to Edmund Cody, Aug. 30, 1863, in Burnett, ed., "Letters of Barnett Hardeman Cody," 372; WCO to WCOJR, Dec. 24, 1900, OFP. Oates's depression resembles in many respects what we now call post-traumatic stress disorder. See Dean, *Shook Over Hell*, esp. 46–69. Oates's condition may have been worsened not only by the loss of his brother and battlefield "shock," but also by the profound effects that the deaths by disease in his regiment had on him during the first year of the war. See also Talbott, "Combat Trauma," 41–47.

13. WCO, *War*, 237; Coddington, *Gettysburg Campaign*, 537–539; Penny and Laine, *Struggle for the Round Tops*, 168–169.

14. Vaughan, "Diary of Turner Vaughan," 589; WCO, *War*, 239, 589–590; Jordan, *Some Events and Incidents*, 46.

15. Lasswell, ed., *Rags and Hope*, 188; WCO, *War*, 247.

16. Penny and Laine, *Struggle for the Round Tops*, 106–107.

17. Coco, *Vast Sea of Misery*, 98; Coco, *Strange and Blighted Land*, 205; Rufus B. Weaver to WCO, Mar. 3, 1909, OFP.

18. Coco, *Vast Sea of Misery*, 98–99; Coco, *Strange and Blighted Land*, 206.

19. Patterson, *Debris of Battle*, 57–58; Coco, *Vast Sea of Misery*, 99, 183; WCO, *War*, 226–227, 674; [J]. A. E. Reed to WCO, Nov. 20, 1896, in ibid., 674–675. For the treatment of prisoners, see Linderman, *Embattled Courage*, 236–239; Mitchell, "Our Prison System," 565–585. On medical care for wounded prisoners, from the Confederate point of view, see Cunningham, *Doctors in Gray*, 127–133; there is no comparable account of Union treatment of wounded Confederates, although most accounts of Gettysburg's aftermath discuss the medical care given Confederate prisoners by Union doctors, civilian personnel of the volunteer commissions, and local residents. Oates incorrectly recorded the doctor's initials as "G. A. E." The identity of Miss Lightner has not been established. She may have been a relative of the Nathaniel Lightner family of Gettysburg. Apparently William Oates later corresponded with her, for he knew that she had died when he published his memoirs in 1905. See WCO, *War*, 227.

20. WCO, *War*, 239–240; Stocker, ed., *From Huntsville to Appomattox*, 113–115; Vaughan, "Diary of Turner Vaughan," 589–590; Jordan, *Some Events and Incidents*, 48; Laine and Penny, *Law's Alabama Brigade*, 125; Lasswell, ed., *Rags and Hope*, 189; Pfanz, "Gettysburg Campaign after Pickett's Charge," 118–124.

21. Register of Sick and Wounded Confederates, July 22, 1863, CSR (Barnett H. Cody).

22. Reed to WCO, Nov. 20, 1896, in WCO, *War*, 675; Medical Record, July 25, 1863, CSR (JAO); Weaver to WCO, Mar. 3, 1909, OFP.

23. OA, chap. 1. About his mother's extrasensory perception, William C. Oates noted: "Afterwards it was ascertained to a certainty that he [John] died about the time our mother had said that she saw him die. She was twelve hundred miles away from him, had not heard of the battle, or that he was wounded, but notwithstanding she knew of his death at the very hour it occurred." On Civil War dreams and their importance, see Royster, *Destructive War*, 244–246.

24. WCO, *War*, 252; McClendon, *Recollections*, 181–182; Jordan, *Some Events and Incidents*, 49; Vaughan, "Diary of Turner Vaughan," 593–595; Polley, *Hood's Texas Brigade*, 197–198; James Crowder to family, Aug. 26, 1863, in Mathis, *In the Land of the Living*, 58–59; Simpson, *Hood's Texas Brigade*, 294.

25. WCO, *War*, 671; Jordan, *Some Events and Incidents*, 46; McClendon, *Recollections*, 29.

26. WCO, *War*, 724; McClendon, *Recollections*, 182.

27. On the seasoning of soldiers, see Linderman, *Embattled Courage*, 113–133, 169–179; Hess, *Union Soldier*, 143–157.

28. WCO, *War*, 227.

29. WCO to Edmund Cody, Aug. 30, 1863, in Burnett, ed., "Letters of Barnett Hardeman Cody," 372–373. On the terms used to describe depression during the Civil War, see Dean, *Shook over Hell*, 115–116. For another analysis of Oates's letter of condolence to Cody, see also LaFantasie, *Twilight at Little Round Top*, 225–227.

30. James Crowder to family, Aug. 26, 1863, in Mathis, *In the Land of the Living*, 59; McClendon, *Recollections*, 181–182.

31. Lonn, *Desertion*, 18, 32; Freeman, *R. E. Lee*, 3: 163–164; Freeman, *Lee's Lieutenants*, 3:217–219; Dean, *Shook over Hell*, 127–128; WCO, *War*, 429–430, 715. See also Martin, *Desertion of Alabama Troops*. On the role played by honor in discouraging desertion, particularly how honor worked to convince some soldiers, especially those who came from yeomen backgrounds, that their real duty lay to their women and families back home, see Weitz, *A Higher Duty*, 177–179.

32. McPherson, *Ordeal by Fire*, 321; McPherson, "From Limited to Total War, 1861–1865," 66–86; Catton, *Stillness at Appomattox*, 2, 16, 19–21; Catton, *America Goes*

to War, 14–27, 68–86; Donald, *Liberty and Union*, 121–122, 144–148. Bruce Catton eloquently makes the case that the Emancipation Proclamation was the real turning point of the Civil War and, by means of its military measures, transformed the limited war into a total war. See, for example, Catton, *Terrible Swift Sword*, 461–470; Catton, *Never Call Retreat*, 49–50, 276–277.

33. Foote, *The Civil War*, 641–642.

34. Faust, *Creation of Confederate Nationalism*, 22–40; Beringer et al., *Why the South Lost the Civil War*, 82–102; Lincoln, Second Inaugural Address, Mar. 4, 1865, in Basler, ed., *Collected Works*, 8:332–333; Constitution of the Confederate States of America, in McPherson, *Ordeal By Fire*, A–1; Thomas, "God and General Lee," 15–24; Stowell, "Stonewall Jackson and the Providence of God," in Miller et al., eds., *Religion and the American Civil War*, 187–207.

35. Robertson, *Soldiers Blue and Gray*, 186–187; Wiley, *Life of Johnny Reb*, 174–184; Vaughan, "Diary of Turner Vaughan," 591; Laine and Penny, *Law's Alabama Brigade*, 137. On the spring revival that took place among Lee's soldiers camped along the Rappahannock, see Sears, *Chancellorsville*, 42–43.

36. General Orders No. 83, Aug. 13, 1863, reprinted in Harwell, ed., *Confederate Reader*, 224.

37. Beringer et al., *Why the South Lost the Civil War*, 268–272; Faust, "Christian Soldiers," 88–109; Norton, "Revivalism in the Confederate Armies," 410–424; Robertson, *Soldiers Blue and Gray*, 187; Wiley, *Life of Johnny Reb*, 183–184; Berends, "'Wholesome Reading Purifies and Elevates the Man,'" in Miller et al., eds., *Religion and the American Civil War*, 131–166; Mitchell, "Christian Soldiers?" in ibid., 297–309; Jones, *Christ in the Camp*, 337. On the cultural morphology of religious revivals and awakenings in general, see Wallace, "Revitalization Movements," 264–281; McLoughlin, *Revivals, Awakenings, and Reform*, 1–23.

38. Laine and Penny, *Law's Alabama Brigade*, 137; Vaughan, "Diary of Turner Vaughan," 591, 593, 595; WCO, *War*, 602.

39. Jones, *Christ in the Camp*, 338–339; Jordan, *Some Events and Incidents*, 49–50; Vaughan, "Diary of Turner Vaughan," 593–595; L. S. Knowles to Father, Aug. 17, 1863, reprinted in *Southern Advertiser*, Oct. 14, 1863; Laine and Penny, *Law's Alabama Brigade*, 137.

40. WCO, *War*, 277.

41. WCO, *War*, 247.

42. Tribute of Respect, ca. Aug. 30, 1863, reprinted in Burnett, ed., "Letters of Barnett Hardeman Cody," 373–375.

43. WCO, *War*, 226; WCO to JBB, Mar. 29, 1876, in Ladd and Ladd, eds., *Bachelder Papers*, 1:464; MOLC interview; Coco, *Wasted Valor*, 130–131. For years, the book of poems remained in the hands of the Oates family as a treasured heirloom, but sometime during the late twentieth century it was pilfered—along with several Civil War mementoes once belonging to William Oates—from the library at the family's estate in Montgomery, Alabama. The book was listed in an inventory of the Oates library compiled in the 1930s. See Inventory of Books Contained in the Oates Library—Belvoir, 1937, OFP.

Chapter 7: Gone to Flickering

1. Cozzens, *This Terrible Sound*, 53–60, 85–90. On Gettysburg as a turning point, see Kinsel, "From Turning Point to Peace Memorial," 203–222.

2. Jordan, *Some Events and Incidents*, 50; WCO, *War*, 253–254; Stocker, ed., *From Huntsville to Appomattox*, 133–134; Laine and Penny, *Law's Alabama Brigade*, 143; Cozzens, *This Terrible Sound*, 90, 102–103, 119–120; WCO to A. P. Stewart, Dec. 23, 1890, OFP (another copy of this letter is located in the Ezra Ayers Carman Papers, NYPL). Stewart, who served as a major general in Buckner's corps at Chickamauga, later became a commissioner of the Chickamauga and Chattanooga National Military Park. Oates wrote a report on his regiment's participation in the battle and submitted it to headquarters, but he never saw the document again, and it was not included among the Confederate papers printed in the *O.R.* Oates remarked rather tartly that General Law, whom he otherwise considered an able officer and a fine fighter, paid little attention to army paperwork and usually only sent casualty reports to his superior officers. See WCO, *War*, 261. Nearly thirty years later, Oates intended his letter to Stewart as a belated substitution for his lost battle report.

3. Cozzens, *This Terrible Sound*, 119–138.

4. WCO, *War*, 254; Jordan, *Some Events and Incidents*, 50–51; Stocker, ed., *From Huntsville to Appomattox*, 134–135; WCO to Stewart, Dec. 23, 1890, OFP; Laine and Penny, *Law's Alabama Brigade*, 144–148.

5. WCO, *War*, 254–255; WCO to Stewart, Dec. 23, 1890, OFP; Jordan, *Some Events and Incidents*, 51; Laine and Penny, *Law's Alabama Brigade*, 148–151.

6. WCO, *War*, 255; WCO to Stewart, Dec. 23, 1890, OFP.

7. Laine and Penny, *Law's Alabama Brigade*, 157.

8. Cozzens, *This Terrible Sound*, 300–302, 305, 368–375, 384; Laine and Penny, *Law's Alabama Brigade*, 161; WCO, *War*, 255–256; Jordan, *Some Events and Incidents*, 51; WCO to Stewart, Dec. 23, 1890, OFP. On the independent streak in Southern soldiers, see Donald, "Confederate as Fighting Man," 178–193; Catton, "Confederate Legend," 9–23.

9. WCO to Stewart, Dec. 23, 1890, OFP; WCO, *War*, 256; Jordan, *Some Events and Incidents*, 51.

10. WCO, *War*, 256–258; WCO to Alexander, Aug. 25, 1868, E. P. Alexander Papers, SHC; WCO to Stewart, Dec. 23, 1890, OFP; Samuel K. McSpadden to E. F. Travis, Oct. 5, 1863, in *O.R.*, Ser. 1, 30, Pt. 2, 334. Major General Thomas C. Hindman, commanding a division in Longstreet's left wing, also reported that "the Fifteenth Alabama Regiment, of General Law's command, which had lost its direction, fired on [Brigadier General Zachariah C.] Deas' right, but upon discovering the mistake, moved up and fought gallantly with him." Deas, however, who commanded the brigade that included the 19th Alabama, only praised Oates and the 15th Alabama for "behaving with great gallantry" during the battle. See T. C. Hindman to G. Moxley Sorrel, Oct. 25, 1863, in *O.R.*, Ser. 1, 30, Pt. 2, 303; Z. C. Deas to J. P. Wilson, Oct. 9, 1863, in ibid., 332. Historians have not been able to discern whether the 15th Alabama actually fired into McSpadden's ranks or not. Laine and Penny conclude that "it is likely that before Oates could get his men's attention some shots were accidentally fired into the 19th Alabama." Laine and Penny, *Law's Alabama Brigade*, 172. Cozzens states flatly that the 15th Alabama did indeed fire into the rear of the 19th Alabama, but the evidence is not as conclusive as he implies. See Cozzens, *This Terrible Sound*, 384–385.

11. WCO, *War*, 257–258; WCO to Stewart, Dec. 23, 1890, OFP; Jordan, *Some Events and Incidents*, 51–52. Lytle was already dead when Oates dragged his body under

the trees. WCO to Alexander, Aug. 23, 1868, E. P. Alexander Papers, SHC. Oates later learned that Lytle had composed the famous poem, "Antony and Cleopatra," with its "beautiful and pathetic" (as Oates called it) opening line, "I am dying, Egypt, dying." WCO, *War*, 258.

12. WCO, *War*, 259–261; WCO to Stewart, Dec. 23, 1890, OFP.

13. WCO to Alexander, Aug. 25, 1868, E. P. Alexander Papers, SHC; WCO to Stewart, Dec. 23, 1890, OFP; WCO, *War*, 262. See also Cozzens, *This Terrible Sound*, 426–427.

14. WCO, *War*, 262–263.

15. WCO, *War*, 263–264; Jordan, *Some Events and Incidents*, 52–53; Laine and Penny, *Law's Alabama Brigade*, 173; WCO to Alexander, Aug. 23, 1868, E. P. Alexander Papers, SHC; WCO to Stewart, Dec. 23, 1890, OFP.

16. See Joseph B. Kershaw to James M. Goggin, Oct. 15, 1863, in *O.R.*, Ser. 1, 30, Pt. 2, 504.

17. Laine and Penny, *Law's Alabama Brigade*, 176, 180–181; James Crowder to Mother, Sept. 29, 1863, in Mathis, *In the Land of the Living*, 76; WCO, *War*, 269.

18. Evander M. Law to [War Department], Sept. 28, 1863, CSR (Alexander A. Lowther); WCO to A. M. Baldwin, Sept. 28, 1863, OFP.

19. For many years, the certificate was displayed, neatly framed, in Oates's library at his house behind the state capitol in Montgomery, Alabama, and years later in his son's home, Belvoir, on the outskirts of that same city. Unfortunately the certificate was stolen, with other valuable Oates memorabilia, in 1995. I saw the certificate and took notes from it in 1992, during a visit to Montgomery.

20. Jordan, *Some Events and Incidents*, 55; Stocker, ed., *From Huntsville to Appomattox*, 139; WCO, *War*, 270; Laine and Penny, *Law's Alabama Brigade*, 181. The artillery belonged to a section of Captain Overton W. Barrett's Missouri Battery. Laine and Penny, *Law's Alabama Brigade*, 181. Oates said the guns were from a Louisiana battery. WCO, *War*, 270.

21. Houghton and Houghton, *Two Boys*, 39; Vaughan, "Diary of Turner Vaughan," 597–598; Jordan, *Some Events and Incidents*, 55–56; WCO, *War*, 270–273.

22. Cozzens, *Shipwreck*, 4, 7, 51; Jordan, *Some Events and Incidents*, 56; WCO, *War*, 272–273, 275.

23. WCO, *War*, 275–276; Jordan, *Some Events and Incidents*, 57–59; Evander M. Law to R. M. Simms, Nov. 3, 1863, in *O.R.*, Ser. 1, 31, Pt. 1, 224.

24. WCO, *War*, 276–278; Evander M. Law, "Lookout Valley: Memorandum of Gen. E. M. Law," Nov. 3, 1878, Ezra Carmen Papers, NYPL.

25. WCO, *War*, 278–280; Jordan, *Some Events and Incidents*, 59–60; WCO, *Speech of Governor William C. Oates*, 5; Law to Simms, Nov. 3, 1863, in *O.R.*, Ser. 1, 31, Pt. 1, 225; James L. Sheffield to L. A. Terrell, Nov. 3, 1863, in ibid., 228–231; Law, "Lookout Valley: Memorandum of Gen. E. M. Law," Nov. 3, 1878, Carmen Papers, NYPL; Laine and Penny, *Law's Alabama Brigade*, 184, 186–194.

26. WCO, *War*, 337, 745.

27. Walker, *Backtracking in Barbour County*, 310–312; "Heirs of Richardson Burge Toney," undated typescript, OFP; Georgia Oates Gossler, "Notes on Roseland," undated, OFP; Obituary, *Eufaula Times*, ca. June 16, 1875; Washington Toney to Edmund Cody, Jan. 8, 1860 (photostat), OFP; Toney to Cody, June 17, 1861, in Burnett, ed., "Some Confederate Letters," 189–192; Obituary (signed "Watkins"), unidentified news clipping, ca. June 16, 1875, Bound Leather Book of Manuscripts, Notes, and News Clippings, OFP.

28. Obituary, *Eufaula Times*, ca. June 16, 1875; Walker, *Backtracking in Barbour County*, 311–312, 317; Gossler, "Notes on Roseland," undated, OFP; *Eufaula Daily Inquirer-Sun*, Jan. 6, 1895.

29. Walker, *Backtracking in Barbour County*, 311–312; Gossler, Notes on Roseland, undated, OFP.

30. Walker, *Backtracking in Barbour County*, 195, 313–314; *MA*, Jan. 16, 1939. For Sallie Toney's correct birth date, sometimes erroneously given as 1863, see inscription in Oates family Bible (photocopy), Old Settlers' Records, AML.

31. WCO, *War*, 338.

Chapter 8: The End of Chivalry

1. WCO, *War*, 338.

2. WCO, *War*, 338–340; Laine and Penny, *Law's Alabama Brigade*, 177–180, 197–198, 206–208, 217–224.

3. Rhea, *Battle of the Wilderness*, 42–59, 74–87, 102–129, 271–282.

4. WCO, *War*, 343; Rhea, *Battle of the Wilderness*, 283–326.

5. Laine and Penny, *Law's Alabama Brigade*, 236; Oates, *War*, 344.

6. Perry, "Reminiscences," 52–53; Laine and Penny, *Law's Alabama Brigade*, 238–240, 245–246.

7. Perry, "Reminiscences," 54; WCO, *War*, 347; Laine and Penny, *Law's Alabama Brigade*, 241–244, 246.

8. WCO, *War*, 348–349; Laine and Penny, *Law's Alabama Brigade*, 248–250; Rhea, *Battle of the Wilderness*, 351–366, 370–371.

9. WCO, *War*, 349–350; Perry, "Reminiscences," 58–63; Laine and Penny, *Law's Alabama Brigade*, 250–252; Rhea, *Battle of the Wilderness*, 399–401.

10. Charles Francis Adams, Jr., to Henry Adams, July 27, 1864, in Ford, ed., *A Cycle of Adams Letters*, 2:168.

11. WCO, *War*, 357–358; Laine and Penny, *Law's Alabama Brigade*, 255–258.

12. WCO, *War*, 358; Laine and Penny, *Law's Alabama Brigade*, 258–262; Rhea, *Battles for Spotsylvania Court House*, 45–88.

13. WCO, *War*, 358–359; Rhea, *Battles for Spotsylvania Court House*, 232–307; Muffly, ed., *Story of Our Regiment*, 859–860.

14. WCO, *War*, 359; Laine and Penny, *Law's Alabama Brigade*, 262.

15. WCO, *War*, 363–365; Laine and Penny, *Law's Alabama Brigade*, 263.

16. WCO, *War*, 365; Furgurson, *Not War But Murder*, 113–114, 121–123, 167–168, 236–242.

17. WCO, *War*, 365–367; McClendon, *Recollections*, 210–211; Jordan, *Some Events and Incidents*, 82–83; Laine and Penny, *Law's Alabama Brigade*, 271–276.

18. Catton, *A Stillness at Appomottox*, 163; Grant, *Memoirs and Selected Letters*, 588.

19. Furgurson, *Not War But Murder*, 210–219, 277–280. The casualty figures for the 15th Alabama during the Cold Harbor campaign are from Jones, comp., "The 15th Alabama Volunteer Infantry Regiment," http://www.tarleton.edu/activities/pages/facultypages/jones/#4, accessed Dec. 28, 1996. On Lowther's wound, see Laine and Penny, *Law's Alabama Brigade*, 275.

20. WCO, *War*, 366.

21. Laine and Penny, *Law's Alabama Brigade*, 280–284; Oates, *War*, 368–369.

22. Register of Appointments, CSR (Alexander A. Lowther). Lowther submitted supporting documents written by James Cantey, the former colonel of the 15th

Alabama, and John F. Treutlen, the former lieutenant colonel of the regiment, to prove that Lowther by seniority deserved the colonelcy and command of the regiment. See Cantey to Samuel Cooper, Feb. 2, 1864, CSR (Lowther); Treutlen to Cooper, Feb. 10, 1864, CSR (Lowther); Cantey, Facts Concerning A. A. Lowther's Seniority, Feb. 11, 1864, CSR (Lowther). On Lowther's ailments, see the medical certificates dated May 21, 1863 and July 8, 1863, in CSR (Lowther). He seems also to have contracted tuberculosis, which Lowther's doctors referred to as "phthisis pulmo." Register of General Hospital No. 4, Richmond, June 21, 1864, CSR (Lowther).

23. WCO, *War*, 369–371; Laine and Penny, *Law's Alabama Brigade*, 277–278; James L. Pugh to Samuel Cooper, June 11, 1864, CSR (WCO); Pugh to Jefferson Davis, June 13, 1864, CSR (WCO); William F. Perry to Cooper, June 15, 1864, CSR (WCO); Endorsement by Charles W. Field on Perry's letter to Cooper, June 15, 1864, CSR (WCO); John B. Hood to Cooper, June 24, 1864, CSR (WCO).

24. WCO, *War*, 371.

25. Cooper to WCO, June 21, 1864, CSR (WCO); Lowther to Cooper, July 12, 1862, CSR (Alexander A. Lowther). Laine and Penny state that Isaac Trimble was responsible for revoking Lowther's resignation. Laine and Penny, *Law's Alabama Brigade*, 23.

26. Perry to Cooper, June 28, 1864, CSR (WCO); WCO, Reasons for Declining Temporary Command of the 48th Alabama, July 20, 1864, CSR (Alexander A. Lowther); WCO, *War*, 371–372; Laine and Penny, *Law's Alabama Brigade*, 278.

27. WCO, *War*, 371–373; Laine and Penny, *Law's Alabama Brigade*, 287–288.

28. WCO, *War*, 792, 796. On the 48th Alabama regiment, see Taylor, *History of the 48th Alabama*.

29. WCO, *War*, 373–376; Laine and Penny, *Law's Alabama Brigade*, 287–295. Lowther's severe wound at Fussell's Mill resulted in an extended furlough. He did not return to duty until the winter of 1865. Inspection Report of Law's Brigade, Jan. 27, 1865, CSR (Alexander A. Lowther).

30. WCO, *War*, 375–377; Laine and Penny, *Law's Alabama Brigade*, 295–297.

31. WCO, *War*, 377–378.

32. WCO, *War*, 379–383.

33. The skin color and age of Sallie Vandalia, who by 1880 had married and become Sallie Knight, is revealed in U.S. Population Census, Polk County, Texas, 1880. See also WCO, Statement Concerning Claude Oates, Jan. 5, 1896, OFP. On Oates's interest in women of color, see OA, chap. 5.

34. WCO, *War*, 383; MOLC interview.

35. WCO, *War*, 383; MOLC interview.

36. WCO, *War*, 428–429.

37. WCO, *War*, 430–431.

38. Pugh to Davis, Jan. 27, 1865, CSR (WCO); WCO to Samuel W. Mellon, Feb. 2, 1865, CSR (WCO); Oates to Davis, Feb. 2, 1865, CSR (WCO); Pugh to Davis, Feb. 2, 1865, CSR (WCO); Mellon to James A. Seddon, Feb. 3, 1865, CSR (WCO); Register of Appointments, Feb. 23, 1865, CSR (WCO). Long after the war, Oates maintained that General John Bell Hood, while commander of the Army of the Tennessee, had requested the War Department to commission him a brigadier general at a time when Oates had still not recovered from the amputation of his arm. See WCO, *War*, 341. If this were so, Hood apparently did not make the request formally or submit the necessary paperwork to the War Department, for no such petition exists in Oates's compiled service record.

39. WCO, *War*, 431–432, 501–503, 538.
40. WCO, *War*, 432, 711; Laine and Penny, *Law's Alabama Brigade*, 333.
41. WCO, *War*, 227, 432.
42. On regimental loyalties, see Prokopowicz, *All for the Regiment*; McPherson, *For Cause and Comrades*; Dunkelman, *Brothers One and All*.

Chapter 9: Before the Bar

1. WCO, *War*, 533.
2. On Oates's legal practice during the war, see, for example, Order to Convey Lands (typescript), July 14, 1862, OFP. He may have formed a partnership with several other Abbeville attorneys during the war years. See, for instance, Warren, *Henry*, 108.
3. On attorneys' fees in criminal cases, see *Brown et al. v. The State*, 46 Ala. 148 (1871 Ala. LEXIS 147).
4. The case involving the split decision was *Reddick et al. v. Long*, 124 Ala. 260; 27 So. 402 (1899 Ala. LEXIS 222). For his Supreme Court case, see *Oates v. National Bank*, 100 U.S. 239; 25 L. Ed. 580; 10 Otto 239 (1879 U.S. LEXIS 1827).
5. *Ex Parte Norton & Shields*, 44 Ala. 177 (1870 Ala. LEXIS 27); *Stikes v. Swanson et al.*, 44 Ala. 633 (1870 Ala. LEXIS 115); *Chisholm v. Coleman*, 43 Ala. 204 (1869 Ala. LEXIS 31). On Alabama legal thought in the postwar era, see McLaughlin, "A 'Mixture of Race and Reform,'" 284–309. Peters served as chief justice of the Alabama Supreme Court during the 1873–1874 term.
6. *Cantelou v. Doe*, 56 Ala. 519 (1876 Ala. LEXIS 580); *Green et al. v. The State*, 59 Ala. 68 (1877 Ala. LEXIS 56); Wallenstein, "Race, Marriage, and the Law of Freedom," 433–434; McLaughlin, "A 'Mixture of Race and Reform,'" 294–306.
7. For these cases, see *Sowell v. Sowell's Administrator*, 40 Ala. 243 (1866 Ala. LEXIS 53); *Arrington et al. v. Roach*, 42 Ala. 155 (1868 Ala. LEXIS 56); *Alabama Conference M. E. Church South v. Price, Executor, &c.*, 42 Ala. 39 (1868 Ala. LEXIS 34).
8. *Roach, Adm'r, v. Gunter et al.*, 44 Ala. 209 (1870 Ala. LEXIS 33).
9. *Gunter v. Dale County*, 44 Ala. 639 (1870 Ala. LEXIS 117); *Dale County v. Gunter*, 46 Ala. 118 (1871 Ala. LEXIS 145).
10. *Montgomery v. The State*, 40 Ala. 684 (1867 Ala. LEXIS 57); *Crawford v. The State*, 44 Ala. 45 (1870 Ala. LEXIS 8); *Crawford v. The State*, 44 Ala. 382 (1870 Ala. LEXIS 85).
11. For Oates's law library, see Inventory of Books Contained in the Oates Library—Belvoir, 1937, OFP.
12. Memorial Resolution of Atlas Insurance Company Board of Directors, ca. Oct. 15, 1910, OFP.
13. WCO, Record Book of Personal and Political Letters, 1877–1886, OFP; WCO, Account Book, 1878–1907, OFP; Oates Family Bible (photocopy), Old Settlers' Records, AML; WCO, Statement Concerning Claude Oates, Jan. 5, 1896, OFP.
14. Deed, Catharine Howard to WCO et al., July 5, 1861; Deed, James W. Deese and Mary Deese to William L. Pelham, Jan. 1, 1861; Deed, William L. Pelham to WCO, Dec. 22, 1877; Contract, WCO and S. E. Daugey, Nov. 30, 1875; M. J. Hart, Deposition Concerning the Estate of Thomas Howard, Oct. 3, 1927; U.S. Land Grant to Coleman Barns, Sept. 20, 1839; U.S. Land Grant to James Ward, Dec. 10, 1841; Alabama Land Grant to James Ward, Jan. 27, 1845; U.S. Land Grant to Lee R. Miller, July 15, 1853; U.S. Land Grant to Nathaniel Hesters, March 3, 1854; U.S. Land Grant to John Marick, Jr., July 1, 1858; U.S. Land

Grant to Seaborn J. Johnson, Sept. 1, 1858; U.S. Land Grant to Jason Yates, Nov. 1, 1858; U.S. Land Grant to Green B. Pitts, Nov. 1, 1858; U.S. Land Grant to Thomas Howard, Nov. 1, 1858—all OFP.

15. William Oates Long to WCOJR, Feb. 8, 1926, OFP; *Birmingham News*, Sept. 9, 1910; *Mobile Register*, Sept. 10, 1910.

16. *Mobile Register*, Sept. 10, 1910; *National Cyclopaedia of American Biography*, 2:244; Contract, WCO and S. E. Daugey, Nov. 30, 1875, OFP; WCO, Notebook, ca. 1885, unpaginated (entry for "Ellis' Cotton Seed"), OFP; M. J. Hart, Deposition Concerning the Estate of Thomas Howard, Oct. 3, 1927, OFP; WCOJR to Warren Andrews (First National Bank, Montgomery), Oct. 30, 1932, OFP; WCOJR, Circular Letter Concerning Alabama Timber Lands for Sale, ca. late 1932, OFP. On sharecropping and the cotton economy of the South in the postwar years, see Cooper and Terrill, *American South*, 426–430, 433–438; Foner, *Reconstruction*, 173–174, 211, 392–395, 404–409. The *National Cyclopaedia* sketch of Oates's life was written by a Colonel Avery of Georgia who let Oates see the text and correct it before publication. See "Personal Data" (WCO/Governor), ca. May 1, 1901, Governors' Vertical Files, ADAH.

17. Rogers et al., *Alabama*, 225–227.

18. Lincoln, Proclamation of Amnesty and Reconstruction, Dec. 8, 1863, in Basler, ed., *Collected Works*, 7:53–56; Foner, *Reconstruction*, 35–37, 60–62; WCO, *War*, 533.

19. Donald, *Liberty and Union*, 158–159; McPherson, *Ordeal by Fire*, 513–514; Donald, *Lincoln*, 581–585, 589–592; Wills, "Lincoln's Greatest Speech?" 60–70.

20. Foner, *Reconstruction*, 179–197; Rogers et al., *Alabama*, 230–233; WCO to Alexander, Aug. 25, 1868, E. P. Alexander Papers, SHC; Editorial, *MA*, Sept. 10, 1910.

21. Foner, *Reconstruction*, 185, 196, 228–280; Cooper and Terrill, *American South*, 398–403; McPherson, *Ordeal by Fire*, 555–566. On the Freedmen's Bureau in Alabama, see White, "Black Lives, Red Tape," 241–258.

22. Cooper and Terrill, *American South*, 393–398, 409–411; Rogers et al., *Alabama*, 229, 242–243, 247, 250–251. On the Klan's activities in Alabama, see Trelease, *White Terror*, 49–55, 81–88, 246–273, 302–310, 392–393. See also Rable, *But There was No Peace*, 1–15.

23. Editorial, *MA*, Sept. 10, 1910; Warren, *Henry*, 105–110; Certificate of Membership, Fraternity of Ancient Freemasons, Henry Lodge No. 91, June 9, 1866, OFP; Hoyt M. Warren, "Henry's Heritage: Architectural Legacy," *Abbeville Herald*, Nov. 13, 1980; Oates Family Bible (photocopy), Old Settlers' Records, AML.

24. U.S. Population Census, Henry County, Alabama, 1860, 1870; Oates Family Bible (photocopy), Old Settlers' Records, AML. Lucy Hickman was the daughter of Daniel Edward Hickman (born in Georgia, ca. 1802; died in Louisiana, ca. 1855) and Sarah Ann G. Calk (born in South Carolina). See Family Search Ancestral File, Lucy Hickman (AFN: VX8K-T9), http://www.familysearch.org, accessed June 13, 2005. On Poe's marriage, see Quinn, *Edgar Allan Poe*, 219–224, 252–254. See also Freedman, "Sexuality in Nineteenth-Century America," *Reviews in American History*, 10 (December 1982), 196–215.

25. Oates Family Bible (photocopy), Old Settlers' Records, AML.

26. *Nugent v. The State*, 19 Ala. 540 (1851 Ala. LEXIS 117). For the pertinent Alabama laws on rape, see Walker, comp., *Revised Code of Alabama*, Sections 3361–3367, 3670, and 4194.

27. *Lewis v. The State*, 35 Ala. 380 (1860 Ala. LEXIS 5). In this decision, the Alabama Supreme Court reversed the conviction of a slave for rape.

28. *Lewis v. The State*, 35 Ala. 380 (1860 Ala. LEXIS 5); U.S. Population Census, Henry County, Alabama, 1860. On historical attitudes toward rape, particularly in nineteenth-century America, see Donat and D'Emilio, "Feminist Redefinition of Rape and Sexual Assault," 9–22; Bardaglio, "Rape and the Law in the Old South," 749–772; Sommerville, "Rape Myth in the Old South Reconsidered," 481–518; Bardaglio, *Reconstructing the Household*, 176–214; *Gendered Strife and Confusion*, 8–9; Sommerville, "'I Was Very Much Wounded,'" 136–177; Block, "Rape Without Women," 849–868; Krause, "'Infamous Outrage and Prompt Retribution,'" 182–203; Block, "Bringing Rapes to Court," http://commonplace.dreamhost.com//vol-03/no-03/block/index.shtml; Sommerville, *Rape and Race*, 1–19, 200–218, 223–260. On Southern women who lacked male providers, see Bynum, *Unruly Women*. In modern parlance, Oates possibly committed what is known as "family rape" or "acquaintance rape," depending on the nature of his relationship with Lou Hickman.

29. On Southern misogyny, see Sommerville, *Race and Rape*, 5–7, 10–11, 15, 27, 69, 71, 86, 88, 96, 101, 179, 182, 201.

30. For the psychological effects of amputation, see Williamson et al., "Social and Psychological Factors,"249–268; Williamson and Walters, "Perceived Impact of Limb Amputation," 221–230. On social expectations during the nineteenth century that the natural condition of adult males was to become husbands, see Rose, *Victorian America*, 145–162; Bertolini, "Fireside Chastity," 707–737.

31. Mitchell, *Vacant Chair*, 3–19, 71–114, 151–166; Faust, *Mothers of Invention*, 248–257; Rable, *Civil Wars*, 1–30, 50–72, 112–138; Whites, "Civil War," 3–21; Christ, "Victorian Masculinity," 146–162; Berry, *All That Makes a Man*, 193–196.

32. See, for example, Coviello, "Poe in Love," 875–901; Faust, *James Henry Hammond*, 241–245; Kincaid, *Child-Loving*; Bardaglio, *Reconstructing the Household*, 39–48.

33. On average marriage ages, which are difficult to determine for the nineteenth century, see Presser, "Age Differences Between Spouses," 190–205; Monahan, *Pattern of Age*, 72–73, 99–112; Rothman, *Hands and Hearts*, 283, 287–288.

34. Berry, *All That Makes a Man*, 40–42, 116–117; Mayfield, "'The Soul of a Man!'" 477–500. On the cavalier ethic, see also Taylor, *Cavalier and Yankee*; Dawson, "The Puritan and the Cavalier," 597–614; Wyatt-Brown, *Southern Honor*; Genovese, *Slaveholders' Dilemma*; Stowe, *Intimacy and Power*.

35. For the marketplace and its impact on the cavalier ideal, see Oakes, *Ruling Race*; Escott, *Many Excellent People*; Shore, *Southern Capitalists*; Johnson, *The Men and the Vision*. On Lee as a model cavalier, see Gallagher, "An Old-Fashioned Soldier," 295–321; Fellman, *Making of Robert E. Lee*.

36. U.S. Population Census, Polk County, Texas, 1880 (Sallie Knight).

37. U.S. Population Census, Henry County, Alabama, 1870, 1880; U.S. Population Census, Dale County, Alabama, 1900; Ruth Oates, Untitled School Paper on William C. Oates, ca. 1961, typewritten copy in the possession of Charlton Oates Pingel, Enon, Ohio (1992); Oates Family Bible (photocopy), Old Settlers' Records, AML; MOLC interview.

38. Warren, *Henry*, 110–111; WCO, Speech on Confederate Soldiers, undated (typescript with handwritten emendations), OFP.

Chapter 10: The One-Armed Hero of Henry County

1. Warren, *Henry*, 111; Obituary, *MA*, Sept. 10, 1910; Obituary, *Birmingham Ledger*, Sept. 9, 1910; Farmer, "William Calvin Oates," in Johnson and Malone,

eds., *DAB*, 7:605; Jim Reisler, "One-Armed Hero Legend Lives On," *Dothan Eagle*, Feb. 21, 1982.

2. Warren, *Henry*, 111; Wakeman, comp., *Official Proceedings*, 31–32, 37–39, 75, 152–160. On Seymour, see Mitchell, "Horatio Seymour," in Johnson and Malone, eds., *DAB*, 9:6–9.

3. WCO, Speech on Effects of the Civil War, ca. 1893, OFP; Obituary, *Chicago Post*, Sept. 9, 1910.

4. Rogers et al., *Alabama*, 250–251; *National Cyclopaedia of American Biography*, 2:244; *MA*, Oct. 27, 1962. On Jacksonian attitudes toward equality, see Pessen, "The Egalitarian Myth," 989–1034; Ashworth, "The Jacksonian as Leveller," 407–421; Ashworth, *Slavery, Capitalism, and Politics*, 323–350; Stewart, "Emergence of Racial Modernity," 181–217.

5. *National Cyclopaedia of American Biography*, 2:244; Obituary, *Birmingham Ledger*, Sept. 9, 1910; Obituary, *Mobile Register*, Sept. 10, 1910.

6. *Henry County Register*, Aug. 5, 1871; OA, chap. 1.

7. WCO, *War*, 383; OA, chap. 3; Hoyt M. Warren, "Henry's Heritage: James B. Long," *Abbeville Herald*, Nov. 16, 1978; U.S. Population Census, Henry County, Abbeville, Alabama, 1880. Oates assumed the role of legal guardian of his sister's children. See *Watson v. Oates*, 58 Ala. 647 (1877 Ala. LEXIS 297). Concerning Oates's place of domicile, a later court decision describes Oates as a Eufaula resident in 1873. See *Oates v. National Bank*, 100 U.S. 239; 25 L. Ed. 580; 10 Otto 239 (1879 U.S. LEXIS 1827).

8. Walker, *Backtracking in Barbour County*, 225, 307, 312–314; MOLC interview; *MA*, Jan. 16, 1939. Examples of Sallie Toney's poems, sketches, short fiction, and other works may be found in the Oates Family Papers. Clippings of her poems from the Eufaula papers are located in Bound Leather Book of Manuscripts, Notes, and News Clippings, OFP.

9. Miriam Brewer Richardson, "A Day in Old Montgomery," *MA*, Sept. 19, 1937.

10. WCO to Alexander, Aug. 25, 1868, E. P. Alexander Papers, SHC.

11. WCO, "Gettysburg—The Battle on the Right," 172–182.

12. Going, *Bourbon Democracy in Alabama*, 10–18; Rogers, *The One-Gallused Rebellion*, 41–55; Rogers et al., *Alabama*, 252–258; Wiggins, *Scalawag in Alabama Politics*, 97, 101; Foner, *Reconstruction*, 552–553; Fleming, *Civil War and Reconstruction in Alabama*, 708–709; Smartt, *History of Eufaula*, 102–107; Rable, *But There was No Peace*, 114–117. The best account of the Eufaula riot is Hennessey, "Reconstruction Politics and the Military," 112–125, but see also Owens, "Eufaula Riot of 1874," 224–238. On the 1874 election, see Williams, "Alabama Election of 1874," 210–218. For the influence of the Klan on Alabama elections, see Sloan, "Ku Klux Klan," 113–124; Granade, "Violence," 181–202.

13. WCO, Some Thoughts on the Negro Enfranchisement, ca. 1888, OFP.

14. Wiggins, *Scalawag in Alabama Politics*, 97–99; Rogers et al., *Alabama*, 262–264; Foner, *Reconstruction*, 552–553.

15. Rogers et al., *Alabama*, 266–267; McMillan, *Constitutional Development*, 175–188, 189–191; Obituary, *Birmingham Ledger*, Sept. 9, 1910.

16. McMillan, *Constitutional Development*, 191–210, 216; Rogers et al., *Alabama*, 266–268; Going, *Bourbon Democracy in Alabama*, 20–26; Jones, "William Calvin Oates," 341–342; "Personal Data" (WCO/State Constitutional Convention), ca. Oct. 1901, Governors' Vertical Files, ADAH; Alabama Constitution of 1875, http://www.legislature.state.al.us/misc/history/constitutions/1875/1875_6.html, accessed Sept. 23, 2000.

17. Mortgage Deed, M. A. Bell to WCO, June 7, 1870; Mortgage Deed, John M. B. Kelly and S. A. Kelly to WCO, Jan. 6, 1872; Mortgage Deed, Berrien Saunders to WCO, May 28, 1874; Deed, William L. Pelham to WCO, Dec. 22, 1877; OA, chap 1—all OFP. For a sampling of the cases handled by Oates and his brother Wyatt, see *Bottoms & Powell v. Brewer & Brewer*, 54 Ala. 288 (1875 Ala. LEXIS 92); *Matthews et al. v. Dowling and Wife*, 54 Ala. 202 (1875 Ala. LEXIS 69); *Early & Lane v. Owens*, 68 Ala. 171 (1880 Ala. LEXIS 388).

18. *Raines v. Raines's Executors*, 51 Ala. 237 (1874 Ala. LEXIS 61).

19. *McElvain v. Mudd, Administrator*, 44 Ala. 48 (1870 Ala. LEXIS 9); *Bryan v. Hendrix*, 57 Ala. 387 (1876 Ala. LEXIS 454). For some of Oates's cases that dealt less substantively with the issue of Confederate currency, see *Hudgens et al. v. Cameron's Administrator*, 50 Ala. 379 (1874 Ala. LEXIS 228); *Gamble v. Jordan et al.*, 54 Ala. 432 (1875 Ala. LEXIS 113); *Calloway v. Kirkland*, 57 Ala. 476 (1876 Ala. LEXIS 476). On the legal issues surrounding contract payments made in Confederate currency, see also McLoughlin, "'A Mixture of Race and Reform,'" 300–301.

20. *Oates v. National Bank*, 100 U.S. 239; 25 L. Ed. 580; 10 Otto 239 (1879 U.S. LEXIS 1827).

21. For obituaries of Washington Toney, see Bound Leather Book of Manuscripts, Notes, and News Clippings, OFP. The handwritten manuscripts of a short story, "The Rivals," and a novella, "Leoline," by Sarah (Sallie) Toney are also to be found in OFP.

22. STO, "May the Sunlight of Happiness Ever Attend" ("My wife's Poem to me when she was but 14 years old"), ca. 1876, OFP.

23. WCO to WCOJR, Dec. 24, 1900, OFP.

24. On Bachelder, see Sauers, "John B. Bachelder," 115–127. For the early preservation efforts at Gettysburg, see Vanderslice, *Gettysburg*, 202–320; Harrison, "'A Fitting and Expressive Memorial,'" GNMP; Patterson, "From Battle Ground to Pleasure Ground," 128–157.

25. WCO to JBB, Mar. 29, 1876, in Ladd and Ladd, eds., *Bachelder Papers*, 1:463–469; WCO, *War*, 705; John F. Treutlen to WCO, Aug. 24, 1879, in the possession of Dr. Jack Anderson, Enterprise, Ala. (1994). Bachelder corresponded with a good number of other former Confederates—including Longstreet, Law, Alexander, and Kershaw—around this time. See Ladd and Ladd, eds., *Bachelder Papers*, 1:449–458, 462–479, 483–499.

26. WCO, Notebook, 1879, OFP. On Oates's extensive land holdings in Texas, see Texas Lands of WCO, ca. 1895; Description of Property in Hale County, Texas, owned by WCOJR, Feb. 15, 1936—both OFP. The Panhandle lands were worked by tenant farmers who grew cotton and wheat.

27. On Oates's skill at networking, see, for example, the numerous entries in Record Book of Political and Personal Letters, ca. 1877–1886, OFP; and WCO to Colonel [?], July 4, 1880, Oates Papers, 1880–1904, ADAH.

28. Obituary, *Birmingham Ledger*, Sept. 9, 1910; *National Cyclopaedia of American Biography*, 2:244.

29. U. S. House of Representatives, *Testimony and Papers in the Contested Election Case of A. A. Mabson vs. W. C. Oates*, Misc. Doc. No. 18, 47th Cong., 1st Sess., Dec. 30, 1881, 1–10, 54–55. Oates later publicly admitted to participating in fraudulent schemes by which he had been elected to various offices. See *Official Proceedings of the Constitutional Convention*, 3:2788–2789.

30. STO Diary, May 20, 1930, OFP; "Personal Data" (WCO/State Constitutional Convention), ca. Oct. 1901, Governors' Vertical Files, ADAH; WCO to Marcus J. Wright, Jan. 25, 1882, Wright Papers, HL.

31. On the delay that took place between the end of the war and the reawakening of interest in the conflict and its participants, see Linderman, *Embattled Courage*, 266–297; McConnell, *Glorious Contentment*, 167–180.

32. U.S. Population Census, Henry County, Abbeville, Alabama, 1880; Ruth Oates, Untitled School Paper on William C. Oates, ca. 1961, typewritten copy in the possession of Charlton Oates Pingel, Enon, Ohio (1992); U.S. Population Census, Dale County, Alabama, 1900. Lucy Hickman remained in Abbeville until sometime after 1880, when she moved to Dale County and lived with Josh. In 1878, she gave birth to a daughter, Ola, who later took her mother's last name. There is no record of the father's identity. Sometime between 1900 and 1910, Lucy and Ola Hickman moved to Graceville in Jackson County, Florida, where the two worked as farm laborers. Lucy Hickman died between 1910 and 1920. See U.S. Population Census, Dale County, Alabama, 1900; U.S. Population Census, Jackson County, Florida, 1910. During the first decade of the twentieth century, Josh Oates seems to have given up the practice of medicine to become a fireman. In 1910, he appears on the federal census as a fireman residing at the Central Fire Department in Birmingham, Alabama. Perhaps he had taken on duties as the resident physician of the firehouse. There is no entry for him in the 1920 federal census. See U.S. Population Census, Jefferson County, Birmingham, Alabama, 1910.

33. Garraty, *New Commonwealth*, 231–235.

34. *Cong. Rec.*, 47th Cong., 1st sess., 1881–1882, Vol. 13, pt. 1, 89, 238, 275, 724, 742, 796, 876, 990, 1059, 1131, 1143, 1602.

35. *Cong. Rec.*, 47th Cong., 1st sess., 1881–1882, Vol. 13, pt. 1, 1695, 2426; "Married," unidentified news clipping, ca. Mar. 28, 1882, in Bound Leather Book of Manuscripts, Notes, and News Clippings, OFP; STO Diary (1930), n.d. (entry on back cover); Walker, *Backtracking in Barbour County*, 314.

36. *Cong. Rec.*, 47th Cong., 1st sess., 1881–1882, Vol. 13, pt. 1, 2658.

37. Woodward, ed., *Mary Chesnut's Civil War*, 9; Presser, "Age Differences Between Spouses," 190–205; Monahan, *Pattern of Age*, 72–73, 99–112; Rothman, *Hands and Hearts*, 283, 287–288. Lack of reliable data makes generalizations about average marriage ages for males and females before the twentieth century very difficult to calculate. See Monahan, *Pattern of Age*, 136. One can judge the tremendous gap in age between Oates and T by noting the difference in age among some other couples of the Civil War era: for example, John C. Frémont was eleven years older than his wife Jesse; George E. Pickett was eighteen years older than LaSalle, his second wife; and Jefferson Davis was nineteen years older than Varina. Oates, of course, was twenty-nine years older than T.

38. On "falling in love" and ideal love, see Rothman, *Hands and Hearts*, 102–107, 198–200; on self-awareness, companionate and patriarchal relationships, and separate spheres, see Lystra, *Searching the Heart*, 34–36, 192–193, 214, 208–210, 230–231; Welter, "Cult of True Womanhood," 151–74; on domesticity in the postwar South, see Edwards, *Scarlett Doesn't Live Here Anymore*, 182–183. Historian Lawrence Stone uses the term "companionate marriage" to describe the voluntary marriages, as opposed to parentally arranged marriages, that became more common in England during the early nineteenth century. See Stone, *Family, Sex, and Marriage in England*.

39. For the emergence of the "new woman" in the South, particularly among the younger generation born, like T, between 1850 and 1870, see Censer, *Reconstruction*

of White Southern Womanhood, 10–97; Bardaglio, *Reconstructing the Household*; Edwards, *Gendered Strife and Confusion*; Hunter, *How Young Ladies Became Girls*; Thomas, *New Woman in Alabama*; Bleser, ed., *In Joy and in Sorrow*, 15–31, 135–175, 215–232; Thomas, ed., *Stepping out of the Shadows*, 75–94. On Alabama elite women and social clubs, see Thomas, *New Woman in Alabama*, 1–68.

40. For male attitudes toward marriage during the Victorian era, see Rotundo, *American Manhood*, 129–166; Rothman, *Hands and Hearts*, 153–154; Lystra, *Searching the Heart*, 129–130, 136, 194–195. Southern male patriarchal attitudes toward women and marriage are examined in McKean, "Southern Patriarch," 376–389; Richards, "'And He Shall Rule Over Thee,'" 317–346; Scott, "Women's Perspective," 52–64; Faust, *Mothers of Invention*, 4, 59, 121–123, 133–134, 252–253; Whites, *Civil War*, 8–11, 59–60, 133–137, 174–175; Edwards, *Gendered Strife and Confusion*, 107–144; Bardaglio, *Reconstructing the Household*, 3–36; Bleser and Heath, "The Clays of Alabama," 135–153; Wiggins, "A Victorian Father," 233–252; Censer, *Reconstruction of White Southern Womanhood*, 31–32. On work and male self-identity, particularly what E. Anthony Rotundo calls "self-made manhood," see Rotundo, *American Manhood*, 3–4, 167–193. See also Kimmel, *Manhood in America*, 81–116; Griswold, *Fatherhood in America*, 10–33. Historians tend to agree that American marriages became less patriarchal during the course of the nineteenth century, but there is less consensus on when the shift took place from the hierarchical model to "companionate" marriages. See, for example, Rotundo, *American Manhood*, 163–164; Lystra, *Searching the Heart*, 227–237; Degler, *At Odds*, 8–65.

41. For hierarchical gender distinctions, see Scott, *Southern Lady*, 43–44; Rotundo, *American Manhood*, 134–140, 164–166; Lystra, *Searching the Heart*, 230–237. Rotundo argues that companionate marriage "grew up alongside the hierarchical concept of marriage without really supplanting it." Rotundo, *American Manhood*, 130. On the perpetuation of patriarchy in the realm of legal domestic relations, see Grossberg, *Governing the Hearth*, 27.

42. For marital conflicts caused by the clash between companionate and patriarchal conceptions of marriage, see Fox-Genovese, "Family and Female Identity, 15–31; Censer, *Reconstruction of White Southern Womanhood*, 32, 276; Rotundo, *American Manhood*, 130–134. On the importance of candor and the achievement of intimacy, see Rothman, *Hands and Hearts*, 113–114, 227–230; Lystra, *Searching the Heart*, 32–35. Insightful discussions of mutuality and mutual identification in nineteenth-century marriages may be found in Rotundo, *American Manhood*, 150–157; Rothman, *Hands and Hearts*, 107, 247–248; Lystra, *Searching the Heart*, 9, 248–249.

43. "Biographical Sketch of Hon. Wm. C. Oates," typescript, ca. 1892; WCO, "Some Things I Have Done While a Member of Congress," typescript, ca. 1891—both OFP. On the tariff, see Taussig, *Tariff History of the United States*; Kaplan and Ryley, *Prelude to Trade Wars*.

44. Ellis Spear, "A Visit to Gettysburg," *Lincoln County News*, June 9, 1882; *Gettysburg Star and Sentinel*, June 21, 1882; *Gettysburg Compiler*, June 21, 1882. Bachelder mentioned Oates's attendance at the reunion in an unrelated newspaper article: Bachelder, "General Farnsworth's Death," *Philadelphia Weekly Times*, Dec. 30, 1882. William Swallow mistakenly thought that Oates had attended a reunion in 1880. See Hoke, *Great Invasion*, 329.

45. *MA*, Jan. 16, 1939. On invitations to the White House, see, for example, those dated Mar. 9, 1886, June 15, 1886, Jan. 27, 1887, Feb. 21, 1887—all OFP.

46. WCO to WCOJR, Feb. 28, 1905; WCO to WCOJR, Mar. 16, 1901; WCO to WCOJR, Nov. 25, 1900; WCO to WCOJR, Dec. 20, 1903—all OFP.

47. "Hon. William C. Oates' Interview with the *Mobile Register*" (pamphlet), July 7, 1892, p. 1 (copy in SUL); WCO to WCOJR, Dec. 13, 1900; WCO to WCOJR, May 7, 1905; WCO, Notebook, ca. 1885; STO to WCO, Sept. 4, 1901; STO to WCO, Oct. 25, 1901—all OFP.

48. WCO to WCOJR, Apr. 9, 1905; STO to WCO, Sept. 22, 1901; WCO to STO, Sept. 17, 1903—all OFP.

49. *Eufaula Daily Bulletin*, July 15, 1884; WCO to WCOJR, Sept. 2, 1888; WCOJR to STO, ca. Sept. 14, 1900—both OFP.

50. Oates Family Bible, Old Settlers' Records, AML.

51. WCO to WCOJR, Sept. 16, 1900; WCO to WCOJR, Jan. 1, 1901; WCO to WCOJR, Sept. 2, 1900; WCO to WCOJR, Oct. 7, 1900 —all OFP.

52. WCO to WCOJR, May 20, 1891; STO to WCO, Dec. 10, 1901; STO to WCO, Oct. 25, 1901—all OFP.

53. On the bonds between mothers and sons in the nineteenth century, see Rothman, *Hands and Hearts*, 116–117; Rotundo, *American Manhood*, 28–30, 49–52, 141–142.

54. WCO, *War*, 264.

55. WCO, "Some Things I Have Done While a Member of Congress," typescript, ca. 1891, OFP; WCO, "Speech on Refund of Direct Tax of 1861," Apr. 3, 1888, *Cong. Rec.*, 19, Pt. 10 (1888), 21–25; WCO, "Speech on Refund of the Direct Tax," Dec. 6, 1888, ibid., 20, Pt. 3 (1889), 5–7; WCO, "Speech on Direct Tax Bill," Feb. 24, 1891, ibid., 22, Pt. 4 (1891), 251–254; Obituary, *Washington Post*, Sept. 11, 1910.

56. WCO, "Speech on Fitz John Porter," February 1, 1884, *Cong. Rec.*, 15, Pt. 6 (1884), 11–13. For the congressional debate on the case, see ibid., Pt. 1 (1884), 800–840; ibid., Pt. 5 (1884), 5251–5252. On the details surrounding Porter's dismissal from the army, see Sears, "The Court-Martial of Fitz John Porter," in *Controversies and Commanders*, 51–73. The bill to reinstate Porter to the rank of colonel in the regular army was finally passed by Congress and signed into law by President Grover Cleveland in 1886.

57. M. F. Maury, "A Vindication of Virginia and the South," *SHSP*, 1 (1876), 49–61. In his memoirs, Oates reprinted Maury's essay in its entirety. See WCO, *War*, 40–48.

Chapter 11: Striking to Hurt

1. WCO, *War*, 199–200; *MA*, Sept. 18, 1910; *National Cyclopaedia of American Biography*, 2:244; *Chicago Post*, Sept. 9, 1910; "Biographical Sketch of Hon. Wm. C. Oates," typescript, ca. 1892, OFP; WCO, "Some Things I Have Done While a Member of Congress," typescript, ca. 1891, OFP. On American xenophobia after the Civil War, see Higham, *Strangers in the Land*; Curran, *Xenophobia and Immigration*; Daniels, *Guarding the Golden Door*.

2. Brewer, *Alabama*, 280; "Biographical Sketch of Hon. Wm. C. Oates," typescript, ca. 1892, OFP; Memorial Resolutions for WCO from Atlas Insurance Company, Oct. 15, 1910, OFP; *Birmingham News*, Sept. 11, 1910; *MA*, Sept. 10, 1910. On the changes in American language influenced by the war, see the literary estimates in Wilson, *Patriotic Gore*, 636–654; Delbanco, "To the Gettysburg Station," 31–38.

For slang words that came out of the war and, in many cases, endured beyond Appomattox, see Wiley, *Life of Billy Yank*, 186–187; Monaghan, "Civil War Slang and Humor," 125–133; Robertson, *Soldiers Blue and Gray*, 106–107; Garrison and Garrison, eds., *Encyclopedia of Civil War Usage*.

3. WCO, "Congressional Campaign Speech," ca. 1892 (typescript); WCO, Statement on Negro Votes and Re-election to Congress, 1888 (typescript); WCO, Some Thoughts About the Negro Enfranchisement, ca. 1888 (typescript)—all OFP. For Oates's collection of anecdotes and jokes, see WCO, Notebook [ca. 1885]; WCO, Notebook [ca. 1894]—both OFP.

4. WCO, Congressional Campaign Speech, ca. 1892 (typescript), OFP.

5. Rogers, *The One-Gallused Rebellion*, 121–164; Rogers, "The Farmers' Alliance in Alabama," in Wiggins, comp., *From Civil War to Civil Rights*, 162–172; Rogers et al., *Alabama*, 298–299. On Kolb and his early career, see Rogers, "Reuben F. Kolb," 109–119; Rogers, *The One-Gallused Rebellion*, 99–101, 109–110, 115–120. On the Southern Populist movement, see Goodwyn, *Populist Moment*; Palmer, *"Man over Money"*; McMath, *Populist Vanguard*.

6. WCO, "Some Things I Have Done While a Member of Congress," typescript, ca. 1891, OFP; WCO, "The Homestead Strike," *North American Review*, 155 (1892), 355–364; "Hon. William C. Oates' Interview with the *Mobile Register*" (pamphlet), July 7, 1892, 3 (copy in SUL).

7. Washington, *Up from Slavery*, 63; Rogers, *One-Gallused Rebellion*, 165–167, 209–210; Rogers et al., *Alabama*, 305–309. On disunity in the Democratic Party during the postwar period, see Going, *Bourbon Democracy in Alabama*, 41–49.

8. Rogers, *One-Gallused Rebellion*, 171–172; WCO, "Congressional Campaign Speech," ca. 1892 (typescript), OFP; WCO, "Some Things I Have Done While a Member of Congress," typescript, ca. 1891, OFP; William C. Oates, "Speech on Free Coinage of Silver, Repeal of the Sherman Law, and the 10 Percent Tax on State Bank Notes," Sept. 1893, *Cong. Rec.*, 25, Pt. 3 (1893), 152–157. On free silver, see Dieterich and Willson, "The Dimensions of Political Discourse," 13–18; Rodabaugh, "Fusion, Confusion, Defeat, and Disfranchisement," 131–153; Weaver, "John Sherman and the Politics of Economic Change," 7–19; Gramm and Gramm, "The Free Silver Movement in America," 1108–1129. See also DeVine, "Free Silver and Alabama Politics."

9. "Hon. William C. Oates' Interview with the *Mobile Register*" (pamphlet), July 7, 1892, 7 (copy in SUL); Rogers, *One-Gallused Rebellion*, 141–146, 229–231.

10. WCO, Congressional Campaign Speech, ca. 1892 (typescript), OFP; Rogers et al., *Alabama*, 308–311. On Jones, see Aucoin, "Thomas Goode Jones"; Aucoin, "Thomas Goode Jones and African American Civil Rights," 257–271. For the election of 1892, see Rodabaugh, "'Kolbites' Versus Bourbons," 275–321.

11. *Eufaula Daily Bulletin*, July 15, 1884; WCO to WCOJR, May 20, 1891, OFP; WCO to Thomas G. Jones, May 11, 1892, Jones Papers, ADAH; WCO to WCOJR, Aug. 15, 1889, OFP; *Eufaula Tribune*, June 4, 1930. While they took in Naples and all its sights, Oates and his family met Senator John Sherman, the former secretary of the treasury and the brother of the general, who was making his own grand tour with his wife. Sherman was amused by a happenstance involving a German man and Oates while they all stayed at the same hotel in Naples. According to Sherman, a passerby asked: "Is that not John Sherman?" Oates replied: "Yes, that is Sherman," and added as a compliment, "He was a good watchdog in the treasury." A German named Eichmann, catching the word "watchdog" and thinking it an insult, repeated it to Sherman. That man, said

Eichmann pointing to Oates, "was not your friend." As Sherman remembered the incident, "I had great difficulty in persuading him what a 'watchdog' meant, [and] that it was intended as a compliment, not as an insult." Sherman, *Recollections*, 2:1043.

12. WCO to JBB, Sept. 16, 1888, in Ladd and Ladd, eds., *Bachelder Papers*, 3:1556–1558; WCO to JBB, Sept. 22, 1888, in ibid., 3:1558–1560; WCO to JBB, Nov. 9, 1889, in ibid., 3:1676; "Personal Data" (WCO/Governor), ca. May 1, 1901, Governors' Vertical Files, ADHA; "Hon. William C. Oates' Interview with the *Mobile Register*" (pamphlet), July 7, 1892, 1 (copy in SUL). Oates often wrote notes on the flyleaves of many of the Civil War books in his personal library.

13. Oates Family Bible (photocopy), Old Settlers' Records, AML; OA, chap. 1; WCO, Sketch of Myself, Aug. 4, 1857, OFP.

14. WCO, "Speech on Refund of Direct Tax of 1861," Apr. 3, 1888, *Cong. Rec.*, 19, Pt. 10 (1888), 21–25; *National Cyclopaedia of American Biography*, 2:244; WCO, "Some Things I Have Done While a Member of Congress," typescript, ca. 1891, OFP; "Biographical Sketch of Hon. Wm. C. Oates," typescript, ca. 1892, OFP.

15. WCO, "The Homestead Strike," *North American Review*, 155 (1892), 355–364. On the strike, see Serrin, *Homestead*, 66–95; Demarest, *"The River Ran Red."* For Oates's definition of "class legislation," see *National Cyclopaedia of American Biography*, 2:244.

16. *National Cyclopaedia of American Biography*, 2:244; WCO, "Some Things I Have Done While a Member of Congress," typescript, ca. 1891, OFP; WCO, Campaign Speech at Birmingham, 1894 (typescript), OFP. On the depression of 1893, see Faulkner, *Politics, Reform and Expansion*, 141–147, 163–164; Brands, *The Reckless Decade*, 39–40, 73–74.

17. Rogers, *The One-Gallused Rebellion*, 236–237; Rogers et al., *Alabama*, 311–312.

18. Rogers, *The One-Gallused Rebellion*, 245, 271–272; Sparkman, "Kolb-Oates Campaign of 1894," 13–18.

19. Unidentified news clipping, n.d., Scrapbook, Maud McLure Kelly Collection, Alabama Series, Box 10, SUL; "Hon. William C. Oates' Interview with the *Mobile Register*" (pamphlet), July 7, 1892, pp. 2, 8 (copy in SUL); WCO to Thomas G. Jones, Jan. 11, 1894, Jones Papers, ADAH.

20. WCO to Jones, Jan. 27, 1894, Jones Papers, ADAH; MOLC interview.

21. WCO to Elihu Root, June 2, 1903, OC. On the establishment of the Chickamauga and Chattanooga National Military Park, see Boynton, comp., *Dedication of the Chickamauga and Chattanooga National Military Park*, 1–22; Boynton, "The National Military Park," 703–708. For the creation of the Gettysburg National Military Park and its commission, see Harrison, "'Patriotic and Enduring Efforts,'" 53–74; Harrison, "'A Fitting and Expressive Memorial,'" GNMP; Patterson, "From Battle Ground to Pleasure Ground," 128–157.

22. Rogers, *The One-Gallused Rebellion*, 276–277; Fry, *John Tyler Morgan*, 121–123; Sparkman, "Kolb-Oates Campaign of 1894," 8–13. For a good, but dated, account of the gubernatorial campaign, see Moore, *History of Alabama*, 632–638. See also Hackney, *Populism to Progressivism*, 34, 52–68; Nolan, "William Henry Skaggs," 116–134.

23. WCO, Campaign Speech at Birmingham, 1894 (typescript), OFP; Rogers, *The One-Gallused Rebellion*, 245–246.

24. Jones, "William Calvin Oates," 343; WCO, Campaign Speech at Birmingham, 1894 (typescript), OFP; Sparkman, "Kolb-Oates Campaign of 1894," 19–20; Rogers, *The One-Gallused Rebellion*, 281–282.

25. Rogers, *The One-Gallused Rebellion*, 277–278; WCO, Campaign Speech at Birmingham, 1894 (typescript), OFP.

26. Rogers, *The One-Gallused Rebellion*, 278–279, 282–283; WCO, Campaign Speech at Birmingham, 1894 (typescript), OFP; Sparkman, "Kolb-Oates Campaign of 1894," 24–25.

27. Sparkman, "Kolb-Oates Campaign of 1894," 26–28, 36; Rogers, *The One-Gallused Rebellion*, 282–283.

28. Rogers, *The One-Gallused Rebellion*, 283–285; Sparkman, "Kolb-Oates Campaign of 1894," 41–42; Rogers et al., *Alabama*, 314.

29. WCO, *Inaugural*, 1–7 [first pagination]; Rogers, *The One-Gallused Rebellion*, 291–292. A typewritten draft of the address, with handwritten emendations, is in OFP.

30. WCO, *Inaugural*, 1–20 [second pagination].

31. Oates's voluminous administrative files for his term as governor are located in ADAH. On the election contest law, see Rogers et al., *Alabama*, 315.

32. Rogers, *The One-Gallused Rebellion*, 295–296; Charles S. Fairchild to WCO, July 5, 1895, OAF; General Statement of the Alabama State Treasury (typescript), Dec. 31, 1895, OAF; news clipping, *MA*, ca. early Jan. 1896, OFP; news clipping, *Birmingham News*, ca. Aug. 1896, OFP.

33. WCO, "Industrial Development," 566–574.

34. Hackney, *Populism to Progressivism*, 73–75, 83–84; Webb, *Two Party Politics*, 140; WCO to WCOJR, May 20, 1891, OFP. On the convict lease system, see Ward and Rogers, "'Punishment Seven Times More,'" 20–33; Curtin, *Black Prisoners and Their World*.

35. MOLC interview.

36. Harlan, *Booker T. Washington*, 231–232, 258; STO to WCO, Nov. 3, 1901, OFP. On Washington's dinner with Roosevelt, and the nation's shocked reaction, see Harlan, *Booker T. Washington*, 311–324.

37. Durr, *Outside the Magic Circle*, 160; MOLC interview.

38. Ruth Oates, Untitled School Paper on William C. Oates, ca. 1961, typewritten copy in the possession of Charlton Oates Pingel, Enon, Ohio (1992); U.S. Population Census, Dale County, Alabama, 1900; WCO, Statement Concerning Claude Oates, January 5, 1896, OFP.

39. Claude Oates to WCO, ca. Jan. 1896; WCO, Statement Concerning Claude Oates, Jan. 5, 1896; G. B. Hudson to WCO, Dec. 31, 1892—all OFP. For Sallie Vandalia Knight Allen's other children, most of whom seem to have been fathered by her estranged husband, the otherwise unidentified Mr. Knight, see U.S. Population Census, Polk County, Texas, 1880.

40. Thomas F. Turner to WCO, Nov. 12, 1892; Turner to WCO, Dec. 27, 1894; Turner to WCO, Feb. 27, 1895; Texas Lands of WCO, ca. 1895—all OFP.

41. Turner to WCO, Feb. 27, 1895; S. V. Allen to WCO, Mar. 9, 1895; Allen to WCO, Aug. 1, 1895; Allen to WCO, Aug. 15, 1895; Allen to WCO, Sept. 6, 1895; Claude Oates to WCO, ca. Jan. 1896; WCO, Statement Concerning Claude Oates, Jan. 5, 1896—all OFP.

Chapter 12: A Soldier in His Heart

1. Smith and Hayford, eds., *Journals*, 14:206.

2. J. S. Fullerton to WCO, July 26, 1895, OAF; W. H. Bayliss to WCO, Aug. 18, 1895, OAF; WCO to Fullerton, Sept. 13, 1895, in Boynton, comp., *Dedication of*

the *Chickamauga and Chattanooga National Military Park*, 216; WCO to WCOJR, Sept. 17, 1895, OFP.

3. Fullerton to WCO, Sept. 10, 1895, OAF; Boynton, comp., *Dedication of the Chickamauga and Chattanooga National Military Park*, 23–24, 43–79, 154–159, 160–175; *New York Times*, Sept. 21, 1895; Lee, *Origin and Evolution*, 32.

4. Boynton, comp., *Dedication of the Chickamauga and Chattanooga National Military Park*, 175–176. Oates's speech was also privately printed as a pamphlet. See WCO, *Speech of Governor William C. Oates*.

5. Boynton, comp., *Dedication of the Chickamauga and Chattanooga National Military Park*, 180–181.

6. Ibid., 182–183.

7. Ibid., 187–188.

8. *New York Times*, Sept. 21, 1895; Horatio C. King to JFN, Sept. 23, 1895, OC.

9. Thomas M. Owen to WCO, Oct. 24, 1895, OAF; R. S. DesPartes to WCO, Jan. 11, 1896, OFP; WCO to WCOJR, July 8, 1896, OFP. The Owen letter is to be found, misplaced, in the administrative file for November 1895, OAF.

10. Cope, WCO's Visit; WCO to WCOJR, July 8, 1896, OFP; WCO to Root, June 2, 1903, OC. While on Little Round Top, a photographer accompanying the party took a picture of Oates standing on the rock that marked the place where his attacks had gained the greatest ground. Unfortunately the photograph has not survived.

11. For the dedication of the 20th Maine monument, see Miller, ed., *Dedication of the Twentieth Maine Monuments*; Desjardin, *Stand Firm Ye Boys from Maine*, 137–139.

12. *MA*, Jan. 16, 1939; *Eufaula Daily Inquirer-Sun*, Jan. 6, 1895; WCO to WCOJR, Aug. 9, 1895, OFP; Edwards, *Scarlett Doesn't Live Here Anymore*, 20–21.

13. George E. Brewer to WCO, Dec. 11, 1895, OAF; WCO to WCOJR, Jan. 9, 1896, OFP; WCO to STO, Jan. 12, 1896, OFP.

14. STO to WCOJR, Jan. 13, 1896; WCOJR to STO, Jan. 13, 1896; STO to WCOJR, ca. Jan. 17, 1896; STO to WCOJR, ca. Jan. 31, 1896; STO to WCOJR, ca. Feb. 1896; STO to WCOJR, Feb. 6, 1896; STO to WCOJR, Feb. 15, 1896—all OFP.

15. STO to WCOJR, Apr. 25, 1896, OFP; STO to WCOJR, n.d. [summer 1896], OFP; MOLC interview.

16. WCO to H. C. Tompkins, Feb. 14, 1896, OFP; Tomkins to WCO, Mar. 4, 1896, OFP; "Personal Data" (WCO/State Constitutional Convention), ca. Oct. 1901, Governors' Vertical Files, ADAH; *MA*, Sept. 10, 1910; WCO, *Biennial Message*, 6–11, 14–24, 28–33, 37–44, 46, 63, 66–69, 71–76 (copy in SUL); Webb, *Two-Party Politics*, 145. On the 1896 election, see Durden, *Climax of Populism*.

17. Unidentified news clipping, Nov. 24, 1896, OFP; Statement Made by WCO and Filed with Governor Joseph F. Johnston, Jan. 11, 1897, WCO Papers. On Governor Johnston, see Rogers et al., *Alabama*, 316–317, 320–323, 334–337. See also Rodabaugh, "Fusion, Confusion, Defeat, and Disfranchisement," 131–153.

18. MOLC interview.

19. At some point after finishing his term as governor, he began publishing regular features in the *Montgomery Advertiser* that combined his notes and compiled fragments of the 15th Alabama's war record. The newspaper items specifically asked readers to criticize and correct anything he was getting wrong. WCO, comp., "More War Records," *MA*, Feb. 27, 1898.

20. [J.] A. E. Reed to WCO, Nov. 20, 1896, reprinted in WCO, *War*, 675.

21. JLC to WCO, Feb. 27, 1897, JLC Papers, BC. Only this incomplete, one-page typewritten draft of the letter, with Chamberlain's handwritten emendations, survives; Oates's recipient copy is not extant.

22. WCO to JLC, Mar. 8, 1897, SCWC. There is at least one page missing from the extant letter. My thanks to Thomas Desjardin for bringing this important Oates letter to my attention. There is no record that Chamberlain replied to this letter from Oates.

23. WCO to F. A. Dearborn, Mar. 28, 1898, OFP. This handwritten version, retained by Oates, was probably used by a secretary to prepare a formal typewritten reply to Dearborn. The letter has been reprinted in full in LaFantasie, ed., "William C. Oates Remembers Little Round Top," 57–63.

24. *Eufaula Tribune*, June 4, 1930. For Oates's own explanation of the causes of the War with Spain, see WCO, *War*, 545–548. A good scholarly treatment of the diplomatic crisis and public frenzy that led to war is Trask, *War with Spain*, 1–59.

25. WCO to William McKinley, May 18, 1898; Petition from Officers of the 2nd Alabama Regiment, May 31, 1898—both ODF.

26. Oath of Office (WCO), June 2, 1898, ODF; Officer's Commission (WCO), June 3, 1898, ODF; Traxel, *1898*, 64–65, 144; Ayers, *Promise of the New South*, 329, 332; Weigley, *American Way of War*, 183–185, 195; Morison, *Oxford History of the American People*, 799–804.

27. WCO to R. A. Alger, June 3, 1898, ODF; WCO, *War*, 555–558. In Oates's opinion, the Spanish-American War was so closely linked to the Civil War—if only in underscoring how the victorious Union and the dastardly Republicans continued to tread on Southern state loyalty—that he included a chapter recounting his unhappy experiences as a volunteer officer in his later book, *The War Between the Union and the Confederacy* (1905).

28. WCO, *War*, 555–560. An unexpurgated copy of Oates's letter to the president, dated July 2, 1898, is in ODF. The excisions in the printed version are minor.

29. WCO to H. C. Corbin, July 8, 1898, ODF; WCO to Corbin, July 19, 1898, ODF; WCO, *War*, 561.

30. Trask, *War with Spain*, 235–244, 257–269, 286–319, 430–431.

31. Nurses' Record of Treatment for WCOJR, July 27–Aug. 30, 1898, OFP; Special Orders No. 177, July 29, 1898, ODF; WCO to William McKinley, Aug. 8, 1898, ODF; WCO, *War*, 561. On Willie's illness and recovery, see also the correspondence from T's sisters, Clara Houston and Carrie Jackson, to her in the Oates Family Papers.

32. WCO to Corbin, Sept. 7, 1898, ODF; WCO to McKinley, Sept. 7, 1898, ODF; WCO to STO, Sept. 16, 1898, OFP; WCO, *War*, 561. On Camp Meade, see Sauers, *Pennsylvania in the Spanish American War*, 45–52. For the surrender of Manila, see Trask, *War with Spain*, 411–422.

33. WCO, *War*, 562; WCO to STO, Sept. 16, 1898, OFP; WCO to WCOJR, Oct. 8, 1898, OFP.

34. WCO, *War*, 562; WCO to WCOJR, May 20, 1899, OFP; WCO to Root, June 2, 1903, OC.

35. *Gettysburg Star and Sentinel*, Sept. 8, 1898; Emmor B. Cope, Annual Report, 1898, Park Archives, GNMP.

36. William M. Robbins, "Monuments at Gettysburg," *Atlanta Constitution*, Oct. 24, 1898. On Robbins, see also J. H. Hill, "A Sketch of the Late Major Robbins," *Gettysburg News*, September 12, 1905.

37. WCO to S. B. M. Young, Oct. 8, 1898, Young Papers; WCO, *War*, 562; Cosmas, *An Army for Empire*, 131. Oates did not admit in his memoirs that he refused to command black troops; he said only that he was unwilling to submit to the replacement of the 202nd New York with the 9th Ohio. On African Americans in the War with Spain, see Fletcher, "Black Volunteers in the Spanish-American War," 48–53.

38. Henry C. Corbin to Samuel B. M. Young, Oct. 12, 1898, Young Papers; Report of Second Corps Movement from Camp Meade to South Carolina and Georgia, Dec. 10, 1898, Young Papers; WCO, *War*, 562–563. On Ames, see Ames, *Adelbert Ames*.

39. WCO, *War*, 562–563. On the Philadelphia Peace Jubilee, see Sauers, *Pennsylvania in the Spanish American War*, 49.

40. WCO, *War*, 564–565.

41. WCO, *War*, 565; Jones, "William Calvin Oates," 343.

42. WCO to McKinley, Jan. 6, 1899, ODF; WCO to STO, Jan. 6, 1899, OFP; WCO, *War*, 565; Discharge of William C. Oates, Special Orders No. 8, Jan. 11, 1899, ODF; Farewell Order to Division, Special Orders No. 15, Jan. 15, 1899, OFP.

43. WCO, Brief for Complainants, J. B. Long et al. vs. Robert Newman et al., ca. Feb. 1, 1899; WCO to WCOJR, May 20, 1899— both OFP.

44. *MA*, Nov. 3, 1899; *Montgomery Journal*, Mar. 22, 1900; unidentified news clipping, ca. 1900, OFP; *Mobile News*, undated news clipping, ca. 1900, OFP.

45. Morgan to WCO, June 23, 1900, OFP.

46. *MA*, June 10, 1900; *Birmingham News*, June 11, 1900; *Anniston Evening Star*, June 11, 1900; Clara T. Houston to STO, June 11, 1900, OFP.

Chapter 13: Stumbling Toward Equality

1. WMR Journal, Jan. 11, 1899, June 12, 1899, June 13, 1899, June 14, 1899, June 17, 1899, June 24, 1900, July 5, 1900, Sept. 13, 1900, SHC; WCO to Marcus J. Wright, June 24, 1899, Marcus J. Wright Papers, HL. A copy of the Robbins Journal is in the GNMP library. I am grateful to Thomas A. Desjardin for bringing the journal and several entries, including these, to my attention. For a complete account of Oates's attempt to raise a monument on Little Round Top to the 15th Alabama, see LaFantasie, "Conflicting Memories of Little Round Top," 106–130.

2. WCOJR to WCO, Sept. 2, 1900; WCO to WCOJR, Sept. 2, 1900—both OFP. For Willie's letters to his mother, see for example, WCO to STO, ca. Aug. 10, Aug. 19, 1900, OFP.

3. WCOJR to WCO, Oct. 13, 1900; WCO to WCOJR, Oct. 23, 1900; WCOJR to WCO, Nov. 17, 1900; WCO to WCOJR, Nov. 25, 1900—all OFP.

4. WCO to WCOJR, Dec. 24, 1900, OFP.

5. McMillan, *Constitutional Development*, 250–258; Fry, *John Tyler Morgan*, 129.

6. Woodward, *Origins of the New South*, 321–349; Hackney, *Populism to Progressivism*, 147–179; Kousser, *Shaping of Southern Politics*, 139–171; Ayers, *Promise of the New South*, 146–149, 283–309.

7. Woodward, *Origins of the New South*, 330–342; Hackney, *Populism to Progressivism*, 147–150; Kousser, *Shaping of Southern Politics*, 130–138, 165–168; Hyman, *The Anti-Redeemers*, 1–9; Webb, *Two-Party Politics*, 1–10. On the Southern Progressives, see Kirby, *Darkness at the Dawning*.

8. McMillan, *Constitutional Development*, 259–260; Hackney, *Populism to Progressivism*, 147–179; Kousser, *Shaping of Southern Politics*, 139–165.

9. Hackney, *Populism to Progressivism*, 149, 217; *Official Proceedings of the Constitutional Convention*, 4:4956–4957.

10. McMillan, *Constitutional Development*, 261–263; *Official Proceedings of the Constitutional Convention*, 1:3–5.

11. On the "Big Mules" and their Populist opponents, see Grafton and Permaloff, *Big Mules and Branchheads*.

12. McMillan, *Constitutional Development*, 264–265.

13. *Official Proceedings of the Constitutional Convention*, 1:7–9; Flynt, "Alabama's Shame," 67–76.

14. McMillan, *Constitutional Development*, 266; *Official Proceedings of the Constitutional Convention*, 1:101; WCO to WCOJR, May 5, 1901, OFP; WCO to STO, May 29, 1901, OFP; "Personal Data" (WCO/State Constitutional Convention), ca. Oct. 1901, Governors' Vertical Files, ADAH. On T's eye ailment, see also WCO to WCOJR, Mar. 16, 1901, OFP.

15. McMillan, *Constitutional Development*, 263, 267–268; *Official Proceedings of the Constitutional Convention*, 1:9–12.

16. WCO, "Importance of Suffrage Question in Framing Alabama's Constitution," *Birmingham Age-Herald*, Jan. 9, 1901.

17. For the ideological basis of Oates's racial views after 1900, see Grantham, "Progressive Movement and the Negro," 461–477; Gaston, *New South Creed*, 136–144, 207–214; Frederickson, *Black Image in the White Mind*, 283–319. C. Vann Woodward places Oates in the "patrician" tradition of racial attitudes, but Oates was not regarded during his own lifetime as a member of the patrician class. See Woodward, *Origins of the New South*, 339.

18. McMillan, *Constitutional Development*, 273–281; *Official Proceedings of the Constitutional Convention*, 1:1257–1266.

19. *Official Proceedings of the Constitutional Convention*, 1:1257–1264.

20. *Official Proceedings of the Constitutional Convention*, 1:1264–1266; Fry, *John Tyler Morgan*, 151.

21. McMillan, *Constitutional Development*, 283–287.

22. *Official Proceedings of the Constitutional Convention*, 3:2786–2787.

23. *Official Proceedings of the Constitutional Convention*, 3:2787–2788.

24. *Official Proceedings of the Constitutional Convention*, 3:2788–2789. On the motives of white Southerners who wished to implement voter restrictions in the South, see Kousser, *Shaping of Southern Politics*, 1–10, 45–83, 238–266. Kousser incorrectly identifies Oates as supporting suffrage restrictions for whites *and* blacks and as a die-hard foe of the 15th Amendment. Kousser, *Shaping of Southern Politics*, 70, 233. What Kousser fails to take into account is Oates's changing attitudes and opinions over time—what might uncharitably be called his political opportunism—and the shift in the political wind that came with the rise of Populism in the 1890s, which caused cataclysmal schisms in the Alabama Democratic Party that lasted well into the first decade of the twentieth century.

25. Cf. Wood, *Creation of the American Republic*, 70–75, 471–518. On the American creed of equality, see Morgan, "Conflict and Consensus," 289–309; Wood, *Radicalism of the American Revolution*, 232–243. For Jefferson's legacy to the concept of equality, see Maier, *American Scripture*, 189–208; for Lincoln's, see Wills, *Lincoln at Gettysburg*, 37–40, 99–120; Peterson, *Lincoln in American Memory*, 383–384.

26. *Official Proceedings of the Constitutional Convention*, 3:2792.

27. *Official Proceedings of the Constitutional Convention*, 3:2793.

28. *Official Proceedings of the Constitutional Convention*, 3:2794–2795.

29. McMillan, *Constitutional Development*, 294–296, 306.

30. *Official Proceedings of the Constitutional Convention*, 4:4440–4442. On Oates's support for black suffrage, see also Hackney, *Populism to Progressivism*, 194–197.

31. On this "reign of terror" waged against blacks after 1890, see Litwack, *Trouble in Mind*, 280–325; Feldman, "Lynching in Alabama," 114–141; Flynt, "Alabama's Shame," 67–76; Tolnay and Beck, *A Festival of Violence*; Williamson, "Wounds Not Scars," 1221–1253; Bundage, ed., *Under Sentence of Death*; Dray, *At the Hands of Persons Unknown*. For an analysis of Southern racial violence, see Cash, *Mind of the South*, 122–123; Hackney, "Southern Violence," 906–925.

32. *Official Proceedings of the Constitutional Convention*, 4:4441.

33. "Personal Data" (WCO/State Constitutional Convention), ca. Oct. 1901, Governors' Vertical Files, ADAH; McMillan, *Constitutional Development*, 349–352; Webb, *Two-Party Politics*, 2.

34. WCOJR to WCO, Aug. 21, 1901; STO to WCO, Aug. 28, 1901; WCOJR to WCO, Aug. 29, 1900[1901]; STO to WCO, Sept. 4, 1901—all OFP.

35. WCOJR to WCO, Sept. 11, 1901; STO to WCO, Sept. 28, Oct. 15, 1901—all OFP; Walker, *Backtracking in Barbour County*, 316.

36. WCOJR to WCO, Oct. 23, 1901; STO to WCO, Oct. 25, Nov. 3, 1901; STO to WCO, Nov. 13, 1901; WCOJR to WCO, Nov. 13, 1901—all OFP.

37. Quoted in Hall, *Magic Mirror*, 212.

38. *McKissack v. McClendon et al.*, 133 Ala. 558; 32 So. 486 (1901 Ala. LEXIS 163); *Pilcher v. United States*, 113 F. 248 (1902 U.S. App. LEXIS 3954); *Nordan v. the State*, 143 Ala. 13; 39 So. 406 (1904 Ala. LEXIS 102); *Bowdon v. Atlantic Coast Line Ry., Co.*, 148 Ala. 29; 41 So. 294 (1906 Ala. LEXIS 277).

39. Hoyt M. Warren, "Twenty One Beats in Henry," *Abbeville Herald*, Nov. 3, 1983; WCOJR to WCO, ca. Dec. 2, 1901, OFP; STO to WCO, Dec. 3, Dec. 10, 1901—both OFP. The precise time when Oates began writing his unpublished autobiography is not known. From internal evidence, he seems to have worked on it after 1900, and, more likely, following his participation in the constitutional convention of 1901.

40. WCO to WMR, Apr. 1, 1902, OC.

41. WCO, *Letters Written by Gen. Wm. C. Oates*, 1–5.

42. WCO, *Letters Written by Gen. Wm. C. Oates*, 5–12.

43. WCO, *Letters Written by Gen. Wm. C. Oates*, 12–19, 20–27, 29–46.

44. WCO, *Letters Written by Gen. Wm. C. Oates*, 47–50. Based on this statement, Oates would have been greatly displeased by the subtitle of this book, which identifies him not by the highest rank earned during his two military services, but by the rank for which he is most famous—his Confederate colonelcy.

45. WCO, *Letters Written by Gen. Wm. C. Oates*, 50–54.

46. WCO to WCOJR, Aug. 22, 1902, OFP.

47. WCO to WMR, Sept. 24, 1902, OC.

48. WMR to JPN, Sept. 27, 1902, OC.

49. WMR to WCO, Oct. 1902, OC; Linenthal, *Sacred Ground*, 109–110; Sauers, "John B. Bachelder," 124–125; Lang, "The 72nd Pennsylvania," 8, 12, 60–61.

50. WCO to WMR, Oct. 2, 1902, OC.

51. WCO, *War*, 432–436; Hoyt M. Warren, "Confederate Veterans Meet—1902," *Abbeville Herald*, June 30, 1983; Resolution Adopted by Reunion of the Survivors

of the 15th Alabama Infantry Regiment, Nov. 12–13, 1902, OC. After the reunion, Willie wrote to Oates: "I am so glad you had a success of the reunion. It must, indeed, have been a quite unique sensation, for you and all the other members of the old regiment to meet together and talk over the old marches and hardships that you endured together. I would have loved to have been at home to have seen it." WCOJR to WCO, Nov. 19, 1902, OFP.

52. WCO to Gettysburg Commissioners, Dec. 9, 1902; WCO to WMR, Dec. 10, 1902; WMR to WCO, Dec. 16, 1902—all OC; WMR Journal, Dec. 16, 1902, SHC.

53. WMR Journal, Oct. 7, Oct. 13, Oct. 25, Nov. 10, Dec. 16, 1902, SHC. On the commissioners and their work, see *Annual Reports of the Gettysburg National Military Park Commission*, 77–82. See also, Unrau, *Administrative History*, 18–23; Linenthal, *Sacred Ground*, 89–126; Harrison, "'Patriotic and Enduring Efforts,'" 53–74.

54. WCOJR to WCO, Dec. 18, 1902; WCOJR to STO, ca. Dec. 22, 1902—both OFP.

Chapter 14: Requiem

1. WCO to JPN, Jan. 21, 1903; JPN to WCO, Feb. 9, 1903; WMR to JPN, Feb. 11, 1903—all OC; WMR to WCO, Feb. 11, 1903, CF; WMR Journal, Feb. 11, 1903, SHC.

2. WCO to WMR, Feb. 14, 1903, OC.

3. WCO to the Secretary of War, ca. Feb. 15, 1903, OC. On Root, see Leopold, *Elihu Root*.

4. JPN to Schofield, Feb. 26, Feb. 27, 1903—both OC. On Nicholson's presence in Gettysburg at this time, see JPN Journal, Feb. 20, 1903, Park Archives, GNMP.

5. Cadet Records (WCOJR), U.S. Military Academy, West Point, N.Y.; WCO to STO and WCO, [Mar. 9, 1903], OFP; WCOJR to STO, ca. Mar. 11, Mar. 21, Apr. 19, Aug. 25, 1903, OFP.

6. WCO to JPN, May 14, 1903; JNP to WCO, May 26, 1903; WCO to Root, June 2, 1903; Schofield to JPN, June 18, 1903—all OC. Copies of Oates's letter to Root may also be found in the Oates Family Papers; CF; and Joshua L. Chamberlain Papers, LC.

7. On Chamberlain after the war, see Trulock, *In the Hands of Providence*, 334–379; Golay, *To Gettysburg and Beyond*, 304–316, 332–343; Smith, *Fanny and Joshua*, 174–352; Pullen, *Joshua Chamberlain*, passim. For the recollections of Chamberlain's secretary, see Catherine T. Smith, "Brunswick's 'Soldier Statesman,'" *Brunswick Times Record*, Sept. 7, 1976. On Chamberlain's historical reputation after the war, see LaFantasie, "Joshua Chamberlain and the American Dream," 31–55.

8. JPN to JLC, Aug. 6, 1903; JLC to JPN, Aug. 14, Aug. 17, 1903; JPN to JLC, Aug. 21, 1903; JPN to Root, Aug. 26, 1903; JLC to JPN, Sept. 2, 1903—all OC. Oates and Chamberlain had first corresponded in 1897. See Chapter 12.

9. Alabama General Assembly, Senate Joint Resolution No. 530, Oct. 9, 1903, CF.

10. JPN to WCO, Oct. 30, 1903; William R. Houghton, "Gettysburg in 1903," *Birmingham Age-Herald*, ca. late Oct. 1903; Houghton to WMR, Nov. 2, 1903; Houghton to JPN, Nov. 14, 1903; Houghton to Root, Nov. 14, 1903; WMR, "Gettysburg in 1903" (typescript), Nov. 18, 1903; WMR to JPN, Nov. 18, 1903;

WMR, "Historic Gettysburg in 1903" (typescript); Robbins, "Gettysburg 1903," *Selma* [Ala.] *Herald*, Nov. 23, 1903; JPN to Root, Dec. 1, 1903; Houghton, "Gettysburg in 1903: A Reply to Maj. Robbins," *Birmingham Age-Herald*, Dec. 13, 1903—all OC; WCO to Root, Dec. 16, 1903, CF; WMR, "Gettysburg National Park" (typescript), ca. Dec. 1903; WMR, "Gettysburg National Park" (broadside), ca. Dec. 1903; WMR to JPN, Jan. 20, 1904—all OC. On the Houghton brothers, see Houghton and Houghton, *Two Boys in the Civil War*.

11. WCO to JPN, Nov. 4, 1903, OC; WCO to WCOJR, Nov. 8, 1903, OFP; WCO to JPN, Nov. 13, 1903, OC.

12. WCO to WCOJR, Dec. 5, Dec. 20, 1903—both OFP; Charles A. Richardson to JPN, Dec. 28, 1903, Jan. 4, 1904; WMR to JPN, Jan. 13, 1904 [misdated 1903]—all OC. For the commission's other work, including road construction and tree plantings, see *Annual Reports of the Gettysburg National Military Park Commission*, 85–101.

13. Root to Gettysburg Commissioners, Jan. 22, 1904, OC; Root to WCO, Jan. 22, 1904, OC; Root to Clayton, Jan. 22, 1904, CF; Root to Charles W. Thompson, Jan. 22, 1904, CF.

14. WCO to WCOJR, Mar. 14, Mar. 26, 1904, both OFP; Wiley to JPN, Mar. 28, 1904; JPN to Wiley, Mar. 31, 1904; Wiley to JPN, Apr. 4, 1904—all OC.

15. WCO to WCOJR, May 3, May 17, 1904—both OFP. On Walter Neale and his publishing house, see Krick, *Bibliography of Neale Books*, esp. iii–xx.

16. Wiley to JPN (telegrams), July 5, July 9, 1904, OC; WMR, July 11 – 12, 1904, SHC; WCO to WMR, July 18, 1904, OC; WCO to JLC, Apr. 14, 1905, OC. The commissioners did not keep detailed records on the construction of Chamberlain Avenue. The road project is mentioned as having been completed in *Annual Reports of the Gettysburg National Military Park Commission*, 77. Sometime in the 1930s, Chamberlain Avenue was torn up and removed, although the roadbed is still clearly visible today. In successive annual reports, the commissioners maintained that they had "taken great care to preserve as nearly as possible [the battlefield] as it was at the time of the battle." See, for instance, ibid., 96.

17. Oates's account of his walk with Robbins on Little Round Top and the Eagle Hotel meeting is in WCO to JLC, Apr. 14, 1905, OC. Only Robbins kept a record of the day spent with Oates. See WMR Journal, July 12, 1904, SHC.

18. WCO to WMR, July 18, 1904, OC, GNMP.

19. WCO to WMR, Sept. 4, 1904; JPN to WCO, Jan. 3, 1905—both OC.

20. WCO to JPN, Mar. 1, 1905, OC.

21. WCO to WCOJR, Feb. 28, 1905, OFP; *Literary Digest*, Apr. 8, 1905; *Memphis Commercial Appeal*, Mar. 6, 1905.

22. *Chicago News*, Mar. 14, 1905; WCO, *War*, xxiii–xxiv.

23. WCO, *War*, 140.

24. WCO, *War*, 132.

25. WCO to WCOJR, Apr. 9, 1905, OFP. There is no indication of how Oates's disagreements with his publisher fared.

26. JLC to JPN, Mar. 16, 1905, OC. Another copy of Chamberlain's letter is in OFP. What were "facts" to Chamberlain were something else to Oates. In mentioning his official report of the engagement on Little Round Top, Chamberlain was citing his after-action report dated July 6, 1863, and published in the *Official Records*. Everyone who consulted the *Official Records*—including Oates and anyone else—would have no reason to doubt the date of Chamberlain's report or its authenticity. Neither Nicholson nor Oates could know that Chamberlain lied

about when he had written the published report. Documents found in the National Archives now reveal that Chamberlain wrote his "official report" not in 1863 but in 1884, after the editors of the *Official Records* informed him that his original report had been lost and asked him to supply a replacement. He sent them the report that was later included in the volume of official reports for the Army of the Potomac at Gettysburg and told the editors that he had reconstructed his original report from memory. Chamberlain had no more written his published report on the march from Gettysburg than Lincoln had written the Gettysburg Address on the back of an envelope. See JLC to George B. Herenden, July 6, 1863 [i.e., ca. Mar. 15, 1884], Records of the War Records Office, Entry 729, Union Battle Reports, RG 94 (Records of the Adjutant General's Office), NA. My thanks to Thomas A. Desjardin for sharing his discovery of Chamberlain's "reconstructed" official report found among the papers of the *Official Records* project.

27. WCO to JLC, Apr. 14, 1905, OC.
28. JLC to WCO, May 18, 1905, OC.
29. JLC to JPN, May 18, 1905; JPN to JLC, May 22, 1905— both OC.
30. JPN to WCO, Oct. 25, 1905; WCO to Lunsford L. Lomax, Oct. 30, 1905; Lomax to WCO, Nov. 3, 1905; Lomax to JPN, Nov. 7, 1905; Lomax to J. F. C. Talbott, Apr. 3, 1906—all OC. On Robbins's death, see Cope's Report, 1905, p. 1, Park Archives, GNMP; JPN Journal, May 2, 1905, Park Archives, GNMP; P. T. Vaughan et al., "Maj. W. M. Robbins," *Confederate Veteran*, 13 (Aug. 1905), 373–374; J. H. Hill, "A Sketch of the Late Major Robbins," *Gettysburg News*, Sept. 12, 1905.
31. Oliver Wendell Holmes, Jr., "A Soldier's Faith," in Posner, ed., *The Essential Holmes*, 80–87. For the context in which Oates and Chamberlain's memories competed with one another, see Blight, *Race and Reunion*, 140–167, 173–209, 264. On Civil War monuments and their meanings, see also Davis, "Empty Eyes, Marble Hand," 2–21; Savage, *Standing Soldiers*.
32. WCOJR to STO, ca. July 18, 1905; WCO to WCOJR, July 26, 1905—both OFP. For the North Montgomery real estate deal, see the numerous deeds, all dated in June 1905, between J. R. Graves Ivy and Oates, OFP.
33. WCOJR to STO, Sept. 25, Oct. 13, ca. Nov. 11, 1905; WCOJR to WCO, ca. Nov. 17, 1905; WCOJR to STO, Dec. 9, 1905— all OFP.
34. Unidentified news clipping, Aug. 9, 1906, OFP; *MA*, Sept. 10, 1910. On the Senate primary of 1906, see Jones, "Political Reform and Party Factionalism," 3–32.
35. For a brief history of the establishment of the Office of the Commissioner for Locating and Marking Confederate Graves, see the introduction to Register of Confederate Soldiers, Sailors, and Citizens Who Died in Federal Prisons and Military Hospitals in the North, 1861–1865, ca. 1912, Records of the Office of the Commissioner for Locating and Marking Confederate Graves, RG 92 (Records of the Office of the Quartermaster General), NA, Microform Publication M918. On Longstreet and Mosby, see Piston, *Lee's Tarnished Lieutenant*, 110–112, 119–123, 142–143; Ramage, *Gray Ghost*, 275, 280–284, 328–330, 336–340.
36. L. Frank Nye to Mrs. Edgar Marburg, Jan. 12, 1909; WCO to Dickinson, Dec. 9, 1909—both CGC2. For Oates's admiration of Nye's work, see WCO to Dickinson, Nov. 1, 1909, CGC2. On Lafayette Franklin Nye, see Blessing and Hoyes Family Homepage (Robert W. Blessing and Ruth Hoyes Blessing), Sev-

enth Generation, www.cyberenet.net/~rubo/d369.htm, accessed July 29, 2001. Nye—who was born in Hummelstown, Pennsylvania, on Apr. 28, 1876—worked for the War Department for forty-one years. He died in Athens, Ohio, on Oct. 11, 1963.

37. Nye to M. M. Smalley, Oct. 17, 1908; WCO to Mrs. S. B. Grommet, Oct. 29, 1908; WCO to Dick Morgan, Dec. 17, 1908; WCO to United Daughters of the Confederacy, Kansas City, Missouri, Apr. 1, 1909; WCO to Dickinson, Apr. 29, 1909—all CGC2.

38. WCO to J. W. C. O'Neal, Feb. 19, Feb. 23, 1909; WCO to Rufus Weaver, Feb. 23, 1909—all CGC2. On the exhumation of Confederate dead at Gettysburg and their reinterment South, see Coco, *A Strange and Blighted Land*, 133–141; Mitchell, *Hollywood Cemetery*, 70–92; Howard, "Journey of the Dead," 62–65; Richter, "Removal of the Confederate Dead," 113–122.

39. Nye to Weaver, Mar. 2, 1909, CGC2; Weaver to WCO, Mar. 3, 1909, OFP.

40. WCO to Superintendent, Hollywood Cemetery, Mar. 5, 1909; WCO to John R. Hooper, Mar. 8, 1909; WCO to Bettie Ellyson, Mar. 8, 1909—all CGC2.

41. WCO to Ellyson, July 26, 1909, CGC2.

42. WCO to WCOJR, Aug. 30, Sept. 2, 1909; WCOJR to Georgia Whiting Saffold, ca. Sept. 3, ca. Sept. 21, 1909—all OFP.

43. WCO to Ellyson, Jan. 19, 1910; Nye to Hooper, Feb. 11, 1910; Ellyson to WCO, Feb. 18, 1910—all CGC3.

44. WCO to Ellyson, Feb. 19, 1910, CGC2; Ellyson to WCO, Feb. 23, 1910, CGC3.

45. WCO to Ellyson, Mar. 8, 1910, CGC2; Nye to John E. Lamb, May 13, 1910, CGC2; Nye to Ellyson, June 28, July 9, 1910, CGC3.

46. Nye to Van Amringe Granite Company, July 14, July 23, Aug. 13, Aug. 30, 1910, CGC2; WCOJR to Mildred Reynolds Saffold, ca. Aug. 16, 1910, OFP; WCOJR to Georgia Whiting Saffold, Aug. 30, 1910 (first letter), OFP.

47. WCO to Georgia Whiting Saffold, Aug. 30, 1910 (second letter), OFP; Mildred Reynolds Saffold to Georgia Whiting Saffold, Sept. 7, 1910, OFP; WCO to Georgia Whiting Saffold, early Sept. 1910, OFP; *Birmingham Ledger*, Sept. 9, 1910; *MA*, Sept. 10, 1910.

48. *Birmingham News*, Sept. 9, 1910; *MA*, Sept. 10, 1910; *MA*, Sept. 11, 1910; *Birmingham Ledger*, Sept. 11, 1910.

49. *MA*, Sept. 11, 1910; *Birmingham Age-Herald*, Sept. 11, 1910.

50. *MA*, Sept. 12, 1910; *Birmingham Ledger*, Sept. 12, 1910; *Birmingham News*, Sept. 12, 1910; *Montgomery Journal*, Sept. 12, 1910.

51. *Jacksonville Metropolis*, Sept. 23, 1910; Last Will and Testament of WCO, July 21, 1909, OFP.

52. WCOJR to Georgia Whiting Saffold, Sept. 11, 1910, OFP.

53. STO Diary, Apr. 26, 1930, OFP.

54. Obituary, *MA*, July 3, 1933; MOLC Interview, OFP; Faulkner, *Requiem for a Nun*, act 1, sc. 3: Gavin Stevens.

SELECTED BIBLIOGRAPHY

Listed below are the manuscript and printed sources used to write this biography. Numerous additional sources of decidedly narrower focus are cited in full in the Notes.

MANUSCRIPT SOURCES

Abbeville Memorial Library, Abbeville, Ala.
    Oates Family Bible
    Old Settlers' Records
Alabama Department of Archives and History, Montgomery, Ala.
    Oates Family Papers
    15th Alabama Regimental File
    4th Alabama Regimental File
    47th Alabama Regimental File
    48th Alabama Regimental File
    Governors' Vertical Files
    Thomas G. Jones Papers
    William C. Oates Administrative Files
    William C. Oates Papers
Dr. Jack Anderson, Enterprise, Ala.
    Treutlen Letter
Auburn University, Auburn, Ala.
    Kolb-Hume Collection
    James Lawrence Pugh Papers
Hawthorne-Longfellow Library, Bowdoin College, Brunswick, Maine
    Joshua Lawrence Chamberlain Papers
    Elisha Coan Manuscript

Simon Schwob Memorial Library, Columbus College, Columbus, Ga.
    Caspar B. Boyd Letters
Robert W. Woodruff Library, Emory University, Atlanta, Ga.
    John Park Family Papers
Gettysburg National Military Park, Gettysburg, Pa.
    Aftermath Files
    Battlefield Burial Sites
    Berdan's Sharpshooters
    Biographical Information: Gettysburg Commissioners
    Joshua Lawrence Chamberlain
    Civilian Accounts
    Confederate Field Hospitals
    Confederate and Union Field Hospitals
    Confederate Interment Sites
    83rd Pennsylvania Regimental File
    Engineers Department Records: Gettysburg Battlefield Commission
    Farnsworth's Charge and Death
    1st Texas Regimental File
    5th Texas Regimental File
    15th Alabama Regimental File
    4th Alabama Regimental File
    44th New York Regimental File
    47th Alabama Regimental File
    Gettysburg Battlefield Memorial Association Minutes
    Gettysburg Newspaper Clippings
    History of Gettysburg National Military Park Files
    Hood's Division
    Hollywood Cemetery
    July 2, 1863 Files
    Little Round Top Files
    20th Maine Regimental File
    John P. Nicholson Journal
    John P. Nicholson Letters
    William C. Oates Correspondence
    16th Michigan Regimental File
    Union Field Hospitals
    Vincent's Brigade File
Huntington Library, San Marino, Calif.
    John P. Nicholson Papers
    Oates Letters
    Marcus J. Wright Papers
Library of Congress, Washington, D.C.
    Joshua L. Chamberlain Papers
Maine Historical Society, Portland, Maine
    Joshua L. Chamberlain Papers, Collection 10
Maine State Archives, Augusta, Maine
    Civil War Correspondence
James S. Schoff Civil War Collection, William L. Clements Library, University of
    Michigan, Ann Arbor
    Norton Letter
    Oates Letter

National Archives, Washington, D.C.
  RG29: Records of the Bureau of the Census
      Tenth U.S. Population Census, 1880, Henry County, Alabama
      Tenth U.S. Population Census, 1880, Polk County, Texas
  RG92: Records of the Office of the Quartermaster General
      Gettysburg National Military Park Battlefield Commission Records
      Records of the Office of the Commissioner for Locating and Marking Con-
          federate Graves
  RG94: Records of Adjutant General's Office
      William C. Oates Document File (War with Spain)
      Records of the War Records Office
  RG109: War Department Collection of Confederate Records (Compiled Ser-
      vice Records)
      Barnett H. Cody
      Isaac B. Feagin
      Alexander A. Lowther
      John A. Oates
      William C. Oates
New Hampshire Historical Society, Concord, N.H.
  John B. Bachelder Papers
New York Public Library
  Ezra Ayers Carman Papers
Southern Historical Collection, University of North Carolina, Chapel Hill
  E. P. Alexander Papers
  William M. Robbins Journal
Charlton Oates Pingel, Enon, Ohio
  Oates Genealogy and Family History Papers
  Ruth Oates, Untitled School Paper on William C. Oates, ca. 1961
Pejepscot Historical Society, Brunswick, Maine
  Joshua Lawrence Chamberlain Papers
  Alice Rains Trulock Collection
Harwell G. Davis Library, Sanford University, Birmingham, Ala.
  Maud McLure Kelly Collection
  William C. Oates Collection
Abbott Spear, Warren, Maine
  Ellis Spear Papers
University of Texas at Arlington, Arlington, Texas
  Clarence P. Denman Papers
U.S. Army Military History Institute, Carlisle Barracks, Pa.
  Robert L. Brake Collection
  Samuel B. M. Young Papers
U.S. Military Academy, West Point, N.Y.
  Cadet Records (William C. Oates, Jr.)

BOOKS, ARTICLES, THESES, AND INTERNET SOURCES

Note: Dates in Internet citations refer to when the sites were consulted, not when they were created.

Aaron, Daniel. *The Unwritten War: American Writers and the Civil War.* New York, 1973.

Adams, Michael C. C. "Men in America: Two Studies in Gender History." *Reviews in American History,* 22 (1994), 14–19.

Alexander, Edward Porter. *Military Memoirs of a Confederate: A Critical Narrative.* New York, 1907.

Alleman, Tillie (Pierce). *At Gettysburg, or, What a Girl Saw and Heard of the Battle.* New York, 1889.

Allen, Theodore W. *The Invention of the White Race: Volume I—Racial Oppression and Social Control.* London, 1994.

Allen, Theodore W. *The Invention of the White Race: Volume II—The Origin of Racial Oppression in Anglo-America.* London, 1997.

Ames, Blanch Ames. *Adelbert Ames: General, Senator, Governor, 1835–1933.* New York, 1964.

Anbinder, Tyler. *Nativism and Slavery: The Northern Know Nothings and the Politics of the 1850s.* New York, 1992.

Annals of the War. Philadelphia, 1879.

Annual Reports of the Gettysburg National Military Park Commission to the Secretary of War, 1893–1904. Washington, D.C., 1905.

Appleby, Joyce. "Reconciliation and the Northern Novelist, 1865–80." *Civil War History,* 10 (1964), 117–129.

Ashworth, John. "The Jacksonian as Leveller." *Journal of American Studies,* 14 (1980), 407–421.

Ashworth, John. *Slavery, Capitalism and Politics in the Antebellum Republic: Volume I—Commerce and Compromise, 1820–1850.* Cambridge and New York, 1995.

Aucoin, Brent Jude. "Thomas Goode Jones and African American Civil Rights in the New South." *Historian,* 60 (1998), 257–271.

Aucoin, Brent Jude. "Thomas Goode Jones, Redeemer and Reformer: The Racial Politics of a Conservative Democrat in Pursuit of a 'New' South." MA thesis, Miami University, 1993.

Ayers, Edward L. "Legacy of Violence." *American Heritage,* 42 (October 1991), 103–109.

Ayers, Edward L. "Narrating the New South." *Journal of Southern History,* 61 (August 1995), 555–566.

Ayers, Edward L. *The Promise of the New South: Life After Reconstruction.* New York, 1992.

Ayers, Edward L. *Vengeance and Justice: Crime and Punishment in the Nineteenth-Century American South.* New York and Oxford, 1984.

Bachelder, John B. "General Farnsworth's Death." *Philadelphia Weekly Times,* December 30, 1882.

Bachelder, John B. *Gettysburg: What to See, and How to See It.* Boston and New York, 1873.

Bailey, Hugh C. "Disaffection in the Alabama Hill Country, 1861." *Civil War History,* 4 (1958), 183–193.

Bardaglio, Peter W. "Rape and the Law in the Old South: 'Calculated to Excite Indignation in Every Heart.'" *Journal of Southern History,* 60 (1994), 749–772.

Bardaglio, Peter W. *Reconstructing the Household: Families, Sex, and the Law in the Nineteenth-Century South*. Chapel Hill and London, 1995.

Barney, William L. *The Secessionist Impulse: Alabama and Mississippi in 1860*. Princeton, N.J., 1974.

Bartley, Numan V. "In Search of the New South: Southern Politics After Reconstruction." *Reviews in American History*, 10 (December 1982), 150–163.

Barton, Michael. "Painful Duties: Art, Character, and Culture in Confederate Letters of Condolence." *Southern Quarterly*, 17 (winter 1979), 123–134.

Barzizo, Decimus et Ultimus. *The Adventures of a Prisoner of War, 1863–1864*, ed. R. Henderson Shuffler. Austin, 1964.

Basler, Roy P., ed. *The Collected Works of Abraham Lincoln*, 8 vols. New Brunswick, N.J., 1953.

"The Battle Field at Gettysburg." *Berks and Schuylkill Journal* (July 18, 1863).

Beaudot, William J. K. "A Civil War Madness." *Milwaukee History*, 20 (1997), 58–69.

Bederman, Gail. *Manliness and Civilization: A Cultural History of Gender and Race in the United States, 1880–1917*. Chicago, 1995.

Belo, A. H. "The Battle of Gettysburg." *Confederate Veteran*, 8 (1900), 165–168.

Benedict, George G. *Vermont in the Civil War*, 2 vols. Burlington, Ver., 1886–1888.

Berends, Kurt O. "'Wholesome Reading Purifies and Elevates the Man': The Religious Military Press in the Confederacy." In Miller et al., eds., *Religion and the American Civil War*. New York and Oxford, 131–166.

Beringer, Richard E, Herman Hattaway, Archer Jones, and William N. Still, Jr. *Why the South Lost the Civil War*. Athens, Ga., 1986.

Berry, Stephen W. II, *All That Makes a Man: Love and Ambition in the Civil War South*. New York and Oxford, 2003.

Bertolini, Vincent J. "Fireside Chastity: The Erotics of Sentimental Bachelorhood in the 1850s." *American Literature*, 68 (1996), 707–737.

Billman, Calvin J., ed. "Joseph M. Ellison: War Letters (1862). *Georgia Historical Quarterly*, 48 (June 1964), 229–238.

Blatt, Martin H., Thomas J. Brown, and Donald Yacovone, eds. *Hope and Glory: Essays on the Legacy of the 54th Massachusetts Regiment*. Amherst, Mass., 2000.

Bleser, Carol K., and Lesley J. Gordon, eds., *Intimate Strategies of the Civil War: Military Commanders and Their Wives*. New York and Oxford, 2001.

Bleser, Carol K., and Frederick Heath. "The Clays of Alabama: The Impact of the Civil War on a Southern Marriage." In Bleser, ed., *In Joy and in Sorrow*, 135–153.

Bleser, Carol K., ed. *In Joy and in Sorrow: Women, Family, and Marriage in the Victorian South, 1830–1900*. New York and Oxford, 1991.

Blight, David W. *Beyond the Battlefield: Race, Memory, and the American Civil War*. Amherst, Mass., 2002.

Blight, David W. "'For Something Beyond the Battlefield': Frederick Douglass and the Struggle for the Memory of the Civil War." *Journal of American History*, 75 (1989), 1156–1178.

Blight, David W. *Race and Reunion: The Civil War in American Memory*. Cambridge, Mass., 2001.

Block, Sharon. "Bringing Rapes to Court." *Common-Place*, 3 (2003), http://common-place.dreamhost.com//vol-03/no-03/block/index.shtml, accessed June 7, 2005.

Block, Sharon. "Rape Without Women: Print Culture and the Politicization of Rape, 1765–1815." *Journal of American History*, 89 (2002), 849–868.

Boatner, Mark Mayo, III. *The Civil War Dictionary.* New York, 1959.

Boritt, Gabor S., ed. *The Gettysburg Nobody Knows.* New York, 1997.

Botsford,Theophilus F. *A Boy in the Civil War*, 7th ed. Montgomery, Ala., 1914.

Boyd, Minnie Clare. *Alabama in the Fifties: A Social Study.* New York, 1951.

Boynton, Henry V. "The Blue and the Gray United." *Southern Historical Society Papers*, 16 (1888), 339–349.

Boynton, Henry V., comp. *Dedication of the Chickamauga and Chattanooga National Military Park, September 18–20, 1895.* Washington, D.C., 1896.

Boynton, Henry V. "The National Military Park." *Century*, 50 (September 1895), 703–708.

Brands, H. W. *The Reckless Decade: America in the 1890s.* New York,1995.

Brannen, Ralph N. Brannen. "John Gill Shorter: War Governor of Alabama, 1861–1863." M.A. thesis, Auburn University, 1956.

Braude, Ann. *Radical Spirits: Spiritualism and Women's Rights in Nineteenth Century America.* Boston, 1989.

Braudy, Leo. *From Chivalry to Terrorism: War and the Changing Nature of Masculinity.* New York, 2003.

Brewer, Willis. *Alabama: Her History, Resources, War Record, and Public Men.* Montgomery, Ala., 1872.

Brown, Richard Maxwell. "Historical Patterns of Violence in America." In Graham and Gurr, eds., *Violence in America*, 1969, 43–80.

Brundage, W. Fitzhugh, ed. *Under the Sentence of Death: Lynching in the South.* Chapel Hill and London, 1997.

Brundage, W. Fitzhugh, ed. *Where These Memories Grow: History, Memory, and Southern Identity.* Chapel Hill and London, 2000.

Bruner, Gary D. "Up Over Big Round Top: The Forgotten 47th Alabama." *Gettysburg Magazine*, 22 (July 2000), 6–22.

Buck, Paul H. *The Road to Reunion, 1865–1900.* Boston, 1937.

Buechler, John. " 'Give 'em the Bayonet'—A Note on Civil War Mythology." In Hubbell, ed., *Battles Lost and Won*, 135–140.

Burnett, Edmund Cody, ed. "Letters of Barnett Hardeman Cody and Others, 1861–1864." *Georgia Historical Quarterly*, 23 (1939), 265–299, 362–380.

Burnett, Edmund Cody, ed. "Some Confederate Letters: Alabama, Georgia, and Tennessee." *Georgia Historical Quarterly*, 21 (June 1937), 188–203.

Busey, John W., and David G. Martin. *Regimental Strengths and Losses at Gettysburg.* Baltimore, 1994.

Bynum, Victoria E. *Unruly Women: The Politics of Social and Sexual Control in the Old South.* Chapel Hill and London, 1992.

Carmichael, Peter S. *Lee's Young Artillerist: William R. J. Pegram.* Charlottesville, Va., 1995.

Carnes, Mark C., and Clyde Griffen, eds. *Meanings for Manhood: Constructions of Masculinity in Victorian America.* Chicago, 1990.

Carp, Benjamin L. "Nations of American Rebels: Understanding Nationalism in Revolutionary North America and the American Civil War." *Civil War History*, 48 (2002), 5–33.

Carroll, Bret E. *Spiritualism in Antebellum America.* Bloomington, Ind., 1997.

Cash, W. J. *The Mind of the South.* New York, 1941.

Cashin, Joan E. *A Family Venture: Men and Women on the Southern Frontier.* New York and Oxford, 1995.

Cashin, Joan E., ed. *The War Was You and Me: Civilians in the American Civil War.* Princeton and Oxford, 2002.

"Casper W. Boyd, Company I, 15th Alabama Infantry, C.S.A.: A Casualty of the Battle of Cross Keys, Virginia—His Last Letters Written Home." *Alabama Historical Quarterly*, 23 (fall and winter 1961), 291–299.

Catton, Bruce. *America Goes to War: The Civil War and Its Meaning in American Culture.* Middletown, Conn., 1958.

Catton, Bruce. "Brother against Brother." *American Heritage*, 12 (April 1961), 4–7, 89–93.

Catton, Bruce. "The Confederate Legend." In *The Confederacy* [Booklet issued by Columbia Records to accompany the recording, "The Confederacy," by Richard Bales and the National Gallery Orchestra (LS 1004)] (New York, ca. 1955), 9–23.

Catton, Bruce. *Glory Road.* Garden City, N.Y., 1952.

Catton, Bruce. "Hayfoot, Strawfoot!" *American Heritage*, 8 (April 1957), 30–37.

Catton, Bruce. *Never Call Retreat.* Garden City, N.Y., 1965.

Catton, Bruce. *A Stillness at Appomattox.* Garden City, N.Y., 1953.

Catton, Bruce. *Terrible Swift Sword.* Garden City, N.Y., 1963.

Censer, Jane Turner. *The Reconstruction of White Southern Womanhood, 1865–1895.* Baton Rouge, 2003.

Chadwick, Bruce. *The Reel Civil War: Mythmaking in American Film.* New York, 2001.

Chamberlain Association of America. *Joshua Lawrence Chamberlain: A Sketch.* N.p., 1906.

Chamberlain, Joshua L. "Address." In *Dedication of the Twentieth Maine Monuments at Gettysburg, Oct. 3, 1889.* Waldoboro, Maine, 1891, 26–31.

Chamberlain, Joshua L. "The Maine 20th at Gettysburg." *The Maine Farmer*, December 28, 1865.

Chamberlain, Joshua L. *The Passing of the Armies.* New York, 1915.

Chamberlain, Joshua L. "The Twentieth Maine at Gettysburg." *Eastern Argus*, December 20, 1865.

Chamberlain, Joshua L. "Through Blood and Fire at Gettysburg." *Hearst's Magazine*, 23 (June 1913), 894–909.

Chase, David W. "Fort Mitchell: An Archaeological Excavation in Russell County, Alabama." *Special Publications of the Alabama Archaeological Society*, Number 1 (February 1974).

Christ, Carol. "Victorian Masculinity and The Angel in the House." In Vicinus, ed., *A Widening Sphere*, 146–162.

Clarke, Augustus P. "The Sixth New York Cavalry, Its Movements and Service at the Battle of Gettysburg." *United Service Magazine*, 16 (1896), 411–415.

Clinton, Catherine. *The Other Civil War: American Women in the Nineteenth Century.* New York, 1984.

Clinton, Catherine. *Plantation Mistress: Woman's World in the Old South.* New York, 1982.

Clinton, Catherine. *Tara Revisited: Women, War, and the Plantation Legend.* New York, 1995.

Clinton, Catherine, and Nina Silber, eds. *Divided Houses: Gender and the Civil War.* New York and Oxford, 1992.

Cobbs, Nicholas Hamner. "The Night the Stars Fell on Alabama." *Alabama Review*, 22 (1969), 147–157.

Coco, Gregory A. *A Strange and Blighted Land: Gettysburg—The Aftermath of a Battle.* Gettysburg, Pa., 1995.

Coco, Gregory A. *A Vast Sea of Misery: A History and Guide to the Union and Confederate Field Hospitals at Gettysburg, July 1–November 20, 1863.* Gettysburg, Pa., 1988.

Coco, Gregory A. *Wasted Valor: The Confederate Dead at Gettysburg.* Gettysburg, Pa., 1990.

Coddington, Edwin B. *The Gettysburg Campaign: A Study in Command.* New York, 1968.

Connerton, Paul. *How Societies Remember.* Cambridge, 1989.

Connelly, Thomas L. *The Marble Man: Robert E. Lee and His Image in American Society.* Baton Rouge, 1977.

Connelly, Thomas L. and Barbara L. Bellows. *God and General Longstreet: Defeat, the Lost Cause, and the Emergence of the New South, 1865–1913.* Baton Rouge, 1982.

Connor, Seldon et al. *In Memoriam: Joshua Lawrence Chamberlain.* Circular No. 5, Whole Number 328, Military Order of the Loyal Legion of the United States, Commandery of the State of Maine. Portland, Maine, 1914.

Cooper, William J., and Thomas E. Terrill. *The American South: A History.* New York, 1991.

Cormier, Steven A. *The Siege of Suffolk: The Forgotten Campaign, April 11–May 4, 1863.* Lynchburg, Va., 1989.

Cosmas, Graham A. *An Army for Empire: The United States Army in the Spanish-American War.* College Station, Tex., 1998.

Court, Carney. "The Contested Image of Nathan Bedford Forrest." *Journal of Southern History,* 67 (2001), 601–630.

Coviello, Peter. "Poe in Love: Pedophilia, Morbidity, and the Logic of Slavery." *ELH,* 70 (autumn 2003), 875–901.

Cox, Karen Lynne. "Women, the Lost Cause, and the New South: The United Daughters of the Confederacy and the Transmission of Confederate Culture, 1894–1919." Ph.D. Dissertation, University of Southern Mississippi, 1997.

Cox, Robert S. *Body and Soul: A Sympathetic History of American Spiritualism.* Charlottesville, Va., 2003.

Cozzens, Peter. *The Shipwreck of Their Hopes: The Battles for Chattanooga.* Urbana and Chicago, 1994.

Cozzens, Peter. *This Terrible Sound: The Battle of Chickamauga.* Urbana and Chicago, 1992.

Craven, Wayne. *The Sculptures at Gettysburg.* N.p., 1982.

Crews, Frances. *The Memory Wars: Freud's Legacy in Dispute.* New York, 1995.

Cullen, Jim. *The Civil War in Popular Culture: A Reusable Past.* Washington, D.C., 1996.

Cunningham, H. H. *Doctors in Gray: The Confederate Medical Service.* Baton Rouge, 1958.

Curran, Thomas J. *Xenophobia and Immigration, 1830–1930.* Boston, 1975.

Curtin, Mary Ellen. *Black Prisoners and Their World: Alabama, 1865–1900.* Charlottesville, Va., 2000.

Cushman, Stephen. *Bloody Promenade: Reflections on a Civil War Battle.* Charlottesville, Va., 1999.

Custer, Andie. "The Kilpatrick-Farnsworth Argument that Never Happened." *Gettysburg Magazine,* 28 (January 2003), 100–116.

Cutrer, Thomas W., ed. *Longstreet's Aide: The Civil War Letters of Thomas J. Goree.* Charlottesville, Va., 1995.

Daniels, Roger. *Guarding the Golden Door: American Immigration Policy and Immigrants Since 1882.* New York, 2004.

David, Thomas J. "Alabama's Reconstruction Representatives in the U.S. Congress, 1868–1878: A Profile." *Alabama Historical Quarterly*, 44 (spring and summer 1982), 32–49.

Davis, Archie K. *Boy Colonel of the Confederacy: The Life and Times of Henry King Burgwyn, Jr.* Chapel Hill and London, 1985.

Davis, Charles S. *The Cotton Kingdom in Alabama*. Montgomery, Ala., 1939.

Davis, Stephen. "Empty Eyes, Marbel Hand: The Confederate Monument and the South." *Journal of Popular Culture*, 16 (1982), 2–21.

Davis, William C. *Battle at Bull Run*. Garden City, N.Y., 1977.

Davis, William C. *The Cause Lost: Myths and Realities of the Confederacy*. Lawrence, Kan., 1996.

Davis, William C. *Gettysburg: The Story Behind the Scenery*. Las Vegas, Nev., 1983.

Davis, William C. *Jefferson Davis: The Man and His Hour*. New York, 1991.

Davis, William C. *Three Roads to the Alamo: The Lives and Fortunes of David Crockett, James Bowie, and William Barret Travis*. New York, 1998.

Davis, William C. *A Way Through the Wilderness: The Natchez Trace and the Civilization of the Southern Frontier*. New York, 1995.

Dawson, Jan C. "The Puritan and the Cavalier: The South's Perception of Contrasting Traditions." *Journal of Southern History*, 44 (November 1978), 597–614.

Dean, Eric T., Jr. *Shook Over Hell: Post-Traumatic Stress, Vietnam, and the Civil War*. Cambridge, Mass., 1997.

Debo, Angie. *The Road to Disappearance: A History of the Creek Indians*. Norman, Okla., 1941.

Degler, Carl N. *At Odds: Women and the Family in America from the Revolution to the Present*. New York, 1980.

Delbanco, Andrew. "To the Gettysburg Station." *New Republic* (Nov. 20, 1989), 31–38.

Delfino, Susanna, and Michelle Gillespie, eds. *Neither Lady nor Slave: Working Women of the Old South*. Chapel Hill and London, 2002.

Demarest, David P., Jr. *"The River Ran Red": Homestead, 1892*. Pittsburgh, 1992.

Denman, Clarence Phillips. *The Secession Movement in Alabama*. Montgomery, Ala., 1933.

Desjardin, Thomas A. *Stand Firm Ye Boys from Maine: The 20th Maine and the Gettysburg Campaign*. Gettysburg, Pa., 1995.

DeVine, Jerry Wayne. "Free Silver and Alabama Politics, 1890–1896." Ph.D. Dissertation, Auburn University, 1980.

Dieterich, H. R., and John P. Willson. "The Dimensions of Political Discourse: Some Observations on the Free Silver Controversy of the 1890's." *Social Studies*, 61 (1970), 13–18.

Donald, David Herbert. "Died of Democracy." In Donald, ed., *Why the North Won the Civil War*, 77–90.

Donald, David Herbert. "The Confederate as a Fighting Man." *Journal of Southern History*, 25 (May 1959), 178–193.

Donald, David Herbert. *Liberty and Union*. Boston, 1978.

Donald, David Herbert. *Lincoln*. New York, 1995.

Donald, David Herbert, ed. *Why the North Won the Civil War*. Baton Rouge, 1960.

Donat, Patricia L. N., and John D'Emilio. "A Feminist Redefinition of Rape and Sexual Assault: Historical Foundations and Change." *Journal of Social Issues*, 48 (1992), 9–22.

Dorman, Lewy. *Party Politics in Alabama from 1850 through 1860.* Publication of the Alabama State Department of Archives and History, Historical and Patriotic Series No. 13. Wetumpka, Ala., 1935.

Dorsey, Bruce. "History of Manhood in America, 1750–1920." *Radical History Review*, No. 64 (1996), 19–30.

Dray, Philip. *At the Hands of Persons Unknown: The Lynching of Black America.* New York, 2002.

Dunkelman, Mark H. *Brothers One and All: Esprit de Corps in a Civil War Regiment.* Baton Rouge, 2004.

Durden, Robert F. *The Climax of Populism: The Election of 1896.* Lexington, Ky., 1965.

Durden, Robert F. *The Gray and the Black: The Confederate Debate on Emancipation.* Baton Rouge, 1972.

Durr, Virginia Foster. *Outside the Magic Circle: The Autobiography of Virginia Foster Durr.* University, Ala., 1985.

Early, John Cabell. "A Southern Boy at Gettysburg." *Civil War Times Illustrated*, 9 (June 1970), 35–48.

Eaton, Clement. *A History of the Southern Confederacy.* New York, 1954.

Eaton, Clement. "The Role of Honor in Southern Society." *Southern Humanities Review*, special issue (1976), 47–58.

Edel, Leon. "The Figure Under the Carpet." In Pachter, ed., *Telling Lives*, 16–24.

Edwards, Laura F. *Gendered Strife and Confusion: The Political Culture of Reconstruction.* Urbana, Ill., 1997.

Edwards, Laura F. *Scarlett Doesn't Live Here Anymore: Southern Women in the Civil War Era.* Chicago, 2000.

Eicher, David J. *The Longest Night: A Military History of the Civil War.* New York, 2001.

Elmore, Thomas L. "A Meteorological and Astronomical Chronology of the Gettysburg Campaign." *Gettysburg Magazine*, 13 (July 1995), 7–21.

Escott, Paul D. *Many Excellent People: Power and Privilege in North Carolina, 1850–1900.* Chapel Hill and London, 1985.

Fahs, Alice. *The Imagined Civil War: Popular Literature of the North and South, 1861–1865.* Chapel Hill and London, 2001.

Fahs, Alice, and Joan Waugh, eds. *The Memory of the Civil War in American Culture.* Chapel Hill and London, 2004.

Faragher, John Mack. *Sugar Creek: Life on the Illinois Prairie.* New Haven, 1988.

Farmer, Hallie. "William Calvin Oates." In Johnson and Malone, eds., *Dictionary of American Biography*, 7:605.

Farmer, Margaret Pace. *One Hundred Fifty Years in Pike County Alabama, 1821–1971.* Anniston, Ala., 1973.

Faulkner, Harold U. *Politics, Reform and Expansionism, 1890–1900.* New York, 1959.

Faulkner, William. *Requiem for a Nun.* London, 1953.

Faust, Drew Gilpin. "Christian Soldiers: The Meaning of Revivalism in the Confederate Army." In Faust, *Southern Stories*, 88–109.

Faust, Drew Gilpin. "The Civil War Soldier and the Art of Dying." *Journal of Southern History*, 47 (February 2001), 3–38.

Faust, Drew Gilpin. *The Creation of Confederate Nationalism: Ideology and Identity in the Civil War South.* Baton Rouge, 1988.

Faust, Drew Gilpin. *James Henry Hammond and the Old South: A Design for Mastery* Baton Rouge and London, 1982.

Faust, Drew Gilpin. *Mothers of Invention: Women of the Slaveholding South in the American Civil War*. Chapel Hill and London, 1996.

Faust, Drew Gilpin. *"A Riddle of Death": Mortality and Meaning in the American Civil War*. Gettysburg, Pa., 1995.

Faust, Drew Gilpin. *Southern Stories: Slaveholders in Peace and War*. Columbia, Mo., 1992.

Faust, Drew Gilpin. "Southern Violence Revisited." *Reviews in American History*, 13 (1985), 205–210.

Fede, Andrew. "Legitimized Violent Slave Abuse in the American South, 1619–1865: A Case Study of Law and Social Change in Six Southern States." *American Journal of Legal History*, 29 (1985), 93–150.

Feldman, Glenn. "Lynching in Alabama, 1889–1921." *Alabama Review*, 48 (1995), 114–141.

Fellman, Michael. *The Making of Robert E. Lee*. New York, 2000.

Fentress, James and Chris Wickham, *Social Memory*. Oxford, 1992.

Fields, Barbara Jeanne. "Ideology and Race in American History." In Kousser and McPherson, eds., *Region, Race, and Reconstruction*, 143–177.

Fields, Barbara Jeanne. "Slavery, Race, and Ideology in the United States of America." *New Left Review*, 181 (1990), 95–118.

Filene, Peter. "Between a Rock and a Soft Place: A Century of American Manhood." *South Atlantic Quarterly*, 84 (1985), 339–355.

Fitzhugh, George. "Disunion in the Union." *De Bow's Review*, 28, old series (January 1860), 1–7.

Fleming, Walter L. "The Buford Expedition to Kansas." *American Historical Review*, 6 (January 1901), 38–48.

Fleming, Walter L. *Civil War and Reconstruction in Alabama*. New York, 1905.

Fletcher, Marvin. "The Black Volunteers in the Spanish-American War." *Military Affairs*, 38 (April 1974), 48–53.

Fletcher, William A. *Rebel Private: Front and Rear—Memoirs of a Confederate Soldier*. New York, 1995.

Flynt, Wayne. "Alabama's Shame: The Historical Origins of the 1901 Constitution," *Alabama Law Review*, 53 (fall 2001), 67–76.

Foner, Eric. *Reconstruction: America's Unfinished Revolution, 1863–1877*. New York, 1988.

Foner, Eric. "Reconstruction Revisited." *Reviews in American History*, 10 (December 1982), 82–100.

Foote, Shelby. *The Civil War, A Narrative: Fredericksburg to Meridian*. New York, 1963.

Ford, Worthington C., ed. *A Cycle of Adams Letters, 1861–1865*. 2 vols. Boston and New York, 1920.

Förster, Stig, and Jörg Nagler, eds. *On the Road to Total War: The American Civil War and the German Wars of Unification, 1861–1871*. Cambridge and Washington, D.C., 1997.

Foster, Gaines M. *Ghosts of the Confederacy: Defeat, the Lost Cause, and the Emergence of the New South*. New York, 1987.

The Fourth Annual Gettysburg Seminar, Gettysburg National Military Park, March 4, 1995. Gettysburg, Pa., 1995.

Fox-Genovese, Elizabeth. "Family and Female Identity in the Antebellum South: Sarah Gayle and Her Family." In Bleser, ed., *In Joy and in Sorrow*, 15–31.

Fox-Genovese, Elizabeth. *Within the Plantation Household: Black and White Women of the Old South*. Chapel Hill and London, 1988.

Frank, Joseph Allan, and George A. Reeves. *"Seeing the Elephant": Raw Recruits at the Battle of Shiloh*. Westport, Conn., 1989.

Frank, Stephen M. *Life with Father: Parenthood and Masculinity in the Nineteenth-Century North*. Baltimore, 1998.

Franklin, John Hope. *The Emancipation Proclamation*. Garden City, N.Y., 1963.

Franklin, John Hope. *The Militant South*. Cambridge, Mass., 1956.

Franklin, John Hope. *Reconstruction After the Civil War*. Chicago, 1961.

Fredrickson, George M. *The Black Image in the White Mind: The Debate on Afro-American Character and Destiny, 1817–1914*. New York, 1971.

Freedman, Estelle B. "Sexuality in Nineteenth-Century America: Behavior, Ideology, and Politics." *Reviews in American History*, 10 (December 1982), 196–215.

Freeman, Douglas Southall. *Lee's Lieutenants: A Study in Command*. 3 vols. New York, 1942–1946.

Fremantle, Arthur J. L. *Three Months in the Southern States*. New York, 1864.

Fry, Joseph A. *John Tyler Morgan and the Search for Southern Autonomy*. Knoxville, Tenn., 1992.

Furgurson, Ernest B. *Ashes of Glory: Richmond at War*. New York, 1996.

Furgurson, Ernest B. *Chancellorsville 1863: The Souls of the Brave*. New York, 1992.

Furgurson, Ernest B. *Not War But Murder: Cold Harbor, 1864*. New York, 2000.

Gallagher, Gary W. *Jubal A. Early, the Lost Cause, and Civil War History: A Persistent Legacy*. Milwaukee, Wisc., 1995.

Gallagher, Gary W. *Lee and His Generals in War and History*. Baton Rouge, 1991.

Gallagher, Gary W. "An Old-Fashioned Soldier in a Modern War? Robert E. Lee as Confederate General." *Civil War History*, 45 (1999), 295–321.

Gallagher, Gary W., ed. *Fighting for the Confederacy: The Personal Recollections of General Edward Porter Alexander*. Chapel Hill and London, 1989.

Gallagher, Gary W., ed. *The Second Day at Gettysburg: Essays on Confederate and Union Leadership*. Kent, Ohio, 1993.

Gallagher, Gary W., ed. *Lee the Soldier*. Lincoln, Neb., 1996.

Gallagher, Gary W., ed. *The Third Day at Gettysburg and Beyond*. Chapel Hill, N.C., 1994.

Gallagher, Gary W., and Alan T. Nolan, eds. *The Myth of the Lost Cause and Civil War History*. Bloomington, Ind., 2000.

Garraty, John A. *The New Commonwealth, 1877–1890*. New York, 1968.

Garraty, John A., and Mark C. Carnes, eds., *American National Biography*, 24 vols. (New York, 2000)

Garrison, Webb, and Cheryl Garrison, eds. *The Encyclopedia of Civil War Usage*. Nashville, Tenn., 2001.

Gaston, Paul M. *The New South Creed: A Study in Southern Mythmaking*. New York, 1970.

"General M. J. Bulger: An Alabama Hero." *Montgomery Advertiser*, October 2, 1898.

Genovese, Eugene D. *Roll, Jordan, Roll: The World the Slaves Made*. New York, 1974.

Genovese, Eugene D. *The Slaveholders' Dilemma: Freedom and Progress in Southern Conservative Thought, 1820–1860*. Charleston, S.C., 1992.

Gerrish, Theodore. *Army Life: A Private's Reminiscences of the War*. Portland, Maine, 1882.

Gettysburg, July 2, 1863: Col. William C. Oates to Colonel Homer R. Stoughton. Abbeville, Ala., 1888.

Gettysburg Discussion Group website, http://www.gdg.org, accessed March 23, 2000.

Gettysburg National Military Park Library website, http://www.nps.gov/gett/library/ libmain.htm, accessed February 10, 2000.

Gienapp, William E. "The Crime Against Sumner: The Caning of Charles Sumner and the Rise of the Republican Party." *Civil War History*, 25 (1979), 218–245.

Glatthaar, Joseph T. "The Common Soldier of the Civil War." In Simon and Stevens, ed., *New Perspectives*, 119–147.

Glatthaar, Joseph T. *The March to the Sea and Beyond: Sherman's Troops in the Savannah and Carolina Campaigns*. New York, 1985.

Glatthaar, Joseph T. *Partners in Command: The Relationships Between Leaders in the Civil War*. New York, 1993.

Glenn, Myra C. "Political Intrigue and Family Conflict during the Civil War: The Beechers of Elmira." *Biography*, 19 (1996), 41–56.

Going, Allen Johnston. *Bourbon Democracy in Alabama, 1874–1890*. University, Ala., 1951.

Golay, Michael. *To Gettysburg and Beyond: The Parallel Lives of Joshua Lawrence Chamberlain and Edward Porter Alexander*. New York, 1994.

Goldfield, David. *Still Fighting the Civil War: The American South and Southern History*. Baton Rouge, 2002.

Goodwyn, Lawrence. *The Populist Moment: A Short History of the Agrarian Movement in America*. New York, 1978.

Gordon, John B. *Reminiscences of the Civil War*. New York, 1904.

Gordon, Leslie J. *General George E. Pickett in Life and Legend*. Chapel Hill and London, 1998.

Gorn, Elliot J. "'Gouge and Bite, Pull Hair and Scratch': The Social Significance of Fighting in the Southern Backcountry." *American Historical Review*, 90 (February 1985), 18–43.

Grafton, Carl, and Anne Permaloff. *Big Mules and Branchheads: James E. Folsom and Political Power in Alabama*. Athens, Ga., 1985.

Graham, Hugh Davis, and Ted Robert Gurr, eds. *Violence in America: Historical and Comparative Perspectives*. A Report to the National Commission on the Causes and Prevention of Violence, June 1969. New York, 1969.

Gramm, Marshall, and Phil Gramm. "The Free Silver Movement in America: A Reinterpretation." *Journal of Economic History*, 64 (2004), 1108–1129.

Granade, Ray. "Violence: An Instrument of Policy in Reconstruction Alabama." *Alabama Historical Quarterly*, 30 (1968), 181–202.

Grant, Ulysses S. *Memoirs and Selected Letters*. Ed. Mary Drake McFeely and William S. McFeely. New York, 1990.

Grantham, Dewey. "The Progressive Movement and the Negro." *South Atlantic Quarterly*, 54 (October 1955), 461–477.

Grasso, Linda. *The Artistry of Anger: Black and White Women's Literature in America, 1820–1860*. Chapel Hill and London, 2002.

Greenberg, Kenneth S. *Honor and Slavery: Lies, Duels, Noses, Masks, Dressing as a Woman, Gifts, Strangers, Humanitarianism, Death, Slave Rebellions, The Proslavery Argument, Baseball, Hunting, and Gambling in the Old South*. Princeton, N.J., 1996.

Greenberg, Kenneth S. *Masters and Statesmen: The Political Culture of American Slavery*. Baltimore, 1985.

Greenberg, Kenneth S. "The Nose, the Lie, and the Duel in the Antebellum South." *American Historical Review*, 95 (1990), 57–74.

Greenberg, Kenneth S. "Why Masters are Slaves." *Reviews in American History*, 11 (September 1983), 386–389.

Griffith, Lucille. *Alabama: A Documentary History to 1900*. University, Ala., 1968.

Grimsley, Mark. *The Hard Hand of War: Union Military Policy Toward Southern Civilians, 1861–1865*. New York and Cambridge, 1995.

Grimsley, Mark. "Modern War / Total War." In Woodworth, ed., *American Civil War*, 379–389.

Grimsley, Mark. "Surviving Military Revolutions: The U.S. Civil War." In Knox and Murray, eds., *Dynamics of Military Revolution*, 74–91.

Griswold, Robert L. *Fatherhood in America: A History*. New York, 1993.

Grossberg, Michael. *Governing the Hearth: Law and the Family in Nineteenth-Century America*. Chapel Hill, 1985.

Grow, Matthew J. "The Shadow of the Civil War: A Historiography of Civil War Memory." *American Nineteenth Century History*, 4 (summer 2003), 77–103.

Guelzo, Allen C. *Lincoln's Emancipation Proclamation: The End of Slavery in America*. New York, 2004.

Hacking, Ian. *Rewriting the Soul: Multiple Personality and the Sciences of Memory*. Princeton, N.J., 1995.

Hackney, Sheldon. *Populism to Progressivism in Alabama*. Princeton, N.J., 1969.

Hackney, Sheldon. "Southern Violence." *American Historical Review*, 74 (February 1969), 906–925.

Halbwachs, Maurice. *The Collective Memory*. Trans. Francis and Vida Ditter. New York, 1980.

Hale, Grace Elizabeth. *Making Whiteness: The Culture of Segregation in the South, 1890–1940*. New York, 1998.

Hall, Jeffrey C. *The Stand of the U.S. Army at Gettysburg*. Bloomington, Ind., 2003.

Hall, Kermit L. *The Magic Mirror: Law in American History*. New York and Oxford, 1989.

Hamlin, Percy G. *"Old Bald Head" (General R. S. Ewell)*. Strasburg, Va., 1940.

Harlan, Louis R. *Booker T. Washington: The Making of a Black Leader, 1856–1901*. Oxford and New York, 1972.

Harris, Carl V. "Right Fork or Left Fork? The Section-Party Alignment of Southern Democrats in Congress, 1873–1897." *Journal of Southern History*, 42 (November 1976), 471–508.

Harrison, Kathleen Georg. "'A Fitting and Expressive Memorial': The Development of Gettysburg National Military Park," January 1988 (revised 1994), History of the Gettysburg National Military Park File, GNMP.

Harrison, Kathleen Georg. "'Patriotic and Enduring Efforts': An Introduction to the Gettysburg Battlefield Commission." In *The Fourth Annual Gettysburg Seminar*, 53–74.

Hartwig, D. Scott. "Robert E. Lee and the Maryland Campaign." In Gallagher, ed., *Lee the Soldier*, 1996, 331–355.

Harwell, Richard B., ed. *The Confederate Reader*. New York, 1958.

Hassler, William Woods. *Colonel John Pelham: Lee's Boy Artillerist*. Chapel Hill, 1960.

Hegel, Georg Wilhelm Friedrich. *The Phenomenology of Mind*. Trans. J. B. Baillie. New York, 1967.

Henderson, G. F. R. *Stonewall Jackson and the American Civil War*. 2 vols. London, 1898.

Hennessey, Melinda M. "Reconstruction Politics and the Military: The Eufaula Riot of 1874." *Alabama Historical Quarterly*, 38 (summer 1976), 112–125.

Hennessy, John J. *Return to Bull Run: The Campaign and Battle of Second Manassas*. New York, 1993.

Hess, Earl J. *The Union Soldier in Battle: Enduring the Ordeal of Combat.* Lawrence, Kan., 1997.

Higham, John. *Strangers in the Land: Patterns in American Nativism, 1860–1925.* 2nd ed. New Brunswick, N.J., 1988.

Hill, J. H. "A Sketch of the Late Major Robbins." *Gettysburg News*, September 12, 1905.

Hoffert, Sylvia D. *A History of Gender in America: Essays, Documents, and Articles.* Upper Saddle River, N.J., 2003.

Hofstadter, Richard, and Michael Wallace, eds. *American Violence: A Documentary History.* New York, 1970.

Hoganson, Kristin. *Fighting for American Manhood: How Gender Politics Provoked the Spanish-American and Philippine-American Wars.* New Haven, 2000.

Hoke, Jacob. *The Great Invasion of 1863.* Dayton, Ohio, 1887.

Hood, John Bell. *Advance and Retreat.* New Orleans, 1880.

Hoole, William Stanley, ed. *Historical Sketches of the Forty-Seventh Alabama Infantry Regiment, C.S.A.* University, Ala., 1982.

Horwitz, Tony. *Confederates in the Attic: Dispatches from the Unfinished Civil War.* New York, 1999.

Houghton, Mitchell. *From the Beginning Until Now.* Montgomery, Ala., 1914.

Houghton, W. R., and M. B. Houghton. *Two Boys in the Civil War and After.* Montgomery, Ala., 1912.

Howard, Thomas W. "Journey of the Dead." *America's Civil War*, 7 (September 1994), 62–65.

Hubbell, John T., ed. *Battles Lost and Won: Essays from Civil War History.* Westport, Conn., 1975.

Hunter, Jane H. *How Young Ladies Became Girls: The Victorian Origins of American Girlhood.* New Haven, 2002.

Hutton, Patrick. "Recent Scholarship on Memory and History." *The History Teacher*, 33 (August 2000), 533–548.

Hyman, Michael R. *The Anti-Redeemers: Hill-Country Political Dissenters in the Lower South from Redemption to Populism.* Baton Rouge and London, 1990.

Jacobson, Matthew Frye. *Whiteness of a Different Color: European Immigrants and the Alchemy of Race.* Cambridge, Mass., 1998.

Janda, Lance. "Shutting the Gates of Mercy: The American Origins of Total War, 1860–1880." *Journal of Military History*, 59 (1995), 7–26.

Jimerson, Randall C. *The Private Civil War: Popular Thought During the Sectional Conflict.* Baton Rouge, La., 1988.

Johnson, Allan, and Dumas Malone, eds. *Dictionary of American Biography.* 21 vols. New York, 1928–1936.

Johnson, Michael P. "Planters and Patriarchy: Charleston, 1800–1860." *Journal of Southern History*, 46 (February 1980), 45–72.

Johnson, Michael P. *Toward a Patriarchal Republic: The Secession of Georgia.* Baton Rouge and London, 1977.

Johnson, Robert U., and Clarence C. Buel, eds. *Battles and Leaders of the Civil War.* 4 vols. New York, 1884–1889.

Johnson, Rossiter, and John Howard Brown, eds. *The Twentieth Century Biographical Dictionary of Notable Americans.* 10 vols. Boston, 1904.

Johnson, Vicki Vaughn. *The Men and the Vision of the Southern Commercial Conventions, 1845–1871.* Columbia, Mo., 1992.

Johnson, Walter. *Soul by Soul: Life Inside the Antebellum Slave Market.* Cambridge, Mass., 1999.

Jones, Allen W. "Political Reform and Party Factionalism in the Deep South: Alabama's 'Dead Shoes' Senatorial Primary of 1906." *Alabama Review*, 26 (January 1973), 3–32.

Jones, J. William Jones. *Christ in the Camp: Or, Religion in Lee's Army*. Richmond, 1887.

Jones, Kenneth W., comp. "Muster Rolls: 15th Alabama Infantry Regiment." http://www.tarleton.edu/~kjones/15muster.html, accessed March 19, 2000.

Jones, Kenneth W. comp. "The 15th Alabama Volunteer Infantry Regiment." http://www.tarleton.edu/activities/pages/facultypages/jones/#4, accessed December 28, 1996.

Jones, Walter B. "William Calvin Oates." *Alabama Historical Quarterly*, 7 (fall 1945), 338–348.

Jordan, William C. *Some Events and Incidents During the Civil War*. Montgomery, Ala., 1909.

Judson, Amos M. *A History of the Eighty-Third Regiment, Pennsylvania Volunteers*. Eire, Pa., 1865.

Kammen, Michael. "Frames of Remembrance: The Dynamics of Collective Memory." *History and Theory*, 34 (1995), 245–261.

Kammen, Michael. *Mystic Chords of Memory: The Transformation of Tradition in American Culture*. New York, 1991.

Kaplan, Edward S., and Thomas W. Ryley. *Prelude to Trade Wars: American Tariff Policy, 1890–1922*. Westport, Conn., 1994.

Kaser, James A. *At the Bivouac of Memory: History, Politics, and the Battle of Chickamauga*. New York, 1996.

Kaufmann, Eric. "American Exceptionalism Reconsidered: Anglo-Saxon Ethnogenesis in the 'Universal' Nation, 1776–1850." *Journal of American Studies*, 33 (1999), 437–457.

Kenny, Michael G. "A Place for Memory: The Interface between Individual and Collective History." *Comparative Studies in Society and History*, 41 (July 1999), 420–437.

Ketchum, Richard M. "Memory as History. *American Heritage*, 42 (November 1991), 142–148.

Kierner, Cynthia A. *Beyond the Household: Women's Place in the Early South, 1700–1835*. Ithaca, N.Y., 1998.

Kimmel, Michael S. *Manhood in America: A Cultural History*. New York, 1996.

Kincaid, James R. *Child-Loving: The Erotic Child and Victorian Culture*. New York, 1992.

Kinsel, Amy J. "American Identity, National Reconciliation, and the Memory of the Civil War." *Proteus*, 17 (2000), 5–14.

Kinsel, Amy J. "'From These Honored Dead': Gettysburg in American Culture, 1863–1930." Ph.D. Dissertation, Cornell University, 1992.

Kinsel, Amy J. "From Turning Point to Peace Memorial: A Cultural Legacy." In Boritt, ed., *The Gettysburg Nobody Knows*, 203–222.

Kirby, Jack Temple. *Darkness at the Dawning: Race and Reform in the Progressive South*. Philadelphia, 1972.

Klein, Maury. *Edward Porter Alexander*. Athens, Ga., 1971.

Knobel, Dale T. *"America for the Americans": The Nativist Movement in the United States*. New York, 1996.

Knox, MacGregor, and Williamson Murray, eds. *The Dynamics of Military Revolution, 1300–2050*. Cambridge and New York, 2001.

Kousser, J. Morgan. *The Shaping of Southern Politics: Suffrage Restriction and the Establishment of the One-Party South, 1880–1910*. New Haven and London, 1974.

Kousser, J. Morgan, and James M. McPherson, eds. *Region, Race, and Reconstruction: Essays in Honor of C. Vann Woodward*. New York, 1982.

Krause, Susan. "'Infamous Outrage and Prompt Retribution': The Case of *People v. Delny*." In Stowell, ed., *In Tender Consideration*, 182–203.

Krick, Robert K. *A Bibliography of Neale Books and History of the Neale Publishing Company*. Dayton, Oh., 1977.

Krick, Robert K. *Conquering the Valley: Stonewall Jackson at Port Republic*. New York, 1996.

Krick, Robert K. "Introduction." In William C. Oates, *The War Between the Union and the Confederacy and Its Lost Opportunities*. Reprint ed. Dayton, Ohio, 1985. Unpaginated front matter.

Krick, Robert K. *Lee's Colonels: A Biographical Register of the Field Officers of the Army of Northern Virginia*. Dayton, Ohio, 1979.

Krick, Robert K. *Stonewall Jackson at Cedar Mountain*. Chapel Hill, N.C., 1990.

Kross, Gary. "Farnsworth's Charge." *Blue and Gray Magazine*, 13(February 1996), 44–53.

Kurtz, Stephen G., and James H. Hutson, eds. *Essays on the American Revolution*. Chapel Hill, N.C., 1973.

Kushner, Howard I. *Self-Destruction in the Promised Land: A Psychocultural Biology of American Suicide*. Brunswick, N.J., 1989.

Kushner, Howard I. "The Suicide of Meriwether Lewis: A Psychoanalytic Inquiry." *William and Mary Quarterly*, 38 (1981), 464–481.

Ladd, David L., and Audrey J. Ladd, eds. *The Bachelder Papers*. 3 vols. Dayton, Ohio, 1994–1995.

LaFantasie, Glenn W. "Becoming Joshua Lawrence Chamberlain." *North & South*, 5 (February 2002), 29–38.

LaFantasie, Glenn W. "Conflicting Memories of Little Round Top." *Columbiad*, 3 (spring 1999), 106–130.

LaFantasie, Glenn W. "Decimated by Disease." *MHQ: The Quarterly Journal of Military History*, 16 (spring 2004), 86–92.

LaFantasie, Glenn W. "Joshua Chamberlain and the American Dream." In Boritt, ed., *The Gettysburg Nobody Knows*, 31–55.

LaFantasie, Glenn W. "The Other Man [on Little Round Top]." *MHQ: The Quarterly Journal of Military History*, 5 (summer 1993), 69–75.

LaFantasie, Glenn W. "The Classic Regimental Bookshelf." *Civil War Regiments*, 2 (1992), 346–350.

LaFantasie, Glenn W. *Twilight at Little Round Top*. Hoboken, N.J., 2005.

LaFantasie, Glenn W. "William C. Oates and the Death of General Elon Farnsworth." *North & South*, 8 (January 2005), 48–55.

LaFantasie, Glenn W., ed. *Gettysburg: Colonel William C. Oates and Lieutenant Frank A. Haskell*. New York, 1992.

LaFantasie, Glenn W. ed. "William C. Oates Remembers Little Round Top." *Gettysburg Magazine*, 21 (July 1999), 57–63.

Laine, J. Gary, and Morris M. Penny. *Law's Alabama Brigade in the War Between the Union and the Confederacy*. Shippensburg, Pa., 1996.

Lang, Dan. "The 72nd Pennsylvania Fought Two Battles at Gettysburg—A Quarter of a Century Apart." *America's Civil War*, 5 (1992), 8, 12, 60–61.

Lasswell, Mary, ed. *Rags and Hope: The Recollections of Val C. Giles, Four Years with Hood's Brigade, Fourth Texas Infantry, 1861–1865*. New York, 1961.

Latschar, John. "History and Memory: Challenges of Interpreting the Civil War." *Proteus*, 19 (2002), 59–64.

Law, Evander M. "The Struggle for 'Round Top.'" In Johnson and Buel, eds., *Battles and Leaders*, 3:318–330.

Lee, Ronald F. *The Origin and Evolution of the National Military Park Idea*. Washington, D.C., 1973.

Leon, Warren, and Roy Rosenzweig, eds. *History Museums in the United States: A Critical Assessment*. Urbana and Chicago, 1989.

Leopold, Richard W. *Elihu Root and the Conservative Tradition*. Boston, 1954.

Linderman, Gerald. *Embattled Courage: The Experience of Combat in the American Civil War*. New York, 1987.

Linenthal, Edward Tabor. *Sacred Ground: Americans and Their Battlefields*. 2nd ed. Urbana and Chicago, 1993.

Littmann, Mark. *The Heavens on Fire: The Great Leonid Meteor Showers*. New York and Cambridge, 1998.

Litwack, Leon F. *Trouble in Mind: Black Southerners in the Age of Jim Crow*. New York, 1998.

Long, Durwood. "Unanimity and Disloyalty in Secessionist Alabama." *Civil War History*, 11 (1965), 257–273.

Long, E. B., with Barbara Long, *The Civil War Day by Day: An Almanac, 1861–1865*. Garden City, N.Y., 1971.

Long, Jeff. *Duel of Eagles: The Mexican and U.S. Fight for the Alamo*. New York, 1990.

Longacre, Edward G. *The Cavalry at Gettysburg: A Tactical Study of Mounted Operations During the Civil War's Pivotal Campaign, 9 June–14 July 1863*. Rutherford, N.J., 1986.

Longacre, Edward G. *Joshua Chamberlain: The Soldier and the Man*. Conshohocken, Penn., 1999.

Longstreet, James. *From Manassas to Appomattox*. Philadelphia, 1896.

Logue, Larry M. "Who Joined the Confederate Army? Soldiers, Civilians, and Communities in Mississippi." *Journal of Social History*, 26 (spring 1993), 611–623.

Lystra, Karen. *Searching the Heart: Women, Men, and Romantic Love in Nineteenth-Century America*. New York and Oxford, 1989.

McCarthy, Carlton. *Detailed Minutiae of Soldier Life in the Army of Northern Virginia, 1861–1865*. Richmond, 1882.

McClendon, William A. *Recollections of War Times By An Old Veteran While Under Stonewall Jackson and Lieutenant General James Longstreet*. Montgomery, Ala., 1909.

McConnell, Stuart. *Glorious Contentment: The Grand Army of the Republic, 1865–1900*. Chapel Hill and London, 1992.

McCurry, Stephanie. *Masters of Small Worlds: Yeoman Households, Gender Relations, and the Political Culture of the Antebellum South Carolina Low Country*. New York, 1995.

McCurry, Stephanie. "The Politics of Yeoman Households in South Carolina." In Clinton and Silber, eds., *Divided Houses*, 22–38.

McCurry, Stephanie. "The Two Faces of Republicanism: Gender and Proslavery Politics in Antebellum South Carolina." *Journal of American History*, 78 (March 1992), 1245–1264.

McDonald, Archie. *William Barret Travis: A Biography*. Austin, Tex., 1976.

McKean, Keith F. "Southern Patriarch: A Portrait." *Virginia Quarterly Review*, 36 (1960), 376–389.

McLaughlin, Glory. "'A Mixture of Race and Reform': The Memory of the Civil War in the Alabama Legal Mind." *Alabama Law Review*, 56 (fall 2004), 284–309.

McLoughlin, William G. *Revivals, Awakenings, and Reform: An Essay on Religion and Social Change in America, 1607–1977.* Chicago, 1978.

McMath, Robert, Jr. *Populist Vanguard: A History of the Southern Farmers' Alliance.* Chapel Hill, 1975.

McMillan, Malcolm C. *Constitutional Development in Alabama, 1798–1901.* Chapel Hill, N.C., 1955.

McMurry, Richard M. *John Bell Hood and the War for Southern Independence.* Lexington, Ky., 1982

McPherson, James M. *Abraham Lincoln and the Second American Revolution.* New York and Oxford, 1990.

McPherson, James M. *Battle Cry of Freedom: The Civil War Era.* New York and Oxford, 1988.

McPherson, James M. *Drawn with the Sword: Reflections on the American Civil War.* New York and Oxford, 1996.

McPherson, James M. *For Cause and Comrades: Why Men Fought in the Civil War.* New York and Oxford, 1997.

McPherson, James M. "From Limited to Total War, 1861–1865." In McPherson, *Drawn with the Sword,* 66–86.

McPherson, James M. "Liberty and Power in the Second American Revolution." In McPherson, *Abraham Lincoln,* 131–152.

McPherson, James M. *Ordeal by Fire: The Civil War and Reconstruction.* 3rd ed. New York, 1992.

McPherson, James M. *What They Fought For, 1861–1865.* Baton Rouge and London, 1994.

McWhiney, Grady, and Perry D. Jamieson. *Attack and Die: Civil War Military Tactics and the Southern Heritage.* Tuscaloosa, Ala., 1982.

Maier, Pauline. *American Scripture: Making the Declaration of Independence.* New York, 1997.

Maine at Gettysburg: Report of the Maine Commissioners. Portland, Maine, 1898.

Mangan, J. A. "Men, Masculinity, and Sexuality: Some Recent Literature." *Journal of the History of Sexuality,* 3 (1992), 303–313.

Mangan, J. A., and James Walvin, eds. *Manliness and Morality: Middle-class Masculinity in Britain and America, 1800–1940.* New York, 1987.

Marcot, Roy. "Berdan Sharpshooters at Gettysburg." *Gettysburg Magazine,* 1 (July 1989), 35–40.

Martin, Bessie. *Desertion of Alabama Troops from the Confederate Army: A Study in Sectionalism.* New York, 1932.

Martin, David G. *Confederate Monuments at Gettysburg.* Conshohocken, Pa., 1995.

Mathis, Ray. *In the Land of the Living: Wartime Letters by Confederates from the Chattahoochee Valley of Alabama and Georgia.* Troy, Ala., 1981.

Matter, William D. *If It Takes All Summer: The Battle of Spotsylvania.* Chapel Hill, N.C., 1968.

May, Robert E. "Dixie's Martial Image: A Continuing Historiographical Enigma." *Historian,* 40 (1978), 213–234.

Mayfield, John. "The Soul of a Man! William Gilmore Simms and the Myths of Southern Manhood." *Journal of the Early Republic,* 15 (1995), 477–500.

Memorial Record of Alabama. 2 vols. Madison, Wis., 1893.

Merton, Robert K. "The Unanticipated Consequences of Purposive Social Action." *American Sociological Review,* 1 (December 1936), 894–904.

Miers, Earl Schenck, and Richard A. Brown, eds. *Gettysburg.* New Brunswick, N.J., 1948.

Military Order of the Loyal Legion of the United States, Commandery of the State of Pennsylvania. *In Memoriam: John Page Nicholson*. Philadelphia, 1922.

Miller, Randall M., Harry S. Stout, and Charles Reagan Wilson, eds. *Religion and the American Civil War*. New York and Oxford, 1998.

Miller, Samuel, ed. *Dedication of the Twentieth Maine Monuments at Gettysburg, October 3, 1889*. Waldoboro, Me., 1891.

Mitchell, Mary H. *Hollywood Cemetery: The History of a Southern Shrine* (Richmond, 1985).

Mitchell, Reid. "Christian Soldiers? Perfecting the Confederacy." In Miller et al., eds., *Religion and the Civil War*, 297–309.

Mitchell, Reid. *Civil War Soldiers*. New York, 1988.

Mitchell, Reid. "The Infantryman in Combat." *North & South*, 4 (August 2001), 12–21.

Mitchell, Reid. "'Our Prison System, Supposing We Had Any': The Confederate and Union Prison Systems." In Förster and Nagler, eds., *On the Road to Total War*, 565–585.

Mitchell, Reid. *The Vacant Chair: The Northern Soldier Leaves Home*. New York and Oxford, 1993.

Mitchell, Stewart. "Horatio Seymour." In Johnson and Malone, eds., *Dictionary of American Biography*, 9:6–9.

Monahan, Thomas P. *The Pattern of Age at Marriage in the United States*. Philadelphia, 1951.

Monaghan, Jay. "Civil War Slang and Humor." *Civil War History*, 3 (June 1957), 125–133.

Moore, Albert Burton. *History of Alabama*. University, Ala., 1934.

Moore, James Tice. "Redeemers Reconsidered: Change and Continuity in the Democratic South, 1870–1900." *Journal of Southern History*, 44 (August 1978), 357–378.

Morgan, Edmund S. *American Slavery, American Freedom: The Ordeal of Colonial Virginia*. New York, 1975.

Morgan, Edmund S. "Conflict and Consensus." In Kurtz and Hutson, eds., *Essays on the American Revolution*, 289–309.

Morgan, James. "Who Saved Little Round Top?" http://www:gdg.org/flash.html, accessed Jan. 16, 2003.

Morison, Samuel Eliot. *The Oxford History of the American People*. New York, 1965.

Muffley, Joseph W. ed. *The Story of One Regiment: A History of the 148th Pennsylvania Vols*. Des Moines, 1904.

Mumford, Lewis. "The Task of Modern Biography." *The English Journal*, 23 (January 1934), 1–9.

Murrell, Amy E. "Union Father, Rebel Son: Families and the Question of Civil War Loyalty." In Cashin, ed., *The War was You and Me*, 358–391.

Nash, Eugene A. *A History of the Forty-Fourth Regiment New York Volunteer Infantry in the Civil War, 1861–1865*. Chicago, 1911.

The National Cyclopedia of American Biography. 80+ vols. New York, 1892– .

Neely, Mark E., Jr. "Was the Civil War a Total War?" *Civil War History*, 37 (1991), 5–28.

Neely, Mark E., Jr. "'Civilized Belligerents': Abraham Lincoln and the Idea of 'Total War.'" In Simon and Stevens, ed., *New Perspectives*, 3–23.

Nevins, Allan. *Grover Cleveland: A Study in Courage*. New York, 1933.

Nolan, Alan T. *Lee Considered: General Robert E. Lee and Civil War History*. Chapel Hill and London, 1991.

Nolan, Terence Hunt. "William Henry Skaggs and the Reform Challenge of 1894." *Alabama History Quarterly*, 33 (1971), 116–134.

Norton, Herman. "Revivalism in the Confederate Armies." *Civil War History*, 6 (December 1960), 410–424.

Norton, Oliver W. *The Attack and Defense of Little Round Top*. New York, 1913.

Nye, Russel Blaine. *Society and Culture in America, 1830–1860*. New York, 1974.

Nye, Wilbur S. *Here Come the Rebels!* Baton Rouge, 1965.

Oakes, James. *The Ruling Race: A History of American Slaveholders*. New York, 1982.

Oates, Stephen B. *The Fires of Jubilee: Nat Turner's Fierce Rebellion*. New York, 1975.

Oates, William C. *Biennial Message of Hon. William C. Oates, Governor of Alabama, 1896*. [Montgomery, Ala., 1896].

Oates, William C. "Gettysburg—The Battle on the Right." *Southern Historical Society Papers*, 6 (1878), 172–182.

Oates, William C. "The Homestead Strike." *North American Review*, 155 (1892), 355–364.

[Oates, William C.]. *Inaugural Address and First Message of William C. Oates, Governor of Alabama to the General Assembly of Alabama*. [Montgomery, 1894].

Oates, William C. "Industrial Development of the South." *North American Review*, 161 (1895), 566–574.

Oates, William C. *Letters Written by Gen. Wm. C. Oates While Traveling in Europe, 1902*. N.p., n.d.

Oates, William C. *Speech of Governor William C. Oates of Alabama Delivered at Chattanooga, Tenn., September 20th, 1895, on the Battles of Chickamauga and Chattanooga*. Montgomery, Ala., 1895.

Oates, William C. *The War Between the Union and the Confederacy and Its Lost Opportunities*. New York and Washington, D.C., 1905.

Official Proceedings of the Constitutional Convention of the State of Alabama, May 21st, 1901, to September 3rd, 1901. 4 vols. Wetumpka, Ala., 1940.

Olick, Jeffrey K., and Joyce Robbins. "Social Memory Studies: From 'Collective Memory' to the Historical Sociology of Mnemonic Practices." *Annual Review of Sociology*, 24 (1998), 105–140.

Olmsted, Frederick Law. *A Journey in the Seaboard Slave States in the Years 1853–1854*. 2 vols. New York and London, 1904.

Onwood, Maurice. "Impulse and Honor: The Place of Slave and Master in the Ideology of Planterdom." *Plantation Society in the Americas*, 1 (1979), 31–56.

O'Reilly, Francis A. *The Fredericksburg Campaign: Winter War on the Rappahannock*. Baton Rouge, 2003

O'Reilly, Frank A. *"Stonewall Jackson" at Fredericksburg: The Battle of Prospect Hill, December 13, 1862*. 2nd ed. Lynchburg, Va., 1993.

Osterweis, Rollin G. *The Myth of the Lost Cause, 1865–1900*. Hamden, Conn., 1973.

Owen, T. M. *History of Alabama and Dictionary of Alabama Biography*. 4 vols. Chicago, 1921.

Owens, Harry P. "The Eufaula Riot of 1874." *Alabama Review*, 16 (1963), 224–238.

Owsley, Frank Lawrence. *Plain Folk of the Old South*. Baton Rouge, La., 1949.

Pachter, Marc., ed. *Telling Lives: The Biographer's Art*. Philadelphia, 1985.

Palmer, Bruce. *"Man over Money": The Southern Populist Critique of American Capitalism*. Baton Rouge, 1980.

Pardoe, Rosemary. "John A. Oates: 'No Brothers Loved Each Other Better.'" http://www.users.globalnet.co.uk/~pardos/JohnOates.html, accessed March 17, 2000.

Parsons, H. C. "Farnsworth's Charge and Death." In Johnson and Buel, eds., *Battles and Leaders*, 3:393–396.

Parsons, M. B. "Violence and Caste in Southern Justice." *South Atlantic Quarterly*, 60 (1961), 455–468.

Patterson, Gerard A. *Debris of Battle: The Wounded of Gettysburg*. Mechanicsburg, Pa., 1997.

Patterson, John S. "From Battle Ground to Pleasure Ground: Gettysburg as a Historic Site." In Leon and Rosenzweig, eds., *History Museums in the United States*, 128–157.

Patterson, John S. "A Patriotic Landscape: Gettysburg, 1863–1913." *Prospects*, 7 (1982), 315–333.

Penny, Morris M., and J. Gary Laine. *Struggle for the Round Tops: Law's Alabama Brigade at the Battle of Gettysburg, July 2–3, 1863*. Shippensburg, Pa., 1999.

Perkins, Bradford. "Impressions of Wartime." *Journal of American History*, 77 (September 1990), 563–568.

Perman, Michael. *Struggle for Mastery: Disfranchisement in the South, 1880–1908*. Chapel Hill and London, 2001.

Perry, Mark. *Conceived in Liberty: Joshua Chamberlain, William Oates, and the American Civil War*. New York, 1997.

Perry, William F. "Reminiscences of the Campaign of 1864 in Virginia." *Southern Historical Society Papers*, 7 (1879), 49–63.

Pessen, Edward. "The Egalitarian Myth and the American Social Reality: Wealth, Mobility, and Equality in the 'Era of the Common Man.'" *American Historical Review*, 76 (October 1971), 989–1034.

Peskin, Allan. "Was There a Compromise of 1877?" *Journal of American History*, 60 (June 1973), 63–75.

Peterson, Merrill D. *Lincoln in American Memory*. New York, 1994.

Pettegrew, John. "'The Soldier's Faith': Turn-of-the-Century Memory of the Civil War and the Emergence of Modern American Nationalism." *Journal of Contemporary History*, 31 (1996), 49–73.

Peterson, Merrill D. *Lincoln in American Memory*. New York and Oxford, 1994.

Pfanz, Donald C. *Richard S. Ewell: A Soldier's Life*. Chapel Hill, N.C., 1998.

Pfanz, Harry W. *Gettysburg: The Second Day*. Chapel Hill, N.C., 1987.

Pfanz, Harry W. "The Gettysburg Campaign after Pickett's Charge." *Gettysburg Magazine*, 1 (July 1989), 118–124.

Pierrepont, Alice V. D. *Reuben Vaughan Kidd: Soldier of the Confederacy*. Petersburg, Va., 1947.

Pindell, Richard. "The True High-Water Mark of the Confederacy." *Blue & Gray*, 1 (December 1983–January 1984), 6–15.

Piston, William Garrett. *Lee's Tarnished Lieutenant: James Longstreet and His Place in Southern History*. Athens, Ga., 1987.

Polk, J. M. *The North and South American Review*. Austin, 1914.

Pollard, Edward A. *The Lost Cause: A New Southern History of the War of the Confederates*. New York, 1866.

Polley, J. B. *Hood's Texas Brigade: Its Marches, Its Battles, Its Achievements*. New York, 1910.

Polley, J. B. *A Soldier's Letters to Charming Nellie*. New York and Washington, D.C., 1908.

Poole, W. Scott. "Never Surrender: The Lost Cause and the Making of Southern Conservatism in the South Carolina Upcountry, 1850–1903." Ph.D. Dissertation, University of Mississippi, 2001.

Posner, Richard A., ed. *The Essential Holmes: Selections from the Letters, Speeches, Judicial Opinions, and Other Writings of Oliver Wendell Holmes, Jr.* Chicago, 1992.

Potter, David M. *The Impending Crisis, 1848–1861*. New York, 1976.

Powell, R. M. "With Hood at Gettysburg." *Philadelphia Weekly Times*, December 13, 1884.

Power, J. Tracey. *Lee's Miserables: Life in the Army of Northern Virginia from the Wilderness to Appomattox*. Chapel Hill and London, 1998.

Presser, Harriet B. "Age Differences between Spouses: Trends, Patterns and Social Implications." *American Behavioral Scientist*, 19 (1975), 190–205.

Prokopowicz, Gerald J. *All for the Regiment: The Army of the Ohio, 1861–1862*. Chapel Hill and London, 2001.

Pugh, David G. *Sons of Liberty: The Masculine Mind in Nineteenth-Century America*. Westport, Conn., 1983.

Pullen, John J. *Joshua Chamberlain: A Hero's Life and Legacy*. Mechanicsburg, Pa., 1999.

Pullen, John J. *The Twentieth Maine: A Volunteer Regiment in the Civil War*. Philadelphia, 1957.

Pyron, Darden Asbury. "Lawlessness and Culture in the Antebellum South." *Virginia Quarterly Review*, 61 (1985), 741–751.

Quinn, Arthur Hobson. *Edgar Allan Poe: A Critical Biography*. New York, 1941.

Rable, George C. *But There was No Peace: The Role of Violence in the Politics of Reconstruction*. Athens, Ga., 1984.

Rable, George C. *Civil Wars: Women and the Crisis of Southern Nationalism*. Chicago, 1989.

Rable, George C. *The Confederate Republic: A Revolution Against Politics*. Chapel Hill and London, 1994.

Rable, George C. *Fredericksburg! Fredericksburg!* Chapel Hill and London, 2002.

Ramage, James A. *Gray Ghost: The Life of Colonel John Singleton Mosby*. Lexington, Ky., 1999.

Reardon, Carol. *Pickett's Charge in History and Memory*. Chapel Hill and London, 1997.

Reed, John Shelton. "To Live—and Die—in Dixie: A Contribution to the Study of Southern Violence." *Political Science Quarterly*, 86 (1971), 429–443.

Rhea, Gordon C. *Cold Harbor: Grant and Lee, May 26–June 3, 1864*. Baton Rouge and London, 2002.

Rhea, Gordon C. *The Battle of the Wilderness, May 5–6, 1864*. Baton Rouge and London, 1994.

Rhea, Gordon C. *The Battles for Spotsylvania Court House and the Road to Yellow Tavern, May 7–12, 1864*. Baton Rouge and London, 1997.

Rhea, Gordon C. *To the North Anna River: Grant and Lee, May 13–25, 1864*. Baton Rouge and London, 2000.

Rice, Edmond Lee, comp. *Civil War Letters of James McDonald Campbell of the 47th Alabama Infantry Regiment*. Waynesville, N.C., n.d.

Richards, Mary Stovall. "'And He Shall Rule Over Thee': Patriarchy in Two Nineteenth-Century American Subcultures." *Journal of Mississippi History*, 63 (2001), 317–346.

Richter, Edward G. J. "The Removal of the Confederate Dead from Gettysburg." *Gettysburg Magazine*, 2 (January 1990), 113–122.

Riemer, Jeffrey W. "Durkheim's 'Heroic Suicide' in Military Combat." *Armed Forces and Society*, 25 (1998), 103–120.

Robbins, William M. "Monuments at Gettysburg." *Atlanta Constitution*, October 24, 1898.

Roberts, Frances Roberts. "William Manning Lowe and the Greenback Party in Alabama." In Wiggins, comp., *From Civil War to Civil Rights*, 145–161.

Robertson, James I. *Soldiers Blue and Gray*. Columbia, S.C., 1988.

Robertson, James I. *Stonewall Jackson: The Man, the Soldier, the Legend*. New York, 1997.

Rodabaugh, Karl Louis. "Fusion, Confusion, Defeat, and Disfranchisement: The 'Fadeout of Populism' in Alabama." *Alabama History Quarterly*, 34 (1972), 131–153.

Roediger, David R. *Towards the Abolition of Whiteness: Essays on Race, Politics, and Working Class History*. London, 1994.

Roediger, David R. *The Wages of Whiteness: Race and the Making of the American Working Class*. London, 1991.

Rogers, William Warren. *The One-Gallused Rebellion: Agrarianism in Alabama, 1865–1896*. Baton Rouge, 1970.

Rogers, William Warren. "The Farmers' Alliance in Alabama." In Wiggins, comp., *From Civil War to Civil Rights*, 162–172.

Rogers, William Warren. "Reuben F. Kolb: Agricultural Leader of the New South." *Agricultural History*, 32 (1958), 109–119.

Rogers, William Warren, Robert David Ward, Leah Rawls Atkins, and Wayne Flynt. *Alabama: The History of a Deep South State*. Tuscaloosa and London, 1994.

Roland, Charles P. "The Ever-Vanishing South." *Journal of Southern History*, 48 (1982), 3–20.

Rorabaugh, W. J. "Who Fought for the North in the Civil War? Concord, Massachusetts, Enlistments." *Journal of American History*, 73 (December 1986), 695–701.

Rothman, Ellen K. *Hands and Hearts: A History of Courtship in America*. New York, 1984.

Rotundo, E. Anthony. *American Manhood: Transformation in Masculinity from the Revolution to the Modern Era*. New York, 1993.

Royster, Charles. *The Destructive War: William Tecumseh Sherman, Stonewall Jackson, and the Americans*. New York, 1991.

Russell, William Howard. *My Diary, North and South*. Burnham, Eng., 1863.

Samuel, Raphael. *Theaters of Memory: Past and Present in Contemporary Culture*. London, 1994.

Samuels, Shirley. *Facing America: Iconography and the American Civil War*. New York and Oxford, 2004.

Sauers, Richard A. "John B. Bachelder: Government Historian of the Battle of Gettysburg." *Gettysburg Magazine*, 3 (July 1990), 115–127.

Sauers, Richard A. *Pennsylvania in the Spanish American War: A Commemorative Look Back*. [Harrisburg, Pa., 1998].

Savage, Kirk. *Standing Soldiers, Kneeling Slaves: Race, War, and Monument in Nineteenth-Century America*. Princeton, N.J., 1997.

Schacter, Daniel L. *Memory Distortion: How Minds, Brains, and Societies Reconstruct the Past*. Cambridge, Mass., 1997.

Schacter, Daniel L. *The Seven Sins of Memory: How the Mind Forgets and Remembers*. Boston and New York, 2002.

Schultz, Jane E. "Healing the Nation: Condolence and Correspondence in Civil War Hospitals." *Proteus*, 17 (fall 2000), 33–41.

Schwartz, Barry. *Abraham Lincoln and the Forge of National Memory.* Chicago, 2000.

Scott, Anne Firor. *The Southern Lady: From Pedestal to Politics, 1830–1930.* Chicago, 1970.

Scott, Anne Firor. "Women's Perspective on the Patriarchy in the 1850s." *Journal of American History,* 61 (June 1974), 52–64

Scott, Mrs. Marvin. *History of Henry County, Alabama.* Pensacola, Fla., 1961.

Sears, Stephen W. *Chancellorsville.* Boston and New York, 1996.

Sears, Stephen W. *Controversies and Commanders: Dispatches from the Army of the Potomac.* Boston and New York, 1999.

Sears, Stephen W. *Gettysburg.* Boston and New York, 2003.

Sears, Stephen W. *Landscape Turned Red: The Battle of Antietam.* New York, 1983.

Sears, Stephen W. "The Last Word on the Lost Order." *MHQ: The Quarterly Journal of Military History* (spring 1992), 66–74.

Sears, Stephen W. *To the Gates of Richmond: The Peninsula Campaign.* New York, 1992.

Sellers, James Benson. *Slavery in Alabama.* University, Ala., 1950.

Serrin, William. *Homestead: The Glory and Tragedy of an American Steel Town.* New York, 1992.

Sherman, John. *Recollections of Forty Years in the House, Senate, and Cabinet.* 2 vols. New York, 1895.

Shevchuk, Paul M. "The 1st Texas Infantry and the Repulse of Farnsworth's Charge." *Gettysburg Magazine,* 2 (January 1990), 81–90.

Shore, Laurence. *Southern Capitalists: The Ideological Leadership of an Elite, 1832–1885.* Chapel Hill and London, 1986.

Siepel, Kevin H. *Rebel: The Life and Times of John Singleton Mosby.* New York, 1983.

Silber, Nina. *The Romance of Reunion: Northerners and the South, 1865–1900.* Chapel Hill and London, 1993.

Silbey, Joel H. "The Southern National Democrats, 1845–1861." *Mid-America,* 47 (1965), 176–190.

Simon, John Y., and Michael E. Stevens, eds. *New Perspectives on the Civil War: Myths and Realties of the National Conflict.* Madison, Wisc., 1998.

Simpson, John A. "The Cult of the 'Lost Cause.'" *Tennessee Historical Quarterly,* 34 (1975), 350–361.

Simpson, Harold B. *Hood's Texas Brigade: Lee's Grenadier Guard.* Waco, Tex., 1970.

Sinha, Manisha. "The Caning of Charles Sumner: Slavery, Race, and Ideology in the Age of the Civil War." *Journal of the Early Republic,* 23 (2003), 233–262.

Sinha, Manisha. *The Counterrevolution of Slavery: Politics and Ideology in Antebellum South Carolina.* Chapel Hill and London, 2000.

Sinha, Manisha. "Revolution or Counterrevolution? The Political Ideology of Secession in Antebellum South Carolina." *Civil War History,* 46 (2000), 205–226.

Sizer, Lyde Cullen. *The Political Work of Northern Women Writers and the Civil War, 1850–1872.* Chapel Hill and London, 2000.

Sloan, John Z. "The Ku Klux Klan and the Alabama Election of 1872." *Alabama Review,* 18 (April 1965), 113–123.

Smartt, Eugenia Persons. *History of Eufaula, Alabama.* N.p., 1933.

Smith, Diane Monroe. *Fanny and Joshua: The Enigmatic Lives of Frances Caroline Adams and Joshua Lawrence Chamberlain.* Gettysburg, Pa., 1999.

Smith, Mark M. *Mastered by the Clock: Time, Slavery, and Freedom in the American South.* Chapel Hill, N.C., and London, 1997.

Smith, Merril D., ed. *Sex Without Consent: Rape and Sexual Coercion in America.* New York, 2001.

Smith, Susan Sutton, and Harrison Hayford, eds. *The Journals and Miscellaneous Notebooks of Ralph Waldo Emerson.* Vol. 14: 1854–1861. Cambridge, Mass., 1978.

Smith-Rosenberg, Carroll. *Disorderly Conduct: Visions of Gender in Victorian America.* New York, 1985.

Sommerville, Diane Miller. "'I Was Very Much Wounded': Rape Law, Children, and the Antebellum South." In Smith, ed., *Sex Without Consent,* 136–177.

Sommerville, Diane Miller. *Rape and Race in the Nineteenth-Century South.* Chapel Hill and London, 2004.

Sommerville, Diane Miller. "The Rape Myth in the Old South Reconsidered." *Journal of Southern History,* 61 (1995), 481–518

Sparkman, John. "The Kolb-Oates Campaign of 1894." M.A. Thesis, University of Alabama, 1924.

Spear, Abbott, et al., eds. *The Civil War Recollections of General Ellis Spear.* Orono, Maine, 1997.

Spear, Ellis. "A Visit to Gettysburg." *Lincoln County News,* June 9, 1882.

Stampp, Kenneth M. *The Peculiar Institution: Slavery in the Ante-Bellum South.* New York, 1956.

Stark, Cruce. "Brothers at/in War: One Phase of Post-Civil War Reconciliation." *Canadian Review of American Studies,* 6 (1975), 174–181.

Statutes Relating to the Protection[,] Control[,] and Use of the Gettysburg National Park and the Regulations Prescribed Therefore by the Secretary of War. N.p., n.d.

Stearns, Carol Zisowitz, and Peter N. Stearns. *Anger: The Struggle for Emotional Control in America's History.* Chicago, 1986.

Steiner, Paul E. *Disease in the Civil War: Natural Biological Warfare in 1861–1865.* Springfield, Ill., 1968.

Stevens, C. A. *Berdan's United States Sharpshooters in the Army of the Potomac, 1861–1865.* St. Paul, Minn., 1892.

Stevens, John W. *Reminiscences of the Civil War.* Hillsboro, Tex., 1902.

Stewart, James Brewer. "The Emergence of Racial Modernity and the Rise of the White North, 1790–1840." *Journal of the Early Republic,* 18 (spring 1998), 181–217.

Stocker, Jeffrey D. ed. *From Huntsville to Appomattox: R. T. Coles's History of 4th Regiment, Alabama Volunteer Infantry, C.S.A., Army of Northern Virginia.* Knoxville, 1996.

Stone, Lawrence. *The Family, Sex, and Marriage in England 1500–1800.* New York, 1977.

Stowe, Steven M. *Intimacy and Power in the Old South: Ritual in the Lives of the Planters.* Baltimore, 1987.

Stowell, Daniel W. "Stonewall Jackson and the Providence of God." In Miller et al., eds., *Religion and the American Civil War,* 187–207.

Stowell, Daniel W., ed. *In Tender Consideration: Women, Families, and the Law in Abraham Lincoln's Illinois.* Urbana, Ill., 2002.

Sutherland, Daniel E. "Abraham Lincoln, John Pope, and the Origins of Total War." *Journal of Military History,* 56 (October 1992), 567–586.

Sutherland, Daniel E. *Fredericksburg and Chancellorsville: The Dare Mark Campaign.* Lincoln, Neb., 1998.

Svenson, Peter. *Battlefield: Farming a Civil War Battleground.* New York, 1992.

Symonds, Craig L. *Joseph E. Johnston: A Civil War Biography.* New York, 1992.

Talbott, John E. "Combat Trauma in the American Civil War." *History Today,* 46 (March 1996), 41–47.

Tanner, Robert G. *Stonewall in the Valley: Thomas J. "Stonewall" Jackson's Shenandoah Valley Campaign, Spring 1862*. Garden City, N.Y., 1976.

Taussig, Frank W. *The Tariff History of the United States*. New York, 1892.

Taylor, John Dykes. *History of the 48th Alabama Volunteer Infantry Regiment, C.S.A.* University, Ala., 1985.

Taylor, William Robert. *Cavalier and Yankee: The Old South and American National Character*. New York, 1963.

Thomas, Emory M. *Bold Dragoon: The Life of J. E. B. Stuart*. New York, 1986.

Thomas, Emory M. "God and General Lee." *Anglican and Episcopal History*, 60 (March 1991), 15–24.

Thomas, Mary Martha. *The New Woman in Alabama: Social Reforms and Suffrage, 1890–1920*. Tuscaloosa, Ala., 1992.

Thornton, J. Mills, III. *Politics and Power in a Slave Society: Alabama, 1800–1860*. Baton Rouge, 1978.

Tolnay, Stewart E., and E. M. Beck. *A Festival of Violence: An Analysis of Southern Lynchings, 1882–1930*. Chicago, 1995.

Trask, David F. *The War with Spain in 1898*. New York, 1981.

Traxel, David. *1898: The Birth of the American Century*. New York, 1998.

Trelease, Allen W. *White Terror: The Ku Klux Klan Conspiracy and Southern Reconstruction*. New York, 1971.

Trudeau, Noah Andre. *Gettysburg: A Testing of Courage*. New York, 2002.

Trulock, Alice Rains. *In the Hands of Providence: Joshua L. Chamberlain and the American Civil War*. Chapel Hill and London, 1992.

Tucker, Glenn. *High Tide at Gettysburg: The Campaign in Pennsylvania*. Indianapolis, Ind., 1958.

Tucker, Phillip Thomas. *Storming Little Round Top: The 15th Alabama and Their Fight for the High Ground, July 2, 1863*. Cambridge, Mass., 2002.

U.S. House of Representatives. *Testimony and Papers in the Contested Election Case of A. A. Mabson vs. W. C. Oates*. Miscellaneous Document No. 18, 47th Congress, 1st Session, December 30, 1881. Washington, D.C., 1881.

U.S. War Department. *The War of the Rebellion: A Compilation of the Official Records of the Union and Confederate Armies*. 70 vols. in 128 parts, index, and atlas. Washington, D.C., 1880–1901.

Unrau, Harlan D. *Administrative History: Gettysburg National Military Park and National Cemetery, Pennsylvania*. Washington, D.C., 1991.

Valliere, Kenneth L. "The Creek War of 1836: A Military History." *Chronicles of Oklahoma*, 57 (1979–1980), 463–485.

Vanderslice, John M. *Gettysburg: A History of the Gettysburg Battle-field Memorial Association*. Philadelphia, 1897.

Vandiver, Frank E. "The Confederacy and the American Tradition." *Journal of Southern History*, 28 (August 1962), 277–286.

Vaughan, P. T., et al. "Maj. W. M. Robbins." *Confederate Veteran*, 13 (August 1905), 373–374.

Vaughan, Turner. "Diary of Turner Vaughan, Co. 'C,' 4th Alabama Regiment, C.S.A." *Alabama Historical Quarterly*, 18 (1956), 573–604.

Vicinus, Martha, ed. *A Widening Sphere: Changing Roles of Victorian Women*. Bloomington, Ind., 1977.

Vinovskis, Maris A. "Have Social Historians Lost the Civil War? Some Preliminary Demographic Speculations." In Vinovskis, ed., *Toward A Social History of the American Civil War*, 1–30.

Vinovskis, Maris A., ed. *Toward a Social History of the American Civil War: Exploratory Essays*. Cambridge and New York, 1990.

von Borcke, Heros, and Justus Scheibert. *The Great Cavalry Battle of Brandy Station, 9 June 1863*. Winston-Salem, N.C., 1976.

Vorenberg, Michael. *Final Freedom: The Civil War, the Abolition of Slavery, and the Thirteenth Amendment*. Cambridge and New York, 2001.

Vorenberg, Michael. "Recovered Memory of the Civil War." *Reviews in American History*, 29 (2001), 550–558.

Wakeman, George, comp. *Official Proceedings of the National Democratic Convention, Held at New York, July 4–9, 1868*. Boston, 1868.

Walker, A. J., comp. *The Revised Code of Alabama*. Montgomery, Ala., 1867.

Walker, Anne Kendrick. *Backtracking in Barbour County: A Narrative of the Last Alabama Frontier*. Richmond, Va., 1941.

Wallace, Anthony F. C. "Revitalization Movements." *American Anthropology*, 58 (1956), 264–281.

Wallace, Willard. *Soul of the Lion: A Biography of Joshua L. Chamberlain*. New York, 1960.

Wallenstein, Peter. "Race, Marriage, and the Law of Freedom: Alabama and Virginia, 1860s–1960s." *Chicago-Kent Law Review*, 70 (1994), 371–437.

Ward, Robert David, and William Warren Rogers. "'Punishment Seven Times More': The Convict Lease System in Alabama." *Alabama Heritage*, 12 (1989), 20–33.

Ward, W. C. "Incidents and Personal Experiences on the Battlefield at Gettysburg." *Confederate Veteran*, 8 (1900), 345–349.

Warner, Ezra J. *Generals in Gray: Lives of the Confederate Commanders*. Baton Rouge and London, 1959.

Warren, Hoyt M. *Henry—The Mother County*. Auburn, Ala., 1976.

Warren, Hoyt M., comp. *Henry's Heritage: A History of Henry County, Alabama*. Abbeville, Ala., 1978.

Warren, Robert Penn. *The Legacy of the Civil War: Meditations on the Centennial*. New York, 1961.

Washington, Booker T. *Up from Slavery*. Ed. William L. Andrews. Oxford and New York, 1995.

Waugh, Charles G., Martin H. Greenberg, and Catherine Clinton, eds. *The Women's War in the South: Recollections and Reflections of the American Civil War*. Nashville, Tenn., 1999.

Wayne, Michael. "An Old South Morality Play: Reconsidering the Social Underpinnings of Proslavery Ideology." *Journal of American History*, 77 (December 1990), 838–863.

Weaver, John B. "John Sherman and the Politics of Economic Change." *Hayes Historical Journal*, 6 (1987), 7–19.

Webb, Samuel L. *Two-Party Politics in the One-Party South, 1874–1920*. Tuscaloosa and London, 1997.

Weigley, Russell F. *The American Way of War: A History of Military Strategy and Policy*. New York, 1973.

Weiner, Marli F. *Mistresses and Slaves: Plantation Women in South Carolina, 1830–1880*. Chicago, 1997.

Weisberg, Barbara. *Talking to the Dead: Kate and Maggie Fox and the Rise of Spiritualism*. San Francisco, 2004.

Weitz, Mark A. *A Higher Duty: Desertion among Georgia Troops during the Civil War*. Lincoln and London, 2000.

Welter, Barbara. "The Cult of True Womanhood: 1820–1860." *American Quarterly*, 18 (1966), 151–74.

Wert, Jeffry D. *General James Longstreet: The Confederacy's Most Controversial Soldier—A Biography*. New York, 1993.

Wert, Jeffry D. *Gettysburg: Day Three*. New York, 2001.

West, John C. *A Texan in Search of a Fight*. Waco, Tex., 1901.

Whan, Vorin E., Jr. *Fiasco at Fredericksburg*. State College, Pa., 1961.

White, Kenneth B. "Black Lives, Red Tape: The Alabama Freedmen's Bureau." *Alabama Historical Review*, 43 (winter 1981), 241–258.

White, Russell C. ed. *The Civil War Diary of Wyman S. White, First Sergeant of Company F, 2nd United States Sharpshooter Regiment, 1861–1865*. Baltimore, 1991.

Whites, LeeAnn. "The Civil War as a Crisis in Gender." In Clinton and Silber, eds., *Divided Houses*, 3–21.

Wiggins, Sarah Woolfolk. *The Scalawag in Alabama Politics, 1865–1881*. University, Ala., 1977.

Wiggins, Sarah Woolfolk. "A Victorian Father: Josiah Gorgas and His Family." In Bleser, ed., *In Joy and in Sorrow*, 233–252.

Wiggins, Sarah Woolfolk, comp. *From Civil War to Civil Rights: Alabama, 1860–1900*. Tuscaloosa and London, 1987.

Wight, W. E., ed. "Sam Lary's 'Scraps from My Knapsack.'" *Alabama Historical Quarterly*, 18 (1956), 499–525.

Wiley, Bell Irvin. *The Life of Johnny Reb*. Indianapolis, Ind., 1943.

Wiley, Bell Irvin. *The Life of Billy Yank*. Indianapolis, Ind., 1952.

Wilkinson, Rupert. *American Tough: The Tough-Guy Tradition and American Character*. Westport, Conn., 1984.

Williamson, Edward C. "The Alabama Election of 1874." *Alabama Review*, 17 (July 1964), 210–218.

Williamson, Joel. "Wounds Not Scars: Lynching, the National Conscience, and the American Historian." *Journal of American History*, 83 (1997), 1221–1253.

Williamson, G. M., and A. S. Walters. "Perceived Impact of Limb Amputation on Sexual Activity: A Study of Adult Amputees." *Journal of Sex Research*, 33 (1996), 221–230.

Williamson, G. M., and R. Schulz, M. Bridges, and A. Behan. "Social and Psychological Factors in Adjustment to Limb Amputation." *Journal of Social Behavior and Personality*, 9 (1994), 249–268.

Wills, Garry. *Lincoln at Gettysburg: The Words that Remade America*. New York, 1992.

Wills, Garry. "Lincoln's Greatest Speech?" *Atlantic Monthly*, 284 (September 1999), 60–70.

Wilson, Charles Reagan. *Baptized in Blood: The Religion of the Lost Cause, 1865–1920*. Athens, Ga., 1980.

Wilson, Edmund. *Patriotic Gore: Studies in the Literature of the Civil War*. New York, 1962.

Wittenberg, Eric J. *Gettysburg's Forgotten Cavalry Actions*. Gettysburg, Pa., 1998.

Wood, Gordon S. *The Creation of the American Republic, 1776–1787*. Chapel Hill, 1969.

Wood, Gordon S. *The Radicalism of the American Revolution*. New York, 1991.

Woodward, C. Vann. *Origins of the New South, 1877–1913*. Baton Rouge, 1951.

Woodward, C. Vann. *Reunion and Reaction: The Compromise of 1877 and the End of Reconstruction*. Rev. ed. Garden City, N.J., 1956.

Woodward, C. Vann, ed. *Mary Chesnut's Civil War*. New Haven and London, 1981.

Woodworth, Steven E. *The American Civil War: A Handbook of Literature and Research*. Westport, Conn., 1996.

Woodworth, Steven E. *Beneath a Northern Sky: A Short History of the Gettysburg Campaign*. Wilmington, Del., 2003.

Wright, James R. "Time On Little Round Top." *Gettysburg Magazine*, 2 (January 1990), 51–54.

Wright, James R. "Vincent's Brigade on Little Round Top." *Gettysburg Magazine*, 1 (July 1989), 41–44.

Wyatt-Brown, Bertram. *Honor and Violence in the Old South*. New York, 1986

Wyatt-Brown, Bertram. *The Shaping of Southern Culture: Honor, Grace, and War, 1760s–1880s*. Chapel Hill and London, 2001.

Wyatt-Brown, Bertram. *Southern Honor: Ethics and Behavior in the Old South*. New York and Oxford, 1982.

Yates, Frances. *The Art of Memory*. Chicago, 1966.

Young, Elizabeth. *Disarming the Nation: Women's Writing and the American Civil War*. Chicago, 1999.

Youngblood, William. "Unwritten History of the Gettysburg Campaign." *Southern Historical Society Papers*, 38 (1910), 312–318.

INDEX

Abbeville Banner, 16

Adams, Francis, Jr., 159

Adrian, John D., 113, 115

African Americans. *See also* race and racism; slavery
  Alabama population, 23
  confrontations with the military, 51
  and the farmers' movement, 226
  and Lost Cause ideology, xxiii
  Oates' opinion of, xviii, xxviii, 9–10, 239–40, 243, 269–70, 274

agrarian interests, 266. *See also* cotton

Alabama Brigade, xxviii

Alabama Constitutional Convention, xviii, 20–21, 283

Alabama General Assembly, 291

Alabama Revised Code, 204

Alabama Supreme Court, 174–78, 201–2, 280

Alabama Third Congressional District, 207

Alexander, Edward Porter, xxiv, xxxi, 198

Alger, Russell A., 254, 255

Allen, Sallie Vandalia Knight, 241–43. *See also* Vandalia, Sarah (Sallie)

American Revolution, 22

Ames, Adelbert, 257

Anderson, George T., 83

Anderson, Richard, 162, 166

Anthony, John, 20

Antietam, 56, 130

Appomattox, xxiii, 66, 170

Archer, James J., 60

aristocracy, 153, 197–98

Army of Northern Virginia. *See also* specific units
  at Antietam, 57
  at Chancellorsville, 330n. 8
  at Cold Harbor, 160
  command changes, 156
  desertions, 127
  at Gaines Mill, 45
  at Gettysburg, 111
  at Harpers Ferry, 55–57
  in Maryland, 55–57
  morale problems, 125
  at Petersburg, 169
  Potomac River crossing, 120–21
  reorganization of, 76
  at Second Manassas, 51
  unit cohesion, 171
  and veterans' reunions, 246
  winter camps, 62–63

Army of the Cumberland, 138
Army of the Potomac. *See also specific
    units*
    at Cold Harbor, 160
    command changes, 73
    at Fredericksburg, 59
    at Gaines Mill, 45
    at Gettysburg, 83, 85, 95, 106
    at Hagerstown, 120
    intelligence gathering, 63
    in Maryland, 56
    at Rapidan River, 156
    at Rappahannock River, 123
    treatment of prisoners, 119
    and veterans' reunions, 246
Army of the Tennessee, 66, 138, 345n.
    38
Army of Virginia (Union), 50
Arthur, Chester A., 210
Ashby, Turner, 41–42
Athens, Georgia, 258
Atkinson, Edmund N., 60
Atlantic Coast Line Railway, 280

Bachelder, John B.
    and battle reconstruction, 216–17,
        229
    on Farnsworth incident, 338–39n. 6
    and Gettysburg monument efforts,
        253, 284
    and Gettysburg Park founding, 206–7
    and veterans' reunions, 216
Bagwell, James, 112
Bagwell, John, 111–12
Bagwell, William, 111–12
Baldwin, Joseph Glover, 2
Banks, Nathaniel P., 50
Baptists, 131–32
Barbour County Chancery Court, 201–2
Bass, Allan, 196
Battles and Leaders of the Civil War
    (Century Magazine Company),
        209
bayonet charges, 46, 102, 252
Bealeton, Virginia, 38–39
Benning, Henry Lewis, 83, 89
Berdan's Sharpshooters, 87
Beverly Ford, 75
bigotry. *See* race and racism

Big Round Top, *84*
    casualties, 106, 107
    described, 83
    15th Alabama's advance on, 88, 89–
        94
    15th Alabama's defense of, 112, 116
    15th Alabama's descent from, 94–97
    15th Alabama's retreat to, 106–9
    Oates' account of, 229
    Oates' tour of, 216
    reconnaissance of, 85
    sharpshooters on, 87
    and veterans' reunions, 248
Bilbo, Theodore Gilmore, xxx
Birmingham Ledger, xvii
Black Belt, 226, 236, 266, 274
black codes, 176, 182
Blair Education bill, 235
Bland-Allison Act (1878), 227
"Bleeding" Kansas, 15–16
Bolivar Heights, 56
Boteler's Ford, 57
Bragg, Braxton, 138, 145
Brainard, Henry, 101, 134, 281
Brandy Station, 75
Breckinridge, John C., 18–19, 169
Breckinridge Democrats, 18–19, 21
Brewer, Miriam, 197
Brewer, Willis, 197
Bridgeport, 149
Brooks, Preston, xxix
Brown, John, xxix, 18, 19
Brown's Ferry, 148–50
Bryan, Lee E., 47
Bryan, William Jennings, 250, 260
Buchanan, James, 14
Buckner, Simon B., 250
Buford, Jefferson, 15–16
Bulger, Michael J.
    at Gettysburg, 90, 91, 94, 95, 98,
        106–7
    inaccurate accounts of, 334n. 14
    surrender, 336–37n. 40
Bullock, Edward, 14, 15
Bull Run. *See* First Manassas; Second
    Manassas
Bull's Gap, 155
Bunker Hill, 57, 59, 131
Burgwyn, Henry K., Jr., xxxi
Burns, Robert, 40, 75

Burnside, Ambrose E., 59, 61, 73
Bushman's Hill, 113
Butler, Matthew C., 254
Buttermilk Rangers, 169

Calhoun, John C., 14
Calvinism, 132–33
Camp Haskell, 258, 259
Camp Holly, 164
Camp Meade, 256, 257
camp meetings, 132. *See also* religion
Cantey, James
  and command changes, 74, 163
  and the 15th Alabama, 31–32
  and Lowther promotion, 344–45n. 22
  personality conflicts, 37
  at Richmond, 45
  at Second Manassas, 49
  and the Valley Campaign, 42, 43
Carnegie, Andrew, 230–31
Carroll, W. H., 131–32
casualties. *See specific battles*
cavalry
  at Beverly Ford, 75–76
  cavalry reviews, 75–76, 331n. 12
  Farnsworth attack, 112–16, 337–38n. 4
  at Gettysburg, 335n. 31, 336n. 35, 337–38n. 4
  Pickett's charge, 112
Cedar Mountain, 50
Cedar Run, 297
cemeteries, 301–5, 306, 308–9
Cemetery Ridge, 83–85, *84*, 284, 337–38n. 4
Centreville, Virginia, 34–35
Chamberlain, Joshua Lawrence
  and Bulger surrender, 336–37n. 40
  correspondence with, xxvii
  and Gettysburg monument efforts, 252–53, 289–90, 294–95, 298–301, 363–64n. 26
  at Little Round Top, xvii, 95, 104
  military career, 257
  monument to, 248
Chambersburg, Pennsylvania, 80
Chancellorsville, 74
Charleston Mercury, 114
Chattanooga, 138, 145–47, 147–50, 233
Chesnut, Mary, 211
Chester Station, 162

Chicago Post, xvii
Chickamauga, 138–45, 148, 233, 237
Chickamauga and Chattanooga Military Park, 245–47, 342n. 2
Circuit Court of the United States for the Middle District of Alabama, 204
citizenship, 70, 90, 275
civil rights legislation, 182
Civil War amendments, 178
clairvoyance, 6–9, 109, 121–22, 340n. 23
Clark, William A., 16
Cleburne, Patrick, 66
Clemm, Virginia, 184
Cleveland, Grover, 225, 229, 232
Cobbs, E. E., 306
Cochran, John, 15, 196
Cocke, Philip St. George, 114
Cody, Barnett "Bud"
  captured, 118–20
  childhood, 5
  death, 121, 126, 134–35, 252
  enlistment, 30, 33
  at Gettysburg, 101, 106, 107, 111
  and John Oates, 35
  on religious revivalism, 58, 134
  remains buried, 303
Cody, Edmund, 126, 152
Cold Harbor, 160–61
commissions and promotions
  in the 15th Alabama, 36, 37
  Grant's promotion, 148, 156
  in the Henry Pioneers, 31–32
  John Oates, 72
  Lowther, 344–45n. 22
  and Lowther conflict, 146–47, 162
  Oates' colonel commission, 74, 147
  and Oates' petitions, 345n. 38
  and the Spanish-American War, 253–54
Committee on Claims, 210
Compromise of 1850, 14
Confederate Congress
  bounty law, 72
  and the Emancipation Proclamation, 66
  and enlistment of slaves, 170
  and Lowther conflict, 146
  and Oates' colonel commission, 74, 147
  and organization of the military, 62

Confederate Constitution, 129–30
Confederate Memorial Day, 308
Confederate Senate, 74
Confiscation Act (1862), 129
Congressional Medal of Honor, 290
Constitutional Convention (Alabama),
        177, 265–78
Control Conservative Club of Henry
        County, 191, 193–94
convict lease system, 238
Cooper, Samuel, 163, 169
Cope, Emmor B., 248
Coppinger, John J., 254
Corbin, Henry Clark, 254, 255–56
cotton, 180, 196, 220, 238
courage, 103–4
Creek War, 4, 152
Crittenden, Catherine, 50
Crittenden, George B., 36
Crittenden, John J., 70
Crockett, David, 2
Cromwell, Oliver, 58
Cross Keys, 42, 43–44, 151
CSS *Alabama*, 282
Cumberland Valley, 80
currency
        Confederate currency disputes, 202
        and Congress, 231–32
        gold standard, 226–27, 229, 232, 238
        silver standard, 226–27, 232, 250–51,
            260
Currens house, 116

Dale County, 177–78
Dancy, John C., 239
Daniel, John W. L., 37
Darbytown Road, 164–65
Davis, Jefferson
        and command changes, 73, 156,
            162–63
        and commissions/promotions, 36,
            146–47
        and desertions, 127
        and the Emancipation Proclamation,
            64, 65, 66
        and enlistment of slaves, 330n. 35
        and General Johnston, 38
        inauguration, 27
        marriage, 351n. 37
        and morale problems, 130

Oates' opinion of, xxii
optimism, 63
public opinion of, 78
and Richmond defense, 72
and secession, 221
speeches, 32
and transfer requests, 169
Davis, Varina, 351n. 37
Dearborn, F. A., 252, 253
Declaration of Independence, 274
deism, 133–34
democracy, 24, 25, 37, 125, 324n. 43
Democratic Party
        and Alabama constitutional conven-
            tion, 269
        "Bourbon Democrats," 199–200,
            226, 228, 232, 234, 266, 274
        Breckinridge Democrats, 18–19
        and congressional elections, 207–8
        and electoral reform, 265
        and the gold standard, 227, 229
        and gubernatorial campaign, 236
        Jeffersonian Democrats, 226–28,
            232–35, 268
        and the Ku Klux Klan, 183
        National Democrats, 18
        and Oates' political career, 193–94,
            195
        and the Porter case, 221
        and Reconstruction, 191
        Redemption Democrats, 176
        and secession, 18–19, 21
        Silver Democrats, 227
        splits in, 20
descendants clause, 271
desertions
        and enlistment of slaves, 64
        at Gettysburg, 82
        and honor, 340n. 31
        Oates' opinion on, 127–28, 169
        and suicide, 339n. 7
Devil's Den, *84*, 86–87, 89, 90, 91, 92
diabetes, 304
Dickerson, Samuel, 45
Dingley Tariff (1897), 216
disease, 10, 34, 39, 255, 256
disfranchisement, xxix, 191, 265–78,
        360n. 24
domesticity, 212–13
Durr, Virginia Foster, 319n. 25

Eagle Hotel, 294
Early, Jubal A., 60, 81, 198, 247
economics
    and currency standards, 226–27, 229,
        232, 238, 250–51, 260
    depression, 238
    and Oates' governorship, 238
    Panic of 1873, 227
    Panic of 1893, 238, 241
    and tariffs, 215–16, 220, 231, 235
    and taxation, 215–16, 265
education
    of Oates' brothers, 18, 201
    Oates' lack of, 8, 12–13, 293, 296
    Oates' political position on, 235, 278
    of Oates' sons, 209, 263, 264, 278,
        283, 285, 288, 297
    and segregation, 200
    and taxation, 276
"The Effigies" (Hemans), 135
Eighteenth Corps (Union), 160
Eighth Circuit Court, 146
83rd Pennsylvania, 95, 97–99, 288, 289,
    290
elections and election fraud
    and Alabama constitutional conven-
        tion, 265–78
    and congressional elections, 207–8
    and the Democratic Party, 228
    and the Farmers' Alliance, 225
    and gubernatorial campaign, 234,
        235–36
    Oates' accused of, 234
    and racial issues, 223, 265–78
    reform, 265–78
Elliott, William, 302, 303
Ellison, Henry, 98, 106, 281
Ellyson, Bettie, 303–4
emancipation, 196, 272
Emancipation Proclamation, 64–67,
    129, 202
Emmitsburg Road, 83–85, *84*, 116–17
England, 282
Essays (Macaulay's), 196
ethnic pluralism, 79
Eufaula, Alabama, 13, 195–96
Eufaula Regency, 153, 197, 226
Europe, 281–82
Ewell, Richard S.
    and command changes, 76

    at Cross Keys, 44
    described, 36
    on enlistment of slaves, 330n. 35
    and Fredericksburg, 60
    at Gaines Mill, 45–46
    at Second Manassas, 51–52
    and slavery, 65
    and the Valley Campaign, 38–39, 40

Fairfield Road, 117–18
Falling Waters, 120
Farmers' Alliance, 225–28, 250, 265–68
Farnsworth, Elon J., xxvii, 113–15, 229,
    337–38n. 4, 338–39n. 6
Faulkner, William, 309
Fayetteville, 81
Feagin, Isaac B.
    promotions, 31, 74, 162
    and proposed memorial, 281
    resignation, 169
    at Second Manassas, 53
    wounded, 57, 90, 118
The Federalist, 274
Field, Charles W., 156, 162, 163, 166
15th Alabama
    at Antietam, 57–59
    at Appomattox, 170–71
    at Brown's Ferry, 148–50
    casualties, 119, 326n. 16, 337n. 41
    at Chattanooga, 145–47
    at Chickamauga, 138–45
    at Cold Harbor, 159–61
    command changes, 36, 49–50, 76
    diseases and health problems, 34,
        36–37, 39
    fighting strength, 337n. 41
    first engagements, 38–44
    formation of, 31–38
    at Fredericksburg, 59–62
    at Gaines Mill, 45–47
    at Gettysburg, 81–82, *84*, 89–94, 94–
        97, 97–99, 99–102, 106–7
    at Hagerstown, 120
    at Harpers Ferry, 55–57
    at Little Round Top, 97–99, 99–102,
        102–6, 335n. 31
    Oates' history of, xxv–xxvi, 220
    organization of, 31–34
    at Petersburg, 169
    at Potomac River crossing, 77–78

15th Alabama (*continued*)
  praise for, 342n. 10
  proposed memorial, 281, 283–85,
    298–301
  at Raccoon Ford, 75
  and religious revivalism, 57–59, 134
  reunions, 284, 291
  at Second Manassas, 49–54
  at Shenandoah Valley, 40–44
  at Suffolk, 72–73, 74
  winter camps, 35, 36, 39, 62–63
15th Amendment
  and the Alabama constitutional con-
    vention, 200, 269, 271–72
  Oates' opinion of, 360n. 24
  resistance to, 178
  and southern state constitutions, 265
15th Maine, 100
Fifth Corps, 119
5th Alabama, 114
5th Texas, 46
filibusters, 230
financial panics, 227, 231–32, 238, 241
First Army Corps, 62
First Manassas, 28, 54, 114
First National Bank of Montgomery,
  203–5
1st Texas, 112
Fiscel, Michael, 119
Fiscel farm, 119, 121, 303
Fitzhugh, George, 19
Flag Mountain, 76
Fleetwood Hill, 75–76
Florida, 9
Flournoy, Thomas, 151
The Flush Times of Alabama and Missis-
  sippi (Baldwin), 2
fog of war, 143, 298
foraging, 78, 80–81
Forney, William H., 233
Fort Mitchell, 30–31
Fort Sumter, 27
48th Alabama
  at Gettysburg, 83, *84*, 89
  at New Market Heights, 164–67
  Oates' command, 163–64
  Oates' commitment to, 171
  at Orange Plank Road, 157
  at Petersburg, 169
44th Alabama, 83, 89, 161

44th New York
  and Bulger's surrender, 336–37n. 40
  at Gettysburg, 98
  and Gettysburg monument efforts,
    288, 289, 290
47th Alabama
  at Gettysburg, 83, *84*, 87, 90, 91, 95,
    96, 98, 106–7
  inaccurate accounts of, 334n. 14
14th Amendment, 178, 182, 272
Fourth Reconstruction Act (1868), 183
4th Alabama
  at Gettysburg, 83, *84*, 93, 94, 95, 98,
    103, 113
  and proposed monuments, 283, 287
4th Texas, *84*
franchise. *See* elections and election
  fraud; suffrage rights
Franklin, Benjamin, 2, 134
Frederick, Maryland, 55
Fredericksburg, Virginia, 59, 63, 123,
  131
Freedmen's Bureau, 182, 183
Fremantle, Arthur J. L., 55, 80
Frémont, Jesse, 351n. 37
Frémont, John C., 42, 43–44, 351n. 37
Frick, Henry Clay, 230–31
Fugitive Slave Law, 14
Fulton, John S., 139
Fussell's Mill, 165, 166

Gaines, William, 45
Gaines Mill, 45–47, 125
gambling, 6, 11
Garfield, James A., 207, 210
Gaston, J. B., 305–6
gender issues
  Oates' relationship with women, 7
  and paternalism, 218–19
  and social structure, 16–17, 24–25,
    30, 249
  and Victorian society, 210–15
Georgia Brigade, 89
Gettysburg
  battle lines, 80–88
  Big Round Top assault, 89–94
  Big Round Top retreat, 106–9
  casualties, 106–8, 116–17, 126, 130,
    132
  cavalry battles, 111–16

current status of monuments, 309
descent from Big Round Top, 94–97
impact on Oates, xx, 137
legacy of, 251
Little Round Top assault, 97–99,
    99–102, 102–6
as military park, 233
military reunions, 216, 229
monument proposals, 237, 252–53,
    257, 263–64, 283–85, 287–89,
    291–95, 298–301, 350n. 25, 363–
    64n. 26
and morale problems, 125
Oates' article on, 198–99
Oates family visit to, 256
prisoners from, 118–20
psychological impact, 111–16
retreats from, 116–18
and total war, 128
Gettysburg Address, 274
Gettysburg Battlefield Memorial Asso-
    ciation, 206–7, 233
Gettysburg National Military Park,
    247, 256, 280–81, 291–92, 293–
    94, 335n. 29
Gilded Age, 231
Gold Democrats, 227
gold standard, 226–27, 229, 232, 238
Gordon, Alexander C., 19, 28
Gordon, John B., 160, 247
Gordonsville, Virginia, 39, 50
Gorgas, Josiah, 129
Graham, James D., 256, 257
grandfather clauses, 268, 271, 276
Grant, Ulysses S.
    and Chamberlain, 289
    at Chattanooga, 150
    at Cold Harbor, 160
    at Laurel Hill, 159
    promotion, 148, 156
    and total war, 129
graves of Confederate soldiers, 301–5
Great Awakening, 6
Greenback Party, 227
Grimsley, Mark, 329n. 33
Groveton, 51
Guerry, Peter, 46
Gunter, William F., 177–78

Hagerstown, Maryland, 120
Hamilton, Alexander, 274

Hamilton's Crossing, 59
Hancock, Winfield Scott, 165, 207
Harlan, John Marshall, 204
Harpers Ferry, xxix, 18, 55–57
Harris, Joel Chandler, 224
Harrisonburg, 41
Hay, John, 255
Hayes, Rutherford B., 220, 289
Haymarket, Virginia, 34, 326n. 16
Hayne, Paul Hamilton, xxx
Hearst, William Randolph, 253
Hegel, Georg Wilhelm, xxviii
Heintzelman, Samuel P., 38
Hemans, Felicia, 135, 196
Henderson, Texas, 12
Hendley, William R., 127
Henry County, Alabama
    African American population, 23
    growth of, 174
    military enlistments, 28
    Oates' land holdings in, 179
    politics of, 191
    and Reconstruction, 183, 191
    slave census, 324n. 40
Henry Grays (company), 28
Henry House Hill, 53
Henry Pioneers (company). *See also*
    15th Alabama
    age of enlistees, 35
    first deployments, 31
    formation of, 28–30
    at Gettysburg, 97
    Oates' biographical sketches, 123
    sibling enlistees, 70
Herr's Ridge, 82, 83
Heth, Henry, 158
Hickman, Lucy ("Lou")
    daughter, 351n. 32
    and Oates' estate, 306
    and Oates' marriage, 212
    Oates' relationship with, 183–91,
        196, 209, 215
Hickman, Melissa Oates, 184, 306
Hickman, Ola, 351n. 32
Hickman, Robert H., 184, 185
Hill, Ambrose P., 56, 60, 76
Hill, Blant, 103, 106
Hill, D. H., 60
Hill's Point, 73
Hindman, Thomas C., 342n. 10

Hoke, Robert F., 60–61
Holloway, William R., 100, 106
Hollywood Cemetery, 303, 304
Holmes, Morris, 70
Holmes, Oliver Wendell, Jr., 300
Holmes, Pulaski, 70
Holmes, William, 70
Homestead Act, 210
Homestead Steel Mill, 230–31, 238
honor
    and command changes, 140
    and desertions, 127–28, 340n. 31
    and military service, 29
    of Oates, xx–xxi, 86, 103–4
    Oates' advice on, 239
    and prisoners of war, 120
    and secession, 20
    and sexuality, 189–90
    and suicide, 115
Hood, John Bell
    at Chickamauga, 138
    and command changes, 74, 162–63
    division makeup, 62
    at Gettysburg, 81, 83, 85–86, 87, 93
    and Oates' promotion, 345n. 38
    and Potomac crossing, 78
    wounded, 148
Hooker, Joseph, 73, 74, 149
Hooper, John R., 304
Hot Springs, Arkansas, 228, 301
Houghton, Fred, 261–62
Houghton, Mitchell, 78, 291
Houghton, William R., 291
House Ways and Means Committee,
    195
Hudson, William O., 150
Hussey, Jefferson, 150

ideology, xxiv, 29, 64–67, 220. *See also*
    Lost Cause ideology
immigration, xx, 78, 223, 231. *See also*
    race and racism
imperialism, 259
industrial interests, 266
inheritance clauses, 271, 276
Interstate Commerce Commission, 220

Jackson, James W., 90
Jackson, Thomas J. "Stonewall"
    and command changes, 62–63, 147,
        163

at Cross Keys, 44
    death, 76
    early victories, 54
    as focus of research, xxxi
    and Fredericksburg, 60, 61
    at Gaines Mill, 45
    at Harpers Ferry, 55
    killed, 157
    leadership style, 40, 124
    marching pace, 56
    Oates' opinion of, xxiii
    and religious revivalism, 58, 130
    at Second Manassas, 51–53
    at Suffolk, 74
    and the Valley Campaign, 40–41
Jay's Mill, 138
Jefferson, Thomas, 25, 134, 274
Jeffersonian Democrats, 226–28, 232–
    35, 268
Jelks, William, 283
Jenkins, Micah, 148, 157
Jerusalem, Virginia, 73
Johnson, Andrew, 181
Johnson, Bushrod R., 138, 142
Johnston, Joseph E., 35–38, 170
Johnston, Joseph F., 233–34, 251, 265
Johnston, Samuel R., 83
Jones, Thomas G., 228, 232, 236–37,
    270, 271
Jordan, William, 123, 149, 150
Judiciary Committee, 230

Kansas-Nebraska Act, 14
Kearny, Philip, 53
Keils, John, 336n. 35
Kershaw, Joseph B., 142, 143, 144, 159
Kilpatrick, H. Judson, 113, 337–38n. 4
King, Horatio, 247
Kirkland, Cicero, 296
Know-Nothing Party, 79
Knox, John B., 268
Kolb, Reuben F.
    and the Farmers' Alliance, 225–26,
        228
    gubernatorial campaign, 233, 234–37
    Oates' battles with, 273
Ku Klux Klan, 183, 194, 199, 235
Kyle, R. B., 293

labor unions, 230–31
Ladies' Memorial Association, 303–4

La Fayette Road, 139, 140–41
Lane, James H., 60
Lary, Samuel D., 33, 34
Laurel Hill, 159
Law, Evander M.
  brigade makeup, 62
  on cavalry actions at Gettysburg,
    336n. 35
  and cavalry battles, 112–13
  at Chickamauga, 140, 144
  at Cold Harbor, 160
  and command changes, 74
  conflicts with Longstreet, 155–56
  at Gettysburg, 81, 83, *84*, 85, 87, 89–
    90, 91, 93, 106
  at Hagerstown, 120–21
  leaves of absence, 148
  Oates' opinion of, 342n. 2
  and Oates' promotions, 146
Lawrenceville Academy, 12–13
Lee, Fitzhugh, 254
Lee, Robert E.
  at Bolivar Heights, 56
  cavalry reviews, 331n. 12
  and command changes, 76, 163
  and desertions, 127
  early victories, 54
  and the Emancipation Proclamation,
    65
  as focus of research, xxxi
  and foraging, 78
  at Fredericksburg, 59, 62
  at Gaines Mill, 45
  at Gettysburg, 82–83, 85, 117, 125,
    129
  at Hagerstown, 121
  at Laurel Hill, 159
  Maryland campaign, 55
  and morale, 127
  Oates' opinion of, xxii, xxiii
  and patriarchal authority, 190
  Pennsylvania invasion, 79
  at Petersburg, 169
  and religion, 130
  at Richmond, 72
  at Second Manassas, 50, 53
  and slavery, 25
  at Suffolk, 73, 74
  surrender, 170
  at Vicksburg, 118
  and winter camps, 63

Leonid meteor showers, 2, 309, 320n. 4
Lightner, Miss, 120, 121
Lincoln, Abraham
  assassination, 173
  commitment to the war, 72, 99–100
  and dreams, 122
  Emancipation Proclamation, 64–67,
    129
  Gettysburg Address, 274
  Oates' opinion of, 29, 246–47
  promotions and commissions, 148,
    156
  public opinion of, 78
  and Reconstruction, 181
  and religion, 129
  and secession, 18, 19, 21
Lingo, Elijah W., 167
Linton, Amanda Oates, 201, 306
literacy tests, 265, 271
Little Round Top, *84*, 97
  casualties, 106, 107, 111–12, 252
  15th Alabama's assault on, 97–99,
    99–102, 102–6
  inaccurate accounts of, 334n. 14
  and John Oates' death, 118–20
  monuments, 256–57, 264, 283–85,
    287–88, 288–90, 293–95, 298–
    301, 309
  as observation point, 83
  scale of battle, 111
  sharpshooters on, 87
  and veterans' reunions, 216–17, 248
Lomax, Lunsford L., 299
Long, Huey, xxx
Long, James B., 167, 195
Long, Mary Jane, 195, 306–7
Longstreet, James
  at Chancellorsville, 330n. 8
  at Chattanooga, 149
  at Chickamauga, 138, 140, 142
  and command changes, 73–74, 76,
    147
  conflicts with subordinates, 155–56
  First Army Corps, 62
  as focus of research, xxxi
  at Gettysburg, 82–85
  honored, 245–46
  and Oates' article, 198–99
  Republican appointments, 302
  at Second Manassas, 53
  at Suffolk, 72–74

Longstreet, James
  at Thoroughfare Gap, 51
  wounded, 157
Lookout Creek, 150
Lookout Mountain, 147
Lookout Valley, 148
Lost Cause ideology
  and African Americans, xxiii
  and Alabama law, 175–76
  and Confederate veterans, 124
  diffusion of, xxiii–xxiv
  and Oates' book, 297
  Oates' commitment to, xxii, xxiii,
    173, 198, 216, 246–47
  and politics, 223, 224
  and proposed monuments, 300
  and reconciliation, 291
  and Reconstruction, 176
  and romanticism, 205
Louisiana, 10, 322n. 20
Lowe, Thaddeus, 63
Lowther, Alexander A.
  at Appomattox, 170
  at Chattanooga, 150
  and command changes, 74, 162–63
  and Fredericksburg, 59
  at Fussell's Mill, 165
  at Gaines Mill, 47
  leaves of absence, 57, 155, 162
  promotions, 31–32, 37, 344–45n. 22
  rivalry with Oates, 124, 145–46
  at Second Manassas, 49–50
  at Thoroughfare Gap, 51
loyalty oaths, 181
Luray, 40–41
lynchings, 237, 277
Lytle, William H., 142
Lytle Hill, 142

Mabson, Algernon A., 207–8
Malone, George Y., 47
Manassas. *See* First Manassas; Second
    Manassas
Manassas Junction, 51
market economy, 190
marriage
  age differences, 351n. 37
  "companionate marriage," 214–15,
    351n. 38, 352n. 41
  Oates' marriage to "T," 210–12
  and patriarchal society, 213–15,
    352n. 40

and social status, xx–xxi
  and Victorian society, 210–15
Marshall, Texas, 11
Martinsburg, Maryland, 56
Marye's Heights, 61
Masons, 183
Massanutten Mountain, 40
Maury, M. F., 221
McClellan, George B., 36, 45, 221
McClendon, William A. "Gus," 30–31,
    37, 46, 60, 123, 280
McElhaney, Loula, 261–62
McElvain v. Mudd, 202
McFadden, Samuel, 144
McJunkin, Samuel B., 131
McKinley, William, 250, 252–56, 258–
    60, 290
McLaws, Lafayette, 56, 81, 83, 138, 155
McPherson's Ridge, 216
McSpadden, Samuel K., 141–42, 342n.
    10
Meade, George Gordon, 120
Meredith, M. E., 149–50
Metropolitan Hotel, 210
Mexican War, 31
Micow, B. H., 202–3
Middleburg, Virginia, 77
Military Order of the Loyal Legion of
    the United States, 247
military service
  black soldiers, 182
  citizen soldiers, 70, 90
  and the Emancipation Proclamation,
    64–67
  end of Oates' career, 259
  Oates' brigadier general commis-
    sion, 253–54
  and racism, 276
  reunions, 207, 216, 280, 291, 361–
    62n. 51
  siblings in service, 69–71
  slaves, 64, 170, 330n. 35
  volunteerism, 28–29
  and voting rights, 276
Missionary Baptist Church, 195
Missionary Ridge, 147
Mobile, Alabama, 10
Montgomery, Alabama, 27
Montgomery, George, 178
Montgomery Advertiser, xvii, 235, 240
Moore, Andrew B., 28

morale, 57–59, 63, 127, 129–35
Morgan, John Tyler, 234, 260, 271
Mosby, John Singleton, xxxi, 302
Murphy, Edgar Gardner, 270
mysticism, 6–7, 8–9. *See also* clairvoyance

Nacogdoches County, 11
National Banking Act (1864), 204
National Democrats, 18
National Hotel, 210
Native Americans, 4–5
Neale, Walter, 293
Newberry, Jimmie, 151
New Guilford, 80, 81
New Market Heights, 164–67
New Model Army, 58
New Orleans, Louisiana, 10
Nicaragua canal bill, 230
Nicholson, John P.
    background, 233
    and Gettysburg monument efforts,
        264, 283, 285, 287, 289, 290, 292,
        295, 298–99, 363–64n. 26
    on Oates' speech, 247
19th Alabama, 141–42, 144, 342n. 10
Ninth Amendment, 221
9th Ohio Colored Battalion, 257
North American Review, 231, 238
North Anna River, 159
Nye, L. Frank, 302–3, 303–4

Oakwood Cemetery, 306, 308, 309
Oates, Claudius (Claude)
    birth, 179
    education, 209
    fraudulent land deal, 241–43
    and Oates' estate, 307
    and Oates' marriage, 211
    and Oates' racism, 192
    Oates' support of, 183, 188, 209
    professional successes, 190
Oates, Georgia Saffold, 320n. 2
Oates, James Wyatt, 195, 201, 281
Oates, John
    account of death, 252
    anniversary of death, 264–65
    captured, 111
    childhood, 5, 8
    death, xxii, xxiii, 117, 118–20, 121,
        126, 134–35, 187
    enlistment, 27–28, 70

    and Farnsworth incident, 338–39n. 6
    at Gaines Mill, 46
    at Gettysburg, 80–83, 86–88, 91–92,
        94, 98, 101, 106–7, 109, 111
    illness, 77, 80, 82–83, 86
    impact of death, 206
    in law practice, 17
    at Little Round Top, 101
    relationship with brother, 69, 71–72,
        145
    and religion, 134
    remains buried, 303
    in Texas, 12
    transfers, 35
Oates, Joshua Cornillus
    birth, 184, 191
    in Dale County, 351n. 32
    education, 209
    medical career, 240–41
    and Oates' estate, 307
    and Oates' marriage, 211
    Oates' support of, 188, 209
Oates, Marion Saffold, 308–9
Oates, Sarah Sellars (mother), 3, 6, 17–
    18, 109, 121–23, 229
Oates, Sarah Toney ("T")
    adolescence, 205–6
    at Camp Haskell, 258
    childhood, 168–69
    death, 308–9
    health problems, 249–50, 254–55,
        255–56, 269, 278–79
    infancy, 153
    intellectual maturity, 208
    and Oates' death, 305–6
    and Oates' estate, 307
    in Paris, 281
    pregnancy, 218–19
    racism, 240
    social life, 217–21, 249, 264, 301
    travels, 248
Oates, William "Bill" (cousin), 11
Oates, William C.
    achievements, xvii–xviii
    aggressiveness, 142–43, 144–45, 174
    ambition, xviii–xix, xx, xxx, 12, 15,
        21, 54, 140, 219
    ancestry, 2
    authorship, xxiv–xxvi, 1–2, 251, 279,
        280, 292, 295–97, 318n. 16, 320n.
        2, 322n. 20

Oates, William C. (*continued*)
  birth date, 2, 320n. 3
  bravery, 101, 261–62, 296
  childhood, 3–5, 5–8
  children, 219
  conservatism, 223–24
  courage, 140–41
  criticism of, 124
  death, 305–6
  depression, 117, 137–38, 140, 143,
    146, 149, 169, 243, 279, 339n. 12
  education, 8, 12–13
  entrepreneurial spirit, 173–74
  family life, xviii–xix, 3–4
  finances and land holdings, 179–80,
    200–201, 207, 241–43, 251, 279–
    80, 301, 306–7, 319n. 25
  funeral, 305–6
  governorship, 233, 234–40
  health problems, 10, 56–57, 105–6,
    228, 263, 301–2, 304–5
  independence, 142–43
  law practice, xxviii, 13–18, 174–79,
    200–5, 208, 259–62, 279–80, 292
  leadership, 33, 39, 69, 123–26, 137,
    143–44
  obituaries, xvii
  and paternalism, 10
  personality, xviii–xix, xxxi
  physical appearance, 7, 17, 197, 228
  political views, 153
  promotions, 72, 74
  public speaking, xxiii, 224, 240
  racism, 191–92
  and religion, 58–59, 118, 132–35
  sentimentality, 40
  sexual proclivities, 167–68, 183–92
  and slavery, xxviii
  temper, 219
  travels, 228, 281–82, 292, 303, 305,
    354n. 11
  and violence, xxi–xxii, 2–3, 6, 8, 239,
    261–62
  war wounds, 50, 53, 56–57, 141,
    149–51, 165–67, 281, 328n. 14
  wealth, 175, 179–80, 200–201, 207,
    241–43, 251, 279–80, 301, 306–7,
    319n.25
  wedding, 210
  and women, 6, 10, 40, 120, 167–68,
    205
  xenophobia, 78–79, 223, 231

Oates, William Calvin, Jr. (son)
  birth, 219
  dismissed form West Point, 288
  education, 263, 264, 278, 283, 285,
    288, 297
  and father's health, 304
  graduation, 301
  health problems, 255, 256
  Oates' advice to, 1, 239
  and Oates' death, 305–7
  in Paris, 281
  resignation from West Point, 269
  travels, 249–50, 254
  and veterans' reunions, 248
Oates, William (father), 2, 4–5, 121–23,
  195, 320–21n. 6
Oates, Wyatt, 11, 248
Oates and Oates (law firm), 17
Oates's Crossroads, 4, 5, 6–7
Oates v. National Bank, 202–5
Ocala Platform, 226–27
O'Connor, Pat, 102
Official Records (U.S. War Department),
  xxvi, 209, 229, 363–64n. 26
O'Neal, John W. C., 303
Orange Plank Road, 156–58
Orchard Knob, 246
Orr, James L., 18
Owen, Thomas M., 248
Ox Hill, 53

Palmer, John L., 250
Panama Canal, 230
Panic of 1873, 227
Panic of 1893, 238, 241
Park, Frank, 103
Parker, Aaron, 261–62
Parks, Isaac, 101
Parsons, Lewis E., 181
paternalism, 10, 24, 195–96, 239, 270
patriarchal society
  and marriage, 352n. 40
  and military service, 30
  and Oates' law practice, 16–17
  and personal ambition, 21
  in postwar south, 190
  and racism, 213–14
  and secession, 21–25
patriotism, 28–29, 130
Peach Orchard, *84*
Peck, E. Wolsey, 176, 202

pedophilia, 189
Pegram, William R. J., xxxi
Pelham, John, xxxi, 59–60
Pemberton, John C., 118
Peninsula Campaign, 45–47, 125
Pennsylvania, 76
Pennsylvania "Bucktail Regiment," 43
Pensacola, Florida, 10
Perry, Edward S., 157
Perry, William F., 139–40, 156–57, 158, 162, 163
Peters, Thomas Minott, 176, 178
Petersburg, Virginia, 72, 162, 169
Pettus, Edmund W., 250, 260, 271
Phillips, W. Hallett, 175, 202
Pickett, George E., 72, 162, 351n. 37
Pickett, LaSalle, 351n. 37
Pickett's charge, 112
Pierce, Franklin, 14
Pike County, Alabama, 3–5, 23
Plum Run, 88, 90, 106, 113
Poe, Edgar Allan, 184
The Poetical Works of Mrs. Felicia Hemans, 135
poetry, 135, 196, 205, 211, 212, 341n. 43
politics. *See also* elections and election fraud
    and Alabama constitutional convention, 265–78
    campaigning, xxiii, xxviii, 220, 223–24
    Democratic Convention, 193–95
    and disfranchisement, xxix, 191, 265–78, 360n. 24
    and the Eiffel Regency, 14
    and the Emancipation Proclamation, 64
    and the Eufaula Regency, 153, 197, 226
    gubernatorial campaign, 234–40
    and law practice, 13–18
    Oates' career summarized, xx
    Oates' congressional career, 229–34
    Oates' dedication to, 210
    and Porter case, 220–21
    and Reconstruction, 191
    and secession, 18–25
    Senate bids, 260, 301
    and social structure, 197–98
    and Washington life, 218

poll taxes, 265, 271
Pope, John, 50, 53
Populists
    and Alabama constitutional convention, 266, 268, 273, 276
    and the Farmers' Alliance, 226
    and gubernatorial campaign, 234–35
    and the Jeffersonian Democrats, 228, 232–33
    Oates' opinion of, 238–40
    and racism, 240
Porter, Fannie, 75
Porter, Fitz John, 220–21
Porter family, 75
Port Lavaca, Texas, 12
Port Republic, 42, 44
Port Royal, 59, 62, 131
Potomac River, 77–78, 120–21
prayer meetings, 51, 58, 134. *See also* religion
precognition. *See* clairvoyance
predestination, 132–33
prisoners of war, 118–20, 302, 340n. 19
Proclamation of Amnesty and Reconstruction, 181
Progressives, 268
promotions. *See* commissions and promotions
Prospect Hill, 60
protective tariffs, 215–16
Protestantism, 130–31, 133
Providence Church Road, 74
Provisional Congress, 27
Pugh, Bullock and Buford, 13–18
Pugh, James L.
    background, 13–14
    congressional bid, 15
    and John Oates, 73
    legal cases with Oates, 176
    and Oates' command dispute, 162
    Senate seat vacated, 250
    and slavery, 65
    and transfer requests, 169
Pulitzer, Joseph, 238, 253

Raccoon Ford, 75
race and racism. *See also* white supremacy
    and Alabama constitutional convention, 265–78
    black codes, 176, 182

race and racism (*continued*)
  and Claudius Oates, 242–43
  and elections, xxix, 191–92, 223,
    265–78
  and the Emancipation Proclamation,
    129
  and immigration, 78–79
  Jim Crow laws, xxx, 224
  and Lost Cause ideology, xxiii–xxiv,
    291
  in the military, 51, 257
  Oates' struggle with, xx, 9, 307
  and paternalism, 239–40, 270
  racial politics, 227–28, 234–35
  racial violence, 182–83, 194, 199,
    235, 236–37
  and secession, 29–30
  segregation, xxix, 200, 224–25, 278
  and slavery, 65–67
  and social structure, 23–24, 24–25
Radical Republicans, 181, 182, 193, 272
railroads, 199, 268
Raines family, 201
Randall, Samuel J., 210
rape, 168, 184–85
Rapidan River, 156
Rapier, James T., 194
Rappahannock River, 123, 127
Rappahannock Station, 38–39
Reconstruction
  and Alabama constitutional conven-
    tion, 276
  alternate schemes for, 180–83
  and Lost Cause ideology, 176
  Oates' resistance to, xix–xx, 178
  and politics, xxix–xxx, 191, 194, 223
  and racism, 182–83, 192
Redemption Democrats, 176, 199–200.
    See also "Bourbon" Democrats
Reed, J. A. E., 119–20, 134–35, 251–52,
    340n. 19
Reilly, James, 85
religion
  deism, 133
  Oates' family, 5–6, 320–21n. 6
  and racism, 79, 275
  religious revivalism, 57–59, 63, 129–
    35
  Spiritualism, 6–7, 8–9, 321n. 16
Republican Party
  and Alabama constitutional conven-
    tion, 266, 269, 276

and electoral campaigns, 225
  and McKinley, 260
  post–Civil War conflicts, 216
  and voting rights, 199–200
reunions
  for Alabama veterans, 280
  and battle reconstruction, 216–17,
    229, 248
  at Chattanooga, 245–47
  at Gettysburg, 207, 248
  and Gettysburg monument efforts,
    284
  Oates' son on, 361–62n. 51
revivalism, 57–59, 63, 128–35
Reynolds, John, 216
Rice, James C., 336–37n. 40
Richardson, Charles, 283, 285, 293
Richardson, William N., 31, 43
Richmond, Virginia, 45–47, 72
Richmond Christian Advocate, 131
Richmond Enquirer, 165
Riley, Turner, 177
Roach, Administrator, v. Gunter et al.,
    177–78, 202
Robbins, William P.
  background, 233
  and Gettysburg monument efforts,
    257, 263, 264, 280, 283, 285,
    287–88, 291–95
Robertson, Jerome Bonaparte, 85, 87,
    89, 155
Roosevelt, Theodore, xviii, 240, 301
Root, Elihu, 287–90, 292
Rosecrans, William S., 138, 140, 145,
    148
Roseland plantation
  Oates' convalescence at, 151–53,
    167–68
  and Oates' marriage, 213
  Oates' time at, 196, 205
  ownership change, 279
  and Reconstruction, 219
  social life, 249
Rosser, Thomas, 254
Russell, William Howard, xxix

Saffold, Benjamin Franklin, 177, 202
Saffold, Georgia Whiting. *See* Oates,
    Georgia Saffold
San Juan Hill, 255

Sauls, John, 296–97
Schofield, John, 288
Scott, Walter, 212
secession, 18–25
   and the Eiffel Regency, 14
   fights over, xxix
   and Lost Cause ideology, 198
   and Oates' book, 297
   Oates' support of, xix, 221
   and slavery, 324n. 42
   and the U.S. Constitution, 19, 21,
     22, 221
Second Army Corps, 160, 256
Second Manassas, 32, 33, 36, 49–53,
   220, 296
2nd U.S. Sharpshooters, 87, 90–92, 100,
   103
Seddon, James A., 72, 73–74, 147, 162
segregation, xxix, 200, 224–25, 278
Seminary Ridge, 83, *84*, 263, 284
Seminole Indians, 9
Semmes, Raphael, 282
Seven Days' campaign, 45–47
7th South Carolina, 142, 143
72nd Pennsylvania, 284
Seward, William Henry, 18
Seymour, Horatio, 194
Shaaf, Francis Key, 95, 105, 336n. 36
Shafter, William, 255
Shakespeare, William, 13
sharecropping, 180
Sharpsburg, 56, 130
sharpshooters
   and Feagin's death, 118
   at Gettysburg, 87, 95, 100, 103, 105,
     112
   at the North Anna River, 159
   at Petersburg, 162
Sheffield, James L., 138–39
Shenandoah River, 77
Shenandoah Valley, 40–44
Sheridan, Philip Henry, 129
Sherman, John, 354n. 11
Sherman, William Tecumseh, xxiv, 129
Sherman Silver Purchase Act, 227, 232
Shields, James, 42, 44
Shorter, Eli S., 15
Shorter, John Gill, 15, 32, 197
Shorter family, 197
Shreveport, Louisiana, 10

Sickles, Daniel E., *84*, 85
Silver Democrats, 227
silver standard, 226–27, 232, 250–51,
   260
16th Mississippi, 36
Sixth Corps (Union), 106, 160
6th Alabama, 28, 35, 37
6th New York Cavalry, 335n. 31, 336n.
   35
6th North Carolina, 36
Slaughter's Mountain, 50
slavery
   and democracy, 324n. 43
   economic impact, 173, 180
   and the Emancipation Proclamation,
     64–67, 129, 202
   enlistment of slaves, 64, 170, 330n.
     35
   impact of, 196
   and the Oates family, 324n. 40
   Oates on, xix, xx, xxviii, 297, 307
   and political campaigns, 225
   and poor whites, 4
   and religion, 131
   and secession, 23
   and sexual exploitation, 167–68
   slave marriages, 176
   and social structure, 23–24, 153
   and southern politics, 14
   and white supremacy, 79
Slyder farm, 88, 106, 109, 118
Smedley, Randolph, 62
Smith, Gustavus W., 36
Snicker's Gap, 77
snipers, 116, 161. *See also* sharpshooters
Snodgrass Hill, 142, 143–44
snowball fights, 63
social life, 196, 217–21, 249, 264, 301
social structure
   and election reform, 275
   and the Emancipation Proclamation,
     64–67
   and farmer's movements, 226
   and gender, 16–17, 24–25, 30, 249
   hierarchical organization, 65, 71,
     129, 214
   and military service, 29–30
   and paternalism, 270
   and plantation economy, 153, 196
   and politics, 197–98

social structure (*continued*)
  in postwar south, 190
  and race, 323n. 30
  and sharecropping, 180
  and status of individuals, xx–xxi,
    xxix–xxx, 23
  and Victorian society, 71, 103–4,
    188, 210–15, 219
  and wealth, 201, 319n. 25
"Somebody's Darling" (song), 108–9
South Carolina, 22
Southern Baptist Convention, 131
Southern Democrats, 231, 266. *See also*
    Democratic Party
Southern Historical Society, 198
Southern Historical Society Papers, 198,
    206–7, 252
Southern Republicanism, 24–25. *See also*
    Republican Party
South Mountain, 81–82, 120
Spanish-American War, xviii, xix, xxviii,
    253–59, 358n. 27
Spear, Ellis, 216
Spencer, G. E., 32
Spiritualism, 6–7, 8–9, 321n. 16
Spotsylvania, 159, 164
St. Louis (ship), 282
Stafford Heights, 59
Stanardsville, Virginia, 39
states' rights, xxiv, 14, 22, 66–67, 194,
    220
Stevens, Isaac I., 53
Stevens, Thaddeus, 81
Stewart, A. P., 342n. 2
Strickland, William, 166–67
strikes, 230–31
Stuart, J. E. B., xxxi, 75, 77, 331n. 12
Styron, William, xxx
Suffolk, Virginia, 72–74
suffrage rights
  and Alabama constitutional conven-
    tion, 265–78
  and disfranchisement, xxix, 191,
    265–78, 360n. 24
  and election fraud, 228
  Oates' support for, xviii, 360n. 24
  and racism, xxviii, 224
  and Reconstruction, 182
  and slavery, 324n. 40
  and violence, 199
suicide, 113–16, 338–39n. 6, 339n. 7

Sumner, Charles, xxix
Sumner, Edwin V., 61
Swallow, William H., 216
Swift Run Gap, 39–40

Taft, William Howard, 299, 301
Tallassee Manufacturing Company of
    Montgomery, 202–3
Tammany Hall, 194
Taneytown Road, 119, 336n. 36
tariffs, 215–16, 220, 231, 235
taxation, 215–16, 265
Taylor, Zachary, 14
Tennessee River, 148–50
Tenth Amendment, 221
Terrell, Leigh R., 93–94, 144, 149
Texas, 11–12, 207, 241–42, 322n. 20
3rd South Carolina, 142, 143
13th Amendment, 178, 182
Thomas, George H., 148
Thoroughfare Gap, 51
timber interests, 180
Tomkins, H. C., 250
Toney, Caroline, 196
Toney, Sarah. *See* Oates, Sarah Toney
    ("T")
Toney, Sarah Bass, 151, 152, 205
Toney, Sterling, 196
Toney, Washington, 151, 152, 196, 205
Toney, William, 42, 151–52
total war, 125, 128, 329n. 33
Travis, William Barret, 11
Treaty of Paris, 258
Treutlen, John, 42, 74, 344–45n. 22
Trimble, Isaac R.
  described, 36
  at Gaines Mill, 45
  at Second Manassas, 49, 52
  and the Valley Campaign, 38, 42,
    43–44
Turner, Nat, 73
Turner's Rebellion, 73
Tuskegee Negro Normal Institute, 226,
    239–40
Twain, Mark, 224
20th Maine
  at Gettysburg, 95–100, 102–3, 105–
    6, 252
  at Little Round Top, 336n. 34, 336n.
    35
  monument to, 256–57, 294, 335n. 29

and proposed monuments, 287, 288–90, 298
and veterans' reunions, 216, 248
28th Maine, 119
21st Georgia, 36, 43
21st North Carolina, 36
26th North Carolina, xxxi
typhoid, 39, 255, 256

Union Church, 41, 42
United Confederate Veterans, 306
United Daughters of the Confederacy, 213, 306
United States Circuit Court, 208
Unitarians, 134
Universalists, 134
University of Alabama, 241, 288, 301
University of Virginia Law School, 301
U.S. Congress
    and currency standards, 231–32
    and family life, 219
    and Gettysburg monument efforts, 291
    House Ways and Means Committee, 195
    and Oates' biography, 322n. 20
    Oates' career in, 229–34
    Oates' election to, 208
    and Reconstruction, 181–82, 193, 194
    and Spanish-American War, 253
    and Washington life, 217–21
U.S. Constitution. *See also specific amendments*
    Civil War amendments, 178
    Oates' support of, 273
    and secession, 19, 21, 22, 221
U.S. Fifth Circuit Court, 174, 280
U.S. House of Representatives, 215, 229–30, 291
U.S. Military Academy (West Point), 259–60, 263, 264, 283
U.S. Senate, xx, xxix, 250, 260, 267, 291, 301
U.S. Supreme Court, 175, 202–5
U.S. War Department, 209
USS *Kearsage*, 282
USS *Maine*, 253

Vaderland (ship), 281
Vaiden, William J., 237

Valley Campaign, 40–44
Valley of Death, 92
Vandalia, Sarah (Sallie). *See also* Allen, Sallie Vandalia Knight
    Oates' affair with, 167–71
    Oates' relationship with, 190–91
    and Oates' self-image, 187
    Oates' support of, 179, 183
    and the Toney family, 196
Vanderbilt University, 191, 241
veteran affairs, 206, 216, 289
Vicksburg, 118, 128
Victorian society, 71, 103–4, 188, 210–15, 219
vigilante violence, 277. *See also* lynchings
"A Vindication of Virginia and the South" (Oates), 221
violence
    on the Alabama frontier, 3–5
    and criminal cases, 201
    labor unrest, 230
    and law troubles, 9, 11
    of Oates, xxi–xxii, 2–3, 6, 8, 239, 261–62, 307
    and politics, 20–21
    racial, 237, 277
    sexual, 168, 184–86
    in Southern culture, xxviii–xxix
    of war, 54
volunteerism, 28–29
voting, 191, 199. *See also* suffrage rights

Waco, Texas, 11–12
Waddell, De Bernie, 78, 102, 105, 210
Walker, John G., 56
The War Between the Union and the Confederacy and Its Lost Opportunities (Oates), xxii, xxv, 123, 293, 295–97, 318n. 16
Ward, William, 80
War Department (Confederacy), 146, 147, 162, 163, 169
War Department (U.S.)
    and military parks, 233, 245, 285
    and Oates' discharge, 259
    and proposed monuments, 287–88, 289, 299–300
Warfield Ridge, 83, 112, 263
War of 1812, 216
Warren, Gouverneur K., 289

Warren, Robert Penn, xxx
Washington, Booker T., 226, 239–40,
    243, 269–70, 274
Washington, D.C., 217–21
Watts, Thomas H., 75
Weaver, James B., 228
Weaver, Rufus B., 303
Weaver, Samuel, 303
Webb, Alexander S., 289
Weems, Lock, 46–47
West Point, 259–60, 263, 264, 283
Wheeler, Joseph, 169, 254, 282
White League, 199
white supremacy
    and Alabama constitutional conven-
        tion, 275, 276–77
    and Democratic Party, 194
    and immigration, 78–79
    Oates' belief in, xx, xxiv, xxx, 153
    and patriarchal dominance, 213–14
    and political campaigns, 223, 227,
        235, 267, 272, 273–74
    and racial violence, 239, 277

and Reconstruction, 192
and secession, 24, 29–30
and slavery, 65
and suffrage, 266
Wilde, Oscar, xxii
Wilderness Campaign, 158, 164
Wiley, Ariosto Appling, 248, 287–88,
    292, 293, 299
Willard Hotel, 210
Williams Island, 148
William (slave), 155
Williamsport, Pennsylvania, 77
women. *See* gender issues
Women's Christian Temperance
    Union, 213
Wright, Richard, xxx
Wright, Tom, 144
Wright Avenue, 293–94

Yancey, William Lowndes, 14, 15, 18,
    20
Young, Samuel B. M., 257

Zouaves regiments, 45

ABOUT THE AUTHOR

GLENN W. LAFANTASIE is the Frockt Family Professor of Civil War History and the Director of the Center for the Civil War in the West at Western Kentucky University. he is the bestselling author of *Twilight at Little Round Top*. He has also written for several magazines and newspapers, including *American History*, *North & South*, *MHQ: The Quarterly Journal of Military History*, *The New York Times Book Review*, *America's Civil War*, *Civil War Times Illustrated*, and *The Providence Journal*. Professor LaFantasie is at work on a microhistory of a farm family from Gettysburg during the Civil War era. He lives with his wife in Bowling Green.